ENFORCEABILITY OF LANDLORD AND TENANT COVENANTS

AUSTRALIA
Thomson, Sydney

CANADA and USA
Carswell
Toronto • Ontario

NEW ZEALAND
Brooker's, Auckland

SINGAPORE and MALAYSIA
Thomson Information (S.E. Asia)
Singapore

ENFORCEABILITY OF LANDLORD AND TENANT COVENANTS

T. M. FANCOURT Q.C.

SECOND EDITION

LONDON
SWEET & MAXWELL
2006

Published in 2006 by
Sweet & Maxwell of
100 Avenue Road, London NW3 3PF
Typeset by Interactive Sciences Ltd, Gloucester.
Printed and bound by Athenaeum Press Ltd.

No natural forests were destroyed to make this product;
only farmed timber was used and replanted

British Library Cataloguing in Publication Data

A CIP catalogue record for this book
is available from the British Library

ISBN 0421–952–903
9780–421–952–904

IN LOVING MEMORY OF DORIS FANCOURT
AND MARY PHOEBE STEVENS

FOREWORD TO THE FIRST EDITION

A book on enforceability of leasehold covenants is very welcome for a number of reasons. First, it is a topic which merits a book in its own right, and, until the publication of this volume, no such book existed. Secondly, there have been a number of recent and important cases where the courts have had to consider the fundamental nature of leasehold covenants. Thirdly, some fundamental changes to the previously existing law have been effected by Parliament when it enacted the Landlord and Tenant (Covenants) Act 1995. Fourthly, as any reader of law reports, and particularly the specialist law reports, will know, leasehold covenants have provided a fertile source of litigation over the past twenty years: any doubts on that score will be put to rest by a quick perusal of the list of cases in this book.

I am therefore confident that any book on the subject should be welcome to barristers, solicitors, surveyors, and indeed many others in the English property world, as well as to academic lawyers.

Having read the final draft of this book, I believe that Timothy Fancourt has done much more than filling a hole in the market. His book satisfies what I believe to be the three main requirements of any first-class legal textbook: in terms of contents, structure and style, it is readable and it is also easy to use so far as the practitioner is concerned; in terms of contents, it deals with the subject fully and intelligently; the author expresses his own views on significant points on which there is no, conflicting, or unsatisfactory authority or on which there is poorly drafted legislation.

Accordingly, I have no hesitation in recommending this book both to practitioners and to academics.

David Neuberger
Royal Courts of Justice
December, 1996

PREFACE TO THE FIRST EDITION

[illegible]

PREFACE TO THE FIRST EDITION

This book was written because the Landlord and Tenant (Covenants) Act came into force on January 1, 1996. Until that time, the law governing the enforceability of leasehold covenants as between lessors and their assigns and lessees and their assigns and any third parties was governed principally by the common law doctrines of privity of contract and privity of estate, with a statutory overlay of a few sections from the 1925 property legislation. That legislation added something of a polished finish to the law established by the old privities; and since 1925, the principles of law governing enforceability of leasehold covenants has become tolerably well defined, if not always simple to apply. It might be thought, therefore, that Parliament was bold indeed to attempt to replace this body of established law with a new code, comprised almost entirely in thirty-odd sections of a new statute. But the political imperative was present, and the Parliamentary draftsman ever willing, and so, on January 1, 1996, with something of a flourish if not a rush, the Landlord and Tenant (Covenants) Act 1995 was with us.

As Chapter 2 of the Text describes, the "old" law continues to apply to all tenancies granted in and before 1995, and also, in exceptional cases, to some tenancies granted on or after January 1, 1996. The existing principles of privity of contract, privity of estate and the relevant sections of the 1925 legislation will, therefore, continue to apply to many tenancies for many years to come. Part II of the Text attempts to summarise the law applying to such tenancies, both in order to provide a concise but connected treatment of that law, and also for the purpose of convenient comparison and contrast with the "new" code. Apart from the exceptional cases just mentioned, all tenancies granted on or after January 1, 1996 will be "new tenancies" within the meaning of section 1 of the Landlord and Tenant (Covenants) Act 1995, and to them the new statutory code will apply. Its provisions are considered in detail in Part III of the Text. A number of the provisions of the Act of 1995 apply both to "old" tenancies and to "new" tenancies. These introduce reforms in the law governing the liability of former tenants and guarantors of former tenants, and they are considered in Part IV. The remaining Parts of the Text deal with the anti-avoidance provisions of the Act, with the important amendment to s.19 of the Landlord and Tenant Act 1927 (Provisions as to covenants not to assign, etc. without licence or consent) which is intended to complement the provisions of the Act of 1995 relating to release of tenants' contractual liabilities and to authorised guarantee agreements, and with other amendments and repeals.

In writing this book, I have been greatly assisted by my colleagues in Falcon Chambers who have been involved, as I have, during the past year in advising on various aspects of the Act of 1995, and who have raised with me a number of interesting points on the true construction and effect of the Act. In particular, I am very grateful to Kim Lewison, Q.C. who, with typical assiduity and mastery of the subject, read the manuscript in a matter of days, and made a considerable number of helpful suggestions from which I have profited in finalising the Text. I should also record here debts which, though less directly reflected in the Text, are no less valuable: Mr Michael Prichard, formerly Senior Tutor and Director of Studies in Law at Gonville and Caius College, who first stimulated an interest in and demanded a rigorous approach to the analysis of the workings of property law; and Sir Robert Megarry, who needs no introduction, but who, over several years of working together on *The Rent Acts*, helped me to grapple with the difficulties of writing a coherent and accurate text about a (in that case) frighteningly complicated subject, and whose own books are, of course, a paragon to which all legal authors aspire. Any failings and infelicities of this book reflect entirely the poorness of the pupil, and not the excellence of the tuition. Finally, I am grateful to Sir David Neuberger, himself a foremost ex-practitioner in the field of landlord and tenant law, for taking time from his new career on the Bench to write the Foreword.

Although this book is a little late for the first anniversary of the Landlord and Tenant (Covenants) Act 1995, to say nothing of its coming into force, I am cheered by the fact that, to date, no case turning on or involving the Act has been reported. I hope that the book may prove of some assistance in the years to come, during which the operation of the Act can be expected to be subjected to close judicial scrutiny.

The Text states the law as at December 1, 1996.

FALCON CHAMBERS T.M.F.
December 1, 1996

PREFACE TO SECOND EDITION

The Landlord and Tenant (Covenants) Act 1995, which made significant changes to the law relating to enforceability of landlord and tenant covenants, came into force over ten years ago, on January 1, 1996. It is ten years too since the first edition of this book was published. The years that have passed have provided answers to some of the uncertainties to which the Act gave rise, but by no means to all of them. Some fundamental issues have apparently not been argued in court, though much debated by academics and practitioners, such as what counts as an equitable assignment, and the relationship between executed guarantee agreements and the anti-avoidance provisions. Only in the last three or four years have cases concerning the machinery of the Act appeared with regularity in the law reports, including one decision of the House of Lords on the effect of consensual release of landlord covenants and several in the Court of Appeal. The frequency appears to be increasing, with one important appeal on the effect of s.17 notices due to be heard by the Court of Appeal in January 2007. These decisions, and all others of which I am aware, are fully addressed in the text, together with changes in the body of statutory law since 1996, including the advent of the Human Rights Act 1998, the Contracts (Rights of Third Parties) Act 1999 and the Land Registration Act 2002. There has, I need hardly say, also been a significant number of cases reported on aspects of the law that applies to old tenancies, which will continue to be of importance for decades to come.

I am grateful to all those who have taken the trouble to bring to my attention errors in the text of the first edition, gaps in its treatment of the subject and issues that I had not previously considered. I hope that this edition can be regarded as an improvement on what was necessarily, in 1996, a tentative explanation of much that was then obscure. The structure of the book is almost exactly the same, except that the Parts previously dealing separately with Anti-avoidance and Assignment of Tenancies have been merged into one, in view of the considerable overlap in practice of their subject-matter, and a new Part dealing with aspects of Enforcement, has been added.

The law is stated as at November 1, 2006.

T.M.F

Falcon Chambers
November 1, 2006.

PREFACE TO SECOND EDITION

The Landlord and Tenant (Covenants) Act 1995, which made significant changes to the law relating to enforceability of landlord and tenant covenants, came into effect on January 1, 1996. [illegible] the first edition of this book was published. The years that have passed have provided answers to some of the uncertainties to which the Act gave rise. But by no means all of them. Some [illegible] issues have apparently not been argued upon or clearly articulated by academics or practitioners, such as what counts as an equitable assignment and the relationship between excluded [illegible] agreements and the anti-avoidance provisions. Only in the last three or four years have cases [illegible] the meaning of the Act appeared with regularity in the law reports, including a decision of the House of Lords on the effect of [illegible] of landlord covenants and several at the Court of Appeal. The frequency appears to be increasing, with one important [illegible] of the Court of Appeal in January 2007. These decisions, and all others of which I am aware, are fully addressed in the text, together with developments in [illegible] law since 1996, including the advent of the Human Rights Act 1998, the Contracts (Rights of Third Parties) Act 1999 and the Land Registration Act 2002. There has, needless to say, also been a significant number of cases reported on aspects of the law which applies to old tenancies, which will continue to be of importance for decades to come.

I am grateful to all those who have taken the trouble of writing to any [illegible] of the first edition [illegible] treatment of the subject and [illegible] that I had not previously considered. I hope that this edition is an improvement [illegible] explanation of [illegible]. The structure of the book is almost exactly the same, except that [illegible] previously dealt with separately [illegible] Anti-avoidance and [illegible] of Tenancies have been merged into one, and [illegible] dealing with [illegible] Enforcement has been added.

The law is stated as at November 1, 2006.

L.M.

Falcon Chambers

November 1, 2006

CONTENTS

PART I
INTRODUCTION

PART II
OLD TENANCIES

PART III
NEW TENANCIES

PART V
ANTI-AVOIDANCE AND ASSIGNMENT OF TENANCIES

PART VII
ENFORCEMENT OF COVENANTS

TABLE OF CASES

AE Realisations (1985) Ltd, Re [1988] 1 W.L.R. 200; [1987] 3 All E.R. 83; [1987] B.C.L.C. 486; [1988] P.C.C. 48; (1988) 85(2) L.S.G. 35; (1988) 132 S.J. 51, Ch D 9.11, 18.13

Aiken v Stewart Wrightson Members Agency Ltd [1996] 2 Lloyd's Rep. 577; [1997] 6 Re. L.R. 79, CA (Civ Div); affirming [1995] 1 W.L.R. 1281; [1995] 3 All E.R. 449; [1995] 2 Lloyd's Rep. 618; [1995] C.L.C. 318; *The Times*, March 8, 1995, QBD (Comm) 20.01

Allied Dunbar Assurance Plc v Fowle [1994] B.C.C. 422; [1994] 2 B.C.L.C. 197; [1994] 25 E.G. 149; *The Times*, February 22, 1994, QBD 9.06

Allied Dunbar Assurance Plc v Homebase Ltd; sub nom. Homebase Ltd v Allied Dunbar Assurance Plc [2002] EWCA Civ 666; [2003] 1 P. & C.R. 6; [2002] L. & T.R. 27; [2002] 2 E.G.L.R. 23; [2002] 27 E.G. 144; [2002] 22 E.G.C.S. 134; (2002) 99(24) L.S.G. 38, CA (Civ Div) 24.05

Allied London Investments Ltd v Hambro Life Assurance Plc (No.2) [1984] 1 E.G.L.R. 62; (1984) 270 E.G. 948 .... 3.03, 7.01, 20.01

Allnatt London Properties Ltd v Newton [1984] 1 All E.R. 423; (1983) 45 P. & C.R. 94; (1983) 265 E.G. 601, CA (Civ Div) 23.14, 24.12

Amec Developments Ltd v Jury's Hotel Management (UK) Ltd [2002] T.C.L.R. 13; (2001) 82 P. & C.R. 22; [2001] 1 E.G.L.R. 81; [2001] 07 E.G. 163; [2000] E.G.C.S. 138; [2000] N.P.C. 125, Ch D 26.16, 26.18

Amsprop Trading Ltd v Harris Distribution Ltd [1997] 1 W.L.R. 1025; [1997] 2 All E.R. 990; [1997] 2 E.G.L.R. 78; [1997] 47 E.G. 127; [1996] N.P.C. 154; *The Times*, November 13, 1996, Ch D 8.01

Arlesford Trading Co v Servansingh [1971] 1 W.L.R. 1080; [1971] 3 All E.R. 113; (1971) 22 P. & C.R. 848; 115 S.J. 507, CA (Civ Div) 4.19, 6.04

Associated British Ports v CH Bailey Plc [1990] 2 A.C. 703; [1990] 2 W.L.R. 812; [1990] 1 All E.R. 929; (1990) 60 P. & C.R. 211; [1990] 16 E.G. 65; [1990] E.G.C.S. 41; (1990) 87(17) L.S.G. 35; (1990) 140 N.L.J. 441; *The Times*, March 23, 1990, HL 26.02

Attorney General v Blake [2001] 1 A.C. 268; [2000] 3 W.L.R. 625; [2000] 4 All E.R. 385; [2000] 2 All E.R. (Comm) 487; [2001] I.R.L.R. 36; [2001] Emp. L.R. 329; [2000] E.M.L.R. 949; (2000) 23(12) I.P.D. 23098; (2000) 97(32) L.S.G. 37; (2000) 150 N.L.J. 1230; (2000) 144 S.J.L.B. 242; *The Times*, August 3, 2000; *Independent*, November 6, 2000 (C.S), HL 26.08, 26.18

Avonridge Property Co Ltd v Mashru; sub nom. London Diocesan Fund v Phithwa; Mashru v Avonridge Property Co Ltd; Avonridge Property Co Ltd v London Diocesan Fund; London Diocesan Fund v Avonridge Property Co Ltd [2005] UKHL 70; [2005] 1 W.L.R. 3956; [2006] 1 All E.R. 127; [2006] 1 P. & C.R. 25; [2006] L. & T.R. 4; [2006] 1 E.G.L.R. 15; [2006] 01 E.G. 100; [2005] 49 E.G.C.S. 88; (2006) 103(1) L.S.G. 16; (2006) 150 S.J.L.B. 28; [2005] N.P.C. 138; *The Times*, December 5, 2005, HL 3.03, 12.30, 14.29, 14.51, 14.55, 23.08, 23.16, 24.12

Ayling v Wade [1961] 2 Q.B. 228; [1961] 2 W.L.R. 873; [1961] 2 All E.R. 399; 105 S.J. 365, CA 8.01, 26.16

BHP Petroleum Great Britain Ltd v Chesterfield Properties Ltd; sub nom. Chesterfield Properties Ltd v BHP Petroleum Great Britain Ltd; BHP Great Britain Petroleum Ltd v Chesterfield Properties Ltd [2001] EWCA Civ 1797; [2002] Ch. 194; [2002] 2 W.L.R. 672; [2002] 1 All E.R. 821; [2002] 2 P. & C.R. 9; [2002] L. & T.R. 18; [2002] 2 E.G.L.R. 121; [2001] 50 E.G.C.S. 88; (2002) 99(5) L.S.G. 29; (2002) 146 S.J.L.B. 5; [2001] N.P.C. 174; [2002] 1 P. & C.R. DG17;

TABLE OF STATUTES

TABLE OF STATUTORY INSTRUMENTS

PART I

Introduction

CHAPTER 1

Introduction to Leasehold Covenants

A covenant, in general usage, is a solemn promise; in its strict and somewhat antique meaning, it is a contract made under seal. It can also mean a particular contractual stipulation in such a contract, i.e. one of the terms or clauses of the contract under seal. It is in the latter sense that the law of landlord and tenant is primarily concerned with covenants. A lease is a contract between a landlord and a tenant, generally made under seal[1] or expressed to be executed as a deed[2]; and a leasehold covenant is therefore one of the contractual obligations of that lease to be observed or performed by either the landlord or the tenant. Although it is strictly incorrect to speak of a covenant of a lease made orally or under hand, or indeed of a covenant of an agreement for lease for more than three years, terms of such leases and equitable leases are regularly spoken of as "covenants"; and, as will be seen, the Landlord and Tenant (Covenants) Act 1995 honours this wider, if inexact, usage. An obligation of a lease on the part of the landlord may conveniently be called a "landlord covenant", and "tenant covenant" bears a corresponding meaning. **1.01**

A covenant may be either express or implied. An express covenant is one made, in the form of an agreement, by an express stipulation in the lease. An implied covenant may be either implicit from the words of the lease,[3] or implicit in that it arises as a matter of law from the mere fact that **1.02**

[1] Though a seal is not now required for the execution of a lease by an individual or by a corporation; the deed must make it clear on its face that it is intended to be a deed and must be signed and delivered as a deed: Law of Property (Miscellaneous Provisions) Act 1989, s.1(1)(b), (2), (2A), (3), below, p.406; Companies Act 1985, ss.36A(3), (4), 36AA, below, pp.395–96; Law of Property Act 1925, s.74A(1), below, p.360, as amended respectively by the Regulatory Reform (Execution of Deeds and Documents) Order 2005 (SI 2005/1906). Moreover, leases taking effect in possession for terms not exceeding three years, reserving the best rent which can reasonably be obtained without taking a fine, may be made orally or under hand.

[2] Law of Property (Miscellaneous Provisions) Act 1989, s.1(2); Companies Act 1985, s.36A(4); Law of Property Act 1925, s.74A(1).

[3] In the sense in which a term may be implied into any contract as being necessary for the proper commercial working of the contract or as representing the clear but unspoken intention of the parties, or both.

the contract in question is one of lease,[4] or implied by statute in the case of a lease of a particular kind.[5]

1.03 The particular significance of landlord and tenant covenants lies in the fact that a lease creates not just a contract between the lessor and the lessee, but also an estate in land,[6] which has an existence and significance going beyond the bargain of the original parties to the lease. The legal estate in land may have a duration of hundreds of years, and therefore will exceed the lifespan of any individual lessor or lessee, as well as that of most corporations. When divested from the original lessor and original lessee, the term of years and the reversionary estate do not continue to exist denuded of all the terms of the original contract; most, if not all, of the landlord and tenant covenants of any given lease are so inherently part of the estate in land that they are said to be "incidents" of the estate, or "imprinted" upon it.[7] Shortly after the time of the Grantees of Reversions Act 1540, it was recognised that the assignee of a lease was bound by those tenant covenants which touched and concerned the land[8]; and a succession of statutes[9] passed to an assignee of the reversion the benefit of those tenant covenants and the burden of those landlord covenants which touched and concerned the land. Successors in title of the lessor and the lessee therefore stand in the shoes of the original contracting parties, and are bound by most of the terms of their agreement.

1.04 Having assigned the lease or the reversion, as the case may be, the lessee or lessor has not washed his hands of the matter, because his original contract with the other party remains and binds him. From the moment of the assignment, therefore, the leasehold covenants have taken on a double significance, both as incidents of the lease or reversion in the hands of the new tenant or landlord, and as a contract binding the original lessor and lessee. Questions then arise as to the respective rights and liabilities of the original parties and their assigns, who are both apparently liable under the same obligations. These questions relate both to the relationship between the assignee and the other party to the lease and to the relationship between the assignor and the assignee.

1.05 Further complications arise when new property interests are created out of the estates of either the landlord or the tenant. If the landlord

[4] e.g. the landlord's implied covenant not to derogate from his grant, and the tenant's implied (if not expressed) obligation to yield up the premises at the expiry of the term.

[5] e.g. the repairing covenants on the part of the landlord which are implied in short leases of dwelling-houses by Landlord and Tenant Act 1985, s.11.

[6] Which will be a legal estate if the necessary formalities for its creation are observed: see Law of Property Act 1925, ss.1(1)(b), 52–54.

[7] See *City of London Corp v Fell* [1993] Q.B. 589, *per* Nourse L.J., [1994] 1 A.C. 458, *per* Lord Templeman.

[8] *Spencer's Case* (1583) 5 Co. Rep. 16a.

[9] The Grantees of Reversions Act 1540; the Conveyancing Act 1881; the Conveyancing Act 1911; and the Law of Property Act 1925.

grants a reversionary lease of the same premises demised to the tenant, or a concurrent lease of his reversion, or even a mortgage, the question arises: who is entitled to the benefit of the tenant covenants of the lease, and who is bound to comply with the landlord covenants? If the tenant grants a sub-tenancy of all or part of the premises demised by the lease, or mortgages them, the questions arise: can the landlord compel the sub-tenant or mortgagee to abide by the terms of the lease, and can the sub-tenant or mortgagee of the tenant hold the landlord to his obligations in the lease? At this stage, enforceability of the leasehold covenants ceases to be a matter only of privity of contract or privity of estate, and becomes tied up with the enforceability in equity of covenants restrictive of the user of land.[10]

The complications that arise where a number of successive assignments of reversion and term have taken place, and where intermediate or subsidiary interests in land have been created in the meantime, can be extreme.[11] The law which applied prior to January 1, 1996 had, by and large, worked out from the basis of the 1925 property legislation answers to most of the problems which arise in practice.[12] In some respects, however, this collection of answers was thought to be unsatisfactory. In particular, the continuing contractual liability of the original lessee on the tenant covenants of the lease had become politically unacceptable in the climate of economic decline and corporate and personal insolvency of the early 1990s. This saw many assignees of leases go to the wall and so become unable to pay the rent under their tenancies. **1.06**

Accordingly, on January 1, 1996, the Landlord and Tenant (Covenants) Act 1995 was brought into force. This far-reaching piece of legislative reform introduced a new system regulating the continuance and enforceability of obligations under leasehold covenants, and other associated matters. It applies in the main only to leases granted after January 1, 1996, though some important new provisions apply to both existing and new leases. For many years to come, the courts will still be concerned with two different legal codes governing the liabilities of landlords and tenants under leasehold covenants; and the identification of which system applies to any given lease is therefore of primary importance. The next chapter is concerned with this issue. **1.07**

Both the old and the new systems for the transmission and enforceability of leasehold covenants have been affected by the Human Rights Act 1998, which came into force on October 2, 2000. Under that Act, legislation must be given effect, so far as it is possible to do so, in a way **1.08**

[10] Under the principle in *Tulk v Moxhay* (1848) 41 E.R. 1143.

[11] For one modest example, see *Selous Street Properties Ltd v Oronel Fabrics Ltd* [1984] 1 E.G.L.R. 50.

[12] Although it is true to say that a number of important cases were only decided in the 1980s and 1990s.

which is compatible with Convention rights.[13] The rights most likely to be engaged in a property law context are the right to respect for private and family life, freedom from discrimination and protection of property.[14] This is a new canon of construction and is a strong adjuration, which may involve adopting a meaning other than the natural and ordinary meaning of the words of a statute.[15] The court must first see whether, on the ordinary construction of the words, the provision is compatible with Convention rights; if not, the court must see whether it is possible, legitimately, to construe the words in such a way as to achieve compatibility. It may be proper to adopt even a strained construction to achieve that purpose, but the court cannot go so far as to distort familiar language or to change the identity of the provision.[16] If it is not possible to achieve compatibility, the court may make a declaration of incompatibility.[17] As has already been demonstrated, the drive for compatibility can now lead the court to depart from long-established meanings of familiar property statutes.[18] But this provision of the Human Rights Act does not have retrospective effect to alter rights and obligations created before October 2, 2000[19] and so in many cases the legislation in question will continue to be construed without regard to the requirement of compatibility.

[13] Human Rights Act 1998, s.3(1).

[14] Convention, arts 8 and 14, and art.1 of the First Protocol.

[15] *R. v D.P.P., Ex p. Kebiline* [2000] 2 A.C. 326, *per* Lord Cooke of Thorndon.

[16] *Clarke v Kato* [1998] 1 W.L.R. 1647, *per* Lord Clyde.

[17] Under Human Rights Act 1998, s.4(2).

[18] *PW & Co v Milton Gate Investments Ltd* [2004] Ch. 142; see below, para.4.06.

[19] *Wilson v First County Trust Ltd (No.2)* [2004] 1 A.C. 816.

CHAPTER 2

Old and New Tenancies

The Landlord and Tenant (Covenants) Act 1995 (hereafter referred to as "the Covenants Act"), which came into force on January 1, 1996, created two classes of tenancy for the purposes of the law concerning the enforceability of the terms of a tenancy as between original parties to the tenancy and/or their successors in title. The first class is all those tenancies which were granted before January 1, 1996 ("old tenancies"); the second class is all those tenancies which were or will be granted on or after that date ("new tenancies"). There are exceptions to this general classification.[1] **2.01**

The question of when a tenancy was granted is therefore of paramount importance for the enforceability of obligations of the parties to the lease and their successors in title. Although the Covenants Act thus classifies tenancies according to when they are "granted",[2] it contains no definition of what amounts to a grant for this purpose. Accordingly, the question falls to be determined by the general law. A tenancy is granted when the lease or tenancy agreement creating the term of years is (in the case of a deed) signed and delivered by both parties[3] or (in the case of a written tenancy agreement for a term of three years or less not purporting to be a deed) signed by both parties. A tenancy for a term of three years or less granted in possession at the best rent which could reasonably be obtained without the taking of a fine can be granted orally,[4] and in such a case the tenancy is "granted" when a binding oral agreement intended to grant exclusive possession of premises for a term is concluded. The requirement for a deed to be delivered means that the tenancy will not be granted until both parties have delivered their respective parts, though in the case of **2.02**

[1] See below, paras 2.09 *et seq*.

[2] Covenants Act, s.1(2).

[3] In the case of an individual, creation of a deed is governed by Law of Property (Miscellaneous Provisions) Act 1989, s.1; in the case of a limited company, by a combination of that section, Law of Property Act 1925, ss.74, 74A and Companies Act 1985, ss.36A, 36AA. As amended (and inserted) by the Regulatory Reform (Execution of Deeds and Documents) Order 2005 (SI 2005/1906), these provisions enable a deed to be executed under hand but reaffirm the common law requirement for a deed to be delivered: see also *Bolton M.B.C. v Torkington* [2004] Ch. 66.

[4] Law of Property Act 1925, s.54(2).

execution by a limited company there is a rebuttable presumption of delivery at the time of execution.[5]

2.03 In the Covenants Act, "tenancy" means any lease or other tenancy, and includes "an agreement for a tenancy".[6] A contract for a tenancy is an equitable lease provided that the agreement is specifically enforceable in equity.[7] For the purposes of the Covenants Act, such an equitable lease will therefore be "granted" when the agreement is made or, if later,[8] when the agreement becomes specifically enforceable. If the agreement for a lease is subsequently superseded by a legal lease, the legal lease will be "granted" within the meaning of the Covenants Act when it is signed and delivered.[9] In each of these cases, the time identified would be the date of the grant, notwithstanding that the term of the tenancy so granted did not commence until a later date.

2.04 Sometimes a tenancy is not created by any express agreement of the parties but by implication of law arising from the payment of a periodic rent as consideration for the exclusive possession of property.[10] Such a tenancy would be taken, for the purposes of the Covenants Act, to have been granted at the time when the implication of grant arises as a matter of law.

2.05 Where the reversion out of which the lease is granted is registered land or the premises are subject to compulsory registration, the time at which the lease is granted will depend on the length of the term of the lease. Where the term exceeds seven years,[11] the grant of the lease is completed by registration in the same way as for a transfer of the reversionary title,[12] and therefore the legal lease is not "granted" for the purposes of the

[5] Companies Act 1985, s.36AA(2); the same presumption applies in the case of any corporation aggregate by virtue of Law of Property Act 1925, s.74A(2).

[6] Covenants Act, s.28(1).

[7] *Walsh v Lonsdale* (1882) 21 Ch.D. 9; "agreement for a tenancy" in Covenants Act, s.28(1) must connote a specifically enforceable agreement within this principle.

[8] e.g. under the law applying to agreements made before September 27, 1989, when a sufficient memorandum or note of the agreement is signed by the party to be charged, or when there is part performance of the agreement: Law of Property Act 1925, s.40(1), (2), now repealed.

[9] If this date is on or after January 1, 1996 but the agreement creating the equitable lease was made before that date, exception (a) (see below, para.2.10) will apply, and the lease will create an old tenancy and not a new tenancy.

[10] The creation of such a tenancy is now less readily inferred that was once the case: see *Javad v Mohammed Aqil* [1991] 1 W.L.R. 1007.

[11] Or if the tenancy falls within any of the other categories specified in Land Registration Act 2002, s.27(2), of which the term taking effect in possession more than 3 months after the date of the grant will be the only common example.

[12] Land Registration Act 2002, ss.12(1)–(4), 27(1), (2), 29(1), Sch.2, para.3. The same applied in the case of leases exceeding 21 years under the Land Registration Act 1925. The Act of 2002 came into force on October 13, 2003.

Covenants Act until the date from which registration takes effect.[13] But a lease for seven years or less is not required to be registered or noted on the register of the reversionary title, and takes effect as if it were a registered disposition immediately on being granted.[14] Where the reversionary title is not registered but the land is in a compulsory registration area, a lease for more than seven years[15] must be registered, and is void so far as regards the creation of a legal estate unless registered within two months from the date of the grant,[16] or within such extended time as the Registrar may allow on application to him.[17]

1. Old tenancies

Tenancies granted before January 1, 1996 are unaffected by most of the provisions of the Covenants Act. Enforceability of obligations in such tenancies, as between the original parties and/or their successors in title, continues to be governed by the common law principles of privity of contract and privity of estate, and by the statutory provisions of ss.78, 79, 141 and 142 of the Law of Property Act 1925. So, for example, the liability of the original tenant under the covenants of the tenancy continues for the duration of the term, notwithstanding his assignment of the tenancy; and obligations that "touch and concern" such tenancies are enforceable by and against successors in title of the original parties, but those that do not are not so enforceable. These familiar principles have applied as a body unchanged since 1926, and in some cases from a much earlier time, but they were frequently the subject of High Court and county court litigation during the recessionary years of the early 1990s. This was the result of the prevalence of corporate and individual insolvency at that time, resulting in guarantors and former tenants being pursued by the landlord for rent arrears, etc., in some cases many years **2.06**

[13] The unregistered lease will, however, be an agreement for a tenancy within the meaning of Covenants Act, s.28(1): see below, para.2.09. As such it is itself a tenancy, and must have been granted when it was executed or signed. Later registration should not affect the category of tenancy for the purposes of the Covenants Act.

[14] Land Registration Act 2002, s.29(4).

[15] Or falling within the the other 4 categories specified: see n.10, above.

[16] Land Registration Act 2002, s.6(1),(4). In such a case, after the two months have expired without registration having been applied for, even if not before, it could not be said that a legal lease was granted; though the lease would still be effective as an enforceable agreement for a tenancy: *ibid.*, s.7(2). But if the lease is duly registered, it is not clear whether it was "granted" when executed (when the equitable lease was created) or when subsequently registered. The better view is probably that the lease was granted when executed.

[17] *ibid.*, s.6(5).

after the former tenant had assigned the lease and ceased to have any real connection with the demised premises. Such issues continue to be litigated notwithstanding the advent of the Covenants Act.

2. New tenancies

2.07 Tenancies granted on or after January 1, 1996 are governed by the new statutory code for enforceability of landlord and tenant covenants contained in ss.3 to 16 of the Covenants Act. These sections provide for the termination of the contractual liability of original lessees and lessors after the assignment of their interests, and for all landlord and tenant covenants other than those expressed (in whatever terms) to be personal to be binding on and enforceable by successors in title of the original parties. The common law principles of privity of contract and privity of estate are therefore overridden, and ss.78, 79, 141 and 142 of the Law of Property Act 1925 have no application to new tenancies.

2.08 In some circumstances, a landlord and a tenant who purport to vary the terms of their tenancy bring about, as a matter of law, a surrender of the existing tenancy and the re-grant of a second tenancy. Whether or not the purported variation amounts to a surrender and re-grant is usually a question of what the parties intended to achieve, such intention to be ascertained on well-established principles by construing the document or words that they have used.[18] But in two cases, the purported variation will effect a surrender and re-grant regardless of the intentions of the parties. These are: (1) where the parties purport to include more land within the same demise, and (2) where the parties purport to extend the length of the term granted. In each case, the purported variation is so fundamental that, as a matter of law, the desired result cannot be achieved without there being implied the grant of a new tenancy.[19] In such cases, and in other cases where as a matter of construction the parties intend to grant a second tenancy, the existing tenancy is surrendered by operation of law in view of the grant of the second tenancy. The question then arises: if the second tenancy came into existence on or after January 1, 1996, is it a new tenancy for the purposes of the Covenants Act? The answer is that such a tenancy is treated in the same way as a tenancy expressly granted after January 1, 1996[20]; i.e. it will be a new tenancy unless the grant of the second tenancy falls within any of the exceptions discussed below.

[18] *Friends Provident Life Office v British Railways Board* [1996] 1 All E.R. 336.

[19] *ibid.*, *The Trustees of JW Childers Will Trust v Anker* [1996] 1 E.G.L.R. 1.

[20] Covenants Act, s.1(5).

3. Exceptions

2.09 There are five exceptions to the classification of new tenancies and old tenancies set out in sections 1 and 2 above.

(a) *Agreements made before January 1, 1996*

2.10 If a tenancy is granted on or after January 1, 1996 in pursuance of an agreement entered into before that date, the tenancy is treated for the purposes of the Covenants Act as an old tenancy and not as a new tenancy.[21] The words "an agreement entered into" must be taken to denote a legally binding agreement.[22] For leases other than leases for three years or less, such a binding agreement (unless made before September 27, 1989) must be in writing and be signed[23] by both parties or on their behalf.[24] Where a legally binding agreement to vary an old tenancy by extending the length of the term or by adding to the premises demised is entered into before January 1, 1996, and the variation is effected pursuant to that agreement on or after January 1, 1996, the second tenancy which is deemed as a matter of law to have been granted[25] is not a new tenancy for the purposes of the Covenants Act.[26] But if the agreement so to vary an old tenancy is made on or after January 1, 1996, the re-granted tenancy which comes into existence subsequently is a new tenancy for the purposes of the Covenants Act.

(b) *Order of a Court made before January 1, 1996*

2.11 If a tenancy is granted on or after January 1, 1996 in pursuance of an order of a court made before that date, the tenancy is treated for the purposes of the Covenants Act as an old tenancy and not as a new tenancy.[27]

[21] *ibid.*, s.1(3)(a).

[22] Were it otherwise, the grant of the tenancy could only truly be said to be in pursuance of the will of both parties on the day of the grant on or after January 1, 1996 (and not in pursuance of the prior non-binding agreement), for either party was legally at liberty to withdraw from the proposed tenancy up to the moment of grant.

[23] See *Firstpost Homes Ltd v Johnson* [1995] 1 W.L.R. 1567.

[24] Law of Property (Miscellaneous Provisions) Act 1989, s.2. Note that an exchange of correspondence signed by both parties will apparently not suffice: *Commission for the New Towns v Cooper (Great Britain) Ltd* [1995] Ch. 259; *McCausland v Duncan Lawrie Ltd* [1997] 1 W.L.R. 38. In the case of an agreement for a lease for more than three years made before September 27, 1989, the agreement to be legally binding must have been evidenced by a signed written memorandum for the purposes of Law of Property Act 1925, s.40, or be supported by part performance.

[25] See above, para.2.08.

[26] Covenants Act, s.1(3)(a), (5).

[27] Covenants Act, s.1(3)(b).

2.12 The usual circumstances in which such a court order will have been made are an application made by a business tenant for a new tenancy under s.24 of the Landlord and Tenant Act 1954. In principle, and subject to anything agreed to the contrary by the parties, the term of the new tenancy so ordered will commence three months and three weeks after the date of the order,[28] but the new lease is often executed some weeks after the court order.[29] Also, the county courts have jurisdiction under the Rent (Agriculture) Act 1976, the Rent Act 1977, the Housing Act 1985 and the Housing Act 1988 to order the grant of a tenancy of suitable alternative accommodation as a condition of making a possession order of a dwelling-house. In principle, such a tenancy granted on or after January 1, 1996 would be a "new" tenancy, unless the court order were made before that date.

2.13 A court may also order the grant of a tenancy in proceedings for specific performance of an agreement for such a grant, but in such cases, if the order is made before January 1, 1996, the enforceable agreement for the tenancy must *ex hypothesi* have been entered into before the order, and so the case falls within exception (a) above. Even if the court order is made after January 1, 1996, if the agreement being specifically enforced was made before that date the tenancy will be an old tenancy because exception (a) applies. Other cases in which a tenancy may be granted in pursuance of an order of a court are a lease granted to a sub-tenant or mortgagee by way of relief against forfeiture pursuant to the Law of Property Act 1925, s.146(4), and a lease granted to satisfy the equity in one party to an action under the doctrine of proprietary estoppel.[30]

(c) *Tenancy granted in pursuance of prior option*

2.14 If a tenancy is granted on or after January 1, 1996 in pursuance of an option granted before that date, the tenancy is treated as falling within exception (a) above, i.e. as having been granted pursuant to an agreement made before January 1, 1996, and accordingly it is not a new tenancy.[31]

[28] Landlord and Tenant Act 1954, ss.36(1), 64; Civil Procedure Rules 1998, r.52.4(2).

[29] The tenant has a statutory right within 14 days of the court order to decline to take the renewal tenancy: Landlord and Tenant Act 1954, s.36(2).

[30] In both these cases, a lease will generally be made pursuant to the court order, and so a lease made on or after January 1, 1996 in pursuance of an order made before that date will create an old tenancy. *Quaere* whether the same result would follow where the Companies or Bankruptcy Court orders the vesting of a disclaimed lease pursuant to Insolvency Act 1986, ss.181(3), 320(3): in such cases it may be that no tenancy is "granted" in pursuance of the order within the meaning of Covenants Act, s.1(3)(b).

[31] This deeming provision was evidently considered necessary in view of the jurisprudential debate as to whether an option is in substance a conditional contract: see *Spiro v Glencrown Properties Ltd* [1991] Ch. 537, *per* Hoffmann J.

This is so whether or not the option was exercised before January 1, 1996.[32] The words "in pursuance of an option granted" must denote: (i) an effectual conferring on the original grantee of a legal right to exercise the option against the original grantor, and (ii) that at the time of exercise of the option it was enforceable as between the option holder and the person against whom it is sought to be exercised.[33] The date of grant of the option is the date when the legal right vested in the original grantee, not the date when any contingency for its exercise was satisfied. The statutory provision does not distinguish between different types of option, and so a put option such as a lessor's right to require a surety to take up a new lease upon a disclaimer, would fall within it.[34]

(d) *Rights of first refusal*

For the purposes of the Covenants Act, "option" is deemed to include a right of first refusal. Thus, a tenancy granted on or after January 1, 1996 in pursuance of a right of first refusal granted before that date, is treated as a tenancy granted pursuant to an agreement entered into before that date. It is accordingly not a new tenancy for the purposes of the Act. **2.15**

But the Act does not specify when a right of first refusal is to be treated as being granted. By analogy with an option, one would expect the date of grant for the purposes of the Act to be the date when the original right was conferred, i.e. when the agreement conferring the right on the original grantee was made. On the other hand, a right of first refusal, unlike an option, confers no immediate right on the grantee[35]; the right to call for the subject matter of the grant depends entirely on a decision of the grantor (which may never be made) to sell. Nevertheless, it is suggested that, in view of the drafting of subss.(6) and (7) of s.1 of the Act, the analogy with contingent options should prevail. So, where (for example) (i) an agreement for a right of first refusal on a lease of certain premises is made in December 1995; (ii) the decision to grant the lease is notified by the grantor in December 1996 and the grantee elects to take it,

[32] Covenants Act, s.1(6).

[33] If it were otherwise, the tenancy could only truly be said to have been granted in pursuance of the wills of both parties on or after January 1, 1996, as the party against whom the option is purportedly exercised could otherwise have declined to perform in accordance with its terms.

[34] See *Swallow Hotels Ltd v I.R.C.* [1999] E.G.C.S. 151, where no distinction was drawn between call and put options in relation to the expression "executed in pursuance of a contract made on or before 2nd July 1997" in Finance (No.2) Act 1997, s.49(6).

[35] And is therefore incapable of substantive registration under the Land Charges Act 1972: see *Pritchard v Briggs* [1980] Ch. 338; *Bircham & Co Nominees (No.2) Ltd v Worrell Holdings Ltd* [2001] 3 E.G.L.R. 83. The position has now changed under the Land Registration Act 2002 for rights of pre-emption created in relation to registered land on or after October 13, 2003: *ibid.*, s.115.

and (iii) the lease is executed in February 1997, the lease is not a "new lease" for the purposes of the Act because the agreement conferring the right was made before January 1, 1996.

(e) *Overriding leases*

2.16 Overriding leases, granted pursuant to s.19 of the Covenants Act to a former tenant or guarantor who has been called upon to discharge liabilities of the current tenant of premises,[36] always follow the class of the tenancy which they override. Thus, an overriding lease granted after January 1, 1996 will only be a new tenancy for the purposes of the Covenants Act if the tenancy under which the existing tenant has defaulted is a new tenancy.[37]

[36] See below, Ch.22.
[37] Covenants Act, s.20(1).

PART II

Old Tenancies

Introduction

As will already be evident, the law relating to enforceability of landlord and tenant covenants as it existed prior to January 1, 1996, both as between the original parties to the tenancy and as between their successors in title, will continue to apply to numerous tenancies for a number of years. Large numbers of residential tenancies were granted before that date under long leases for terms of 99 or 125 or even 999 years, and the main provisions of the Covenants Act providing for the release of the original tenant's contractual liability will never apply to these tenancies.[1] Even commercial leases of an institutional type were generally granted for terms of 20 or 25 years, and there will therefore be tens of thousands of such leases still in existence.

The existing law applying to old tenancies will consequently continue to be of considerable importance; indeed, many cases in this field have been litigated and a good number reported since the Covenants Act came into force. It can reasonably be expected that tenants and guarantors under old tenancies will continue to pursue innovative and technical arguments in an attempt to escape from the wretched consequences of the bargain that they made many years previously.

This Part of the text attempts to set out in some detail the "old" law, namely the law of enforceability of leasehold covenants which applies to all tenancies in existence before January 1, 1996, and which, as stated, will continue to apply to them. Those provisions of the Covenants Act which apply to old tenancies as from January 1, 1996 are discussed in Part IV of the text.[2]

[1] Unless the law is further changed in this regard. Some important provisions of the Act apply to old tenancies as from January 1, 1996, however: see Part IV, below.

[2] Below, pp.213 *et seq.*

CHAPTER 3

Privity of Contract

A lease (or a tenancy agreement, written or oral) is a contract made between the lessor and the lessee. A lease for more than three years is required to be made by deed,[1] and so where executed under seal no other consideration is technically required to support the bargain.[2] Nevertheless, the demise by the lessor is generally expressed to be made in consideration of the covenants made by the lessee; conversely, the lessee's covenants are self-evidently made in consideration of the demise by the lessor and of any covenants expressly made by him. Where a surety for the lessee is also a party to the lease, the lease usually solemnly recites that the demise by the lessor is made at the request of the surety, even if the lessor executes the lease under seal and thereby supplies consideration for the promise of the surety. These formalities underscore the contractual foundations of a lease of land,[3] a matter of some considerable importance in the genesis of the Covenants Act. **3.01**

1. Privity of contract

While the original lessor and original lessee remain landlord and tenant respectively under the tenancy, the obligations in the lease are enforceable between them as a matter of privity of contract, and not merely as incidents of the estate in land created by the lease. For so long as the lease remains in existence, all its terms (unless void or illegal or liable to rectification) are enforceable as a matter of contract between those original parties, irrespective of whether a given covenant touches and **3.02**

[1] Law of Property Act 1925, ss.52(1), 54(2).

[2] A seal is no longer required for execution of a deed by an individual or by a limited company: Law of Property (Miscellaneous Provisions) Act 1989, s.1(1); Companies Act 1985, s.36A(4).

[3] The technicalities of the ancient law of landlord and tenant have recently been deprecated by the Courts in favour of a simpler, contract-based analysis of rights and obligations arising from a lease: see, for example, *Hussein v Mehlman* [1992] 2 E.G.L.R. 287, *Eller v Grovecrest Investments Ltd* [1994] 4 All E.R. 845 (on distress) and *Escalus Properties Ltd v Robinson* [1996] Q.B. 231. There are, however, limits to this approach: *per* Neuberger L.J. in *Edlington Properties Ltd v J.H. Fenner & Co Ltd* [2006] 1 W.L.R. 1583, para.46.

concerns the subject matter of the lease or is expressed to be personal to one of the parties. Similarly, the obligations and rights of "third parties" to the lease such as guarantors and management companies will be fully enforceable as a matter of the law of contract.[4]

So, where a lessee assigns to another the legal estate in land that the lease created, the lessee is divested of his legal estate, but his contractual liability to the lessor is not affected[5] unless the lessor and the lessee either have agreed in the lease that it should be,[6] or so agree upon the assignment. As from the assignment, the lessee's liability to pay the rents and observe the covenants is as direct and primary[7] as it was before the assignment, for it is a matter of pure contract between the lessee and the lessor.[8] The contract does not become one of guarantee of the obligations of the assignee.[9] The lessor is therefore quite entitled to pursue the lessee for rent due, or for performance of the covenants in the lease, without first pursuing the assignee or any guarantor for the assignee.[10] Subject to the law of limitation of actions,[11] an original lessee cannot complain that a landlord has delayed in suing him for rent and contractual interest,[12] though if interest is claimed pursuant to statute on a judgment, the Court can and in an appropriate case does refuse to award it, or awards it at a

[4] For further consideration of such third party covenants, see Ch.10, below.

[5] "... not one jot or tittle": *per* Walton J. in *Allied London Investments Ltd v Hambro Life Assurance Ltd (No.2)* [1984] 1 E.G.L.R. 62, 63E.

[6] A relatively rare occurrence. Even when both landlord and original tenant are bound by a voluntary arrangement of the current tenant's debts under Pt I of the Insolvency Act 1986, the landlord's right to sue the original tenant is not generally affected thereby: *March Estates Plc v Gunmark Ltd* [1996] 2 E.G.L.R. 38; *Johnson v Davies* [1999] Ch. 117.

[7] Vis-à-vis the landlord, though not as between assignor and assignee: see below, Ch.7, paras 7.01, 7.18ff.

[8] *Baynton v Morgan* (1888) 22 Q.B.D. 74. Not only does the lessee remain liable to the lessor, but his contractual liability is automatically transferred from the lessor to the lessor's assignee upon an assignment of the lessor's reversionary estate: see below, Ch.4, para.4.03.

[9] And so the original lessee cannot claim to be released by a variation of the terms of the contract in the same way that a surety might under the rule in *Holme v Brunskill* (1877) 3 Q.B.D. 495. But see below, Ch.21, for the effect of the new provisions of Covenants Act, s.18, which do apply to old tenancies.

[10] *Norwich Union Life Assurance Society v Low Profile Fashions Ltd* [1992] 1 E.G.L.R. 86.

[11] Which imposes a limitation period of six years in relation to a claim for rent or for damages in respect of arrears of rent, regardless of whether the lease is made under seal: Limitation Act 1980, s.19: *Romain v Scuba T.V. Ltd* [1997] Q.B. 887. "Rent" includes sums reserved as rent or recoverable as rent in arrear: *Escalus Properties Ltd v Robinson* [1996] Q.B. 231.

[12] *Allied London Investments Ltd v Hambro Life Assurance Ltd (No.2)* [1984] 1 E.G.L.R. 62 (a case where in fact no provision for contractual interest existed in the lease).

reduced rate, for periods of delay.[13] A landlord is under no duty of care to the tenant, nor is there to be implied into a lease a term for the lessor to take care, to ensure that, in granting consent to assign to a later assignee, that assignee is financially sound and able to pay the rent and perform the obligations under the tenancy.[14]

The lessor, if he assigns his reversionary estate, remains similarly liable on his contract with the lessee throughout the term of the lease, unless either there is express provision in the lease for his release upon assignment[15] or there is an actual release upon the assignment.[16]

The liabilities of the lessee and his assignee (and of the lessor and his assignee) are several, but not cumulative; and so the lessor is only entitled to full satisfaction against one and not both,[17] though he may have judgment against both and seek to execute those judgments against each of them. It follows that full payment by either the lessee or by his assignee discharges any liability of the other, but a release of the assignee does not automatically release the lessee.[18]

2. Extent of liability

The liability of the original lessee being in contract, the extent of his liability is determined by the terms of that contract.[19] So, where the lease provides for the rent payable under it to be reviewed from time to time, and the review is carried out according to the terms of the lease, the original lessee is liable for the increased rent, even though it was agreed without his consent by his assignee (or a subsequent assignee) and the lessor, or determined in proceedings between such parties not involving **3.03**

[13] Compare *Allied London Investments Ltd v Hambro Life Assurance Ltd*, above, with *Estates Gazette Ltd v Benjamin Restaurants Ltd* [1994] 1 W.L.R. 1528 at 1534C–F.

[14] *Norwich Union Life Assurance Society v Low Profile Fashions Ltd* [1992] 1 E.G.L.R. 86.

[15] Not such a rare occurrence: see, e.g. *London Diocesan Fund v Phithwa* [2005] 1 W.L.R. 3956.

[16] In *City and Metropolitan Properties Ltd v Greycroft* [1987] 1 W.L.R. 1085, a lessor who transferred the reversion remained liable for breaches of covenant existing at the date of the transfer. Law of Property Act 1925, s.142(1) does not have an effect similar to *ibid.*, s.141, which automatically transfers accrued rights to transferees of the reversion: see below, paras 4.19, 4.22.

[17] Or partly from one and partly from the other, but at no time can he recover more in total than the amount due under the lease.

[18] *Sun Life Assurance Society v Tantofex Engineers* [1999] L.&T.R. 568, distinguishing *Deanplan Ltd v Mahmoud* [1993] Ch. 151, which was a case on joint and several liability. A voluntary arrangement under the Insolvency Act 1986 is not a release, or an accord and satisfaction, for these purposes: *March Estates Plc v Gunmark Ltd* [1996] 2 E.G.L.R. 38; *Johnson v Davies* [1999] Ch. 117.

[19] i.e. by the terms of the lease itself, and including any variations of the original lease to which the original lessee has consented.

the original lessee.[20] But where an assignee of the term and the landlord agree outside the terms of the lease that additional rent will be payable, the original lessee is not liable for the excess because he did not agree to pay it.[21] In one case, an original lessee was held liable for the increased rent resulting from a rent review even where it was agreed between lessor and assignee of the term otherwise than in accordance with the strict letter of the rent review clause.[22] The *ratio* of that decision, made before the *Friends Provident*[23] case was decided by the Court of Appeal, should now be regarded as doubtful.[24] If the assignee of the term and the landlord have the rent reviewed on some basis other than that which the original lessee agreed, then prima facie the original lessee is not bound to pay it because he did not agree to pay a rent determined on that basis.[25]

Difficulties do arise from this result. First, is the onus on either the lessor or the original lessee to prove that any variation in the basis of the review did or did not affect the amount of the rent, and if so by how much? Or is the original lessee liable to pay only the previously passing rent, or even nothing at all for the review period in question?[26] Secondly, if the lessor cannot rely on the rent as reviewed, is the review machinery exhausted, or is the lessor entitled to have another review as between him

[20] *Centrovincial Estates Ltd v Bulk Storage Ltd* (1983) 46 P. & C.R. 393. This part of the decision is still good law notwithstanding the disapproval of some of the dicta of Harman J. by the Court of Appeal in *Friends Provident Life Office v British Railways Board* [1996] 1 All E.R. 336.

[21] *Friends Provident Life Office v British Railways Board*, above. This result would not obtain where a rent review clause entitled landlord and tenant to agree the new rent and agreement is reached.

[22] *Gus Property Management Ltd v Texas Homecare Ltd* [1993] 2 E.G.L.R. 93.

[23] Above.

[24] Although Beldam L.J., in the *Friends Provident* case, thought that the decision itself could be justified on other grounds.

[25] This view was expressed, *obiter*, by Millett L.J. in *Metropolitan Properties Co. (Regis) Ltd v Bartholomew* [1996] 1 E.G.L.R. 82. A much more difficult case is where the rent is reviewed in accordance with the provisions of the review clause by which the original lessee was bound, but the nature of the demised premises themselves have changed. If alterations have been carried out in accordance with the terms of the lease, then the original lessee should be bound because this was within the scope of the terms of the lease which he agreed and, by assigning the term, he placed the assignee in his shoes for the purpose of benefiting from those terms. (In reality, such alterations will generally be disregarded for the purposes of the rent review.) But where the alterations were carried out unlawfully, and are valued upon review, is the rent being reviewed on terms on which the original lessee did not contract, or is it merely the nature or characteristics of the demised premises which have altered? *Selous Street Properties Ltd v Oronel Fabrics Ltd* [1984] 1 E.G.L.R. 50 is a case where the original lessee was liable for the increased value, but *quaere* whether the result would be the same after *Friends Provident Life Office v British Railways Board*, above.

[26] It is submitted that in the case of a standard "upwards only" review clause, the original lessee is liable for the previously passing rent, at least.

and the original lessee on the terms which bind the original lessee? These difficulties are similar to those which might arise under the new provision of s.18 of the Covenants Act.[27]

The liability of the original lessee depending on the terms of his contract, he is only liable to pay rent and other sums due under the lease for the duration of the term granted and not for any statutory continuation of the term.[28] Of course, the original lessee may contract otherwise[29] and be liable for rent during any statutory continuation of the tenancy; but in the absence of express words, this will be construed as a liability for the rent last payable during the term, and not for any interim rent which the tenant might become liable to pay pursuant to ss.24A to 24D of the Landlord and Tenant Act 1954, as amended.[30]

3. Statutory exceptions

Where a lease is granted which contains a covenant or obligation for perpetual renewal of the term of the lease, it takes effect as a demise for 2,000 years (or, in the case of an underlease, as a demise for a term less in duration by one day than the term out of which it is granted) to commence from the date fixed for the commencement of the lease (or underlease) but free from any obligation for renewal.[31] In such a case, the lessee (or underlessee), notwithstanding any stipulation to the contrary, is liable only for rent accruing and for breaches of covenants or conditions occurring while he or his personal representatives have the term vested in him or them.[32] This exception does not apply to leases for lives or until marriage or the formation of a civil partnership, which are converted by **3.04**

[27] As to which, see below, Ch.21.

[28] Under Pt II of the Landlord and Tenant Act 1954: *City of London Corp v Fell* [1994] 1 A.C. 458. Similar results would follow in the case of a continuing tenancy under Pt I of that Act, a statutory tenancy succeeding a protected tenancy under the Rent Act 1977, and the deemed grant of a new periodic assured tenancy under Pt I of the Housing Act 1988.

[29] One commonly sees covenants to pay the rent during the term and any statutory continuation thereof.

[30] *Herbert Duncan v Cluttons* [1993] Q.B. 589. For a case where the wording of a surety's covenant extended to interim rent, see *Collin Estates Ltd v Buckley* [1992] 2 E.G.L.R. 78. The decisions in these cases will apply equally to the new provisions of the Act of 1954, as substituted by the Regulatory Reform (Business Tenancies) (England and Wales) Order 2003 (SI 2003/3096).

[31] Law of Property Act 1922, s.145, Sch.15, para.5.

[32] *ibid.*, para.11(1). An antique forebear of the Covenants Act, combining a distaste of prolonged contractual liability after assignment of a lease with a recognition of the need to protect the release of the original lessee by an anti-avoidance provision.

statute into leases for 90 years determinable after death or marriage or the formation of the partnership.[33]

4. Liability under negative covenants

3.05 The doctrine of privity of contract is readily applicable to positive covenants, such as covenants to pay rent and service charge or to keep premises in repair. Under such covenants, the original lessee has covenanted to do something, and if it has not been done by him or by some other in his place, and if he has not been released from his covenant, then he is by force of those facts in breach of his contractual obligation. In most modern leases, however, a sizeable percentage of contractual obligations undertaken by the lessee are negative in substance. Covenants "not to assign or sub-let without consent" and "not to alter or add to the demised premises without consent" are typical, if simplified, examples. These are covenants which touch and concern the demised premises, and so bind any assignee of the tenancy or part thereof under the doctrine of privity of estate. Accordingly, if the assignee of the tenancy sub-lets the premises and alters them without asking for the lessor's consent, he is in breach of obligations of the tenancy by which he is bound, and as such is liable in damages to the lessor for any loss suffered.

3.06 But is the original lessee also in breach of his contract? At first blush, the answer appears to be that he is not, for he has neither sub-let the premises nor altered them. The conventional view, however, is that he is in breach, because the effect of the covenants in the lease is that the original lessee warrants to the landlord that neither he nor his successors in title during the term will do any of the forbidden acts.[34] Now this is not how the contract that the original lessee made could conceivably be construed, and it is to the Law of Property Act 1925 that adherents of the conventional view turn for support. Section 79(1) of that Act provides:

> "A covenant relating to any land of a covenantor or capable of being bound by him, shall, unless a contrary intention is expressed, be deemed to be made by the covenantor on behalf of himself his successors in title and the persons deriving title under him or them, and, subject as aforesaid shall have effect as if such successors and other persons were expressed."

The pertinent question is whether the words "on behalf of himself, his successors in title . . . ", etc. mean that any covenant to which that

[33] Under Law of Property Act 1925, s.149(6), as amended by Civil Partnerships Act 2004, s.81, Sch.8, para.1.

[34] See, e.g. *Megarry and Wade's The Law of Real Property* (6th ed.), paras 16-037, 16-038.

subsection applies is to be construed as a covenant by the covenantor "that neither he, nor his successors in title . . . etc., will do [the forbidden act]". If these words were expressed in the covenant, they certainly would have the effect of making the original lessee the warrantor for his assigns; but it is at least doubtful whether the words of the subsection are synonymous with these.

Section 79(1) of the Law of Property Act 1925 applies not only to leasehold covenants, but also to freehold covenants, and therefore the effect of such a construction would be to make a covenantor and his estate liable in perpetuity for any breach of a freehold restrictive covenant by a successor in title, however remote. One requirement for the burden of a freehold covenant to be binding in equity on successors in title of the covenantor[35] is that the covenant must have been intended to run with particular land of the covenantor[36]; and it is this, it is submitted, that the subsection is drafted to achieve.[37] If this is correct, it is in line to some extent, though not fully, with the purpose of s.78(1) of the Law of Property Act.[38] Despite some conflicting dicta from the House of Lords in cases when this specific point was not decided,[39] the better view is that s.79(1) is merely a word-saving provision,[40] and was not intended to alter substantially the law as it then stood,[41] which did not have the effect of making a covenantor automatically liable for the defaults of his assigns.[42] **3.07**

It is therefore suggested that, in the case of negative covenants, an original lessee is not without more in breach of his contract with the lessor if an assignee of the original lessee breaks one of the obligations

[35] Under the principle in *Tulk v Moxhay* (1848) 2 Ph. 774; 41 E.R. 1143.

[36] *Crest Nicholson Residential (South) Ltd v McAllister* [2004] 1 W.L.R. 2409.

[37] For a freehold restrictive covenant actually to bind the covenantor's land in the hands of a successor in title, it will also normally have to have been protected by registration as a land charge under the Land Charges Act 1972 or as an interest affecting a registered estate under the Land Registration Act 2002, as the case may require. (A leasehold restrictive covenant is not registrable, save where it relates to registered land other than the demised premises, and liability will turn on the application of the doctrine of notice: see below, para.8.05.) But the question here is whether the covenant is *capable* of binding successors in title, and this is a different question from whether it actually does so.

[38] Though this section has been held to effect a full statutory annexation of the benefit of a covenant to the covenantee's land, subject to any express or implied contrary intention: *Federated Homes Ltd v Mill Lodge Properties Ltd* [1980] 1 W.L.R. 594; *Crest Nicholson Residential v McAllister*, above.

[39] See *Tophams Ltd v Earl of Sefton* [1967] 1 A.C. 50; *Rhone v Stephens* [1994] 1 A.C. 310.

[40] *Crest Nicholson Residential v McAllister*, above, and *Morrells of Oxford Ltd v Oxford United Football Club Ltd* [2001] Ch. 459.

[41] See *ibid.*

[42] *Hall v Ewin* (1887) 37 Ch.D. 74; *Powell v Hemsley* [1909] 1 Ch. 680, [1909] 2 Ch. 252.

attached to the tenancy.[43] The assignee is liable to have the covenant enforced against him, as a transferee of freehold land is liable to enforcement in equity (but not at law), if he is bound by its burden.[44]

5. Termination of original lessee's liability

3.08 This may be achieved by an express release under seal or for valuable consideration between the lessor (or assignee of the reversion) and the original lessee, or by the landlord releasing the tenant or any intermediate assignee of the tenancy who has given a direct covenant to the landlord in circumstances in which an intention to release the original lessee too can be inferred.[45] Otherwise, the original lessee's liability will terminate with the tenancy itself, and so if the landlord forfeits the lease or exercises a break clause or takes a surrender of the tenancy by deed, the original lessee's further liability will end at the time of termination.

A surrender by operation of law may be inferred where the landlord and the tenant do acts that are inconsistent with the continued existence of the tenancy, for example the tenant delivering and the landlord accepting from the tenant the deed of lease, the landlord accepting the keys to the premises with a view to retaking possession,[46] and the landlord granting a new lease of the premises in possession either to the tenant or with his knowledge and acquiescence. A re-taking of possession may suffice, but it is generally an equivocal act.[47] A surrender by operation of law and re-grant of a new lease will be inferred where the landlord and tenant purport to vary the existing lease by adding additional demised premises or substituting others, or by altering the term granted by the lease[48]; with other variations, the question is whether the landlord and the tenant intended by their variation to substitute a new lease.[49] A surrender of part of the demised premises only will not release the original lessee from his liability.[50]

[43] For a different analysis, see *Megarry and Wade's Law of Real Property* (6th ed. 2000), paras 15-008 and 15-009, though these do not address specifically the case of a negative covenant.

[44] See the *Morrells of Oxford* case, above.

[45] *Sun Life Assurance Society v Tantofex Engineers* [1999] L.&T.R. 568, distinguishing *Deanplan Ltd v Mahmoud* [1993] Ch. 151. As to the effect of direct covenants by assignees, see below, para.5.05.

[46] But the handing of the keys to the landlord does not automatically effect a surrender by operation of law; the question is *quo animo* the keys were taken: see *Proudreed Ltd v Microgen Holdings Plc* [1996] 1 E.G.L.R. 89.

[47] See *Relvok Properties Ltd v Dixon* (1972) 25 P. & C.R. 1, and *Oastler v Henderson* (1877) 2 Q.B.D. 575.

[48] *J. W. Childers Trustees v Anker* [1996] 1 E.G.L.R. 1; *Friends Provident Life Office v British Railways Board* [1996] 1 All E.R. 336.

[49] *ibid.*

[50] *Baynton v Morgan* (1882) 22 Q.B.D. 74.

If the liquidator of the tenant, or his trustee in bankruptcy, disclaims the tenant's interest in the demised premises, the original lessee's liability is not affected thereby.[51]

6. Effect of severance of term or reversion

An assignment of part of premises demised by a lease does not, as against the landlord, create two tenancies unless, perhaps, the landlord concurs in an apportionment of the rent or of the lessee's covenants.[52] The landlord is not bound by any apportionment of rent that the assignor and assignee agree between themselves,[53] and may sue the assignor on his contract to pay the whole of the rent. But if the assignor and the assignee have agreed an apportionment of the rent, there is implied in the conveyance a covenant by the assignee at all times after the conveyance to pay the apportioned rent and to observe and perform all the lessee's covenants so far as they relate to the part assigned[54]; and if the assignor has to pay rent which was apportioned to the part assigned, or any costs, damages, or expenses in respect of a breach of covenant relating to that part, the assignor has a statutory right to distrain on that part in order to recover the amount paid.[55] **3.09**

An assignment of the reversion on part of premises demised by a lease does not create two tenancies.[56] The assignor remains liable on all the covenants in the tenancy on the part of the lessor notwithstanding the assignment of part of the reversion. **3.10**

[51] *Warnford Investments Ltd v Duckworth* [1979] Ch. 127; *Hindcastle Ltd v Barbara Attenborough Associates Ltd* [1997] A.C. 70. For the effect of disclaimer, see below, Ch.9.

[52] *Lester v Ridd* [1990] 2 Q.B. 430.

[53] Law of Property Act 1925, s.190(3).

[54] *ibid.*, s.77(1)(D)(i), Sch.2, Pt X, para.(i).

[55] *ibid.*, s.190(4).

[56] *Jelley v Buckman* [1974] Q.B. 488.

CHAPTER 4

Liability as Between Original Lessee and Assignee of the Lessor's Reversion

When the original lessor transfers his reversionary estate, he does not rid himself of his contractual liability to the original lessee,[1] but he does divest himself of the estate in land out of which the lease was created. The transferee of the reversionary estate takes it subject to the leasehold estate either because the lease, if it is for more than seven years, will have been noted in the charges register of the lessor's registered title, or because, if it is for seven years or less, the lease will be an overriding interest in its own right.[2] (In unregistered conveyancing, the lease is a legal estate in land which binds all purchasers irrespective of notice or registration.) The transferee of the reversion cannot therefore claim to be entitled to vacant possession of the land. But neither is he prima facie entitled to the benefit of the original lessor's contract with the lessee[3] or bound by the burden of such contract (save insofar as he takes subject to the legal estate in land). He does stand in a relationship of privity of estate with the original lessee from the time of the transfer,[4] however, which, as will be seen, amounts to much the same thing. 4.01

1. Nature and origin of the doctrine of privity of estate

The doctrine of privity of estate essentially "imprints" the rights and obligations of the lease "on the term or the reversion, as the case may be, enforceable between the owners thereof for the time being as conditions of the enjoyment of their respective estates".[5] The nature of the doctrine 4.02

[1] See Ch.3, above.

[2] Under Land Registration Act 2002, s.29(2), Sch.3, para.1. If the lease is for more than seven years but is not noted on the lessor's registered title, it will still be capable of protection as an overriding interest under *ibid.*, para.2, if the lessee is in actual occupation.

[3] Subject to the effect of Contracts (Rights of Third Parties) Act 1999, s.1: see below, Ch.10.

[4] Strictly, from the date from which the transfer is registered at the Land Registry: *Brown & Root Technology Ltd v Sun Alliance and London Assurance Co Ltd* [1996] Ch. 51.

[5] *Per* Nourse L.J. in *City of London Corp v Fell* [1993] Q.B. 589, approved by Lord Templeman at [1994] 1 A.C. 458.

was first considered by the courts in 1583,[6] when the Court of King's Bench, by reference to the Grantees of Reversions Act 1540, held that leasehold covenants run with the land and thereby bind all assignees of the term who are privy to the estate in question, i.e. the term of years. As will be seen,[7] the rule in *Spencer's Case* applies only to those leasehold covenants which "touch and concern" the demised premises. Liability under the doctrine of privity of estate necessarily relates only to that period of time when the landlord or the tenant is the owner of the reversion or of the term, as the case may be; for upon a further assignment, the assignor's privity of estate disappears, and save in the cases of the original lessee and original lessor, there is no privity of contract on which a continuing liability can be founded.

It is notable that the case which "founded" the doctrine of privity of estate relied, by way of analogy, on the statutory provisions of the Grantees of Reversions Act 1540, under which the benefit and burden of leasehold covenants which touched and concerned the land ran with the reversion. At all times until January 1, 1996, there were statutory provisions governing the running of leasehold covenants with the reversion existing in parallel with the doctrine of privity of estate.[8] These statutory provisions were considered necessary because, although a covenant could run with a lease at common law, a reversion was not "land" for these purposes.[9] Liability between an assignee of the reversion and the lessee is still governed (in relation to old tenancies) by s.141 of the Law of Property Act 1925 and, in relation to the burden of the lessor's covenants, by s.142 of that Act.

2. The statutory provision: benefit

4.03 Rent reserved by a lease, and the benefit of every covenant or provision therein contained, having reference to the subject-matter thereof, and on the lessee's part to be observed or performed, and every condition of re-entry or other condition therein contained, shall be annexed and incident to and shall go with the reversionary estate in the land, or in any part thereof, immediately expectant on the term granted by the lease. This is so notwithstanding severance of that reversionary estate, and it is without prejudice to any liability affecting any covenantor or his estate.[10] Any such rent, covenant or provision shall be capable of being recovered, received, enforced, and taken advantage of, by the person from time to

[6] *Spencer's Case* (1583) 5 Co. Rep. 16a.

[7] Below, paras 4.09 *et seq.*

[8] After the Grantees of Reversions Act 1540, Conveyancing Act 1881, s.10, and Law of Property Act 1925, s.141.

[9] See *Megarry and Wade's Law of Real Property* (6th ed.), para.16-013.

[10] Law of Property Act 1925, s.141(1).

time entitled, subject to the term, to the income of the whole or any part, as the case may require, of the land leased.[11]

The statutory provision takes effect subject to any term to the contrary effect in the deed of transfer.[12]

3. Application of the statutory provision: benefit

(a) *"Lease"*

For the purposes of the statutory provision, "lease" includes leases made before as well as after January 1, 1926, and includes "an under-lease or other tenancy".[13] There is no reason, therefore, why the provision should not apply to leases validly made in writing or orally,[14] and even to agreements for lease capable of specific performance.[15] **4.04**

(b) *"On the lessee's part"*

The provision applies only to rent payable by the lessee and to covenants and provisions to be performed or observed by the lessee. It therefore does not apply to transfer to an assignee of the reversion the benefit of a covenant by a surety for the lessee, though the benefit of such a covenant may pass at common law.[16] **4.05**

(c) *"The reversionary estate"*

It is this estate with which the benefit of the lessee's covenants etc. goes, and it carries with it an entitlement at law to the income of the demised premises. As enacted, "the reversionary estate" is a reference to the estate out of which the lease was granted, not any estate that would (absent the lease) entitled its owner to possession from time to time. But it is possible, where necessary, to construe these words as including such estates, e.g. the estate of a superior landlord.[17] So where the termination of a headlease might have left the superior landlord unable to enforce the obligations of sub-tenants who remained in possession, the statutory provision would **4.06**

[11] *ibid.*, s.141(2).

[12] *I.R.C. v John Lewis Properties Plc* [2002] 1 W.L.R. 35.

[13] Law of Property Act 1925, s.154.

[14] i.e. leases not requiring to be made by deed by virtue of Law of Property Act 1925, s.54(2).

[15] See *Rickett v Green* [1910] 1 K.B. 253, and *Rye v Purcell* [1926] 1 K.B. 446, cases decided under Conveyancing Act 1881, s.10.

[16] See below, Ch.10.

[17] Such necessity arose under the Human Rights Act 1998, s.3, in *PW & Co v Milton Gate Investments Ltd* [2004] Ch. 142. The conclusion that the reversionary estate may include superior landlords' estates was contrary to all previous understanding of the statutory provision.

have been construed to as to preserve the right to income from the premises.[18] Where a superior estate is deemed to be the reversionary estate, e.g. upon a merger or surrender,[19] rent and the benefit of the tenant covenants pass to the owner of the superior estate; but this will not happen if the underlease terminates before the headlease is surrendered, for then there is no longer a reversion on the underlease.[20]

4.07 An assignment of the reversionary estate or part thereof must be made by deed,[21] unless it is effected by statute or statutory instrument or by operation of law. Thus, a beneficiary under trusts of the reversionary estate is not himself entitled to the benefit of the lessee's covenants by virtue of the provision[22]; but an equitable assignee of the reversion, who has given notice of the assignment to the tenant, is so entitled because he is entitled to the income as such.[23] The assignee does not need to have the whole of the reversionary estate vested in him; so, e.g. where a concurrent lease is granted by the lessor, which takes effect at law as an assignment of the reversionary estate for the duration of the concurrent lease, the concurrent lessee is seised of the reversionary estate and is entitled to the income for the purposes of the provision. Where part only of the reversionary estate is assigned by the lessor, the severance of that estate does not affect the operation of the provision, and the rents, conditions[24] and covenants will be annexed and incident to and go with the several parts. The operation of a severance of the reversionary estate made before January 1, 1926 is not affected by the provision.[25]

(d) *"therein contained"*

4.08 These words of the statutory provision include covenants which are implied into a lease as a matter of law,[26] but not covenants in collateral agreements, although the benefit of such covenants may pass with the land at common law.[27]

[18] *ibid.*, at paras 89 and 129–132. In the event, such a conclusion was not necessary because the sub-tenancies did not survive the termination of the headlease.

[19] Law of Property Act 1925, s.139(1).

[20] *Twogates Properties Ltd v Birmingham Midshires Building Society* (1997) 75 P.&C.R. 386.

[21] Law of Property Act 1925, s.52(1).

[22] *Schalit v Joseph Nadler Ltd* [1933] 2 K.B. 79.

[23] *Scribes West Ltd v Relsa Anstalt (No.3)* [2005] 1 W.L.R. 1847, distinguishing *Schalit v Nadler*, above.

[24] By virtue of Law of Property Act 1925, s.140(1).

[25] *ibid.*, s.141(4)(a).

[26] *Cole v Kelly* [1920] 2 K.B. 106, a decision on Conveyancing Act 1881, s.10(1).

[27] *P&A Swift Investments Ltd v Combined English Stores Ltd* [1989] A.C. 632.

4. The "touching and concerning" requirement

Not all the covenants and provisions contained in the lease and on the lessee's part to be observed or performed are annexed and incident to the reversionary estate by virtue of the statutory provision. Only those covenants and provisions which "have reference to the subject-matter of the lease" go with the reversionary estate. This is the same concept as, in older terminology, covenants that touch and concern the demised premises.[28] What these expressions denote is those covenants which affect "the landlord in his normal capacity as landlord or the tenant in his normal capacity as tenant",[29] and not those which have no real connection with the interest in land to which they are appended. Thus, purely personal or collateral covenants between the lessor and the lessee, which have no lasting significance for the continuing landlord and tenant relationship regardless of the identity of landlord or tenant, do not touch and concern the demised premises, and the benefit of them will not pass to an assignee of the reversion pursuant to the statutory provision. The law relating to covenants which do and do not have reference to the subject-matter of the lease has frequently been criticised as difficult to justify or accurately to summarise, or both.[30] But there is an established body of decisions which, however illogical some of the distinctions may seem, the courts do apply.[31] Fortunately, perhaps, the draftsmen of leases do not seem to have an inexhaustible supply of draft covenants the type or substance of which has not previously been considered by the courts, and so there is some measure of certainty. But occasionally new types of covenant arise,[32] or new arguments are taken,[33] or alternatively the point arises in a slightly different context,[34] and the courts have recourse to first principles in **4.09**

[28] See *Hua Chiao Commercial Bank Ltd v Chiaphua Industries Ltd* [1987] A.C. 99, *per* Lord Oliver at p.106.

[29] *ibid.*, n.107.

[30] See, e.g., the observations of Romer L.J. in *Grant v Edmondson* [1931] 1 Ch. 1 at 28.

[31] See, e.g., the observations of Browne-Wilkinson L.J. in *Kumar v Dunning* [1989] Q.B. 193 at p.205B, who declined to disregard the apparently anomalous decision in *Thomas v Hayward* (1869) L.R. 4 Ex. 311 (landlord's covenant not to allow other premises to be used for a business competing with the tenant's business, which was the only permitted business under the lease, held not to touch and concern the demised premises).

[32] See *Harbour Estates Ltd v HSBC Bank Plc* [2005] Ch. 194 (break clause expressed to be personal to tenant but assignable in some circumstances touched and concerned the premises).

[33] See *Caerns Motor Services Ltd v Texaco Ltd* [1994] 1 W.L.R. 1249.

[34] As, most recently, in the context of surety covenants: see *Kumar v Dunning*, above, n.31; *P & A Swift Investments Ltd v Combined English Stores Ltd*, above; *Coronation Street Industrial Properties Ltd v Ingall Industries Plc* [1989] 1 W.L.R. 304.

attempting to decide whether a given covenant "touches and concerns" or does not.

4.10 In 1808, Bayley J. attempted a definition of a covenant which touched and concerned the demised premises. He considered that the covenant "must either affect land as regards its mode of occupation, or it must be such as *per se*, and not merely from collateral circumstances, affects the value of the land".[35] This definition, which purports to lay down alternative ways in which the requirement could be satisfied, was followed and approved on several occasions subsequently.[36] In *P & A Swift Investments Ltd v Combined English Stores Group Ltd*,[37] Lord Oliver, having flirted with the concept of touching and concerning in a previous case,[38] attempted to lay down a "satisfactory working test". A covenant touches and concerns land so as to run with the reversion if the following three conditions are satisfied:

(1) the covenant benefits only the reversioner for the time being and, if separated from the reversion, ceases to be of benefit to the covenantee;
(2) the covenant affects the nature, quality, mode of use or value of the land of the reversioner;
(3) the covenant is not expressed to be personal (i.e. neither being given only to a specific reversioner nor in respect of the obligations only of a specific tenant).

A fourth principle was added: (4) the fact that a covenant is to pay a sum of money will not prevent it from touching and concerning the land so long as the other three conditions are satisfied and the covenant is connected with something to be done on, to or in relation to the land.

4.11 It is respectfully considered that this working test is of no greater clarity or assistance in pinning down the principle underlying touching and concerning than any of the earlier tests. The first principle of Lord Oliver's test, if it depends to any extent on the words "for the time being", falls into the trap of circularity which he had previously identified,[39] for a covenant benefits only the reversioner for the time being if it does at law run with the reversion. Apart from those words, the principle identifies only a covenant which relates to one person's land and which would not be of value to him were he not the owner of that land. But a covenant regulating the user of the demised premises, or to pay a sum of money in relation to the premises, which do both touch and concern the land, could

[35] *Congleton Corp v Pattison* (1808) 10 East 130 at 138.
[36] e.g. by the Court of Appeal in *Kumar v Dunning*, above, n.31.
[37] Above, n.27.
[38] *Hua Chiao Commercial Bank Ltd v Chiaphua Industries Ltd*, above, n.28.
[39] In the *Hua Chiao* case, above, n.28.

easily be of benefit to a non-reversioner. The third condition is too wide, in the sense that a tenant's covenant which is expressed to be personal to the particular lessee can nevertheless touch and concern the land and be enforceable by an assignee of the reversion against the lessee.[40] Thus, the benefit of a covenant can pass to successors in title of the lessor even if the burden cannot bind successors of the lessee. Further, Lord Oliver's test seems to require all three main principles to be satisfied for a covenant to touch and concern land[41]; yet, despite the saving in the fourth principle, a covenant to pay a sum of money, even though it satisfies the second principle, will not satisfy the first because a covenant to pay money will be of benefit to a covenantee regardless of whether he owns the reversionary estate.

Given that the majority of common covenants found in leases do have reference to the subject-matter of the lease, it seems more profitable to identify those which do not, rather than to try to define what those that do have in common. This is particularly so now that, in relation to new tenancies, the concept of "touching and concerning" is of no relevance.[42] Some categories may be identified: **4.12**

(i) PERSONAL COVENANTS: those that are expressed to be personal to a particular lessor or lessee only,[43] or which by their very nature are personal,[44] or those which involve the lessee performing some personal service for the lessor.

(ii) MONEY COVENANTS: those that require the tenant to make a payment to a third party, which is purely collateral to the lease.[45]

(iii) OPTIONS TO PURCHASE: a covenant by the landlord giving the lessee an option to purchase the reversion[46] or some land adjoining the demised

[40] See *System Floors Ltd v Ruralpride Ltd* [1995] 1 E.G.L.R. 48, 50.

[41] This despite his apparent approval of Bayley J.'s definition, which is alternative in form.

[42] The Covenants Act has savings in respect of covenants which are expressed in some way to be personal to any person: see below, paras 12–03 *et seq*.

[43] e.g. a covenant by the lessee "for so long as XYZ Corporation is the landlord under this lease, to ... [do something], and a break clause expressed to be personal to the original lessee: *Max Factor Ltd v Wesleyan Assurance Society* (1997) 74 P.&C.R. 8. A break clause expressed to be personal to the tenant but assignable in certain circumstances does not fall within this category: *Harbour Estates v HSBC Bank*, above.

[44] e.g. a covenant by the lessee "to lay flowers once a week on the memorial to the lessor's parents in the folly in the gardens of the demised premises".

[45] *Mayho v Buckhurst* (1617) Cro. Jac. 438.

[46] *Woodall v Clifton* [1905] 2 Ch. 257; *Griffith v Pelton* [1958] Ch. 205.

premises[47] (but not a covenant to renew the lease, which does have reference to the subject-matter of the lease).[48]

(iv) OTHER LAND: covenants in respect of lands not included in the demised premises, except where the thing to be done on those lands will directly benefit the demised premises.[49]

(v) PREMIUM: an obligation to pay a premium by instalments,[50] or an additional premium upon a development having been completed.[51]

(vi) CHATTELS: a covenant to replace chattels as opposed to fixtures[52]; a covenant to deliver up at the end of the term chattels used in the lessee's business,[53] and a covenant not to sell hay and other crops grown on the demised premises.[54]

In such cases, even if the covenant purports to be made with or on behalf of successors in title, it is personal or collateral or both, and as such the benefit does not pass to an assignee of the lessor's reversionary estate.

5. The statutory provision: burden

4.13 The obligation under a condition or of a covenant entered into by a lessor with reference to the subject-matter of the lease shall, if and so far as the lessor has power to bind the reversionary estate immediately expectant on the term granted by the lease, be annexed and incident to and go with that reversionary estate, or the several parts thereof, notwithstanding severance of that reversionary estate. Such obligation may be taken advantage of and enforced by the person in whom the term is from time to time vested by conveyance, devolution in law or otherwise. If and in as far as the lessor has power to bind the person from time to time entitled to that reversionary estate, the obligation may be taken advantage of and enforced against any person so entitled.[55] These provisions take effect without prejudice to any liability affecting a covenantor or his estate.[56]

[47] *Collison v Lettsom* (1815) 6 Taunt. 204.

[48] And also needs to be protected by registration if the lessee is not in actual occupation of registered land: *Beesly v Hallwood Estates* [1960] 1 W.L.R. 549; *Webb v Pollmount Ltd* [1966] Ch. 584.

[49] *Dewar v Goodman* [1908] 1 K.B. 94; *Sampson v Easterby* (1829) 9 B.& C. 505.

[50] *Hill v Booth* [1930] 1 K.B. 381.

[51] *First Penthouse Ltd v Channel Hotels & Properties (UK) Ltd* [2004] 1 E.G.L.R. 16.

[52] *Gorton v Gregory* (1862) 3 B. & S. 90.

[53] *Williams v Earle* (1868) L.R. 3 Q.B. 739.

[54] *Lybbe v Hart* (1889) 29 Ch.D. 8.

[55] Law of Property Act 1925, s.142(1).

[56] *ibid.*, s.142(2).

6. Application of the statutory provision: burden

(a) "*Lease*"

For the purposes of the statutory provision, "lease" includes leases made before as well as after January 1, 1926, and includes "an under-lease or other tenancy".[57] There is no reason, therefore, why the provision should not apply to leases validly made in writing or orally,[58] and even to agreements for lease capable of specific performance.[59] **4.14**

(b) "*Condition or covenant*"

Although different from the words "covenant or provision" used in relation to the passing of the benefit, these words have been construed as including any agreement, even if not under seal (and therefore strictly not a covenant), and even if not in the lease itself.[60] Although the point appears not to have been decided, it is thought that implied covenants, such as landlord's repairing obligations in short residential leases,[61] must fall within the words "a covenant entered into by a lessor". **4.15**

(c) "*Reversionary estate*"

This is prima facie a reference to the estate out of which the lease was granted, but where necessary it is possible to construe the statutory provision as referring to any estate that would, in the absence of the lease, entitle its owner to possession from time to time.[62] The assignee does not need to be entitled to the whole of the reversionary estate before the covenant or condition may be enforced against him; so, e.g., where a concurrent lease is granted by the lessor, which takes effect at law as an assignment of the reversionary estate for the duration of the concurrent lease, the concurrent lessee is *pro tempore* entitled to the reversionary estate and is liable to have the covenant or condition enforced against him by the tenant for the time being. Where part only of the reversionary **4.16**

[57] *ibid.*, s.154.

[58] i.e. leases not requiring to be made by deed by virtue of Law of Property Act 1925, s.54(2).

[59] See *Rickett v Green* [1910] 1 K.B. 253, and *Rye v Purcell* [1926] 1 K.B. 446, cases decided under Conveyancing Act 1881, s.10.

[60] See *Weg Motors Ltd v Hales* [1962] Ch. 49 and *Lotteryking Ltd v AMEC Properties Ltd* [1995] 2 E.G.L.R. 13, 14L. Compare the words "every covenant or condition therein contained" in Law of Property Act 1925, s.141(1), above, para.4.08.

[61] Landlord and Tenant Act 1985, ss.11–13.

[62] *PW & Co v Milton Gate Investments Ltd* [2004] Ch. 142, paras 89, 129–132. Such a construction may be necessary to protect such an owner's human rights under the Convention.

estate is assigned by the lessor, the severance of that estate does not affect the operation of the provision, and the obligation under the condition or covenant will be annexed and incident to and go with the several parts. Where the lease was made before January 1, 1882, the operation of a severance of the reversionary estate made before January 1, 1926 is not affected by the provision.[63]

(d) *"With reference to the subject-matter of the lease"*

4.17 The requirement here is the same as under the provisions of the Act relating to the benefit of the lessee's covenants, namely that only the burden of those covenants which touch and concern the demised premises pass to an assignee of the reversionary estate or part thereof.[64] All usual landlord covenants do have reference to the subject-matter of a lease, though there are some exceptions. The most common of these exceptions are set out below:

(1) a covenant to sell the reversion or other property[65];
(2) a covenant by the lessor not to allow other property to be used for a competing use[66];
(3) a covenant to return a rent deposit at the end of the term[67];
(4) a covenant to allow the lessee to display advertising material for the lessee's business on other adjoining premises belonging to the lessor.[68]

7. Effect of the statutory provisions

4.18 Before any transfer of the lessor's reversionary estate, the lessor was entitled to enforce the lessee's obligations and to any right to re-enter the demised premises, and was correspondingly liable to have his covenants and any conditions enforced against him. Upon a transfer of the reversionary estate, there is a question as to his entitlement to and liability for both accrued and future rights and obligations under the lease. The statutory provisions relating to the passing of the benefit and burden of

[63] Law of Property Act 1925, s.142(2).
[64] See s.4, above, for a general consideration of the principle of "touching and concerning". The same principle applies, *mutatis mutandis*, to covenants and conditions made by a lessor.
[65] See above, para.4.12, and note that a covenant to renew the lease does have reference to the subject-matter of the lease.
[66] *Thomas v Hayward* (1869) L.R. 4 Ex. 311; but note the limited *ratio decidendi* of this case, as expounded by Browne-Wilkinson L.J. in *Kumar v Dunning* [1989] Q.B. 193, 205.
[67] *Hua Chiao Commercial Bank Ltd v Chiaphua Industries Ltd* [1987] A.C. 99.
[68] *Re No.1 Albemarle Street* [1959] Ch. 531.

covenants, etc. on an assignment by the lessor govern these matters. They apply equally to equitable leases as to legal terms of years.

(a) *Accrued rights of lessor*

Section 141 of the Law of Property Act 1925 has been held to effect a statutory transfer, together with the reversionary estate, of all the benefit of the lessee's covenants which touch and concern the land. This includes any rights which had accrued to the lessor before he transferred the reversionary estate. Thus the right to sue for unpaid rent which accrued due before the transfer, and the right to sue for damages for breaches of covenant which were complete before the transfer, pass to the transferee.[69] Pursuant to the usual rule for assignment of choses in action, the transferee's right to the rent or damages is subject to all equities that affected the transferor's title, including any right of set-off.[70] But the tenant cannot set off a claim for damages for breach of covenant by the assignor against rent falling due to the transferee after the transfer of the reversion.[71] **4.19**

Unless the lessor expressly provides in the transfer for the right to sue to be reserved to him, he therefore loses all right to sue for such rent or for damages.[72] This effect results from the words of the statute, and is different from the result that the doctrine of privity of estate would have produced. So, where the lease has been terminated before the interest of the landlord is sold, the statute is not applicable, and the right to sue the tenant for accrued breaches remains with the vendor.[73] The same result is achieved where an underlease is terminated before the headlease is surrendered: the head lessor does not become entitled to sue the underlessee.[74] **4.20**

In some circumstances, the assignee's right to recover rent and service charge from a lessee is conditional on his notifying the lessee of the assignment. This is so generally where the assignment is equitable only, **4.21**

[69] *Re King, deceased* [1963] Ch. 459; *Arlesford Trading Co. Ltd v Servansingh* [1971] 1 W.L.R. 1080. In the latter case, this was so despite the fact that the lessee assigned the tenancy before the transfer of the reversion was effected, and so the lessor's assignee had never enjoyed privity of estate with the lessee.

[70] *Muscat v Smith* [2003] 1 W.L.R. 2853.

[71] *Edlington Properties Ltd v J.H. Fenner & Co. Ltd* [2006] 1 W.L.R. 1583.

[72] *Re King, deceased*, above; *I.R.C. v John Lewis Properties Plc* [2002] 1 W.L.R. 35; even, *semble*, if the lessor has already started proceedings, because it would be artificial to regard the rights in the proceedings as different from the rights in the underlying chose in action (*per* Upjohn L.J. in *Re King*).

[73] *Re Lyne-Stephens and Scott-Miller's Contract* [1920] 1 Ch. 472; *Rother District Investments Ltd v Corke* [2004] 1 E.G.L.R. 47 (termination by peaceable re-entry before assignee's title registered).

[74] *Twogates Properties Ltd v Birmingham Midshires Building Society* (1997) 75 P.&C.R. 386.

pending registration.[75] More specifically, upon an assignment of the reversionary estate in premises which consist of or include a dwelling, the assignee is bound[76] to give notice in writing of the assignment, and of his name and address, to the tenant before the next rent day or, if later, within two months of the assignment.[77] If the assignee makes a written demand to a tenant of premises which consist of or include a dwelling[78] for rent or other sums due under a tenancy, the demand must include the name and address of the landlord.[79] If it does not, any amount consisting of service charge[80] or an administration charge[81] is treated for all purposes as not being due to the assignee until such information is furnished by notice.[82] A landlord of such premises is required by notice to furnish the tenant with an address in England and Wales at which notices may be served on him by the tenant[83]; and in default, any rent, service charge[84] or administration charge[85] otherwise due to the assignee is treated for all purposes as not being due to the assignee until such a notice is given to the tenant.[86] Thus, even though the lessor has been divested of his right to the rent, etc. by the assignment, the assignee may not be entitled to it either unless and until he serves the requisite notice.

(b) *Accrued liability of lessor*

4.22 The language of s.142 of the Law of Property Act 1925 does not effect a similar transfer of all the liabilities of the lessor. The assignee of the reversionary estate is only liable for defaults made during the period of his ownership, and he is not liable in respect of any breaches of covenant

[75] *Scribes West Ltd v Relsa Anstalt (No.3)* [2005] 1 W.L.R. 1847.

[76] Upon pain of conviction of a criminal offence.

[77] Landlord and Tenant Act 1985, s.3(1).

[78] Other than premises comprised in a tenancy to which Pt II of the Landlord and Tenant Act 1954 applies.

[79] And, if the address is not in England or Wales, an address therein at which notices may be served on the landlord by the tenant: Landlord and Tenant Act 1987, s.47(1).

[80] Within the meaning of Landlord and Tenant Act 1985, s.18(1).

[81] Within the meaning of Commonhold and Leasehold Reform Act 2002, Sch.11.

[82] Landlord and Tenant Act 1987, s.47(2). There is an exception for when a court- or LVT-appointed receiver or manager has been appointed to receive the service charge, but not for an RTM company under Commonhold and Leasehold Reform Act 2002, Pt II, Ch.1.

[83] Landlord and Tenant Act 1987, s.48(1).

[84] Within the meaning of Landlord and Tenant Act 1985, s.18(1).

[85] Within the meaning of Commonhold and Leasehold Reform Act 2002, Sch.11.

[86] Landlord and Tenant Act 1987, s.48(2). See *Drew-Morgan v Hamid-Zadeh* [1999] L.&T.R. 503. Again, there is an exception in the case of a court- or LVT-appointed receiver or manager, but not for an RTM company.

or condition committed by the lessor prior to the transfer of title to the reversion.[87] Nor can such breaches be enforced against him in monetary terms by means of an equitable set-off, unless the assignee sues as assignee of the debt and not as owner of the reversion.[88] The lessor remains liable for such breaches, and in some circumstances may remain liable for breaches occurring after the transfer of the reversionary estate.[89] These circumstances are where the assignee is bound, but fails, to give notice of the assignment to the lessee.[90] In such a case, the lessor remains liable to the lessee in respect of any breach of any covenant, condition or agreement under the tenancy occurring before the end of a stipulated period (the "relevant period") as if the reversionary estate were still vested in him.[91] The transferee will also be liable for such breaches, and he and the lessor are jointly and severally liable.[92] The relevant period is the period beginning with the date of the assignment and ending on the date when the first of the following happens:

(i) the transferee gives notice in writing of the assignment and of his name and address to the lessee;
(ii) notice in writing of the assignment, and of the transferee's name and last-known address, is given to the lessee by the lessor.[93]

A lessor of premises which consist of or include a dwelling is therefore well-advised to give the lessee immediate notice in terms of (ii), above, upon an assignment of the reversionary estate.[94]

(c) *Accrued right to re-enter*

Where a person becomes entitled by conveyance or otherwise to the whole or any part of the land leased, any rent, covenant or provision may be recovered, received enforced or taken advantage of by him, notwithstanding that he becomes so entitled after the condition or re-entry or forfeiture has become enforceable.[95] But that subsection does not render **4.23**

[87] *Duncliffe v Caerfelin Properties Ltd* [1989] 2 E.G.L.R. 38, approved in *Edlington v Fenner*, above.
[88] See *Edlington v Fenner*, above.
[89] Which will normally be effected upon registration of the transferee at HM Land Registry: *Brown & Root Technology Ltd v Sun Alliance and London Assurance Co. Ltd* [1996] Ch. 51.
[90] See para.4.21, above.
[91] Landlord and Tenant Act 1985 s.3(3A).
[92] *ibid.*
[93] *ibid.*, s.3(3B).
[94] Note that the provisions of Landlord and Tenant Act 1985, s.3 (in contradistinction to Landlord and Tenant Act 1987, ss.47, 48) apply even if the tenancy is one to which Pt II of the Landlord and Tenant Act 1954 applies. "Assignment" does not include the grant of a mortgage or charge: Act of 1985, s.3(4)(b).
[95] Law of Property Act 1925, s.141(3).

enforceable any condition of re-entry waived or released before the transfer.[96] It has been held that the effect of s.141 is to transfer to the assignee of the reversionary estate the right to forfeit the lease, provided that the right had not been waived previously,[97] even if the rent arrears themselves are re-assigned to the assignor so that no money is due to the assignee.[98] It is not generally a pre-condition of the right to re-enter that the transferee give the lessee notice of the transfer,[99] but an equitable assignee must do so before he can re-enter lawfully.[1] But if no notice of the assignment is given to the lessee, he may validly pay rent to the lessor; and the assignment does not render the lessee liable for breach of any covenant to pay rent on account of his failure to pay rent to the assignee before such notice is given.[2]

4.24 It has been suggested that the words "by conveyance or otherwise" in the statutory provision mean that the effect of s.141 is not limited to a case in which the lessor's reversion is assigned, but would include a case where the lessor's interest as mesne landlord terminates but the lessee's tenancy continues.[3] But it seems unlikely that, in such a case, the mesne landlord's right to recover outstanding rent was intended to be passed to the head landlord. Probably the subsection should be regarded as effecting a transfer of existing proprietary rights of re-entry and *future* rights under covenants, in any case where the reversionary estate is not conveyed.[4] At all events, where the lessee's interest is terminated before the mesne landlord's interest is surrendered the superior landlord cannot claim under the covenants in the underlease.[5]

8. Severance of the reversion

4.25 As noted already,[6] ss.141 and 142 of the Law of Property Act 1925, which govern the transmission of the benefit of lessees' covenants and the

[96] *ibid.*

[97] *London & County (A & D) Ltd v Wilfred Sportsman Ltd* [1971] Ch. 764. That case also decided that a transfer of the reversionary estate "subject to and with the benefit of" the lease does not itself waive an accrued right to forfeit as it is, so far as the lessee is concerned, *res inter alios acta.*

[98] *Kataria v Safeland Plc* [1998] 1 E.G.L.R. 39.

[99] *Scaltock v Harston* (1875) 1 C.P.D. 106.

[1] *Scribes West v Relsa Anstalt (No.3)*, above.

[2] Law of Property Act 1925, s.151(1). *Semble*, therefore, an assignee of the reversionary estate must give notice to the lessee before he can safely forfeit for non-payment of rent due to the assignee.

[3] *Electricity Supply Nominees Ltd v Thorn EMI Retail Ltd* [1991] 2 E.G.L.R. 46. In this case, the lessee's interest continued pursuant to Landlord and Tenant Act 1954, Pt II, but the same principle would apply under Law of Property Act 1925, s.139(1) in the case of a surrender or merger of the lessor's reversion.

[4] Thus operating in parallel with Law of Property Act 1925, s.139.

[5] *Twogates v BMBS*, above.

[6] Above, paras 4.07 and 4.16.

burden of lessors' covenants, both specifically provide that the operation of those sections is not affected by a severance of the reversion. An assignee of part of the reversionary estate will therefore have the benefit of the lessee's covenants, and be subject to the lessor's covenants, which touch and concern the part of the premises assigned to him. Upon an assignment of part of the reversion, assignor and assignee can agree an apportionment of the rent as between themselves, but this apportionment will not bind the tenant unless either he has agreed it or the court has made the apportionment.[7] Except in such cases, the tenant, who remains the tenant under one tenancy, may lawfully pay the whole of the rent to the assignor.

Every condition or right of re-entry, and every other condition contained in the lease, is apportioned and annexed to the severed parts of the reversionary estate as if the land comprised in each severed part had alone originally been comprised in the lease.[8] Right of re-entry here includes a right to determine the lease by notice to quit or otherwise.[9] But where such a notice is served by a person entitled to a severed part of the reversion so that it extends to part only of the demised premises, the lessee may within one month determine the lease in regard to the rest of the land by giving to the owner of that land a counter-notice expiring at the same time as the original notice.[10] For these provisions to apply, the severance must be genuine, and not merely colourable.[11] **4.26**

[7] *Swansea Corp v Thomas* (1882) 10 Q.B.D. 48; *Lester v Ridd* [1990] 2 Q.B. 430. In relation to particular categories of tenancy, there is a statutory jurisdiction to apportion rents: see *Woodfall's Law of Landlord and Tenant* (28th ed. (looseleaf)), para.7.128. Such statutory apportionments will also bind tenants.

[8] Law of Property Act 1925, s.140(1).

[9] *ibid.*, s.140(2).

[10] *ibid.* A notice under Landlord and Tenant Act 1954, Pt II is not a notice to quit for this purpose: *Nevill Long & Co. (Boards) Ltd v Firmenich & Co.* (1984) 47 P. & C.R. 59.

[11] *Persey v Bazley* (1984) 47 P. & C.R. 37.

burden of lessors' covenants, but apparently providing that the operation of those sections is not affected by a severance of the reversion [illegible] estate or part of the [illegible] severed estate will therefore have the benefit of the lessee's covenants, and be subject to the lessor's covenants which [illegible] the part of the premises [illegible] assignment of part of the reversion [illegible] themselves, [illegible]

[illegible]

[illegible]

[illegible] *Thomas* (1883) [illegible] [illegible] (1964) [illegible]

[illegible] *Property Act* [illegible]

[illegible] under Landlord and Tenant Act [illegible] for this purpose: [illegible]

[illegible] (1964) [illegible]

CHAPTER 5

Liability as Between Original Lessor and Assignee of the Term

As with an original lessor who assigns his reversionary estate, when the original lessee assigns the term of years created by the lease he does not rid himself of his contractual liability to the original lessor[1]; but he does divest himself of the legal estate in land. This is so, and the assignment is effective to vest the estate in the assignee, even if the assignment is made in breach of a covenant in the lease.[2] To be effective at law, the assignment must be made by deed, even if the lease was validly created orally or in writing[3]; though an informal sub-letting for the residue of the term that takes effect by operation of law as an assignment is nonetheless effective to assign the lease.[4] Prima facie, the assignee of the term is neither entitled to the benefit nor subject to the burden of the original lessee's contract; but, from the time of the assignment,[5] the assignee, who is the owner of the lease, stands in a relationship of privity of estate with the original lessor.[6] From this relationship[7] it follows that the benefit of the lessor's covenants and the burden of the lessee's covenants which touch and **5.01**

[1] See Ch.3, above.

[2] *Old Grovebury Manor Farm v W. Seymour Plant Hire Ltd (No.2)* [1979] 1 W.L.R. 1397. But the breach of covenant will give the lessor a remedy against the lessee in damages for any loss suffered, and may entitle the lessor, if he so wishes, to forfeit the lease. If the assignee knew of the breach, the lessor may seek an injunction to re-assign the lease: *Hemingway Securities Ltd v Dunraven Ltd* [1995] 1 E.G.L.R. 61; *Crestfort Ltd v Tesco Stores Ltd* [2005] 3 E.G.L.R. 25.

[3] *Crago v Julian* [1992] 1 W.L.R. 372; *Camden LBC v Alexandrou (No.2)* (1997) 30 H.L.R. 534.

[4] *Parc (Battersea) Ltd v Hutchinson* [1999] L.&T.R. 554.

[5] Or, if the lease is a registered title, from the date from which the transfer is registered at the Land Registry: see *Brown & Root Technology Ltd v Sun Alliance and London Assurance Co. Ltd* [1996] Ch. 51.

[6] Provided the assignment is made by deed. An equitable assignment may be binding as between assignee and assignor, but it does not vest the estate itself, i.e. the legal term of years, in the assignee, and so no privity of estate with the lessor exists: *Purchase v Lichfield Brewery Co. Ltd* [1915] 1 K.B. 184.

[7] The nature and origins of which are discussed in Ch.4, above, para.4.02, in relation to an assignment of the reversionary estate.

concern the demised premises pass to the assignee of the term because they are "imprinted" on the term vested in him.[8]

5.02 A deed of assignment or transfer of a lease generally uses the words "assign" or "transfer", although there is no requirement to use them if the intended effect is otherwise plain from the terms of the deed. In one exceptional case,[9] a lease may be assigned in the absence of a deed, or even by parol. Where a lessee purports to grant an underlease of the demised premises for the whole of or more than the residue of the term of the lease, the intended underlease takes effect as an assignment of the lease, even though the deed or agreement is in the form of an underlease and reserves a rent to the lessee. This is so even if the residue of the term is small enough to enable an underlease for a term exceeding it to be granted by parol,[10] and so a purported oral or written underlease effects a valid assignment of the residue of the lessee's term.[11] A grant of an underlease for a fixed term of years by a periodic tenant does not fall within this principle[12]; nor does such a grant by a tenant whose tenancy is continuing or will continue under Pt II of the Landlord and Tenant Act 1954,[13] because it cannot be said that the lessee has disposed of the whole of his interest in the premises.

1. Basis of assignee's rights and liabilities

5.03 Unlike the position as between an assignee of the reversionary estate and the original lessee, there is no statutory provision which purports to govern the enforceability of covenants, provisions and conditions of the lease as between the lessor and an assignee of the term.[14] The entitlement of an assignee of the term to enforce the obligations of the lessor, and correspondingly his liability to observe and perform the lessee's obligations, in so far as they touch and concern the demised premises, derive

[8] See *City of London Corp v Fell* [1993] Q.B. 589, *per* Nourse L.J. (affd. and approved by the House of Lords: [1994] 1 A.C. 458). Law of Property Act 1925, ss.62(1), 63(1) do not operate to transfer the benefit of covenants that do not touch and concern the land: *Kumar v Dunning* [1989] Q.B. 193, 198–99; *Harbour Estates Ltd v HSBC Bank Plc* [2005] Ch. 194, 210–11.

[9] Disregarding for these purposes statutory vesting of property.

[10] i.e. a residue of three years or less: Law of Property Act 1925, s.54(2).

[11] *Milmo v Carreras* [1946] K.B. 306; *Grosvenor Estate Belgravia v Cochrane* [1991] 2 E.G.L.R. 83; *Parc (Battersea) Ltd v Hutchinson*, above.

[12] *Oxley v James* (1844) 13 M.& W. 209.

[13] *William Skelton & Son Ltd v Harrison & Pinder Ltd* [1975] Q.B. 361.

[14] Historically, this is because covenants could pass with the land comprised in the leasehold estate at common law, whereas a reversion on a lease was not "land" for these purposes: see *Megarry and Wade's Law of Real Property* (6th ed.), para.15-046. In fact, Law of Property Act 1925, s.142(1) does also provide for the enforcement of obligations against the successor in title of the lessor by successors in title of the lessee.

from the doctrine of privity of estate. This being so, the assignee's entitlement and corresponding liability will only subsist in relation to that time when privity of estate exists. So, in the absence of an express assignment of the chose in action, the assignee has no right to sue the lessor in relation to breaches of the lessor's covenants occurring prior to the assignment of the term. And when the assignee further assigns the term, both his liability and his entitlement will terminate as to future rights and obligations; though he will remain liable for breaches during the period of time when the term was vested in him, and will remain entitled to sue the lessor for breaches of the lessor's obligations occurring during that period. In the case of a lease the title to which is registered, the estate in the lease is not assigned until the disposition is registered.[15]

Although the assignee is not liable for breaches occurring or rent falling due before the assignment to him, in certain cases his position will be such as to make him in effect liable for such matters. In the case of a breach of covenant which is a continuing breach, such as an obligation to keep the demised premises in repair, the assignee will be liable to remedy the breach after the assignment to him, even though the breach had subsisted for some time before it. And the assignee may be sued for any loss suffered by the lessor and caused by his failure to repair. He is also at risk of having his lease forfeited.[16] In the case of unpaid rent, although the assignee is not liable to pay it, the lessor may (unless he has waived the right)[17] forfeit the lease for non-payment of rent, and the assignee will have to discharge the arrears, interest and costs as the price of obtaining relief against forfeiture.[18] The lessor may not distrain against the assignee's chattels for rent unpaid by the assignor.[19] In some cases, the question of whether the lessee or the assignee is liable for rent or other money due is one of nice construction of the lease. Thus, where the amount of reviewed rent payable in respect of a period prior to the assignment became ascertained after the assignment, and the provisions of the Apportionment Act 1870 applied, the assignee was not liable for the 5.04

[15] *Brown & Root Technology Ltd v Sun Alliance and London Assurance Co. Ltd* [1996] Ch. 51.

[16] Subject, in both cases, to the provisions of the Leasehold Property (Repairs) Act 1938.

[17] If the lessor grants licence to assign the lease, he may thereby waive any right of forfeiture which had accrued by the date of that licence (see *Billson v Residential Apartments Ltd (No.1)* [1992] 1 A.C. 494; but if rent had fallen due, e.g. 12 days prior to the licence, but the proviso for re-entry in the lease specified that the rent must be unpaid for 14 or 21 days before the right of re-entry became exercisable, the lessor could validly re-enter after the assignment. On waiver, see *Re a debtor (No.13A/IO/95); Re a debtor (No.14A/IO/95)* [1996] 1 All E.R. 691.

[18] See *Parry v Robinson-Wyllie* [1987] 2 E.G.L.R. 233.

[19] *Wharfland Ltd v South London Cooperative Building Co. Ltd* [1995] 2 E.G.L.R. 21.

additional rent[20]; but if the terms of the lease provided for the lessee —pending determination of the rent review—to continue to pay rent at the rate passing, and to pay any excess due after determination on the rent day following that determination, the assignee is arguably liable for the whole of the excess, even if it related in part to a period before the assignment.

5.05 For many years, it has been the practice[21] of lessors when granting licence to assign to extract from the proposed assignee, as a condition of granting the licence, a direct covenant to pay the rent and observe and perform the covenants on the part of the lessee for the whole of the residue of the term. Notwithstanding the continuing contractual liability of the lessee, and even when a subsequent assignee made the same covenant with the lessor, the first assignee has been held to be liable on his covenant for the whole of the residue of the term.[22] Similarly, a covenant by an assignee "to pay the rents reserved by the Lease at the time and in manner therein provided for . . . " made him liable for the rent for the whole of the residue of the term, notwithstanding a further assignment.[23] A further advantage for the lessor is that the assignee thereupon becomes liable on all the lessee's covenants in the lease, and not just on those which pass under the doctrine of privity of estate because they touch and concern the demised premises.

In this way, a lessor can accumulate a number of contractual obligations to pay the rent, etc. each of which is, so far as the lessor is concerned, a primary liability that he is entitled to enforce. Such covenants by assignees of the term clearly touch and concern the demised premises,[24] and so the benefit of this covenant will pass to successors in title of the lessor at common law.[25] An original lessee or an intermediate assignee cannot complain that the lessor has not first sued the actual tenant or an assignee further down the chain of assigns, and is effectually in the same position as an original lessee who is bound by his contract.

[20] *Parry v Robinson-Wyllie*, above.

[21] Of doubtful validity where the covenant against assignment is qualified by the words "without the consent of the lessor": see *Waite v Jennings* [1906] 2 K.B. 11, *per* Vaughan Williams L.J.

[22] *J. Lyons & Co. Ltd v Knowles* [1943] K.B. 366.

[23] *Estates Gazette Ltd v Benjamin Restaurants Ltd* [1994] 1 W.L.R. 1528, overturning the judge at first instance who had sought to avoid the plain meaning of the words and limit the assignee's liability to that period which privity of estate would have covered.

[24] In so far as they duplicate obligations which themselves touch and concern the land.

[25] Under the principle in *P & A Swift Investments Ltd v Combined English Stores Group Ltd* [1989] A.C. 632, where Lord Templeman equates assignee covenants to surety covenants, though not pursuant to Law of Property Act 1925, s.141 because the covenant in the deed of licence is not "therein contained" within the meaning of s.141(1), nor is it made by the lessee.

2. Equitable leases

An equitable lease is either an agreement for lease which is specifically enforceable,[26] or a lease for more than three years[27] made in writing instead of by deed and therefore ineffective for the purpose of creating a legal estate.[28] Since the liability of an assignee of the term (in the absence of a direct covenant between assignee and lessor) depends on privity of estate existing between him and the lessor, it has been held that the rule in *Spencer's Case* cannot apply in the case of an equitable lease since, presumably, there is not an estate in land to which lessor and assignee are both privy.[29] Thus, although the benefit of a lessor's covenant touching and concerning the demised premises can pass at common law, the assignee of the term is not subject to the burden of the lessee's covenants, except those that can be enforced in equity as restrictive covenants to which the assignee's equitable interest is necessarily subject. **5.06**

A number of arguments have been advanced to obviate this inconvenient result,[30] none of which is wholly convincing, but it seems quite likely that an assignee of an equitable lease who enters into possession of the demised premises, who pays rent, and is accepted by the lessor as the tenant under the lease, would not be able later to dispute his liability under the lessee's covenants of the equitable lease. Of course, the difficulty is obviated if the assignee, as a condition of the lessor's consent to the assignment to him of the equitable lease, covenants directly with the lessor to observe and perform the lessee covenants for the residue of the term.

3. Severance of the term

Liability as between the original lessor and an assignee of the term being governed by the principle of privity of estate,[31] the assignee of part of the demised premises is entitled to the benefit of those covenants of the lessor which touch and concern the part of the premises vested in him; and, conversely, he is liable to the lessor on those covenants of the lessee which touch and concern the same part.[32] As regards rent, assignor and assignee may agree an apportionment which binds them and their successor in title; but the lessor will not be bound by such an apportionment without **5.07**

[26] Under the principle in *Walsh v Lonsdale* (1882) 21 Ch.D. 9.

[27] Or for three years or less but granted in consideration of a fine or at a rent less than the best rent which could reasonably be obtained: Law of Property Act 1925, s.54(2).

[28] *ibid.*, ss.52(1), 53(1)(a).

[29] *Purchase v Lichfield Brewery Co. Ltd* [1915] 1 K.B. 184.

[30] See Dr Gray's *Elements of Land Law* (2nd ed.), pp. 871–873.

[31] See para.5.03, above.

[32] *Stevenson v Lambard* (1802) 2 East 575.

his consent.[33] The lessor is entitled to recover from an assignee a proportionate part of the rent, but not the whole. The proportion would be that part of the rent which the court thought was fairly attributable to the part in question, irrespective of the lessees' apportionment.[34] Anomalously, an assignee of part of the term is vulnerable to a distress levied to recover the full amount of the rent due[35]; but an assignee so distrained upon, or threatened with distress, will be entitled to contribution from the lessee(s) of the other part (or parts) of the premises.[36] Also where, on an assignment of part of the term, an apportionment of rent is agreed between an assignor who conveys and is expressed to convey as beneficial owner and his assignee, there is implied a covenant by the assignor at all times from the assignment to pay the balance of the rent (after deducting the apportioned part or parts) and to observe and perform all the lessee's covenants so far as they relate to the retained part.[37]

[33] Law of Property Act 1925, s.190(3).

[34] *Lester v Ridd* [1990] 2 Q.B. 430, *per* Dillon L.J.

[35] *ibid.* Rent issues out of each and every part of the land.

[36] See *Bonner v Tottenham and Edmonton Permanent Investment Building Society* [1899] 1 Q.B. 161; and *Electricity Supply Nominees Ltd v Thorn EMI (Retail) Ltd* [1991] 2 E.G.L.R. 46.

[37] Law of Property Act 1925, s.77(1)(D)(ii), Sch.2, Pt X, para.(ii).

CHAPTER 6

Liability as Between Assignees of Term and Reversion

Although an assignee of the reversionary estate will have the benefit of 6.01 the original lessee's covenants by statute,[1] and may also have the benefit of a direct covenant made with him by an assignee of the term as a condition of that assignment, mutual enforceability of covenants as between assignees of the term and reversion is otherwise governed by the principle of privity of estate. So, assignees of the reversionary estate and of the term are bound to perform lessor's and lessee's covenants respectively which touch and concern the demised premises. That position, in relation to the burden of the lessor's covenants is mirrored by the following statutory provision in relation to the passing of the benefit and burden of the lessor's covenants:

> "[These covenants] may be taken advantage of and enforced by the person in whom the term is from time to time vested by conveyance, devolution in law or otherwise; and, if and as far as the lessor has power to bind the person from time to time entitled to that reversionary estate, the obligation aforesaid may be taken advantage of and enforced against any person so entitled."[2]

So, as with the position between the original lessor and an assignee of the term, an assignee of the reversionary estate and an assignee of the term are mutually liable only in respect of the period of time when reversion and term are vested in them respectively.

The position can be illustrated by reference to the following series of 6.02 assignments:

		1.		4.		5.	
	L	———	L2	———	L3	———	L4
The lease	|						
	|	2.		3.		6.	
	T	———	T2	———	T3	———	T4

[1] Law of Property Act 1925, s.141(1).
[2] *ibid.*, s.142(1).

L first assigns to L2; then T assigns to T2; then T2 assigns to T3; then L2 assigns to L3; then L3 assigns to L4, and finally T3 assigns to T4. It is assumed that neither T2 nor T3 gives a direct covenant to L2. For a period of time, L2 and T3 stand in a relationship of privity of estate as landlord and tenant respectively. Immediately before that period began, L2 was the landlord of T2; immediately after that period, L3 became the landlord of T3.

6.03 Considered first from the perspective of T3, T3 had no liability in respect of the lessee's covenants prior to becoming the tenant, and he assumed none on being assigned the lease in respect of any time prior to that assignment.[3] Upon the assignment, he became liable to L2 on the lessee's covenants which touch and concern the demised premises; but he had no liability to L because he was never in a position of privity of estate (or of course contract) with him. He therefore was never entitled to the benefit of L's covenants either,[4] but as from the assignment became entitled to enforce against L2 those of the lessor's covenants which touch and concern the demised premises. Upon the further assignment of the reversionary estate from L2 to L3, T3 thenceforth became liable to L3 both in respect of his past breaches of the lessee's covenants or rent arrears[5] and in respect of future breaches of covenant and obligations. From that time also, T3 was only entitled to look to L3 for performance of the lessor's covenants, but he retained his right to sue L2 for any breaches occurring before the assignment to L3.[6] The changes just discussed in relation to the assignment from L2 to L3 recurred upon the further assignment of the reversionary estate from L3 to L4 (so L4 became entitled to sue T3 for any rent arrears from the time of L2's and L3's ownership). Upon the assignment of the term to T4, T3 ceased to be liable as to the future to perform any of the lessee's covenants, but he retained his right to sue L2, L3 or L4 for damages for breaches of the lessor's covenants prior to his assignment to T4; and his liability to L4 in respect of breaches of the lessee's covenants committed by him prior to the assignment to T4 was unaffected.

6.04 Looking at the same series of assignments from the perspective of L3, L3 became entitled to the benefit of T's covenants (in so far as they touch and concern the demised premises) and became entitled to enforce the

[3] See above, para.5.04, for the risk of forfeiture in respect of pre-assignment breaches of covenant or rent arrears.

[4] In the absence of a statutory provision equivalent to Law of Property Act 1925, s.141, which transfers the benefit of the original lessee's covenants to an assignee of the reversionary estate.

[5] *Re King, deceased* [1963] Ch. 459.

[6] T3 cannot set off against his liability to L3 his claim against L2, unless L3 is suing for arrears of rent ante-dating the transfer to L3: *Muscat v Smith* [2003] 1 W.L.R. 2853; *Edlington Properties Ltd v J.H. Fenner & Co. Ltd* [2006] 1 W.L.R. 1583.

same covenants against T3 as from the date of the assignment from L2 to L3. He also became entitled to the benefit of T2's covenants in relation only to the period when T2 was the tenant,[7] even though L3 and T2 never enjoyed privity of estate or contract.[8] But L3 only became liable to T3 (and to no other tenant) from the date of the assignment in respect of the lessor's covenants which touch and concern the demised premises. Upon his further assignment to L4, L3 lost all rights to sue T, T2 and T3 upon the lessee's covenants or for rent,[9] and his liability on the lessor's covenants ceased for the future. But he remained liable to T3 (only) for any losses suffered by T3 caused by a breach of the lessor's covenants during the time when the reversionary estate was vested in him.

In practice, it is very common for a direct covenant to be taken from **6.05** each assignee of the term; and so the landlord to whom that covenant is given, and any successor in title of him,[10] will be able to rely on the direct contractual liability of an assignee of the term, rather than on the doctrine of privity of estate as such. Such a direct covenant will make the assignee liable on all the lessee's covenants in the lease, and not just on those which touch and concern the demised premises.

Once again, in relation to an equitable lease, the burden of the lessee's covenants cannot pass to and bind an assignee of the term[11] under the doctrine of privity of estate. But this difficulty is obviated if the assignee is required to enter into a direct covenant with the landlord to observe and perform the lessee covenants during the residue of the term.

[7] *Re King, deceased*, above.

[8] *Arlesford Trading Co. Ltd v Servansingh* [1971] Ch. 1080.

[9] Unless he expressly reserved those rights to himself in the assignment to L4: see *Re King, deceased*, above.

[10] See *P&A Swift Investments Ltd v Combined English Stores Ltd* [1989] A.C. 632.

[11] See above, paras 5.03, 5.06.

same covenants against T3 as from the date of the assignment to him (T4)[illegible]. He also becomes entitled to the benefit of T['s] covenants in relation to the period when T2 was the tenant. Therefore though T3 and T2 never [illegible] from the date of the assignment [illegible] the lessor's covenants which touch and concern the demised premises [illegible] assignment [illegible] liability [illegible] covenants [illegible] the lessee [illegible] extensive estate [illegible]

6.05 In practice, [illegible] covenant [illegible] the landlord [illegible] assignment [illegible] and [illegible] the [illegible] estate and another [illegible] and [illegible] the demised premises.

[illegible] the [illegible] of the lease [illegible] cannot [illegible] of the [illegible] if the assignee is required to enter into a direct covenant with the landlord to observe and perform the lessee's covenants during the residue of the term.

[illegible] decided above.

[illegible] (1971) Ch. 1080.

[illegible] Unless he expressly reserved [illegible] rights to [illegible] the assignment [illegible] see [illegible] decided above.

[illegible] See [illegible] (1989) [illegible] 637.

[illegible] See above, paras 5.05–5.06.

CHAPTER 7

Rights of Original Lessees and their Assignees *Inter Se*

As has been seen, an original lessee, an intermediate assignee who has covenanted with the lessor to observe and perform the lessee's covenants for the residue of the term, and a subsequent assignee who is actually the tenant under the lease, all have equal and primary liabilities to the lessor for the rent and for performance of the lessee's covenants. The lessor is therefore entitled to sue any of them for the rent or for e.g. failure to comply with the tenant's repairing obligations,[1] although the normal commercial expectation is that the lessor will pursue the actual tenant if and for so long as he is good for the money.[2] **7.01**

If the lessor does sue the actual tenant and makes full recovery from him, the previous tenants will no longer be liable to the landlord for the sums claimed, for the tenant's payment discharges their liabilities.[3] Nor do the previous tenants become liable to reimburse the tenant or contribute to his liability, for, as between them and the actual tenant, he is primarily liable to pay the rent and to perform the lessee's covenants. But if the lessor sues either the original lessee or the intermediate assignee on his contractual obligation to pay, that person will seek to recover from his assignee or (if different) from the actual tenant, or from both, the amount he has paid to the lessor. The exact basis on which such a claim can be made is a mixture of express contract, statutorily implied covenants, covenants implied at common law, and restitutionary principles, and it had been the subject of much litigation before the arrival of the Covenants Act, which made radical changes,[4] on January 1, 1996. This chapter will consider the law relating to rights and liabilities of lessees and assigns *inter se* as it stood before the relevant provisions of the Covenants

[1] Different considerations may arise in the case of a breach of a negative covenant: see above, para.3.05.

[2] *Allied London Investments Ltd v Hambro Life Assurance Ltd* [1984] 1 E.G.L.R. 62, *per* Walton J. at p.63E–F.

[3] The liability is not cumulative, but is otherwise several: see *Sun Life Assurance Society Ltd v Tantofex Engineers* [1999] L.&T.R. 568, distinguishing *Deanplan Ltd v Mahmoud* [1993] Ch. 151, a case on joint and several liability. The position may be different if the landlord compromises his claim for a lesser amount than that due: *Jameson v Central Electricity Generating Board* [2000] 1 A.C. 455.

[4] As to which, see below, Ch.14.

Act came into force, and in doing so will look at the effect of the Law of Property (Miscellaneous Provisions) Act 1994 on covenants on the part of assignors.

1. Terms of assignment of lease

7.02 In order to dispose of the legal estate, an assignment must be made by deed.[5] Such a deed is a mixture of dispositive effect and contract, and it is axiomatic that the parties to a deed of assignment may agree such terms within the law as they think appropriate. It is common for the assignee to covenant with the assignor that he (the assignee) will pay the rent reserved by the lease and will observe and perform the obligations on the part of the lessee for the residue of the term of years. Often, the covenant goes further and includes an agreement by the assignee to indemnify the assignor against the consequences for the assignor of any breach of such obligations or failure to pay the rent. There is nothing remarkable about such a covenant. It reflects the practical understanding of the parties that the assignee is thenceforth taking over in all respects responsibility for the leasehold obligations and that the assignor is no longer interested in the demised premises, while at the same time recognising the significance of the assignor's continuing contractual obligation to the lessor.

In modern times, it has become quite common for such terms as to performance and indemnity not to be expressed in the deed of assignment. This is not because modern-day assignors have become more philanthropic in their outlook but because, in the absence of some exclusionary wording in the deed, similar covenants are implied into legal assignments of leases by the Law of Property Act 1925.[6] Most assignors are content with the statutory wording. The same Act also implied covenants as to title on the part of persons who are expressed to convey as beneficial owners,[7] and these covenants are now implied by the provisions of the Law of Property (Miscellaneous Provisions) Act 1994.[8] For the same reason it is unusual to see covenants as to the assignor's title set out *in extenso* in the deed of conveyance.[9] Deeds of assignment are therefore generally short and unremarkable instruments.

[5] Even where the tenancy was validly created by writing or orally: *Crago v Julian* [1992] 1 W.L.R. 372; *Camden LBC v Alexandrou (No.2)* (1997) 30 H.L.R. 534.

[6] s.77(1)(C), (D).

[7] Or as settlors, trustees, mortgagees or personal representatives: *ibid.*, s.76.

[8] See below, section 2(b).

[9] Although it is very common to see expressed a particular variation of one of the implied covenants, for the further protection of the assignor; see below.

2. The statutory implied covenants on the part of the assignor

(a) *Conveyances made before July 1, 1995*

In any conveyance[10] for valuable consideration (other than a mortgage) executed before July 1, 1995, there was included and implied a covenant by the person who conveyed in terms of Pt I of Sch.2 to the Law of Property Act 1925 (in this section referred to as "the Act"). Part I contains covenants as to the title of the conveying party, his power to convey, the quiet enjoyment of the person to whom the conveyance is made, and further assurance on request. In any conveyance of leasehold property for valuable consideration (other than a mortgage) executed before July 1, 1995, there was included and implied a further covenant by the person who is expressed to convey as beneficial owner in terms of Pt II of Sch.2 to the Act. Part II is in the following terms: 7.03

> "That, notwithstanding anything by the person who so conveys, or any one through whom he derives title, otherwise than by purchase for value, made, done, executed, or omitted, or knowingly suffered, the lease or grant creating the term or estate for which the land is conveyed is, at the time of conveyance, a good, valid, and effectual lease or grant of the property conveyed, and is in full force, unforfeited, unsurrendered, and has in nowise become void or voidable, and that, notwithstanding anything as aforesaid, *all the rents reserved by, and all the covenants, conditions, and agreements contained in, the lease or grant, and on the part of the lessee or grantee and the persons deriving title under him to be paid, observed, and performed, have been paid, observed, and performed* up to the time of conveyance."[11]

That covenant, as it stands, would amount to a warranty that each and every one of the covenants in the lease had been fully performed by the assignor up to the time of the assignment, and so, in order to protect the assignor against the consequences of hidden or unknown breaches, the words in italics were usually qualified,[12] either by referring to matters known to the assignor, or more specifically by excluding the effect of

[10] A conveyance does not include a demise by way of lease at a rent: Law of Property Act 1925, s.76(5); but it does include an assignment of a lease.

[11] Italics added.

[12] Law of Property Act 1925, s.76(6) permits variations or extensions made by deed or assent.

those words in relation to the assignor's compliance with the repairing covenant of the lease.

7.04 In relation to leasehold land the title to which is registered under the Land Registration Acts, similar covenants on the part of assignors are implied under those Acts on the transfer of any leasehold interest in land other than the grant of an underlease.[13] But such covenants are not implied on a transfer of a registered lease which is a new tenancy within the meaning of the Landlord and Tenant (Covenants) Act 1995.[14]

7.05 The benefit of these implied covenants is annexed and incident to and goes with the estate or interest of the implied covenantee, and is capable of being enforced by every person in whom that estate or interest is, for the whole or any part thereof, from time to time vested.[15] Thus, the assignee of the lease and all successive assignees have the benefit of that covenant by the original assignor. Such implied covenants may therefore still be of importance today.

(b) *Dispositions made on or after July 1, 1995—the Law of Property (Miscellaneous Provisions) Act 1994*

7.06 On July 1, 1995, the provisions of the Law of Property (Miscellaneous Provisions) Act 1994 relating to implied covenants on the part of persons effecting or purporting to effect dispositions of property[16] by an instrument[17] came into effect.[18] In relation to dispositions of property made on or after July 1, 1995, these provisions replace the covenants which were implied under the Law of Property Act 1925[19] or the Land Registration Act 1925[20] on the part of a person who conveyed and was expressed to convey *inter alia* as beneficial owner. The provisions relating to the old implied covenants are repealed subject to transitional provisions and exceptions.[21] Unlike the 1925 provisions, the new provisions under the Act of 1994 apply to the creation of a term of years,[22] as well as to an assignment of an existing lease.

[13] Previously under Land Registration Act 1925, s.24(1)(a), (2), now under Land Registration Act 2002, s.134(2), Sch.12, paras 20(1)(a), (b)(i), (3).

[14] *ibid.*, para.20(5).

[15] *ibid.*, s.76(6).

[16] "Property" includes a thing in action, and any interest in real or personal property: *ibid.*, s.1(4).

[17] "Instrument" includes an instrument which is not a deed: *ibid.*

[18] Law of Property (Miscellaneous Provisions) Act 1994, s.23(1); The Law of Property (Miscellaneous Provisions) Act 1994 (Commencement No.2) Order 1995 (SI 1995/1317), art.2.

[19] By s.76, repealed on July 1, 1995, subject to transitional provisions.

[20] By s.24(1)(a), repealed on July 1, 1995, subject to transitional provisions.

[21] Below.

[22] Law of Property (Miscellaneous Provisions) Act 1994, s.1(4).

(i) TRANSITIONAL PROVISIONS

The enforcement of a covenant implied by either section 76 of the Law of Property Act 1925 or s.24(1)(a) of the Land Registration Act 1925 on a disposition before July 1, 1995 is unaffected by the repeal of those sections.[23] 7.07

(ii) EXCEPTIONS

In two cases, the old-form covenants are implied on dispositions made on or after July 1, 1995. 7.08

(1) Section 76 of the Law of Property Act 1925 applies in relation to a disposition of property made on or after July 1, 1995 in pursuance of a contract entered into before that date where three conditions are satisfied. First, the contract contains a term providing for a disposition to which that section would have applied if the disposition had been made before July 1, 1995. Secondly, the existence of the contract and of that term is apparent on the face of the instrument effecting the disposition. Thirdly, there has not been an intervening disposition of the property expressed, in accordance with the new provisions of Pt I of the Act of 1994, to be made with full title guarantee.[24]
(2) Similarly, s.24(1)(a) of the Land Registration Act 1925 applies[25] in relation to a disposition of a leasehold interest in land made on or after July 1, 1995 in pursuance of a contract entered into before that date where three conditions are satisfied. First, the covenant specified in that provision would have been implied on the disposition if it had been made before that date. Secondly, the existence of the contract is apparent on the face of the instrument effecting the disposition. Thirdly, there has been no intervening disposition of the leasehold interest expressed, in accordance with Pt I of the Act of 1994, to be made with full title guarantee.[26]

An "intervening disposition" for the purposes of these two exceptions means a disposition on or after July 1, 1995 to, or to a predecessor in title of, the person by whom the disposition in question is made.[27] Where, in order for the two exceptions above to apply, it is necessary for certain matters to be apparent on the face of the instrument effecting the

[23] *ibid.*, s.10(1), (2), not repealed or amended by Land Registration Act 2002.
[24] *ibid.*, s.11(1).
[25] Notwithstanding its repeal by Land Registration Act 2002.
[26] Law of Property (Miscellaneous Provisions) Act 1994, s.11(2).
[27] *ibid.*, s.11(3).

disposition, the contract is deemed to contain an implied term that they should so appear.[28] For the purposes of these exceptions, in relation to a disposition of property made in accordance with an option granted before July 1, 1995 but exercised on or after that date, the contract for the disposition shall be deemed to have been entered into on the grant of the option.[29]

7.09 Where the exceptions above do not apply only because there has been an intervening disposition expressed to be made with full title guarantee, the effect of the terms of the contract is varied by statute.[30] A contract which contains a term that the person making the disposition shall do so as beneficial owner shall be construed as requiring that person to do so by an instrument expressed to be made with full title guarantee.[31] A contract which contains a term that the person making the disposition shall do so as settlor, or as trustee or mortgagee or personal representative, shall be construed as requiring that person to do so by an instrument expressed to be made with limited title guarantee.[32] A contract for the disposition of a leasehold interest in land entered into at a time when the title to the leasehold interest was registered shall be construed as requiring the person making the disposition for which it provides to do so by an instrument expressed to be made with full title guarantee.[33] Where the contract provides that any of the terms to be implied by virtue of s.76 of the Law of Property Act 1925 or s.24(1)(a) of the Land Registration Act 1925 shall be implied in a modified form, the contract shall be construed as requiring a corresponding modification of the covenants implied under Pt I of the Act of 1994 by virtue of the above variations of the effect of the contract.[34]

(iii) The new implied covenants

7.10 Where an instrument effecting or purporting to effect a disposition of property is made on or after July 1, 1995 and the exceptions in (b) above do not apply, there are implied covenants on the part of the person making the disposition, and the nature of these depends on whether the disposition is expressed to be made with full title guarantee or with limited guarantee.[35] If the disposition is not expressed to be made with full title guarantee, or with limited title guarantee, no covenants on the

[28] *ibid.*, s.11(4).
[29] *ibid.*, s.13.
[30] By *ibid.*, s.12(1).
[31] *ibid.*, s.12(2).
[32] *ibid.*, s.12(3).
[33] *ibid.*, s.12(4).
[34] *ibid.*, s.12(5).
[35] *ibid.*, s.1(1), (2). The covenants are not implied, or are modified, in some cases: for these, see below.

part of the disponor are implied. The covenants are implied whether or not the disposition is for valuable consideration.[36] Where in an instrument effecting or purporting to effect a disposition of property a person is expressed to direct the disposition, Pt I of the Act of 1994 applies to him as if he were the person making the disposition.[37]

(1) *Dispositions expressed to be made with full title guarantee.* In such case, the covenants in ss.2, 3(1), (2), 4 and 5 of the Act of 1994 are implied.[38] These covenants are set out in section (iv) below.

(2) *Dispositions expressed to be made with limited title guarantee.* In such cases, the covenants in ss.2, 3(3), 4 and 5 of the Act of 1994 are implied.[39] These covenants are set out in section (iv) below.

(iv) THE TERMS OF THE COVENANTS

(1) *Section 2:* **7.11**

(a) A covenant that the person making the disposition has the right (with the concurrence of any other person conveying the property) to dispose of the property as he purports to; and
(b) a covenant that he will at his own cost do all that he reasonably can to give the person to whom he disposes of the property the title he purports to give.[40]

The obligation under s.2(b) includes, in relation to a disposition of an interest in land the title to which is registered, doing all that he reasonably can to ensure that the person to whom the disposition is made is entitled to be registered as proprietor with at least the class of title registered immediately before the disposition.[41] In relation to a disposition of an interest in land the title to which is required to be registered by virtue of the disposition, the obligation under s.2(b) includes giving all reasonable assistance fully to establish to the satisfaction of the Chief Land Registrar the right of the person to whom the disposition is made to be registered as proprietor.[42]

[36] *ibid.*, s.1(1).
[37] *ibid.*, s.8(3).
[38] *ibid.*, s.1(2)(a).
[39] *ibid.*, s.1(2)(b).
[40] *ibid.*, s.2(1).
[41] *ibid.*, s.2(2)(a).
[42] *ibid.*, s.2(2)(b).

In the case of a disposition of an existing interest in land, a number of presumptions apply, subject to the terms of the instrument, in ascertaining for the purposes of the covenants implied by s.2 what the person making the disposition purports to dispose of. These are:

(1) that where the title to the land is registered, the disposition is of the whole of that interest;
(2) that where the title to the interest is not registered and it appears from the instrument that the interest is a leasehold interest, the disposition is of the property for the unexpired portion of the term of years created by the lease; and
(3) that in any other case where the title to the interest is not registered, the disposition is of the fee simple.[43]

7.12 (2) *Section 3(1), (2).* A covenant that the person making the disposition is disposing of the property free from all charges and incumbrances (monetary or not) and from all other rights exercisable by third parties; but this covenant does not extend to charges, incumbrances and rights which the person making the disposition does not and could not reasonably be expected to know about.[44] This implied covenant extends generally to liabilities imposed and rights conferred by or under any enactment. But it does not so extend to the extent that any such liabilities and rights are not such as to constitute defects in title by reason of being, at the time of the disposition, only potential liabilities and rights in relation to the property, or by reason of being liabilities and rights imposed on or conferred in relation to property generally.[45]

7.13 (3) *Section 3(3).* A covenant that the person making the disposition has not since the last disposition for value:

(a) charged or incumbered the property by means of any charge or incumbrance which subsists at the time when the disposition is made, or granted third party rights in relation to the property which so subsist; or
(b) suffered the property to be so charged or incumbered or subjected to any such rights, and that he is not aware that anyone else has done so since the last disposition for value.[46]

7.14 (4) *Section 4.* Where the disposition is of leasehold land, covenants that the lease is subsisting at the time of the disposition, and that there is no

[43] *ibid.*, s.2(3).
[44] *ibid.*, s.3(1).
[45] *ibid.*, s.3(2).
[46] *ibid.*, s.3(3).

subsisting breach of a condition or tenant's obligation, and nothing which at that time would render the lease liable to forfeiture.[47] If the disposition is the grant of an underlease, the covenants are that the lease out of which the underlease is created is subsisting at the time of the disposition, and that there is no subsisting breach of a condition or tenant's obligation under that superior lease, and nothing which would render that lease liable to forfeiture.[48]

(5) *Section 5.* Where the disposition is a mortgage of property subject to a rentcharge, a covenant that the mortgagor will fully and promptly observe and perform all the obligations under the instrument creating the rentcharge that are for the time being enforceable with respect to the property by the owner of the rentcharge in his capacity as such.[49] Where the disposition is a mortgage of leasehold land, a covenant that the mortgagor will fully and promptly observe and perform all the obligations under the lease subject to the mortgage that are for the time being imposed on him in his capacity as tenant under the lease.[50] Where the disposition is of a mortgage of a commonhold unit, a covenant that the mortgagor will fully and promptly observe and perform all the obligations under the commonhold community statement that are for the time being imposed on him in his capacity as a unit-holder or as a joint unit-holder.[51] **7.15**

In these cases, "mortgage" includes charge, and "mortgagor" is to be construed as including chargor.[52]

(v) EFFECT OF THE NEW COVENANTS

The operation of any of these new covenants which are implied in an instrument can be limited or extended by a term of that instrument.[53] So, for example, the covenant under s.4(1)(b) can be limited by a term stating that it does not apply to any repairing or decorating covenant on the part of the tenant in the lease, in the same way as the old implied covenants were usually so limited.[54] The person making the disposition is not liable under the covenants implied by virtue of s.2(1)(a) (right to dispose), s.3 (charges, incumbrances and third party rights) or s.4 (validity of lease) in respect of any particular matter to which the disposition is expressly **7.16**

[47] *ibid.*, s.4(1).
[48] *ibid.*, s.4(2).
[49] *ibid.*, s.5(1), (2).
[50] *ibid.*, s.5(1), (3).
[51] *ibid.*, s.5(1),(3A), inserted by Commonhold and Leasehold Reform Act 2002, s.68, Sch.5, para.7; SI 2004/1832.
[52] Law of Property (Miscellaneous Provisions) Act 1994, s.5(4).
[53] *ibid.*, s.8(1).
[54] See above, para.7.03.

made subject.[55] Nor is that person liable under any of those covenants for anything to which the disposition is not expressly made subject, but which at the time of the disposition is within the actual knowledge of the person to whom the disposition is made, or which is a necessary consequence of facts that are then within that person's knowledge.[56] For this purpose, s.198 of the Law of Property Act 1925 (deemed notice by virtue of registration) is disregarded.[57] Nor is the person making the disposition so liable where title to the interest disposed of is registered under the Land Registration Act 2002 and the matter in question is at the time of the disposition entered in the register of title of the interest.[58]

The benefit of any covenant implied by virtue of Pt I of the Act of 1994 is annexed and incident to and goes with the estate or interest of the person to whom the disposition is made, and is capable of being enforced by every person in whom that interest or estate is (in whole or in part) for the time being vested.[59]

(c) *Transfer of Part of Land held under Registered Lease*

7.17 In the relatively unusual case of a transfer (at any time) of part only of the land comprised in a registered lease, if the transferor continues to hold land under the lease there is implied on his part a covenant that he and the persons deriving title under him will—

- (a) where the rent reserved by the lease is apportioned, pay the rent apportioned to the part retained,
- (b) comply with the covenants and conditions contained in the lease so far as affecting the part retained, and
- (c) keep the transferee and the persons deriving title under him indemnified against all actions, expenses and claims on account of any failure to comply with (a) and (b) above.[60]

No such covenant is implied where the registered lease is a new tenancy within the meaning of the Landlord and Tenant (Covenants) Act 1995.[61]

[55] Law of Property (Miscellaneous Provisions) Act 1994, s.6(1).
[56] *ibid.*, s.6(2).
[57] *ibid.*, s.6(3).
[58] *ibid.*, s.6(4), inserted by Land Registration Act 2002, s.133, Sch.11, para.31(1), (2).
[59] Law of Property (Miscellaneous Provisions) Act 1994, s.7.
[60] Land Registration Act 2002, s.134(2), Sch.12, para.20(1)(b)(ii), (4), replacing Land Registration Act 1925, s.24(2), which applied to similar effect prior to October 13, 2003.
[61] *ibid.*, para.20(5).

3. The statutory implied covenants on the part of the assignee

7.18 In addition to the implied covenants on the part of the assignor of a lease, there are deemed by statute to be included and implied covenants on the part of the assignee in the following cases.[62] In a conveyance[63] for valuable consideration, other than a mortgage, of the entirety of the land comprised in a lease, for the residue of the term or interest created by the lease, a covenant by the assignee with the conveying party in terms of Pt IX of Sch.2 to the Law of Property Act 1925.[64] That Part is in the following terms:

> "That the assignees, or the persons deriving title under them, will at all times from the date of the conveyance or other date therein stated, duly pay all rent becoming due under the lease creating the term or interest for which the land is conveyed, and observe and perform all the covenants, agreements and conditions therein contained and thenceforth on the part of the lessee to be observed and performed:
>
> And also will at all times, from the date aforesaid, save harmless and keep indemnified the conveying parties and their estate and effects, from and against all proceedings, costs, claims and expenses on account of any omission to pay the said rent or any breach of any of the said covenants, agreements and conditions."

(A similar type of implied covenant is provided for in the case of a conveyance for valuable consideration, other than a mortgage, of part of the land comprised in the lease for the residue of the term or interest created by the lease at an apportioned rent, and it imposes mutual obligations to pay the apportioned parts of the rent and perform and observe the covenants of the lease in relation to each respective part of the land.)[65] Such a covenant is construed as a covenant of indemnity only, and will not entitle the assignor to compel the assignee to perform the covenants in the lease in a case where the lessor has not threatened the assignee with proceedings,[66] nor *semble* to enter the demised premises to

[62] *ibid.*, s.77(1).
[63] Conveyance does not include a demise by way of lease at a rent: *ibid.*, s.77(3); but it does include an assignment of a lease.
[64] *ibid.*, s.77(1)(C).
[65] *ibid.*, s.77(1)(D), Sch.2, Pt X.
[66] *Harris v Boots Cash Chemists Ltd* [1904] 2 Ch. 376. Before there is a specific obligation on the assignee, the covenant must be in clear and unmistakable terms to that effect: *ibid.*

perform the obligations of which the assignee is in default.[67] The covenant is not a covenant of guarantee.[68]

7.19 In relation to leasehold land the title to which is registered under the Land Registration Acts, similar covenants on the parts of assignees are implied on the transfer of any leasehold interest in land under those Acts other than by way of the grant of underleases.[69] The indemnity implied by the Land Registration Act 1925 has been construed as requiring a causative connection between the breach of covenant and the losses claimed, and such causation was found even where the lessee claimed in respect of rent payments that were not strictly due to the lessor.[70] But such covenants are not implied on a transfer of a registered lease which is a new tenancy within the meaning of the Landlord and Tenant (Covenants) Act 1995.[71]

7.20 The Law of Property Act provides that the benefit of such implied covenants shall be annexed and incident to and go with the estate or interest of the implied covenantee,[72] and under the Land Registration Acts the implied covenants are made with the assignor and the persons deriving title under him.[73] In the case of an assignment by a lessee of the whole of the lease for the residue of the term, that provision necessarily has limited effect because the assignee has disposed of the whole of his estate, and therefore the benefit of the implied covenant is effectively personal to the lessee. Such implied covenant may be varied or extended by deed,[74] but in practice it rarely is. The statutory covenant is only implied into conveyances made after December 31, 1925.[75]

4. Implied agreement of assignee apart from statute

7.21 Apart altogether from the statutory implied covenants just considered, there is implied at common law an agreement on the part of each and every assignee of a lease to indemnify the original lessee against breaches

[67] *Stroude v Beazer Homes Ltd* [2006] 2 P.&C.R. 6, para.62.
[68] *Scottish & Newcastle Plc v Raguz (No.1)* [2004] L.&T.R. 11.
[69] Previously Land Registration Act 1925, s.24(1)(b), (2), and now Land Registration Act 2002, s.134(2), Sch.12, paras 20(1)(a), (b)(i), (2), (3).
[70] *Scottish & Newcastle Plc v Raguz (No.3)* [2006] EWHC 821 (Ch) (no valid notice under Covenants Act, s.17 served on lessee). The appeal against this decision is due to be heard by the Court of Appeal in early 2007.
[71] Land Registration Act 2002, Sch.12, para.20(5).
[72] Law of Property Act 1925, s.77(5).
[73] Land Registration Act 1925, s.24; Land Registration Act 2002, Sch.12, para.20.
[74] Law of Property Act 1925, s.77(6).
[75] *ibid.*, s.77(8).

of covenant committed by that assignee during the time when the lease is vested in him.[76] This implied obligation is more limited than the statutory implied covenant, in that it does not extend to breaches occurring after the assignee has further assigned the lease, but it is independent of it.[77] So, where the statutory covenant is expressly excluded, it was held that the more limited implied agreement was not thereby excluded.[78] The reason for the implied agreement is that, as between the lessee and the actual tenant, the liability of the actual tenant is primary and that of the lessee secondary.[79] Today, it is more likely that this implied agreement would be categorised as an obligation to reimburse under the law of restitution, because the original lessee has been obliged to pay money for the sole benefit of the tenant,[80] who would otherwise be unjustly enriched.[81] An original lessee who is called upon to pay rent which should have been, but was not, paid by a remote assignee ("T3") therefore has a direct claim against T3. But if T3 has assigned on to T4, and the "primary" default was by T4, the original lessee has no claim against T3 under this principle.[82] But it is considered that this same principle must apply in the law of restitution where an intermediate assignee, who was liable to the lessor under a direct covenant with the lessor made on the assignment to him, paid the rent or other sums due to the lessor. As between him and the tenant, the tenant was primarily liable to pay, and so the assignee is entitled to recoup his expenditure from the tenant to prevent the unjust enrichment of the tenant.[83]

[76] *Baynton v Morgan* (1888) 22 Q.B.D. 74, 82; *Re Poole and Clarke's Contract* [1904] 2 Ch. 173.

[77] *Moule v Garrett* (1872) L.R. 7 Ex. 101, 103; *Selous Street Properties Ltd v Oronel Fabrics Ltd* [1984] 1 E.G.L.R. 50.

[78] *Re Healing Research Trustee Co. Ltd* [1992] 2 All E.R. 481.

[79] See *Re Downer Enterprises Ltd* [1974] 1 W.L.R. 1460; *Becton Dickinson U.K. Ltd v Zwebner* [1989] Q.B. 208.

[80] See Goff and Jones, *The Law of Restitution* (6th ed.), Ch.15. *Sed quaere* whether a remedy of recoupment would go as far as a right to an indemnity, for example in relation to legal costs incurred: see *op. cit.*, para.13-003, n.10.

[81] But there is at least one material difference in effect: a right of recoupment or subrogation only entitles the party secondarily liable to recover from the tenant the sums which he paid to the lessor; it is not so extensive as an obligation to indemnify, under which the lessee would be entitled to all expenses and costs to which he was put by reason of the breach or non-payment of the tenant.

[82] If it were otherwise, the plaintiff in *R.P.H. Ltd v Mirror Group (Holdings) Ltd* (1992) 65 P. & C.R. 252, would not have had to seek the innovative remedy of an order against his immediate assignee, T2, to pursue the next assignee down the line, T3.

[83] Note that it is the tenant and not the lessor who is unjustly enriched, because the liability of all co-obligors to the lessor is satisfied by the payment by the assignee.

5. Effect of implied covenants and implied agreement on part of assignees

7.22 Whether the lessee has the benefit of an express covenant of indemnity or of the statutorily implied covenant of indemnity, the effect is that if and whenever the lessee is sued on his contract in respect of unpaid rent or breaches of covenant by the tenant, he is as a matter of contract entitled to be indemnified by his immediate assignee. If the statutory covenant has been excluded, and no express covenant of indemnity made, the lessee is entitled to look to the actual defaulting tenant to be indemnified or reimbursed; but this will rarely be of benefit because, generally, the reason for the lessor's pursuing the lessee is that the tenant is insolvent or otherwise unable to pay the lessor's claim.

7.23 Much more difficult questions arise as between the lessee and a remote intermediate assignee,[84] and as between the lessee and a guarantor for any of the assignees or for the actual tenant,[85] where the actual tenant is insolvent. In such cases, there is no express or statutorily implied covenant of which the lessee can avail himself because he did not assign to those persons; and the implied agreement[86] will not serve against persons who were not the actual tenant at the relevant time. Essentially, the questions are: (a) whether the lessee is entitled to be reimbursed because the other persons are "nearer" to the primary obligation than he is; or (b) whether such persons are properly to be regarded as *aequali jure* and therefore all liable to contribute rateably and to contribution from each other; and (c) whether a guarantor, whose liability is of its nature secondary,[87] is in a better position relatively than any of those with primary liabilities to the lessor.

(a) *Proximity to primary obligation*

7.24 In a case where, as between the original lessee and successive assignees of the lease, all are directly and primarily liable to the lessor by reason of covenants made by each assignee with the lessor, it is tempting to suggest that any one of them is entitled to an indemnity, alternatively recoupment, from any other who is closer in the line of assignees to the actual tenant. So, for example, in the case of successive assignments discussed in

[84] i.e. an assignee who is neither the actual tenant nor the person to whom the lessee assigned the lease.

[85] The same issues arise where, in (say) a chain of five assignments, T2, who has given a direct covenant to the lessor, wishes to pursue T4 or T5, or a guarantor for T3, T4, T5 or T6.

[86] i.e. the *Moule v Garrett* principle (para.7.21, above).

[87] Although a surety covenant might well be drafted to impose on the surety a "primary" liability to the landlord.

relation to the liability of assigns of the reversion and of the term (but assuming this time that each of T2 and T3 did make a covenant with L2 upon the assignments of the lease to them):

		1.		4.		5.	
	L	———	L2	———	L3	———	L4
The lease	|						
		2.		3.		6.	
	T	———	T2	———	T3	———	T4

T would be able to recover from T3 as well as from T2 and T4 any sum which he had to pay to L4, even though he did not assign to T3 and T3 was not the tenant at the time when the arrears arose. And a surety for T4 would be *a fortiori* liable to indemnify T because of his proximity to the actual tenant. But this argument does not seem logical, and neither is it the law. If T is claiming to be indemnified, he must be able to prove some express or implied covenant of indemnity; but there is none vis-à-vis T3 except during the time when the lease was actually vested in T3.[88] If T is claiming some relief in quasi-contract or restitution, he must be able to show that he made some compulsory payment (which he admittedly did) and made it for the benefit of T3, and which therefore gives rise to the implied obligation on the part of T3 to repay T, and conversely a right in T to recoup his expenditure. But the payment made by T was not for the benefit of T3 as such, because T3 was not in possession of the demised premises. The payment by T did have the effect of terminating T3's liability for the same sum; but this will be the case with any non-cumulative, several obligation, and it is not the law that a joint and several obligor is entitled to be repaid by another simply because he has, by payment, satisfied the liability of that other.[89] If the "proximity to the tenant" rule did apply, the plaintiff in *R.P.H. Ltd v Mirror Group Holdings Ltd*[90] would not have had to try to obtain an order from the court that the first assignee of the lease pursue his right of indemnity against the second assignee, or alternatively assign to the plaintiff his right of action. It is submitted, therefore, that this argument has no substance.[91]

[88] Above, para.7.06.

[89] Though, in the case of non-cumulative co-obligors, he will be entitled to a contribution.

[90] (1992) 65 P. & C.R. 252. In that case, it was held that an original lessee, who had a right of indemnity from his assignee, had no right to compel that assignee to sue the next assignee for an indemnity, nor to require the first assignee to assign to the original lessee his right of action against the second assignee.

[91] And two first instance decisions, which can be read as suggesting that this is a factor—*Selous Street Properties Ltd v Oronel Fabrics Ltd* [1984] 1 E.G.L.R. 50 and *Becton Dickinson U.K. Ltd v Zwebner* [1989] Q.B. 208—should not be so interpreted.

(b) *Aequali jure*

7.25 The true position in the example given above is that T is entitled to be indemnified by T2, and is entitled to an indemnity or to recoupment from T4[92]; but that as between him and T3 there is no basis on which to distinguish their equal primary liabilities to L4. If T2 is insolvent, and T4 is thought to be unable to pay, T is entitled to a contribution from T3 at common law because they are severally liable in respect of the same debt or damage. T can therefore claim from T3 a percentage of his liability: one half of the sum that he paid to L4 from T3 or, if T4 is solvent, one third of that sum.

(c) *Guarantors*

7.26 For the reasons given in (a) above, it is submitted that the argument that a surety for the actual tenant is liable to indemnify the lessee and other assignees because of his proximity to the tenant is misconceived. In two first instance decisions,[93] it has been held that a lessee is entitled to an indemnity from a guarantor of the tenant because, although there is no contract between the guarantor and the lessee and the guarantor does not have the lease vested in him, the guarantor's liability to the lessor is closely related to that of the tenant, and the tenant's liability is "primary" as between him and the lessee. So the Court has been able to conclude that the guarantor is more liable—by implication, more culpable—than the lessee. It is easy to see how the Court, in a particular case, could want to come to that conclusion[94]; but it is submitted that it is at least doubtful whether it has any sound basis in law. In both the first instance decisions referred to, dicta of Pennycuick J. in *Re Downer Enterprises Ltd*[95] concerning rights of subrogation were relied on in support of the conclusion reached. In that case, an intermediate assignee who had paid the rent to the lessor was held to be entitled, by way of subrogation to the lessor's right, to claim it from the tenant as an expense of the tenant's

[92] See above, para.7.21.

[93] See above, n.91.

[94] In *Becton Dickinson U.K. Ltd v Zwebner*, above, n.91, for example, the judge found as a fact that the assignment to the tenant would not have proceeded unless the surety had guaranteed to the lessor the obligations of the tenant. And in *Kumar v Dunning* [1989] Q.B. 193 at p.201A, Sir Nicolas Browne-Wilkinson V.-C. opined, *obiter*, that such a conclusion was consistent with justice and common sense. *Sed quaere*: this comment was made in the context of deciding whether the surety's covenant touched and concerned the land of the landlord and therefore whether the benefit of it passed at common law to the assignee of the reversion.

[95] [1974] 1 W.L.R. 1460.

liquidation, and therefore in priority to the general creditors. But in that case, the entitlement of the intermediate assignee to an indemnity already existed because, as between the assignee and the tenant in liquidation, the liability of the latter to pay was primary. So subrogation was available as an additional remedy to prevent the unjust enrichment of the company. Subrogation is not a right, but a remedy[96]; and for it to operate as a remedy, there must be a pre-existing right of indemnity, recoupment or contribution. The lessee's entitlement to an indemnity or recoupment as against the tenant's surety cannot therefore be justified on the grounds of a "right" of subrogation alone. The relevant question is whether, as between the lessee and the surety, the surety's liability to pay the lessor is primary and the lessee's is secondary (or alternatively, for there to be a right of contribution, that they are *aequali jure*).

An argument that the surety's liability is primary or equal has to start from the unpromising proposition that, vis-à-vis the lessor, the lessee's liability is unquestionably primary, as it is based on a direct contract, and the surety's is secondary. The surety has given a covenant to the lessor only, guaranteeing the liability of the tenant, a covenant which prima facie sounds in damages for breach.[97] The giving of that covenant will, in many cases,[98] have nothing to do with the lessee at all. There is no express or statutorily implied right of indemnity; and the justification for the implied obligation of the type in *Moule v Garrett*,[99] namely that the payment by the lessee is for the benefit of the tenant in that it is the latter who gets the benefit of the payment by enjoying possession of the land, does not exist: the surety has no right to possession as against the tenant. For the same reason, the surety cannot be said to have been unjustly enriched at the expense of the lessee, although the tenant unquestionably has been. For these reasons, it is submitted that a surety is in a better position than any person directly and primarily liable to the lessor, and that the decisions in *Selous Street Properties Ltd v Oronel Fabrics Ltd*[1] and *Becton Dickinson v Zwebner*[2] might not be followed in a higher **7.27**

[96] See Goff and Jones, *The Law of Restitution* (6th ed.), paras 3-001 *et seq.*

[97] See *Moschi v Lep Air Services Ltd* [1973] A.C. 331. Most surety covenants made in connection with leases go on to provide that, in the event that the assignee fails to pay the rent, the surety will pay it and/or make good to the lessor all losses occasioned thereby. The intention of such provision is to give the lessor a claim against the surety in debt rather than damages; but it does not detract from the position that the surety has a secondary liability. Of course, the surety covenant can be drafted so as to impose a primary liability to the lessor.

[98] i.e. where there is an intermediate assignee between the lessee and the tenant.

[99] Above, para.7.21.

[1] Above, n.91.

[2] *ibid.*

court.[3] To avoid any doubt, the assignor could seek from the guarantor a guarantee of the assignee's express or implied covenant with the assignor, but this will be of no avail to the assignor upon a further assignment of the lease, with which he will not be involved.

6. The Covenants Act

7.28 Consequent on the provisions of the Covenants Act that release an assigning tenant from further liability under the tenant covenants of the lease, the covenants previously implied on the part of the assignee of a term of years[4] (and on the part of the assignor of part of the land comprised in the lease)[5] are no longer implied on an assignment of a new tenancy.[6] In an appropriate case, such covenants may be expressly made in the deed of assignment or transfer; and the limited obligation to reimburse implied at common law[7] probably applies in any event.[8] But the Covenants Act has also provided for the Civil Liability (Contribution) Act 1978 to apply, to provide a jurisdiction to enable persons, where they are jointly and severally liable under a covenant by virtue of the Covenants Act, to claim contribution from each other.[9]

7. Liability as between assignees of the reversion

7.29 The position of the original lessor and his assigns is not dissimilar to that of the original lessee and assignees of the term: several, non-cumulative liability. On assignments made before July 1, 1995 and expressed to be made as beneficial owner, there are implied covenants for title, etc., on the part of the assignor in terms of s.76(1)(A) of and Pt I of Sch.2 to the Law

[3] This particular point was conceded and not argued in *Kumar v Dunning*, above, n.94. In the *Selous Street* case, Hutchison J. also decided that a surety for the lessee was entitled in his own right to be indemnified by the surety for the tenant. It is submitted that, as a secondary obligor himself, the surety for the lessee would be entitled to be indemnified by the tenant (by subrogation to the lessee's right to be so indemnified); but that the two sureties, both of whom have guaranteed the obligation of someone with a primary liability to the lessor, are *aequali jure* and entitled to contribution from each other at common law in respect of any liability in debt and under the Civil Liability (Contribution) Act 1978 in respect of any liability in damages.

[4] See above, para.7.18.

[5] Above, para.7.17.

[6] Covenants Act, ss.14, 30(2), (3); Land Registration Act 2002, s.134(2), Sch.12, para.20(5).

[7] Above, para.7.21.

[8] Following the reasoning in *Re Healing Research Trustee Co. Ltd* [1992] 2 All E.R. 481. It will be of importance where the assigning tenant is not released, i.e. on an unlawful or involuntary assignment.

[9] Covenants Act, s.13(3). See below, paras 16.06, 16.11.

of Property Act 1925.[10] For assignments made on or after July 1, 1995 expressed to be made with full or limited title guarantee, covenants on the part of the assignor are implied under the Law of Property (Miscellaneous Provisions) Act 1994.[11] But there is no statutorily implied covenant by the assignee to perform the landlord's covenants in the lease, or to indemnify the assignor. An express covenant in such terms is often included upon the transfer of a reversion. Otherwise, a lessor who remains liable to the original lessee by reason of privity of contract and who is compelled to expend money or pay damages to the tenant is in principle probably entitled to recoupment from the owner from time to time of the reversionary estate, on the principle in *Moule v Garrett*.[12]

[10] Note that the implied covenants in Pt II of Sch.2 are not implied in this case unless the reversion is itself a lease.

[11] Subject to the transitional provisions and exceptions: see above, paras 7.07, 7.08. Note that the covenants under s.5 are not implied unless the reversion is itself a lease.

[12] (1872) L.R. 7 Ex. 101: see above, paras 7.21 *et seq*.

CHAPTER 8

Rights of Original Lessor and Assignees of the Reversion Against Sub-tenants and Mortgagees of the Term

1. The general principle: no privity

Unlike the relationship between assignees of the term and of the reversion, between the head landlord (called here "the landlord") and his assigns and the sub-tenant there is neither privity of contract nor privity of estate. The sub-tenant's contract is invariably[1] made with the tenant, and the estate is that created by the demise in the underlease to which the landlord is not privy. The landlord cannot therefore sue the sub-tenant on the terms of the sub-lease, and neither can his assigns. Neither can a sub-tenant sue the landlord on the covenants in the headlease, whether directly or by requiring the tenant to sue.[2] To this general principle there are a number of specific exceptions (or quasi-exceptions), and these are considered below. 8.01

[1] It is conceivable that the sub-tenant's covenants might be expressed to be made with the tenant *and* with the landlord, in which circumstances the landlord could take the benefit of those covenants under Law of Property Act 1925, s.56 or Contracts (Rights of Third Parties) Act 1999. This hypothetical situation is to be contrasted with the one, often seen, where the sub-tenant covenants with the tenant to perform the tenant's covenants in the headlease (other than the covenant to pay rent) in so far as they relate to the premises sub-demised: here the covenant is only purportedly made *with* the tenant, albeit the subject-matter of that covenant is by reference to the terms of the headlease. See also *Amsprop Trading Ltd v Harris Distribution Ltd* [1997] 1 W.L.R. 1025. But where the lessor under the sub-lease covenants with the sub-tenant to observe and perform the lessee's covenants in the headlease, the sub-tenant can compel the lessor to observe and perform them, for such a covenant is not a mere covenant of indemnity: *Ayling v Wade* [1961] 2 Q.B. 228. See also *Stroude v Beazer Homes Ltd* [2006] 2 P.&C.R. 6, para.62, on implied rights of concurrent obligors to enter to perform obligations, and compare *Harris v Boots Cash Chemists Ltd* [1904] 2 Ch. 376; above, para.7.18, n.66.

[2] See *South of England Dairies Ltd v Baker* [1906] 2 Ch. 631.

2. The exceptions

(a) *Sub-letting for whole term of headlease*

8.02 A purported sub-lease of the whole (or part) of the premises demised by the headlease for the residue of (or more than) the term of the headlease amounts in law to an assignment of the tenant's interest in the whole (or that part) of the premises.[3] Thus, from the date of the purported sub-lease, landlord and intended sub-tenant stand in a relationship of privity of estate, and those covenants of the headlease which touch and concern the land comprised in the purported sub-lease may be enforced by either landlord or intended sub-tenant, as the case might be. The tenant in effect drops out of the picture so far as the premises comprised in the purported sub-lease are concerned, although he may retain his liability (and rights) as the originally contracting lessee, and anomalously he does have the right to sue the intended sub-tenant[4] for any element of profit rent in the purported sub-lease.[5] This is not really a case of an exception, in that the intended sub-lease never comes into existence.

(b) *Surrender or merger*

8.03 Where a reversion expectant on a lease of land is surrendered or merged, the estate or interest which as against the lessee for the time being confers the next vested right to the land, is deemed the reversion for the purpose of preserving the same incidents and obligations as would have affected the original reversion had there been no surrender or merger thereof.[6] Thus, where a headlease is surrendered by the tenant to the landlord, the sub-tenancy continues in accordance with its terms, and the landlord is entitled to enforce the conditions and tenant's covenants of the sub-tenancy against the sub-tenant.[7] Correspondingly, the landlord becomes bound by any of the landlord's covenants of the sub-tenancy. Once again, this is not a true exception in that a privity of estate is created by statute as from the time when the headlease is surrendered or merged. The statute does not apply if the underlease terminates before the headlease.[8]

[3] *Beardman v Wilson* (1868) L.R. 4 C.P. 57; *Milmo v Carreras* [1946] K.B. 306; *Parc (Battersea) Ltd v Hutchinson* [1999] L.&T.R. 554.

[4] Though not to distrain for it.

[5] *Milmo v Carreras*, above.

[6] Law of Property Act 1925, s.139(1).

[7] *Bromley Park Garden Estates Ltd v George* (1991) 23 H.L.R. 441.

[8] *Twogates Properties Ltd v Birmingham Midshires Building Society* (1997) 75 P.&C.R. 386.

(c) *Statutory continuation or deeming*

Where a business sub-tenancy continues by virtue of Pt II of the Landlord and Tenant Act 1954 beyond the duration of the interest of the landlord under the sub-tenancy, the provision of the Law of Property Act 1925 considered in (b) above applies as if it had provided for the coming to an end of the reversion for any reason other than surrender or merger.[9] The head landlord therefore becomes the landlord of the sub-tenant on the terms of the sub-tenancy as from the expiration of the headlease, and is thenceforth entitled to enforce the conditions of the sub-tenancy. The same applies in relation to residential long tenancies at low rents.[10] **8.04**

Statutory codes affording security of tenure to residential tenants also make provision for the continuation of a sub-tenancy beyond the termination of the head tenancy, and for the enforceability of the obligations incident to the sub-tenancy in such cases.[11]

(d) *Restrictive covenants*

A landlord may be entitled in equity to enforce some of the covenants in the headlease against a sub-tenant. For the reasons given,[12] this cannot be achieved as a matter of contract; but equitable remedies may lie against a sub-tenant who takes the sub-tenancy subject to restrictive covenants in the headlease. The position is governed by the doctrine of notice in unregistered land, because a restrictive covenant made between a lessee and a lessor is not registrable under the Land Charges Act 1925 as a Class D(ii) land charge[13] or otherwise. Only equity's darling, the purchaser of a legal estate without notice, will take free from the restrictive covenant. Although the sub-tenant purchases a legal estate,[14] he has constructive notice of any restrictive covenant in the tenant's lease because he is entitled to call for that lease and inspect it.[15] He will therefore be bound by a restrictive covenant in the headlease and, in principle, be liable to **8.05**

[9] Landlord and Tenant Act 1954, s.65(2).

[10] By virtue of Local Government and Housing Act 1989, s.186, Sch.10, para.20(4).

[11] Rent Act 1977, s.137; Housing Act 1988, s.18.

[12] Above, para.8.01.

[13] Land Charges Act 1972, s.2(5)(ii). See *Dartstone v Cleveland* [1969] 1 W.L.R. 1807.

[14] Unless the underlease is for more than three years and is not made under seal, or unless, in the case of an underlease for three years or less not made under seal, a premium is paid or less than the best rent is reserved: Law of Property Act 1925, ss.52(1), 54(2).

[15] Under Law of Property Act 1925, s.44(2), (4), (5); *Teape v Douse* (1905) 92 L.T. 319.

have it enforced against him by equitable relief, and in particular the grant of an injunction.[16]

Where the title to the tenant's land is registered and the restrictive covenant relates to that land, the sub-tenant is bound by the restrictive covenant, whether his sub-tenancy is registered or not.[17] The leasehold restrictive covenant is an incident of the registered leasehold title and so does not require substantive registration as an "interest affecting a registered estate".[18] But if the tenant's land is not registered, because either it was granted before October 13, 2003 for a term exceeding 21 years and has not been assigned since that date or it was granted for a term not exceeding seven years,[19] the doctrine of constructive notice applies as in the case of unregistered land.[20] Where the restrictive covenant relates to land other than the demised premises, it will be unenforceable against a sub-tenant unless registered.[21]

(e) *Indirect enforcement by forfeiture*

8.06 Where a landlord validly forfeits his tenant's lease, any inferior interests in the nature of mortgages or sub-tenancies also terminate unless either the tenant, or the mortgagee or sub-tenant as the case may be, obtains relief against the forfeiture. If the tenant obtains relief, the mortgage or sub-tenancy is automatically reinstated; if the mortgagee or sub-tenant himself has to apply for and obtain relief, the order for relief will usually be for the vesting of a new lease in him,[22] though the sub-tenant has the right, under statute and at common law, to apply for relief in the name of the tenant.[23] As a term of granting relief to a sub-tenant, the Court will generally require the sub-tenant to remedy the breach of covenant which entitled the landlord to forfeit the headlease,[24] because the overriding

[16] See, e.g. *Parker v Whyte* (1863) 1 H. & M. 167; and *Clements v Welles* (1865) L.R. 1 Eq. 200.

[17] By virtue of Land Registration Act 2002, ss.27(2), 29(4), 33(c).

[18] Within the meaning of ibid., ss.28(1), 29(1). Although the intending sub-tenant is entitled to see the lease and therefore is fixed with notice of its terms, constructive notice has no part to play in registered conveyancing under the Land Registration Act 2002.

[19] Nor within any of the other exceptional categories of *ibid.*, s.27(2)(ii) to (v).

[20] The landlord has to produce his own lease to prove title and Law of Property Act 1925, s.44 is not disapplied in such a case.

[21] Land Registration Act 2002, ss.29(2), 33(c).

[22] See *Escalus Properties Ltd v Robinson* [1996] Q.B. 231, in which it was held that a sub-tenant or mortgagee could in some circumstances seek relief in the name of the tenant.

[23] *Bland v Ingram's Estates (No.1)* [2001] Ch. 767, extending the principle to an equitable chargee.

[24] *A fortiori* where the breach, for example non-repair, was in fact the breach of the sub-tenant under the terms of the sub-tenancy.

principle is that the landlord, who has exercised a legal right, is entitled (if relief is to be granted) to be placed in the same position as if no breach of covenant had occurred.[25] In this way, the terms of the headlease may be capable of indirect enforcement against the sub-tenant.

Where the sub-tenancy comes into existence as a result of a breach of covenant by the tenant known to the sub-tenant at the time of grant, the sub-tenancy may be ordered to be surrendered.[26]

(f) *Indirect enforcement by levying distress*

Although the sub-tenant is not liable to pay rent due under the headlease,[27] his chattels on the demised premises are liable to be distrained upon by the landlord in the event that the tenant does not pay the rent under the headlease. In this respect, at common law the sub-tenant was in no different position from any stranger to the headlease whose goods happened to be found on the demised premises.[28] The matter is now governed by the Law of Distress Amendment Act 1908. A lawful sub-tenant whose rent is the full value of the premises comprised in the sub-tenancy and who pays rent at least quarterly may declare that the goods distrained upon are his, and that he is willing to pay his rent directly to the landlord until the landlord's arrears are paid off, and tender any arrears owed by him to the tenant.[29] By so doing, the landlord is effectually precluded from proceeding further with the distress against the goods of the sub-tenant.[30] As an alternative, the landlord is given the right to serve a notice on the sub-tenant stating the amount of the arrears under the headlease and requiring the sub-tenant to pay his rent directly to the landlord until the arrears are discharged.[31] In this way, a landlord can seek to take the benefit, to the extent permitted, of the sub-tenant's obligation to pay rent to the tenant despite the absence of privity of contract or estate as between landlord and sub-tenant. 8.07

[25] See *Egerton v Jones* [1939] 2 K.B. 702.

[26] The sub-tenant has knowingly procured a breach of contract by the tenant: *Hemingway Securities Ltd v Dunraven Ltd* (1995) 71 P.&C.R. 30; *Crestfort Ltd v Tesco Stores Ltd* [2005] 3 E.G.L.R. 25.

[27] Nor is he liable to make a contribution to, or to repay, rent paid by the original lessee to the landlord upon the insolvency of the assignee of the headlease, even if the sub-tenant exclusively enjoys possession of the premises demised by the headlease: *Bonner v Tottenham and Edmonton Permanent Investment Building Society* [1899] 1 Q.B. 161.

[28] Such a person had a right of recoupment against the tenant on the basis that he had compulsorily discharged a liability which was the tenant's, thereby unjustly enriching the tenant: *Exall v Partridge* (1799) 8 T.R. 308.

[29] Law of Distress Amendment Act 1908, ss.1, 5.

[30] *ibid.*, s.2.

[31] *ibid.*, s.6. See *Rhodes v Allied Dunbar Pension Services Ltd* [1989] 1 W.L.R. 800.

3. Mortgagees of leases

8.08 A post-1925 legal mortgage of a lease can only be effected by a subdemise for a term of years absolute, less by one day at least than the term of the lease and subject to a provision for cesser on redemption, or by a charge by deed expressed to be by way of legal mortgage.[32] Of these, the second is by far the most common in standard commercial lending. The effect of such a charge by deed is that the mortgagee has the same protection, powers and remedies as if a sub-term less by one day than the term of the lease had been thereby created in favour of him.[33]

The position of the mortgagee is similar in some respects to that of the sub-tenant, although in fact and in law a sub-term is not created by a charge by way of legal mortgage. The mortgagee never becomes liable to the landlord under any terms of the lease or of the mortgage; though in order to preserve his security the mortgagee will have to ensure that the rent, etc. under the lease is duly paid. Even if the mortgagee takes possession of the demised premises, he does so under his own deemed sub-lease, and not as the tenant or as an assignee of the tenant. In one respect at least, however, the mortgagee is in a better position than the sub-tenant: most mortgages provide that, in circumstances of default by the mortgagor, the mortgagee can act and take proceedings in the name of the mortgagor, and so the mortgagee can in such circumstances (in the name of the mortgagor) enforce the landlord's obligations in the lease.

8.09 An equitable mortgagee or chargee of leasehold land obtains no legal estate or interest in the land. It is *a fortiori* that the mortgage or charge is something contractual between the tenant and the chargee to which the landlord is not privy, and under which he therefore has no rights.

8.10 All mortgagees and chargees are vulnerable to the two means of indirect enforcement against them of the tenant's covenants,[34] though the position of a mortgagee or chargee is different in relation to the remedy of distress, in that the mortgagee or chargee is not an "undertenant" for the purposes of the Law of Distress (Amendment) Act 1908, and so cannot be served with a notice to pay any sums to the landlord. The landlord may, however, still effectually serve such a notice on a sub-tenant in a case where the tenant has charged the demised premises, whether by a fixed or a floating charge.[35]

[32] Law of Property Act 1925, s.86(1).
[33] *ibid.*, s.87(1)(b).
[34] Above, paras 8.06 and 8.07.
[35] *Rhodes v Allied Dunbar (Pension Services) Ltd* [1989] 1 W.L.R. 800.

CHAPTER 9

Insolvency and Disclaimer

1. Insolvency of individuals

On the appointment of a trustee of the estate of a bankrupt, or upon the Official Receiver becoming trustee, the estate of the bankrupt vests in the trustee or in the Official Receiver.[1] That estate will include leasehold property previously vested in the bankrupt,[2] unless the lease is held on trust for any other person,[3] or unless the lease is one of the following types of tenancy: 9.01

(1) an assured tenancy or assured agricultural occupancy within the meaning of the Housing Act 1988, the terms of which inhibit an assignment as mentioned in s.127(5) of the Rent Act 1977;

(2) a protected tenancy, within the meaning of the Rent Act 1977 in respect of which, by virtue of any provision of Pt IX of that Act, no premium can lawfully be required as a condition of assignment[4];

(3) a tenancy of a dwelling-house by virtue of which the bankrupt is, within the meaning of the Rent (Agriculture) Act 1976, a protected occupier of the dwelling-house, and the terms of which inhibit an assignment as mentioned in s.127(5) of the Rent Act 1977[5]; and

(4) a secure tenancy, within the meaning of Pt IV of the Housing Act 1985, which is not capable of being assigned except in the cases mentioned in s.91(3) of that Act, as amended.

[1] Insolvency Act 1986, s.306.

[2] But not a statutory tenancy or a right to remain in possession on the expiry of a long lease protected by Pt I of the Landlord and Tenant Act 1954: see *de Rothschild v Bell* [2000] Q.B. 33, and n.4, below.

[3] Insolvency Act 1986, s.283(3)(a).

[4] A statutory tenant under the Rent Act has no property in the demised premises capable of vesting in his trustee, merely a status of irremovability (see *Megarry's The Rent Acts* (11th ed.), Vol.1, pp.252 *et seq.*).

[5] A statutory tenant under the Rent (Agriculture) Act has no property in the demised premises capable of vesting in his trustee, merely a status of irremovability (see *Megarry's The Rent Acts* (11th ed.), Vol.1, p.302).

In these four cases, the tenancy does not automatically vest in the trustee, but the trustee can serve a notice in writing on the bankrupt which causes such a tenancy to vest in the trustee as part of the estate, and the vesting relates back to the commencement of the bankruptcy.[6]

9.02 When a lease is vested in the trustee as part of the bankrupt's estate, the trustee becomes liable under the covenants in the lease which touch and concern the demised premises, including the payment of rent. A covenant against assignment expressed to be made by the bankrupt and his successors in title will bind the trustee,[7] although the statutory vesting in the trustee will not amount to a breach of that covenant. The trustee can only get rid of his personal liability from the date of the vesting of the lease in him by disclaiming it[8]; though he can terminate the lease, and thereby limit his continuing liability, by any of the means (e.g. a notice to quit) by which the bankrupt could have terminated it. If the trustee assigns the lease, his liability will terminate from that time forward, privity of estate having then ceased to exist, and there being no contractual liability as between the landlord and the trustee.

9.03 Where it is the landlord and not the tenant who becomes bankrupt, the trustee of the estate of the landlord will have the right to enforce all the tenant's covenants in the lease which touch and concern the demised premises, and correspondingly will be bound to perform all the covenants on the part of the landlord which do so.

2. Corporate insolvency

9.04 When a limited company goes into liquidation, whether compulsory or voluntary, its property, including leasehold property, remains vested in it, and does not vest in its liquidator.[9] The company in liquidation remains liable on its covenants, including the covenant to pay rent, but enforcement of such covenants is restricted by the Insolvency Act 1986.[10] A

[6] Insolvency Act 1986, s.308A.

[7] *Re Wright, Ex p. Landau v The Trustee* [1949] Ch. 729.

[8] See below.

[9] The Court has power to order the vesting of such property, but this is rarely sought: see Insolvency Act 1986, s.145.

[10] *ibid.*, s.126(1) (before winding-up order) and s.130(2) (after winding-up order). After a winding-up order, the leave of the Companies Court is required to bring proceedings against the company in liquidation. In a voluntary winding-up, leave is not required, but the Court would, it is submitted, use its inherent jurisdiction to stay proceedings whose sole object was to try to give the claimant a fuller recovery than that to which he would be entitled by proving for his debt or by enforcing his security. Where proceedings are not so directed, e.g. where the landlord seeks to prevent the company, by its liquidator, using the demised premises in breach of a restrictive covenant in the lease, leave should be granted to allow the action to continue; and where the landlord seeks on clear grounds to forfeit the lease and recover possession, the Companies Court routinely grants an order of leave to sue and summary possession, known as a "Blue Jeans" order,

liquidator, who in certain respects is no more than an agent of the company, is bound by the company's covenant not to assign the lease without the consent of the landlord.[11] A liquidator of a company also has power under the Insolvency Act to disclaim the lease,[12] and he may, on behalf of the company, terminate the lease in any way in which the company could have terminated it. The same applies in principle to a limited liability partnership.[13]

3. Disclaimer

This section is concerned in particular with the effect of a disclaimer by a liquidator or trustee in bankruptcy on the enforceability of the covenants in the lease. It does not purport to give a full analysis of all aspects of the statutory provisions relating to disclaimer. **9.05**

(a) *Introduction*

The power to disclaim in the event of insolvency is conferred on trustees in bankruptcy and liquidators of limited companies by the Insolvency Act 1986.[14] Where a lease is vested in a bankrupt or in a company in liquidation, the trustee in bankruptcy or liquidator, as the case may be, can disclaim the bankrupt's or company's interest in the lease, and particular requirements for a disclaimer of a lease are specified in the Act[15] and in the Insolvency Rules 1986. The effect of a disclaimer is to determine, as from the date of the disclaimer, the rights, interests and **9.06**

where it is clear that the company cannot pay the rent arrears (*Re Blue Jeans Sales Ltd* [1979] 1 W.L.R. 362). Where the landlord claims that he is entitled to continuing rent for the premises as an expense in the liquidation (see *Re Downer Enterprises Ltd* [1974] 1 W.L.R. 1460), an application in the Companies Court would be the better procedure.

[11] *Re Farrow's Bank* [1921] 2 Ch. 164.

[12] See below.

[13] The Limited Liability Partnership Regulations 2001 (SI 2001/1090), regs. 4 and 5.

[14] ss.315–321 in respect of individual insolvency, and ss.178–182 in respect of insolvent companies. Equivalent powers are conferred on liquidators of limited liability partnerships: The Limited Liability Partnership Regulations 2001, reg.5. Also, where a company or LLP is dissolved, and is at the time of dissolution the tenant of leasehold property, the tenancy vests in the Crown as *bona vacantia* under Companies Act 1985, s.654, and the Crown has a similar right to disclaim under s.656 of that Act. Where the Crown does disclaim, the effect is as if the liquidator of the company or LLP had disclaimed under the Insolvency Act immediately before the dissolution of the company. This section therefore does not consider further disclaimers under the Companies Act, but for a full consideration and analysis, see *Allied Dunbar Assurance Plc v Fowle* [1994] B.C.C. 422.

[15] ss.179, 317.

liabilities of the company or the bankrupt and his trustee in the lease.[16] Any person suffering loss as a result of the disclaimer is deemed a creditor to the extent of the loss suffered, and can prove for the loss in the winding up, or as a bankruptcy debt, as the case may be.[17] Property cannot be disclaimed under the statutory provisions unless it is property of some value,[18] but in all cases a lease will satisfy this test because it carries with it a right to possession of land or to receipt of rents and profits of the land.

9.07 A lease cannot be disclaimed as to part of the demised premises, but has to be disclaimed as a whole or not at all.[19] But where, as a result of a severance, only a part of premises demised had been assigned to the bankrupt or company, or where the bankrupt or company had assigned away part of the demised premises and remained the tenant of part only, it is considered that the trustee or liquidator could disclaim the whole of the interest vested in the bankrupt or company, even though that was not the whole of the premises originally demised by the lease, at all events where the severance had been concurred in by the landlord. In such a case, the obligations of the lessee and the landlord in relation to the other part or parts of the demised premises would be unaffected by the disclaimer of the bankrupt's interest in his part.

(b) *Effect of disclaimer on leasehold covenants*

9.08 Where no person other than the bankrupt, the trustee and the landlord (or the company in liquidation and the landlord) is interested in the lease or subject to any of the leasehold obligations, whether as principal or surety, the disclaimer will terminate the lease for the future for all purposes.[20] As between the landlord and the bankrupt, the lease is deemed to have been surrendered.[21] This will be the case where the bankrupt (or company) is the original lessee and there is no guarantor for his obligations. No one else is bound by the tenant's obligations, and there is no one in whom the lease can be vested.[22]

[16] *ibid.*, ss.178(4)(a), 315(3)(a). In the case of a disclaimer by a trustee in bankruptcy, the disclaimer also discharges the trustee from all personal liability under the lease as from the commencement of his trusteeship: s.315(3)(b).

[17] *ibid.*, ss.178(6), 315(5).

[18] A contract that consists only of valueless obligations will not be property for these purposes: *Re SSSL Realisations (2002) Ltd* [2005] 1 B.C.L.C. 1.

[19] *Ex p. Allen, re Fussell* (1882) 20 Ch.D. 341; and see *MEPC v Scottish Amicable* [1993] 2 E.G.L.R. 93.

[20] See the discussion in *Warnford v Duckworth* [1979] Ch. 127.

[21] See *Hindcastle v Barbara Attenborough Associates Ltd* [1997] A.C. 70.

[22] Under Insolvency Act 1986, ss.181, 182, or ss.320, 321.

But if the bankrupt (or company) is an assignee of the lease, or if he is the original lessee but a guarantor of his liabilities under the lease exists, or where a sub-tenancy exists, the lease is deemed not wholly to have disappeared from the picture. A disclaimer under the Insolvency Act does not, except so far as is necessary for releasing the bankrupt and his estate and the trustee (or the company) from any liability, affect the rights or liabilities of any other person.[23] **9.09**

Therefore, the liabilities of the bankrupt's (or company's) guarantor, and of any original lessee and intermediate assignees of the term who gave direct covenants to the landlord, are not terminated.[24] The guarantor remains liable on his own contract, made by reference to the obligations of the bankrupt under the lease, but the original lessee and any qualifying intermediate assignee are liable under the covenants of the lease. To that extent, therefore, the leasehold covenants remain enforceable, notwithstanding the disclaimer by or on behalf of the actual tenant.

The guarantor or any of the original tenant and qualifying intermediate assignees will be entitled to apply for the residue of the term of the lease to be vested in them.[25] Until a vesting order is made, the lease is non-existent, but in so far as the rights and obligations of others are concerned it is deemed to remain in existence.[26] The landlord may forfeit the lease for non-payment of rent or for any other breach of covenant entitling him to re-enter. Upon such forfeiture, the lease is treated by the landlord as terminated for the future for all purposes, and the guarantor's, original lessee's and intermediate assignees' liabilities are then terminated. **9.10**

Where a sub-tenancy exists, the effect of the disclaimer is to terminate the contractual relationship (or relationship of obligations existing by virtue of privity of estate) as between the bankrupt (or company) and the sub-tenant[27]; but the sub-tenant's interest in the sub-demised premises is not terminated, and he is *pro tempore* entitled to remain in possession as **9.11**

[23] Insolvency Act 1986. ss.178(4)(b), 315(3). This means the liability of the bankrupt under pre-existing rights, capable of being terminated by the disclaimer, and not the statutory liability to compensate for loss caused by the disclaimer: see *Hindcastle Ltd v Barbara Attenborough Associates Ltd*, above.

[24] *Hindcastle*, above, overruling *Stacey v Hill* [1901] 1 K.B. 660 in relation to the liability of a surety.

[25] It had previously been held that a guarantor was not entitled to apply for a vesting order (*Re No.1 London Ltd* [1991] B.C.L.C. 501; *Re Yarmarine (I.W.) Ltd* [1992] B.C.C. 28), but these decisions were made before *Stacey v Hill* was overruled in *Hindcastle*, and on the basis that the guarantor's liability ended with the principal's. *Hindcastle* has now conclusively established that this is not the case, and the guarantor's continuing liability is a "liability in respect of the demised premises" within the meaning of the Act, entitling him to apply for the lease to be vested in him.

[26] *Hindcastle*, above.

[27] *Re A.E. Realisations Ltd* [1988] 1 W.L.R. 200.

against the landlord.[28] He is not liable to be sued on the covenants in his sub-lease by the landlord,[29] but he is vulnerable to a forfeiture of the headlease, and may have to apply for a vesting order to protect his interest. Indeed, the landlord can put the sub-tenant (or a mortgagee) to his election by applying for a vesting order. If the sub-tenant or mortgagee declines to accept an order vesting the lease in him, he is excluded thenceforth from all interest in the property.[30] His rights and liabilities are ended if a vesting order is made in favour of some other person.[31]

[28] *Smalley v Hardinge* (1881) 7 Q.B.D. 524; *Hindcastle*, above.

[29] Nor can he enforce the obligations of the lessee against the landlord.

[30] Insolvency Act 1986, ss.182(4), 321(4); and see *Re A.E. Realisations Ltd*, above.

[31] See *Re A.E. Realisations Ltd*, above. But the right to possession of a statutory tenant under the Rent Act 1977 cannot be so affected: *Re Vedmay* [1994] 1 E.G.L.R. 74. The Court was able to reach this distinction on the ground that a statutory tenant has no proprietory interest in the demised premises.

CHAPTER 10

Third Party and Non-Party Covenants

Most commonly, leases are made by two parties, the landlord and the tenant. But two other parties to deeds of lease are regularly encountered: a surety for the obligations of the tenant, and a management company to which some or all of the obligations of the landlord are allotted. A consideration of the scope and enforceability of their obligations casts some light on the law relating to enforceability of covenants in old tenancies as a whole, although, particularly in the case of the surety, some aspects of their obligations are best regarded as *sui generis*. 10.01

This Chapter then considers recent statutory provisions enabling non-parties to a lease to take the benefit, and even become subject to the obligations, of the covenants of one or more parties to the lease.[1]

1. Sureties

(a) *Sureties for original lessees*

A surety for the obligations of the original lessee is invariably a party to the deed by which the lease is made. There are generally two forms of covenant of guarantee: one, whereby the surety covenants that the lessee will perform all his obligations under the lease, and the other, whereby the surety covenants to pay rent, etc. and to perform the covenants in the event that the tenant does not. The first is a classic guarantee covenant, whose effect is that the surety is in breach of his covenant the moment the tenant is in default,[2] and which gives rise to a remedy against the surety in damages for breach of covenant.[3] The second is in the nature of a covenant of indemnity, rather than of guarantee, and gives rise to a remedy in debt in the event that the surety fails to pay. It is very common to see both these formulations together in modern leases; the second has the advantage that the surety can be sued in debt and, in an appropriate case, summary judgment recovered for the full amount of the debt, rather than a judgment for damages to be assessed. A third limb is also often 10.02

[1] Below, paras 10.10 *et seq.*

[2] Because the obligation of the surety is to "see to it" that the lessee performs his obligations: *Cerium Investments Ltd v Evans* (1991) 62 P. & C.R. 203.

[3] See *ibid.* and *Moschi v Lep Air Services Ltd* [1973] A.C. 331.

seen: a covenant by the surety to take up a new lease on the same terms in the event of a disclaimer of the existing lease by the liquidator or trustee in bankruptcy of the lessee.[4]

10.03 The surety's covenant is made with the lessor, and the lessor can sue on the direct covenant between them. But if the landlord assigns the reversion, and does not expressly assign the benefit of the surety's covenant, the assignee enjoys neither privity of contract[5] nor privity of estate with the surety. Can the assignee of the reversion call on the surety in the event of the tenant's default? The assignee of the reversion cannot rely on s.141 of the Law of Property Act 1925 because the covenant is not a covenant "on the lessee's part to be observed or performed" within the meaning of that section.

This problem was considered and resolved by the House of Lords in *Swift (P & A) Investments Ltd v Combined English Stores Group Ltd*,[6] in which it was held that, because the covenant touched and concerned the land,[7] the benefit of it passed with the land at common law. It was subsequently held that the benefit of a surety's covenant to take a new lease in the event of a disclaimer similarly passed to an assignee of the reversion.[8] It would seem, therefore, that the benefit of a covenant by a third party which touches and concerns the demised land will be capable of enforcement by successors in title of the landlord or tenant, as the case may be.

10.04 It has long been established that a surety will be entitled to treat himself as released from his contract of guarantee if the obligations which he has guaranteed are varied by the principals without his consent in such a way

[4] After some uncertainty, it was considered that this obligation survived the disclaimer and consequential release of the surety himself (as was then perceived to be the effect of a disclaimer by the liquidator of an original lessee): *Re Yarmarine (I.W.) Ltd* [1992] B.C.C. 28. But this aspect of a surety's liability has been overtaken by the decision of the House of Lords in *Hindcastle v Barbara Attenborough Associates Ltd* [1997] A.C. 70, holding that a surety is not released in such circumstances. Now, the only benefit to the landlord of this third limb seems to be to enable the surety to be put into legal possession of the demised premises, which may effectually absolve the landlord from statutory or common law liabilities which depend on possession, occupation or control of the premises.

[5] Unless the surety's covenant purports to be made with the assignee, or the covenant purports to confer a benefit on the assignee (or all assignees) of the covenant, in which case the Contracts (Rights of Third Parties) Act 1999, if not excluded, will apply so as to enable the assignee to enforce the guarantee. See below, paras 10.10 *et seq*.

[6] [1989] A.C. 632.

[7] Because it increased the value of the reversion: see the discussion of Lord Oliver's four-part test for touching and concerning, above, paras 4.10 and 4.11.

[8] *Coronation Street Industrial Properties Ltd v Ingall Industries Plc* [1989] 1 W.L.R. 304.

that it cannot be said, without factual inquiry, that the surety could not be prejudiced by the variation.[9] Where a surety is so released from his guarantee obligations, he is also released from subsidiary obligations that he enters into as principal, such as the obligation to take a new lease in the event of a disclaimer.[10]

(b) *Sureties for assignees of the lease*

Some alienation covenants in leases expressly provide for the landlord to be entitled to require the provision of a guarantor for the obligations of an assignee of the term; in other cases, it may be a reasonable condition for the landlord to impose, or something that he is entitled to impose,[11] on the giving of consent to the proposed assignment. In such cases, it has become standard practice for the assignee to covenant with the landlord in the licence to assign to observe and perform the tenant's covenants for the residue of the term[12]; and the surety will usually guarantee this obligation of the assignee. It is considered that the covenant of such a surety will pass with the reversionary estate at common law in the same way as the covenant of the surety for the original lessee.[13] **10.05**

On its true construction, the covenant of such a surety may be one of guarantee of the new, direct covenant of the assignee with the landlord, and not a guarantee of the terms of the lease itself. Where, therefore, the assignee further assigns the lease with the landlord's consent, and the landlord and the further assignee agree to vary the terms of the lease for the duration of that assignee's ownership of the lease, the covenant of the first assignee (which was made by reference to the terms of the lease as they then were) was not varied, and the surety for him not released.[14] The suggestion in some cases[15] that a lessee is bound by variations of the lease made by his assignees, has now been conclusively rejected by the Court of Appeal.[16] In considering whether a surety has been released by a

[9] *Holme v Brunskill* (1877) 3 Q.B.D. 495. See also *Selous Street Properties Ltd v Oronel Fabrics Ltd* [1984] 1 E.G.L.R. 50; *West Horndon Industrial Park Ltd v Phoenix Timber Group Ltd* [1995] 1 E.G.L.R. 77; *Howard de Walden Estates v Pasta Place Ltd* [1995] 1 E.G.L.R. 79, and *Metropolitan Properties Co. (Regis) Ltd v Bartholomew* [1995] 1 E.G.L.R. 65, [1996] 1 E.G.L.R. 82.

[10] *Howard de Walden Estates v Pasta Place Ltd*, above.

[11] Under Landlord and Tenant Act 1927, s.19(1A): see below, para.24.05.

[12] See *Estates Gazette Ltd v Benjamin Restaurants Ltd* [1994] 1 W.L.R. 1528.

[13] See above, para.10.03.

[14] *Metropolitan Properties Co. (Regis) Ltd v Bartholomew* [1996] 1 E.G.L.R. 82. That was so even though the first assignee was a party to the deed by which *inter alia* the variation of the lease was effected.

[15] *Centrovincial Estates Ltd v Bulk Storage Plc* (1983) 46 P. & C.R. 393; *Selous Street Properties Ltd v Oronel Fabrics Ltd* [1984] 1 E.G.L.R. 50.

[16] *Friends Provident Life Office v British Railways Board* [1996] 1 All E.R. 336.

variation in the contract guaranteed, therefore, it is necessary to identify exactly the contract or covenant which the particular surety has guaranteed, and to see whether *its* terms have been varied without the surety's consent.

2. Management companies

10.06 Quite commonly, in leases of units on trading or industrial estates and in long leases of flats, a management company (which may or may not be owned by the lessees) is a party to the leases of the units on the estate or the flats in the building. In such cases, the structure of the relevant obligations in the lease is generally as follows. The lessee covenants with the lessor and with the management company to pay his rent and the service charge to the management company[17]; the management company covenants to insure and to carry out repairs to the common parts of the estate, or the common parts and structure and exterior of the building, as the case may be; and the lessor's covenant is limited to a covenant for quiet enjoyment. In effect, therefore, the management company takes over some of the lessor's obligations in return for the payment by the lessee of its proportion of the costs incurred in carrying out those obligations.

The ability to be able to ensure that the management company does carry out its obligations is self-evidently of importance and value to the lessees of the estate or building. As between the original lessee and the company, the matter is governed by privity of contract, and no difficulty arises in principle. But what happens when the lessee assigns his lease, and what happens if the management company is wound up or purports to assign its functions to another? These matters are addressed in the following paragraphs.

(a) *Assignment of lease*

10.07 It has been seen[18] that an assignee of the term is bound by those tenant covenants, and is entitled to the benefit of those landlord covenants, in the lease that touch and concern the demised premises, because they are incidental to, or "imprinted on", the leasehold estate. But the enforceability of such covenants as between the lessor and his successors in title on the one hand and the assignees of the term on the other depends on the existence of an estate in land to which they are both privy; and no such

[17] The other lessee's covenants, e.g. the covenant to use the premises for the specified purposes only, are usually made with the lessor only.

[18] Above, para.5.03.

estate exists between a management company and an assignee of the term. The management company's position is generally one of pure contract.[19]

The problem can be overcome by the company being a party to the licence to assign, and covenanting with the assignee in terms of its covenants in the lease in return for the assignee's covenant with it.[20] But in the absence of such direct covenants, there are doubts about the company's ability to sue the assignee for the service charges, etc. The benefit of the company's covenant will pass to the assignee of the term at common law, by analogy with the case of *Swift (P & A) Investments Ltd v Combined English Stores Group Ltd*,[21] in that the covenant touches and concerns the demised premises; but the burden of the covenant cannot pass on equivalent principles. If the lessee's covenant to pay the service charge to the management company was made with the lessor as well as with the company, the burden of the lessee's covenant with the lessor will pass to the assignee of the term on the principle of privity of estate, and so the assignee's obligation to pay the management company will be capable of enforcement by the lessor (or his assignee) in an action for damages for breach of covenant or indirectly by forfeiture proceedings. But where there was no such covenant in the lease, and no direct covenant is made in the licence to assign, there is no clear principle on which the assignee can be made directly liable to pay the service charge, etc. to the company, though the lessee remains liable to pay under its contract.[22]

Where a management company exists as a party to the lease, therefore, it is good practice for the lessee's covenants with the company to be made also with the lessor, or alternatively for the assignee of the term to covenant with the lessor that it will comply with its obligations to the company.

[19] It is possible for a management company to have common parts vested in it over which lessees enjoy legal easements appurtenant to their leases, but it is submitted that this will not be sufficient to make all lessees' covenants with the company enforceable by it against successors in title of the lessee.

[20] Or indeed the assignee's covenant with the landlord could be expressed to be made also with or for the benefit of the management company, and the benefit of the covenant would enure for the company under Law of Property Act 1925, s.56(1) or Contracts (Rights of Third Parties) Act 1999, s.1, even though it was not a party to the lease. But this will not give the assignee the benefit of the company's covenants.

[21] [1989] A.C. 632 (surety's covenant with lessor passes at common law to assignee of the reversion).

[22] Having paid, the lessee would be entitled to be indemnified by the assignee under the covenant implied by Law of Property Act 1925, s.77(1)(C), or to recoupment under the restitutionary principle in *Moule v Garrett* (1872) L.R. 7 Ex. 101.

(b) *End of management company*

10.08 The fact that a lessor is a limited company is of no particular concern to a lessee or assignee of the term because the land vested in the company will always be vested in someone,[23] even if the lessor becomes insolvent and is dissolved. In whomever the reversionary estate is vested, the owner will be liable to perform those landlord covenants in the lease which touch and concern the demised premises. But the same does not apply to a management company, which does not own the reversion and which has only contractual rights and obligations under the leases of the estate or building and no proprietary rights. In a case where the lessor has no obligation to maintain the common parts and keep the structure and exterior in repair, the continuance of the management company is therefore of some importance to lessees. But the continuance of the company's obligations is uncertain: there is no privity of estate with the lessees, and the burden of the company's covenants cannot be effectually assigned to another company without the consent of that other and all the lessees.

10.09 In these circumstances, if the management company goes into liquidation, the liquidator can simply decline to perform the company's obligations or even disclaim the unprofitable contract, and the lessees will be left to prove for the loss which they have suffered by reason of the company's breach of contract or the disclaimer. The right to prove will, in most cases, be virtually worthless. Prima facie, the lessees cannot compel performance of the company's obligations, and the machinery for performance of the maintenance and repair obligations under the leases will have broken down. In the case of long lessees of residential flats, Pts II, III and IV of the Landlord and Tenant Act 1987 provide some recourse where the management of the building has broken down. Part II[24] enables such lessees to apply to a leasehold valuation tribunal for the appointment of a manager; Pt III[25] enables them, in cases of serious default, to acquire the freehold or leasehold reversion; and Pt IV gives a leasehold valuation tribunal jurisdiction to vary long leases of flats if they fail to make satisfactory provision for any of a number of matters, including the repair or maintenance of the building containing the flat.[26] In the case of leases which do not attract the provisions of the Act of 1987,[27] the High Court has jurisdiction to appoint a receiver or manager whenever it is just and

[23] Ultimately the Crown, as *bona vacantia*.

[24] Landlord and Tenant Act 1987, ss.21–24.

[25] *ibid.*, ss.25–34.

[26] *ibid.*, s.35, as amended by Commonhold and Leasehold Reform Act 2002, ss.162, 163.

[27] i.e. premises which are not residential flats, and leases to which Pt II of the Landlord and Tenant Act 1954 applies (business tenancies).

convenient to do so.[28] But subject to these matters, there is real difficulty in enforcing the covenants of a defunct management company.

3. Non-parties

(a) *The Contracts (Rights of Third Parties) Act 1999*

Prior to November 11, 1999, the question of whether a non-party to any contract (other than an assignee of one of the parties) could take the benefit of it depended on whether the contract purported to be made with him.[29] In no circumstances short of a contractual novation could such a non-party become subject to the burden of a contract. But in the case of a contract entered into after May 10, 2000,[30] a person who is not a party to a contract has been able, subject to various limitations, to enforce a term of a contract in his own right if either the contract expressly provides that he may or the term purports to confer a benefit on him.[31] **10.10**

A term does not purport to confer a benefit on a non-party if, on a proper construction of the contract, it appears that the parties to the contract did not intend the term to be enforceable by the non-party.[32] There is considerable overlap between the considerations relevant to this question and those relevant to whether or not the term purports to confer a benefit on a person.[33] But if the contract is neutral as to question of the parties' intentions as to enforceability, the court can still conclude that the term purports to confer a benefit on a non-party.[34] For these provisions to apply, the non-party must be expressly identified in the contract by name, as a member of a class or as answering a particular description, but need not be in existence when the contract is entered into.[35] For the purposes of exercising a right to enforce a term, the non-party has any remedy that would have been available to him in an action for breach of contract had he been a party. The rules relating to damages, injunctions, **10.11**

[28] Supreme Court Act 1981, s.37(1).

[29] Law of Property Act 1925, s.56(1); *Beswick v Beswick* [1968] A.C. 58. Broader principles have historically applied in relation to deeds of guarantee: see *Moody v Condor Insurance Ltd* [2006] 1 W.L.R. 1847.

[30] Contracts (Rights of Third Parties) Act 1999, ss.1(1), 10(2) (Royal Assent: Nov. 11, 1999)

[31] *ibid.* A contract entered into between Nov. 11, 1999 and May 10, 2000 is subject to the same provisions if it expressly provides for the application of the Act.

[32] Contracts (Rights of Third Parties) Act 1999, s.1(2).

[33] *Laemthong International Lines Co. Ltd v Artis* [2005] 2 All E.R. (Comm) 167, para.49.

[34] *Nisshin Shipping Co. Ltd v Cleaves & Co. Ltd* [2004] 1 All E.R. (Comm) 481, para.23.

[35] Contracts (Rights of Third Parties) Act 1999, s.1(3).

specific performance and other relief apply accordingly.[36] The Act does not distinguish between leases and other contracts to which its provisions might apply. Nor does it make any provision for a non-party to become subject to any contractual obligation.

10.12 Since the provisions of the Act cannot apply to contracts made before November 11, 1999, they will be of very limited application to old tenancies. In practice, the Act is rarely used in any event. The main debate generated has been as to the appropriate language in which its unintentional effect should be excluded.[37] Its possible application in relation to new tenancies is considered in Ch.17.

(b) *RTM Companies*

10.13 Under the Commonhold and Leasehold Reform Act 2002,[38] management functions of the landlord and any other party to a lease, other than the tenant, can be divested from them and vested in a right to manage company (RTM company) created by the tenants for that purpose. Management functions for these purposes are functions with respect to services, repairs, maintenance, improvements, insurance and management.[39] The right to manage applies only in relation to self-contained buildings or parts of buildings containing two or more residential flats owned by qualifying tenants of long residential leases.[40] These provisions came into effect on September 30, 2003 and apply to leases granted before as well as after that date.[41]

10.14 The functions that may become vested in RTM companies under the Act of 2002 include obligations as well as rights, and where so vested the obligations and rights cease to be obligations or rights of the landlord or other party unless so agreed with the RTM company.[42] Thus, where the right to manage has been conferred on the RTM company, the obligations and rights of the landlord and any management company that is a party to a qualifying lease are statutorily transferred to the RTM company. The obligations thereupon binding the RTM company are owed to the tenants

[36] *ibid.*, s.1(5). Accordingly, the rule that specific performance will not be granted in favour of a volunteer is presumably overridden by the Act: "a party to the contract" must mean a party from whom consideration has moved.

[37] So as to exclude only the operation of the Act and not the effect of the common law or of other statutes.

[38] Pt 2, Ch.1.

[39] Commonhold and Leasehold Reform Act 2002, s.96(5). But functions relating to flats or other units not held by qualifying tenants and functions relating to forfeiture and re-entry are excluded: s.96(6).

[40] *ibid.*, ss.72, 75, 76.

[41] The Commonhold and Leasehold Reform Act 2002 (Commencement No.2 and Savings) (England) Order 2003 (SI 2003/1986), arts 1(2), 2.

[42] Commonhold and Leasehold Reform Act 2002, ss.96(4), 97(2).

and to the landlord.[43] Tenant covenants of a lease that remain enforceable by the landlord, notwithstanding the conferring of the right to manage, are also enforceable by the RTM company in the same manner. This right extends to rights to enter the demised premises to inspect them, but not to rights of forfeiture or re-entry.[44] For the purposes of giving effect to the right to manage, numerous statutory provisions in the Landlord and Tenant Acts 1927, 1985, 1987 and 1988 are deemed to apply with amendments in relation to the RTM company and the new regime for management functions.[45]

[43] *ibid.*, s.97(1).
[44] *ibid.*, s.100.
[45] *ibid.*, s.102, Sch.7.

PART III

New Tenancies

CHAPTER 11

Landlord and Tenant Covenants

The main provisions of the Covenants Act[1] fundamentally altered the law relating to enforceability of landlord and tenant covenants. The essential changes are that: tenants are released from their contractual obligations on an assignment of the tenancy; landlords are entitled to apply for release on an assignment of the reversion and will be so released if either the tenant agrees or the court considers it reasonable for the landlord to be released, and obligations and rights under landlord and tenant covenants pass to the respective assignees, regardless of whether they touch and concern the demised premises. **11.01**

As its name suggests, the Covenants Act is specifically concerned with landlord and tenant covenants, though these are given an extended meaning and there is some overlap with the general law of restrictive covenants in particular.[2]

1. Meaning of "landlord covenant" and "tenant covenant"

The provisions of the Covenants Act apply (with three exceptions) to a "landlord covenant" and a "tenant covenant" of a tenancy.[3] Strictly, a covenant is a written promise made in a deed under seal,[4] and therefore is inapposite to describe a term of a parol agreement. But for the purposes of the Act, "covenant" includes a term, condition and obligation, and therefore the Act applies in principle to parol agreements which are tenancies.[5] In the Act, "tenancy" means any lease or other tenancy, including a sub-tenancy and an agreement for a tenancy,[6] but not including a mortgage term.[7] Further, references in the Act to a covenant **11.02**

[1] ss.3–16 and 21.

[2] See below, paras 12.25 *et seq*.

[3] Covenants Act, s.2(1).

[4] See above, Ch.1, para.1.01.

[5] Covenants Act, s.28(1).

[6] Agreements for tenancies only fall within the Act if they comply with the necessary formalities (see Law of Property (Miscellaneous Provisions) Act 1989, s.2), otherwise they are not binding contracts and equity cannot treat the agreement as being a tenancy, save where a constructive trust or proprietary estoppel exists.

[7] Covenants Act, s.28(1).

(or any description of covenant) of a tenancy include a covenant (or a covenant of that description) contained in a collateral agreement.[8] In other words, terms, conditions and obligations contained in any agreement supplemental to or qualifying the terms of the tenancy agreement, and whether made before or after the tenancy was created, may be "covenants" within the meaning of the Act.

11.03 The Covenants Act does not apply to any "covenants", but only to "landlord covenants" and "tenant covenants". "Landlord covenant" in relation to a tenancy means a covenant falling to be complied with by the landlord of premises demised by the tenancy; similarly, "tenant covenant" in relation to a tenancy means a covenant falling to be complied with by the tenant of premises demised by the tenancy.[9] "Landlord" and "tenant" in relation to a tenancy mean the person for the time being entitled to the reversion expectant on the term of the tenancy and the person entitled to that term respectively.[10] Thus, where a covenant is expressed to be personal, or is necessarily to be complied with prior to the grant of the lease or by the lessor only, it cannot be a "landlord covenant" for the purposes of the Act, for it does not fall to be complied with by the person for the time being entitled to the reversion.[11] On this basis, a covenant by a lessee in a collateral agreement to grant a sub-lease to the lessor is not a "tenant covenant".[12] Although all covenants expressed to be performed by the lessor or lessee personally will therefore necessarily not be landlord or tenant covenants respectively, expressly personal obligations are not the only type of covenant that cannot be a landlord or tenant covenant.[13] The question of whether a covenant is expressed to be personal, which as we shall see is of importance for the transmissibility provisions of the Act, is therefore in principle a different question from that of whether it is or is not a landlord or tenant covenant.[14]

[8] *ibid.*

[9] *ibid.*

[10] *ibid.*

[11] *BHP Petroleum Great Britain Ltd v Chesterfield Properties Ltd* [2002] Ch. 12 (personal obligation to remedy construction defects); *Edlington Properties Ltd v J.H. Fenner & Co. Ltd* [2006] 1 W.L.R. 1583 (obligation to build factory, on completion of which lease to be granted).

[12] *First Penthouse Ltd v Channel Hotels & Properties (UK) Ltd* [2004] 1 E.G.L.R. 16.

[13] See, e.g. *Edlington v Fenner* and *First Penthouse v Channel Hotels*, above.

[14] It may be doubted whether the decision in *BHP v Chesterfield*, above, intended this distinction to be drawn and whether Parliament intended it. It tends to re-introduce the distinction between covenants that do and do not touch and concern the demised premises, contrary to the purpose of the Act: see *per* Neuberger J. in *Oceanic Village Ltd v United Attractions Ltd* [2000] Ch. 234. The Court of Appeal in *BHP v Chesterfield* was concerned not with the question of whether the burden of the lessor's covenant passed to its successor in title but whether the lessor was released from the burden, pursuant to the release provisions of the Act. Accordingly, the answer was not simply that the covenant

Where two or more persons jointly constitute either the landlord or the tenant in relation to a tenancy, references in the Act to "the landlord" or "the tenant" are references to both or all of the persons who jointly constitute the landlord or the tenant, as the case may be.[15] **11.04**

2. Type of landlord covenants and tenant covenants to which the Covenants Act applies

The Covenants Act applies to all landlord and tenant covenants (as defined above), with only three exceptions. In particular, it applies to landlord and tenant covenants whether or not any such covenant has reference to the subject matter of the tenancy, i.e. whether or not the covenant touches and concerns the land of the covenantee.[16] The Act applies whether such a covenant is express, implied or imposed by law.[17] Thus, important implied covenants such as a landlord's obligations not to derogate from his grant and to keep the structure and exterior of dwelling-houses let under short residential tenancies in good repair, and a tenant's obligations to use the demised premises in a tenant-like manner and to yield up the demised premises with vacant possession at the end of the term, are within the scope of the Act. So too are any terms of the tenancy which must be implied as a matter of law to give business efficacy to the tenancy. **11.05**

3. The exceptions

The three exceptions to the application of the Covenants Act referred to above are: **11.06**

(1) any covenant imposed in pursuance of ss.35 or 155 of the Housing Act 1985 (covenants for repayment of discount given on purchase of houses if an early disposal is made, such covenants being binding on purchaser or secure tenant and his successors in title);

was expressed to be personal (thereby excepting it from the transmission provisions of the Act), although it would have been a remarkable result for the burden of the covenant to be non-transmissible yet for the lessor to be released. It is suggested that the same result would have been achieved by holding that covenants that are expressed to be personal are not landlord covenants. However, the distinction between covenants that cannot be landlord (or tenant) covenants and expressly personal covenants is now firmly established, as described in the text.

[15] *ibid.*, s.28(4). So, *semble*, an obligation on one or some only cannot be a "landlord covenant" or "tenant covenant".

[16] *ibid.*, s.2(1)(a).

[17] *ibid.*, s.2(1)(b).

(2) any covenant imposed in pursuance of para.1 of Sch.6A to the Housing Act 1985 (covenants by secure tenant, also binding successors in title of the secure tenant, to make a payment to redeem the landlord's share of the value of the dwelling-house); and

(3) any covenant imposed in pursuance of ss.11 or 13 of the Housing Act 1996[18] or of paras 1 or 3 of Sch.2 to the Housing Associations Act 1985 (covenants for repayment of discount given on purchase of houses if an early disposal is made, such covenants being binding on purchaser or secure tenant and his successors in title, or covenants restricting further disposal of houses in National Parks, etc.).[19]

These are very limited and particular exceptions to the application of the Covenants Act. They are intended to prevent the covenantor from being released from the burden of his covenant to make a repayment to a local housing authority or a housing association upon an assignment of a leasehold house bought at a discount or, in one case, to prevent the further disposal of a house of a particular character.

[18] Inserted with effect from October 1, 1996, by the Housing Act 1996 (Consequential Provisions) Order 1996 (SI 1996/2325), art.5, Sch.2, para.22.

[19] Covenants Act, s.2(2), as amended.

CHAPTER 12

Transmission of Benefit and Burden of Landlord Covenants and Tenant Covenants

1. Transmission

The benefit of all landlord covenants and the burden of all tenant covenants of a new tenancy are annexed and incident to the whole of the premises demised by the tenancy and to each and every part of those premises. Correspondingly, the benefit of all tenant covenants and the burden of all landlord covenants of a new tenancy are annexed and incident to the whole of the reversion in the demised premises and to each and every part of the reversion.[1] The reversion in the demised premises is that interest expectant on the termination of the tenancy of them.[2] The benefit and burden of all landlord and tenant covenants of a tenancy pass in accordance with s.3 of the Act upon an assignment of the whole or any part of the premises demised by the tenancy or upon an assignment of the whole or any part of the reversion in them.[3] But as has already been seen,[4] covenants not falling to be performed by the person from time to time entitled to the term or the reversion, as the case may be, are not tenant covenants or landlord covenants, and so their benefit and burden do not pass in this way. **12.01**

Accordingly, on a transfer of the reversion, the lessor ceases to be entitled to the benefit of the tenant covenants for the future, notwithstanding the terms of the contract in the lease, and his assignee becomes bound by the landlord covenants. And on a transfer of the demised premises the lessee ceases to be bound by the tenant covenants for the future[5] and his assignee becomes entitled to the benefit of the landlord covenants. It may therefore be critical to know exactly when the assignment of the demised premises or of the reversion takes place for the purposes of the Covenants Act. There are exceptions to this principle of transmission which are considered below.

[1] Covenants Act, s.3(1)(a).
[2] *ibid.*, s.28(1).
[3] *ibid.*, s.3(1)(b).
[4] Above, para.11.03.
[5] See below, Ch.14.

12.02 To the extent that there remains in force any rule of law by virtue of which the burden of a covenant whose subject matter is not in existence at the time when it is made does not run with the land affected unless the covenantor covenants on behalf of himself and his assigns, that rule of law is abolished in relation to new tenancies.[6]

2. Exceptions

(a) *Personal covenants*

12.03 The principle of transmission outlined in section 1, above does not apply in the case of a covenant which, in whatever terms, is expressed to be personal to any person. Section 3 of the Act does not operate to make such a covenant enforceable by or (as the case may be) against any other person:

> "Nothing in this section shall operate—
> (a) in the case of a covenant which (in whatever terms) is expressed to be personal to any person, to make the covenant enforceable by or (as the case may be) against any other person . . . ."[7]

This provision comprises two elements which require some analysis.

12.04 (i) MEANING OF "(IN WHATEVER TERMS) IS EXPRESSED TO BE PERSONAL TO ANY PERSON". Under the old law, covenants which did not touch and concern the demised premises or the reversion, as the case may be, did not bind successors in title of the covenantor and could not be enforced by successors in title of the covenantee.[8] There are essentially three types of such covenants. First, those which are expressed to be personal. Such covenants need not use the word "personal": e.g. "for so long as the landlord is the XYZ Corporation, the tenant will not sell lemons at the demised premises" is a covenant expressed to be personal because the benefit of it is limited to the covenantee.[9] Secondly, those which by their very nature are personal, although not expressed in any terms to be so. An

[6] Covenants Act, s.3(7). The rule of law in question is one of the principles in *Spencer's Case* (1583) 5 Co.Rep. 16a; 1 Sm.L.C. (13th ed.), p.51, an anomaly of the Grantees of Reversions Act 1540, but already abolished in relation to covenants touching and concerning the land of the covenantee or covenantor by Law of Property Act 1925, ss.78(1), 79(1). Covenants Act, s.3(7) abolishes any remnant of the rule which might now apply to covenants in new tenancies.

[7] Covenants Act, s.3(6)(a).

[8] See above, para.4.09.

[9] Similarly, a covenant by the tenant "here meaning XYZ Corporation only" is expressed to be personal: cf. *Max Factor Ltd v Wesleyan Assurance Society* (1996) 74 P.&C.R. 8 (break clause exercisable by "the Lessee here meaning Max Factor only").

example is: "the tenant will sing holy mass at least once a week at the Church of St Radegund, Dillchester". These two types of covenant do not touch and concern the reversion in the demised premises because they are of personal interest to the particular covenantee only.[10] But a third type of covenant, although not obviously personal in that sense, nevertheless does not touch and concern the demised premises or the reversion. For example, a landlord's covenant which benefits only the advantageous carrying on of a particular trade on the demised premises and does not benefit the demised premises per se,[11] and a landlord's covenant to sell the reversion or to give the tenant a right of first refusal.[12] None of these three types of covenant was capable of binding successors in title of the covenantor or of being enforced by successors in title of the covenantee under the previous law.

With the exceptions of the specific statutory covenants which are set out in Ch.11, above, and subject to exception (ii) below, the effect of s.3 of the Act is that the benefit and burden of a landlord or tenant covenant will pass unless the covenant is expressed, in whatever terms, to be personal to any person. It appears likely, therefore, that only covenants of the first type outlined above will fall within these statutory words and will not be enforceable by or, as the case may be, against another person. It is considered that only covenants which either specifically state that they are personal to a given person, or which in terms limit their applicability to the interest of a given person, can be said to be expressed in any terms to be personal, though any express terms conveying such intention will suffice.[13] The second and third types of covenant identified above cannot truly be said to be expressed in any terms to be personal. *Semble*, therefore, the Covenants Act has widened the class of landlord and tenant covenants capable of binding or being enforced by successors in title of lessors and lessees. **12.05**

(ii) MEANING OF "ENFORCEABLE BY (OR AS THE CASE MAY BE) AGAINST ANY OTHER PERSON". A further difficulty arises from the wording of the **12.06**

[10] See *First Penthouse Ltd v Channel Hotels and Properties (UK) Ltd* [2004] 1 E.G.L.R. 16 (personal covenant in collateral agreement to pay commission to third party).

[11] See *Thomas v Hayward* (1869) L.R. 4 Ex. 311; *Kumar v Dunning* [1989] Q.B. 193 at 205. *Sed quaere*: this decision is perhaps difficult to reconcile with the decision in *Caerns Motor Services Ltd v Texaco Ltd* [1994] 1 W.L.R. 1249.

[12] *Woodall v Clifton* [1905] 2 Ch. 257; *Sherwood v Tucker* [1924] 2 Ch. 440; *Charles Frodsham & Co. v Morris* (1972) 229 E.G. 961.

[13] In the *First Penthouse* case, above, it was held that for these purposes an intention that a covenant be personal could be "expressed" explicitly or implicitly by the lease as a whole. *Sed quaere*: s.3(6)(a) requires the covenant to be expressed (in whatever terms) to be personal. But a covenant that is not a "landlord covenant" at all does not have to be expressed to be personal in order to escape the transmission provisions of the Act.

Act. It provides that a covenant expressed (in whatever terms) to be personal to any person shall not have the effect of making the covenant enforceable "by or (as the case may be) against any other person". Suppose an assignment of the tenancy is made by the tenant who gave the lemon-selling covenant in the first example above. Although the landlord who had the benefit of the covenant remains unchanged, and accordingly the covenant would not be enforced *by* any other person, the identity of the tenant has changed and the covenant would be enforced *against* another person. The Act could be said to apply so that the new tenant is not bound by the personal covenant, because the covenant would otherwise be enforced against another person. But the covenant was expressed to be personal to the landlord, not personal to the tenant[14]; and the identity of the landlord has not changed. It is probable that the words "by or (as the case may be) against any other person" should be applied distributively so that where the covenant is personal to the covenantee, an assignee of the covenantor will be bound, and where the covenant is personal to the covenantor an assignee of the covenantee will take the benefit.[15] But there is a problem with this approach: a covenant that is personal to the covenantor will not be a "landlord covenant" or "tenant covenant" at all[16] and so on this construction the statutory exception will only apply to covenants expressed to be personal to a covenantee and the words "or (as the case may be) against" are superfluous.[17]

(b) *Non-registration under the Land Registration Act 1925 or the Land Charges Act 1972*

12.07 The principle of transmission outlined in section 1 above does not apply in the case of a covenant which, for the purpose of binding a successor in title of the covenantor, requires to be registered under either the Land Registration Act 2002 or the Land Charges Act 1972 but has not been registered:

> "Nothing in this section shall operate—

[14] "... for so long as the landlord is the XYZ Corporation, the tenant will not ...".

[15] The possibility of a covenant being personal to one party but not to the other was recognised and accepted in *System Floors Ltd v Ruralpride Ltd* [1995] 1 E.G.L.R. 48 (benefit of term expressed to be personal to original tenant, but assignee of reversion bound).

[16] Above, para.11.03.

[17] The difficulty is, perhaps, another indication that Parliament did not intend the definitions of "landlord covenant" and "tenant covenant" to carry the significance that was attributed to them in *BHP Petroleum Great Britain Ltd v Chesterfield Properties Ltd* [2002] Ch. 12.

(b) to make a covenant enforceable against any person if, apart from this section, it would not be enforceable against him by reason of its not having been registered under the Land Registration Act 2002 or the Land Charges Act 1972."[18]

Generally, landlord and tenant covenants are not void for non-registration because such covenants do not fall within the types of interest which are registrable as interests affecting a registered estate under the Land Registration Act 2002 (in the case of registered land) or as land charges under the Land Charges Act 1972 (in the case of unregistered land). The main exceptions to this are a tenant's covenant to offer to surrender his term[19] and a landlord's covenant to offer to renew the tenancy[20] or to sell the reversion.[21] In each of these cases, the covenant creates an estate contract which is a registrable interest under each Act and must be protected by notice against the registered title in the case of registered land and by a Class C(iv) land charge against the name of the estate owner in the case of unregistered land. If the benefit of such covenants is not registered, they are void as against registered transferees of the title or purchasers for money or money's worth of a legal estate in the land on familiar conveyancing principles.[22] In such a case, s.3 of the Act does not apply to make the covenant enforceable against such a transferee or purchaser or his successors in title. In the case of a registrable landlord's covenant to renew or sell the reversion, if the title to the reversion is registered, the tenant's right to renew or purchase will be protected as an overriding interest by his actual occupation of the demised premises, even if not registered. In such case, the covenant remains enforceable and the transmission principle of s.3 of the Act does apply. **12.08**

Before October 13, 2003, a covenant by a lessor not to use other property that he owned for a particular use was not registrable (being a covenant between a lessor and a lessee).[23] Although the covenant might bind successors in title to the lessor's reversion, it would not bind successors in title to the other property, at least where the lease was not **12.09**

[18] Covenants Act, s.3(6)(b), as amended by Land Registration Act 2002, s.133, Sch.11, para.33(1),(2).

[19] *Greene v Church Commissioners* [1974] Ch. 467.

[20] *Phillips v Mobil Oil* [1989] 1 W.L.R. 888.

[21] *Beesly v Hallwood Estates* [1960] 1 W.L.R. 549.

[22] Land Registration Act 1925, ss.20(1), 23(1); Law of Property Act 1925, s.199(1); Land Charges Act 1972, s.4(6).

[23] *Dartstone Ltd v Cleveland Petroleum Co. Ltd (No.2)* [1969] 1 W.L.R. 1807; *Oceanic Village Ltd v United Attractions Ltd* [2000] Ch. 234.

registered against the landlord's title to that property.[24] But since that date, such a restrictive covenant is registrable, in so far as it relates to land other than the demised premises,[25] and so failure to register it will prevent the covenant being enforced against the transferee of the reversion.

3. Effect of transmission on future liabilities

(a) *Assignment by tenant*

12.10 As from the assignment[26] by the tenant under a tenancy, the assignee becomes bound by the tenant covenants of the tenancy except to the extent that (i) immediately before the assignment they did not bind the assignor, or (ii) they fall to be complied with in relation to any demised premises not comprised in the assignment.[27] Correspondingly, as from the assignment, the assignee becomes entitled (to the exclusion of the assignor) to the benefit of the landlord covenants of the tenancy except to the extent that they fall to be complied with in relation to any demised premises not comprised in the assignment.[28] The words "to the extent that" are of particular importance. There are thus two exceptions here to the assignee's succeeding in full to the tenant's rights and obligations, and these are considered in the following paragraphs.

Unless the context otherwise requires, "assignment" includes equitable assignment, assignment in breach of a covenant of a tenancy, and assignment by operation of law. One of the main, unresolved problems of the Act is at what point in time, where there is a contract for the assignment of a lease (or indeed of a reversion), the "assignment" has taken place. It is difficult to conceive that the draftsman intended the benefit and burden of covenants to pass, and the release of continuing liabilities to take effect, at the moment when an unconditional contract for the assignment of the lease (or reversion) is made; yet the contract is in one sense, between the parties to the contract, an equitable assignment. It is difficult to say that the context, as distinct from common sense and legal principles established under the old law, requires otherwise.[29] An executed but as yet unregistered transfer would be an assignment for these purposes. The law governing the execution and presumed delivery of instruments by individuals and by corporations has recently been

[24] *Oceanic Village v United Attractions*, above.

[25] Land Registration Act 2002, s.33(c).

[26] Covenants Act, s.28(1).

[27] *ibid.*, s.3(2)(a).

[28] *ibid.*, s.3(2)(b).

[29] The definitions in *ibid.*, s.28(1) are expressed to apply "unless the context otherwise requires".

clarified by a series of statutory amendments,[30] though the amendments only apply to instruments executed before September 15, 2005.[31]

(i) COVENANTS NOT BINDING THE ASSIGNOR BEFORE ASSIGNMENT. In determining whether any covenant bound the assignor immediately before the assignment, any waiver or release of the covenant which (in whatever terms) is expressed to be personal to the assignor shall be disregarded.[32] It is considered that the waiver or release must be one binding on the covenantee at the time in question, but subject to that, "waiver" and "release" should be widely construed. Thus, for example, a covenant by the tenant to keep the demised premises in repair which is qualified by a proviso that "for so long as ABC Limited is the Tenant the Tenant shall not be obliged to put the demised premises into any better condition than they were in at the date hereof" will inure in the hands of the assignee as a full repairing covenant.[33] Similarly, a letter written by the landlord several years after the date of grant waiving further compliance by ABC Ltd only with the restrictive user covenant will not prevent the covenant from applying with full force to the assignee. **12.11**

A release or waiver of a contractual obligation undertaken in a deed need no longer be made by deed, or even in writing, to be effective.[34] But to come within the terms of the statutory provision, the release or waiver must be: (i) express, and (ii) expressed (in whatever terms) to be personal. It is doubtful, therefore, whether a waiver which is implied from conduct, or a waiver in the sense of a quasi-estoppel by acquiescence[35] or a full estoppel by representation or conduct, can be disregarded in considering to what extent covenants did not bind the assignor immediately before the assignment. It does at first blush seem odd that a documented release or waiver will preserve the full force of the covenant upon an assignment but that a less formal waiver may release the assignee, and hence all future **12.12**

[30] The Regulatory Reform (Execution of Deeds and Documents) Order 2005 (SI 2005/1906) ("the Order"). The relevant provisions of Law of Property Act 1925, ss.74, 74A, Companies Act 1985, ss.36A, 36AA and Law of Property (Miscellaneous Provisions) Act 1989, s.1, all as amended by the Order, are printed below, Appendix 2, pp.358–60, 395–97, 406–08.

[31] In relation to instruments executed before that date, the statutory provisions as to due execution and delivery of deeds and other instruments apply without the amendments introduced by the Order: art.1(2).

[32] Covenants Act, s.3(4).

[33] *Semble*, a reassignment of the tenancy to ABC Ltd may not entitle ABC Ltd to re-take the benefit of this concession: *Max Factor Ltd v Wesleyan Assurance Society* (1996) 74 P.&C.R. 8; and see *BP Oil UK Ltd v Lloyds TSB Bank Plc* [2005] 1 E.G.L.R. 61. This is because, as a matter of construction, the qualification is limited to the time of the tenant's original tenancy, not because the qualification is not "expressed to be personal" within the meaning of the Act.

[34] *Mitas v Hyams* [1951] 2 T.L.R. 1215.

[35] *Willmott v Barber* (1880) 15 Ch.D. 96.

assignees, of the term or reversion as the case may be from compliance with the express terms of the covenant. Further, a waiver in the sense of a promissory estoppel (which will normally be express) is never extinctive of the right of the party waiving compliance, but merely suspends his right to rely on it.[36] Yet if a landlord waives compliance with a repairing covenant in terms which are not expressed to be personal, and the tenant then assigns the tenancy, the effect of the Act would seem to be that the assignee is not bound by the covenant: for immediately before the assignment, the repairing covenant did not bind the assignor on account of the waiver, yet the waiver was not expressed in any terms to be personal to the assignor, which would entitle one to disregard the waiver for the statutory purposes.

12.13 Thus, it seems, could an assignment of the term or reversion under a new tenancy convert a promissory estoppel, under which rights as against the representee are merely suspended, into a permanent release of all his successors in title from the rights of the representor. A landlord whose licence to an assignment is required should be astute to avoid this possible pitfall. He should do so by inserting terms appropriate to withdraw any temporary waiver of rights, or by giving notice to the assignor prior to the assignment. The answer to this apparent oddity may be that the estoppel inures for the benefit of the assignee until the representor by notice resumes his strict legal rights; for the exception applies only "to the extent that" covenants did not bind the assignor. If this is correct, the Covenants Act can have the effect that covenants may become binding on assignees at some future time.

12.14 (ii) COVENANTS FALLING TO BE COMPLIED WITH IN RELATION TO DEMISED PREMISES NOT COMPRISED IN THE ASSIGNMENT. Save in relation to covenants to pay money, a covenant falls to be complied with in relation to demised premises not comprised in the assignment if either: (a) it in terms applies to that part of the demised premises, or (b) in its practical application it can be attributed to that part of the premises, whether or not it can also be attributed to other individual parts of the demised premises.[37]

It is considered that limb (a) connotes an exclusive application in terms to that non-assigned part of the premises. Limb (b) is to deal with covenants of general application. To the extent that any covenant falls to be complied with in relation to non-assigned premises, the assignee is not bound by the covenant to that extent, i.e. the assignee is bound by the covenant in so far as it affects (if at all) the part of the demised premises

[36] See *Hughes v Metropolitan Ry. Ltd* (1877) 2 App.Cas. 439; *Brikom Investments Ltd v Carr* [1979] Q.B. 467.

[37] Covenants Act, s.28(2).

assigned to him. But he is not bound insofar as it relates to other parts of the demised premises. If a given covenant either in terms applies or in its practical application can be attributed solely to a part of the demised premises not comprised in the assignment, then the assignee is not bound by it at all.

So far as covenants to pay money are concerned, such a covenant falls **12.15** to be complied with in relation to demised premises not comprised in the assignment if either (a) it in terms applies to such premises, or (b) the amount of the payment is determinable specifically by reference to such premises or (in the case of a tenant covenant) by reference to anything falling to be done by or for a person as tenant or occupier of such premises or (in the case of a landlord covenant) by reference to anything falling to be done by or for a person as landlord of such premises.[38]

Alternative (a) should present little difficulty in practice. It is considered that this alternative connotes an exclusive application in terms to the non-assigned premises. Alternative (b) is somewhat opaque, but the words "determinable specifically by reference to" must be taken to imply a quantification by reference solely to the non-assigned part of the premises or to something done by someone as the tenant, occupier or landlord of that part alone.

The purpose of the Act seems to be that an assignee of the tenancy will **12.16** only be exonerated wholly from compliance with a tenant covenant, or correspondingly will only lose entirely the benefit of the landlord covenant, in cases where the covenant either in terms applies only to or is specifically and solely linked to a non-assigned part of the demised premises. That is entirely logical. In cases where this is not so, two situations will arise. First, in relation to covenants other than money covenants, the assignee will not be bound by the covenant, or correspondingly will lose the benefit of the covenant, only *to the extent that* it falls to be complied with in relation to the non-assigned premises. Second, in relation to a covenant to pay money, the covenant, being entirely general as to the premises to which it relates, does not for this limited statutory purpose[39] "fall to be complied with" in relation to the non-assigned premises *at all*, and so the assignee will be fully bound by or derive the full benefit of the covenant (as the case may be). Thus, for example, an assignee who takes an assignment of a one-third part of premises demised by a five-year lease at a fixed rent will prima facie be liable for the whole of the rent. In this way, the words "to the extent that" only have a significant effect where a non-money covenant, e.g. a covenant to repair, is of general application as respects various parts of the

[38] *ibid.*, s.28(3).
[39] By virtue of Covenants Act, s.28(3).

demised premises, including the non-assigned part. In all other cases, the assignee will either not be bound at all (because the covenant relates solely to the non-assigned premises) or be bound in full (either because the non-money covenant applies only to the assigned part or because the money covenant was not in terms, or in the quantification of the money, applicable solely to the non-assigned premises).[40]

12.17 For the purposes of the Covenants Act, any assignment (however effected) consisting in the transfer of the whole of the tenant's interest in any premises demised by a tenancy shall be treated as an assignment by the tenant of those premises, even if that assignment is not effected by the tenant.[41] "Assignment" here, as elsewhere, includes an assignment in breach of a covenant in the tenancy, and an assignment by operation of law.[42] Thus, the provisions of the Act as to transmission of benefit and burden of tenant covenants apply where the whole of the tenant's interest in any demised premises is assigned by operation of law (for example, upon the bankruptcy of the tenant) or by another person who has the power to effect the assignment. But an assignment of the equitable interest only in the tenancy is not an assignment of the whole of the tenant's interest, so it appears that the context here excludes an equitable assignment that is not effected by the tenant himself from the effects of the transmission provisions of the Act.

(b) *Assignment by landlord*

12.18 As from the assignment[43] of the reversion by a landlord under a tenancy, the assignee becomes bound by the landlord covenants of the tenancy except to the extent that (a) immediately before the assignment they did not bind the assignor, or (b) they fall to be complied with in relation to any demised premises not comprised in the assignment.[44] Correspondingly, as from the assignment, the assignee becomes entitled (to the exclusion of the assignor) to the benefit of the tenant covenants of the tenancy except to the extent that they fall to be complied with in relation to any demised premises not comprised in the assignment.[45] Accordingly, a term in a transfer reserving to the assignor the right to future rent under

[40] In this important case, the provisions of Covenants Act, ss.9 and 10 relating to apportionment of covenants binding both assignor and assignee come into play: see Ch.15, below.

[41] Covenants Act, s.28(6)(b).

[42] *ibid.*, s.28(1), the context of Covenants Act, s.28(6)(b) not requiring otherwise.

[43] See above, para.12.10.

[44] Covenants Act, s.3(3)(a).

[45] *ibid.*, s.3(3)(b).

the lease has been held to purport to modify the operation of the transmission provisions of the Act and so be void.[46]

In general terms, the commentary under "(a) *Assignment by tenant*"[47] applies equally to an assignment by a landlord of the reversion in the whole or part of the demised premises, the statutory provisions[48] being *mutatis mutandis* identical. So the same question of when the reversion has been "assigned" for the purposes of the Act will arise.[49] Further, the exceptions discussed in "2. Exceptions"[50] also apply, namely:

(1) nothing in section 3 of the Act operates, in the case of a covenant which is expressed (in whatever terms) to be personal to any person, to make such covenant enforceable by or (as the case may be) against any other person[51];
(2) nothing in section 3 operates to make a covenant enforceable against any person if, apart from that section, it would not be enforceable against him by reason of its not having been registered under the Land Registration Act 1925 or the Land Charges Act 1972.[52]

It should be noted, however, that unlike the effect of an assignment of the reversion of an old tenancy, the assignee of the reversion on a new tenancy becomes bound by the landlord covenants for the duration of the term of the lease, subject only to the release provisions of the Act. This is because the assignee is not only liable under the principle of privity of estate but pursuant to the scheme of the Covenants Act, under which the assignee becomes bound by the covenants but can apply for release on further assignment of the reversion.[53]

These provisions of the Covenants Act, as to the effect of an assignment **12.19**
by the landlord, only apply if the landlord assigns the whole of his interest (as owner of the reversion) in the whole or in part of the demised premises,[54] and not if he grants a concurrent lease of his reversion in the

[46] Under the anti-avoidance provisions of the Act: *Property Co. v Inspector of Taxes* [2005] S.T.C. (SCD) 59. For the anti-avoidance provisions, see below, Ch.23.

[47] Paras 12.10–12.17, above.

[48] Covenants Act, s.3(2), (3).

[49] See above, at para.12.10.

[50] Paras 12.03–12.09, above.

[51] Covenants Act, s.3(6)(a).

[52] *ibid.*, s.3(6)(b).

[53] See below, Ch.14, section 2.

[54] Covenants Act, s.28(5). Before January 1, 1996, the grant of a concurrent lease of the reversion was, for the purposes of preserving the obligations of landlord and tenant in the pre-existing lease as between the concurrent lessee and the tenant, effective as an assignment of the landlord's reversion for the duration of the term of the concurrent lease.

whole or in part of the demised premises for a term of years. The effect of the grant of such a concurrent lease by the landlord is now doubtful because nothing in ss.78, 79, 141 or 142 of the Law of Property Act 1925 applies in relation to new tenancies[55]; nor do the transmission provisions of the Covenants Act apply because the landlord has not assigned his full interest. The concurrent lessee must rely on the right conferred by the Covenants Act[56] to enforce the tenant covenants; but it is at least doubtful whether this entitles the concurrent lessee to sue in respect of breaches of covenant by the tenant committed before the grant of the concurrent lease[57]; and moreover the Act does not preclude the landlord (i.e. the concurrent lessor) from suing the tenant on, e.g. his covenant to pay the rent. These are difficulties which are not fully resolved by the Covenants Act, nor have they been resolved to date by judicial interpretation.[58] For present purposes, however, it is sufficient to note that the transmission provisions of the Act do not apply unless the landlord assigns the whole of his reversionary estate in the demised premises, or in part of such premises as the case may be.

12.20 For the purposes of the Covenants Act, any assignment (however effected) consisting in the transfer of the whole of the landlord's interest (as owner of the reversion) in premises demised by a tenancy shall be treated as an assignment by the landlord of the reversion in those premises, even if that assignment is not effected by the landlord.[59] "Assignment" here, as elsewhere, includes an assignment in breach of a covenant in the tenancy, and an assignment by operation of law.[60] Thus, the provisions of the Act as to transmission of benefit and burden of landlord covenants apply where the whole of the landlord's interest in the reversion in any demised premises is assigned by operation of law (e.g. upon the bankruptcy of the landlord) or by another person who has the power to effect the assignment. But an assignment of the equitable interest only in the reversion is not an assignment of the whole of the landlord's interest, so the context here seems to exclude an equitable assignment not effected by the landlord himself from the effect of the transmission provisions of the Act.

[55] By virtue of Covenants Act, s.30(4).

[56] s.15(1).

[57] Which was the position under Law of Property Act 1925, s.141 (*Re King, Robinson v Gray* [1963] 1 W.L.R. 459; *Muscat v Smith* [2003] 1 W.L.R. 2853), but is not generally the effect of an assignment of a new tenancy (*Edlington Properties Ltd v J.H. Fenner & Co. Ltd* [2006] 1 W.L.R. 1583): see below, paras 12.21–12.23.

[58] See the discussion of the problem, *obiter*, in *First Penthouse Ltd v Channel Hotels & Properties (UK) Ltd* [2004] 1 E.G.L.R. 16, paras 53–56.

[59] Covenants Act, s.28(6)(a).

[60] *ibid.*, s.28(1), the context of Covenants Act, s.3 not requiring otherwise.

(c) *Pre-assignment rights and liabilities*

(i) THE LAW FOR OLD TENANCIES.[61] Upon an assignment of the reversion, the assignee is not liable to the tenant for any breaches of covenant committed by his predecessors in title prior to the assignment,[62] and the assignor remains liable.[63] But the assignee is, to the exclusion of the assignor (unless the assignment otherwise provides), entitled to sue the tenant for breaches occurring before the assignment.[64] **12.21**

Upon an assignment of the term, the assignee is not liable to the landlord for any breaches of covenant committed prior to the assignment or for rent falling due before it,[65] nor is he entitled to sue the landlord for breaches occurring before the assignment. The assignor remains liable for breaches before the assignment and is entitled to pursue rights which accrued to him prior thereto.

(ii) THE STATUTORY PROVISION. The Covenants Act provides that where, as a result of an assignment and by virtue of the Act, a person becomes bound by or entitled to the benefit of a covenant, he does not by virtue of the Act have any liability or rights under the covenant in relation to any time falling before the assignment.[66] But this does not preclude the person in question having any such rights expressly assigned to him.[67] **12.22**

(iii) COMPARISON. The position of an assignee tenant is unchanged under the Act from the position which would result (in the absence of express contrary provision) on the assignment of an old tenancy. But the landlord's position is materially altered. Instead of automatically receiving (in the absence of express contrary provision) the benefit of any rights relating to the tenancy which arose prior to the assignment, the assignee landlord of a new tenancy receives no such rights unless the assignor expressly assigns them to him. Thus, in the case of non-payment of a rental instalment falling due before the date of the assignment of the **12.23**

[61] This subject is considered in some detail in Pt II of the text, and the brief restatement here is only for the purposes of convenient comparison with the statutory provision in the Covenants Act.

[62] *Duncliffe v Caerfelin Properties Ltd* [1989] 2 E.G.L.R. 38; *Muscat v Smith*, above. Where the breach is a continuing breach, however, the assignee will become liable in his own right unless he remedies the breach.

[63] *City and Metropolitan Properties Ltd v Greycroft* [1987] 1 W.L.R. 1085.

[64] *Re King, Robinson v Gray* [1963] 1 All E.R. 781.

[65] Though if the landlord forfeits the tenancy, the assignee may have to remedy the breach or pay the rent arrears as a condition of obtaining relief against forfeiture. Also, if the breach is a continuing breach, the assignee will become liable in his own right unless he remedies the breach.

[66] Covenants Act, s.23(1).

[67] *ibid.*, s.23(2).

reversion,[68] the assignor landlord retains the right to sue the tenant for the rent[69]; but he has no right to forfeit the tenancy on account of the rent arrears because the right of re-entry passes to the assignee landlord.[70] The assignee landlord on the other hand can forfeit the tenancy for non-payment of rent, but has no right to sue for the arrears. Yet payment of the rent arrears is invariably a pre-condition of relief against forfeiture for non-payment of rent, and generally the only condition for relief (other than payment of costs and interest) which the court will impose.[71] An even more difficult scenario could arise if the assignor landlord sues the tenant for damages for breach of his repairing obligations. The breach being a continuing one, there is nothing to prevent the assignee landlord from suing for damages too, or seeking to forfeit the tenancy, or both.[72]

The new statutory provision summarised in para.12.22, above, includes the words "shall not *by virtue of this Act* have any liability or rights . . . " (emphasis added). As ss.78, 79, 141 and 142 of the Law of Property Act 1925 do not apply in relation to new tenancies, it is difficult to see how, other than by an express assignment of the chose in action, an assignee can acquire *aliunde* any rights under covenants in relation to a time before the assignment. The words were doubtless included to forestall any argument that a purported assignment of accrued rights was void as modifying the operation of the Act[73]; but they may be of some significance in relation to the position of an assignee becoming bound by the tenant covenants. Nothing in the Act imposes any liability on the assignee in relation to a time before the assignment; but upon a forfeiture, the assignee tenant might still be required by the court, as a condition of the grant of relief against forfeiture, to remedy breaches occurring before the assignment.

12.24 The statutory provision leaves open the question of whether an assignee, landlord or tenant, may expressly take on liabilities in relation to a time before the assignment. It is submitted that such an agreement would not infringe the anti-avoidance provisions of the Act[74] because the

[68] Hence the importance of identifying the date of the assignment: see above, para.12.10.

[69] Even if the assignor landlord is released from his obligations pursuant to Covenants Act, ss.6–8 (as to which see below, Ch.14, paras 14.12 *et seq.*): *ibid.*, s.24(4).

[70] *ibid.*, s.23(3). See Ch.13, below.

[71] See *Gill v Lewis* [1956] 2 Q.B. 1. To whom should the arrears of rent, interest and costs be paid by the tenant in order to obtain relief against forfeiture? What if the assignor landlord is satisfied with the terms obtained on the assignment and is uninterested in further involvement, or is untraceable? These are difficulties that the court must work out on a pragmatic basis.

[72] All on the assumption that the Leasehold Property (Repairs) Act 1938 does not apply to restrict such rights.

[73] See Ch.23, below.

[74] Covenants Act, s.25; see below, Ch.23.

statutory provision is limited ("... shall not by virtue of this Act...") to identifying the effect of the Act itself. It was no purpose of the Act to prevent assignees from assuming voluntarily liabilities to which, under the general law as it previously stood, they would not have become subject by virtue of an assignment.

4. Restrictive covenants

Restrictive covenants are a different case from general landlord or tenant covenants because of their proprietary effect. As has been seen, the Act does not make a restrictive covenant bind an assignee if it would otherwise not be enforceable by reason of non-registration.[75] But assuming that a restrictive covenant can (or will) bind an assignee of the term or the reversion, who else will be bound? Two cases call for consideration. First, an assignee of part only of the landlord's interest in the reversion (e.g. an equitable assignee or a concurrent lessee) or of the tenant's interest in the lease (e.g. an equitable assignee or a sub-tenant). Secondly, a purchaser of other property also owned by the landlord (or by the tenant), where the covenant relates to that other property. **12.25**

(a) *Incomplete assignee of reversion or term*

(i) REVERSION. An assignee of part only of the landlord's interest in the reversion is not an assignee within the meaning of the Act,[76] so an equitable assignee[77] or concurrent lessee is not as such bound by a restrictive covenant. A covenant between lessor and lessee is not registrable if it relates to the demised premises themselves[78] and so the covenantee's rights are prima facie vulnerable. Accordingly, the Covenants Act expressly provides that any landlord or tenant covenant that is restrictive of the user of land is capable of being enforced also against any other person who is the owner or occupier of any demised premises to which the covenant relates, whether or not the tenancy expressly so provides.[79] But this provision only applies to restrictions on use of the premises demised by the tenancy in question, not to restrictions on use of other property owned by the landlord.[80] So an equitable assignee and a concurrent lessee would both be bound by a covenant relating to the demised premises, though such a landlord covenant is not commonly encountered. As shown below,[81] the purchaser of an interest in other **12.26**

[75] Above, para.12.07.
[76] Covenants Act, s.28(5).
[77] See above, para.12.20.
[78] Land Registration Act 1925, s.33(c).
[79] Covenants Act, s.3(5).
[80] *Oceanic Village Ltd v United Attractions Ltd* [2000] Ch. 234.
[81] Below, para.(b).

property will not be bound unless the burden of the covenant is registered by the tenant.

12.27 (ii) TERM. Unlike the case just considered, an equitable assignee of the tenant's interest under a lease is an assignee within the meaning of the Act,[82] and so an assignee of part only of the tenant's interest in the premises is bound by the restrictive covenant as such.[83] A sub-tenant is not an assignee, but will be bound by the restrictive covenant by virtue of the express statutory provision considered under (i) above.

(b) *Purchaser of other property*

12.28 As from October 13, 2003, a covenant made between a lessor and a lessee is registrable to the extent that the covenant relates to land other than the demised premises.[84] If unregistered, a purchaser will take free from the covenant: the purchaser is not the assignee of the landlord's or tenant's interest in the demised premises and the extended statutory provision considered under (a) above has no application.

(c) *Benefit of restrictive covenant*

12.29 The benefit of a restrictive covenant will, it is considered, pass together with the benefit of other covenants on an assignment of the term or of the reversion, as the case may be. Where there is no assignment within the meaning of the Covenants Act, the benefit may pass according to the extended provisions of the Act in the case of mortgagees and concurrent lessees,[85] but otherwise will pass according to the normal rules for annexation or assignment of the benefit of such covenants capable of running with land.[86]

5. Anti-avoidance

12.30 The provisions of the Covenants Act relating to transmission of benefit and burden of covenants in new tenancies and their enforcement are, like other provisions of the Act, subject to anti-avoidance provisions. Briefly, any agreement relating to a tenancy is void to the extent that it would exclude, modify or otherwise frustrate the operation of any provision of the Act or impose on the tenant some disadvantage in the event of the

[82] Covenants Act, s.28(1); above, para.12.10.

[83] Though an involuntary assignment of a partial interest might not be an "assignment": *ibid.*, s.28(6)(b); above, para.12.17.

[84] n.78, above.

[85] Covenants Act, s.15.

[86] As comprehensively reviewed and explained by Chadwick L.J. in *Crest Nicholson Residential (South) Ltd v McAllister* [2004] 1 W.L.R. 2409.

operation of any of the provisions of the Act.[87] But nothing in the Act is to be read as preventing a party to a tenancy from releasing a person from a landlord covenant or a tenant covenant of the tenancy.[88] Thus, an agreement in a lease that upon assignment of the reversion the assignee is to be released from certain landlord covenants would be void as excluding the effect of the transmission provisions of the Act,[89] but an actual release entered into between tenant and assignee of the reversion to similar effect would be perfectly valid.[90] The anti-avoidance provisions of the Covenants Act are considered fully in Chapter 23.

The statutory provision just considered,[91] which negates the assumption by the assignee of liability or rights relating to a time before the assignment, leaves open the question of whether an assignee, landlord or tenant, may expressly take on liabilities in relation to a time before the assignment. It is submitted that such an agreement would not infringe the anti-avoidance provisions of the Act[92] because the statutory provision is limited (" . . . shall not by virtue of this Act . . . ") to identifying the effect of the Act itself. It was no purpose of the Act to prevent assignees from assuming voluntarily liabilities to which, under the general law as it previously stood, they would not have become subject by virtue of an assignment. And nothing in the Act itself prevents the express assignment of rights. **12.31**

[87] Covenants Act, s.25(1), considered fully in Ch.23, below.

[88] *ibid.*, s.26(1)(a).

[89] *Aliter* an agreement to release the assignor: *London Diocesan Fund v Phithwa* [2005] 1 W.L.R. 3956.

[90] The same distinction between a void agreement that something shall be done in the future and a lawful doing of the something in question exists in Pt II of the Landlord and Tenant Act 1954 in relation to contracting out of security of tenure for business tenants: see Woodfall's *Law of Landlord and Tenant* (28th ed. (looseleaf)), para.22–038.

[91] Above, para.12.22.

[92] Covenants Act, s.25; see below, Ch.23.

CHAPTER 13

Transmission of Rights of Re-Entry

A right of re-entry is itself an interest in land capable of existing independently at law.[1] But for new tenancies, the benefit of a landlord's right of re-entry is statutorily annexed and incident to the whole, and to each and every part, of the reversion in the premises demised by the tenancy.[2] The benefit of such a right of re-entry passes on an assignment of the whole or any part of the reversion in the demised premises.[3] The combined effect of ss.4(b) and 28(5) of the Covenants Act makes clear that the statutory transmission of the benefit of the landlord's right of re-entry under the tenancy only occurs where the landlord assigns the whole of his interest in the reversion in the whole or part of the demised premises, as the case may be. The significance of this appears to be that on the grant of a concurrent lease a right of re-entry will be exercisable by both the landlord and the concurrent lessee, equivalent to the regime for the statutory transmission of the benefit and burden of covenants.[4] No distinction is made depending on whether the term of the tenancy ends before or after the term of the concurrent lease. How this right will operate in practice, where the landlord seeks to re-enter, is unclear. **13.01**

Where as a result of an assignment a person becomes, by virtue of the Covenants Act, entitled to a right of re-entry contained in a tenancy, that right is exercisable in relation to a breach of a covenant in the tenancy which occurred before the assignment as in relation to one occurring afterwards. In this regard the law relating to new tenancies is the same as that relating to old tenancies.[5] Similarly, the assignee of the reversion on a new tenancy is not so entitled to a right of re-entry in respect of a pre-assignment breach if, by reason of any waiver or release, it was not exercisable immediately before the assignment.[6] The concept of "waiver" **13.02**

[1] Law of Property Act 1925, s.1(2)(e). See *London & County (A. & D.) Ltd v Wilfred Sportsman Ltd* [1971] Ch. 764.

[2] *ibid.*, s.4(a).

[3] *ibid.*, s.4(b).

[4] *ibid.*, s.15(1) makes provision for a concurrent lessee to enforce such tenant covenants; and it also provides for a right of re-entry to be so enforceable.

[5] See *Kataria v Safeland Plc* [1998] 1 E.G.L.R. 39; above, para.4.23.

[6] Covenants Act, s.23(3).

in relation to forfeiture of a lease is familiar and well-defined.[7] In particular, by statute, a waiver of a right to forfeit does not operate as a general waiver of the covenant which was broken or not observed.[8] The word "release" is less precise, but perhaps, consistently with the approach to the words "waiver or release" in connection with the transmission of the benefit and burden of covenants,[9] it should be construed widely as including any act by or on behalf of the landlord other than a "waiver" which would have prevented the landlord from lawfully exercising the right of re-entry.

13.03 It is submitted that the effect of transmission of a right of re-entry under the Act is indistinguishable from the position established in relation to old tenancies.

[7] See *Woodfall's Law of Landlord and Tenant* (28th ed. (looseleaf)), para.17.092 ff.

[8] Law of Property Act 1925, s.148(1); *Broomleigh Housing Association v Hughes* [1999] E.G.C.S. 134.

[9] In Covenants Act, s.3(4); above, paras 12.11 and 12.12.

CHAPTER 14

Release of Covenants on Assignment

Sections 5 to 8 of the Covenants Act effect the most far-reaching (and best publicised) reform in the law of landlord and tenant since 1927. During the recession of the late 1980s and early 1990s, and even before that time, considerable resentment had developed among tenants who found themselves sued on their original covenants in medium-length leases because the individuals or companies to which they had assigned their leases had become insolvent. In many cases, the assignment had taken place some 10–20 years before a very substantial claim for arrears of rent and service charge was brought by the landlord, or even by a successor-in-title of the landlord, of whom the original lessee had never heard. In many cases, a claim for several years' contractual interest under the lease was added to the landlord's claim. **14.01**

In 1988, the Law Commission recommended[1] that the principle of privity of contract in relation to leases should be reformed, though it stopped short of recommending complete abrogation. The Commission's recommendations lay dormant for some years before a Private Member's Bill was introduced in the House of Commons. The first Bill was blocked, but a second, arising from a compromise negotiated by the British Retail Consortium and the British Property Federation, was passed with Government backing on July 19, 1995.

The provisions relating to release of liability of assignors are intended to dovetail with the provisions for the transmission of the benefit and burden of covenants, considered in Ch.12. Under those provisions, almost all landlord covenants and tenant covenants in new tenancies become enforceable by and against assignees of the term and the reversion. Like those provisions, the provisions for release of liability under the covenants apply only to new tenancies. The Covenants Act provides for the automatic release from further liability of a tenant who assigns the whole or part of premises of which he is the tenant; but a landlord must apply to be released on assigning the reversion, unless the lease makes express provision for his liability to end. **14.02**

[1] Report on Landlord and Tenant Law: Privity of Contract and Estate (Law Com. No.174).

1. Assignment of demised premises by tenant

14.03 If a tenant assigns the whole of premises demised to him under a tenancy, he is released from the tenant covenants of the tenancy and ceases to be entitled to the landlord covenants of the tenancy, both as from the assignment.[2] This applies even if the tenant is no longer the tenant of the whole of the premises comprised in the tenancy,[3] i.e. even if he has already surrendered part, or if he has already assigned part of the premises to another. In principle, an equitable assignment suffices to bring the subsection into effect[4]; but an assignment in breach of a covenant of the tenancy or by operation of law (both of which are "excluded assignments") does not.[5] And an equitable assignment, in the sense of an assignment binding between assignor and assignee but not binding on the landlord for want of formality, may well be an "excluded assignment", depending on the terms of the alienation covenant in the lease.

14.04 The release from the tenant covenants and loss of entitlement to the benefit of the landlord covenants are both effective "as from the assignment". This presumably means the date of the deed of conveyance,[6] or (in the case of a lease the title to which is registered) the date of the deed of transfer, and not the date from which the transfer is registered because an equitable assignment suffices. It is doubtful whether a binding contract to assign is an "assignment" within the meaning of the section, despite the definition of "assignment",[7] and despite the purchaser under such a contract having equitable rights over the property until completion and the right to specific performance of the agreement. If such an

[2] Covenants Act, s.5(2). For the meaning of "tenant covenant" and "landlord covenant", see Ch.11, above. The time when the assignment takes place is therefore of crucial importance to the operation of the Act. Unless the context otherwise requires, "assignment" includes equitable assignment, assignment in breach of a covenant of a tenancy, and assignment by operation of law: Covenants Act, s.28(1). One of the unresolved problems of the Act is at what point in time, where there is a contract for the assignment of a lease (or of a reversion), the "assignment" has taken place. It is difficult to conceive that the draftsman intended the benefit and burden of covenants to pass and the release of continuing liabilities to take effect at the moment where an unconditional contract for the assignment of the lease (or reversion) is made, yet the contract is in one sense an equitable assignment. It is difficult to say that the context requires otherwise. An executed but as yet unregistered transfer is probably an assignment for these purposes. See para.12.10, above, at nn.29–31 for the law regarding execution and delivery of deeds of transfer.

[3] Covenants Act, s.5(4).

[4] *ibid.*, s.28(1). But see above, n.2.

[5] *ibid.*, s.11(1),(2). For excluded assignments, see Ch.16, below.

[6] A deed is required for an assignment at law of a tenancy of any length: see *Crago v Julian* [1992] 1 W.L.R. 372; *Camden L.B.C. v Alexandrou (No.2)* (1997) 74 P.&C.R. D33.

[7] Covenants Act, s.28(1).

assignment were an "assignment" for these purposes, there would, on completion, have been two "assignments" for the purposes of the Act.[8] In the case of an equitable assignment by writing, the relevant time will be the date when the writing was made.

If a tenant assigns part only of the premises demised to him, then as from the assignment he is released from the tenant covenants of the tenancy, and ceases to be entitled to the benefit of the landlord covenants of the tenancy, only to the extent that those covenants fall to be complied with in relation to that part of the demised premises.[9] Once again, this applies whether or not the tenant is tenant of the whole of the premises comprised in the tenancy.[10] Thus, a tenant can derive the benefit of the statutory release *pro tanto* on each of a number of successive assignments of parts of the premises demised to him. **14.05**

Save in relation to covenants to pay money, a covenant falls to be complied with in relation to demised premises comprised in the assignment if either (a) it in terms applies to that part of the demised premises, or (b) in its practical application it can be attributed to that part of the premises whether or not it can also be attributed to other individual parts of the demised premises.[11] It is considered that limb (a) connotes an exclusive application in terms to that assigned part of the premises. Limb (b) provides for covenants of more general application. To the extent that any covenant falls to be complied with in relation to such assigned premises, the assignor is not bound by the covenant to that extent, i.e. the assignor remains bound by the covenant in so far as it affects (if at all) the part of the demised premises retained by him, but he is no longer bound insofar as it relates to the part of the demised premises assigned. If a given covenant either in terms applies, or in its practical application can be attributed solely, to a part of the demised premises comprised in the assignment, then the assignor is not bound by it any longer. **14.06**

So far as covenants to pay money are concerned, such a covenant falls to be complied with in relation to demised premises comprised in the assignment if either (a) it in terms applies to such premises, or (b) the amount of the payment is determinable specifically by reference to such premises or (in the case of a tenant covenant) by reference to anything falling to be done by or for a person as tenant or occupier of such premises or (in the case of a landlord covenant) by reference to anything falling to be done by or for a person as landlord of such premises.[12] **14.07**

[8] It is considered that equitable assignments are, for these purposes, limited to assignments intended to be effective at law, but formally defective or dependent on registration for legal effect, and assignments of equitable leases which, of necessity, are equitable assignments.

[9] Covenants Act, s.5(3).

[10] *ibid.*, s.5(4).

[11] *ibid.*, s.28(2).

[12] *ibid.*, s.28(3).

Alternative (a) should present little difficulty in practice. It is considered that this alternative connotes an exclusive application in terms to the assigned premises. Alternative (b) is somewhat opaque, but the words "determinable specifically by reference to" must be taken to imply a quantification by reference solely to the assigned part of the premises or to something done by someone as the tenant, occupier or landlord of that part alone.

14.08 The purpose of the Act seems to be that an assignor of the tenancy will only be exonerated wholly from compliance with a tenant covenant, or correspondingly will only lose entirely the benefit of the landlord covenant, in cases where the covenant either in terms applies only, or is specifically and solely linked, to an assigned part of the demised premises. In cases where this is not so, two situations will arise. First, in relation to covenants other than money covenants, the assignor will be released from the covenant, or correspondingly will lose the benefit of the covenant, only to the extent that it falls to be complied with in relation to the assigned premises. Secondly, in relation to a covenant to pay money, the covenant, being entirely general as to the premises to which it relates, does not for this limited statutory purpose "fall to be complied with" in relation to the assigned premises *at all*,[13] and so the assignor will be fully bound by or derive the full benefit of the covenant (as the case may be). Thus, for example, an assignor who assigns a one-third part of premises demised by a five-year lease at a fixed rent will prima facie be liable for the whole of the rent. The words "to the extent that"[14] therefore only have a significant effect where a non-money covenant, e.g. a covenant to repair, is of general application as respects various parts of the demised premises including the assigned part. In all other cases, the assignor will either be released entirely (because the covenant relates solely to the assigned premises) or be bound in full (either because the non-money covenant relates only to the non-assigned premises or because the money covenant was not in terms, or in the quantification of the money, applicable solely to the assigned premises). In the latter case, the apportionment provisions of the Act can come into play.[15]

14.09 Where a tenant is released from a covenant by virtue of these provisions, his liability arising from a breach of the covenant occurring before the release is unaffected.[16] Similarly, where he ceases thereby to be entitled to the benefit of a covenant, this does not affect any rights of his arising from a breach of the covenant occurring before he ceases to be so entitled.[17] These provisions might give rise to interesting questions in

[13] By virtue of *ibid.*, s.28(3).
[14] In *ibid.*, s.5(2).
[15] See below, Ch.15.
[16] Covenants Act, s.24(1).
[17] *ibid.*, s.24(4).

connection with repairing covenants. A tenant ("T") who was in breach of his repairing obligations lawfully assigns the tenancy to A. T remains liable to be sued for damages[18] in respect of all the disrepair at the date of the assignment; A can also be sued in due course for the same damage arising from (essentially) the same breach of covenant. Does the landlord ("L") have to give credit for sums which might be recovered from A, or is T liable in full? Conversely, if L was in breach of his repairing obligations at the date of the assignment and remains so thereafter, is L separately liable in damages to both T and A?

Where a tenant is released from a covenant to any extent by virtue of the Act, any guarantor of the tenant's obligations under that covenant is released from his covenant to the same extent.[19] **14.10**

2. Assignment of reversion by landlord

Unlike the case of an assignment by the tenant under a tenancy, the Covenants Act does not provide for automatic release of any continuing landlord's contractual liability upon an assignment of the whole or part of the reversion. Landlords are given a right to apply to be released from landlord covenants by service on the tenant of a notice requesting such release. In cases where the tenant promptly objects to the release of the landlord's continuing liability, the court must decide whether it is reasonable for that liability to be released. The reason for the difference in treatment is that under the terms of the lease landlords generally have some control over assignments by tenants, entitling them to refuse consent where the intended assignee is unsuitable; tenants usually have no control over landlords' entitlement to assign the reversion. The right to apply for a release is important, however: absent a contractual or statutory release, a landlord under a new tenancy will remain liable on the landlord covenants for the duration of the tenancy. **14.11**

(a) *Landlord's entitlement to apply for release*

Where a landlord assigns the reversion in the whole or in part only of premises of which he is the landlord under a tenancy, he may apply to be released from landlord covenants in the tenancy in accordance with the s.8 procedure.[20] If the reversion in part only of the premises is assigned by the landlord, he may only apply by the s.8 procedure to be released from the landlord covenants to the extent that they fall to be complied with in relation to that part of those premises.[21] A landlord is entitled to apply for **14.12**

[18] Subject to the provisions of the Leasehold Property (Repairs) Act 1938.
[19] Covenants Act, s.24(2).
[20] *ibid*, s.6(2)(a), (3)(a). For the procedure, see below.
[21] *ibid*., s.6(3)(a).

release whether or not he is the landlord of the whole of the premises comprised in the tenancy.[22] Thus, a landlord may dispose of his reversion in several parts and at different times and apply for a release *pro tanto* on the occasion of each disposal of part of his reversionary interest. The right to apply for release only applies to "landlord covenants" within the meaning of the Act.[23] So covenants that are expressed to be personal to the lessor, or which fall to be performed before the grant of the lease or before any assignment of the reversion, are not within the scope of the release provisions because they cannot be "landlord covenants".[24] Pursuant to the Act, [25] the Lord Chancellor has prescribed appropriate forms of notices requesting release by statutory instrument.[26] The Regulations so made are referred to hereafter as the "Notices Regulations 1995".

14.13 Save in relation to covenants to pay money, a landlord covenant falls to be complied with in relation to demised premises the reversion on which is assigned if either (a) it in terms applies to that part of the demised premises, or (b) in its practical application it can be attributed to that part of the premises whether or not it can also be attributed to other individual parts of the demised premises.[27] It is considered that limb (a) connotes an exclusive application in terms to the part of the premises the reversion on which is assigned. Limb (b) is for covenants of more general application. To the extent that any covenant falls to be complied with in relation to such part of the premises, the landlord may apply to be released to that extent, i.e. the landlord may apply for release in-so-far as the covenant affects the part of the demised premises the reversion on which is assigned, but he is not entitled to apply for release insofar as it relates to other parts of the demised premises. If a given covenant either in terms applies, or in its practical application can be attributed solely to the part of the demised premises the reversion on which is assigned, then the landlord may apply for total release from it.

14.14 So far as covenants to pay money are concerned, such a covenant falls to be complied with in relation to demised premises the reversion on which is being assigned if either (a) it in terms applies to such premises, or (b) the amount of the payment is determinable specifically by reference to such premises or by reference to anything falling to be done by or for a person as landlord of such premises.[28] Alternative (a) should present little difficulty in practice. It is considered that this alternative connotes

[22] *ibid.*, s.6(4).

[23] *ibid.*, s.28(1).

[24] *BHP Petroleum Great Britain Ltd v Chesterfield Properties Ltd* [2002] Ch. 12; *Edlington Properties Ltd v JH Fenner & Co. Ltd* [2006] 1 W.L.R. 1583.

[25] Covenants Act, s.27(1).

[26] The Landlord and Tenant (Covenants) Act 1995 (Notices) Regulations 1995 (SI 1995/2964), below.

[27] Covenants Act, s.28(2).

[28] *ibid.*, s.28(3).

an exclusive application in terms to the premises the reversion on which is being assigned. Alternative (b) is somewhat opaque, but the words "determinable specifically by reference to" must be taken to imply a quantification by reference solely to that part of the premises or to something done by someone as the tenant, occupier or landlord of that part alone.

The purpose of the Act seems to be that an assignor of the reversion will only be exonerated wholly from compliance with a landlord covenant, or correspondingly will only lose entirely the benefit of the tenant covenant, in cases where the covenant either in terms applies only to, or is specifically and solely linked to, the part of the demised premises the reversion on which is assigned. In cases where this is not so, two situations will arise. First, in relation to covenants other that money covenants, the assignor will be entitled to apply for release only to the extent that the covenant falls to be complied with in relation to the part of the demised premises the reversion on which is assigned. Secondly, in relation to a covenant to pay money, the covenant, being entirely general as to the premises to which it relates, does not for this limited statutory purpose "fall to be complied with" in relation to the assigned part at all,[29] and so the landlord will remain fully bound by the covenant. Thus, the words "to the extent that" in s.6(3)(a) only have a significant effect where a non-money covenant, e.g. a covenant to repair, is of general application as respects the various parts of the demised premises. In all other cases, the landlord will either be entitled to apply for a full release (because the covenant relates solely to that part of the premises the reversion on which is assigned) or be disentitled to apply for release at all (either because a non-money covenant relates solely to a non-assigned part or because the money covenant was not in terms, or in the quantification of the money, applicable solely to that part of the demised premises).[30] **14.15**

(b) *Procedure for application by landlord for release*

An application by an assigning landlord for the release of a covenant to any extent (i.e. either in full or to the extent that such covenant falls to be complied with in relation to the part of the premises the reversion on which is being assigned)[31] is made by serving on the tenant a notice informing him of the proposed assignment or (as the case may be) the fact that the assignment has taken place, and of the request for the covenant to be released to that extent.[32] Such notice must be served on the tenant **14.16**

[29] By virtue of Covenants Act, s.28(3).

[30] In this important case, the provisions of Covenants Act, ss.9 and 10, relating to apportionment of covenants binding both assignor and assignee, come into play: see Ch.16, below.

[31] See above.

[32] Covenants Act, s.8(1).

either before or within a period of four weeks beginning with the date of the assignment in question.[33] For these purposes, "the tenant" means the tenant of the premises comprised in the assignment in question or, if different parts of those premises are held under the tenancy by different tenants, each of those tenants.[34] Thus, where a tenant has assigned (e.g.) three parcels of the demised premises to three different individuals and retained the last parcel himself, a landlord who has assigned (or who wishes to assign) part of his reversion and wishes to be released from the landlord covenants to that extent must serve notice pursuant to the s.8 procedure on each of the four tenants who is the tenant of any part of the premises the reversion on which has been (or is to be) assigned by the landlord.

14.17 The form of any notice to be served for the purposes of s.8 is prescribed by statutory instrument.[35] The Act stipulated that any regulations made should require an initial notice to include—

> "(a) an explanation of the significance of the notice and the options available to the person on whom it is served;
> (b) a statement that any objections to the proposed release . . . must be made by notice in writing served on the person or persons by whom the initial notice is served within the period of four weeks beginning with the day on which the initial notice is served; and
> (c) an address in England and Wales to which any such objections may be sent."[36]

The forms prescribed by the Notices Regulations 1995 for a landlord's initial notice are Form 3 (in the case of a landlord applying to be released from all the landlord covenants of the tenancy on assignment of his entire interest) and Form 4 (in the case of a landlord applying to be released from the landlord covenants of the tenancy to the appropriate extent on assignment of part only of his interest) in the Schedule to the Notices Regulations 1995, or forms substantially to the like effect.[37] In view of the complexities of the prescribed forms, it is unlikely that anything less than forms in the Schedule to the Notices Regulations 1995, or such forms with very minor omissions or immaterial typographical errors, will be held to be substantially to the like effect. If any notice purporting to be served for the purposes of s.8(1) of the Covenants Act is not in the

[33] *ibid.*, s.8(1).
[34] *ibid.*, s.8(4)(a).
[35] Notices Regulations 1995, reg.2(b)(c), Forms 3,4.
[36] Covenants Act, s.27(2).
[37] Notices Regulations 1995, reg.2(b), (c). See *Megarry's Assured Tenancies* (2nd ed.), paras 8-25 and 13-31 on the application of similar words in relation to notices under the Housing Acts 1985 and 1988.

prescribed form or a form substantially to the like effect, the notice shall not be effective for the purposes of that section.[38]

(i) Form of prescribed notices. The prescribed forms are set out in Appendix 3.[39] Both Form 3 and Form 4 are in two parts: the first is to be completed by the landlord requesting release; the second is for the response (if any) of the tenant. Part I of both Form 3 and Form 4 tells the tenant served with the notice that if he does *not* consider it reasonable for the landlord to be released, he must notify the landlord within the period of four weeks beginning with the giving of the notice by using Pt II of the Form. Part I of the Forms tells the tenant that he may withdraw an objection to release at any time. Note 6 to Pt I advises the tenant to bear in mind that in the event of late withdrawal of objection, or if the court finds it reasonable for the landlord to be released, the tenant might have to pay costs. Apart from that warning, the tone of the language of the forms tends to suggest to an uninformed tenant that he has nothing much to lose by objecting. One can readily imagine that such a tenant, served with a notice which does not explain to him that the assignee landlord will be liable to perform the landlord covenants in the tenancy from the date of the assignment in place of the previous landlord, will regard it as unreasonable for the landlord to be released, and therefore serve a notice of objection. Once landlords become more familiar with the procedure, county courts can therefore expect to be quite busy with landlords' consequential applications for declarations that it is reasonable for the landlord to be released.[40] **14.18**

(ii) Service of notices. The Act requires the notice to be served on the tenant (as defined) within the period of four weeks beginning with the date of the assignment in question, or before the assignment. The statutory time limit must be strictly applied. The period of four weeks begins on the date of the assignment, and so the last date for service of the notice is 27 days after the day on which the assignment is made. For example, if the reversion on a lease granted on February 2, 1996 is assigned on March 2, 2006, the last day for service is March 29, 2006 (not March 30, 2006). Section 23 of the Landlord and Tenant Act 1927 applies in relation to the service of a landlord's notice under s.8 requesting a release.[41] The notice is therefore validly served if it is: **14.19**

[38] Covenants Act, s.27(4).
[39] See below, App.3, pp.439–46.
[40] For this procedure, see below, para.14.24.
[41] Covenants Act, s.27(5).

(a) served personally on the tenant;
(b) left for the tenant at his last known place of abode in England or Wales;
(c) sent through the post in a registered letter addressed to the tenant at such last known place of abode; or
(d) in the case of a local or public authority or a statutory or a public utility company, sent through the post in a registered letter addressed to the secretary or other proper officer at the principal office of such authority or company.

A registered letter includes recorded delivery post.[42] The last known place of abode of a company can be its registered office.[43]

14.20 The effect of service by one of these prescribed modes is that service is deemed to have been effected if the landlord can prove compliance with one of them, even if in fact the tenant was not served at all.[44] Thus posting of the notice by recorded delivery post is good service, even if the letter is never delivered. Moreover, in the case of service by post, service is effected when the letter is posted; the contrary conclusion is not required by the Human Rights Act 1998 and the provisions of the Interpretation Act 1978 and other provisions as to time of service have no application.[45] The risk of non-service is statutorily placed on the intended recipient of the notice.[46] A landlord may choose to serve the tenant by some other mode, and provided that the notice is received such service is perfectly valid; but the risk of non-service is then on the landlord.

(c) *Effect of timeous application by landlord for release*

14.21 Where an application by the landlord for the release of a covenant is made in time and in the correct form, the covenant is released to the extent mentioned in the notice in three different sets of circumstances:

(1) if the tenant does not, within the period of four weeks beginning with the day on which the notice is served, serve on the landlord a notice in writing objecting to the release;
(2) if the tenant does serve such a notice but the court, on the application of the landlord, makes a declaration that it is reasonable for the landlord to be so released; or

[42] Recorded Delivery Service Act 1962, s.1.
[43] *National Westminster Bank Ltd v Betchworth Investments Ltd* [1975] 1 E.G.L.R. 57.
[44] *Galinski v McHugh* (1988) 57 P. & C.R. 359; *Commercial Union Life Assurance Co. Ltd v Moustafa* [1999] 2 E.G.L.R. 44; *Blunden v Frogmore Investments Ltd* [2002] 2 E.G.L.R. 29.
[45] *Beanby Estates Ltd v Egg Stores (Stamford Hill) Ltd* [2003] 3 E.G.L.R. 85; *C A Webber (Transport) Ltd v Railtrack Plc* [2004] 1 E.G.L.R. 49.
[46] *ibid.*

(3) if the tenant serves on the landlord a notice in writing consenting to the release and, if he has previously served a notice objecting to it, stating that that notice is withdrawn.[47]

The extent mentioned in the notice will be either a total release in the event of a transfer of the whole of the landlord's interest (Form 3) or a release to the extent that the obligations under the covenant fall to be complied with in relation to the part of the landlord's interest transferred (Form 4). Each of the three sets of circumstances in which release will occur must be separately considered.

(i) FAILURE BY TENANT TO SERVE NOTICE OBJECTING. A notice in writing objecting to the release of the landlord must be in the prescribed form, or in a form substantially to the like effect.[48] The prescribed form is, where a landlord has served a notice in Form 3 (total release), Pt II of that Form, and where a landlord has served a notice in Form 4 (partial release), Pt II of that Form.[49] If the tenant does not serve on the landlord a notice objecting to the release within the period of four weeks beginning with the day on which the landlord's notice applying for release was served, the landlord is released from the covenant(s) to the extent mentioned in the notice. The statutory time limit must be strictly applied.[50] The period of four weeks starts on the day on which the landlord's notice was served on the tenant, and so the last day for service of the tenant's notice of objection is the 27th day after the day of service of the landlord's notice.[51] **14.22**

Identifying the day on which the landlord's notice was served can give rise to a number of difficulties. It is noteworthy that para.5 of Pt I of both of the landlord's notice prescribed forms (Forms 3 and 4) states: **14.23**

> "If you do **not** consider it reasonable for me/us to be released, you **must** notify me/us of your objection, using Part II of this Form, within the period of **FOUR WEEKS** beginning with the giving of this notice . . . ."

The forms prescribed by statutory instrument therefore appear to equate service of the landlord's notice with the giving of it, although note 4 to Pt I of both Forms warns the tenant that "the date of giving of the notice may not be the date written on the notice or the date on which you actually saw it. It may, for instance, be the date on which the notice was

[47] Covenants Act, s.8(2).
[48] Notices Regulations 1995, reg.2(b)(ii), 2(c)(ii).
[49] *ibid.*
[50] See n.3 in Pt II of Forms 3 and 4 in the Schedule to the Notices Regulations 1995.
[51] See, by analogy, the example given above, para.14.19.

delivered through the post to your last address known by the landlord". In view of the statutory presumptions of service in s.23 of the Landlord and Tenant Act 1927 which are applied under the Covenants Act, this warning is apposite, though probably insufficient.[52] Service of a landlord's notice applying for release is deemed to be effected by, inter alia, leaving the notice for the tenant at his last known place of abode, in which case the notice is served on the day on which it was so left, or by sending it to him at such address by a registered or recorded delivery letter, in which case the notice is served when it is posted.[53] In the case where the landlord sends his notice to the tenant by ordinary pre-paid post, on the other hand, there is no presumption of service,[54] and it is considered that the tenant could seek to prove that he did not in fact receive the notice either at all or until a later day, and that accordingly as a matter of law it was not served on or not served before the later day, as the case may be.

Once the tenant has identified the day of service of the landlord's notice, he can calculate the day by which his notice of objection must be served. Section 23 of the Landlord and Tenant Act 1927 applies also to the service of such a notice,[55] and accordingly the tenant may take advantage of the presumptions of service which apply if the notice is sent in one of the prescribed ways.[56] If the landlord is not served by the end of the 27th day after the service on the tenant of the landlord's notice, the landlord is without more released from the covenant(s) to the extent specified in the landlord's notice, i.e. fully if the landlord transferred the whole of his reversionary interest and served a Form 3 notice, or to the extent that the covenant(s) fell to be complied with in relation to the part transferred if he disposed of part of his reversionary interest and served a Form 4 notice. It is considered that service by a landlord of a Form 4 notice in a case where he has transferred (or proposes to transfer) all his interest, and similarly service of a Form 3 notice in a case where he has transferred (or proposes to transfer) part of his interest, will be held not to be a "form substantially to the like effect" to the prescribed form in each case.

14.24 (ii) COURT DECLARATION. If the tenant does serve on the landlord in time and in the correct form a notice of objection to the proposed release, the

[52] See the criticisms of the Court of Appeal in relation to similar warning information prescribed for notices under the Landlord and Tenant Act 1954: *Sun Alliance and London Assurance Co. Ltd v Hayman* [1975] 1 W.L.R. 177 (notice given and received when posted).

[53] *Webber v Railtrack*, above.

[54] The Covenants Act does not itself authorise a notice to be served by post (other than by registered or recorded delivery post) and so the presumption of service in due course of post under Interpretation Act 1978, s.7 will not apply to a notice sent by ordinary pre-paid post.

[55] Covenants Act, s.27(5).

[56] See above, paras 14.19 and 14.20.

landlord is not without more released from the covenant(s). The onus is passed back to the landlord, who may either accept that he will not be released, or apply to the county court[57] for a declaration, or wait and hope that the tenant changes his mind. If the landlord does nothing, and the tenant does not change his mind, the landlord is not released. If the landlord wishes to take further steps to secure his release, he must apply to the county court for a declaration that it is reasonable for the covenant to be released to the extent mentioned in the landlord's notice. Neither the Covenants Act nor the Civil Procedure Rules prescribe the form or necessary contents of any such application.[58] The application falls to be made by the landlord, but there is no provision limiting the time within which the application has to be made.

On an application by the landlord, the county court must apparently determine whether or not "it is reasonable for the covenant to be so released".[59] The word "so" relates back to the words "released to the extent mentioned in the notice", and it appears therefore that the court does not have jurisdiction to release the covenant(s) to a lesser extent than that sought in the notice, but only to determine whether it is reasonable or not for the covenant(s) to be released to that extent. Although it might be thought, consistently with the general policy underlying the Covenants Act, that absent any special circumstances it would be reasonable for the landlord to be released, the application falls to be made by the landlord and the onus of proof thus prima facie falls on him.[60] Nevertheless, it is considered that once the landlord adduces sufficient evidence to show that there are no special circumstances surrounding the assignment, the evidential onus will pass to the tenant to persuade the court that it should not, for some reason, make the declaration that the landlord seeks. This balance is hinted at in the rubric under the heading "IMPORTANT" in Forms 3 and 4 in the Schedule to the Notices Regulations 1995, which states: **14.25**

> "IF YOU CONSIDER THAT THERE IS GOOD REASON FOR YOUR LANDLORD **NOT** TO BE RELEASED, YOU MUST ACT QUICKLY."

It is also suggested by the fact that a release, once notified to the tenant, takes effect unless the tenant serves notice on the landlord stating that he

[57] Covenants Act, s.8(4)(c).

[58] Such an application should probably be brought as a Pt 8 claim: CPR 56PD, 2.1.

[59] Covenants Act, s.8(2)(b).

[60] Compare Landlord and Tenant Act 1988, s.1, where the onus is statutorily imposed on a landlord to show that it was reasonable to refuse consent to an assignment, etc. or to show that any conditions subject to which consent was granted were reasonable conditions.

objects to the release. The word "reasonable" connotes an objective test, and requires the court to balance the interests of landlord and tenant. The test is *not* whether the tenant has a reasonable argument for objecting to a release.

14.26 If the court, on the landlord's application, does not make the declaration sought, the covenant(s) is (are) not released (subject to appeal) unless either the tenant subsequently serves a notice consenting to the release[61] or the release is effected upon a later transfer by the new landlord.[62]

14.27 (iii) SERVICE OF TENANT'S NOTICE CONSENTING TO RELEASE. At any time after the service of a landlord's notice in Form 3 or Form 4 seeking release of landlord covenants, the tenant may serve a notice on the landlord consenting to the release. Part II of Forms 3 and 4 provides, in one of the alternative paragraphs numbered 4, a form of words to that effect. But there is no requirement for a tenant's notice of this type to be in a prescribed form; all that is required is a notice in writing consenting to the release. Upon service on the landlord of such a notice, the covenant(s) is (are) released to the extent mentioned in the landlord's notice. If the tenant has previously served on the landlord a notice objecting to release,[63] he may still serve on the landlord a notice in writing consenting to the release. In such a case, the form prescribed is simply a notice in writing stating that the tenant is now consenting and that the notice of objection is withdrawn.[64] Upon service on the landlord of such a notice in writing, the covenant(s) is (are) released to the extent mentioned in the landlord's notice.

(d) *Time and effect of release*

14.28 Any release from a landlord covenant in accordance with the s.8 procedure, whether because the tenant does not serve a notice of objection or because the court declares it to be reasonable or because the tenant serves notice consenting to the release, is regarded as occurring at the time when the assignment in question takes place.[65] Thus, even if the landlord applies after several years to the court for a declaration and the

[61] See below.

[62] For this procedure, see below, paras 14.32 *et seq*.

[63] Presumably only a written notice in the prescribed form under Covenants Act, s.8(2)(a), and not any other notice objecting to release, as this latter type of notice would not be of any effect to prevent release of the landlord covenant(s) pursuant to the prescribed form landlord's notice.

[64] Covenants Act, s.8(2)(c); Notices Regulations 1995, reg.2(b)(iii), 2(c)(iii). The tenant will, *ex hypothesi*, already have sent Pt II of the landlord's notice in Form 3 or Form 4 back to him.

[65] Covenants Act, s.8(3).

declaration is made,[66] or if the tenant after several years gives written notice consenting to release and withdrawing his notice of objection, the release is still treated as having been effected on the date of the assignment of the landlord's interest. What the effect is if the landlord has in the meantime been sued on the landlord's covenants for breaches occurring after the assignment is unclear.

A release of a landlord from a landlord covenant by virtue of these statutory provisions does not affect any liability of the landlord arising from a breach of the covenant occurring before the release (i.e. before the date of the assignment of the landlord's interest).[67]

If the landlord is released from the landlord covenants, he ceases to be entitled to the benefit of the tenant covenants of the tenancy as from the assignment.[68] Similarly, if the landlord is released from the landlord covenants to the extent that they fall to be complied with in relation to the part of the premises assigned, he ceases to be entitled to the benefit of the tenant covenants of the tenancy but only to the extent that they fall to be complied with in relation to that part.[69] Such loss of the benefit of tenant covenants does not affect any rights of the landlord arising from a breach of such covenants occurring before the date of the assignment.[70]

All these provisions point up the importance of identifying the date on which the assignment takes place. Unfortunately, by reason of the definition of "assignment" as including an equitable assignment, there is an element of doubt. For example, which of a series of three events: binding contract for assignment of reversion, execution of deed of transfer, and registration of transferee at H.M. Land Registry, is the date of the assignment?[71]

(e) *Other provisions relating to release of landlords*

(i) CONSENSUAL RELEASE. Nothing in the Covenants Act is to be read as **14.29**
preventing a party to a tenancy from releasing a person from a landlord covenant of the tenancy.[72] Such release need not be under seal or even in writing, but if not under seal and in the form of an agreement, it must be supported by valuable consideration. Moreover, an agreement, as a term of the tenancy, that the landlord is released upon assignment of the whole of his interest in the reversion does not infringe the anti-avoidance

[66] Delay to this degree could be a significant factor when the court decides whether it is reasonable for the covenant(s) to be released, *if* the court is to consider reasonableness at the time when it hears the landlord's application.

[67] Covenants Act, s.24(1).

[68] *ibid.*, s.6(2)(b).

[69] *ibid.*, s.6(3)(b).

[70] *ibid.*, s.24(4).

[71] Probably execution of the deed. See above, para.14.03, n.2.

[72] Covenants Act, s.26(1)(a).

provisions in s.25 of the Act.[73] The provisions of the Covenants Act therefore apply to the extent that there is no consensual machinery for release of the landlord.

14.30 (ii) LANDLORD AND TENANT ACT 1985, s.3. Under this section, if the interest of the landlord under a tenancy of premises which consist of or include a dwelling is assigned, the new landlord must give notice in writing of the assignment and of his name and address to the tenant not later than the next day on which rent is payable under the tenancy or, if that is within two months of the assignment, by the end of that period of two months.[74] "Tenancy" here includes a sub-lease or sub-tenancy and an agreement for a lease or tenancy (or sub-lease or sub-tenancy)[75]; "assignment" here includes any conveyance other than a mortgage or charge,[76] and so the passing of an equitable interest under a contract for sale will not qualify. Even if the demised premises consist of or include a dwelling, the provisions of s.3 do not apply if Pt II of the Landlord and Tenant Act 1954 applies to the tenancy.[77] Section 3 further provides[78] that the person who was the landlord under the tenancy immediately before the assignment ("the old landlord") is liable to the tenant in respect of any breach of covenant, condition or agreement under the tenancy occurring before the end of a specified period after the assignment in like manner as if the interest assigned were still vested in him.[79] The specified period starts on the date of the assignment and ends on the date when either—

(a) notice in writing of the assignment and of the new landlord's name and address is given to the tenant by the new landlord (whether in compliance with the above duty to provide it or not), or
(b) notice in writing of the assignment and of the new landlord's name and last-known address is given to the tenant by the old landlord,

whichever happens first.[80] Where an old landlord and a new landlord are both liable to the tenant in respect of any breach occurring during the specified period, they are jointly and severally liable in respect of it.[81]

[73] *London Diocesan Fund v Phithwa* [2005] 1 W.L.R. 3956. For the anti-avoidance provisions, see below, Ch.23.
[74] Landlord and Tenant Act 1985, s.3(1).
[75] *ibid.*, s.36(2).
[76] *ibid.*, s.3(4)(b).
[77] *ibid.*, s.32(1).
[78] By amendment pursuant to Landlord and Tenant Act 1987, s.50.
[79] Landlord and Tenant Act 1985, s.3(3A).
[80] *ibid.*, s.3(3B).
[81] *ibid.*, s.3(3A).

Under these provisions, there is thus the potential for a landlord who assigns his interest in premises demised by a tenancy to remain liable to the tenant as if the reversion were still vested in him. This would otherwise conflict with the release provisions of the Covenants Act, and so the latter specifically provides that nothing in it affects the operation of the provisions of s.3(3A) of the Landlord and Tenant Act 1985.[82] Of course, there is no automatic release on assignment of the landlord's interest under the Covenants Act, and such release cannot take place (in the absence of an express release) without a notice in the appropriate prescribed form having been served on the tenant; but the prescribed form notices do not give all the particulars specified in Landlord and Tenant Act 1985, s.3(3B), and so it is quite possible for the liability of an assigning landlord of premises comprising or including a dwelling to continue by virtue of that statutory provision, notwithstanding the requirements for a release as from the date of the assignment under the Covenants Act having been satisfied.

(f) *Effect of non-release*

Where a landlord assigns the whole or part of his reversionary interest but is not released by virtue of the Act from the landlord covenant(s), the assignment does not affect any liability of his arising from a breach of the covenant(s) occurring before the assignment.[83] The effect of non-release is further that the landlord remains liable to perform the landlord covenants in the tenancy after the date of the assignment. It is considered doubtful that this makes the landlord liable for the defaults of his assignee under negative landlord covenants.[84] Under the law relating to old tenancies, an original lessor who assigns the reversion would remain liable throughout the term to the original tenant, but not, from the date of the assignment, to any assignee of the term. This is because there was no privity of contract (in relation to the landlord covenants) with any such assignee nor, from the date of the assignment of the reversion, was there privity of estate. Under the provisions of the Covenants Act, however, the benefit of the landlord covenants is statutorily annexed to the term,[85] and so the original lessor's obligations become fully enforceable by an assignee of the term and will remain so notwithstanding an assignment of the reversion upon which the assigning landlord is not released. In this respect, the position of an original lessor under a new tenancy has materially worsened from his legal position under an old tenancy. **14.31**

[82] Covenants Act, s.26(2).
[83] *ibid.*, s.24(3).
[84] See above, paras 3.05 *et seq.*
[85] See above, para.12.01.

3. Right of former landlord to apply for release

14.32 Where a landlord under a new tenancy is not released under the procedures described above[86] upon his assigning the whole or part of his interest, he has in certain circumstances the right to apply for release at a later time if and when a successor in title of his further assigns the landlord's interest. This right is conferred and governed by s.7 of the Covenants Act.

Section 7 applies where a landlord assigns the reversion in premises of which he is the landlord under a tenancy, and immediately before the assignment a former landlord of the premises remains bound by a landlord covenant of the tenancy.[87] The landlord covenant by which the former landlord remains bound is referred to in s.7 as "the relevant covenant". Unlike s.6, which speaks of applying for release from the landlord covenant*s*, s.7 refers to the former landlord remaining bound by *a* landlord covenant. There appears to be no significance in this other than that a former landlord who assigned the reversion in parts may have been released from the landlord covenants in relation to some parts of the demised premises but not others, and therefore may no longer be bound by all the landlord covenants of the tenancy. Section 7 applies whether or not the landlord making the assignment is landlord of the whole of the premises comprised in the tenancy,[88] i.e. even if a third person is landlord of part of the premises comprised in the tenancy, or even if the former landlord is still landlord of such part. But it is unclear whether it applies if the new landlord assigns part only of his reversion.[89]

(a) *Former landlord's entitlement to apply for release*

14.33 If, immediately before the assignment by the landlord, the former landlord does not remain the landlord of any other premises demised by the tenancy, he may apply to be released from the relevant landlord covenant under s.8 of the Act.[90] This clearly covers the case where the former landlord assigned the whole of his interest to the landlord and the landlord now assigns that interest to a new assignee. But *semble*, on the wording of the Act, it also covers the case where the landlord is not

[86] Above, paras 14.11–14.31.
[87] Covenants Act, s.7(1).
[88] *ibid.*, s.7(6)(a).
[89] *ibid.*, s.7(1)(a),(3). Compare the express provision for assignment of the reversion in part only in s.6(3). Why Parliament might have intended the former landlord to lose his right to apply for release if the new landlord assigns part only of the reversion is not clear. Arguably the difference in drafting has no such significance.
[90] *ibid.*, s.7(2). Once again, a covenant that is not a "landlord covenant" will not be subject to this provision: see above, para.14.12.

the landlord of the whole of the premises comprised in the tenancy but is assigning the whole of his interest and the former landlord has before the date of that assignment disposed of the remainder of his reversionary interest elsewhere. So, provided the former landlord is no longer the current landlord of any part of the premises demised by the tenancy, the former landlord may apply for total release from the landlord covenants of the tenancy, even though the assigning landlord may only be assigning part of the reversion. If this is correct, provided the former landlord is no longer the actual landlord of any premises demised by the tenancy, he may apply for total release from the landlord covenants on any occasion when a landlord assigns his interest in any part of the demised premises. But this construction of s.7, which seems incontrovertible on the wording of the section, is not reflected in the forms prescribed for notices to be served on the tenant by a former landlord seeking release,[91] nor does it sit happily with s.8 itself, which requires, inter alia, that the notice of request for release be served on the tenant of the premises comprised in the assignment in question, and not on all tenants under the tenancy.[92]

The former landlord may apply for release whether or not he has previously applied to be released from the relevant covenant, either upon an assignment by himself (i.e. pursuant to s.6) or upon a previous assignment by a successor in title of his (i.e. pursuant to s.7).[93] Thus, there is no restriction on the number of successive applications pursuant to s.7 which a former landlord may make, and it is no bar that he previously applied for release pursuant to s.6 when he assigned part or all of his reversionary interest. **14.34**

But if the former landlord does, immediately before the assignment, remain the landlord of another part (or the remainder) of the premises demised by the tenancy, he may only apply under s.8 of the Act to be released from the relevant covenant to the extent that it falls to be complied with in relation to any premises comprised in the assignment.[94] Thus, if the former landlord has assigned two one-third parts of his reversionary interest to different assignees and retains the other one-third himself, upon a further assignment by one of his assigns of a one-third interest, the former landlord may only apply to be released from the **14.35**

[91] See below, para.14.37.

[92] The section could be made to operate more satisfactorily if the words "the landlord of" in s.7(2) were read as "bound by a landlord covenant of the tenancy in relation to", but this seems too much of a liberty in construction in view of the express use of that phraseology in s.7(1)(b) and similar wording in s.7(4). It seems that the draftsman must surely have had clearly in mind the difference between being the landlord of given premises and being bound by a landlord covenant in relation to such premises.

[93] Covenants Act, s.7(6)(b).

[94] *ibid.*, s.7(3).

landlord covenants to the extent that they fall to be complied with in relation to the premises comprised in that one-third interest.[95]

(b) *Procedure for application by former landlord for release*

14.36 An application by a former landlord for the release of a covenant to any extent (i.e. either in full or to the extent that such covenant falls to be complied with in relation to the part of the premises further assigned) is made by serving on the tenant a notice informing him of the proposed assignment or (as the case may be) the fact that the assignment has taken place, and of the request for the covenant to be released to that extent.[96] Such notice must be served on the tenant either before or within a period of four weeks beginning with the date of the assignment in question.[97] For these purposes, "the tenant" means the tenant of the premises comprised in the assignment in question or, if different parts of those premises are held under the tenancy by different tenants, each of those tenants.[98] It is significant that only those tenants of premises comprised in the assignment by the landlord are required to be served with notice by the former landlord; this suggests that only they will be affected by the release.[99]

14.37 The form of any notice to be served for the purposes of s.8 is prescribed by statutory instrument.[1] The forms prescribed by the Notices Regulations 1995 for a former landlord's initial notice are Forms 5 and 6 in the Schedule to those Regulations, or a form substantially to the like effect.[2] It is here that the difficulties of construction of s.7 are seen to their fullest effect.

The Regulations made by the Lord Chancellor pursuant to the requirement of s.27(1) of the Act prescribe different forms for two different purposes. Form 5 is prescribed for a former landlord applying to be released from all the landlord covenants of the tenancy on a subsequent assignment of the landlord's interest. This appears to have been intended to marry with s.7(2) of the Act, where the former landlord does not remain the landlord of any premises demised by the tenancy; and it suggests that "the relevant covenant", i.e. a landlord covenant by which

[95] For an analysis of when covenants for the purposes of the Act "fall to be complied with" in relation to a particular part of premises, and its application to the release of a landlord from covenants affecting such part, see above, paras 14.13–14.15.

[96] Covenants Act, s.8(1).

[97] *ibid.*

[98] *ibid.*, s.8(4)(a).

[99] But see above, para.14.33

[1] Notices Regulations 1995, reg.2.

[2] *ibid.*, reg.2(d),(e). See Megarry's *Assured Tenancies* (2nd ed.), paras 8-25, 13-31 on the application of similar words in relation to notices under the Housing Acts 1985 and 1988.

the former landlord remains bound, is to be equated with all the landlord covenants of the tenancy. Form 6 is prescribed for a former landlord "who assigned part only of his interest applying to be released from the landlord covenants of the tenancy to the appropriate extent on a subsequent assignment of the landlord's interest".[3] The distinction drawn by the prescribed forms is thus between, on the one hand, a case where the former landlord originally assigned part only of his reversionary interest, and on the other hand, a case where the former landlord originally assigned the whole of his interest, with Form 6 applying in the former case and Form 5 in the latter. But this is not the distinction drawn by s.7: subs.(2) applies where immediately before the assignment by the landlord the former landlord does not remain the landlord of any part of the premises demised by the tenancy, and subs.(3) applies in all other cases. Thus, the prescribed forms do not appear to cater for a former landlord who disposed of the whole of his reversion in successive parts. Nor do the Act and the Regulations together satisfactorily provide for the case where the former landlord disposes of all his interest in successive parts but is not released from the landlord's covenants under s.6 in respect of more than one such part. In such a case, he is apparently entitled as a former landlord to apply for a full release upon a further assignment by one of his assignees, but is only required to serve notice requesting such release on the tenant(s) of the part the reversion to which is being further assigned. It is suggested that an amendment to s.7(2) of the Covenants Act is required to remedy this problem.

In view of the complexities of the prescribed forms, it is unlikely that **14.38** anything less than forms in the Schedule to the Notices Regulations 1995, or such forms with very minor omissions or immaterial typographical errors, will be held to be substantially to the like effect. If any notice purporting to be served for the purposes of s.8(1) of the Covenants Act is not in the prescribed form or a form substantially to the like effect, the notice is not effective for the purposes of that section.[4]

(i) Form of prescribed notices. The prescribed forms are set out in **14.39** Appendix 3.[5] Both Form 5 and Form 6 are in two parts: the first is to be completed by the former landlord requesting release; the second is for the response (if any) of the tenant. Part I of both Form 5 and Form 6 tells the tenant served with the notice that if he does *not* consider it reasonable for the former landlord to be released, he must notify the landlord within the period of four weeks beginning with the giving of the notice by using Pt II of the Form. Part I of the Forms tells the tenant that he may withdraw an objection to release at any time. Note 6 to Pt I advises the tenant to

[3] Notices Regulations 1995, reg.2(e)(i).
[4] Covenants Act, s.27(4).
[5] See below App.3, pp.447–54.

bear in mind that in the event of late withdrawal of objection, or if the court finds it reasonable for the former landlord to be released, the tenant might have to pay costs. Apart from that warning, the forms tend to suggest to an uninformed tenant that he has nothing much to lose by objecting. One can readily imagine that such a tenant, served with a notice which does not explain to him that the assignee landlord will be liable to perform the landlord covenants in the tenancy from the date of the assignment and that the existing landlord also remains liable unless he applies to be released, might regard it as unreasonable for the former landlord to be released, and so serve a notice of objection. Once former landlords of new tenancies become more familiar with the procedure, county courts can therefore expect to be quite busy with former landlords' applications for declarations that it is reasonable for them to be released.[6]

14.40 (ii) SERVICE OF NOTICES. The Act requires the notice to be served on the tenant (as defined) within the period of four weeks beginning with the date of the assignment in question or before the assignment. The assignment in question is that made or to be made by the actual landlord. The statutory time limit must be strictly applied. The period of four weeks begins on the date of the assignment, and so the last date for service of the notice is 27 days after the day on which the assignment is made, e.g. if the reversion vested in the landlord is assigned on August 6, 2006, the last day for service is September 2, 2006 (not September 3, 2006). Section 23 of the Landlord and Tenant Act 1927 applies in relation to the service of a former landlord's notice under s.8 requesting a release.[7] The notice is therefore validly served if it is:

(a) served personally on the tenant;
(b) left for the tenant at his last known place of abode in England or Wales;
(c) sent through the post in a registered letter addressed to the tenant at such last known place of abode; or
(d) in the case of a local or public authority or a statutory or a public utility company, sent through the post in a registered letter addressed to the secretary or other proper officer at the principal office of such authority or company.

A registered letter includes recorded delivery post.[8] The last known place of abode of a company can be its registered office.[9]

[6] See below, para.14.45.
[7] Covenants Act, s.27(5).
[8] Recorded Delivery Service Act 1962, s.1.
[9] *National Westminster Bank Ltd v Betchworth Investments Ltd* [1975] 1 E.G.L.R. 57.

The effect of service by one of these prescribed modes is that service is deemed to have been effected if the former landlord can prove compliance with one of them, even if in fact the tenant was not served at all.[10] Thus posting of the notice by recorded delivery post is good service, even if the letter is never delivered. Moreover, in the case of service by post, service is effected when the letter is posted; the contrary conclusion is not required by the Human Rights Act 1998 and the provisions of the Interpretation Act 1978 and other provisions as to time of service have no application.[11] The risk of non-service is statutorily placed on the intended recipient of the notice.[12] A former landlord may choose to serve the tenant by some other mode, and provided that the notice is received such service is perfectly valid; but the risk of non-service is then on the former landlord. **14.41**

(c) *Effect of timeous application by former landlord for release*

Where an application by the former landlord for the release of a covenant is made in time and in the correct form, the covenant is released to the extent mentioned in the notice in three different sets of circumstances: **14.42**

(1) if the tenant does not, within the period of four weeks beginning with the day on which the notice is served, serve on the former landlord a notice in writing objecting to the release;
(2) if the tenant does serve such a notice but the court, on the application of the former landlord, makes a declaration that it is reasonable for the former landlord to be so released; or
(3) if the tenant serves on the former landlord a notice in writing consenting to the release and, if he has previously served a notice objecting to it, stating that that notice is withdrawn.[13]

The extent mentioned in the notice will be either a total release in the event of the former landlord's no longer being the landlord of any part of the premises demised by the tenancy (Form 5), or a release to the extent that the obligations under the covenant fall to be complied with in relation to the premises comprised in the assignment (Form 6). Each of the three sets of circumstances in which release will occur must be separately considered.

[10] *Galinski v McHugh* (1988) 57 P. & C.R. 359; *Commercial Union Life Assurance Co. Ltd v Moustafa* [1999] 2 E.G.L.R. 44; *Blunden v Frogmore Investments Ltd* [2002] 2 E.G.L.R. 29.

[11] *Beanby Estates Ltd v Egg Stores (Stamford Hill) Ltd* [2003] 3 E.G.L.R. 85; *C A Webber (Transport) Ltd v Railtrack Plc* [2004] 1 E.G.L.R. 49.

[12] *ibid.*

[13] Covenants Act, s.8(2).

14.43 (i) FAILURE BY TENANT TO SERVE NOTICE OBJECTING. A notice in writing objecting to the release of the former landlord must be in the prescribed form, or in a form substantially to the like effect.[14] The prescribed form is, where a former landlord has served a notice in Form 5 (total release), Pt II of that Form, and where a former landlord has served a notice in Form 6 (partial release), Pt II of that Form.[15] If the tenant does not serve on the former landlord a notice objecting to the release within the period of four weeks beginning with the day on which the former landlord's notice applying for release is served, the former landlord is released from the covenant(s) to the extent mentioned in the notice. The statutory time limit must be strictly applied.[16] The period of four weeks starts on the day on which the former landlord's notice was served on the tenant, and so the last day for service of the tenant's notice of objection is the 27th day after the day of service of the former landlord's notice.[17]

14.44 Identifying the day on which the former landlord's notice was served can give rise to a number of difficulties. It is noteworthy that para.5 of Pt I of both of the former landlord's notice prescribed forms (Forms 5 and 6) states:

> "If you do **not** consider it reasonable for me/us to be released, you **must** notify me/us of your objection, using Part II of this Form, within the period of **FOUR WEEKS** beginning with the giving of this notice . . . ."

The forms prescribed by statutory instrument equate service of the former landlord's notice with the giving of it, although note 4 to Pt I of both forms warns the tenant that "the date of the giving of the notice may not be the date written on the notice or the date on which you actually saw it. It may, for instance, be the date on which the notice was delivered through the post to your last address known to the person giving the notice". In view of the statutory presumptions of service in s.23 of the Landlord and Tenant Act 1927, which are applied under the Covenants Act, this warning is apposite though probably insufficient.[18] Service of a former landlord's notice applying for release is deemed to be effected by, inter alia, leaving the notice for the tenant at his last known place of abode, in which case the notice is served on the day on which it was so

[14] Notices Regulations 1995, reg.2(d)(ii), 2(e)(ii).

[15] *ibid.*

[16] See n.3 in Pt II of Forms 5 and 6 in the Schedule to the Notices Regulations 1995.

[17] See, by analogy, the example given above, para.14.40.

[18] See the criticisms of the Court of Appeal in relation to similar warning information prescribed for notices under the Landlord and Tenant Act 1954: *Sun Alliance and London Assurance Co. Ltd v Hayman* [1975] 1 W.L.R. 177 (notice given and received when posted).

left, or by sending it to him at such address by a registered or recorded delivery letter, in which case the notice is served when it is posted.[19] In the case where the former landlord sends his notice to the tenant by ordinary pre-paid post, on the other hand, there is no presumption of service,[20] and it is considered that the tenant could seek to prove that he did not in fact receive the notice either at all or until a later day, and that accordingly as a matter of law it was not served on him or not served before the later day, as the case may be.

Once the tenant has identified the day of service of the former landlord's notice, he can calculate the day by which his notice of objection must be served. Section 23 of the Landlord and Tenant Act 1927 applies also to the service of such a notice,[21] and accordingly the tenant can take advantage of the presumptions of service which apply if the notice is sent in one of the prescribed ways.[22] If the former landlord is not served by the end of the 27th day after the service on the tenant of the former landlord's notice, the former landlord is without more released from the covenant(s) to the extent specified in the former landlord's notice, i.e. fully if the former landlord was not immediately before the assignment landlord of any part of the premises demised by the tenancy and served a Form 5 notice, and otherwise to the extent that the covenant(s) fall to be complied with in relation to that part of the premises the reversion on which is further assigned if the former landlord served a Form 6 notice. It is considered that service by a former landlord of a Form 6 notice in a case where he has transferred all his interest in the reversion, and similarly service of a Form 5 notice in a case where he remains landlord of part of the premises demised by the tenancy, will be held not to be a "form substantially to the like effect" to the prescribed form in each case.

(ii) COURT DECLARATION. If the tenant does serve on the former landlord in time and in the correct form a notice of objection to the proposed release, the former landlord is not without more released from the covenant(s). The onus is passed back to the former landlord, who may either accept that he will not be released, or apply to the county court[23] for a declaration, or wait and hope that the tenant changes his mind. If the former landlord does nothing, and the tenant does not change his mind, the former landlord is not released. If the former landlord wishes to take further steps to secure his release, he must apply to the county court for **14.45**

[19] *Webber v Railtrack*, above.

[20] The Covenants Act does not itself authorise a notice to be served by post (other than by registered or recorded delivery post) and so the presumption of service in due course of post under the Interpretation Act 1978, s.7 will not apply to a notice sent by ordinary pre-paid post.

[21] Covenants Act, s.27(5).

[22] See above, para.14.40.

[23] Covenants Act, s.8(4)(c).

a declaration that it is reasonable for the covenant to be released to the extent mentioned in the former landlord's notice. Neither the Covenants Act nor the Civil Procedure Rules prescribe the form or necessary contents of any such application.[24] The application is to be made by the former landlord, but there is no provision limiting the time within which the application has to be made.

14.46 On an application by the former landlord, the county court must apparently determine whether or not "it is reasonable for the covenant to be so released".[25] The word "so" relates back to the words "released to the extent mentioned in the notice", and it appears therefore that the court does not have jurisdiction to release the covenant(s) to a lesser extent than that sought in the notice, but only to determine whether it is reasonable or not for the covenant(s) to be released to that extent. Although it might be thought, consistently with the general policy underlying the Covenants Act, that absent any special circumstances it would be reasonable for the former landlord to be released, the application falls to be made by the former landlord and the onus of proof thus prima facie falls on him.[26] Nevertheless, it is considered that once the former landlord adduces sufficient evidence to show that there are no special circumstances surrounding the assignment, the evidential onus will pass to the tenant to persuade the court that it should not, for some reason, make the declaration that the former landlord seeks. This balance is hinted at in the rubric under the heading "IMPORTANT" in Forms 5 and 6 of the Schedule to the Notices Regulations 1995, which states:

> "IF YOU CONSIDER THAT THERE IS GOOD REASON FOR THE FORMER LANDLORD **NOT** TO BE RELEASED, YOU MUST ACT QUICKLY."

It is also suggested by the fact that a release, once the assignment and request for release are notified to the tenant, takes effect unless the tenant serves notice on the former landlord stating that he objects to the release. The word "reasonable" connotes an objective test, and requires the court to balance the interests of former landlord and tenant. The test is *not* whether the tenant has a reasonable argument for objecting to a release.

14.47 If the court, on the former landlord's application, does not make the declaration sought, the covenant(s) is (are) not released (subject to appeal) unless either the tenant subsequently serves a notice consenting to the

[24] Such an application should probably be brought as a Pt 8 claim: CPR 56PD, 2.1.

[25] Covenants Act, s.8(2)(b).

[26] Compare Landlord and Tenant Act 1988, s.1, where the onus is statutorily imposed on a landlord to show that it was reasonable to refuse consent to an assignment, etc. or to show that any conditions subject to which consent was granted were reasonable conditions.

release,[27] or unless the release is effected pursuant to the same procedure upon a later transfer by the new landlord.

(iii) SERVICE OF TENANT'S NOTICE CONSENTING TO RELEASE. At any time after the service of a former landlord's notice in Form 5 or Form 6 seeking release of landlord covenants, the tenant may serve a notice on the former landlord consenting to the release. Part II of Forms 5 and 6 provides, in one of the alternative paragraphs numbered 4, a form of words to that effect. But there is no requirement for a tenant's notice of this type to be in a prescribed form; all that is required is a notice in writing consenting to the release. Upon service on the former landlord of such a notice, the covenant(s) is (are) released to the extent mentioned in the former landlord's notice. If the tenant has previously served on the former landlord a notice objecting to release,[28] he may still serve on the former landlord a notice in writing consenting to the release. In such a case, the form prescribed is simply a notice in writing stating that the tenant is now consenting and that the notice of objection is withdrawn.[29] Upon service on the former landlord of such a notice in writing, the covenant(s) is (are) released to the extent mentioned in the former landlord's notice. **14.48**

(d) *Time and effect of release*

Any release from a landlord covenant in accordance with the s.8 procedure, whether because the tenant does not serve a notice of objection or because the court declares it to be reasonable or because the tenant serves notice consenting to the release, is regarded as occurring at the time when the assignment in question takes place.[30] Thus, even if the former landlord applies after several years to the court for a declaration and the declaration is made,[31] or if the tenant after several years gives written notice consenting to release and withdrawing his notice of objection, the release is still treated as having been effected on the date of the further assignment of the landlord's interest. What the effect is if the **14.49**

[27] See below.

[28] Presumably only a written notice in the prescribed form under Covenants Act, s.8(2)(a) and not any other notice objecting to release, as this latter type of notice would not be of any effect to prevent release of the landlord covenant(s).

[29] Covenants Act, s.8(2)(c); Notices Regulations 1995, reg.2(d)(iii), 2(e)(iii). The tenant will, *ex hypothesi*, already have sent Pt II of the former landlord's notice in Form 5 or Form 6 back to him.

[30] Covenants Act, s.8(3). The assignment in question is the new assignment, not the assignment made by the former landlord.

[31] Delay to this degree could be a significant factor when the court decides whether it is reasonable for the covenant(s) to be released, *if* the court is to consider reasonableness at the time when it hears the former landlord's application.

former landlord has in the meantime been sued on the landlord's covenants for breaches occurring after the further assignment is unclear.

A release of a former landlord from a landlord covenant by virtue of these statutory provisions does not affect any liability of the former landlord arising from a breach of the covenant occurring before the release (i.e. before the date of the further assignment of the landlord's interest).[32]

14.50 If the former landlord is released in accordance with s.8 of the Act from every landlord covenant by which he remained bound immediately before the assignment, he ceases to be entitled to the benefit of the tenant covenants of the tenancy.[33] Similarly, if the former landlord is so released from every such landlord covenant to the extent that it falls to be complied with in relation to any premises comprised in the further assignment, he ceases to be entitled to the benefit of the tenant covenants of the tenancy to the extent that they fall to be so complied with.[34] Such loss of the benefit of the tenant covenants does not affect any rights of the former landlord arising from breaches of such covenants occurring before the date of the further assignment.[35]

All these provisions point up the importance of identifying the date on which the assignment takes place. Unfortunately, by reason of the definition in the Act of "assignment" as including an equitable assignment, there is some doubt about it. If there are three successive events, namely: a binding contract for an assignment of the reversion, execution of a deed of transfer, and registration of the transferee at H.M. Land Registry, which is the date of the assignment for the purposes of the Act?[36]

(e) *Other provisions relating to release of former landlords*

14.51 (i) CONSENSUAL RELEASE. Nothing in the Covenants Act is to be read as preventing a party to a tenancy from releasing a person from a landlord covenant of the tenancy.[37] Such release need not be under seal or even in writing, but if not under seal and in the form of an agreement, it would need to be supported by valuable consideration. Moreover an agreement as a term of the tenancy that on assignment (or further assignment) the

[32] Covenants Act, s.24(1).
[33] *ibid.*, s.7(4); presumably also from the date of the assignment.
[34] *ibid.*, s.7(5); presumably also from the date of the assignment.
[35] *ibid.*, s.24(4).
[36] Probably the execution of the deed: see above, para.14.03, n.2.
[37] *ibid.*, s.26(1)(a).

lessor will be released from further liability under the landlord covenants does not infringe the anti-avoidance provisions in s.25 of the Act.[38]

(ii) LANDLORD AND TENANT ACT 1985, s.3. As has been seen,[39] the effect of this section may be to continue the liability of a previous landlord of certain premises who has assigned his reversionary interest, notwithstanding that the procedure under the Covenants Act for a release of the relevant covenants has been followed. Although it is unlikely to occur frequently in practice, it is technically possible for the liability of a former landlord to be continued in this way, even though the requirements and procedure under ss.7 and 8 of the Covenants Act have been satisfied and followed respectively. This could arise in the following circumstances. The former landlord assigns his reversionary interest to A1, but does not apply for or obtain a release upon that assignment. A1 then assigns to A2, and the former landlord serves the appropriate notice applying for a release and is "released" pursuant to it. Neither the former landlord nor A1 nor A2 has notified the tenant of the name *and address* of A1 or A2 (the former landlord's Form 5 notice not having this effect), and so the relevant period under s.3 of the Landlord and Tenant Act 1985[40] has not ended. The Act of 1985 is, in this respect, given precedence over the Covenants Act.[41] The provisions and effect of this section are considered more fully above,[42] in connection with the first assignment of the reversion, where in practice they are more likely to arise. **14.52**

(f) *Effect of non-release*

Where a person bound by a landlord covenant of a tenancy assigns the whole or part of his reversionary interest but is not released by virtue of the Act from the landlord covenant(s), the assignment does not affect any liability of his arising from a breach of the covenant(s) occurring before the assignment.[43] Thus, if a former landlord's application for release is unsuccessful, any liabilities of his which arose before the assignment by the landlord are, as one would expect, unaffected. The effect of non-release is further that the former landlord remains liable to perform the landlord covenants in the tenancy after the date of the assignment by the landlord. It is considered doubtful that this makes the landlord liable for the defaults of his assignee under negative landlord covenants.[44] Under **14.53**

[38] *London Diocesan Fund v Phithwa* [2005] 1 W.L.R. 3956. For the anti-avoidance provisions, see below, Ch.23.

[39] Above, para.14.30.

[40] As defined in Landlord and Tenant Act 1985, s.3(3B); above, para.14.30.

[41] Covenants Act, s.26(2).

[42] Above, para.14.30.

[43] Covenants Act, s.24(3).

[44] See above, paras 3.05 *et seq.*

the law relating to old tenancies, an original lessor who assigns the reversion would remain liable throughout the term to the original tenant, but not, from the date of the assignment of the reversion, to any assignee of the term. This is because there was neither privity of contract (in relation to the landlord covenants) with any such assignee nor, from the date of the assignment of the reversion, was there privity of estate. Under the provisions of the Covenants Act, however, the benefit of the landlord covenants is statutorily annexed to the term,[45] and the original lessor's obligations become fully enforceable by an assignee of the term and will remain so notwithstanding successive assignments of the reversion upon which the original landlord is not released. In this respect, the position of an original lessor under a new tenancy has been materially worsened from the position under old tenancies.

4. Anti-avoidance

14.54 The provisions of the Covenants Act relating to release of tenant and landlord covenants on assignment of landlords' and tenants' interests under new tenancies are, like other provisions of the Act, subject to anti-avoidance provisions. Briefly, any agreement relating to a tenancy is void to the extent that it would exclude, modify or otherwise frustrate the operation of any provision of the Act, or imposes on the tenant some disadvantage in the event of the operation of any of the provisions of the Act.[46] But nothing in the Act is to be read as preventing a party to a tenancy from releasing a person from a landlord covenant or a tenant covenant of the tenancy.[47] Thus an agreement in a lease that upon assignment of the reversion the assignee is to be freed from certain non-personal covenants would be void as excluding the effect of the transmission provisions of the Act; but a release actually entered into between tenant and assignee of the reversion to similar effect would be perfectly valid.[48]

14.55 Similarly, it has now been authoritatively determined that a term of the tenancy to the effect that the lessor is released on assignment of the reversion from further liability under the tenant covenants does not offend the anti-avoidance provisions.[49] This is because it was not the

[45] See above, para.12.01.

[46] See Covenants Act, s.25 for the detailed anti-avoidance provisions, considered fully in Ch.23, below.

[47] Covenants Act, s.26(1)(a).

[48] The same distinction between a void agreement that something shall be done in the future and a lawful doing of the something in question exists in Landlord and Tenant Act 1954, Pt II, in relation to contracting out of security of tenure for business tenants: see *Woodfall's Law of Landlord and Tenant* (28th (looseleaf) ed.), para.22–038.

[49] *London Diocesan Fund v Phithwa* [2005] 1 W.L.R. 3956.

purpose of the Covenants Act to prevent consensual release but to provide for release where the parties to the lease would otherwise not have been released.[50] There is perhaps a fine line in terms of effect between such an agreed release (valid) and an agreement that if the landlord applies under the Act to be released the tenant will not object (clearly invalid, as excluding a right conferred by the Act).[51] But there is a difference in principle between making a contract to which the provisions of the Act in question have no application and agreeing that provisions of the Act that do apply shall not be effective, or that one party will do something to exclude their application. It has not, however, yet been held (nor was it argued in the *Avonridge* case) that the anti-avoidance provisions only apply to executory agreements. The provisions are considered more fully in Ch.23.

[50] *ibid.*, *per* Lord Nicholls of Birkenhead at paras 16, 17.
[51] See [2006] 70 Conv. 79 (Dixon)

CHAPTER 15

Apportionment

Where a tenant or a landlord assigns only part of his interest under a tenancy, some of the tenant or landlord covenants (as the case may be) will, as from the assignment, fall to be complied with in relation to both the assigned part and the retained part. Some of these covenants, e.g. a landlord's covenant to repair the structure and exterior of the premises, will fall to be complied with by the owner of each part of the severed interest in relation to his part, and no further specific statutory provision is necessary[1] to divide up such liability. Other covenants, e.g. a tenant's covenant to use a part of the demised premises for a particular use only, will fall to be complied with only by the owner of that part. But a third category is those covenants where something falls to be done by the tenant or the landlord (as the case might be) and where the obligation is not in its practical application attributable to any particular part of the premises, and so it is not possible without more to divide up the liability to perform it between various parts of the demised premises. The paradigm case is the tenant's obligation to pay rent, which issues out of each part of the demised premises. In relation to old tenancies, a landlord was entitled to the full rent of the premises from a tenant who retained part unless he (the landlord) agreed to be bound by an apportionment between the tenants.[2] **15.01**

In relation to new tenancies, the Covenants Act enables application to be made for such apportionments, agreed between assignor and assignee tenants, or between assignor and assignee landlords, to become binding on the other party to the tenancy. It seems likely[3] that the draftsman of **15.02**

[1] Law of Property Act 1925, s.140(1) makes provision for apportionment of obligations in the nature of conditions between severed parts of the reversionary estate: above, para.4.25. Covenants Act, s.3 provides for the benefit and burden of tenant covenants or landlord covenants (as the case may be) to pass to assignees of part except to the extent that such covenants fall to be complied with in relation to premises not comprised in the assignment. See Ch.12, above.

[2] See above, para.5.07.

[3] A conclusion that is far from clear from the Act itself, and is only expressed here with some diffidence and after considerable reflection.

the Act only intended the apportionment provisions to apply in relation to general covenants (by landlord or tenant) either to pay money or to do something else unconnected with the demised premises, that is to say covenants compliance with which is not specifically referable to any particular part or parts of the demised premises. In order to arrive at this relatively straightforward result, however, an unnecessarily tortuous drafting process involving the application of multiple defined phrases has been used, which can only leave some element of doubt as to the true ambit of these apportionment provisions.

1. The right to apply for an apportionment

15.03 The right to apply for an apportionment to become binding on the person or persons benefited by the covenant (called "the appropriate person" in the Act) arises where the assignor and assignee tenants, or assignor and assignee landlords, agree between themselves how liability under the tenant covenants, or landlord covenants (as the case may be), of the tenancy of a specified type are to be apportioned between themselves. The right arises only where a tenant assigns part only of the premises demised to him by a tenancy,[4] or where a landlord assigns the reversion in part only of the premises of which he is the landlord under a tenancy,[5] both of which are relatively rare occurrences under modern leases. The right therefore does not arise where, e.g. a landlord and his assignee of the reversion in the whole of the demised premises are jointly and severally liable under the landlord covenants, or where a tenant and his sub-tenant agree who is to perform the tenant covenants of the tenancy. The specified type of covenant is defined by the Act as a "non-attributable tenant covenant" or a "non-attributable landlord covenant", and the right to apply for an apportionment to become binding arises only where, after the assignment in question, both the tenant (or landlord) and his assignee are to be bound by a non-attributable tenant (or landlord) covenant of the tenancy.[6]

(a) *Meaning of "non-attributable" covenant*

15.04 For the purposes of these apportionment provisions, a covenant is, in relation to an assignment, a "non-attributable" covenant if it does *not* fall to be complied with in relation to any premises comprised in the

[4] Covenants Act, s.9(1)(a).
[5] *ibid.*, s.9(2)(a).
[6] *ibid.*, s.9(1)(b), (2)(b).

assignment.[7] A covenant other than a covenant to pay money falls to be complied with in relation to such premises if—

(1) it in terms applies to them; or
(2) in its practical application it can be attributed to them, whether or not it can also be attributed to other individual parts of the demised premises.[8]

Thus, for covenants other than covenants to pay money, a non-attributable covenant is one which neither in terms applies to the premises comprised in the assignment nor, in its practical application, can be attributed to them. This means that only those non-money covenants (1) that in terms apply to, or fall to be complied with solely in relation to, non-assigned premises and (2) that do not in terms apply to, or fall to be complied with in relation to, *any* particular demised premises[9] are "non-attributable" covenants within the definition of the Act. Clearly, only the second of these categories is capable of binding both assignor and assignee, for liability under the first category would not pass to the assignee tenant or landlord in any event under the transmission provisions of s.3 of the Act.[10] So there will be relatively few non-money, non-attributable covenants by which both assignor and assignee are to be bound after the assignment because the majority of covenants will have practical application to at least part of the assigned part of the demised premises.[11]

In relation to covenants to pay money, on the other hand, such a covenant of a tenancy falls to be complied with in relation to an assigned part of the demised premises if— **15.05**

(1) it in terms applies to that part; or

[7] *ibid.*, s.9(6). It is prima facie unclear whether this definition connotes a covenant not falling to be complied with at all in relation to premises comprised in the assignment or one which does not fall fully and exclusively to be complied with in relation to such premises. The answer (the former) is only found by referring to another and distant definition section, Covenants Act, s.28.

[8] *ibid.*, s.28(2).

[9] e.g. a tenant covenant to notify the landlord of any planning notice served on it.

[10] *ibid.*, s.3(2),(3); above, paras 12.10 *et seq.*

[11] Even an amateur draftsman could have conceived of a better way of providing for this result, if the result was intended. The obscurity of the drafting makes it possible that the result was not intended, but it is extremely difficult to make better sense of the apportionment provisions of the Act. It is considered that the analysis in the 1st ed. of this work (para.15.04), which left only money covenants within the scope of the provisions, is less likely to be the true effect of the Act than the analysis suggested here.

(2) the amount of the payment is determinable specifically by reference—
   (i) to that part; or
   (ii) to anything falling to be done by or for a person as tenant or occupier of that part (if it is a tenant covenant); or
   (iii) to anything falling to be done by or for a person as landlord of that part (if it is a landlord covenant).[12]

It is considered that this definition is concerned with an exclusive application to,[13] or determination by reference to,[14] the part in question. Thus, if the covenant to pay money does not in terms apply (only) to the part assigned, and the amount of the payment is not determinable specifically by reference (only) to that part, etc. (as defined in (2) above), the covenant does not fall to be complied with in relation to that part and the covenant is a "non-attributable" covenant for the purposes of the apportionment provisions of s.9 of the Act. Thus, only non-specific covenants to pay money, such as a tenant's covenant to pay rent or service charge, fall within the apportionment provisions of the Act. The benefit or burden of money covenants that in terms apply, or whose amount is determined specifically by reference, to non-assigned parts of the premises will not pass to the assignee in any event.[15]

(b) *Meaning of "covenant to pay money"*

15.06 It is unclear how restrictively "a covenant to pay money" will be construed. Doubtless, a tenant's covenant to pay money such as rent and service charge to his landlord will be included; but it is not clear whether a secondary and contingent liability, such as a tenant's obligation to repay to his landlord the costs of his landlord entering the premises to carry out works to remedy breaches of covenant by the tenant,[16] is "a covenant to pay money". The primary obligation under the lease, the covenant to repair, is not a "non-attributable" covenant, and until the default occurs it will not be clear whose obligation has been broken and therefore who is contingently liable to pay. Also, a covenant to pay interest is a covenant to pay money, as is a covenant to pay to the landlord his costs of and incidental to the preparation and service of a notice pursuant to s.146 of the Law of Property Act 1925; but it is hard to believe that the draftsman intended such covenants to be apportionable. In relation to landlords' obligations, covenants to pay money in a primary sense are more unusual.

[12] Covenants Act, s.28(3).
[13] Pt (1) of the definition.
[14] Pt (2) of the definition.
[15] n.10, above.
[16] Such a claim is a claim in debt and not in damages: see *Jervis v Harris* [1996] Ch. 195.

A landlord's covenant to lay out insurance moneys in rebuilding damaged premises could be construed as a covenant to pay money, yet it is hard to imagine that the draftsman had such a covenant in mind. If not this, it is difficult to see what landlords' covenants to pay money he did have in mind. And it is also unclear whether tenants' (or landlords') covenants to pay money to third parties are apportionable under these provisions.

(c) *The agreement*

The third precondition for a tenant and his assignee, or a landlord and his assignee, to apply to the appropriate person for an apportionment to become binding on him is that the tenant and his assignee, or the landlord and his assignee, agree that from the assignment liability under the covenant is to be apportioned between them in such manner as is specified in the agreement.[17] Any such agreement between assignor and assignee may apportion liability in such a way that a party to the agreement is exonerated from all liability under a covenant.[18] Although there is no express requirement to such effect, the wording of the section seems to imply that the "agreement" between the assignor and the assignee must be in writing.[19] In an ordinary case, a contract for an assignment of part of a tenant's or landlord's interest would have to be in writing and signed by both parties or their agents,[20] and one would expect any apportionment to be agreed in it; but the "agreement" that the Act contemplates could be made orally at the time of, or even after, the assignment itself. Arguably, therefore, an oral "agreement" would suffice. There seems to be no need to imply a restriction that the "agreement" be binding as between assignor and assignee before the application to the appropriate person is made. The prescribed form notices of application[21] are required to be signed by the assignor and the assignee, and to include details of the apportionment proposed, and so the notice itself could be an agreement binding the assignor and assignee. When such agreement has been made, the parties to it may apply for the apportionment to become binding on the appropriate person in accordance with the procedure in s.10 of the Act.[22] 15.07

[17] Covenants Act, s.9(1)(c), (2)(c).

[18] *ibid.*, s.9(3): i.e. the other party is wholly responsible for the payment in question, or the two other parties are each liable for one half.

[19] And n.3 in Forms 7 and 8 in the Schedule to the Notices Regulations 1995 suggests that a copy of the agreement be attached to the notice.

[20] Law of Property (Miscellaneous Provisions) Act 1989, s.2.

[21] Notices Regulations 1995, Schedule, Forms 7, 8.

[22] Covenants Act, s.9(4).

2. Who is to be bound by the apportionment

15.08 "The appropriate person" means, in the case of a tenant's application, the landlord of the entire premises demised to the assignor tenant by the tenancy (or, if different parts of those premises are held under the tenancy by different landlords, each of those landlords); and in the case of a landlord's application, it means the tenant of the entire premises of which the assignor landlord is the landlord under the tenancy (or, if different parts of those premises are held under the tenancy by different tenants, each of those tenants).[23] Thus, where a tenant proposes to assign part of the premises of which he is the tenant, the appropriate person may be all the landlords of different parts of the premises, even if the tenant proposes to assign a part of the premises of which one of the landlords only is the landlord. Similarly, where a landlord assigns part of his reversion, the appropriate person is all the tenants of the whole of the demised premises of which the landlord is the reversioner, even if some of these tenants are not tenants of the part of the demised premises, the reversion to which is being assigned.

15.09 In any case where assignor and assignee apply for their agreed apportionment to become binding on the appropriate person, they may also apply for it to become binding on any person other than the appropriate person who is for the time being entitled to enforce the covenant in question.[24] One obvious such person might be a management company, entitled under the terms of a long lease of a residential flat or under a lease of commercial premises to recover from the tenant his contribution to service charge.[25] But other examples of such persons exist within the Covenants Act itself. Thus, tenant and assignee may apply for their apportionment to become binding on any concurrent lessee who comes into existence and who is for the time being entitled to the rents and profits under the tenancy[26]; or on any mortgagee in possession of the reversion in the demised premises.[27] Similarly, landlord and assignee may apply for their appportionment to become binding on any mortgagee in possession of any premises demised by the tenancy under a mortgage granted by the tenant.[28] It seems that such a person must be entitled to enforce the covenant in question at the time when the application is made ("who *is* for the time being entitled . . . "), and so, in the case of an

[23] *ibid.*, s.9(7).
[24] *ibid.*, s.9(5).
[25] See Notices Regulations 1995, Form 7, n.1.
[26] See Covenants Act, s.15(1)(a).
[27] See *ibid.*, s.15(1)(b).
[28] See *ibid.*, s.15(3).

application in respect of a mortgagee, the mortgagee must be in possession at that time.[29] The procedure in s.10 of the Act applies in relation to an application for the apportionment to become binding on such a person as it applies to an application made with regard to the appropriate person.[30] It seems that a separate application has to be made.

3. The procedure

The apportionment agreement in question between assignor and assignee relating to a non-attributable covenant will generally arise before or at the time of the assignment of part of the demised premises or of the reversion. The parties to an apportionment agreement (i.e. the landlord and his assignee, or the tenant and his assignee, as the case may be) apply for an apportionment to become binding on the appropriate person[31] within the meaning of the Act if, by a stipulated time, they serve on the appropriate person a notice in the prescribed form containing particular information. The same procedure must be followed in a case where the parties seek to have their agreement become binding on any other person who is for the time being entitled to enforce the covenant in question.[32] **15.10**

(a) *Time for service*

The stipulated time is either before or within the period of four weeks beginning with the date of the assignment in question.[33] If the notice is served later than that time, the application is invalid, the right to have the apportionment become binding on the appropriate person has been lost, and the appropriate person can disregard the application. The Act **15.11**

[29] *Quaere* whether a mortgagee not in possession at the time when an application is made is bound by an apportionment which becomes binding on the appropriate person if he subsequently goes into possession. This must depend on the effect of an apportionment becoming binding under the s.10 procedure. It seems arguable that such an existing mortgagee would not be bound, as s.10(2) states only that the application becomes binding on the appropriate person; yet the prescribed forms of notices proposing apportionments assume that successors-in-title will be bound. If the assignor and assignee must make a separate application when the mortgagee goes into possession, in most cases the time limit for such applications will have expired. On ordinary principles of the law of mortgage, one would not expect the mortgagee of land to be bound unless he consented or unless statute so provided; but the Covenants Act does not state who is to be bound by such apportionments.

[30] Covenants Act, s.9(5).

[31] Or such other person to whom they are entitled to apply under s.9(5): see above.

[32] *ibid.* In such a case the procedural requirements set out in the following paragraphs apply in the same way in relation to a notice served on such a person.

[33] Covenants Act, s.10(1).

requires the notice to be served on the appropriate person (as defined) within the period of four weeks beginning with the date of the assignment in question or before the assignment. The statutory time limit must be strictly applied. The period of four weeks begins on the date of the assignment, and so the last date for service of the notice is 27 days after the day on which the assignment is made. So, if part of the reversion on a lease granted on April 2, 1996 is assigned on May 2, 2006, the last day for service is May 29, 2006 (not May 30, 2006). Section 23 of the Landlord and Tenant Act 1927 applies in relation to the service of a notice under s.10 applying for an apportionment to become binding.[34] The notice is therefore validly served if it is:

(a) served personally on the appropriate person;
(b) left for the appropriate person at his last known place of abode in England or Wales;
(c) sent through the post in a registered letter addressed to the appropriate person at such last known place of abode; or
(d) in the case of a local or public authority or a statutory or a public utility company, sent through the post in a registered letter addressed to the secretary or other proper officer at the principal office of such authority or company.

A registered letter includes recorded delivery post.[35] The last known place of abode of a company can be its registered office.[36]

15.12 The effect of service by one of these prescribed modes is that service is deemed to have been effected if compliance with one of them can be proved, even if in fact the appropriate person was not served at all.[37] Thus posting of the notice by recorded delivery post is good service, even if the letter is never delivered. Moreover, in the case of service by post, service is effected when the letter is posted; the contrary conclusion is not required by the Human Rights Act 1998 and the provisions of the Interpretation Act 1978 and other provisions as to time of service have no application.[38] The risk of non-service is statutorily placed on the appropriate person as intended recipient of the notice.[39] The parties seeking an apportionment may choose to serve the appropriate person by some

[34] *ibid.*, s.27(5).

[35] Recorded Delivery Service Act 1962, s.1.

[36] *National Westminster Bank Ltd v Betchworth Investments Ltd* [1975] 1 E.G.L.R. 57.

[37] *Galinski v McHugh* (1988) 57 P. & C.R. 359; *Commercial Union Life Assurance Co. Ltd v Moustafa* [1999] 2 E.G.L.R. 44; *Blunden v Frogmore Investments Ltd* [2002] 2 E.G.L.R. 29.

[38] *Beanby Estates Ltd v Egg Stores (Stamford Hill) Ltd* [2003] 3 E.G.L.R. 85; *C A Webber (Transport) Ltd v Railtrack Plc* [2004] 1 E.G.L.R. 49.

[39] *ibid.*

other mode and, provided that the notice is received, such service is perfectly valid; but the risk of non-service is then on the parties rather than on the appropriate person.

(b) *Form of notice*

The notice must inform the appropriate person of the following matters: (i) the proposed assignment or, as the case might be, the fact that the assignment has taken place; (ii) the prescribed particulars of the agreement, and (iii) the request of the persons who have agreed the apportionment that the apportionment should become binding on him.[40] The Act requires the form of any notice to be served for the purposes of s.10 to be prescribed by regulations made by statutory instrument,[41] and further stipulates that the regulations require any notice served for the purposes of s.10(1) to include: **15.13**

(a) an explanation of the significance of the notice and of the options available to the appropriate person;
(b) a statement that any objections to the proposed binding effect of the apportionment must be made by notice in writing served on the persons by whom the s.10(1) notice was served within the period of four weeks beginning with the day on which the s.10(1) notice was served; and
(c) an address in England and Wales to which any such objections may be sent.

If any notice purporting to be served for the purposes of s.10(1) is not in the prescribed form, or in a form substantially to the same effect, the notice is ineffective.[42]

The forms prescribed for the purposes of s.10(1) of the Act are the forms numbered 7 and 8 in the Schedule to the Landlord and Tenant (Covenants) Act 1995 (Notices) Regulations 1995,[43] or in each case a form substantially to the like effect.[44] In view of the complicated nature of Form 7 and Form 8 and of their prescribed contents, it seems unlikely that any form of notice other than Form 7 or Form 8 will be valid, save perhaps for one of those Forms containing only minor typographical errors or inconsequential omissions. **15.14**

[40] Covenants Act, s.10(1).
[41] *ibid.*, s.27(1); any such statutory instrument shall be subject to annulment in pursuance of a resolution of either House of Parliament: s.27(6).
[42] Covenants Act, s.27(4).
[43] SI 1995/2964, referred to hereafter as the Notices Regulations 1995. For the Notices Regulations 1995 and Forms 7 and 8, see below, App.3, pp.455–64.
[44] Notices Regulations 1995, reg.2(f)(i), (g)(i).

Form 7 is the form of notice prescribed for a joint notice by a tenant and his assignee for a binding apportionment of liability under non-attributable tenant covenants of a tenancy on assignment of part of the property. It is in two parts: Pt I to be completed by the tenant and his assignee, and Pt II for the response, if any, of the landlord.[45] Part I requires the tenant and his assignee to attach a schedule to the notice specifying the nature of the obligation, the term or condition of the lease or other instrument under which it arises, and the manner in which the liability to perform it is divided under the agreement they have made. Footnotes to the form suggest that the apportionment agreement might be attached to the notice.[46] The form must be signed by or on behalf of both the tenant and his assignee.

Form 8 is the form of notice prescribed for a joint notice by a landlord and his assignee for a binding apportionment of liability under non-attributable landlord covenants of a tenancy on an assignment of part of the reversion. It also is in two parts, and the contents are essentially the same as Form 7.[47] Form 8 must be signed by or on behalf of both the landlord and the assignee.

4. Circumstances in which apportionment becomes binding

15.15 Where an application for an apportionment of liability under a non-attributable covenant to become binding has been made in time and in due form, the apportionment will become binding on the appropriate person in any of three events.

(a) *No notice of objection*

15.16 The apportionment will become binding on the appropriate person if he does not, within the period of four weeks beginning with the day on which the notice of application is served on him, serve on the parties to the agreement[48] a notice in writing objecting to the apportionment becoming binding on him.[49] A notice in writing objecting to the apportionment becoming binding must be in the prescribed form or a form substantially to the like effect.[50] The prescribed form is where a tenant and his assignee have served a notice in Form 7 Pt II of that Form; and where a landlord and his assignee have served a notice in Form 8

[45] Or other person for the time being entitled to enforce the obligation in question.

[46] See above, para.15.07.

[47] See below, App.3.

[48] i.e. the persons who served the notice on him.

[49] Covenants Act, s.10(2)(a).

[50] Notices Regulations 1995, reg.2(f)(ii), 2(g)(ii).

Pt II of that Form.[51] Part II of each Form provides for the appropriate person to state either that he agrees to be bound by the apportionment agreement or that he does not consider it reasonable that he should be bound and objects to being so bound. The statutory time limits must be strictly applied.[52] The period of four weeks starts on the day on which the notice was served on the appropriate person, and so the last day for service of the notice of objection is the 27th day after the day of service of the notice.[53]

Identifying the day on which the notice was served can give rise to a number of difficulties. It is noteworthy that para.5 of Pt I of both of the prescribed forms (Forms 7 and 8) states: **15.17**

> "If you do **not** consider it reasonable for you to be bound by this agreement, you **must** notify both of us of your objection, using Part II of this Form, within the period of **FOUR WEEKS** beginning with the giving of this notice . . . ."

The Forms prescribed by statutory instrument therefore equate service of the notice with the giving of it, and note 4 to Pt I of both Forms warns the tenant that "the date of the giving of the notice may not be the date written on the notice or the date on which you actually saw it. It may, for instance, be the date on which the notice was delivered through the post to your last address known to the person giving the notice." In view of the statutory presumptions of service under s.23 of the Landlord and Tenant Act 1927 which are applied under the Covenants Act,[54] this warning is apposite but not sufficiently precise.[55] Service of a notice applying for an agreed apportionment to become binding is deemed to be effected by, inter alia, leaving the notice for the appropriate person at his last known place of abode, in which case the notice is served on the day on which it was left, or sending it to him at such address by a registered or recorded delivery letter, in which case the notice is served when it posted, even if it is never delivered.[56] In the case where the notice is sent to the appropriate person by ordinary pre-paid post, on the other hand,

[51] *ibid.*

[52] See n.3 in Pt II of Forms 7 and 8 in the Schedule to the Notices Regulations 1995.

[53] See the example above, para.15.11.

[54] By s.27(5).

[55] See the criticisms of the Court of Appeal in *Sun Alliance and London Assurance Company Ltd v Hayman* [1975] 1 W.L.R. 177.

[56] *Blunden v Frogmore Investments Ltd* [2002] 2 E.G.L.R. 29; *Beanby Estates Ltd v Egg Stores (Stamford Hill) Ltd* [2003] 3 E.G.L.R. 85; *C A Webber (Transport) Ltd v Railtrack Plc* [2004] 1 E.G.L.R. 49.

there is no presumption of service,[57] and it is considered that the appropriate person could seek to prove that he did not in fact receive the notice either at all or until a later day, and that accordingly, as a matter of law, it was not served on him at all or not before the later day, as the case may be.

Once the appropriate person has identified the day of service of the notice, he can calculate the day by which his notice of objection must be served. Section 23 of the Landlord and Tenant Act 1927 applies also to the service of such a notice,[58] and accordingly the appropriate person may take advantage of the presumptions of service which apply if the notice is sent in one of the prescribed ways.[59] If the parties to the agreement are not served by the end of the 27th day after the service of the notice of application on the appropriate person, the apportionment without more becomes binding on the appropriate person.

15.18 It will be recalled that "the appropriate person" for these purposes may well be two or more persons, e.g. where different parts of the reversion in the premises demised by the tenancy are vested in different landlords, or where two or more persons are tenants of premises of which the landlord is the reversioner.[60] In such cases, for the apportionment to become binding, all the persons who together constitute "the appropriate person" will have to be served with a notice in the prescribed form (or a form substantially to the like effect) by the end of the period of four weeks beginning with the date of the assignment in question. If one or more of the landlords or tenants (as the case may be) who together constitute "the appropriate person" are not so served, the requirements of the Act have not been complied with, and the right to apply for an apportionment to become binding has been lost.

A similar problem may arise where the several persons who together constitute "the appropriate person" have been validly served with the initial notice. Any notice objecting to the proposed apportionment must be served by "the appropriate person", and so it seems that a notice of objection timeously served by one only of such persons will not suffice to prevent the apportionment from becoming binding if the other such persons do not serve a notice of objection in time.[61] Also, a notice of objection given by the appropriate person must be served timeously and in due form on "the parties to the agreement", i.e. on both tenant and

[57] The Covenants Act does not itself authorise a notice to be served by post (other than by registered or recorded delivery post) and so the presumption of service in due course of post under Interpretation Act 1978, s.7 will not apply to a notice sent by ordinary pre-paid post.

[58] Covenants Act, s.27(5).

[59] See above, para.15.11. One of the ways would be by recorded delivery post to the address given in the Form 7 or Form 8 notice.

[60] See above, para.15.08.

[61] Covenants Act, ss.9(7), 10(4).

assignee (or landlord and assignee, as the case may be) who gave the initial notice; again, it seems that a failure to serve one of those persons in time or in due form will prevent the objection from taking effect and will result in the apportionment becoming binding. Clearly, some care is required in the service of notices relating to apportionments under the Covenants Act.

(b) *Court declaration*

The apportionment will become binding on the appropriate person if he does duly serve a notice of objection, but the court, on the application of the parties to the agreement, makes a declaration that it is reasonable for the apportionment to become binding on him.[62] Thus, if the appropriate person does serve in time and in the correct form a notice of objection to the proposed apportionment becoming binding on him, he is not without more bound by the proposed apportionment. The onus is passed back to the parties to the agreement, who may do one of the following: accept that the apportionment that they have agreed will not become binding on the appropriate person, apply to the county court[63] for a declaration, or wait and hope that the appropriate person changes his mind. If the parties to the agreement do nothing, and the appropriate person does not change his mind, the apportionment does not bind the appropriate person. If the parties to the agreement do wish to take further steps to make the apportionment binding, they must apply to the county court for a declaration that it is reasonable for the apportionment to become binding on the appropriate person. Neither the Covenants Act nor the Civil Procedure Rules prescribe the form or necessary contents of any such application,[64] but it is clear that an application made by just one of the parties to the agreement will be incompetent. There is no provision limiting the time within which the application has to be made. **15.19**

On an application by the parties to the agreement, the county court must apparently determine whether or not it is reasonable for the apportionment to become binding on the appropriate person.[65] Prima facie, an apportionment of an obligation to pay money agreed between a tenant and his assignee on a fair basis, according to their respective interests in the demised premises where part has been lawfully assigned, is one by which it will be reasonable for the landlord(s) to be bound; however, the application in such a case falls to be made by the tenant and **15.20**

[62] Covenants Act, s.10(2)(b).
[63] *ibid.*, s.10(4).
[64] The application should probably be a Pt 8 application: CPR Pt 56PD, 2.1 by analogy.
[65] Covenants Act, s.10(2)(b).

his assignee and so the onus of proof falls on them.[66] Nevertheless, it is considered that once the tenant and his assignee adduce sufficient evidence to show that there are no special circumstances surrounding the assignment and that the above matters are satisfied, the evidential onus will shift to the landlord(s) to persuade the court that it should not, for some particular reason or reasons, make the declaration sought. This balance is hinted at in the rubric under the heading "IMPORTANT" in Forms 7 and 8 of the Schedule to the Notices Regulations 1995 which states:

> "IF YOU CONSIDER THAT THERE IS GOOD REASON WHY YOU SHOULD **NOT** BE BOUND BY THEIR AGREEMENT, YOU MUST ACT QUICKLY."

It is also suggested by the fact that the apportionment, once notified to the appropriate person, binds him unless he serves notice on the parties to the agreement stating that he objects to be bound. On the other hand, an apportionment which seeks to release one of the parties to the agreement from all responsibility under the money or other non-attributable covenant in question,[67] or which proposes an apportionment which is in fact disproportionate, might well be open to objection on substantial grounds. The word "reasonable" connotes an objective test, and requires the court to balance the interests of the parties. The test is not whether the tenant, or landlord as the case may be, has a reasonable argument for objecting to the agreed apportionment.

15.21 If the court, on the application, does not make the declaration sought, the appropriate person is not bound by the apportionment (subject to appeal) unless the appropriate person subsequently serves a notice on the parties to the agreement consenting to be bound.[68] If the court does make the declaration sought, the apportionment binds the appropriate person as from the time when the assignment in question took, or takes, place.[69]

(c) *Consent of appropriate person*

15.22 The third way in which an apportionment can become binding is where, at any time after the service by the parties to an apportionment agreement of a notice in Form 7 or Form 8 seeking to have the appropriate person

[66] Compare Landlord and Tenant Act 1988, s.1, where the onus is statutorily imposed on a landlord to show that it was reasonable to refuse consent to an assignment, etc., or to show that any conditions subject to which consent was granted were reasonable conditions.

[67] As it may do: Covenants Act, s.9(3).

[68] See below.

[69] Covenants Act, s.10(3); see below.

bound by the apportionment, the appropriate person serves a notice on the parties to the agreement consenting to be bound by it. Part II of Forms 7 and 8 provides, in one of the alternative paragraphs numbered 4, a form of words to that effect. But there is no requirement for a notice of this type to be in a prescribed form; all that is required is a notice in writing consenting to the apportionment becoming binding on him.[70] Upon service of such a notice on the parties to the agreement,[71] the apportionment becomes binding on the appropriate person. If the appropriate person has previously served on the parties to the agreement a notice objecting to becoming bound,[72] he may still serve on them a notice in writing consenting to become bound. In such a case, the form prescribed is simply a notice in writing stating that the appropriate person is now consenting and that the notice of objection is withdrawn.[73] Upon service on the parties to the agreement of such a notice in writing, the appropriate person becomes bound by the apportionment proposed in the initial notice.

5. Time and effect of appropriate person becoming bound

Where any apportionment becomes binding in accordance with the s.10 procedure, whether because the appropriate person does not serve a notice of objection in time or because the court declares it to be reasonable for him to be bound or because the appropriate person serves notice consenting to become bound, this is regarded as occurring at the time when the assignment in question takes place.[74] Thus, even if the parties to the agreement apply after several years to the court for a declaration and the declaration is made, or if the appropriate person after several years gives written notice consenting to become bound and withdrawing his notice of objection, the apportionment is still treated as having become binding on the date of the assignment.[75] **15.23**

The prescribed form notices proceed on the assumption that, where an apportionment becomes binding on the appropriate person, it will also **15.24**

[70] *ibid.*, s.10(2)(c).

[71] i.e. both of them.

[72] Presumably only a written notice in the prescribed form under Covenants Act, s.9(2)(a) and not any other notice objecting to release, as this latter type of notice would not be of any effect to prevent the apportionment binding the appropriate person.

[73] Covenants Act, s.9(2)(c); Notices Regulations 1995, reg.2(f)(iii), 2(g)(iii).

[74] Covenants Act, s.10(3).

[75] Delay to this degree could be a significant factor when the court decides whether it is reasonable for the appropriate person to be bound by the apportionment agreed, if the court is to consider reasonableness at the time when it hears the application.

bind successors-in-title of the appropriate person.[76] Although there is nothing in the Covenants Act expressly to this effect, it seems that the binding apportionment may act as a variation of the lease or tenancy agreement either by consent (where the appropriate person serves notice consenting to be bound) or by operation of law (where no notice of objection is served, or where the county court declares it reasonable for the appropriate person to be bound by the apportionment). One difficult area in this regard is where there is a mortgage of the tenant's or landlord's interest granted before the date of the assignment when the apportionment is regarded as occurring, but where the mortgagee is not in possession and therefore is not amenable to the apportionment procedure.[77] It would be an odd result, and contrary to the principles of the law of mortgages, for an existing mortgagee of the landlord's interest to be bound in that way by an apportionment making a tenant of (e.g.) one-third of the demised premises responsible for all the rent under the tenancy to the exclusion of the tenant of two-thirds.

6. Other provisions relating to apportionment

(a) *Consensual apportionments*

15.25 Nothing in the Covenants Act is to be read as preventing the parties to a tenancy from agreeing to an apportionment of liability under a landlord covenant or a tenant covenant of the tenancy.[78] An agreement to enter into an apportionment agreement, however, as distinct from an executed agreement, might infringe the anti-avoidance provisions in s.25 of the Act. These are considered in detail later.[79]

(b) *Effect of other enactments*

15.26 No apportionment which has become binding in accordance with s.10 of the Covenants Act shall be affected by any order or decision made under or by virtue of any enactment not contained in the Covenants Act which relates to apportionment.[80]

[76] See Notices Regulations 1995, Schedule, Forms 7 and 8, Pt I, n.1; Pt II, n.1.

[77] See above, para.15.09.

[78] Covenants Act, s.26(1)(b).

[79] Below, Ch.23.

[80] Covenants Act, s.26(3).

CHAPTER 16

Excluded Assignments

1. Meaning of "excluded assignment"

The application of the provisions of the Covenants Act relating to release of covenants on assignment and apportionment of liability between assignor and assignee[1] is modified by s.11 of the Covenants Act in relation to what are termed "excluded assignments". An excluded assignment is an assignment of the term of years or of the reversion in breach of a covenant of a tenancy, or such an assignment by operation of law.[2] It is clear from the terms of s.11 that an assignment of part of the premises demised by a tenancy, or an assignment of part of the reversion on demised premises, made in breach of a covenant of the tenancy or by operation of law, is also an excluded assignment for the purposes of s.11. **16.01**

(a) *Assignments in breach of a covenant*

"Covenant" has its usual wide meaning under the Covenants Act and includes term, condition and obligation; it is not restricted to a written agreement in a document under seal. So, e.g. an obligation of an orally agreed tenancy for less than three years is a "covenant" for the purposes of the Act. Further, a covenant of a tenancy includes, for these and other purposes of the Act, a covenant (as defined) contained in a collateral agreement.[3] An agreement made after the grant of the tenancy (supported by valuable consideration) that varies the tenancy, or which imposes some further obligation in relation to it, is therefore a covenant of a tenancy for the purposes of the Act. So too would be a term of an earlier agreement to grant a lease, for covenant is not limited to those covenants that are "landlord covenants" or "tenant covenants", as defined by the Act.[4] **16.02**

[1] Covenants Act, ss.5–10; see above, Chs 14 and 15.

[2] Covenants Act, s.11(1).

[3] *ibid.*, s.28(1); though a "collateral agreement" is an agreement collateral to the tenancy and so the term of the collateral agreement in question must relate in some way to the tenancy.

[4] See above, para.11.03. So, e.g. an assignment in breach of a personal right of pre-emption would be an excluded assignment.

Section 11 does not otherwise define the type of covenant in breach of which the assignment is made thereby making it an excluded assignment, though by necessary implication it will be a covenant in some way limiting or qualifying the right of the landlord or tenant to assign his interest or part of it. Two difficulties of interpretation arise here.

16.03 First, when is the assignment taken to be made for the purposes of this section? As the provisions of this section are intended to dovetail with the provisions of ss.5–7 of the Act, "assignment" must bear the same meaning here as in those sections. Although "assignment" is defined for the purposes of the Act as including an equitable assignment unless the context otherwise requires,[5] it is considered that the time with which the section is concerned is the date of the deed of conveyance,[6] or (in the case of a lease the title to which is registered) the date of the deed of transfer, and not the date from which the transfer is registered, because an equitable assignment suffices. So a binding contract to assign, where some formal completion of the agreement is contemplated, is not an "assignment" within the meaning of the section (even if the purchaser under such a contract has equitable rights over the property until completion) because the completion of the agreement to assign will be the "assignment" for the purposes of the Act. In the case of an equitable assignment by writing, the relevant time will be the date when the writing was made.

16.04 Secondly, and in view of the conclusion just drawn, it is unclear whether "a covenant" in s.11 means only a covenant which is broken at the time of the assignment, or whether it also embraces a covenant which is broken after the assignment. A tenant's covenant that permits assignment, subject only to the requirement that the tenant register the assignment with the landlord within one month of the assignment, will be broken if the tenant does not register the assignment within the month; but at the time of the assignment itself there was no breach of covenant. It is considered that s.11 is concerned only with a breach at the time of the assignment. In the case of an assignment by a landlord, time for the assignor landlord to apply for release starts to run from the date of the assignment; it must therefore have been intended that the assignment could be characterised as "excluded" or not at the time of the assignment.[7]

[5] Covenants Act, s.28(1).

[6] A deed is required for an assignment at law of a tenancy of any length: see *Crago v Julian* [1992] 1 W.L.R. 372; *Camden LBC v Alexandrou (No.2)* (1997) 74 P.&C.R. D33. See *Parc (Battersea) Ltd v Hutchinson* [1999] L.&T.R. 554 for an anomalous exception.

[7] If the assignment were "excluded", the right to apply for release would not exist: see Covenants Act, s.11(3), and below.

(b) *Assignments by operation of law*

An assignment by operation of law occurs where the interest or part of the interest of the landlord or tenant under a tenancy passes to another without any assignment having been effected *inter partes*. So, e.g. on the bankruptcy of an individual who is solely beneficially entitled to a tenancy or a reversion, the interest vests in the trustee in bankruptcy.[8] If the bankrupt holds the property in question on trust (whether express, implied, statutory,[9] constructive or resulting), the property itself will not vest in the trustee in bankruptcy because it will not be part of the bankrupt's estate,[10] though any beneficial interest solely owned by the bankrupt will so vest.[11] Other common cases are where property vests in the Crown as *bona vacantia* on the dissolution of a limited company or of a limited liability partnership,[12] and where property vests in personal representatives on the death of a testator[13] or in the public trustee on the death of an intestate.[14] Probably a vesting of trust property in new or continuing trustees under ss.40(1)(b) or 40(2)(b) of the Trustee Act 1925 will be an assignment by operation of law for these purposes, as it takes effect automatically on the appointment of a new trustee or on the retirement of an existing trustee. There does not seem to be any convincing reason why the vesting of jointly owned property in the surviving owners, upon the death of one of them, pursuant to the law of survivorship should not also be an excluded assignment for these purposes. **16.05**

2. Effect of excluded assignment of tenant's interest

In the case of an excluded assignment of the interest (or part thereof) of a tenant under a tenancy, the tenant is not released from the tenant covenants of the tenancy, and does not cease to be entitled to the benefit **16.06**

[8] Insolvency Act 1986, s.306(1),(2).

[9] i.e. under a trust of land pursuant to the Trusts of Land and Appointment of Trustees Act 1996.

[10] Insolvency Act 1986, s.283(3)(a).

[11] Note that there are categories of property which will not, in the absence of some further step taken by the trustee in bankruptcy, or at all, vest in the trustee: Insolvency Act 1986, ss.283(2), (3)(b), (3A) and 308A. Of these, tenancies under the Rent Act 1977, the Rent (Agriculture) Act 1976, the Housing Act 1985 and the Housing Act 1988 are of particular importance here.

[12] Companies Act 1985, s.654(1), as also applied in the case of the dissolution of an LLP by The Limited Liability Partnership Regulations 2001 (SI 2001/1090), reg.4(1), Sch.2, Pt I.

[13] Administration of Estates Act 1925, s.1(1).

[14] *ibid.*, s.9, as substituted with effect from July 1, 1995 by Law of Property (Miscellaneous Provisions) Act 1994, s.14(1).

of the landlord covenants of the tenancy,[15] as from that assignment.[16] The tenant is so released, however, and does so lose the benefit of the landlord covenants, as from the next assignment (if any) of the premises assigned by him that is not an excluded assignment.[17] Thus, instead of being released as from the date of the first assignment, the tenant will only be released if there is a subsequent assignment that is not an excluded assignment, and only with effect from the date of that subsequent assignment. If the subsequent assignment is of part only of the premises assigned by the tenant on the excluded assignment, the release and the loss of the benefit of the landlord covenants upon that subsequent assignment only has effect to the extent that the covenant or covenants in question fall to be complied with in relation to that part of the premises.[18] If the other part or parts of the premises assigned by the tenant on the excluded assignment are later assigned, a further partial release and loss of benefit of the landlord covenants takes place, on the occasion of each such assignment, in relation to such part or parts.[19]

(a) *Joint and several liability*

16.07 Until the subsequent assignment or assignments take place resulting in a later release of the tenant's liability, the tenant and the assignee under the excluded assignment will be jointly and severally liable under the tenant covenants of the tenancy,[20] and each will be entitled to the benefit of the landlord covenants. In the event of either the tenant or the assignee being released, for example because the landlord agrees with the assignee to release him from accrued and continuing liabilities in consideration of a one-off payment, the other is not released from his liability under the covenants of the tenancy.[21]

16.08 On an assignment of the premises (or part of the premises) demised by a tenancy which is *not* a new tenancy, there is an implied covenant of

[15] As would otherwise be the case pursuant to Covenants Act, s.5(2), (3).

[16] Covenants Act, s.11(2)(a).

[17] *ibid.*, s.11(2)(b).

[18] *ibid.*, s.11(7)(a). For the meaning of a covenant falling to be complied with in relation to a part of premises demised by a tenancy, see above, paras 14.06 *et seq*.

[19] *ibid.*, s.11(7)(b).

[20] *ibid.*, s.13(1).

[21] *ibid.*, s.13(2), overruling in relation to new tenancies the effect of the decision in *Deanplan Ltd v Mahmoud* [1993] Ch. 151, where it was held that a release agreed with the assignee necessarily released the original tenant to the same extent. Since then, the decisions in *Johnson v Davies* [1999] Ch. 117 and *Sun Life Assurance Society Plc v Tantofex (Engineers) Ltd* [1999] 2 E.G.L.R. 135 have disapproved *Deanplan v Mahmood* in relation to several, non-cumulative liabilities of lessees and their assigns, as distinct from cases of joint and several liability.

indemnity by the assignee or assignees in favour of the assignor that the assignee(s) will pay the rent reserved by the tenancy and comply with all the tenant's covenants for the remainder of the term, and keep the assignor indemnified against the consequences of non-compliance.[22] Those statutory covenants are not implied in the case of assignments of new tenancies.[23] Instead, and to the extent required, the Covenants Act provides a statutory basis for a claim for contribution as between persons jointly and severally liable under the same covenants by virtue of the Act. For these purposes, the Civil Liability (Contribution) Act 1978 has effect as if liability to a person under a covenant were liability in respect of damage suffered by that person. References to damage in that Act are accordingly to include a breach of a covenant of a tenancy, and s.7(2) of that Act is, for these purposes, treated as omitted.[24]

The non-application to new tenancies of statutory implied indemnity covenants should make no difference in practice to the entitlement in principle of an assignor tenant to be indemnified by his assignee. In the first place, an express covenant of indemnity could be made; and this would not appear to infringe the anti-avoidance provisions of the Covenants Act.[25] Secondly, an assignment which is unlawful is still fully effective to vest the tenancy in the assignee,[26] and as a matter of quasi-contract or restitutionary law an obligation to repay or indemnify would be implied in favour of the assignor who retained no beneficial interest in the demised premises or in the part assigned.[27] In addition, the assignor tenant would have the extra remedy of being subrogated to the landlord's claim against the assignee.[28]

(b) *Apportionment*

In the case of an excluded assignment, the apportionment provisions of the Covenants Act[29] do not apply to enable the tenant and his assignee to **16.09**

[22] Law of Property Act 1925, s.77(1)(C), (D); Land Registration Act 1925, s.24(1)(b), (2); Land Registration Act 2002, s.134(2), Sch.12, para.20(1)(a), (b)(i), (3).

[23] Covenants Act, ss.14, 30(2), Sch.2. Where the tenant is released, no indemnity is required.

[24] *ibid.*, s.13(3). The Civil Liability (Contribution) Act 1978 is set out in App.2, below.

[25] It being no purpose of the Act to maintain the liability of an assignor at the expense of his assignee. See below, Ch.23.

[26] *Old Grovebury Manor Farm v W. Seymour Plant Sales & Hire (No.2)* [1979] 1 W.L.R. 1379.

[27] See *Moule v Garrett* (1872) L.R. 7 Ex. 101; *Becton Dickinson UK Ltd v Zwebner* [1989] Q.B. 208. Even where the statutory covenants were expressly excluded from a conveyance, the *Moule v Garrett* principle still applied: *Re Healing Research Trustee Co Ltd* [1992] 2 All E.R. 481.

[28] See *Re Downer Enterprises Ltd* [1974] 1 W.L.R. 1460.

[29] Covenants Act, s.9; above, Ch.15.

apply[30] for an agreed apportionment to become binding as from the excluded assignment. But the apportionment provisions will apply on the next assignment (if any) of the premises assigned by the tenant that is not an excluded assignment, so as to enable the tenant and his assignee under the excluded assignment to apply for the agreed apportionment to become binding as from that subsequent assignment.[31] Where, in these circumstances, the apportionment provisions do apply upon the subsequent assignment, references in the provisions of the Act to the assignment, or to the assignee under it, are references to the excluded assignment and the assignee under that assignment.[32] Thus, e.g. the requirement that both tenant and assignee are to be bound after the assignment by a non-attributable covenant of the tenancy[33] must be satisfied in relation to the position after the excluded assignment, and not the position after the subsequent non-excluded assignment; and the application for the apportionment to become binding must be made by the parties to the excluded assignment. However, references to the assignment or proposed assignment in s.10 of the Covenants Act, as it applies in relation to an application for apportionment made in these deferred circumstances, are references to the subsequent non-excluded assignment.[34] Thus, the time limit for serving the prescribed form notice[35] runs from the date of the subsequent non-excluded assignment; the notice must inform the landlord of that assignment, not the earlier excluded assignment; and if the apportionment becomes binding pursuant to the apportionment procedure it is taken to have done so at the time when the subsequent non-excluded assignment took place.

16.10 If the subsequent assignment is of part only of the premises assigned by the tenant on the excluded assignment, the apportionment provisions of s.9 of the Covenants Act only have effect to the extent that the covenant or covenants in question fall to be complied with in relation to that part of the premises.[36] The apportionment provisions of s.9 only come into play at all (in relation to a tenant) where a tenant assigns part only of the premises demised to him; and so this further qualification applies where the assignee under the excluded assignment (or a successor excluded assignee of his) subsequently assigns or proposes to assign part only of

[30] Under Covenants Act, s.10.
[31] *ibid.*, s.11(5).
[32] *ibid.*, s.11(6)(a).
[33] *ibid.*, s.9(1)(b). See above, para.15.04, for the meaning of this.
[34] *ibid.*, s.11(6)(b).
[35] See above, para.15.11.
[36] Covenants Act, s.11(7)(a). For the meaning of a covenant falling to be complied with in relation to a part of premises demised by a tenancy, see above, paras 15.04 and 15.05.

the part that was first assigned to him.[37] In such circumstances, the right to apply for an apportionment to become binding is limited to an apportionment related to that part that was subsequently assigned. If the other part (or other parts) of the premises assigned by the tenant on the excluded assignment are later assigned on non-excluded assignments, a further apportionment application (or further applications) may be made in relation to that part (or those parts) on the occasion of each such non-excluded assignment.[38] But as there is no requirement that the liability in question be apportioned in a *pro rata* way,[39] in practice the original assignor and assignee could apply to have their apportionment agreement become binding even where the original assignee only further assigns part of what was assigned to him.[40]

3. Effect of excluded assignment of landlord's interest

In the case of an excluded assignment of the interest (or part thereof) of a landlord under a tenancy, the landlord or a former landlord[41] is not entitled to apply for release from the landlord covenants of the tenancy as from that assignment.[42] The landlord or a former landlord is, however, entitled to apply for release upon and as from the next assignment (if any) of the reversion assigned by the landlord which is not an excluded assignment.[43] Thus, instead of being entitled to apply for release as from the date of the first assignment, the landlord (or a former landlord) will only be entitled to apply for release if there is a subsequent assignment that is not an excluded assignment, and the release (if it happens) will only be with effect from the date of that subsequent assignment. If the subsequent assignment is of part only of the reversion assigned by the landlord on the excluded assignment, the right to apply for release upon the subsequent assignment only exists to the extent that the covenant or covenants in question fall to be complied with in relation to that part of the premises.[44] If the other part or other parts of the reversion assigned by **16.11**

[37] This is unlikely to occur frequently in practice. Despite the relatively large proportion of the Covenants Act which addresses the consequences of assignments of part of the demised premises or part of the reversion, these are quite rarely seen. Most alienation covenants prohibit the tenant from assigning or parting with possession of part only of the demised premises.

[38] Covenants Act, s.11(7)(b).

[39] See *ibid.*, s.9(3); above, para.15.07.

[40] A manifestly unequal apportionment might give the county court grounds for finding that it would be unreasonable for the apportionment to become binding on the appropriate person, however: see above, para.15.20.

[41] See above, para.14.32.

[42] Covenants Act, s.11(3)(a).

[43] *ibid.*, s.11(3)(b).

[44] *ibid.*, s.11(7)(a). For the meaning of a covenant falling to be complied with in relation to a part of premises demised by a tenancy, see above, paras 14.13 *et seq.*

the landlord on the excluded assignment are later assigned, a further right to apply for release will arise on the occasion of each such assignment to the extent that covenants fall to be complied with in relation to such part or parts.[45]

Where, by virtue of the foregoing provisions, a right to apply for release under ss.6 or 7 (in the case of a former landlord) of the Covenants Act does arise on a subsequent non-excluded assignment, whether on a subsequent assignment of the whole or a part of the reversion assigned on the excluded assignment, any reference (with one exception) to the assignment in ss.6 or 7 is a reference to the excluded assignment.[46] The exception is where the reference to the assignment relates to the time as from which the release takes effect.[47] In that one exceptional case, and in s.8 of the Covenants Act (procedure for seeking release from a covenant)[48] as it applies by virtue of these provisions relating to excluded assignments, any reference to the assignment or proposed assignment is a reference to the subsequent non-excluded assignment giving rise to the right to apply for release.[49] Thus, the application must be made within the specified time of the subsequent assignment, the tenant must be informed of that assignment, and the release (if any) takes effect as from the subsequent assignment, not from the earlier excluded assignment.[50]

(a) *Joint and several liability*

16.12 Until the subsequent non-excluded assignment or assignments take place and the landlord or former landlord (as the case might be) is released from liability pursuant to his application, the landlord (or former landlord) and the assignee under the excluded assignment will be jointly and severally liable under the landlord covenants of the tenancy,[51] and each will be entitled to the benefit of the tenant covenants. In the event of either the landlord (or former landlord) or the assignee being released, for example because the tenant agrees with the assignee to release him from some of his repairing obligations for some valuable consideration, the other is not released from his liability under the covenants of the tenancy.[52]

[45] Covenants Act, s.11(7)(b).
[46] *ibid.*, s.11(4)(a).
[47] i.e. the words "as from the assignment" in s.6(2)(b), (3)(b).
[48] See above, para.14.16.
[49] Covenants Act, s.11(4)(b).
[50] See *ibid.*, s.8(1), (3); and above, para.14.28.
[51] *ibid.*, s.13(1).
[52] *ibid.*, s.13(2), excluding in relation to new tenancies the effect of the decision in *Deanplan Ltd v Mahmoud* [1993] Ch. 151, where it was held that a release agreed with the assignee of the term necessarily released the original tenant to the same extent.

In most cases, an express covenant will be taken from an assignee of a reversion by the assignor to comply with any obligations affecting the land conveyed and to keep the assignor indemnified against any breach of such obligations. As a result of the Covenants Act, either the assignor will be released pursuant to the Act or, if joint and several liability exists, there is a new statutory basis for a claim for contribution as between persons jointly and severally liable under the same covenants by virtue of the Act. For these purposes, the Civil Liability (Contribution) Act 1978 has effect as if liability to a person under a covenant were liability in respect of damage suffered by that person. References to damage in that Act are accordingly to include a breach of a covenant of a tenancy, and s.7(2) of that Act is, for these purposes, treated as omitted.[53] In principle, the assignor landlord can expect to be indemnified by his assignee, for the benefit of the tenant covenants (and more particularly the right to receive the rent as from the assignment) has passed to the assignee notwithstanding the assignment being an excluded assignment.[54] **16.13**

(b) *Apportionment*

In the case of an excluded assignment, the apportionment provisions of the Covenants Act[55] do not apply to enable the landlord and his assignee to apply[56] for an agreed apportionment of liability to become binding as from the excluded assignment. But they will apply on the next assignment (if any) of the reversion assigned by the landlord which is not an excluded assignment, so as to enable the landlord and his assignee under the excluded assignment to apply for the agreed apportionment to become binding as from that subsequent assignment.[57] Where, in these circumstances, the apportionment provisions do apply upon the subsequent assignment, references in these provisions of the Act to the assignment or to the assignee under it are references to the excluded assignment and the assignee under that assignment.[58] So, e.g. the requirement that both landlord and assignee are to be bound after the assignment by a non-attributable landlord covenant of the tenancy[59] must be satisfied in relation to the position after the excluded assignment, and not the position after the subsequent non-excluded assignment; and the application for the apportionment to become binding must be made by the parties to the excluded assignment. However, references to the assignment **16.14**

[53] *ibid.*, s.13(3). The Civil Liability (Contribution) Act 1978 is set out in App.2, below.

[54] Covenants Act, ss.3(3)(b), 28(1) (definition of "assignment").

[55] *ibid.*, s.9; above, Ch.15.

[56] Under *ibid.*, s.10.

[57] *ibid.*, s.11(5).

[58] *ibid.*, s.11(6)(a).

[59] *ibid.*, s.9(2)(b).

or proposed assignment in s.10 of the Covenants Act, as it applies in relation to an application for apportionment made in these deferred circumstances, are references to the subsequent non-excluded assignment.[60] Thus, the time limit for serving the prescribed form notice[61] runs from the date of the subsequent non-excluded assignment; the notice must inform the tenant(s) of that assignment, not the earlier excluded assignment; and if the apportionment becomes binding it is taken to have done so at the time when the subsequent, non-excluded assignment takes place.

16.15 If the subsequent assignment is of part only of the reversion which was assigned by the landlord on the excluded assignment, the apportionment provisions of the Act only have effect to the extent that the covenant or covenants in question fall to be complied with in relation to that part of the premises.[62] The apportionment provisions only come into play at all (in relation to a landlord) where a landlord assigns part only of the reversion that was vested in him; and so this further qualification applies where the assignee under the excluded assignment (or a successor excluded assignee of his) subsequently assigns or proposes to assign part only of the part of the reversion that was first assigned to him. In such circumstances (likely to be rare in practice), the right to apply for an apportionment to become binding is limited to an apportionment related to that part that was subsequently assigned. If the other part or parts of the reversion, assigned by the landlord, on the excluded assignment, are later assigned on non-excluded assignments, a further apportionment application (or applications) may be made in relation to that part (or parts) on the occasion of each such non-excluded assignment.[63] But as there is no requirement that the liability in question be apportioned *pro rata*,[64] in practice the original assignor and assignee could apply to have their apportionment become binding even where the original assignee only further assigns part of what was assigned to him.[65]

[60] *ibid.*, s.11(6)(b).

[61] See above, para.15.11.

[62] Covenants Act, s.11(7)(a). For the meaning of a covenant falling to be complied with in relation to a part of premises demised by a tenancy, see above, paras 15.04 and 15.05.

[63] *ibid.*, s.11(7)(b).

[64] *ibid.*, s.9(3); above, para.15.07.

[65] A manifestly unequal apportionment might give the county court grounds for finding that it would be unreasonable for the apportionment to become binding on the appropriate person, however: see above, para.15.20.

CHAPTER 17

Third Party and Non-Party Covenants, Rights and Obligations

Quite often in long residential leases, and sometimes in commercial leases, a person other than the tenant, the landlord, and any guarantor(s) for such persons is a party to the deed of lease for certain purposes. The most common example is a management company, which may have rights against either landlord or tenant (or both), such as the right to be paid a service charge, and may correspondingly have obligations to either landlord or tenant (or both), e.g. the responsibility to keep the structure and exterior of the building in repair. For the scheme of the lease and other such leases to operate satisfactorily for the length of the terms granted, the rights of such a third party need to be enforceable against successors in title of the landlord and tenant, and its obligations must similarly be enforceable by such successors in title.[1] Section 12 of the Covenants Act makes provision for this and for other matters related to covenants of such third parties, where under a covenant of the tenancy such a person is liable to discharge a function relating to the demised premises and in that regard rights are conferred on, or are exercisable against, him. These provisions are considered in section 2 of this Chapter. They do not apply in the case of a surety, who is the most common third party in commercial leases. His position under a new tenancy is addressed first in section 1. **17.01**

Before November 11, 1999 the question of whether a person who is not a party to a contract (other than an assignee of the demised premises or of the reversion) could take the benefit of its terms depended on whether or not the contract purported to be made with him. Since that time, the same possibility may arise pursuant to the provisions of the Contracts (Rights of Third Parties) Act 1999, which applies a slightly different test. In practice, this Act is little used; its effect is regularly excluded by parties to commercial contracts including commercial leases. But its potential effect in relation to new tenancies is considered in section 3, below. **17.02**

Apart from the law relating to proprietary rights such as restrictive covenants and easements, there is no equivalent provision, whether of the **17.03**

[1] The law relating to old tenancies failed to achieve this: see above, paras 10.06 *et seq*.

common law or of statute, that has the general effect of making non-parties subject to a contractual obligation. However, the Covenants Act does so in relation to new tenancies in three important respects, making landlord and tenant covenants enforceable against (as well as by) concurrent lessees of the reversion and mortgagees, and also against other owners and occupiers of the demised premises. These are considered in section 4, below.

1. Sureties

17.04 The general law relating to sureties for the lessee or his assignees has been considered in relation to old tenancies,[2] and what is said there applies equally to sureties for lessees and assignees of new tenancies. Although s.141 of the Law of Property Act 1925 has no application to new tenancies,[3] the benefit of a surety covenant did not pass with the reversion to an old tenancy under that provision but at common law; and it is considered that the same should apply in relation to new tenancies. The surety covenant is not a tenant covenant because it does not fall to be performed by the tenant for the time being[4]; nor is it a "third party covenant" within the meaning of that expression in the Covenants Act,[5] and so that Act does not require a covenant by a surety for the lessee (or for an assignee) to be treated differently from under the old law.[6] The same would apply in relation to the benefit of any surety for the landlord, though such a person is not commonly encountered. Where the Act does make a difference is when the former tenant (or *his* surety) is required to be a surety for an assignee. This is dealt with in detail in later Chapters,[7] as are the new principles introduced by the Covenants Act (which apply to old tenancies and new tenancies alike) to limit the liability of sureties for the tenant.[8]

17.05 Where, under the provisions of the Covenants Act, a tenant is released from further liability under tenant covenants of the lease, any surety for the tenant is released to the same extent.[9] No equivalent express provision is made for the (rare) case of a surety for a landlord who is released from the landlord covenants under the Act, though at common law the same

[2] Above, paras 10.02 to 10.05.
[3] Covenants Act, s.30(4)(b).
[4] Within the definitions of *ibid.*, s.28(1).
[5] *ibid.*, s.12(1)(b).
[6] The disapplication of Law of Property Act 1925, s.141 is not an obstacle to the use of the common law principle identified in *Swift (P&A) Investments Ltd v Combined English Stores Group Ltd* [1989] A.C. 632: the surety covenant is not a covenant by the tenant and the Covenants Act does not require it to be treated as such.
[7] Below, Chs 18, 23.
[8] Below, Chs 20–22.
[9] Covenants Act, s.24(2).

result would obtain if the surety was truly a guarantor and not a person with a primary liability in relation to the landlord covenants.[10] Where, under the Act, a landlord ceases to be entitled to the benefit of the tenant covenants,[11] the benefit of any surety's covenant will have passed (for the future) at common law and not pursuant to the Act to the assignee of the reversion, unless assignor and assignee otherwise provide.

2. Third Party Covenants

(a) *Meaning of third party covenant*

A third party for the purposes of the Covenants Act is a person other than the landlord or tenant (or a surety) who is, under a covenant of a tenancy, liable (as principal) to discharge any function with respect to all or any of the demised premises.[12] Such liability might be imposed by a covenant of the lease itself, or by a term, condition or obligation of a tenancy agreement, or by any covenant, term, condition or obligation contained in a collateral agreement.[13] The subject matter of the liability is drafted in the widest terms ("any function with respect to all or any of the demised premises"), and is termed "the relevant function" by the Act. But the liability does not extend to a liability in the nature of a guarantee or any other financial liability referable to the performance or otherwise of a covenant of the tenancy by another party to it.[14] Thus, the liability of a third party to pay a liquidated sum or damages in the event of the failure of the tenant to comply with an obligation of the tenancy is not a relevant third party covenant for the purposes of the Act. Where the prescribed liability as principal under a third party covenant of a tenancy exists,[15] the provisions of s.12 of the Act described below apply in relation to the covenant. It is important to note that these provisions only apply where the third party is *liable* to discharge a function under a covenant of the tenancy. They therefore have no application where, e.g. a superior landlord only has the benefit of tenant covenants. In such a case the person benefited falls to be treated as a non-party.[16] **17.06**

(b) *Transmission of benefit of third party covenant*

The Covenants Act provides for the benefit of such third party covenants **17.07**
to pass in the same way as the benefit of tenant covenants and landlord

[10] See above, para.10.02.
[11] Under Covenants Act, s.6(2)(b), (3)(b) or s.7(5).
[12] *ibid.*, s.12(1)(a).
[13] *ibid.*, s.28(1).
[14] *ibid.*, s.12(1)(b).
[15] i.e. exists in principle under the terms of the covenant.
[16] See below, paras 17.12 *et seq.*

covenants pass under the Act on an assignment. To the extent that any covenant of the tenancy[17] confers any rights against the third party with respect to the relevant function, then for the purposes of the transmission of the benefit of the covenant in accordance with the Act it is treated as if it were either a landlord covenant of the tenancy or a tenant covenant of the tenancy. To the extent that the rights against the third party in respect of the relevant function are exercisable by the landlord, the covenant is treated as a tenant covenant (and so the benefit of the covenant passes, as does the benefit of a tenant covenant, on an assignment by the landlord of the whole or part of his reversionary interest); to the extent that the rights against the third party in respect of the relevant function are exercisable by the tenant, the covenant is treated as a landlord covenant.[18] The words "to the extent that" suggest that the same covenant may be treated in different ways; for example, a covenant by a management company with both tenant and landlord under the lease to provide a 24-hour security presence in the building will be treated for transmission purposes as a landlord covenant to the extent that the covenant is made with the tenant, and as a tenant covenant to the extent that it is made with the landlord. So both an assignee of the term and an assignee of the reversion will be entitled to enforce the covenant (or sue for damages for breach, as the case may be) against the third party.

There is no corresponding provision for the burden of the third party's covenant to bind successors-in-title of the third party,[19] for the third party's covenant is only treated as a tenant covenant or a landlord covenant (as the case may be) "for the purposes of the transmission of the benefit of the covenant in accordance with this Act", and not for the purpose of the transmission of the burden of the covenant.[20]

(c) *Transmission of burden of covenant with third party*

17.08 The Act also makes provision for the burden of covenants made by landlord or tenant under the lease with such a third party to bind their successors in title, in accordance with the transmission principles of the Act. Thus, to the extent that any covenant of the tenancy confers any rights exercisable *by* the third party with respect to the relevant function, for the purposes of the transmission of the burden of that covenant in accordance with the Act the covenant is treated as either a landlord

[17] As widely defined by the Covenants Act, s.28(1); and see above.

[18] *ibid.*, s.12(2).

[19] Usually, such a third party will not have any title to which others could succeed.

[20] See Covenants Act, s.12(2).

covenant of the tenancy or as a tenant covenant of the tenancy.[21] It is treated as a tenant covenant of the tenancy to the extent that the third party's rights are exercisable against the tenant (so that, as with a tenant covenant made with the landlord, the burden of the covenant binds successors in title of the tenant); and it is treated as a landlord covenant to the extent that the third party's rights are exercisable against the landlord. So successors in title of both tenant and landlord are bound to the same extent as their assignors were bound by the covenant. Again, the use of the words "to the extent that" means that, where both landlord and tenant are bound by the same covenant in favour of a third party, successors in title of both landlord and tenant will be bound by the covenant upon an assignment of the whole or part of the interest of each assignor.

(d) *Release*

The Act also makes similar provision for the release of obligations of landlord and tenant under covenants made by either (or both) of them with a third party (though not for the release of obligations of the third party). So, to the extent that any covenant of a tenancy confers rights exercisable by the third party with respect to the relevant function, then, for the purposes of any release from the covenant in accordance with the Covenants Act, it is treated as either a landlord covenant of the tenancy or a tenant covenant of the tenancy.[22] It is treated as a tenant covenant of the tenancy to the extent that those rights are exercisable against the tenant. So, upon a non-excluded assignment, the tenant is released from the obligation which is the subject of the third party rights just as he is released from obligations enforceable by the landlord.[23] The covenant is treated as a landlord covenant of the tenancy to the extent that the rights exercisable by the third party are exercisable against the landlord. So, upon a non-excluded assignment, the landlord has the right to apply for release from the obligation which is the subject of third party rights, just as he has the right to apply for release from covenants enforceable against him by the tenant.[24] 17.09

In relation to release of the landlord from any covenant with a third party that is treated as a landlord covenant, the procedure for seeking release from a covenant under s.8 of the Covenants Act applies as if any reference in that section to the tenant were a reference to the third party.[25] 17.10

[21] *ibid.*, s.12(3). It is not clear why such a covenant, conferring rights exercisable by the third party against either tenant or landlord (or both), needs to be treated as a tenant covenant or landlord covenant, as it would appear to fall within the definitions of "tenant covenant" or "landlord covenant" in s.28(1) in any event.

[22] Covenants Act, s.12(3), (4)(b).

[23] See Ch.14, above.

[24] See Ch.14, above.

[25] Covenants Act, s.12(5).

Thus, the application for release must be made within the prescribed period by serving notice on the third party, and the third party may serve a notice objecting to release. The same procedure and consequences follow as in the case of an application by the landlord for release which is served on the tenant.[26] It seems that the Act contemplates the service of a notice in the prescribed form,[27] although none is prescribed specifically as the form applicable to a notice served under ss.12 and 8, and the wording of the prescribed forms is not always appropriate to receipt by a third party rather than by a tenant.[28] If the covenant is to be treated as a landlord covenant,[29] there appears to be no reason why, if the landlord is not released from the covenant conferring rights on the third party upon his assigning the reversion or part of it, he should not have the right to apply to the third party for release upon a subsequent assignment of the interest which he assigned.[30] Because a landlord must serve a separate notice on a third party, it is perfectly possible for him to be released from his liability to the tenant, for example because the tenant does not within the specified time serve notice of objection, yet not from his liability to the third party, even though the same covenant is made with both.

(e) *Apportionment*

17.11 To the extent that any covenant of the tenancy confers any rights exercisable by the third party with respect to the relevant function, then, for the purposes of apportionment of liability in respect of the covenant in accordance with the Act, the covenant is treated as either a landlord covenant or a tenant covenant of the tenancy.[31] It is treated as a landlord covenant to the extent that those rights are exercisable against the landlord (so that upon an assignment of part of the reversion the landlord has the right to apply to have an agreed apportionment of a non-attributable covenant become binding on the third party); it is treated as a tenant covenant to the extent that those rights are exercisable against the tenant (so that upon an assignment of part of the premises comprised in the tenancy, the tenant has the right to apply to have an agreed

[26] See generally above, paras 14.16 *et seq*.

[27] i.e. Forms 3 or 4 in the Schedule to the Notices Regulations 1995.

[28] e.g. Form 3, Pt I, para.2 ("... of which you are the tenant"). Probably an amendment of the prescribed form to make it specifically applicable to a third party rather than to the tenant would be "a form substantially to the like effect" in the case of a notice to be given to a third party; indeed, it would be likely to be less misleading to the third party.

[29] See n.21, above.

[30] *sc.* the right of the "former landlord" to apply under the Covenants Act, s.7 for release: see above, paras 14.32 *et seq*. The wording of Covenants Act, s.8(1), which applies by virtue of the Covenants Act, s.12(5), includes both s.6 and s.7 within its scope.

[31] Covenants Act, s.12(3), (4)(b).

apportionment of a non-attributable covenant become binding on the third party).[32]

The third party is for these purposes nevertheless not treated as being either the tenant (in the case of a non-attributable landlord covenant) or the landlord (in the case of a non-attributable tenant covenant); any application for the apportionment to become binding is therefore served on the third party and not on the "appropriate person", as defined for the purposes of the apportionment provisions,[33] but it may, if thought appropriate, also be served on such person.[34] The procedure for having an apportionment become binding is considered in Ch.15, and applies in principle to an agreed apportionment of a liability to a third party.

3. Non-parties

As noted above, the Covenants Act itself does not provide for cases where a non-party to the tenancy is expressed to have the benefit of one or more covenants of the tenancy,[35] e.g. where a tenant covenants with the landlord and with a superior landlord or with the other tenants in the building. This is a category of covenant which is neither the case of a third party having a liability under a covenant of the tenancy,[36] nor the case of specified persons automatically having the benefit or burden of the covenants of the tenancy.[37] Such covenants are not prohibited by the Act, but if they are tenant covenants of the tenancy,[38] as both these examples would be, upon an assignment of the reversion the benefit of the covenant would pass to the assignee landlord, apparently exclusively,[39] unless it is implicit that only tenant covenants made with the landlord are annexed to and pass with the reversion. Similarly, if the covenant is a landlord covenant of the tenancy, upon an assignment of the term the benefit of the covenant would seem to pass to the assignee tenant.[40] There must therefore be a question over what happens to such covenants made with non-parties upon an assignment of the term or of the reversion, as the case may be. **17.12**

[32] Again, it is unclear why there is a need for such covenants to be treated as landlord or tenant covenants: see n.21, above.
[33] Covenants Act, s.10(7).
[34] *ibid.*, s.10(4), (5).
[35] Above, paras 17.02, 17.08.
[36] section 2, above.
[37] section 4, below.
[38] Within the meaning of Covenants Act, s.28(1), which does not limit the definition to covenants made *with* the landlord.
[39] *ibid.*, s.3(1), (3); above, para.12.18.
[40] *ibid.*, s.3(1), (2); above, para.12.10.

In the case of covenants that are expressed to be personal to the covenantor (and which therefore cannot be tenant or landlord covenants),[41] so far as the Covenants Act is concerned the burden remains with the covenantor and arguably the benefit remains with the covenantee.[42] In reality, such covenants are left out of the statutory transmission scheme of the Act, as compared with a covenant that is expressed to be personal to the covenantee only, which will be a landlord or tenant covenant and so is within the scheme of the Act. As such, it is considered that an agreement by the covenantor, that the benefit of his personal covenant may be enjoyed by such persons as may be specified (cumulatively or sequentially), is not void under the anti-avoidance provisions of the Covenants Act.[43]

(a) *The Contracts (Rights of Third Parties) Act 1999*

17.13 Prior to November 11, 1999, the question of whether a non-party to any contract (other than an assignee of one of the parties) could take the benefit of it depended on whether the contract purported to be made with him.[44] In no circumstances short of a contractual novation could such a non-party become subject to the burden of a contract. But in the case of a contract entered into after May 10, 2000,[45] a person who is not a party to a contract has been able, subject to various limitations, to enforce a term of a contract in his own right if either the contract expressly provides that he may or the term purports to confer a benefit on him.[46]

For these purposes, a term does not purport to confer a benefit on a non-party if, on a proper construction of the contract, it appears that the parties to the contract did not intend the term to be enforceable by the non-party.[47] For these provisions to apply, the non-party must be expressly identified in the contract by name, as a member of a class or as answering a particular description, but need not be in existence when the contract is entered into.[48] For the purposes of exercising a right to enforce a term, the non-party has any remedy that would have been available to him in an action for breach of contract had he been a party. The rules

[41] See *BHP Petroleum Great Britain Ltd v Chesterfield Properties Ltd* [2002] Ch.12; above, para.11.03.

[42] See the discussion at para.12.06, above.

[43] As to which, see below, Ch.23.

[44] Law of Property Act 1925, s.56(1); *Beswick v Beswick* [1968] A.C. 58.

[45] Contracts (Rights of Third Parties) Act 1999, ss.1(1), 10(2) (Royal Assent: Nov. 11, 1999)

[46] *ibid.* A contract entered into between Nov. 11, 1999 and May 10, 2000 is subject to the same provisions if it expressly provides for the application of the Act.

[47] Contracts (Rights of Third Parties) Act 1999, s.1(2).

[48] *ibid.*, s.1(3).

relating to damages, injunctions, specific performance and other relief apply accordingly.[49] The Act does not distinguish between leases and other contracts to which its provisions might apply. Nor does it make any provision for a non-party to become subject to any contractual obligation.

In practice the Act seems to be little used. Its application is regularly excluded by an express term of the lease, and the main debate generated has been as to the appropriate language in which any unintentional effect should be excluded.[50] But if the effect of the Act is not excluded, a tenant covenant made with the landlord and the other tenants of the building, or a landlord covenant made with the tenant and the other tenants of the building, would be enforceable, at least prior to any assignment of the counterparty's interest, under the terms of the Act by those other tenants. Similarly, a tenant covenant made with the landlord and any superior landlord would at least initially be enforceable by any superior landlord. Such enforcement would be possible by an order of specific performance, even though no consideration had moved from the non-party for the covenant in question. As noted above, a difficult question arises upon assignment of the counterparty's interest as to whether the benefit of the covenant necessarily passes to the assignee only, thereby divesting the non-party of his contractual benefit. **17.14**

Leases regularly define the parties as including their successors in title, or alternatively stipulate that the covenants are made on behalf of the covenantor and his successors in title with the covenantee and his successors in title. Such language is no longer needed to effect a transfer of the benefit or burden of landlord and tenant covenants under the Covenants Act: such a covenant that is not intended to benefit or bind successors in title needs to be expressed (in whatever terms) to be personal otherwise it will automatically do so.[51] But it is to be expected that the traditional language of leases will continue to be used by draftsmen notwithstanding. What therefore is the effect under the Contracts (Rights of Third Parties) Act of a covenant expressed to be made by a tenant with the landlord and its successors in title to the reversion? **17.15**

In relation to covenants that are tenant covenants within the meaning of the Covenants Act (i.e. those intended to be performed by the tenant for the time being under the lease), there will be no difference because the benefit of the covenant will pass in any event under the transmission provisions of the Act. But where the covenant is expressed (in whatever

[49] *ibid.*, s.1(5). Accordingly, the rule that specific performance will not be granted in favour of a volunteer is presumably overridden by the Act: "a party to the contract" must mean a party from whom consideration has moved.

[50] So as to exclude only the operation of the Act and not the effect of the common law or of other statutes.

[51] Above, paras 12.03 *et seq.*

terms) to be personal to the tenant, or if it is otherwise clear that the obligation is not to be performed by the tenant for the time being under the tenancy but only be the original lessee,[52] such a covenant cannot be a tenant covenant and so its benefit will not pass under that Act to successors in title of the lessor. In such a case, the benefit of the covenant may still pass to the successor landlord under the Contracts (Rights of Third Parties) Act. At common law, the benefit of a covenant touching and concerning land (including for these purposes a reversionary estate) could pass with the reversion[53]; but one purpose of the Covenants Act was to abolish the difficult distinction between covenants that do and do not touch and concern demised premises.[54] So the Contracts (Rights of Third Parties) Act combined with the traditional language of leasehold conveyancing may perform an important function in relation to new tenancies by enabling a successor landlord to enforce a personal covenant of the tenant, or indeed a successor tenant to enforce a personal covenant of the landlord.[55] The concept of a covenant that is personal to one of the parties but not both was well established before the Covenants Act[56] and is of continuing importance.

(b) *RTM Companies*

17.16 Under the Commonhold and Leasehold Reform Act 2002,[57] management functions of the landlord and any other party to a lease other than the tenant can be divested from them and vested in a right to manage company (RTM company) created by the tenants for that purpose. Management functions for these purposes are functions with respect to services, repairs, maintenance, improvements, insurance and management.[58] The right to manage applies only in relation to self-contained buildings or parts of buildings containing two or more residential flats owned by qualifying tenants of long residential leases.[59] These provisions

[52] See the *BHP Petroleum Great Britain* case, above.

[53] See above, para.10.03.

[54] Above, para.11.03. It would accordingly be dubious to have recourse to such a doctrine to transfer the benefit of covenants in new tenancies.

[55] The potential difficulty may also be resolved by the language of Covenants Act, s.3(6)(a), as to which see above, para.12.03. If it is the old conveyancing language that saves such covenants, this is not considered to offend the anti-avoidance provisions of Covenants Act, s.25 because the Act provides for transmission except (in effect) where the parties stipulate otherwise, by making their covenants personal and non-assignable.

[56] *System Floors Ltd v Ruralpride Ltd* [1995] 1 E.G.L.R. 48.

[57] Part 2, Ch.1.

[58] Commonhold and Leasehold Reform Act 2002, s.96(5). But functions relating to flats or other units not held by qualifying tenants and functions relating to forfeiture and re-entry are excluded: s.96(6).

[59] *ibid.*, ss.72, 75, 76.

came into effect on September 30, 2003 and apply to leases granted before as well as after that date.[60]

The functions that may become vested in RTM companies under the Act of 2002 include obligations as well as rights. Where so vested, the obligations and rights cease to be obligations or rights of the landlord or other party unless so agreed with the RTM company.[61] Thus, where the right to manage has been conferred on the RTM company, the obligations and rights of the landlord and any management company that is a party to a qualifying lease are statutorily transferred to the RTM company. The obligations thereupon binding the RTM company are owed to the tenants and to the landlord.[62] Tenant covenants of a lease that remain enforceable by the landlord, notwithstanding the conferring of the right to manage, are also enforceable by the RTM company in the same manner. This right extends to rights to enter the demised premises to inspect them, but not to rights of forfeiture or re-entry.[63] For the purposes of giving effect to the right to manage, numerous statutory provisions in the Landlord and Tenant Acts 1927, 1985, 1987 and 1988 are deemed to apply with amendments in relation to the RTM company and the new regime for management functions.[64]

No issue under the anti-avoidance provisions of the Covenants Act applies because the de-annexation and transfer of the burden and benefit of landlord and tenant covenants is effected by statute and court (or LVT) order, not by agreement.

4. Third party rights and obligations

(a) *Enforcement of covenants by persons other than landlord and tenant*

Absent an assignment of the tenancy or of the reversion, landlord and tenant are entitled to enforce the tenant's covenants and the landlord's covenants respectively as a matter of privity of contract. The Covenants Act makes specific provision for others (apart from assignees of the parties) to be entitled to enforce such covenants, and indeed for others to have such covenants enforced against them. In some respects, the Act achieves a welcome clarification of the pre-existing law[65]; in other respects, it introduces new difficulties. There are three categories of person with whom the Act is principally concerned. **17.17**

[60] The Commonhold and Leasehold Reform Act 2002 (Commencement No.2 and Savings) (England) Order 2003 (SI 2003/1986), arts 1(2), 2.

[61] Commonhold and Leasehold Reform Act 2002, ss.96(4), 97(2).

[62] *ibid.*, s.97(1).

[63] *ibid.*, s.100.

[64] *ibid.*, s.102, Sch.7.

[65] See above, Ch.8.

17.18 (i) CONCURRENT LESSEES. A landlord under an old tenancy could grant a further lease of his reversionary interest in the demised premises. This had the effect that the subsequent lessee became the landlord of the tenant under the existing tenancy, to the exclusion of the lessor, for the duration of the term created by the concurrent lease. In such circumstances, the concurrent lessee was, in connection with enforcement of the tenant's covenants, in the position of an assignee of the landlord's reversionary interest for the duration of the term of the concurrent lease,[66] and thereby entitled to the exclusion of the landlord to claim in relation to any outstanding breaches of the tenant's obligations under the tenancy.

The transmission provisions of the Covenants Act do not apply to the case of the grant of a concurrent lease[67]; nor does s.141 of the Law of Property Act 1925 apply. The Act therefore makes separate provision for the case of the grant of a concurrent lease. It provides that where any tenant covenant of a tenancy, or any right of re-entry contained in a tenancy, is enforceable by the reversioner in respect of any premises demised by the tenancy, it is also so enforceable by any person (other than the reversioner) who, as the holder of the immediate reversion in those premises, is for the time being entitled to the rents and profits under the tenancy in respect of those premises.[68] "Reversioner" is defined for the purposes of this provision as the holder for the time being of the interest of the landlord under the tenancy.[69] This must mean the landlord who granted the tenancy or the current holder of that landlord's interest in the premises, because if it meant the person who for the time being stands in the position of landlord in relation to the tenancy, the provision would fail to distinguish between the "reversioner" and the "person (other than the reversioner)". So, where a tenant covenant or a right of re-entry is in principle enforceable by the reversioner in respect of demised premises, it will also be enforceable by any person who, as concurrent lessee, is for the time being entitled to the rents and profits under the tenancy in respect of such premises.[70] Unlike the position under old tenancies, the tenant covenant appears not to be exclusively enforceable by the concurrent lessee, for the wording of the Act is: "it shall also be enforceable by". The

[66] See above, para.4.07.
[67] See above, para.12.19.
[68] Covenants Act, s.15(1)(a).
[69] *ibid.*, s.15(6).
[70] The provision is circular. Under the old law, a concurrent lessee was entitled to the rents and profits because of the effect of Law of Property Act 1925, s.141, as applying to the *pro tanto* assignment of the reversion. It is difficult to see how a "person other than the reversioner" can be entitled to the rents and profits in a case where that section has no application and where there is no assignment. The Covenants Act assumes what it seeks to effect.

Act thus creates the spectre of two different persons being entitled to enforce the covenants in a tenancy at the same time.[71]

The position is apparently the same in relation to rights of re-entry, for the statutory provision does not distinguish between enforcement of tenant covenants and rights of re-entry. The result is curious, to say the least, for a right of re-entry is a species of interest in property at law,[72] and cannot be owned in the same right by different persons unless they are joint owners. Although a right of re-entry can exist in favour of persons other than landlords,[73] experience of superior landlords forfeiting sub-tenancies is rare indeed.[74]

The Covenants Act makes similar provision for enforcement of landlord covenants. Where any landlord covenant of a tenancy is enforceable against the reversioner in respect of any premises demised by the tenancy, it shall also be enforceable against a person in the position of a concurrent lessee.[75] But this time the Act does not specify by whom the landlord covenant in question was enforceable against the reversioner, though presumably it is by the tenant. The landlord covenant appears to be enforceable against both the original landlord (or his assign, as the case may be) and the concurrent lessee. **17.19**

(ii) Mortgagees. Under the law relating to old tenancies, it was at best unclear whether, and in what circumstances, a mortgagee in possession of the interest of a landlord or tenant was bound by or could enforce obligations of the tenancy.[76] The Covenants Act makes express provision for covenants to be enforceable in certain cases both by and against mortgagees in possession. In these provisions, the words "mortgagee" and "mortgage" include "chargee" and "charge" respectively.[77] **17.20**

Where any tenant covenant of a tenancy, or any right of re-entry contained in a tenancy, is enforceable by the reversioner in respect of any premises demised by the tenancy, it is also enforceable by any mortgagee in possession of the reversion in those premises who is entitled to the **17.21**

[71] A spectre that, in respect of old tenancies, the Law of Property Act 1925, s.141(1) had prevented from arising. See *First Penthouse Ltd v Channel Hotels & Properties (UK) Ltd* [2004] 1 E.G.L.R. 16, paras 53–56, for a discussion of the difficulties that arise in practice.

[72] Law of Property Act 1925, s.1(2)(e).

[73] *Shiloh Spinners Ltd v Harding* [1973] A.C. 691.

[74] In relation to old tenancies, the Law of Property Act 1925, s.141(3) effectually transferred the right of re-entry to the concurrent lessee in such circumstances.

[75] Covenants Act, s.15(2).

[76] See above, Ch.8.

[77] Covenants Act, s.15(6).

rents and profits under the tenancy.[78] Once again, "the reversioner" must refer to the original landlord or his assign, as the case may be. But the mortgagee in possession must, to fall within this statutory provision, be in receipt of the rents and profits of the tenancy, and so a mortgagee in possession of the reversioner's interest, where a concurrent lease is in existence, may fall outwith the section. If the concurrent lessee is in receipt of the rents and profits, the spectre of dual rights of enforcement is again present here. The statutory provision does, however, apply in favour of a mortgagee of the reversioner where no concurrent lease exists.

Mortgagees in possession of landlords' interests do not get it all their own way under the Act. A mortgagee in possession of the interest of a reversioner, entitled to the rents and profits under the tenancy, is liable to have the landlord covenants in the tenancy enforced against him.[79]

17.22 Similar provision is made in relation to mortgagees in possession of the interest of a tenant under a tenancy. Where any landlord covenant in a tenancy is enforceable by the tenant in respect of any premises demised by the tenancy, it is also so enforceable by any mortgagee in possession of those premises under a mortgage granted by the tenant.[80] Similarly, where any tenant covenant of a tenancy, or any right of re-entry contained in a tenancy, is enforceable against any tenant in respect of any premises demised by the tenancy, it is also so enforceable against any such mortgagee.[81] Given the definition of "tenant" in the Act,[82] being the person for the time being entitled to the term of years, a mortgagee in possession of the interest of a sub-tenant could not enforce the landlord covenants in the tenancy nor, by virtue of the Act at least, have the tenant covenants enforced against it; nor, it seems, could a mortgagee in possession under a mortgage granted by the tenant's predecessor in title.

17.23 (iii) OWNERS AND OCCUPIERS OF THE DEMISED PREMISES. Any landlord or tenant covenant of the tenancy that is restrictive of the user of land is capable of being enforced against any other person who is the owner or occupier of any demised premises to which the covenant relates. This is so even though there is no express provision of the tenancy to that effect.[83] The language in which this provision is couched, and the reference to the absence of express provision of the tenancy, suggests that it is intended to

[78] *ibid.*, s.15(1)(b).
[79] *ibid.*, s.15(2).
[80] *ibid.*, s.15(3).
[81] *ibid.*, s.15(4).
[82] *ibid.*, s.28(1).
[83] *ibid.*, s.3(5).

being such owners and occupiers *potentially* within the scope of the covenant rather than make them without more liable. This would then be to the same effect as the word-saving provisions of s.79(1) of the Law of Property Act 1925 (which do not apply to new tenancies[84]).[85] So, e.g. such an owner would not be bound if, apart from the Covenants Act, the covenant would not be enforceable for want of registration.[86]

17.24 This provision only applies where the owner or occupier in question is the owner or occupier of any of the premises demised by the tenancy in question. Thus, where a landlord covenants with the tenant not to allow other property owned by him to be used for a competing use, a subsequent lessee of that other property is not bound by the covenant by virtue of the provision of the Covenants Act under consideration.[87] The provision therefore necessarily has little practical application in the case of a landlord covenant: it is rare for a landlord to make a covenant with his tenant not to use the demised premises in a particular way. Moreover, in most cases, the tenant will be in occupation of the demised premises and a concurrent lessee of the reversion will be bound by the landlord covenants of the tenancy, including restrictive covenants, in any event.[88] It will, however, operate to make tenant covenants that are restrictive of the user of the demised premises enforceable by the landlord against any sub-tenants or licensees of the tenant, and against trespassers on the demised premises. Such covenants are not registrable in their own right[89] and now derive protection under the Covenants Act.

Restrictive covenants made between a lessor and a lessee are only registrable where the covenant relates to registered land other than the demised premises.[90] Where such a covenant is registered, its enforceability against owners and occupiers of that land depends on established principles relating to (freehold) restrictive covenants, not on any provision of the Covenants Act. Moreover, the fact that such a restrictive covenant made between the parties to a lease is now registrable means that even an assignee of the covenantor's interest will not be bound by the covenant under the lease unless the covenant is registered.[91]

[84] *ibid.*, s.30(4)(a).

[85] As explained in *Morrells of Oxford Ltd v Oxford United Football Club Ltd* [2001] Ch. 459.

[86] Covenants Act, s.3(6)(b).

[87] *Oceanic Village Ltd v United Attractions Ltd* [2000] Ch. 234.

[88] By virtue of Covenants Act, s.15(2).

[89] See below.

[90] Land Registration Act 2002, s.33(c). cf. Land Registration Act 1925, s.50(1), applying before October 13, 2003, and Land Charges Act 1972, s.2(5)(ii), applying to unregistered land, as explained in *Oceanic Village v United Attractions*, above.

[91] Covenants Act, s.3(6)(b); see above, para.12.07.

(b) *Exceptions*

17.25 There are two exceptions to the principles set out in this section, both of which have been seen as exceptions to the general principle of transmission of the benefit and burden of landlord and tenant covenants. First, nothing in the above provisions operates in the case of a covenant which (in whatever terms) is expressed to be personal to any person to make such covenant enforceable by or (as the case may be) against any other person.[92] Thus, e.g. a concurrent lessee of the original landlord cannot enforce against the tenant a covenant which is expressed to be personal to the original landlord.[93] Secondly, nothing in the above provisions operates to make a covenant enforceable against any person if, apart from those provisions, it would not be enforceable against him by reason of its not having been registered under the Land Registration Act 2002 or the Land Charges Act 1972.[94] Thus, e.g. a mortgagee in possession under a mortgage granted by the tenant could not enforce an unregistered covenant of renewal against an assignee of the landlord's interest (as indeed the tenant could not).[95]

[92] *ibid.*, ss.15(5)(a), 3(6)(a).

[93] *Quaere* whether the covenant could be enforced by the concurrent lessee if it was expressed to be personal to the tenant: see above, para.12.04.

[94] Covenants Act, ss.15(5)(b); 3(6)(b).

[95] See above, para.12.08.

CHAPTER 18

Authorised Guarantee Agreements

One of the principal provisions of the Covenants Act in relation to new tenancies is the automatic termination, upon a non-excluded assignment of the term of years, of the tenant's continuing contractual liability to his landlord. This provision is shored up by the anti-avoidance provisions of the Act, which (in this regard) prevent a landlord from exerting pressure on a would-be tenant to agree that his contractual liability will continue for the duration of the term,[1] notwithstanding the automatic termination provision of the Act. The price exacted by the British Property Federation for withdrawing its objection to this provision was the right in certain circumstances for a landlord to require an assigning tenant, as a condition of the grant of a licence to assign, to guarantee the obligations of his assignee. **18.01**

1. The right to make an authorised guarantee agreement

Where, on an assignment, a tenant is to any extent released from a tenant covenant of a tenancy by virtue of the Covenants Act, nothing in the Act (and in particular the anti-avoidance provisions of s.25) precludes the tenant from entering into an authorised guarantee agreement with respect to the performance of that covenant by the assignee.[2] The words "to any extent" connote a release *pro tanto* of a tenant's obligations under a covenant upon an assignment of part of the demised premises. Specific provision is made too for the case where a tenant is released pursuant to the Act upon a later lawful assignment *inter vivos* following an excluded assignment by the tenant.[3] An agreement of guarantee would, but for these provisions, be a clear infringement of the anti-avoidance provisions in so far as it purported to provide that the tenant's liability would not or **18.02**

[1] And sometimes longer: it has become quite common to see tenants (and assignees) covenanting to pay the rent, etc. during the remainder of the term granted by the lease and during any statutory continuation thereof. Express wording to that effect became necessary, if the landlord's objective was to be achieved, as a result of the decisions in *City of London Corporation v Fell* [1994] A.C. 458 and *Estates Gazette Ltd v Benjamin Restaurants Ltd* [1994] 1 W.L.R. 1528.

[2] Covenants Act, s.16(1).

[3] See below, para.18.15.

might not terminate upon a non-excluded assignment of the demised premises.

The Act is drafted in terms of release from *a* tenant covenant, and of an agreement with respect to the performance of *that* covenant by the assignee, but there is nothing in the section to suggest that the Act must be construed so as to exclude the general presumption that the singular includes the plural[4]; indeed, the general expectation must be that a tenant will be released from a whole raft of covenants, i.e. all the tenant's covenants in the lease, when he assigns the demised premises, and that therefore any authorised guarantee agreement will cover the same range of individual covenants.[5]

18.03 The provisions of the Covenants Act, entitling a landlord to have an authorised guarantee agreement, apply even in the following circumstances in which insolvency has played a part: first, even if the tenant has already made an authorised guarantee agreement in respect of a previous assignment by him of the tenancy in question, and as a result of this obligation the tenancy was subsequently re-vested in him following a disclaimer on behalf of the previous assignee; secondly, even if the tenancy in question is a new tenancy entered into by the tenant in pursuance of a previous authorised guarantee agreement.[6]

2. Meaning of "authorised guarantee agreement"

18.04 For the purposes of the Covenants Act, an agreement is an authorised guarantee agreement if three conditions are satisfied. First, it is an agreement under which the tenant guarantees the performance by the assignee to any extent of the obligation or obligations ("the relevant covenant") from which the tenant is otherwise released upon assignment.[7] Secondly, it is entered into in specified circumstances.[8] Thirdly, its

[4] Interpretation Act 1978, s.6(c).

[5] Although it could, of course, be resticted to individual covenants, e.g. a covenant to pay rent. Such a restriction would affect the question of whether the condition of an authorised guarantee agreement was lawfully imposed at all (see below), though such a limited form of guarantee agreement has not been typical of property dealings before January 1, 1996. Perhaps the only common occurrence of a similar type of requirement is a stipulation for a rent deposit as a condition of the grant of a licence to assign.

[6] Covenants Act, s.16(7). An authorised guarantee agreement may provide for a liability to take a new lease or for the original tenancy to be revested in the tenant following a disclaimer by the liquidator or trustee in bankruptcy of the assignee: see below.

[7] Covenants Act, s.16(2)(a).

[8] *ibid.*, s.16(2)(b); see below.

provisions conform with specified criteria.[9] The first of these requirements has already been considered; a closer analysis of the other two is now needed.

(a) *The specified circumstances*

The circumstances are threefold. First, that by virtue of a covenant against assignment (whether absolute or qualified) the assignment cannot be effected[10] without the consent of the landlord under the tenancy, or some other person. Secondly, that the requisite consent is given subject to a condition (lawfully imposed) that the tenant is to enter into an agreement guaranteeing the performance of the covenants by the assignee. Thirdly, that the agreement is entered into by the tenant in pursuance of that condition.[11] Thus, an authorised guarantee agreement cannot arise unless the landlord[12] lawfully stipulated for the giving of an authorised guarantee agreement as a condition of granting consent to the assignment. Except in a case where, pursuant to s.19(1A) of the Landlord and Tenant Act 1927, the alienation covenant in the lease stipulates that the landlord may require an intending assignor to enter into an authorised guarantee agreement,[13] this apparently circular rationale depends on two assumptions: that the landlord is not obliged to grant consent without the imposition of conditions at all[14]; and that a guarantee of the assignee's obligations is a reasonable condition for the landlord to impose. **18.05**

The question of whether or not a guarantee is a reasonable condition gives rise to some difficulty because, prior to the advent of "new tenancies" under the Covenants Act, no occasion for the imposition of such a condition would have arisen. This is because the tenant's contractual liability would have continued concurrently with the obligations of the assignee; or, alternatively because, in a case where the lease provided for the release of the tenant upon an assignment of the term, it would have been manifestly unreasonable for a landlord to require a guarantee contrary to the express provision for release. It is not, therefore, easy to judge the reasonableness (and therefore lawfulness) of such a condition in the light of the law as it existed and was applied prior to the Covenants Act. Of course, if the alienation covenant contains an absolute **18.06**

[9] *ibid.*, s.16(2)(c); see below.
[10] This must mean lawfully effected.
[11] Covenants Act, s.16(3).
[12] It is unclear whom the draftsman of the Act might have had in mind as being "some other person" whose consent to an assignment is required, but s.16 is unspecific as to whom the authorised guarantee agreement is to be made with; such person could include a superior landlord.
[13] As to which, see below, Ch.24.
[14] As he might be if the proposal was to assign the lease to Marks & Spencer Plc.

prohibition against assignment,[15] there is no question but that it is lawful for the landlord to stipulate for a guarantee as a condition of granting consent to that which he is not even obliged to consider. But if the covenant is qualified in the usual way, a landlord may only withhold consent to the proposed assignment, or make the grant of consent conditional on some matter, if it is reasonable to do so.

So in what circumstances will it be reasonable for the landlord to require an authorised guarantee agreement within the meaning of the Act? The difficulty is that those are, *inter alia*, the circumstances in which an agreement *is* an authorised guarantee agreement for the purposes of the Act. This question defies any exercise of mere statutory interpretation; the most that can be said in general is that the condition requiring such a guarantee will not be lawfully imposed, and the agreement will therefore not be an authorised guarantee agreement for the purposes of the Act, if the proposed assignee is such a good covenant that no guarantor could reasonably be required.[16] An authorised guarantee agreement made by a tenant in receivership is a valid agreement, and the landlord is not entitled to require the receivers to assume personal liability under the agreement.[17] The requirement that the authorised guarantee agreement be lawfully required appears to mean that a guarantor can contend retrospectively that his agreement is not valid, the requirement for such a guarantee not having been lawfully imposed, and that the intended authorised guarantee agreement is accordingly void under the anti-avoidance provisions of the Act.[18]

18.07 The third required circumstance, that the agreement be entered into pursuant to the condition imposed on granting consent to the assignment, might be construed as requiring the agreement to be entered into not later than the time when the assignment is made, on the basis that if the guarantee agreement was a true condition of the granting of consent, it should have been put in place before or at the time that the assignment took place. However, the Act does not so specify, and it is therefore considered that, provided that there is some causal connection between the landlord's consent, the assignment and the making of the authorised guarantee agreement, the precise timing should not matter.

[15] i.e. not one qualified by the words "without the consent of the lessor", or equivalent words.

[16] See *Wallis Fashion Group Ltd v CGU Life Assurance* (2001) 81 P.&C.R. 28.

[17] *Legends Surf Shops Plc (in administrative receivership) v Sun Life Assurance Society Plc* [2005] 3 E.G.L.R. 43.

[18] For these, see below, Ch.23. The requirement that the AGA be lawfully required, and the possibility of its lawfulness being reviewed, may suggest that the anti-avoidance provisions do not only apply to executory agreements.

(b) *The specified criteria*

The Act specifies both limits on the extent to which an agreement can be an authorised guarantee agreement, and matters for which an authorised guarantee agreement may provide. **18.08**

(i) THE LIMITS. An agreement is not an authorised guarantee agreement to the extent that it purports (a) to impose on the tenant any requirement to guarantee in any way the performance of the relevant covenant by any person other than the assignee; or (b) to impose on the tenant any liability, restriction or other requirement (of whatever nature) in relation to any time after the assignee is released from that covenant by virtue of the Act.[19] An authorised guarantee agreement may therefore only impose an obligation in relation to the immediate assignee's liabilities, and may not extend in its effect beyond the time of the release of that assignee pursuant to the Act. The words "to the extent that" imply that an agreement will not be disqualified from being an authorised guarantee agreement *in toto* because some of its terms infringe the limits specified; rather, the offending parts will be struck down by the anti-avoidance provisions of the Act, leaving the guarantee of the immediate assignee's liabilities to stand as the authorised guarantee agreement.[20] So, e.g. an agreement whereby the tenant guarantees the obligations of the assignee and the next immediately succeeding assignee will stand as an authorised guarantee agreement in relation to the first assignee only, and will be void pursuant to the anti-avoidance provisions of the Act insofar as it purports to impose a greater liability. **18.09**

(ii) THE PERMITTED CONTENTS. The Act stipulates four matters which an authorised guarantee agreement may do or provide for, subject to the overriding effect of the two limits set out above. These four matters are now considered. **18.10**

(A) First, it may impose on the tenant any liability as sole or principal debtor in respect of any obligation owed by the assignee under the relevant covenant.[21] The wording of this provision is surprising, for it appears to say that an authorised guarantee agreement may impose on the tenant an obligation which is in no sense the obligation of a guarantor. A liability as sole or principal debtor is not prima facie a secondary liability in the nature of a covenant of guarantee. If the "relevant covenant" is a covenant to pay the rent, it seems that an equivalent primary obligation to pay the rent may be imposed on the tenant under the authorised **18.11**

[19] Covenants Act, s.16(4).

[20] The wording of the anti-avoidance provisions of the Act (s.25(1)) is similar, and is intended to dovetail with the provisions of s.16 now under consideration.

[21] Covenants Act, s.16(5)(a).

guarantee agreement, for that is a liability in respect of the assignee's obligation to pay the rent. It might be argued that what this provision contemplates is a lesser obligation, in the sense of an obligation which is a smaller part of the whole liability of the assignee: the statutory provision is worded as an obligation owed by the assignee under a relevant covenant—a tenant covenant—of the tenancy, and the tenant might have a liability in respect of any part of the obligation owed by the assignee under that covenant. But the draftsman of the Act chose particularly opaque language if that was his intended meaning; and the Act must be taken to contemplate the case of a "guarantee agreement" relating to all the assignee's liabilities under the tenancy.[22] It is therefore difficult to see how this provision in the Act can be construed so as to exclude imposition on the tenant of a primary liability identical to the liabilities of the assignee, which liability would be commensurate with the liability of a tenant under an old tenancy save that the continuing liability would be limited to the duration of the immediate assignee's liability. Presumably, this provision was intended to entitle the landlord to extract from the tenant a covenant of indemnity, rather than of guarantee strictly so called.

18.12 (B) Secondly, the authorised guarantee agreement may impose on the tenant liabilities as guarantor in respect of the assignee's performance of the relevant covenant. These liabilities must be no more onerous than those liabilities to which the tenant would be subject in the event of his being liable as sole or principal debtor in respect of any obligation owed by the assignee under that covenant.[23] A true guarantee is a covenant by the guarantor that the principal debtor will perform his obligations; the guarantor's covenant is broken when the principal fails to perform, and the breach gives rise to a liability in damages.[24] The standard form of surety covenant in a lease goes further than this, and imposes on the surety an obligation in the event of default by the principal to pay all sums due and make good to the landlord any losses suffered by the landlord as a result of the principal's breach. This is in the nature of a covenant of indemnity and has the advantage that a claim in debt can be brought against the surety; but it is still a true surety liability in the sense that liability under the surety covenant is contingent on default by the principal.[25] In view of the wording of the statute, the more onerous surety

[22] See para.18.02 at n.5, above. Indeed, this would be the paradigm case.

[23] Covenants Act, s.16(5)(b).

[24] See *Moschi v Lep Air Services Ltd* [1973] A.C. 331, and *Cerium Investments Ltd v Evans* (1991) 62 P. & C.R. 203.

[25] And therefore such a covenant is vulnerable to defences to liability available only to sureties and not to principal debtors, such as a variation in the terms of the principal contract which could conceivably disadvantage the surety releasing the surety from his liability: see, e.g. *Howard de Walden Estates Ltd v Pasta Place Ltd* [1995] 1 E.G.L.R. 79.

covenant would be permissible, although a covenant to (e.g.) indemnify the landlord against all losses caused by the assignee's failure to comply with the covenants might well be more onerous than the liability of the assignee himself, and therefore be beyond what is permitted as an authorised guarantee agreement.

(C) Thirdly, an authorised guarantee agreement may require the tenant, **18.13**
in the event of the tenancy assigned by him being disclaimed, to enter into a new tenancy of the premises comprised in the assignment. This tenancy must be for a term expiring not later than the term of the disclaimed tenancy and whose tenant covenants are no more onerous than the tenant covenants of the disclaimed tenancy.[26] This provision, too, is oddly drafted. On a disclaimer by the liquidator or trustee in bankruptcy of an assignee (or indeed by the Crown, where the tenancy of a dissolved assignee corporation vests in it as *bona vacantia*), the tenancy is terminated, albeit deemed to remain in existence for so far as the rights and obligations of others are concerned.[27] The effect of the disclaimer is not to extinguish the liability of any other person who may have a liability under the tenancy.[28] The release of the liability of the assignee is not pursuant to the Covenants Act but pursuant to the Insolvency Act 1986, and so the liability of former tenants, whether as principal or as guarantor, would not terminate until either the landlord elected to terminate the tenancy by forfeiture or the tenancy became vested in another person who had an interest or was under some liability in relation to it.[29] Despite this,[30] the Act provides that an authorised guarantee agreement may require the tenant in the event of a disclaimer to enter into a new tenancy. The effect of this will be that the tenant assumes a new liability which, in the absence of a further assignment, will enure for the remainder of the term. In this case, therefore, a tenant's liability under an authorised guarantee agreement is apparently not limited in effect to the period of the assignee's interest in the demised premises.

(D) Fourthly, an authorised guarantee agreement may make provision **18.14**
incidental or supplementary to any provision made under (A) to (C), above. These words are wide indeed, though circumscribed somewhat by the two limits set out above.[31]

[26] Covenants Act, s.16(5)(c). This is subject to the restriction in Covenants Act, s.16(4) that no liability may be imposed by an authorised guarantee agreement in relation to any time after the assignee is released from his obligations under the Act, so if the disclaimer is after the further assignment of the demised premises by the assignee, the tenant cannot be bound to take up a new lease.

[27] *Hindcastle Ltd v Barbara Attenborough Associates Ltd* [1997] A.C. 70.

[28] *ibid.*; and Insolvency Act 1986, ss.178(4)(b), 315(3).

[29] *Hindcastle Ltd v Barbara Attenborough Associates Ltd*, n.27, above; *Re A. E. Realisations Ltd* [1988] 1 W.L.R. 200.

[30] The Covenants Act was drafted and passed before the speeches of the House of Lords in *Hindcastle* were delivered.

[31] Above, para.18.09.

3. The position of "former tenants"

18.15 In most if not all cases of excluded assignments,[32] the landlord's consent to the assignment will not have been obtained and so, one assumes, no authorised guarantee agreement will have been entered into as a condition of the grant of a licence to assign. Because the assignment was an excluded assignment, the tenant will not have been released from his covenants pursuant to the Act; but on the next non-excluded assignment of the premises comprised in the excluded assignment (or part of them), the tenant will be released (or released *pro tanto*).[33] The Covenants Act preserves to the landlord the right to require the assignor under the excluded assignment ("the former tenant") to enter into an authorised guarantee agreement (where lawful to do so) upon the subsequent non-excluded assignment of the demised premises.

18.16 So, where the former tenant is to any extent released from a covenant of a tenancy by virtue of s.11(2) of the Act[34] as from the subsequent assignment, and the assignor enters into an authorised guarantee agreement with the landlord[35] with respect to the performance of that covenant by the assignee under the subsequent assignment, the landlord may require the former tenant too to enter into an agreement.[36] That agreement is one under which the former tenant guarantees, on terms corresponding to those of that authorised guarantee agreement, the performance of that covenant by the assignee under the subsequent assignment.[37] The trigger for the right of the landlord to require such an agreement with the former tenant is thus the assignment giving rise to the release of the former tenant, or the making of the authorised guarantee agreement with the assignor, if that is later. It seems that, in this case, the right of the landlord would have to be enforced (if necessary) by injunction.

The nature of the agreement to be entered into is one under which the former tenant guarantees the performance by the assignee of the covenants from which he has become released; yet, puzzlingly, it is also on terms corresponding to those of the authorised guarantee agreement entered into between the assignor and the landlord. It having been seen that an "authorised guarantee agreement" can comprise or include an obligation in the nature of a principal liability and not just the obligation of a guarantor, it is unclear here whether the agreement to be made between the former tenant and the landlord is one of guarantee *simpliciter* (relating to performance by the assignee of the terms of the covenant from

[32] For these, see above, Ch.16.
[33] See above, para.16.05.
[34] See *ibid.*
[35] Note, not with "some other person": compare Covenants Act, s.16(3)(b).
[36] *ibid.*, s.16(6).
[37] *ibid.*, s.16(6)(a).

which the former tenant has been released), or one which mirrors the terms of the agreement already made between assignor and landlord. It is further provided that, *if* the terms of the agreement between the former tenant and the landlord comply with the requirements of the Covenants Act,[38] any such agreement is an authorised guarantee agreement for the purposes of the Act. It is difficult to see, on any basis, how the terms of such agreement could not comply with those subsections, for either the terms of the agreement "correspond" with the terms of the authorised guarantee agreement between the assignor and the landlord (in which case those subsections must have been complied with, any offending terms being void), or the agreement is just a guarantee of the obligations of the assignee under the covenants from which the former tenant has been released (which falls squarely within subs.(5)(b)).[39] In the application of s.16 to any such agreement, various provisions of that section are omitted and altered to make them fit the particular circumstances of a guarantee by a former tenant.[40]

4. The law relating to guarantee agreements generally

The Act specifically declares that the rules of law relating to guarantees (and in particular those relating to the release of sureties)[41] are, subject to its terms, applicable in relation to any authorised guarantee agreement as in relation to any other guarantee agreement. In this respect, therefore, authorised guarantee agreements are treated no differently from other guarantee agreements; authorised guarantee agreements may specifically exclude the effect of the law relating to release of sureties, just as standard guarantees of lessees' liabilities always have done, to some extent.[42] If sureties' liabilities are to be retained notwithstanding changes in the terms of the principal contract which are not self-evidently non-detrimental to the surety, clear and specific words to this effect will be needed, and some general rubric about preserving sureties' liabilities will probably not **18.17**

[38] *ibid.*, s.16(4),(5): limits and permitted terms; see above.

[39] Perhaps the draftsman was providing for the case where a landlord "encourages" a former tenant to sign an agreement which goes beyond what the former tenant is liable to sign. If so, it is unclear whether such an agreement which exceeds the terms of an authorised guarantee agreement is void as to the whole agreement, or just as to the offending parts: subss.(4) and (6)(b) do not sit happily together.

[40] Subss.(2)(b), (c) and (3) are omitted, and any reference to the tenant or to the assignee shall be read as a reference to the former tenant or the assignee under the assignment: Covenants Act, s.16(6)(c).

[41] See *Holme v Brunskill* (1878) 3 Q.B.D. 495; *Metropolitan Properties Co (Regis) Ltd v Bartholomew* [1996] 1 E.G.L.R. 82.

[42] The most common being to stipulate that the liability of the surety is not released on account of any time given to the lessee to pay.

suffice.[43] The words "subject to its terms" therefore enable the terms of an authorised guarantee agreement to exclude what would be the usual legal incidents of a contract of guarantee. But this raises questions as to whether it could be a reasonably (and therefore lawfully) imposed condition of a licence to assign that the assignor enter into a guarantee in such terms. If not a reasonable condition, the guarantee agreement is not entered into in the circumstances set out in subs.(3) of s.16 of the Act, and the agreement is not an authorised guarantee agreement to that extent.[44]

5. Guarantors of liabilities under authorised guarantee agreements

18.18 One particular issue relating to authorised guarantee agreements has troubled the property industry since shortly after the Covenants Act came into force. It is whether or not a guarantee of the former tenant's liability under an authorised guarantee agreement can lawfully be required from the guarantor of that tenant's obligations under the lease. This could be required either by being prescribed in advance by the terms of the lease as a permitted condition subject to which consent to an assignment may be granted,[45] or (where not so prescribed) by being requested by the landlord as a term of a consent actually granted. In either case, the question is the same: is such a requirement unenforceable by virtue of the anti-avoidance provisions of the Act[46] because it would have effect to frustrate the release of tenants and those with secondary liabilities from the tenant covenants of the lease? Remarkably, despite many articles written on the subject and calls for clarificatory amendment of the Act, no reported authority on the question exists more than 10 years after the Act came into force.

The reason why a landlord would want such a subordinate guarantee is easy to discern. Leases are often granted to single purpose vehicles (SPVs) that have no substantial assets other than the lease. The lease is only granted to the SPV because its substantial parent company (or other suitable person) stands as surety for the obligations of the SPV under the lease. On assignment of the lease, an authorised guarantee agreement

[43] See *Howard de Walden Estates Ltd v Pasta Place Ltd*, n.25, above, and *West Horndon Industrial Park Ltd v Phoenix Timber Group Plc* [1995] 1 E.G.L.R. 77.

[44] Covenants Act, s.16(2)(b).

[45] i.e. for the purposes of Landlord and Tenant Act 1927, s.19(1A); below, para.24.05. The contractual requirement is often bolstered by an express agreement with the guarantor to stand as surety to any AGA made by the tenant.

[46] Below, Ch.23.

made by the SPV alone would be worthless. The "value" of the SPV's covenant was only ever made up by the parent's guarantee. So it would be logical to allow the landlord to have the full value of the covenant under an authorised guarantee agreement too. But is it lawful?

The Covenants Act provides that a tenant's guarantor is released from liability under the tenancy to the same extent as the tenant is released upon an assignment of the term of years.[47] The landlord's right (in certain circumstances) to have the tenant guarantee the liabilities of the assignee under the tenant covenants is an exception to the principle of release, and as such is specifically excluded from the ambit of the anti-avoidance provisions of the Act.[48] There is no express provision in the Act for a tenant's guarantor to make a new guarantee in relation to the liabilities of the assignee. Thus, it is argued, any requirement for the guarantor to provide a new guarantee would offend the anti-avoidance provisions and be void. Certainly, this would be right in relation to any requirement for the guarantor to guarantee the liabilities of the assignee directly, i.e. a guarantee collateral to that of the former tenant, because the assignee's liability is under the tenant covenants, from which the assignor and his guarantor are to be released upon the assignment. But a requirement for the guarantor to guarantee the former tenant's guarantee, i.e. a sub-guarantee, is arguably in a different position vis-à-vis the anti-avoidance provisions. The tenant and his guarantor are only released under the Act from the tenant covenants, which by definition are those obligations of the tenancy falling to be complied with by the tenant for the time being. The authorised guarantee agreement itself is not a tenant covenant but a personal covenant of guarantee, albeit with reference to the subject-matter of the tenant covenants. A requirement for a guarantor to guarantee such a covenant does not, therefore, offend the principle that the tenant and any guarantor be released, subject to the authorised guarantee agreement itself. 18.19

The argument to the contrary is that the reason why an authorised guarantee agreement is expressly exempted from the anti-avoidance provisions is that it does preserve a liability under the tenant covenants[49]; and so a guarantee of such a liability can be said to be a liability under such covenants. But then again, it can be said that the tenant is not fully released from the tenant covenants (to the extent that he has been lawfully required to enter into an authorised guarantee agreement) and so the 18.20

[47] Above, para.17.05.

[48] Covenants Act, ss.16(1), 25(3).

[49] *ibid.* Since an AGA may impose a principal liability under the tenant covenants (para.18.11, above), it cannot be said that it does not impose on the assignor a liability under the tenant covenants, even though an AGA is a new contract.

guarantor cannot expect to be released to any greater extent. It is easy to see why commentators are divided on this issue,[50] even though a purposive construction of the Act would suggest that a sub-guarantee should not be objectionable.

[50] Some reliance has been placed on the terms of Covenants Act, ss.17(3), 18(3) as supporting the argument in favour of a sub-guarantee. It is not wholly clear that those subsections necessarily apply to the circumstances stated in ss.17(1)(a) and 18(1)(a) respectively. Alternatively, they may lend support to an argument that the anti-avoidance provisions only avoid executory agreements: see below, para.23.18.

CHAPTER 19

Forfeiture and Disclaimer

1. Forfeiture of a severed tenancy: the law for old tenancies

As has already been seen, it is possible (subject to the terms of the alienation covenant in any given lease) for the tenant to sever the term by assigning his interest in part or parts only of the premises demised by the lease, as distinct from the whole of them. The effect in law was that, in the absence of the agreement of the landlord to the severance, two or more separate tenancies of the separate holdings are not created,[1] notwithstanding an agreement between the assignor and the assignee(s) apportioning the rent. The landlord is not bound by any such apportionment, although it binds the assignor and assignee(s) *inter se*.[2] Although there is some authority for the proposition that, where parts of demised premises are physically separate from each other, a landlord may forfeit a tenancy only in respect of that part of the premises affected by a breach of covenant,[3] any such principle cannot apply in respect of non-payment of rent. It follows from the landlord not being bound by any apportionment of rent as between assignor and assignee(s) that the landlord can only forfeit the whole of the tenancy for non-payment of rent. In some cases, this may be disadvantageous to the landlord; in others, it will clearly be disadvantageous to the tenant of part who is not in default.[4] **19.01**

2. Forfeiture of part: new tenancies

The Covenants Act makes specific provision for the right of forfeiture of a severed tenancy to be exercisable *only* in respect of the part where the default has occurred. **19.02**

[1] See *Lester v Ridd* [1990] 2 Q.B. 430.
[2] Law of Property Act 1925, s.190(3).
[3] *G.M.S. Syndicate Ltd v Gary Elliott Ltd* [1982] Ch. 1.
[4] Although such a person does, by statute, have remedies against the premises of the defaulting tenant in respect of losses he suffers (Law of Property Act 1925, s.190(4)), this remedy will be illusory if the premises are forfeited and relief is not granted in respect of the defaulting tenant's premises.

(a) *The circumstances*

19.03 This right of limited forfeiture arises where three conditions are satisfied. First, a person must be the tenant of part only of premises demised by a tenancy as a result of one or more assignments. This includes an assignment in breach of covenant and an assignment by operation of law.[5] Secondly, there must be under a proviso or stipulation in the tenancy a right of re-entry or forfeiture for a breach of a tenant covenant of the tenancy. Thirdly, the right must be, apart from the effect of the new statutory provision in question, exercisable in relation to the part of the demised premises and other land demised by the tenancy.[6] Thus, the new statutory provision will not apply (and is not needed) where the right of re-entry is otherwise only exercisable in respect of the part of the premises in question. It has been seen that one of the preconditions for the operation of the new statutory provision is that the tenancy provides a right of re-entry or forfeiture for a breach of the tenant covenant in question. Thus, in the rare case where the reddendum is not reinforced by a tenant's covenant to pay the rent reserved, it is arguable that the statutory provision cannot apply, even though the proviso for re-entry is in standard terms and includes failure to pay the rent within a specified number of days of its becoming due. This is because there is no breach of covenant by the person who is tenant of part of the demised premises.[7] Also, where a proviso entitles the landlord to re-enter in the event of the tenant company going into liquidation etc. the new statutory provision may not apply because the tenant is not in breach of a covenant of the tenancy.[8]

(b) *The limitation*

19.04 Where the three conditions above are satisfied, the right of forfeiture, which would otherwise have been exercisable in relation to more than the part of the premises vested in the tenant in question, is nevertheless only exercisable in relation to that part in connection with a breach of any such covenant (for which a right of re-entry is provided) by the person who is the tenant of the part.[9] So, where part of a tenancy containing a standard tenant's repairing covenant is assigned (lawfully or not) and the assignee

[5] Covenants Act, s.28(1).

[6] *ibid.*, s.21(1).

[7] But this argument may take too narrow a view of the meaning of "covenant", for by Covenants Act, s.28(1) it includes an obligation and a condition, and the tenant is obligated to pay the rent whilst the term is vested in him independently of covenant to pay rent.

[8] But see above, n.7.

[9] Covenants Act, s.21(1).

defaults, the landlord cannot forfeit the tenancy of the part retained by the assignor.

It is not wholly clear what the position is where, in breach of the alienation covenant, a tenant assigns part of the demised premises. Under the law applicable to old tenancies, an assignment in breach of covenant is effective to vest the tenancy in the assignee, but the assignee is liable to have the tenancy forfeited pursuant to a notice served on *him* under Law of Property Act 1925, s.146.[10] Under the new statutory provision, the three preconditions apply in relation to the assignor, and so the landlord's right to forfeit appears to be limited to the part of the demised premises which remains vested in the assignor; the three preconditions also apply in relation to the assignee, but the assignee has not himself committed any breach of covenant, and so the new statutory provision does not apply to him. This curious result appears to follow: that part of the premises which remains lawfully vested in the assignor is liable to forfeiture, but the part vested in the assignee as a result of the unlawful assignment is immune from forfeiture. This result cannot have been intended. It can be avoided if "a breach of any such covenant by that person" is construed as being limited to a breach committed by a person when he has become the tenant of part only of the demised premises. Then, the breach of covenant occurred at the time when the assignor was the tenant of the whole, the new statutory provision has no application, and the whole of the tenancy is liable to be forfeited.[11] 19.05

3. Disclaimer

As has been seen,[12] a liquidator of a company or a limited liability partnership and a trustee in bankruptcy of an individual both have the power to disclaim a lease vested in the company or in the bankrupt, as the case may be, as onerous property. This power is expressly conferred in both cases by the Insolvency Act 1986. The disclaimer operates to determine, as from the date of the disclaimer, the rights, interest and liabilities of the company (or individual) in or in respect of the property disclaimed.[13] An old case decides that a lease which is vested in a company (or in a trustee in bankruptcy) cannot be disclaimed in part: it must be 19.06

[10] *Old Grovebury Manor Farm v W. Seymour Plant Hire Ltd (No.2)* [1979] 1 W.L.R. 1397.

[11] The only remaining problem is: on whom should the s.146 notice be served? On the assignor alone, or on both assignor and assignee? This difficulty is not answered by case law on old tenancies, but in principle it is submitted that it should be served on both, as the unlawful severance does not bind the landlord and there is therefore only one tenancy with, now, two tenants.

[12] See above, Ch.9.

[13] Insolvency Act 1986, s.178(4)(a), 315(3).

either wholly disclaimed or not disclaimed at all.[14] But in that case the court had not been required to decide whether a severed old tenancy could be disclaimed as to only that part vested in the company or the bankrupt. It is submitted that it must have been possible. The severance was effective to vest property in the assignee, albeit the landlord was not bound to accept two tenancies of separate holdings unless he concurred in the severance or in an apportionment of rent. If the liquidator or trustee in bankruptcy were not able to disclaim the part assigned to the company or the bankrupt, as the case may be, the statutory objective of the insolvency legislation, namely to release the company or bankrupt from onerous continuing liabilities, would be frustrated. Further, as noted, the effect of a disclaimer is not more than to release the rights, interest and liabilities of the company or bankrupt; it does not except so far as is necessary for the statutory purpose affect the rights or liabilities of any other person. The landlord could therefore continue to treat the assignor as the tenant of the whole. The same position arguably obtains where the company or bankrupt has assigned part but retained part of the demised premises, but it is then more difficult to judge whether the landlord could require the liquidator or trustee to disclaim the whole.

19.07 In relation to new tenancies, in such circumstances as those considered above, the right of disclaimer is limited to the severed part of the premises vested in the company or in the trustee in bankruptcy. The Covenants Act specifies that where a company which is being wound up, or a trustee in bankruptcy, is as a result of one or more assignments the tenant of part only of premises demised by a tenancy, the power of the liquidator or trustee under the Insolvency Act to disclaim property demised by the tenancy is exercisable only in relation to that part.[15] That provision is apposite to cover both the case where the company or bankrupt was the assignee and the case where it or he was the assignor, and it applies whether the assignment or assignments of part of the demised premises were lawful or not.[16]

[14] *Ex p. Allen, Re Fussell* (1882) 20 Ch.D. 341.
[15] Covenants Act, s.21(2).
[16] *ibid.*, s.28(1).

PART IV

Restrictions on Liability of Former Tenants and Guarantors

CHAPTER 20

Fixed Charges

Perhaps the next most significant change (after the automatic termination of a tenant's contractual liability) to the law of landlord and tenant made by the Covenants Act is that requiring a landlord to notify a former tenant and a guarantor of a former tenant promptly if he wishes to be able to look to them for the payment of sums due under a tenancy. Previously, subject to the law of limitation of actions,[1] an action against an original tenant or a previous assignee of the tenancy, or against a guarantor for any of them, might be started many years after the rent (or other sum) had accrued due and the tenant had defaulted in paying it. The former tenant or guarantor had no defence to the landlord's claim on the grounds of delay in bringing the action; he would even be liable to pay any contractual interest which had become due under the lease.[2] **20.01**

The changes made by the Covenants Act in this regard apply both to claims made against former tenants and their guarantors under old tenancies and to claims made under authorised guarantee agreements[3] or against unreleased former tenants or their guarantors[4] in respect of new tenancies. The provisions are contained in s.17 of the Covenants Act, and **20.02**

[1] Under which the limitation period for actions for rent, or for damages in respect of arrears of rent, was six years, regardless of whether the lease was made under seal: Limitation Act 1980, s.19; *Romain v Scuba T.V. Ltd* [1997] Q.B. 887. Rent includes sums payable under the lease which are reserved as rent and sums which are stated to be recoverable as if they were rent in arrears (*Escalus Properties Ltd v Robinson* [1996] Q.B. 231), and also includes sums which a guarantor becomes liable to pay upon default by the tenant: *Romain v Scuba*, above. Otherwise, the limitation period is 12 years for leases under seal, which are specialties for the purposes of the Limitation Act: see, by analogy, *Aiken v Stewart Wrightson Members Agency Ltd* [1995] 1 W.L.R. 1281.

[2] But where a lease made no provision for interest and the claim for interest is pursuant to the Supreme Court Act 1981 or the County Courts Act 1984, the court can exercise its discretion to refuse interest for the period of the delay in the landlord's bringing his action: compare *Allied London Investments Ltd v Hambro Life Assurance Ltd* [1984] 1 E.G.L.R. 62 with *Estates Gazette Ltd v Benjamin Restaurants Ltd* [1994] 1 W.L.R. 1528.

[3] See above, Ch.18.

[4] See above, paras 16.06 *et seq.*

apply only in relation to claims to sums which are defined by the section as "fixed charges".

1. Application of the new provisions

20.03 The new provisions apply where a person, called "the former tenant", is as a result of an assignment no longer a tenant under a tenancy[5] but nevertheless has a continuing liability in relation to it. This continuing liability exists either because, in the case of a tenancy which is a new tenancy, the former tenant has under an authorised guarantee agreement guaranteed the performance by his assignee of a tenant covenant of the tenancy under which any "fixed charge" is payable, or because, in the case of a new tenancy or an old tenancy, the former tenant remains bound by such a covenant.[6] In either case, there must exist a liability on the part of the former tenant in respect of a covenant under which any fixed charge is payable; the new provisions only operate to restrict the right of the landlord to recover from the former tenant or a guarantor for the former tenant a fixed charge which has become due. "Landlord" for these purposes includes any person who has a right to enforce payment of the fixed charge,[7] and therefore includes, e.g. a mortgagee in possession of the landlord's interest under a new tenancy.[8]

20.04 Section 17 does not apply where the former tenant has assigned part or parts of the premises demised by the tenancy without the agreement of the landlord and remains the tenant of another part, for here there is only one tenancy and he remains a tenant under that tenancy. It seems that the section will partially apply if the assignment of part was lawfully made with the landlord's consent and the landlord consented to an apportionment of rent; for then there are two separate tenancies,[9] and the former tenant is, as a result of the assignment, no longer a tenant under the tenancy of the part assigned. The effect of these provisions is therefore that the former tenant derives the benefit of the s.17 restrictions only if his assignment of part is lawfully made.

[5] They therefore do not apply where a landlord seeks to sue the guarantor of a tenant whose liquidator has disclaimed the tenant's interest in the premises.

[6] Covenants Act, s.17(1). In the case of a new tenancy, this will only arise because the assignment, or one of the assignments, was an excluded assignment and therefore the automatic release of the tenant from further liability under the tenant covenants did not take effect.

[7] *ibid.*, s.17(6). Despite some opinions expressed shortly before June 30, 1996, it is considered that this is not apt to include a claim by an assignor of a lease for an indemnity from the former tenant. See below, para.20.14, n.24.

[8] *ibid.*, s.15(1)(b).

[9] See *Lester v Ridd* [1990] 2 Q.B. 430.

2. Meaning of "fixed charge"

"Fixed charge" in relation to a tenancy for these purposes means any of three types of sum payable: rent, service charge, and a third category of liquidated sums. **20.05**

(a) *Rent*

Rent is not defined for the purposes of the Act, but it is clear that it here connotes a sum of money in the nature of rent payable by the tenant to the landlord pursuant to the lease or tenancy agreement. In view of the specific provision for service charge, it is doubtful whether even a service charge properly reserved by the reddendum clause of the lease is "rent" for these purposes. Equally, non-monetary services which can in some circumstances be treated as rent[10] cannot have been intended to be rent here. **20.06**

(b) *Service charge*

"Service charge" is defined by s.18 of the Landlord and Tenant Act 1985 as being an amount payable by a tenant of a dwelling as part of or in addition to the rent which is payable, directly or indirectly, for services, repairs, maintenance, improvements, insurance or the landlord's costs of management, the whole or part of which varies or may vary according to the costs incurred in connection with the matters for which the service charge is payable. That definition is adopted for the purposes of the Covenants Act, save that the words "of a dwelling" in the section are disregarded.[11] **20.07**

(c) *Liquidated sums*

This category comprises any amount payable under a tenant covenant of the tenancy providing for the payment of a liquidated sum in the event of a failure to comply with any such covenant.[12] It is not clear whether the words "any such covenant" refer to a tenant covenant of the tenancy, i.e. any such covenant at all, or to a tenant covenant of the tenancy providing for the payment of a liquidated sum, etc. It is submitted that the former wider construction is more likely, otherwise the definition is somewhat circular and the category would comprise only those covenants which, within the form of one covenant, imposed a primary obligation and also **20.08**

[10] See, e.g. *Bostock v Bryant* [1990] 2 E.G.L.R. 101, a case under the Rent Acts.

[11] Covenants Act, s.17(6)(b).

[12] *ibid.*, s.17(6)(c).

imposed a secondary obligation to pay a liquidated sum in the event of default in compliance with the primary obligation.[13] If the wider construction is the correct one, a covenant such as that to repay to the landlord any costs incurred by him in the preparation and service of a notice pursuant to s.146 of the Law of Property Act 1925 would fall within the definition of "fixed charge": the tenant covenant not complied with is that specified in the notice, and the amount payable under the tenant covenant providing for the payment of a liquidated sum is the costs of the notice. It matters not that the primary obligation and the secondary obligation are contained in different covenants. It is submitted that this is consistent with the apparent policy of the section, namely to impose a time limit for making claims against certain persons for sums of money payable under tenancies. The words "liquidated sum" do not connote a sum of money fixed and identified in the terms of the covenant, but relate to a covenant which, in its practical application, will give rise to a demand for payment of an ascertained sum, the amount of the sum depending on the circumstances in any given case. It is implicit in the operation of s.17 that, by the time the landlord serves the notice of intention to recover, the sum is (subject to any later determination of the final amount of the liability)[14] capable of being specified in the notice.

3. The restriction on liability of former tenants

20.09 Where the conditions as to applicability above are satisfied, the former tenant is not liable under the authorised guarantee agreement, or (as the case may be) under the covenant by which he remains bound, to pay any amount in respect of any fixed charge payable under the covenant unless the landlord takes certain steps.[15] These are that, within the period of six months beginning with the date when the charge becomes due, the landlord serves on the former tenant a notice informing him that the charge is now due and that, in respect of the charge, the landlord intends

[13] Such covenants are not unknown: the most common is a covenant imposing on the tenant an obligation within a specified time to carry out such works in the nature of repair as the landlord shall specify in a notice prepared for that purpose with, in case of default made by the tenant in carrying out the works, a right for the landlord to enter to do the works, and a secondary obligation on the tenant to refund to the landlord the cost of doing them: see *Jervis v Harris* [1996] Ch. 195. Although this bundle of rights and obligations is often drafted in the form of a single numbered or lettered clause amongst the tenant's covenants, it clearly need not be. If it were not, and if the narrower construction of s.17(6)(c) were adopted, the obligation to repay to the landlord would not be covered by that subclause.

[14] See below, paras 20.23 *et seq.*

[15] "Landlord", in relation to a fixed charge, includes any person who has a right to enforce payment of the charge: Covenants Act, s.17(6); para.20.14, below.

to recover from the former tenant such amount as is specified in the notice and (where payable) interest calculated on such basis as is so specified.[16]

(a) *"Any amount"*

The Act provides that the former tenant is not liable to pay any amount in respect of the fixed charge. This must include, in addition to the whole of the fixed charge itself, any interest on the fixed charge and any other costs, expenses or losses which the landlord has suffered by reason of the non-payment of the fixed charge by the tenant, and which might otherwise be recoverable from the former tenant in an action for (in the case of a new tenancy) damages for breach of the guarantee agreement, or (in the case of an old tenancy or a new tenancy where the tenant was not released) damages for breach of the covenant by which the former tenant remains bound. These would, it is submitted, be amounts "in respect of" the fixed charge payable within the meaning of the section. **20.10**

(b) *"Under the covenant"*

The section restricts the former tenant's liability under both an authorised guarantee agreement and any relevant covenant by which he remains bound. It does not restrict the right of a former tenant's assignor to sue the former tenant on any express or implied indemnity covenant by which the former tenant is bound.[17] Thus, where L is the landlord, T the original tenant (under an old tenancy), FT the first assignee (the former tenant within the meaning of the section, who gave the usual direct covenant to L to pay the rent during the residue of the term) to whom T assigned, and A the current tenant to whom FT assigned, L cannot sue T or FT for rent due from A more than six months previously unless he gave a s.17 notice to T or FT within the period of six months from the rent becoming due. But if L did give a timeous notice to T and T is subsequently held liable to L, T can seek to be indemnified by FT even though neither L nor T gave notice in time to FT.[18] This is because T is suing FT on his covenant of indemnity, and not on a tenant covenant of the tenancy under which any fixed charge is payable. The same analysis will apply in principle where the tenancy is a new tenancy if T was not released from further liability on his assignment to FT and entered into an **20.11**

[16] Covenants Act, s.17(2).

[17] *MW Kellogg Ltd v Tobin* [1999] L.&T.R. 513.

[18] In one case, FT was held liable to indemnify T even though T was not served with a valid s.17 notice before he paid the fixed charge: *Scottish & Newcastle Plc v Raguz (No.3)* [2006] EWHC 821 (Ch). At the date of publication, an appeal is pending.

authorised guarantee agreement upon FT's assignment to A.[19] In such a case, although there is no indemnity covenant implied under the Law of Property Act upon T's assignment to FT,[20] the legal effect in terms of a claim by T against FT is probably the same.[21]

(c) *"The date when the charge becomes due"*

20.12 This will be governed by the terms of the tenancy under which the fixed charge is payable. The only difficult case is likely to be in respect of the third category of fixed charges, other liquidated sums.[22] Where a landlord incurs costs as a result of the tenant's failure to comply with a tenant covenant of a tenancy, which the tenant is liable to pay, the tenant's liability to pay may arise upon the expenditure being incurred by the landlord, upon demand being made by the landlord, or upon service of a notice upon the tenant. Which of these it is must be a matter of construction of the tenancy; but it is not always easy to identify which, and time is implicitly of the essence in relation to the service of the s.17 notice.

(d) *Time for service*

20.13 The period of six months for service of the notice begins with the date when the charge becomes due. It is submitted that the corresponding date rule applies, and not the rule whereby one half of one year's notice to quit is calculated by reference to the gale days. Thus, where rent falls due on March 25, the last day of the period of six months is September 24, and not September 29 or 28. If the notice is served on the former tenant after the period of six months has expired, the former tenant is not liable under the covenant or under the authorised guarantee agreement (as the case may be) to pay any amount in respect of the fixed charge in question, or indeed in respect of any other fixed charges which became due more than six months previously and in respect of which no s.17 notice was served. Transitional provisions applied to fixed charges which became due prior to January 1, 1996.[23]

(e) *The landlord*

20.14 A s.17 notice must be served by the landlord. "Landlord" in relation to a fixed charge includes any person who has the right to enforce payment of

[19] Under Covenants Act., s.16(6).
[20] See *ibid.*, s.14.
[21] See above, para.16.08.
[22] Above, para.20.08.
[23] See below, para.20.39.

the charge.[24] So, where the landlord has assigned the reversion to an old tenancy, the assignor landlord loses the right to serve a s.17 notice as entitlement to the pre-assignment rent arrears passes with the reversion.[25] But in the case of a new tenancy, the assignor retains the right to pre-assignment rent arrears,[26] and the Act enables him (as well, apparently, as the assignee) to serve a notice after the assignment and recover the arrears of rent. As will be seen,[27] this may trigger difficulties concerning the prima facie entitlement to an overriding lease of a former tenant or guarantor who makes full payment pursuant to the s.17 notice.

(f) *Service of notice*

The Act requires a s.17 notice to be *served* on the former tenant within the specified period of time. Section 23 of the Landlord and Tenant Act 1927 is applied in relation to the service of a notice under s.17.[28] The notice is therefore validly served if it is: **20.15**

(1) served personally on the former tenant;
(2) left for the former tenant at his last known place of abode in England or Wales;
(3) sent through the post in a registered letter addressed to the former tenant at such last known place of abode, or
(4) in the case of a local or public authority or a statutory or a public utility company, sent through the post in a registered letter addressed to the secretary or other proper officer at the principal office of such authority or company.

A registered letter includes recorded delivery post.[29] The last known place of abode of a company can be its registered office.[30]

The effect of service by one of these prescribed modes is that service is deemed to have been effected if the landlord can prove compliance with one of them, even if in fact the tenant was not served at all.[31] Thus, **20.16**

[24] Covenants Act, s.17(6). A suggestion in *Kellogg v Tobin*, above, that a lessee can be a "landlord" for these purposes is surely erroneous, and the decision did not turn on this point. The contrary appears to have been decided in a county court decision: *Fresh (Retail) Ltd v Emsden* [1999] C.L.Y. 3693.

[25] Under Law of Property Act 1925, s.141(1), subject to express agreement to the contrary.

[26] Covenants Act, s.23(1).

[27] Below, paras 22.18 *et seq.*

[28] Covenants Act, s.27(5).

[29] Recorded Delivery Service Act 1962, s.1.

[30] *National Westminster Bank Ltd v Betchworth Investments Ltd* [1975] 1 E.G.L.R. 57.

[31] *Galinski v McHugh* (1988) 57 P. & C.R. 359; *Commercial Union Life Assurance Co. Ltd v Moustafa* [1999] 2 E.G.L.R. 44; *Blunden v Frogmore Investments Ltd* [2002] 2 E.G.L.R. 29.

posting of the notice by recorded delivery post is good service, even if the letter is never delivered. Moreover, in the case of service by post, service is effected when the letter is posted; the contrary conclusion is not required by the Human Rights Act 1998 and the provisions of the Interpretation Act 1978 and other provisions as to time of service have no application.[32] The risk of non-service is statutorily placed on the intended recipient of the notice.[33] A landlord may choose to serve the tenant by some other mode, and provided that the notice is received such service is perfectly valid; but the risk of non-service is then on the landlord.

(g) *Form of notice*

20.17 The Act requires the s.17 notice to inform the former tenant (i) that the charge is now due, and (ii) that in respect of the charge the landlord intends to recover from the former tenant such amount as is specified in the notice and (where payable) interest calculated on such basis as is so specified. The Act further provides that the form of any notice to be served for the purposes of s.17 shall be prescribed by regulations made by the Lord Chancellor by statutory instrument.[34] Such regulations must require any notice served for the purposes of s.17 to include an explanation of the significance of the notice.[35] If any notice purporting to be served for the purposes of s.17 is not in the prescribed form, or in a form substantially to the same effect, the notice shall not be effective for the purposes of s.17.[36]

20.18 A form for a s.17 notice is prescribed by the Landlord and Tenant (Covenants) Act 1995 (Notices) Regulations 1995.[37] It is Form 1 in the Schedule to the Notices Regulations 1995, or a form substantially to the like effect.[38] In view of the detailed information in this prescribed form, it seems unlikely that a form different from Form 1 will be held to be a form substantially to the like effect, except perhaps in the case of typographical errors in or minor inconsequential omissions from the prescribed form. Form 1 is appropriate for service on former tenants and on guarantors of former tenants.[39] The prescribed form requires details of the fixed charges in respect of which the notice is given to be set out in an attached schedule. The schedule must be in writing, and must indicate in relation to each item the date on which it became payable, the amount

[32] *Beanby Estates Ltd v Egg Stores (Stamford Hill) Ltd* [2003] 3 E.G.L.R. 85; *C A Webber (Transport) Ltd v Railtrack Plc* [2004] 1 E.G.L.R. 49.
[33] *ibid.*
[34] Covenants Act, s.27(1).
[35] *ibid.*, s.27(3).
[36] *ibid.*, s.27(4).
[37] SI 1995/2964; referred to hereafter as the Notices Regulations 1995.
[38] Notices Regulations 1995, reg.2(a)(i).
[39] For guarantors, see paras 20.36 *et seq.*, below.

payable, and whether it is rent, service charge or a fixed charge of some other kind (in which case particulars of the nature of the charge should be given).[40] Form 1 includes an optional clause dealing with interest payable on the fixed charge. In a case where no interest is contractually payable, the clause may be deleted. Where interest is so payable on the fixed charge, the schedule to the prescribed form must state the basis on which interest is calculated,[41] e.g. rate of interest, date from which it is payable, and provision of the lease or other document under which it is payable. It is not necessary to state the precise amount of the interest claimed, just the basis on which it is calculated. Where interest is contractually payable but the landlord does not claim it, it is considered that, despite the wording of the statute,[42] it is not necessary to specify in the notice the basis on which interest is due; the landlord can omit it and claim only the fixed charge. On the other hand, there is no need to specify in the schedule to Form 1 discretionary interest which will be claimed pursuant to statute[43] on any debt for which judgment is entered by the court, e.g. where there is no contractual entitlement to interest under the lease or any other document. Thus, there is no apparent bar to a landlord waiving his claim to contractual interest by not specifying it in his Form 1 notice, but claiming statutory interest on the judgment sum.[44] The prescribed form contains an optional clause dealing with the case where a fixed charge has accrued due but with the possibility that the exact sum payable will be revised to an increased amount at a later date. This aspect is considered in detail below.

(h) *Effect of notice*

Where the landlord has duly served on the former tenant a s.17 notice in the prescribed form, the amount (exclusive of interest) which the former tenant is liable to pay in respect of the fixed charge in question shall not exceed the amount specified in the notice unless (amongst other requirements) the landlord has, in the notice, warned the former tenant that the amount might be increased. If the former tenant does not, upon receipt of the notice, pay the landlord, the amount of the fixed charge and interest up to the date of judgment may be recovered by the landlord in proceedings. The notice having been duly served, there is no further bar **20.19**

[40] Notices Regulations 1995, Schedule, Form 1, n.4.

[41] See Covenants Act, s.17(2)(b).

[42] *ibid.*

[43] Supreme Court Act 1981, s.35A; County Courts Act 1984, s.69.

[44] It might be attractive to do so where base rates are lower than the court judgment rate. It may be, however, that the Court could be persuaded to exercise its discretion to refuse interest to the date of the judgment, or at least to limit it to the contractual rate, in a case where it seems clear that a landlord has sought to gain a financial advantage in this way.

on the landlord suing for the money due except the provisions of the Limitation Act 1980. Thus for rent, or for damages in respect of arrears of rent, there is a six year limitation period, regardless of whether the lease was made under seal.[45] Rent here includes sums payable which are stated to be reserved as rent or recoverable as rent in arrears.[46] The limitation period probably runs from the date on which the fixed charge originally became due,[47] and not the date on which the s.17 notice was served.[48] Where sums not properly due are included in a s.17 notice, such inclusion does not invalidate the notice in relation to other specified sums that are due.[49]

(i) *Effect of failure to serve notice*

20.20 As has been seen, the former tenant is not liable to pay any amount in respect of the fixed charge unless within the specified period the landlord serves a s.17 notice on him. Even if the landlord brings proceedings, and they are heard within six months of the fixed charge becoming due, the clear wording of the Act[50] makes the former tenant not liable unless the requisite notice has been served. If no notice has been served by the end of the period of six months, therefore, there is no liability and the landlord has no prospect of success in any action brought against the former tenant.[51]

20.21 It may be a question of some importance in day-to-day litigation whether the landlord then has no cause of action, or whether the former tenant has a defence to any action brought. Where the landlord has failed to serve a s.17 notice and brings proceedings after the end of the six months period to recover the fixed charge, it seems clear that the proceedings should be struck out, if not on the ground that the claim discloses no cause of action, then on the ground that the proceedings are an abuse of process,[52] or otherwise (in the High Court) pursuant to its

[45] Limitation Act 1980, s.19; *Romain v Scuba T.V. Ltd* [1997] Q.B. 887.

[46] See *Escalus Properties Ltd v Robinson* [1996] Q.B. 231.

[47] Or from the demand in the case of a guarantor liable to pay on demand: *Re J. Brown's Estate, Brown v Brown* [1893] 2 Ch. 300.

[48] See paras 20.21, 20.22, below.

[49] *Commercial Union Life Assurance Co Ltd v Moustafa* [1999] 2 E.G.L.R. 44, 48H.

[50] Covenants Act, s.17(2); and see *ibid.*, s.17(5), which makes a transitional provision in respect only of proceedings instituted by the landlord before January 1, 1996.

[51] *Bloomfield v Williams* (Feb. 22, 1999, unrep., CA), which did not address the subtler issues in the next paras.

[52] By analogy with a business tenant's claim for a new tenancy, where he ceases to occupy the premises for business purposes: *Domer v Gulf Oil (Great Britain) Ltd* (1975) 119 S.J. 392. Now under CPR r.3.4.

inherent jurisdiction. In principle, it is clear that the limitation on liability provided by s.17 of the Covenants Act is different from the procedural bar on bringing proceedings which the Limitation Act 1980 provides. But is the effect of s.17 to make service of a notice a necessary ingredient of the landlord's cause of action?

At first blush, this seems unlikely. The landlord's cause of action will in most cases be debt. It seems improbable that the Covenants Act should introduce a new cause of action for debts arising under tenant covenants in leases, with different ingredients from a common law action for debt, when no such cause of action was needed.[53] On the other hand, if the failure to serve a s.17 notice only gives the former tenant a defence to any claim of the landlord, two consequences at least seem to follow. First, there is no need for a landlord who brings proceedings to plead in his Particulars of Claim that a s.17 notice was served on the defendant; and the defendant could not therefore apply to strike out the landlord's action for failure to disclose a cause of action, but would have to adduce evidence in support of an application on the ground of abuse of process. Secondly, and following from the first consequence, where the six months period had not expired by the time the landlord started his action, he could correct his oversight by serving a s.17 notice before the action was heard, without any need to amend.[54] Thus, if a landlord were extremely prompt in bringing proceedings against the former tenant, the former tenant would have to await the final hearing of the action (or the expiry of the six months, if earlier) before he could be certain that the claim of the landlord would fail. In effect, the tenant would have to come to Court on the hearing of the landlord's application for summary judgment armed with affidavit evidence that, to that date, no s.17 notice had been served on him.[55] There is thus much to be said for a construction of the Act which makes service of the notice a pre-requisite to the bringing of any proceedings; but it is doubtful whether the Act achieves this.[56] **20.22**

[53] The notice requirements were considered to be procedural only in *Cheverell Estates Ltd v Harris* [1998] 1 E.G.L.R. 27.

[54] If the service of a s.17 notice is not an ingredient in the cause of action, the cause of action was already complete when the proceedings were started, and the proceedings are not invalidated by the later service of a notice.

[55] Faced with such evidence, the landlord might seek an adjournment for the purposes of serving a s.17 notice.

[56] If a landlord sued a guarantor of a former tenant in 1995 for rent falling due in 1995, the proceedings were properly constituted then. But on January 1, 1996, it became necessary to serve a s.17 notice on the guarantor by June 30, 1996 if the liability of the guarantor was to be preserved and judgment entered in the existing proceedings: Covenants Act, s.17(5). It cannot have been the intention of Parliament that such proceedings would have to be aborted and new proceedings started after service of the s.17 notice.

(j) *Liability for greater amount*

20.23 The liability of the former tenant in respect of the fixed charge is limited to the sum specified in the s.17 notice unless three conditions are satisfied. First, the amount of the liability in respect of the fixed charge must subsequently be determined to be for a greater amount[57]; secondly, the s.17 notice must have informed the former tenant of the possibility that that liability would be so determined,[58] and thirdly, within the period of three months beginning with the date of the determination, the landlord must have served on the former tenant a further notice informing him that the landlord intends to recover that greater amount from him (plus interest, where payable).[59] These three conditions must now be examined in turn, though here in their chronological order.

20.24 (1) Information in the original section 17 notice. The prescribed form s.17 notice contains an optional paragraph in the following terms:

> "4. There is a possibility that your liability in respect of the fixed charge(s) detailed in the Schedule will subsequently be determined to be for a greater amount."

A footnote indicates that the paragraph should be deleted if it is not applicable, and that, if applicable to only one or more charges of several in the schedule, the schedule should specify which. If, in the case of a schedule containing several charges only one or some of which are liable to be determined at a later date in a higher sum, the schedule does not identify which are liable to be so determined, it would seem arguable that the s.17 notice did not sufficiently inform the former tenant of the possibility, within the meaning of the Act, in respect of the one or some, because it did not sufficiently identify them.

20.25 (2) Subsequent determination for a greater amount. Note 4 in Form 1, intended for the assistance of the recipient of the notice, suggests that the purpose of the optional paragraph 4 is for cases where "the amount cannot be finally determined within six months after it is due", and then it gives some examples. The problems with the grammar of this extract, and also the difficulty with the words "his liability",[60] point up the difficulty in interpreting the requirement that "his liability in respect

[57] Covenants Act, s.17(4)(a). The paragraph refers to "*his* liability" (emphasis added), but this must be read as referring to the liability of the tenant because the liability of the former tenant has, unless and until increased by service of the further notice, been limited to the amount specified in the first s.17 notice.

[58] Covenants Act, s.17(4)(b).

[59] *ibid.*, s.17(4)(c).

[60] In Covenants Act, s.17(4)(a): see n.57, above.

of the charge is subsequently determined to be for a greater amount". The effect, if the three conditions are met, is undoubtedly that the amount of the liability of the former tenant is increased; but it is clearly not the former tenant's liability which is subsequently determined to be for a greater amount, as the examples given in note 4 of Form 1 illustrate. It is necessary to return to basics here.

The liability of the former tenant is either as guarantor of the liabilities of his assignee, under an authorised guarantee agreement, or as an original (or earlier) covenantor not released upon his assignment of the lease.[61] The person primarily liable[62] under the tenant covenants of the tenancy is the tenant in whom the term is currently vested; the former tenant is secondarily liable[63] for matters for which the tenant is liable, but the former tenant is not the tenant who has, e.g. the conduct of any rent review negotiations or process of determination.[64] What the Covenants Act is therefore seeking to provide is machinery for the landlord to preserve his right to sue a former tenant for the full amount of a charge payable under the tenancy (primarily by the tenant) in circumstances where the charge becomes payable by the tenant, but is liable to be adjusted in its amount, possibly upwards, at a date more that six months after the original charge became due. It is therefore the tenant's liability (for which the former tenant may be liable) which is subsequently determined to be for a greater amount within the meaning of the Act. The relevant questions here are: what liability; and what is "it" within the meaning of the words of note 4?[65] The only easy answer to these difficulties is that the Act has not been particularly well drafted in this respect. **20.26**

It may be the case that the machinery for service of a second notice is inapplicable in most cases. This is because in most cases, often including the two examples provided by note 4, the tenant will, as a matter of construction of the lease, be liable to pay one fixed charge when the provisional or basic sum becomes payable, and a second fixed charge in the form of a balancing or further payment (and crucially not the same charge increased but notionally due in full at the earlier time) at the later time. If he wishes to preserve his rights of recovery from a former tenant in respect of fixed charges, the landlord has to serve a s.17 notice in respect of each fixed charge within six months of that charge becoming due. If therefore, pending a determination of a rent review, the tenant is liable under the lease to pay rent at the rate passing at the review date, and is then liable upon the review having been determined to pay a further **20.27**

[61] *ibid.*, s.17(1).
[62] As between tenant, former tenant(s) and guarantor(s).
[63] See n.62, above.
[64] See *City of London Corp v Fell* [1993] Q.B. 589.
[65] See above, para.20.25.

sum in respect of the excess for the period from the review date until the date of determination,[66] there are probably two separate fixed charges payable by the tenant. One, the rent due on the quarter day at the passing rate[67]; the other, the sum by way of additional rent due when the review is determined, or on the following quarter day.

20.28 In the first edition of this work, it was suggested that whether (a) a s.17 notice warning the former tenant of a future increase in the amount of the fixed charge and then a notice informing him of the amount of the increase, or (b) two successive s.17 notices, was appropriate depended on the true construction and effect of the rent provisions of the particular lease in the factual circumstances. Only where the lease makes no provision for rent to be paid at the rate passing or for any additional rent to be paid on or after determination will it be likely to be appropriate to adopt course (a) rather than course (b). But in a recent case, it has been held that the purposes of the Act are best served by construing the Act as requiring course (a) to be adopted, even if at the time of service of the s.17 notice the rent then payable has been paid in full.[68] The effect of this is to require a landlord, as a precaution, always to serve on former tenants a s.17 notice, stating that no rent is unpaid and that the landlord intends to recover nothing from the former tenant, despite the fact that the tenant is solvent and paying the rent under the lease as it falls due.[69]

20.29 The position is similar where service charges are concerned. Most leases provide for payment on the usual quarter days of equal proportions of the estimated service charge liability for that year, with a balancing payment to become due on production some time after the end of the service charge year of the end of year accounts. In most cases, as a matter of construction of the lease, each of the four quarterly advance payments will be a separate fixed charge within the meaning of the Act; and a further fixed charge will become due on service of the year end accounts. It is submitted that a s.17 notice including paragraph 4 would be inappropriate for each of these advance payments. Only, e.g. if the lease

[66] Or until the next quarter day: both of these are the most common provisions found in rent review clauses in leases.

[67] And similarly for any subsequent quarter days which arrive while the process of determination of the reviewed rent is unconcluded.

[68] *Scottish & Newcastle Plc v Raguz (No.3)* [2006] EWHC 821 (Ch) (wrong type of s.17 notice served in respect of arrears arising from delayed rent review). At the date of publication an appeal is pending.

[69] If, instead, a s.17 notice were only served, if needed, in respect of the arrears arising from the later determination of the reviewed rent, the former tenant would not know until that later time that he was liable to be called on, since the conduct of the rent review was not in his control. It is respectfully suggested that the policy of the Act does not point strongly either way, and that the determining factor should be what the lessee agreed under the terms of the lease. It is not clear from the first instance judgment exactly what the lease in *Scottish & Newcastle v Raguz*, above, did provide.

provided that one quarter of the actual service charge expenditure should be paid on each of the quarter days falling in the service charge year, with no provision for a separate balancing payment at a later date, would it be appropriate to serve such a notice.[70]

So far as the third category of fixed charges is concerned,[71] it is possible that a tenant may become liable to pay a substantial sum by way of a liquidated debt in respect of repairs carried out by the landlord following the tenant's default in complying with a notice to carry out repairs, and that these repairs may take an extended period of time to complete. In such a case, depending on the precise wording of the tenant covenant in question, it may be appropriate to serve a s.17 notice in respect of the costs incurred to a given date, and then to serve a further notice in respect of the greater amount of costs subsequently determined on completion of the works. **20.30**

On the whole, unless the policy underlying the decision in *Scottish & Newcastle v Raguz (No.3)* is upheld on appeal, it is difficult to see that s.17 notices including paragraph 4, providing for a Form 2 notice to be served in respect of increased amounts at a later date, will be commonly used. But it is a matter of some importance to ensure that the correct procedure is used. Although a s.17 notice would not be invalid because it included paragraph 4 where that paragraph was inapplicable, a further notice in the prescribed form appropriate for such a notice[72] is unlikely to be held to be a form substantially to the same effect as the main s.17 notice,[73] and the right to recover the subsequent fixed charge from the former tenant would therefore be lost unless a Form 1 notice were also served in time. A failure to complete paragraph 4 where it is required will, however, be fatal to the recovery of any additional amount later calculated.[74] **20.31**

(3) SERVICE OF A FURTHER NOTICE. As has been seen, the Act provides that the form of any notice to be served for the purposes of s.17 shall be prescribed by regulations made by the Lord Chancellor by statutory instrument,[75] and that such regulations must require any notice served for **20.32**

[70] Such crude service charge provisions are now uncommon save in the oldest or simplest leases; much more usual is the form described previously in the text.

[71] See above, para.20.08.

[72] Form 2. See para.20.33, below.

[73] *sc.* Form 1. Form 2 does not contain a good deal of the important information for the recipient contained in the notes to Form 1, including the information about the right to an overriding lease, and information about the six months time limit for such a notice. Note that the Act itself, and not the secondary legislation, requires the prescribed form to include an explanation of the significance of the notice: Covenants Act, s.27(3).

[74] *Scottish & Newcastle Plc v Raguz*, above.

[75] Covenants Act, s.27(1).

the purposes of s.17 to include an explanation of the significance of the notice.[76] If any notice purporting to be served for the purposes of s.17 is not in the prescribed form, or in a form substantially to the same effect, the notice shall not be effective for the purposes of s.17.[77]

20.33 A form for a further notice pursuant to s.17 has been prescribed by the Notices Regulations 1995. It is Form 2 in the Schedule to the Notices Regulations 1995, or a form substantially to the like effect.[78] In view of the detailed information in this prescribed form, it seems unlikely that a form different from Form 2 will be held to be a form substantially to the like effect, except perhaps in the case of typographical errors in or minor inconsequential omissions from the prescribed form. Form 2 is appropriate for service on former tenants and on guarantors of former tenants.[79] The Form requires a schedule to be attached, setting out the details of the fixed charges which have been determined for a greater amount than that specified in the original s.17 notice. The schedule is required to indicate, in relation to each item, the date on which it was revised, the revised amount payable, and whether it is rent, service charge or a fixed charge of some other kind (in which case particulars of the nature of the charge should be given).[80] Like Form 1, Form 2 contains an optional clause for interest payable on the fixed charge, if applicable. Even if the original s.17 notice gave the required particulars of the basis on which the interest was claimed, it seems that the further notice must do the same.[81]

If the revised amount due in respect of the fixed charge is lower than the amount specified in the original s.17 notice, there is no need to serve a further notice specifying the reduced amount, but nevertheless the landlord is only entitled to recover that lesser amount in respect of the fixed charge from the former tenant.

20.34 The further notice must be served on the former tenant within the period of three months beginning with the date when the charge is determined to be in a greater amount. The date when this occurs may not always be easily identifiable, least of all to the former tenant who receives the notice. If a further notice is appropriate in the case of a rent review, and the amount of the reviewed rent is determined by an arbitrator, is the date on which the charge is determined to be for a greater amount the date on which the award is signed off by the arbitrator, the date on which it is

[76] *ibid.*, s.27(3).
[77] *ibid.*, s.27(4).
[78] Notices Regulations 1995, reg.2(a)(ii).
[79] For guarantors, see below, para.20.36.
[80] Notices Regulations 1995, Schedule, Form 2, para.4, n.4.
[81] See Covenants Act, s.17(4)(c); Notices Regulations 1995, Schedule, Form 2, para.4, n.5. For further analysis of the interest requirement, see above, para.20.18.

"published",[82] the date when the parties receive the award, or the date on which the parties execute a rent review memorandum? Which of these is the relevant date for the purposes of the Covenants Act can be of crucial importance, because time is implicitly of the essence of the requirement that the further notice be served within the specified period of three months; the statutory time limit must be strictly applied. The commentary above[83] relating to time of service and method of service apply, *mutatis mutandis*, to the service of a landlord's further notice under s.17(4) of the Covenants Act as they apply to the service of the principal s.17 notice.

Where the further notice is duly served on the former tenant, the landlord is no longer limited to recovering from the tenant the amount specified in the original s.17 notice, and the former tenant is thenceforth liable, subject to any other defence to liability which the former tenant may have,[84] for the greater amount specified in the further notice, together with any interest the basis of which is specified in the further notice. If a further notice is not duly served by the landlord, the former tenant is not liable to pay more than the amount(s) (exclusive of interest) specified in the original s.17 notice for the fixed charge(s) in respect of which that notice was served.[85] **20.35**

4. Restriction on liability of guarantors

Where the conditions as to applicability[86] are satisfied and a person, here called "the guarantor", has agreed to guarantee the performance by the former tenant of a tenant covenant of a tenancy under which any fixed charge is payable, the guarantor is not liable under the agreement to pay any amount in respect of any fixed charge payable under the covenant unless the landlord takes certain steps.[87] These are that, within the period of six months beginning with the date when the charge becomes due, the landlord serves on the guarantor a notice informing him that the charge is now due and that, in respect of the charge, the landlord intends to recover from the guarantor such amount as is specified in the notice and **20.36**

[82] For the purposes of the Arbitration Acts 1950–1979, an award was published when the arbitrator informed the parties that the award was ready for collection. Under Arbitration Act 1996, s.54, first the parties and then the arbitrator are given power to decide what is to be taken as the date on which the award is made, and in default it is the date on which the arbitrator signs the award.

[83] Paras 20.13, 20.15, 20.16.

[84] See, in particular, Ch.21, below, dealing with the restriction on liability of former tenants where the tenancy is subsequently varied.

[85] Covenants Act, s.17(4).

[86] Above, paras 20.03, 20.04.

[87] "Landlord", in relation to a fixed charge, includes any person who has a right to enforce payment of the charge: Covenants Act, s.17(6).

(where payable) interest calculated on such basis as is so specified.[88] The provisions for "guarantors" are thus identical to those relating to former tenants.[89] It is important to note that this restriction on the liability of a guarantor does *not* apply in the case of a guarantor of the existing tenant.[90]

20.37 The persons who are "guarantors" for the purposes of this provision are, in the case of old tenancies, the guarantors of the original tenants and any intermediate assignees of the lease who remain bound by privity of covenant or by the effect of s.141 of the Law of Property Act 1925; and, in the case of new tenancies, the guarantors of such former tenants who have not been released pursuant to the automatic release provisions of the Covenants Act and guarantors of former tenants' obligations where such former tenants have entered into obligations as sole or principal debtor under authorised guarantee agreements.[91] A person who, *semble*, is not a guarantor for these purposes is the former tenant who has entered into a guarantee agreement upon the further assignment of a lease by his assignee to a second subsequent assignee.[92] This is because such a former tenant guarantees the performance of the tenant covenant(s) by the subsequent assignee, i.e. the new tenant, and not the former tenant within the meaning of s.17. Indeed, such a person appears to slip through the restrictions on liability in s.17 entirely, for neither is he himself a former tenant within the meaning of that section. He has not guaranteed the performance by his assignee of the tenant covenant in question; nor does he remain bound by that covenant because, by virtue of Covenants Act, s.11(2), he is released from continuing liability upon the second subsequent assignment. This loophole may not have been intended: it imposes an unfairly onerous liability on the original assignor under an excluded assignment (as compared with that of the second assignor), who

[88] *ibid.*, s.17(3).

[89] Above, paras 20.09 *et seq.*

[90] So, a guarantor of a company in liquidation can, subject to the law of limitation of actions, be sued at any time in respect of rent, etc. not paid by the liquidator. But the position of a guarantor of a bankrupt would be different, and be governed by Covenants Act, s.17, because the statutory vesting of the lease in the trustee in bankruptcy is an "assignment" for the purposes of the Act (*ibid.*, s.28(1)), and the bankrupt is thereafter a former tenant.

[91] Covenants Act, s.16(5)(a) enables a landlord, if it is lawful to impose such a condition, to require an assigning tenant to enter into an authorised guarantee agreement under which he is liable as sole or principal debtor in respect of any obligation owed by the assignee under a tenant covenant: see above, Ch.18. It is doubtful whether a landlord is entitled to require a guarantor for liabilities under an authorised guarantee agreement (i.e. in effect a guarantor for the guarantor): see above, paras 18.18 *et seq.* Arguably, the attempt would be void as infringing the anti-avoidance provisions of Covenants Act, s.25. See below, Ch.23. Nevertheless, such guarantees do undoubtedly exist and will therefore fall within the terms of *ibid.*, s.17(3).

[92] Covenants Act, s.16(6).

is later required to enter into an agreement guaranteeing the performance of the second assignee.

20.38 The position of a "guarantor", for the purposes of s.17 of the Covenants Act, is generally identical, *mutatis mutandis*, to that of the former tenant. The commentary above[93] therefore applies equally to guarantors. Forms 1 and 2 in the Schedule to the Notices Regulations 1995 contain alternative clauses for the cases of former tenant and guarantor, and that which is inappropriate to the particular circumstances should be deleted. A s.17 notice does not, however, need to be served on the former tenant too, whose obligations the guarantor has guaranteed, before the landlord can seek to recover the fixed charge under the terms of the guarantee.[94]

5. Transitional provisions

20.39 For the purposes of the provisions restricting the liability of former tenants and guarantors for fixed charges, any fixed charge which had become due before January 1, 1996 was treated, with one exception, as having become due on that date.[95] The effect of this provision was that landlords had until June 30, 1996 to serve a s.17 notice in respect of any fixed charge which had accrued due before the Covenants Act came into force, regardless of how long before. The exception is in relation to any fixed charge which had become due before January 1, 1996 and in respect of which, before January 1, 1996, proceedings had been instituted by the landlord for the recovery from the former tenant of any amount in respect of it. In such a case, neither of subss.(2) or (3) of s.17 applied to any such charge.[96] So, where (say) rent became due on December 25, 1995 and proceedings for the rent were started against a former tenant on December 28, 1995, the landlord could continue the proceedings against the former tenant without having to serve a s.17 notice on him, and could start proceedings against a guarantor of the former tenant at any subsequent time (subject to the Limitation Act) without having to serve a notice on the guarantor at all. But if, instead of starting proceedings against the former tenant, the landlord had sued the guarantor, the landlord would have had to serve a s.17 notice on the guarantor before judgment could be entered (or by June 30, 1996 at the latest) and would have had to serve a s.17 notice on the former tenant by June 30, 1996 at the latest if he wished to preserve his right to sue him. Why there should be such a difference is wholly unclear.

[93] Paras 20.09 to 20.35.

[94] *Cheverell Estates Ltd v Harris* [1998] 1 E.G.L.R. 27. *Obiter dicta* in *City of Westminster Assurance Co Ltd v Registrar of Companies* (June 28, 1996, unrep., CA) suggesting the contrary should not be followed.

[95] Covenants Act, s.17(5).

[96] *ibid.*

is later required to enter into an agreement guaranteeing the performance of the assignee's obligations.

[illegible]

Additional protection

[illegible]

[illegible]

CHAPTER 21

Variation in Tenant Covenants After Assignment

As has already been seen, a tenancy granted by a landlord to a tenant for a term of years creates a legal estate in land as well as a binding contract between landlord and tenant. The position of the original tenant under his contract, where he has lawfully assigned the term of years, was the primary object of the reforms made by the Covenants Act. Now, under a new tenancy, where the original tenant (or a subsequent tenant by assignment) lawfully assigns the premises demised under the tenancy for the remainder of the term, he is automatically released from further liability under the tenant covenants of the tenancy.[1] In some circumstances, as we have seen, such a tenant is not released from his liability, or he may be required as a condition of the landlord's consent to the assignment to enter into an authorised guarantee agreement under which some liability is preserved. And the provisions of the Covenants Act for automatic release of tenants do not apply at all to tenants under old tenancies, whose contractual liability remains for the residue of the term. For all of these tenants, despite the restriction on liablity introduced by s.17 of the Covenants Act, whereby notice of intention to recover fixed charges from such former tenants must be served within six months of the charge having become due if their liability is to be preserved, there is the risk of liability at some future time during the residue of the term if the tenant in whom the tenancy is vested defaults. **21.01**

For most such tenants with continuing liabilities, the uneasiness about future liability was aggravated by the feeling that conduct of matters relating to the tenancy, such as compliance with covenants and negotiation of rent reviews, was out of their control, being in the hands of the actual tenant. The former tenant had put the actual tenant into his shoes so far as the future conduct of matters relating to the tenancy was concerned. In particular, it was for the actual tenant to agree with the landlord, if he so wished and if the latter concurred, variations in the terms of the tenancy, such as a widening of a restrictive user covenant. **21.02**

Until a landmark decision of the Court of Appeal in 1995,[2] there was no clear authority on the extent and nature of the liability of an original

[1] See above, paras 14.03 *et seq.*

[2] *Friends Provident Life Office v British Railways Board* [1996] 1 All E.R. 336.

tenant for matters which the actual tenant, as his assignee, had agreed with the landlord subsequently to the assignment. There were even some strong judicial pronouncements that the original tenant (or an intermediate assignee liable under a direct covenant with the landlord) was liable for anything that the assignee, as in effect his agent for all purposes relating to the residue of the term, might do or agree with the landlord to do.[3] The issue arose prominently in cases where an original tenant disputed his liability for an increased rent agreed or determined upon a post-assignment review[4]; but the same principle would arise in the case of any variation in the terms of a lease negotiated by an assignee. The principle would affect not just original tenants and intermediate assignees of the tenancy, but also guarantors for any such persons.[5]

21.03 The Covenants Act introduces, at s.18, a further reform in the law restricting the liability of former tenants or their guarantors where tenant covenants of a tenancy are varied after the assignment by the former tenant. This section applies to old tenancies as well as to new tenancies, but nothing in it applies to any variation of the tenant covenants of a tenancy effected before January 1, 1996.[6]

1. Application of the new provisions

21.04 The new provisions apply where a person, called "the former tenant", is as a result of an assignment no longer a tenant under a tenancy but nevertheless has a continuing liability in relation to it. This continuing liability exists either because, in the case of a tenancy which is a new tenancy, the former tenant has under an authorised guarantee agreement guaranteed the performance by his assignee of any tenant covenant of the

[3] "[T]he basic answer which any real property lawyer would give to a question about an assignee's power to deal with a tenancy interest is that each assignee is the owner of the whole estate and can deal with it so as to alter it or its terms. The estate as so altered then binds the original tenant, because the assignee has been put into the shoes of the original tenant and can do all such acts as the original tenant could have done": *Centrovincial Estates Plc v Bulk Storage Ltd* (1983) 46 P. & C.R. 393, *per* Harman J. at p.396.

[4] *ibid.*; and *Gus Property Management Ltd v Texas Homecare Ltd* [1993] 2 E.G.L.R. 63.

[5] Although the law of sureties entitles a guarantor to treat himself as released from his contract of guarantee where the principals, without his consent, agree a variation in the terms of the contract that he has guaranteed that could conceivably prejudice him (see *Holme v Brunskill* (1878) 3 Q.B.D. 495), the application of this rule to a case where an assignee of a lease agrees a variation is far from straightforward: see *Metropolitan Properties Co (Regis) Ltd v Bartholomew* [1996] 1 E.G.L.R. 82, discussed above, para.10.05.

[6] Covenants Act, s.18(6).

tenancy, or because, in the case of a new tenancy[7] or an old tenancy, the former tenant remains bound by such a covenant.[8] The section does not apply where the former tenant has assigned part or parts of the premises demised by the tenancy without the agreement of the landlord and remains the tenant of another part, for here there is only one tenancy and he remains a tenant under that tenancy. But it seems that the section will apply if the assignment of part was lawfully made with the landlord's consent and the landlord consented to an apportionment of rent, for then there are two separate tenancies,[9] and the former tenant is, as a result of the assignment, no longer a tenant under the tenancy of the part assigned. The effect of these provisions is that the former tenant only derives the benefit of the section applying, thereby potentially limiting any sums for which he is liable, if his assignment of part was lawfully made.

2. The restriction on liability of former tenants

Where the conditions as to applicability, above, are satisfied, the former tenant will not be liable under the covenant or under his authorised guarantee agreement, as the case may be, to pay any amount in respect of the covenant to the extent that the amount is referable to any relevant variation of the tenant covenants of the tenancy effected after the assignment.[10] **21.05**

(a) *Any amount in respect of the covenant*

The Act provides that the former tenant is not liable to pay any amount in respect of the covenant to the specified extent, and is concerned with the payment of sums of money due under the tenant covenant of the tenancy by which he remains bound or which he has guaranteed. The wording is wide enough to include, in addition to the principal sum due under the covenant itself, any interest on that sum and any other costs, expenses or losses which the landlord has suffered by reason of the non-payment or non-performance by the tenant, and which might otherwise be recoverable from the former tenant in an action for (in the case of a new tenancy) damages for breach of the guarantee or (in the case of an old tenancy or a new tenancy where the tenant was not released) damages for breach of the covenant by which the former tenant remained bound. **21.06**

[7] In the case of a new tenancy, this will only be because the assignment, or one of the assignments, was an excluded assignment and therefore the automatic release of the tenant from further liability under the tenant covenants did not take effect.

[8] Covenants Act, s.18(1).

[9] See *Lester v Ridd* [1990] 2 Q.B. 430.

[10] Covenants Act, s.18(2).

These are, it is suggested, amounts "in respect of" the covenant within the meaning of the section.

(b) *To the extent that*

21.07 Unlike the common law principle whereby sureties may be wholly released from their obligations as sureties by a variation in the principal contract,[11] s.18 of the Covenants Act only provides for the restriction of a former tenant's liability if and insofar as that liability has been increased by the variation in question. To that extent only, and no further, the former tenant is not liable under the covenant; but he remains liable for any sum which is not referable to such variation, i.e. he is liable to the same extent that he would have been had there been no such variation if the liability has not thereby been increased. Although the Act uses the phrase "referable to" any relevant variation, it seems clear that it is concerned with increases in the amount payable under the covenant caused by a relevant variation. Where a relevant variation in the tenant covenants of the tenancy has resulted in (e.g.) a lower rent becoming payable, in one sense the lower rent is an amount referable to the variation, but it is doubtful whether Parliament intended the word "referable" to bear this wider meaning.

(c) *Any relevant variation*

21.08 In s.18, "variation" means a variation whether effected by deed or otherwise.[12] This definition is wide enough to include a variation made by oral agreement, if such may be achieved in law. An oral tenancy agreement may be so varied; but an agreement which, as a matter of law, is required to be made in writing or by deed, or evidenced by writing, cannot be varied (as opposed to rescinded) otherwise than by writing.[13] It is now established that an agreement made by deed can be varied by a written document not under seal.[14] The variation with which the Act is here concerned is a variation of "the tenant covenants of the tenancy". Such covenants are those covenants falling to be complied with by the

[11] See above, n.5.

[12] Covenants Act, s.18(7).

[13] *Goss v Lord Nugent* (1833) 5 B. & Ad. 58; *Morris v Baron & Co.* [1918] A.C. 1. This requirement is effectually preserved in relation to contracts for the disposition of an interest in land required to be made in writing under Law of Property (Miscellaneous Provisions) Act 1989, s.2, by the decision of the Court of Appeal in *McCausland v Duncan Lawrie Ltd* [1997] 1 W.L.R. 38. See also *Kilcarne Holdings Ltd v Targetfellow (Birmingham) Ltd* [2005] 2 P.&C.R. 8.

[14] *Mitas v Hyams* [1951] 2 T.L.R. 1215; *Berry v Berry* [1929] 2 K.B. 316.

tenant for the time being of premises demised by the tenancy.[15] The use of the plural is deliberate. The section applies where the former tenant has guaranteed the performance of or remains bound by "any tenant covenant", and it is with liability in respect of or under that covenant which the section is concerned. But the section restricts liability in respect of or under *that* covenant where there has been a relevant variation in *any* of the tenant covenants effected at the specified time, i.e. not just in the particular covenant under which the liability of the former tenant arises. The restriction on liability is to the extent that liability under the particular covenant has been increased by a variation in any of the tenant covenants. One example would be where the rent on review is higher than it would otherwise be as a result of a variation whereby a restrictive user covenant was relaxed. Provided that the variation is a "relevant variation" within the meaning of the Act and is effected after the assignment by the former tenant, the former tenant is not liable under or in respect of the covenant to pay rent to the extent that the rent has been increased above what would otherwise have been payable. The practical difficulties arising from this and other instances are considered below.

For the purposes of s.18 of the Covenants Act, a variation of the tenant covenants of a tenancy is a "relevant variation" if either of the following two conditions are satisfied. **21.09**

(i) RIGHT TO REFUSE. The first of these conditions is if the landlord has, at the time of the variation, an absolute right to refuse to allow it.[16] Thus, using the example given above, if the restrictive user covenant is not qualified by words such as "not without the consent of the landlord which consent shall not be unreasonably delayed or withheld", the landlord would have an absolute right to refuse to allow any request by the tenant for a variation in the covenant, for no such qualification is implied by statute.[17] But if the qualifying words were present in the covenant, the landlord would only have the right to refuse the tenant's application if, at the time, it would be reasonable to do so.[18] It is perhaps doubtful whether this first condition is satisfied if, in any given case, it would in fact at the time have been reasonable for the landlord to have **21.10**

[15] Covenants Act, s.28(1). "Covenant" is given a wide definition by the same subsection, and includes obligations in a collateral agreement. The use of "tenant covenants", as defined, avoids the difficult conceptual argument whether it is the lease itself which is varied by a variation agreed between the landlord and an assignee of the term, or merely the assignee's contract.

[16] *ibid.*, s.18(4)(a).

[17] See Landlord and Tenant Act 1927, s.19(3).

[18] Case law has defined this as meaning that a reasonably minded landlord could take the view that consent should be withheld. It is therefore necessary for the tenant to prove that any reasonable landlord would have given consent if it is to be adjudged to have been unreasonably withheld. See, generally, Woodfall, *Law of Landlord and Tenant* (28th (looseleaf) ed.), para.11.141.

withheld his consent, and not just if the covenant was unqualified. In that sense, too, the landlord had an absolute right to refuse. The Act states that, in determining whether the landlord has or would have had such a right at any particular time, regard should be had to all the circumstances, including the effect of any provision made by or under any enactment.[19]

21.11 The difference between these rival interpretations lies in a case where the covenant is qualified, where it is reasonable for the landlord to refuse his consent, but where he does nevertheless gives his consent. If the test is merely whether the covenant is unqualified, the variation, if effected, is not a relevant variation for the purposes of s.18 because the covenant was qualified. But if the test is whether in the particular case the landlord could lawfully have withheld his consent, the variation is a relevant variation for those purposes because the landlord could lawfully have withheld consent but nonetheless gave it. It seems likely that the latter was the intention of Parliament, and that a variation made by a landlord when it was reasonable to refuse to allow it is a relevant variation.[20]

21.12 The purpose of the definition of "relevant variation" was presumably to exclude those variations to which the landlord had legally to consent; they were variations already provided for in advance by the terms of the tenant covenant by which the former tenant agreed to be bound and he, by assigning his lease, chose to put his assignee into the position where that provision could be exploited. Although in such a case the landlord does not have an absolute right of refusal, in the sense that he must consider whether or not it is reasonable to refuse his consent, at the time when the variation was made he had as a matter of law either the right to refuse or the duty to consent. It is that time to which the first condition is directed. To exclude from the definition those variations where the landlord could reasonably have withheld consent, but chose not to, would significantly limit the protection which s.18 is seeking to afford the former tenant; for in an extreme case it makes no legal difference whether a covenant is qualified or absolute: the landlord in both cases is clearly entitled to refuse. It is the use of the word "absolute" which creates doubt here, but it is considered that the direction to have regard to all the circumstances including statutory provision sufficiently clearly indicates that reasonableness of refusal is brought into play. In some cases, statute overrides even covenants which, in terms, give the landlord an absolute

[19] Covenants Act, s.18(5).

[20] There is an intellectual difficulty with this first condition: in a case where, on its facts, some landlords would reasonably have refused to allow the variation, but others, including the actual landlord, would have agreed to make it, can it be said that there was an "absolute right" to refuse it on the basis that some, but not all, would have done so?

right to refuse.[21] But the effect is that where the former tenant is sued for rent arrears and raises a s.18 defence that the rent was increased by a relevant variation, the courts will be required to embark on a collateral inquiry, namely whether in all the circumstances the landlord could reasonably have withheld his consent to the variation at the time, before it assesses the extent (if any) to which the reviewed rent was attributable to such variation.[22] This in itself may suggest that Parliament had a more limited protection in mind.

(ii) PRIOR VARIATION DEPRIVED LANDLORD OF RIGHT TO REFUSE. The second condition is supplementary to the first. The "relevant variation" test is satisfied if the landlord would have had an absolute right to refuse to allow the variation if the variation had been sought by the former tenant immediately before the assignment by him but, between the time of that assignment and the time of the variation, the tenant covenants of the tenancy have been so varied as to deprive the landlord of such a right.[23] This second condition extends the first by attempting to cover the situation where the first condition was not satisfied by reason of an earlier variation of the tenant covenants of the tenancy, made after the assignment by the former tenant but before the relevant variation. It prevents a two-stage variation of the tenant covenants which would have had the effect of circumventing the protection which s.18 was intended to afford a former tenant. It clearly covers the case where (e.g.) an unqualified covenant restricting the use of the demised premises is first qualified by the use of the standard words of qualification, and then varied again to permit a different use or wider class of uses. By the time of the second variation, the landlord had divested himself of his absolute right to refuse to allow any variation. But the Act requires one to look at the time immediately before the former tenant's assignment, when the covenant was unqualified and when the landlord had an absolute right to refuse to allow the second variation, because the tenant covenants of the tenancy were so varied by the first variation as to deprive the landlord of that right. **21.13**

The condition is more difficult to apply, however, where the covenant was, before the assignment, subject to a proviso that consent could not be unreasonably withheld, and then, after the assignment, was varied, e.g. by stipulating particular circumstances in which consent could not be withheld. Where the landlord then further varies the covenant by permitting a different use in the circumstances in which his consent could not be withheld, the first question is whether, if the covenant had **21.14**

[21] *e.g.* Landlord and Tenant Act 1927, s.3; Fire Precautions Act 1971, s.28; Disability Discrimination Act 1995, s.16.

[22] As to which, see para.21.20, below.

[23] Covenants Act, s.18(4)(b).

remained a standard qualified covenant, the landlord would have been obliged to consent to the second variation. If so, the landlord was not in fact deprived of the right to refuse to allow the second variation because he would have been bound to consent anyway; if not, the first variation did deprive him of the right to refuse to allow the second, but the question then is whether, if the second variation had been sought by the former tenant immediately before the assignment by him when the covenant was qualified, the landlord could at *that* time reasonably have withheld consent. Such a case may therefore call for inquiry into what the position would have been, but for the first variation, both at the time of the second variation and at the time of the assignment by the former tenant. The latter requires inquiry into circumstances which *ex hypothesi* did not arise; and at that time the surrounding circumstances in which the variation was hypothetically sought might have been quite different from those which obtained when the second variation was in fact sought. If it would have been unreasonable to refuse the variation at the earlier time, the second variation is not a relevant variation within the definition in s.18 because the landlord would not at the earlier time have had the right to refuse to allow the second variation.

3. The restriction on guarantors' liability

21.15 At common law, a surety will generally be released from all liability under his contract of guarantee where there is a variation in the terms of the principal contract, made without his consent, in such circumstances that it is not self-evident without factual inquiry that the variation cannot prejudice him.[24] The Covenants Act does not in any way affect the application of this principle,[25] but it provides an additional restriction on the liability of a guarantor of a former tenant where such a person is not wholly released from his liability by a variation of the principal contract. The restriction is of a different type from the common law release referred to, but is directly analogous to the restriction on liability of a former tenant just considered.[26] Like that restriction, it applies alike to guarantors of former tenants under old and new tenancies, though only in respect of variations of the tenant covenants of a tenancy effected on or after January 1, 1996.

21.16 Where the conditions as to applicability relating to the former tenant[27] are satisfied, a person ("the guarantor") who has agreed to guarantee the performance by the former tenant of a tenant covenant of the tenancy will

[24] *Holme v Brunskill* (1877) 3 Q.B.D. 495.

[25] Which may not in any event operate so clearly in the case of a guarantor of a former tenant of a lease which has been assigned: see *Metropolitan Properties Co (Regis) Ltd v Bartholomew* [1996] 1 E.G.L.R. 82.

[26] Above, paras 21.05 to 21.14.

[27] Above, para.21.04.

(where his liability to do so is not wholly discharged) not be liable under the agreement to pay any amount in respect of the covenant to the extent that the amount is referable to any relevant variation of the tenant covenants of the tenancy effected after the assignment.[28] These provisions for "guarantors" are identical to those relating to former tenants previously discussed,[29] and the commentary there applies, *mutatis mutandis*. It is important to note that this restriction on the liability of a guarantor does *not* apply in the case of a guarantor of the existing tenant.

The persons who are "guarantors" for the purposes of this provision are, in the case of old tenancies, the guarantors of the original tenants and any intermediate assignees of the lease who remain bound by privity of covenant, or by the effect of s.141 of the Law of Property Act 1925; and, in the case of new tenancies, the guarantors of such former tenants who have not been released pursuant to the automatic release provisions of the Covenants Act.[30] A guarantor for the actual tenant does not fall within the statutory provision, and his protection must come, if at all, from the application of the rule in *Holme v Brunskill*.[31] Another person who is not a guarantor for these purposes is the former tenant who has entered into a guarantee agreement upon the further assignment of a lease by his assignee to a second, subsequent assignee.[32] This is because such a former tenant guarantees the performance of the tenant covenant(s) by the subsequent assignee, i.e. the new tenant, and not the former tenant within the definition in s.18 of the Covenants Act. Indeed, such a person appears to slip through the restrictions on liability in s.18 entirely, for neither is he himself a former tenant within the meaning of that section. He has not guaranteed the performance by his assignee of the tenant covenant in question; nor does he remain bound by that covenant because, by virtue of s.11(2) of the Covenants Act, he is released from continuing liability upon the second subsequent assignment. **21.17**

It is important to note that the only "relevant variations" which can have the effect of restricting the guarantor's liability are variations of the tenant covenants[33] of the tenancy effected after the assignment by the former tenant. These are, by definition, those covenants falling to be complied with by the actual tenant, i.e. the assignee of the former tenant. Such variations are, however, those which will, insofar as they increase any monetary liability of the tenant, give rise to the equivalent statutory **21.18**

[28] Covenants Act, s.18(3).

[29] Above, paras 21.05 to 21.14.

[30] There appears to be a difference in wording in Covenants Act, s.18(3) as compared with *ibid.*, s.17(3), which would exclude protection under these provisions for any guarantor of a former tenant's AGA: an AGA is not a tenant covenant of the tenancy. See above, para.20.37.

[31] See above, n.24.

[32] Pursuant to Covenants Act, s.16(6).

[33] See n.15, above.

restriction on the former tenant's liability.[34] The guarantor's liability falling within the statutory provisions can only be a liability secondary to that of the former tenant, and so if the former tenant's liability is restricted by the Act, the guarantor's is of necessity limited too, and the express statutory provision for guarantors may be superfluous. Furthermore, if the surety is otherwise potentially liable for an increased amount in respect of a tenant covenant of the tenancy the performance of which he has guaranteed, it is difficult to see how he could not be released from liability under the rule in *Holme v Brunskill*.[35] One possible reason why that rule would not apply is that the surety has consented to the variation, but then can he possibly avail himself of the statutory restriction? It is surely implicit in the drafting of s.18 of the Covenants Act that the former tenant or guarantor (as the case may be) has not agreed to the relevant variation which was made after the assignment by the former tenant. Another possibility is that the surety for the former tenant is not released under the rule in *Holme v Brunskill*[36] because the variation is of the obligations of the assignee, and not of the obligations of the former tenant, which are enshrined in a separate contract[37]; but even then the variation is of a "tenant covenant" for the purposes of the Act, and so the former tenant's liability would itself be restricted under the Act, thereby restricting the guarantor's liability to an equivalent extent.

4. Practical implications

21.19 The restrictions on liability effected by s.18 of the Covenants Act are concerned with additional money payable under a tenant covenant by reason of a relevant variation. Such amounts are likely to fall into four categories: rent, service charge and insurance moneys, interest, and other specific sums payable.

(a) *Rent*

21.20 The amount payable as rent under a standard commercial lease is generally fixed for five-year periods during the term of the lease. A relevant variation in the terms of the lease will therefore not affect the amount of rent payable until the next review is determined or, in the absence of rent reviews, at all. Upon a rent review, the rent will generally be determined upon the basis of the varied terms of the actual tenancy,

[34] Under Covenants Act, s.18(2).
[35] Above, n.24.
[36] Above.
[37] See *Metropolitan Properties Co. (Regis) Ltd v Bartholomew* [1996] 1 E.G.L.R. 82.

unless either the review clause stipulates some other hypothesis or the variation is expressed to be a term personal to the particular assignee. If the rent is determined at a rate higher than it would have been but for the relevant variation, the former tenant and any guarantor of a former tenant will not be liable for the extra amount. But that extra amount will rarely be quantified by the rent review process. The amount of the former tenant's or guarantor's liability will therefore be undetermined and, except to the extent of the previous rental level in the case of an "upwards only" rent review clause, there will be no straightforward debt claim available to the landlord against the former tenant or guarantor. There is no authority for the proposition that the rent can or should be reviewed *de novo* and on different terms as between a former tenant (much less a guarantor) and the landlord; but there is some authority for the court intervening to prevent a breakdown in the machinery which has been put in place.[38] In truth, the machinery has not broken down, because the rent review as between the tenant and the landlord has taken place; what has to be determined is the cap on the former tenant's or guarantor's liability pursuant to the provisions of the Act. The court will have to determine the amount at which the reviewed rent would have been agreed or determined but for the relevant variation.

An alternative analysis is that the landlord is entitled to recover the rent **21.21** from the former tenant or guarantor except to the extent of the overage attributable to the relevant variation, and that the onus of proof in respect of that exception is on the defendant.[39] This would have the advantage of enabling straightforward debt proceedings to be issued and might be justifiable in the majority of cases where, perhaps, a variation has no impact on the level of market rent agreed or determined upon review. The former tenant or guarantor would, in effect, have to accept liability for the full amount of the rent or have the courage to advance a case based on a specified amount of overage. By doing so, and absent any other defence, liability would be admitted for some quantified part of the landlord's claim, and the landlord could then elect, at risk of costs, whether to pursue the action for the overage. It is submitted that this analysis presents a simple and workable system for dealing with what might be a sizeable number of such claims which will be brought in the county courts and in the High Court. Whether it is an approach that will be adopted by the courts must await future resolution. It would, to some extent, mark a departure from the traditional rigour with which the courts expect a claim against a guarantor to be established and proved.

[38] *R & A Millett (Shops) Ltd v Leon Allan International Fashions Ltd* [1989] 1 E.G.L.R. 138.

[39] As is common where a person relies on a statutory exception or exclusion.

(b) *Service charge and insurance*

21.22 So far as service charge and insurance moneys are concerned, it might be expected that service charge liability will, of its nature, identify specific sums expended by the landlord in respect of particular services or works, with the result that any additional expenditure incurred in relation to a variation in the tenant covenants (e.g. a redistribution as between landlord and tenant of liability for repairs and decorations) can be identified. In other cases, however, and in particular with lump sum insurance monies, it will not prove possible to exclude sums specifically attributable to the relevant variation, and in principle the way of dealing with rental increases discussed above could apply.

(c) *Interest*

21.23 Interest is, by its nature, a contingent liability, and its incidence in any given case will depend on the amount and nature of the principal debt. It should, therefore, present no additional difficulty in practice beyond the complicated arithmetic to which litigants in this field have long since become accustomed.

(d) *Other sums*

21.24 So far as other specific sums are concerned, it is difficult to generalise, but these may be either sums solely attributable to provisions of the tenancy which are relevant variations, or they may be sums increased by relevant variations (e.g. the cost of compiling a schedule of dilapidations or of reinstating premises at the end of the term) beyond the amounts which would otherwise have been due. Difficulties are only likely to arise in the latter category.

21.25 Despite some judicial hesitation on this subject, the liability of a former tenant or of a guarantor for a former tenant is only, as from the time of the assignment by the former tenant, based on the contract made by that former tenant, and is not a liability under the terms of the lease or tenancy agreement itself regardless of how much those terms may subsequently be varied.[40] If an assignee agrees subsequently to the assignment to be bound by new obligations, there is no doubt but that the former tenant (and hence any surety for such former tenant) is not liable in respect of such obligations. But if the assignee and the landlord agree variations in one or some tenant covenants which have the effect of increasing the liability under or of making more onerous the performance of other covenants by which the former tenant is bound (such as the liability under covenants to

[40] See *Friends Provident Life Office v British Railways Board* [1996] 1 All E.R. 336.

pay the rent and to keep the demised premises in repair, respectively), it was unclear before January 1, 1996 whether the liability of the former tenant on his covenants extended to any such increased or more onerous obligations.[41] Thus, the new statutory provisions in s.18 of the Covenants Act might not radically have altered the law relating to former tenants' and their guarantors' liability under tenant covenants, but they have established that, in respect of relevant variations effected on or after January 1, 1996 at least, such liability does not extend to any increase in amount in covenanted payments referable to such variations.

[41] Although persuasive *dicta* from the Court of Appeal suggest that the former tenant would not be liable for any increased liability: see *Metropolitan Properties Co (Regis) Ltd v Bartholomew* [1996] 1 E.G.L.R. 82, *per* Millett L.J.

CHAPTER 22

Overriding Leases

For the further protection of former tenants and their guarantors who are called upon to make payments to the landlord in respect of fixed charges payable under tenant covenants of a tenancy, the Covenants Act gives such persons the right to call for the grant of an overriding lease of the premises demised by the tenancy. The provisions of the Covenants Act for the grant of an overriding lease in such circumstances apply, as from January 1, 1996, in the case of both old and new tenancies. An overriding lease is a concurrent lease of the demised premises granted by the landlord; it makes the former tenant or guarantor the immediate landlord of the defaulting tenant. In effect, it gives the former tenant or guarantor the opportunity to take steps, if he thinks fit, to terminate the tenancy of the defaulting tenant, and to occupy the demised premises himself, or to re-market them to a new tenant; alternatively, it gives the former tenant or guarantor the right to exercise or threaten to exercise the more extensive remedies for non-payment of rent or other money due under tenant covenants which are available to a landlord. Once the overriding lease is granted, the former tenant or guarantor, as the immediate reversioner of the demised premises entitled to the rents and profits, is entitled to enforce the tenant covenants of and any right of re-entry contained in the tenancy.[1] **22.01**

1. Meaning of "overriding lease"

For the purposes of the Covenants Act, "overriding lease" means a tenancy of the reversion expectant on the relevant tenancy, which is granted for a term and contains provisions as stipulated in the Act.[2] The relevant tenancy is any tenancy in respect of which the former tenant or his guarantor ("the claimant") makes a payment of a fixed charge pursuant to s.17 of the Covenants Act.[3] The premises demised by the overriding lease are the same premises as are demised by the relevant tenancy.[4] **22.02**

[1] By virtue of Law of Property Act 1925, s.141 in relation to old tenancies, and Covenants Act, s.15(1) in relation to new tenancies.

[2] Covenants Act, s.19(2).

[3] *ibid.*, s.19(1); for detailed commentary on s.17, see Ch.20, above.

[4] *ibid.*

(a) *Term*

22.03 An overriding lease is granted to the claimant for a term equal to the remainder of the term of the relevant tenancy plus three days; or, if that term will wholly displace the landlord's reversionary interest expectant on the relevant tenancy,[5] for a term equal to the remainder of the term of the relevant tenancy plus the longest period less than three days that will not wholly displace that interest, as the case may require.[6] Thus, if the landlord's reversion extends for two days only beyond the termination date of the relevant tenancy, the overriding lease will be for the remainder of the term of the relevant tenancy plus one day; and possibly, in the case of a one-day reversion, for the remainder plus one half of one day, although the law does not generally have regard to parts of a day. There may be difficulties here in the event of the landlord's reversion being a nominal one, because, as will be seen, there can in principle be a number of successive overriding leases, though only one granted by each landlord.[7]

(b) *Provisions*

22.04 Subject to the exceptions considered below and to any modifications which may be agreed by the claimant and the landlord, the overriding lease contains the same covenants as the relevant tenancy, as they have effect immediately before the grant of the overriding lease.[8] Thus, apart from the exceptions and any agreed modifications, the overriding lease will be, *mutatis mutandis*, in the same terms as the terms of the relevant tenancy effective at the date of grant. The exceptions are as follows.

22.05 (i) PERSONAL COVENANTS. The overriding lease is not required to reproduce any covenant of the relevant tenancy to the extent that the covenant is, in whatever terms, expressed to be a personal covenant between the landlord and the tenant under that tenancy.[9] Unlike the similar provision of the Covenants Act for personal covenants in relation

[5] i.e. because the landlord only has three days' or fewer reversion beyond the end of the relevant tenancy.

[6] Covenants Act, s.19(2)(a).

[7] Below, para.22.19.

[8] Covenants Act, s.19(2)(b). Although the Act refers to "any modifications" agreed, it might be thought that there comes a point when the modifications are so extensive that it can no longer truly be said that the new lease granted was an overriding lease granted pursuant to the Act. If this is correct, what would otherwise be an old tenancy might in law be a new tenancy: for this, see below, para.22.11.

[9] *ibid.*, s.19(3).

to the transmission of covenants,[10] this provision in relation to overriding leases is qualified by the words "to the extent that"; perhaps this is to make it clear that a part of a single covenant, which part only is expressed to be personal, may be excised for the purposes of the overriding lease.[11] There is a further difference in wording from the provision in relation to transmission of covenants: that provision makes unenforceable against any other person a covenant which is expressed (in whatever terms) to be personal to *any person*; this provision for overriding leases is in relation to a covenant which is expressed (in whatever terms) to be a personal covenant between the landlord and the tenant under the relevant tenancy. This seems to be a different test, but it is unclear how, if at all, this will differ in its practical application.[12]

What is clear is that, for the covenant of the relevant tenancy not to become incorporated in the overriding lease, it must be *expressed* in some way to be personal between landlord and tenant. Under the law applying to old tenancies, covenants which did not touch and concern the demised premises or the reversion, as the case may be, did not bind successors in title of the covenantor and could not be enforced by successors in title of the covenantee. There are essentially three types of such covenants. First, those that are expressed to be personal. Such covenants need not use the word "personal": e.g. "for so long as the landlord is the XYZ Corporation, the tenant will not sell lemons at the demised premises" is a covenant expressed to be personal because the benefit of it is limited to the covenantee.[13] Secondly, those that by their very nature are personal, although not expressed in any terms to be so, e.g. "the tenant will sing holy mass at least once a week at the Church of St Radegund, Dillchester". These two types of covenant do not touch and concern the reversion in the demised premises because they are of personal interest to the particular covenantee only.[14] But a third type of covenant, although **22.06**

[10] *ibid.*, s.3(6)(a); see above, para.12.03.

[11] It is difficult to see why, in principle, the Act should provide for a different effect for assignees than for overriding lessees.

[12] Arguably, a covenant which is expressed, in whatever terms, to be personal to one of the parties to the tenancy (and so is capable of binding successors in title of the other) will not satisfy this test: see *System Floors Ltd v Ruralpride Ltd* [1995] 1 E.G.L.R. 48 for the effect, under the law relating to old tenancies, of covenants personal to one party.

[13] Similarly, a covenant by the tenant "here meaning XYZ Corporation only" is expressed to be personal: cf. *Max Factor Ltd v Wesleyan Assurance Society* (1996) 74 P.&C.R. 8 (break clause exercisable by "the Lessee here meaning Max Factor only").

[14] See *First Penthouse Ltd v Channel Hotels and Properties (UK) Ltd* [2004] 1 E.G.L.R. 16 (personal covenant in collateral agreement to pay commission to third party).

not obviously personal in that sense, nevertheless does not touch and concern the demised premises or the reversion, e.g. a landlord's covenant which benefits only the advantageous carrying on of a particular trade on the demised premises and does not benefit the demised premises per se,[15] and a landlord's covenant to sell the reversion or to give the tenant a right of first refusal.[16] None of these three types of covenant was capable of binding successors in title of the covenantor or of being enforced by successors in title of the covenantee under the previous law.

22.07 It appears likely, therefore, that only covenants of the first type outlined above will fall within the words "... is (in whatever terms) expressed to be a personal covenant ...", and so will not be duplicated in the overriding lease. It is considered that only covenants that either specifically state that they are personal to a given person, or in terms limit their applicability to the interest of a given person, can be said to be expressed in any terms to be personal, though any express terms conveying such intention will suffice.[17] The second and third types of covenant identified above cannot truly be said to be expressed in any terms to be personal. It seems,.therefore, that covenants that under an old tenancy would not bind or be enforceable by successors in title of the original parties may yet become terms of an overriding lease. Of course, where a claimant is entitled to call for an overriding lease, there must have been an assignment of the tenancy by the original tenant, and so any personal covenants made between the original parties will no longer be enforceable under the relevant tenancy immediately before the grant of the overriding lease; but new personal covenants could have been created upon the assignment to the current tenant(s).

22.08 (ii) SPENT COVENANTS. If any right, liability or other matter arising under a covenant of the relevant tenancy falls to be determined or otherwise operates by reference to the commencement of that tenancy, the corresponding covenant of the overriding lease shall be so framed that the right, liability or matter falls to be determined or otherwise operates by reference to that tenancy; but the overriding lease shall not be required to

[15] See *Thomas v Hayward* (1869) L.R. 4 Ex. 311; *Kumar v Dunning* [1989] Q.B. 193 at 205. *Sed quaere*: this decision is perhaps difficult to reconcile with the decision in *Caerns Motor Services Ltd v Texaco Ltd* [1994] 1 W.L.R. 1249.

[16] *Woodall v Clifton* [1905] 2 Ch. 257; *Sherwood v Tucker* [1924] 2 Ch. 440; *Charles Frodsham & Co v Morris* (1972) 229 E.G. 961.

[17] In the *First Penthouse* case, above, it was held that for these purposes an intention that a covenant be personal could be "expressed" explicitly or implicitly by the lease as a whole. *Sed quaere*: s.3(6)(a) requires the covenant to be expressed (in whatever terms) to be personal. A covenant that is not a "landlord covenant" at all does not have to be expressed to be personal.

reproduce any covenant of that tenancy to the extent that it has become spent by the time that the overriding lease is granted.[18] The intention here is to keep the relevant tenancy and the overriding lease operating in tandem, so that at any given time the overriding lease is merely duplicating the obligations subsisting under the relevant tenancy.[19] But the inclusion of terms specifying contractual obligations on dates prior to the date of grant of the overriding lease might nonetheless create contractual obligations between the parties to the overriding lease,[20] and so the overriding lease is not required to reproduce covenants of the relevant tenancy to the extent that these are spent by the date of grant. So, for example, a covenant to pay rent for the period from (say) October 17, 1986 to December 24, 1986 upon grant of the relevant tenancy, and thereafter to pay rent quarterly in advance, would not be reproduced in the overriding lease to the extent that it had been complied with up to the date of grant of the overriding lease.[21] Similarly, a tenant's covenant to fit out, which had been performed at the start of the relevant tenancy, would not be reproduced in the overriding lease.

Compliance, whether on time or late, must mean that the covenant is to **22.09** that extent and by that time "spent" within the meaning of the Act. Since the right to take up an overriding lease will only arise in a case where a former tenant or a guarantor for a former tenant has been called upon to pay and has paid a fixed charge under the relevant tenancy, a payment made pursuant to a s.17 notice by such a person must also mean that the covenant is "spent" to the extent of that payment, otherwise the former tenant or guarantor might have to pay twice. What is less clear is if, when the former tenant or guarantor calls for an overriding lease, various obligations under covenants in the relevant tenancy have not been complied with by the date of grant of the overriding lease. Presumably, these covenants are not to that extent "spent" merely because time for compliance with them has passed, because the landlord under the relevant tenancy can still seek to enforce compliance with them; "spent" must connote performance, release or waiver by the date of grant of the

[18] Covenants Act, s.19(4).

[19] So, e.g. rent review dates under the overriding lease will be the same as those under the relevant tenancy, taking place on every fifth anniversary (or as the case may be) of the commencement of the relevant tenancy; and any break clause exercisable by notice at the expiration of a given number of years from the commencement of the relevant tenancy will be similarly timed under the overriding lease.

[20] See *Bradshaw v Pawley* [1980] 1 W.L.R. 10 for a lucid analysis by Megarry J. of the position as between landlord and tenant where a lease is made on a date later than the expressed commencement date of the term.

[21] The covenant in the overriding lease would be reworded insofar as necessary to exclude a contractual obligation to that extent.

overriding lease.[22] The lessee under an overriding lease may, depending on the wording of the covenants of the relevant tenancy, become liable under the lease to perform obligations outstanding under the relevant tenancy notwithstanding that these accrued before the date of grant of the overriding lease. So, e.g. a covenant to decorate in the third, sixth, ninth, etc. years of the term of the relevant tenancy will be "framed" in the overriding lease as obligations to decorate during the same years from the date of grant of the relevant tenancy, and will only be excluded from the terms of the overriding lease if those decorating obligations had become spent by the date of grant.

22.10 (iii) THIRD PARTY COVENANTS. Although not expressly stated, it seems implicit that the overriding lease will contain only the covenants and terms of the relevant tenancy that apply as between the landlord and the tenant. So a surety covenant of a third party will not be reproduced in the overriding lease, nor will the claimant be required to procure an equivalent guarantee of his obligations under the overriding lease. Difficulties might arise where, e.g. the relevant tenancy is a long lease of a residential flat to which a management company is a party, covenanting to provide services to the building. There is no warrant in the Covenants Act to require such a person to covenant with the claimant in terms of its obligations in the relevant tenancy, though the management company might be able to take the benefit of the claimant's covenants in the overriding lease, e.g. to pay service charge to the management company, reproducing the tenant covenants under the relevant tenancy.[23] Given that an overriding lease may be an old or a new tenancy,[24] there is no warrant for limiting the terms of the lease to the "landlord covenants" and "tenant covenants" of the relevant tenancy; and so a covenant that does not fall to be performed by the landlord or tenant for the time being can be a term of the overriding lease provided that it is is not excluded as falling within either of the exceptions (i) and (ii), above.

[22] The word "spent" was used in a similar way by the Court of Appeal in *Bass Holdings Ltd v Morton Music Ltd* [1988] Ch. 493 in relation to breaches of covenant. In that case, a tenant's option to break a lease could not be validly exercised if there were subsisting breaches of covenant; but the Court of Appeal held that past breaches which had been fully remedied, or where compliance had been waived by the landlord, were "spent" and therefore not breaches relevant to the option. "Spent" is not a word which features heavily in other landlord and tenant legislation. The concept is the contractual principle of discharge by performance.

[23] The benefit might pass under Law of Property Act 1925, s.56(1) or under Contracts (Rights of Third Parties) Act 1999, s.1; see above, paras 17.13 *et seq.*

[24] See below.

(c) *Other contents*

For the purposes of the Covenants Act, an overriding lease is a new tenancy only if the relevant tenancy is a new tenancy,[25] even if made after January 1, 1996. Every overriding lease is required to state two matters. First, that it is a lease granted under s.19 of the Covenants Act; secondly, whether it is or is not a new tenancy for the purposes of s.1 of the Covenants Act.[26] Any such statement in an overriding lease must comply with such requirements as may be prescribed by land registration rules under the Land Registration Act 2002.[27] The only requirement prescribed is that the statement be in the following form[28]: **22.11**

> "This lease is granted under section 19 of the Landlord and Tenant (Covenants) Act 1995, and is (*or* is not) a new tenancy for the purposes of section 1 of that Act."

2. Entitlement to overriding lease

Where in respect of any tenancy ("the relevant tenancy") any person ("the claimant") makes full payment of an amount which he has been duly required to pay in accordance with s.17 of the Covenants Act, together with any interest payable, he shall be entitled to have the landlord under that tenancy grant him an overriding lease of the premises demised by the tenancy. That entitlement is subject to and in accordance with s.19 of the Covenants Act.[29] It follows that only a former tenant of the premises demised by a relevant tenancy, or a guarantor for such former tenant, is entitled, upon making full payment pursuant to a s.17 notice, to have an overriding lease granted to him. As has been seen,[30] a s.17 notice could specify a large number of different fixed charges which have become due under the tenancy.[31] It is not clear whether the claimant must make full payment in respect of a given fixed charge (and any interest on it, where payable) or full payment of all the fixed charges (and interest, where payable) specified in a given notice. The better view is probably that payment in full of *a* fixed charge will suffice. Section 17 of the Covenants **22.12**

[25] Covenants Act, s.20(1).
[26] *ibid.*, s.20(2).
[27] *ibid.*, as amended by Land Registration Act 2002, s.133, Sch.11, para. 33(1), (3); SI 2003/1725.
[28] The Land Registration (Overriding Leases) Rules 1995 (SI 1995/3154); the full wording of which is set out in App.3, below.
[29] Covenants Act, s.19(1).
[30] Above, para.20.18.
[31] e.g. many years of rent arrears accrued before January 1, 1996. After that date, the number of fixed charges which can be validly specified in one notice will, in practice, be restricted by the requirement to give notice within six months of each charge becoming due.

Act speaks of an amount being specified in the notice in respect of a fixed charge; and s.19(1) specifies full payment of *an* amount which he has been required to pay, not *the* amounts.[32] *Semble*, two different former tenants, or a former tenant and his guarantor, who together make up the full payment of a fixed charge, are not entitled jointly to an overriding lease; but two or more persons who are jointly a former tenant should be so entitled. A claim to exercise the right to have an overriding lease must be made to the landlord; there is no automatic entitlement to an overriding lease.

3. The claim to an overriding lease

22.13 Once any person ("the claimant") has become entitled to the grant of an overriding lease by making a full payment to the landlord,[33] he must consider carefully whether he wishes such a lease to be granted to him. Whether it is a desirable step in any given case will depend on the precise facts of that case,[34] and a claimant would be very well advised to take specific legal advice[35] on the consequences of taking an overriding lease and the consequences of not taking one. If the claimant decides to take an overriding lease, he must set the procedure in motion by notifying the landlord of his desire.

22.14 A claim to exercise the right to an overriding lease is made by the claimant making a request for such a lease to the landlord. Any such request must be in writing, and must specify the payment by virtue of which the claimant claims to be entitled to the lease ("the qualifying payment").[36] Although the request must be in writing, there is no form prescribed for such a request for the purposes of the Act. The written request must be made at the time of making the qualifying payment, or within the period of 12 months beginning with the date of that payment.[37] The Act specifically provides that any request for an overriding lease under s.19 may be sent by post.[38] The effect of this specific provision is that the presumption of due service by post in s.7 of the Interpretation Act 1978 applies to a request for an overriding lease sent by post. That section provides:

[32] This view is reinforced if the effect of grant of an overriding lease on non-spent obligations of the relevant tenancy, as discussed at para.22.09, above, is correct.

[33] See above.

[34] Some of the possible advantages are mentioned at para.22.01, above.

[35] And possibly also a surveyor's advice as to, e.g. the claimant's prospect of disposing of the overriding lease to an acceptable assignee in the open market.

[36] Covenants Act, s.19(5)(a).

[37] *ibid.*, s.19(5)(b).

[38] *ibid.*, s.19(10).

> "Where an Act authorises or requires any document to be served by post (whether the expression "serve" or the expression "give" or "send" or any other expression is used) then, unless the contrary intention appears, the service is deemed to be effected by properly addressing, pre-paying and posting a letter containing the document and, unless the contrary is proved, to have been effected at the time at which the letter would be delivered in the ordinary course of post."

Thus, unless a landlord can affirmatively prove that the written request did not reach him by showing what did happen to it,[39] service is presumed to have been effected on the landlord in the ordinary course of post.[40] The last date for making the request to the landlord is the end of the period of 12 months beginning with the date of the qualifying payment. Thus, if the qualifying payment was made on August 17, 2006, the last day for making the request will be August 16, 2007. The statutory time limit must be strictly observed, and so it is important to consider two matters further: the identification of the date of the qualifying payment, and the time at which the claimant's request to the landlord is made.

(a) *Date of qualifying payment*

22.15 The qualifying payment is the full amount of the fixed charge (and any interest claimed and payable) specified in the landlord's s.17 notice. So if the claimant has paid the charge in instalments, the date is the date on which the last instalment is paid. Where a payment is made in cash, the date is clearly that on which the money is received by the landlord or his authorised agent. But if the payment is made by cheque, the payment is strictly not made until cleared funds reach the bank account of the landlord or his authorised agent. In cases under the Agricultural Holdings Act 1986 and the Housing Act 1988, the court has been prepared to hold that a notice to pay rent was complied with by posting a cheque before the expiry of the period of two months from the date of the notice, where that was the established method of payment, provided that the cheque

[39] See *Lex Service Plc v Johns* [1990] 1 E.G.L.R. 92. In view of the later decisions of the Court of Appeal in *Blunden v Frogmore Investments Ltd* [2002] 2 E.G.L.R. 29 and *C A Webber (Transport) Ltd v Railtrack Plc* [2004] 1 E.G.L.R. 49, which were not concerned with this section, it may be that only the presumption as to the *time* of service can be displaced by evidence as to when the letter actually arrived.

[40] As to which, see *Practice Direction (Q.B.D.: Postal Service)* [1985] 1 W.L.R. 489. Note that this presumption as to the time of service does not apply if registered post or recorded delivery post is used, for in such a case the letter is delivered at the time at which there is a person at the address who signs a receipt for it: *Stephenson & Sons v Orca Properties Ltd* [1989] 2 E.G.L.R. 129.

was subsequently cleared on first presentation.[41] It remains to be seen whether a similar principle will be applied under the Covenants Act. One point in favour of it is that it is the claimant who has to make the request within the specified time, and he can only know the date when the cheque was given or posted to the landlord, and not when the order to pay was honoured and the funds paid into the landlord's bank account.[42]

(b) *Time of claimant's request*

22.16 The Act is concerned with the time at which the claimant's written request is made to the landlord. Subject to the statutory presumption of service by post, it must be assumed that the request is made when the landlord actually receives it.[43] Thus, unless the claimant hands the request to the landlord personally, risk of non-receipt of the request is on the claimant. In particular, the provisions of s.196 of the Law of Property Act 1925 and of s.23 of the Landlord and Tenant Act 1927 do not apply to the making of a claimant's request, so leaving the request for the landlord at his last known address, or posting it to him there, is not deemed to be good service.[44]

4. Effect of claim to overriding lease

22.17 Where the claimant duly makes a request for an overriding lease, the landlord is obliged to grant and the claimant is obliged to take an overriding lease unless one or more of three exceptions is satisfied.[45] If none of those exceptions is satisfied, the landlord shall grant and deliver to the claimant an overriding lease of the demised premises[46] within a reasonable time of the request being received by the landlord, and the claimant shall thereupon deliver to the landlord a counterpart of the lease duly executed by the claimant.[47] Thus, the position is as if an open contract for the grant of an overriding lease had been made between landlord and claimant, save that the terms of the overriding lease are

[41] See *Luttenberger v North Thoresby Farms Ltd* [1993] 1 E.G.L.R. 3; *Hannaford v Smallcombe* [1994] 1 E.G.L.R. 9.

[42] A further argument is that Covenants Act, s.19(5)(b) seems to assume that the making of the payment and the request can be contemporaneous.

[43] See the language of Covenants Act, s.19(6)(a), which suggests that this was the intention of Parliament.

[44] Though in most cases, e.g. where the request is left at the registered office of a property company, it will be good service in fact. For the difficulties that can arise where service or the date of receipt have to be proved, see *Warborough Investments Ltd v Central Midlands Estates Ltd* [2006] EWHC 1459, (Ch).

[45] See below.

[46] i.e. the premises demised by the relevant tenancy.

[47] Covenants Act, s.19(6)(a), (b)(i).

governed by the statutory provisions. After a reasonable time has expired, either party can specify a further reasonable time for completion of the lease and make time of the essence for completion by the expiry of that reasonable time. What is a reasonable time within which the landlord is to grant and deliver the lease must depend on the precise factual circumstances of any given case; but in a case which presents no particular difficulties or complicating factors, 21 days may be thought to be reasonable. In most cases in which the landlord does not dispute the claimant's entitlement to the overriding lease, it will be in the landlord's interest to proffer the lease for completion earlier rather than later. The landlord's obligation to grant and deliver the overriding lease is to be performed within a reasonable time "of the request being received by the landlord". There does not appear to be intended to be any difference between this time and the time when the request is "made to the landlord".[48] Time is necessarily not of the essence for the landlord to grant the lease because no exact date is specified. The Act seems to contemplate that the landlord's obligation and the claimant's obligation to execute and deliver to the landlord a counterpart upon the landlord's delivering the lease are sequential. No doubt, exchange of lease and counterpart being contemplated by the statutory provisions, the delivery by the landlord of the lease is not fully effective to grant the lease before the claimant has delivered his executed part.[49] Indeed, the Act specifically provides that, if the claimant fails to deliver an executed counterpart to the landlord, the claimant shall not be entitled to exercise any of the rights which would otherwise be exercisable by him under the overriding

[48] Perhaps the reason for the difference in the language used is that the obligation to grant the lease is looked at from the landlord's perspective: he would know that he had received the request on a particular date. But in some circumstances (see above, para.14.23, in relation to the giving of prescribed form notices requesting release from liabilities etc.) the date of receipt and the date on which a notice is served will not necessarily be the same. And if the claimant posts his request for an overriding lease to the landlord, such that the presumption of due service in Interpretation Act 1978, s.7 applies, can the landlord nevertheless say that he did not receive it at all, and that therefore for these purposes he is not bound to deliver an overriding lease? This can hardly have been intended to be the result.

[49] A cautious landlord might seek to impose a condition on the delivery of the lease, namely that the claimant should execute and deliver the counterpart, thus making the lease an escrow until the claimant has performed his part of the duties. It is suggested that this would still be compliance by the landlord with his statutory obligation to "grant and deliver" the overriding lease. In practice, no doubt, exchange will take place in the time honoured fashion, and the strict letter of the statute will be more honoured in the breach. It may well be the case that the Act is construed as imposing only correlative, and not sequential, obligations.

lease.[50] The claimant is liable for the landlord's reasonable costs of and incidental to the grant of the lease.[51]

5. The exceptions

(a) *Relevant tenancy determined*

22.18 The landlord is not under an obligation to grant an overriding lease of the demised premises under s.19 of the Covenants Act at a time when the relevant tenancy has been determined.[52] Therefore, if (say) eight months after a claimant has discharged liabilities of the tenant under the relevant tenancy the landlord agrees with the tenant and takes a surrender of the tenancy, a subsequent request for an overriding lease will be of no avail. "Determination" of the tenancy is apt to include a case where the landlord has re-entered, either peaceably or by the service of forfeiture proceedings. Since service of the proceedings effects the re-entry, subject only to proof of the entitlement to forfeit (if disputed) at trial.[53] A forfeiture of the tenancy will exonerate the landlord from the obligation to grant an overriding lease. But if it is later proved that the landlord had not validly forfeited the lease, or that the tenant was entitled to be relieved against such forfeiture, the landlord's obligation to grant an overriding lease will be revived, subject to the 12-month time limit. It seems that a landlord will be exonerated where, even if the tenancy still subsisted at the time when the request for an overriding lease was made, it was determined before the landlord became obliged to deliver the executed lease.[54] Difficult cases could arise, in theory, where the relevant tenancy was determined at a time when the landlord was already in breach of his obligation to grant the overriding lease within a reasonable time. But since in most cases the claimant will be pleased rather than disappointed that the relevant tenancy has been determined, it is difficult to envisage this interesting point being litigated.

[50] Covenants Act, s.20(3).

[51] *ibid.*, s.19(6)(b)(ii).

[52] *ibid.*, s.19(7).

[53] *Canas Property Co. Ltd v K. L. Television Services Ltd* [1970] 2 Q.B. 433.

[54] So an astute landlord, who wishes to call on the former tenant or guarantor for the undischarged liabilities of the tenant, will be able to avoid having to grant an overriding lease to that former tenant or guarantor provided that there are always rent arrears in respect of which he can forfeit, should a request for an overriding lease be made. In view of the need to serve a s.17 notice within six months of the fixed charge becoming due, however, this ability to avoid an overriding lease (should it ever be desired) would have to be carefully managed. If implemented, the strategy would involve his putting an end to the continuing liability of the former tenant or guarantor by forfeiting the lease, and so might not be desirable.

(b) *Overriding lease already granted*

The same landlord can only grant one overriding lease in respect of the same relevant tenancy. Thus, a claimant is not entitled to the grant of an overriding lease if, at the time when he makes his request, the landlord has already granted such a lease and that lease remains in force.[55] This exception was doubtless intended to cover the case where, between the time of payment pursuant to the s.17 notice and the making of the request, an overriding lease has been granted to someone else. The exception is of simple application where there has been no change in the landlord the grant of a further concurrent lease by the same landlord is excluded. But complications arise where there has been a change in the landlord. 22.19

It is important to note that there is no prohibition in the Covenants Act on the grant of successive overriding leases, in the sense of a different former tenant or guarantor being subsequently entitled to an overriding lease from the existing overriding lessee, if the former is served with a s.17 notice by the latter and makes full payment.[56] The intention of the statutory procedure is that the claimant always becomes the immediate landlord of the tenant under the relevant tenancy by the grant of the overriding lease. If the same landlord were liable to grant a second overriding lease (e.g. because he served one s.17 notice on the former tenant in respect of the March quarter's rent and then a second s.17 notice on the former tenant's guarantor in respect of the June quarter's rent), he would only be able to grant a concurrent lease of *his* reversion, i.e. the second overriding lessee would become the landlord of the first overriding lessee. This the Act does not allow.

But what of a case where, in between the service of a s.17 notice and the claimant's claim to an overriding lease, the landlord assigns his interest? Here it is necessary to distinguish between old tenancies and new tenancies.

(i) OLD TENANCIES. Under an old tenancy, the assignment of the reversion would (unless otherwise stated) carry with it the right to recovery of any rent arrears ante-dating the assignment,[57] and so payment pursuant to the s.17 notice would have to be made to the assignee.[58] In that way, the assignee inherits the benefit and consequences of the s.17 notice. The assignee would, it is suggested, be liable to grant the overriding lease once full payment is made to him because the conditions 22.20

[55] Covenants Act, s.19(7)(a).

[56] *ibid.*, s.19(11).

[57] *Re King; Robinson v Gray* [1963] 1 All E.R. 781.

[58] The s.17 notice does not create a liability; it removes a bar to recovery and imposes a limit to liability: see above, paras 20.20 *et seq.*

precedent of s.19(1) of the Covenants Act have been fulfilled. But what if the claimant made payment to the previous landlord, who assigned the reversion after receipt of the payment but before the claimant had made his claim? In principle the same result should be reached because, again, the conditions precedent of s.19(1) have been fulfilled.[59] That subsection does not specify to whom the payment pursuant to the s.17 notice must have been paid; but "the landlord" for the purposes of the obligation to grant the overriding lease means the person for the time being entitled to the reversion expectant on the term of the tenancy.[60]

22.21 Suppose now that the previous landlord had served two (or more) s.17 notices on different persons and that, consequent on one of them, an overriding lease was granted to a former tenant or guarantor who made full payment under one of the notices and claimed an overriding lease. If the landlord then assigns the reversion, the assignee becomes entitled to the benefit of and is subject to the overriding lease; but the right to any further arrears of rent under the relevant tenancy and the benefit of the other s.17 notice(s) has passed to the overriding lessee and not to the assignee landlord.[61] If the amount due under another s.17 notice is then paid to the overriding lessee, and a claim to an overriding lease is made, is the overriding lessee bound to grant a further overriding lease? He is certainly the "landlord" under the relevant tenancy, and all the conditions precedent under s.19(1) have been satisfied. But it seems improbable that Parliament intended this result, as this exception and exception (c)[62] are intended to give the prior right to an overriding lease, whereby the lessee becomes the landlord of the tenant under the relevant tenancy, to the first claimant. But it is impossible to construe "the landlord" as including all prior landlords under the relevant tenancy, and thereby exclude the right to a further overriding lease, because the Act expressly provides that two or more such overriding leases may be granted.[63] The position is, at best, unclear.

22.22 (ii) NEW TENANCIES. In relation to new tenancies, the assignment of the reversion does not (in the absence of an express assignment) carry with it the right to arrears of rent, etc. accrued due before the date of the assignment.[64] Thus, the previous landlord remains entitled to all rent arrears antedating the assignment, and payment pursuant to any s.17 notice must be made to him. Taking the three examples considered above

[59] An intending purchaser of a reversion should therefore ensure that he makes inquiry of the vendor as to whether the vendor has served any s.17 notices relating to tenancies of any part of the premises comprised in the reversion.

[60] Covenants Act, s.28(1), and see *ibid.*, s.19(1).

[61] See above, nn.57 and 59.

[62] See below, para.22.27.

[63] Covenants Act, s.19(11).

[64] *ibid.*, s.23(1); see above, paras 12.21 *et seq.*

in relation to old tenancies, the legal effect for new tenancies seems to be as follows.

First, where payment has not been made before the assignment: here the payment when made seems to entitle the claimant to an overriding lease from the assignee landlord, for he is "the landlord" under the relevant tenancy. Thus, although no payment had been made prior to the assignment of the reversion, and although the previous landlord and not the assignee landlord is paid the amount in the s.17 notice, the assignee landlord is liable to grant an overriding lease. What the position is if the previous landlord had not, prior to the assignment of the reversion, served a s.17 notice at all, is unclear. The previous landlord is, in principle, still entitled to any rent arrears antedating the assignment. In order to be entitled to recover those arrears from a former tenant or guarantor, a s.17 notice must be served by "the landlord". The previous landlord is still entitled to serve a s.17 notice because the definition of "landlord" for the purposes of s.17 includes him.[65] But does this entitle the former tenant or guarantor who makes full payment to claim an overriding lease from the assignee landlord? The position is unclear.[66] **22.23**

Secondly, where payment has already been made prior to the assignment. Here, the same result must obtain, as all the preconditions of s.19(1) are satisfied, and "the landlord" under the relevant tenancy is the assignee. **22.24**

Thirdly, where more than one s.17 notice was served by the previous landlord, and one claim was made to an overriding lease. Where such lease was granted by the previous landlord, the assignment of the reversion will make the assignee the landlord under the overriding lease, but the right to any further arrears in existence as at the date of the grant of the overriding lease will not have passed to the assignee landlord.[67] But who, as between the previous landlord and the overriding lessee, is entitled to the further arrears? This depends on whether the grant of an overriding lessee for a term less than the landlord's interest takes effect, for the purposes of the Act, as an assignment of the landlord's reversion. If so, the previous landlord remains entitled to the arrears because, although the concurrent lessee becomes entitled to enforce the tenant covenants of the relevant tenancy,[68] he does not obtain any rights relating to a time before the grant **22.25**

[65] *ibid.*, s.17(6).

[66] If it does so entitle him, the intending purchaser of a reversion who, for whatever reason, does not wish the spectre of overriding leases to appear must ensure that he takes suitable covenants from his assignor in this respect. But a covenant not to serve a s.17 notice would effectually deprive the assignor of his right to any arrears of rent, etc. The best solution might be for the assignor to assign the right to the rent arrears with the reversion in return for an adjustment to the purchase price.

[67] Covenants Act, s.23(1).

[68] By *ibid.*, s.15(1).

of the overriding lease.[69] But the grant of a concurrent lease does not, apparently, have the same effect as under the law relating to old tenancies[70]; and if it is not an assignment for the purposes of the Act, it is unclear who has the right to the rent arrears.[71] Assuming the previous landlord to have that right, the question then arises whether, if one of the other s.17 notices is satisfied, either the overriding lessee or the assignee landlord becomes liable, upon request, to grant a further overriding lessee. For the reasons given above, it is submitted that the assignee landlord cannot be so liable: he is no longer the "landlord" under the relevant tenancy. But it is even more improbable that Parliament intended the new overriding lessee to be liable to grant a further overriding lease in a case where he is not even the recipient of the amount due under the s.17 notice in question. The acceptable result is that an overriding lessee is only himself liable to grant an overriding lease in the case of, and pursuant to, a s.17 notice served by him as landlord under the relevant tenancy; but arriving at this conclusion as a matter of statutory construction is not an easy task. The position in this regard must remain unclear for the present.

22.26 What is tolerably clear is that the same landlord may be bound to grant a second overriding lease of the demised premises if the first such lease does not remain in force.[72] Thus, e.g. if the first overriding lessee defaults on his rental obligations and the landlord agrees to and takes a surrender of the overriding lease, he again becomes the landlord under the relevant tenancy.[73] If he then serves a s.17 notice on another former tenant or guarantor, and that person pays and claims a new tenancy, the landlord is bound to grant him one (provided that the relevant tenancy has not been determined and provided that exception (c) below does not apply).

(c) *Another request for an overriding lease already made*

22.27 A claimant is not entitled to the grant of an overriding lease if, at the time when he makes his request, another person has already duly made a request for such a lease to the landlord and that request has been neither withdrawn nor abandoned by that person.[74] The due making of the prior request for an overriding lease connotes a valid application made within the time limited by the Act by a former tenant or guarantor of a former tenant who has made full payment of a fixed charge pursuant to a s.17

[69] *ibid.*, s.23(1).

[70] It is for this reason that the provision in s.15(1) of the Covenants Act was required.

[71] Because s.23(1) only applies where, as a result of an assignment, a person becomes entitled by virtue of the Act to the benefit of a covenant.

[72] Covenants Act, s.19(7)(a).

[73] Law of Property Act 1925, s.139(1).

[74] Covenants Act, s.19(7)(b).

notice. This provision contains two elements which must be considered in more detail: the timing of the successive requests, and withdrawal or abandonment of a request.

(i) TIMING. As has been seen,[75] a request for an overriding lease is made when received by the landlord, and a statutory presumption of due service in the course of post might apply. Difficult questions of priority might arise where, e.g. a former tenant posts a request on one day and the guarantor of another former tenant hands the landlord a request the following day. The Act does not give further assistance in this respect; but it does provide two rules for determining the priority of two or more requests which are duly made to the landlord on the same day. First, a request made by a person who was liable for the qualifying payment as a former tenant is treated as made before a request made by a person who was so liable as a guarantor.[76] Secondly, a request made by a person whose liability in respect of the covenant commenced earlier than any such liability of another person is treated as made before a request made by that other person.[77] Thus, a request by the former tenant who assigned the lease to the current defaulting tenant will have priority over a request made on the same day by the guarantor of the original lessee; but he will not have priority over a request made on the same day by the former tenant who assigned the lease to him (It should be noted that these priority rules do *not* apply where one person makes his request at least one day before any others' requests.). **22.28**

(ii) WITHDRAWAL OR ABANDONMENT. For the purposes of s.19 of the Covenants Act, a claimant's request for an overriding lease is withdrawn by the claimant notifying the landlord in writing that he is withdrawing his request.[78] This notification may be sent by post,[79] and accordingly the statutory presumption of due service applies.[80] For the purposes of s.19, a claimant is to be regarded as having abandoned his request if (a) the landlord has requested the claimant in writing to take, within such reasonable period as is specified in the landlord's request, all or any of the remaining steps required to be taken by the claimant before the overriding lease can be granted, and (b) the claimant fails to comply with the landlord's request.[81] The landlord's written request to comply may be **22.29**

[75] Above, para.22.16.
[76] Covenants Act, s.19(8)(a).
[77] *ibid*., s.19(8)(b).
[78] *ibid*., s.19(9)(a).
[79] *ibid*., s.19(10).
[80] Interpretation Act 1978, s.7; see above, para.22.14.
[81] Covenants Act, s.19(9)(b).

sent by post,[82] and accordingly the statutory presumption of due service applies.[83] The claimant is to be regarded as having abandoned his request at the time when the reasonable period specified in the landlord's written request expires.[84] Thus if, in accordance with these principles, an existing request for an overriding lease has been neither withdrawn nor abandoned when a claimant makes his request, that later claimant shall not be entitled to the grant of an overriding lease. Even if the existing request is later abandoned or withdrawn, the later claimant's request is still of no effect because, at the time when he made the request, the first request was still extant.[85]

22.30 Where the landlord's interest is assigned before the landlord grants the overriding lease, the entitlement of the claimant who has made a request to be granted such a lease, and the rights of other subsequent claimants, will depend on registration of the first claimant's request under the Land Registration Act 2002 or the Land Charges Act 1972, as the case may be.[86]

6. Status of request for overriding lease

22.31 As has been seen, a valid request for an overriding lease gives rise (where none of the exceptions apply) to mutual obligations on the part of claimant and landlord akin to the position under an open contract for the grant of a concurrent lease of the premises demised by the relevant tenancy. Such tenancy is not itself registrable under the Land Charges Act 1972, nor taken to be an estate contract within the meaning of that Act, by reason of any right or obligation that *might* arise under s.19 of the Covenants Act.[87] That is to say that a tenant, former tenant or guarantor cannot register his contingent interest in the grant of an overriding lease in the expectation that, at some future time, he will be entitled to such a lease. Equally, if the title to the premises is registered under the Land Registration Act 2002, the contingent interest is not an unregistered interest capable of overriding a registered disposition,[88] nor is it registrable as an interest in the land in order to protect its priority. Even the service of a s.17 notice does not give rise to a registrable interest. But when a valid request is made for an overriding lease, the claimant then has an interest in the land in the nature of an estate contract.

[82] *ibid.*, s.19(10).
[83] Interpretation Act 1978, s.7; above, para.22.14.
[84] Covenants Act, s.19(9)(b).
[85] *ibid.*, s.19(7).
[86] See below.
[87] Covenants Act, s.20(6).
[88] Within the meaning of s.29(2) of and Sch.3 to that Act.

The Covenants Act provides[89] that no right arising from a request for an overriding lease[90] shall be an overriding interest within the meaning of the Land Registration Act, but that any such request shall be registrable under the Land Charges Act or be the subject of a notice under the Land Registration Act 2002 as if it were an estate contract. Thus, to be binding on successors in title of, or purchasers from, the landlord, the rights arising from the request for an overriding lease must be registered, in the case of unregistered land as a Class C(iv) land charge against the name of the landlord, and in the case of registered land, as a notice in the charges register of the registered title.[91] Non-registration in either case is likely to mean that an assignee of the landlord's interest and a concurrent lessee take their interests free from the claimant's entitlement to an overriding lease. If, on the other hand, the claimant's entitlement is protected by registration, any such assignee or lessee will be bound by the claimant's rights, and will be bound to grant him an overriding lease. It must follow that, for the purposes of determining priority as between competing claimants to an overriding lease,[92] a request validly made to a previous landlord which has been registered, and has not been withdrawn or abandoned, is a request previously made to the landlord[93] and disentitles any later claimant to the grant of an overriding lease. **22.32**

7. Withdrawal and abandonment of request

In one respect, the rights of claimant and landlord arising from the making of a request for an overriding lease are unlike a contract freely entered into between them for such a concurrent lease. The claimant apparently has the right to withdraw his request, and thereupon is not bound to take the overriding lease. The claimant's right to withdraw is nowhere expressly stated, but the method and consequences of withdrawal are provided for; and the right of the claimant to withdraw (on terms which protect the landlord) seems consistent with the intention behind the whole concept of overriding leases, namely to afford the former tenant or guarantor some additional protection and rights if he wants to avail himself of them. **22.33**

[89] s.20(6), as amended by Land Registration Act 2002, s.133, Sch.11, para. 33(1), (4); SI 2003/1725.

[90] Under Covenants Act, s.19.

[91] Nothing in the Covenants Act requires the landlord to co-operate in the registration of a notice in the charges register and so the notice may have to be a unilateral notice.

[92] See above.

[93] Within the meaning of Covenants Act, s.19(7)(b).

(a) *Withdrawal*

22.34 A claimant's request is withdrawn by the claimant notifying the landlord in writing that he is withdrawing his request.[94] A claimant cannot withdraw once the overriding lease has been granted. There is no prescribed form or words for such notification, but the notification must be in writing. The Act specifically provides that the notification may be sent by post,[95] and the purpose of this provision is that a statutory presumption of due service in the usual course of post applies to any notification sent by post.[96] Thus, a claimant can be reasonably sure, if he posts his notification pre-paid and correctly addressed, that his claim has been withdrawn with effect from two or four days after the posting.[97] The presumption of due service can only be rebutted by the landlord alleging non-service and showing what in fact happened to the letter.[98]

(b) *Abandonment*

22.35 The converse of the claimant's right to withdraw is that the landlord is entitled to have the claimant comply with the necessary steps for grant of the overriding lease, and have the lease completed within a reasonable time or not at all. If the claimant unreasonably delays, he is in some circumstances deemed to have abandoned his request. For the purposes of s.19,[99] a claimant is to be regarded as having abandoned his request if (i) the landlord has requested the claimant in writing to take, within such reasonable period as is specified in the landlord's request, all or any of the remaining steps required to be taken by the claimant before the lease can be granted, and (ii) the claimant fails to comply with the landlord's request.[1] There is no prescribed form of words for the landlord's request, but it must be in writing. The Act specifically provides that such a request

[94] Covenants Act, s.19(9)(a).

[95] *ibid.*, s.19(10).

[96] Interpretation Act 1978, s.7. See above, para.22.14.

[97] See *Practice Direction (Q.B.D.: Postal Service)* [1985] 1 W.L.R. 489.

[98] *Lex Services Plc v Johns* [1990] 1 E.G.L.R. 92, though this decision is best regarded as doubtful in the light of later decisions of the Court of Appeal in *Blunden v Frogmore Investments Ltd* [2002] 2 E.G.L.R. 29 and *C A Webber (Transport) Ltd v Railtrack Plc* [2004] 1 E.G.L.R. 49. It may be only the date of receipt that is capable of proof contrary to the presumption.

[99] It is not clear whether these words are intended to restrict the withdrawal or abandonment to certain consequences only, i.e. the entitlement of others to claim an overriding lease and the liability of the claimant for the reasonable costs of the landlord, but it is submitted that that cannot have been the intention of Parliament. A claimant cannot notify the landlord of his withdrawal and then seek to compel the grant of an overriding lease provided no other claimants make requests.

[1] Covenants Act, s.19(9)(b).

may be sent by post,[2] and so a statutory presumption of due service in the usual course of post applies to any request sent by post.[3] Thus, a landlord can be reasonably sure, if he posts his request pre-paid and correctly addressed, that the claimant's period for compliance with the request will commence two or four days after the posting.[4] The request must specify a period within which the remaining steps must be taken, and the period must be a reasonable one. What period is reasonable must depend on the steps required to be taken by the claimant in any given case, but it seems unlikely that these will be many or time-consuming. If the period specified is reasonable, and the claimant fails within the specified period to take the steps which the request required him to take, the claim to an overriding lease is treated as having been abandoned by the claimant at the time when the period expires.[5]

(c) *Costs*

Where a claimant who has duly made a request for an overriding lease under s.19 subsequently withdraws or abandons the request before he is granted such a lease by the landlord, the claimant is liable for the landlord's reasonable costs incurred in pursuance of the request down to the time of its withdrawal or abandonment.[6] This provision accordingly does not apply in a case where the request for an overriding lease was not a valid request, e.g. where the claimant did not make full payment pursuant to the s.17 notice. Also, it is submitted, it does not apply where either the landlord was under no obligation to grant an overriding lease because the relevant tenancy had been determined, or the claimant was not entitled to an overriding lease on account of an existing overriding tenancy or a prior extant request.[7] It is for the landlord to satisfy himself whether he is liable to grant an overriding lease. **22.36**

8. Validity and effect of overriding lease

(a) *As against lessor*

An overriding lease under s.19 of the Covenants Act is always a concurrent lease, and as such takes effect subject to the relevant tenancy under which the claimant had a liability. As has been seen, the terms of the overriding lease generally mirror the terms of the relevant tenancy,[8] and **22.37**

[2] *ibid.*, s.19(10).
[3] Interpretation Act 1978, s.7. See above, para.22.14.
[4] See *Practice Direction (Q.B.D.: Postal Service)* [1985] 1 W.L.R. 489.
[5] Covenants Act, s.19(9)(b).
[6] *ibid.*, s.19(9).
[7] See Covenants Act, s.19(7).
[8] See above, paras 22.04–22.11.

therefore will generally include a covenant restricting the alienation of the premises demised by the lease. For the avoidance of doubt, the Act specifically provides that the existence of the relevant tenancy will not be a breach of any covenant restricting alienation in the overriding lease.[9] The fact that an overriding lease takes effect subject to the relevant tenancy does not constitute a breach of any covenant of the overriding lease against subletting or parting with possession of the premises demised by the lease or any part of them.[10]

(b) *As against mortgagee*

22.38 Where a landlord's interest is mortgaged, his right to grant leases of his interest which bind the mortgagee is restricted by statute.[11] Very often, his right is further restricted by the terms of the mortgage.[12] Such statutory or contractual restrictions do not, however, restrict the ability of the mortgagor to grant a lease of his interest which binds him and his lessee by estoppel; it is just that the lease so granted does not bind the mortgagee unless granted in compliance with the statutory (and any contractual) provisions.[13] In the ordinary course, a concurrent lease to be granted by a mortgagor would have to comply with the strict statutory restrictions, and possibly also be granted with the written consent of the mortgagee, in order to create a lease which bound the mortgagee. The Covenants Act dispenses with both such requirements. In doing so, it may inadvertently have created a situation where the security of thousands of mortgagees could be prejudiced.

22.39 (i) THE MAIN STATUTORY PROVISION. An overriding lease shall be deemed to be authorised as against the persons interested in any mortgage of the landlord's interest (however created or arising) and shall be binding on any such persons.[14] "Mortgage" includes "charge",[15] and so includes an

[9] It is considered that, where a sub-tenancy is already in existence at the date of grant of a concurrent lease, the continued existence of that sub-tenancy could not be a breach of the covenant not to sub-let or part with possession in the concurrent lease, though arguably it could be a continuing breach of a covenant not to share possession or occupation. But where a landlord has waived a right to forfeit in respect of a breach of the covenant not to sub-let, an associated breach of covenant, which is a continuing breach, will also be taken to have been waived: *Downie v Turner* [1951] 2 K.B. 112.

[10] Covenants Act, s.20(5)(a).

[11] Law of Property Act 1925, s.99.

[12] e.g. a provision that the mortgagor shall not exercise any statutory powers of leasing without the prior written consent of the mortgagee.

[13] See *Taylor v Ellis* [1960] Ch. 368.

[14] Covenants Act, s.20(4).

[15] *ibid.*, s.20(7)(a).

equitable mortgage and any valid agreement for mortgage and any statutory charge.

(ii) THE SUPPLEMENTARY STATUTORY PROVISIONS. If any person interested in any mortgage of the landlord's interest is by virtue of such a mortgage entitled to possession of the documents of title relating to that interest, the landlord is obliged, within one month of the execution of the overriding lease, to deliver to that person the counterpart of the lease executed and delivered to the landlord by the claimant.[16] If the landlord fails to do so, the instrument creating or evidencing[17] the mortgage applies as if the obligation to deliver the counterpart were included in the terms of the mortgage as set out in that instrument.[18] Thus, an event of default under the mortgage will have occurred and the mortgagee's remedies under the mortgage will be triggered. But by virtue of the main statutory provision,[19] the mortgagee's remedies may already have been affected by the grant of the overriding lease. **22.40**

(iii) EFFECT OF THE DEEMED AUTHORISATION. The deemed authorisation means that the mortgagee is bound by the lease and cannot, e.g. take physical possession of the mortgaged property, cannot sell with vacant possession, and cannot grant a lease of the property in possession. Instead, the mortgagee can go into possession of the mortgaged property by demanding and receiving the rent under the overriding lease, can sell the landlord's interest subject to and with the benefit of the overriding lease, and can grant leases in reversion to the overriding lease. If the overriding lease is one which satisfies the strict requirements of s.99 of the Law of Property Act as to rent and terms, the mortgagee is in theory in no worse position; that is why the mortgagor has the statutory powers of leasing. But in many cases the overriding lease will not satisfy those requirements; in some cases it may fall very far short of them. This is because the overriding lease is, save as provided by the Covenants Act and save to the extent that the landlord and claimant may agree otherwise, on the same terms as the relevant tenancy.[20] But whereas the relevant tenancy did not bind the mortgagee unless it satisfied the statutory requirements, or was granted with the consent of the mortgagee, or both, the overriding **22.41**

[16] *ibid.*, s.20(4)(i).

[17] After *United Bank of Kuwait Plc v Sahib* [1997] Ch. 107, it is clear that any agreement to create a mortgage made after September 27, 1989 must comply with the requirements of Law of Property (Miscellaneous Provisions) Act 1989, s.2, and so, inter alia, must be made in writing and be signed by or on behalf of both parties. This requirement can, in some circumstances, be displaced by a constructive trust: *Kinane v Mackie-Conteh* [2005] EWCA Civ 45.

[18] Covenants Act, s.20(4)(ii).

[19] Above.

[20] Covenants Act, s.19(2)(b).

lease is binding on the mortgagee. So, if the mortgagor without the consent of the mortgagee granted a 10-year lease of the premises at a substantial premium and at a relatively low rent, and if a former tenant claims an overriding lease after having discharged (say) arrears of service charge, the landlord's mortgagee will be bound by the overriding lease at less than market rent, and his security will be worth less as a result. Where he could have washed his hands of the relevant tenancy, the mortgagee is bound by the overriding lease on essentially the same terms. The Covenants Act ought to have provided, but has failed to provide, that a mortgagee is only bound by an overriding lease to the extent that he was bound by the relevant tenancy. The receipt by the mortgagee of the counterpart of the overriding lease, or alternatively his entitlement to take possession because of the mortgagor's default in supplying it,[21] will be scant consolation to a mortgagee whose security has become seriously devalued by the grant of the overriding lease which binds him.

(c) *Generally*

22.42 For most purposes, a tenancy under an overriding lease is treated as any other tenancy. One exception already noted is that for the purposes of the Act an overriding lease is a new tenancy only if the relevant tenancy is a new tenancy.[22] Thus, some leases (being overriding leases) which are granted well into the twenty-first Century will still be old tenancies for the purposes of the Act. Otherwise, the provisions of the Act will apply to such tenancies, as they apply to other new tenancies or old tenancies, as the case may be. In particular, the provisions of the Act relating to authorised guarantee agreements,[23] restrictions on liability of former tenants and guarantors for fixed charges,[24] and restrictions on liability of former tenants and guarantors where the tenancy is subsequently varied,[25] apply where the tenancy in question is an overriding lease as they apply in other cases[26]; and if the lessee under an overriding lease serves a s.17 notice on another former tenant of the relevant tenancy (or on a guarantor for such a person), that lessee may himself be the object of a claim to another overriding lease.[27]

22.43 Further (although, as seen, the Covenants Act expressly validates an overriding lease as against a mortgagee of the landlord's interest, and expressly provides that the existence of the relevant tenancy will not be a breach of the covenants of the overriding lease), there is no provision

[21] Under the supplementary statutory provisions, above.
[22] Covenants Act, s.20(1).
[23] *ibid.*, s.16.
[24] *ibid.*, s.17.
[25] *ibid.*, s.18.
[26] *ibid.*, s.20(5)(b).
[27] *ibid.*, s.19(11); see above, para.22.19.

which validates the grant of the overriding lease as against any superior landlord. The landlord cannot escape his statutory obligation to grant the overriding lease even if the superior landlord refuses his consent to such underletting, and so the provisions of s.19 of the Covenants Act may cause the landlord to commit a breach of covenant under the headlease. Arguably, the alienation covenant in the headlease is void, pursuant to s.25 of the Act, to the extent that it imposes a liability for grant of an overriding lease; but it is very odd that the Act makes no appropriate provision for this case.

9. Liability of landlord for failure to grant overriding lease

Where a claimant duly makes a request for an overriding lease and none of the exceptions applies,[28] the landlord is obligated to grant and deliver the overriding lease within a reasonable time.[29] A failure by the landlord to grant that lease promptly may occasion loss to the claimant, and the Covenants Act provides a remedy for any such loss suffered. A claim that a landlord has failed to comply with the obligation to grant and deliver an overriding lease within a reasonable time can be made the subject of civil proceedings in like manner as any claim in tort for breach of statutory duty.[30] Thus, provided the claimant has suffered some loss,[31] he may seek to recover this in damages from the landlord. But it might not always be straightforward to prove that a landlord is in breach of his statutory duty. The landlord's obligation to grant the overriding lease is necessarily dependent on some degree of cooperation from the claimant, for example supplying details of his address or registered office, and responding to the terms of a draft lease which the landlord proposes should be granted.[32] The Act itself contemplates that the claimant may be taken to have abandoned his claim to an overriding lease in consequence of failure to take steps which need to be taken before the lease can be granted.[33] Thus, even where no overriding lease has as a matter of fact been granted, there may be questions as to whether the landlord has become exonerated from his duty to grant it, or as to whether, in view of the claimant's delay, a reasonable time from the request for the overriding lease had elapsed. And in any claim for damages, the precise time at which the reasonable time elapsed, and the landlord thereupon became in breach of duty, may 22.44

[28] For the exceptions to the obligation of the landlord to grant an overriding lease, see above, paras 22.18 *et seq*.

[29] Covenants Act, s.19(6)(a).

[30] *ibid.*, s.20(3).

[31] Loss is a necessary ingredient of any cause of action in tort except trespass, which is actionable per se.

[32] The overriding lease will not merely duplicate all the terms of the relevant tenancy: see Covenants Act, s.19(2)(b), (3), (4)(b).

[33] *ibid.*, s.19(9)(b).

be material. These are factual matters not unlike the issues which can arise where a landlord, in breach of statutory duty,[34] unreasonably withholds or delays giving consent to a proposed assignment or sub-letting of a lease.[35]

[34] Under Landlord and Tenant Act 1988, s.1.

[35] For examples of such factual issues arising, see *Midland Bank Plc v Chart Enterprises Inc.* [1990] 2 E.G.L.R. 59, *Dong Bang Minerva (UK) Ltd v Davina Ltd* [1996] 31 E.G. 87 and *NCR Ltd v Riverland Portfolio No.1 Ltd (No.2)* [2005] 2 E.G.L.R. 42.

PART V

Anti-avoidance and Assignment of Tenancies

CHAPTER 23

Anti-avoidance

The provisions of the Covenants Act releasing tenants from their contractual liability on assignment, restricting the liability of former tenants and guarantors and entitling such persons to take overriding leases would be of less significance if a landlord could persuade a tenant, as a condition of granting him a lease, to agree to exclude the effect of some or all of these provisions. At most stages in the economic cycle, landlords are generally in a stronger negotiating position than prospective tenants; and tenants who need to rent the premises in question might easily be persuaded to forgo some of the benefits of the Act in order to secure a lease of them. The same commercial pressure that led tenants to take up old tenancies for 20 or 25 year terms would be likely to lead them to agree to exclude the release provisions of the Act. The Covenants Act therefore includes an important and far-reaching anti-avoidance section, whose purpose was clearly to prevent a landlord from circumventing the principal provisions of the Act,[1] though it will apply equally to prevent a tenant from doing so. It does so by making void any agreement that has the effect of excluding, restricting or otherwise fettering the application of any provision of the Act. As such, the provision appears to have been modelled on a similar provision in the Landlord and Tenant Act 1954 designed to protect business tenants' security of tenure,[2] a fact which may be relevant on the question of how exactly the anti-avoidance provision in the Covenants Act has effect. **23.01**

1. The anti-avoidance provision

Any agreement relating to a tenancy is void to the extent that— **23.02**

(1) it would (apart from the anti-avoidance provision) have effect to exclude, modify or otherwise frustrate the operation of any provision of the Covenants Act;
(2) it provides for—
  (i) the termination or surrender of the tenancy, or

[1] Covenants Act, s.25.
[2] Landlord and Tenant Act 1954, s.38(1).

(ii) the imposition on the tenant of any penalty, disability or liability,

in the event of the operation of any provision of the Covenants Act, or

(3) it provides for any of the matters referred to in (2)(i) or (2)(ii) above and does so, whether expressly or otherwise, in connection with, or in consequence of, the operation of any provision of the Covenants Act.[3]

These three limbs are individually considered in paragraphs 23.06–23.10, below.

2. General scope of the provision

23.03 It is apparent that the provision is one whose scope is, and is intended to be, very wide. It applies to "any agreement" which has the effect of, or provides for, limiting in some way the operation of any of the provisions of the Act, whether that effect is intended or not. It applies equally for the benefit of landlord and tenant, though in most cases it will secure benefits to tenants rather than to landlords. Although there are express statutory exceptions to the otherwise far-reaching provision, the language of the provision is so wide that it is possible to construe it so as to make void agreements which the draftsman probably did not intend to come within its scope. The view of the Court of Appeal that it could not "see anything in the 1995 Act to fetter the freedom of contracting parties to place a contractual limit on the transmissibility of the benefit or burden of obligations under a tenancy"[4] was made in the context of obligations expressed to be personal to one or other party of the tenancy and clearly was not intended to, and could not in the light of the anti-avoidance provisions, have more general application. In construing the anti-avoidance provision, it is necessary to bear in mind not just its origin in the similar provision relating to business tenancies,[5] but also the breadth of the principal statutory provisions contained in the Covenants Act that the anti-avoidance provision is intended to protect and the interrelationship of the provision and the amendments to the Landlord and Tenant Act 1927 made by the Covenants Act governing assignments of leases,[6] which was an important part of the "package" of reforms that the Covenants Act

[3] Covenants Act, s.25(1).

[4] *BHP Petroleum Great Britain Ltd v Chesterfield Properties Ltd* [2002] Ch. 12, para.62.

[5] Above, n.2.

[6] Landlord and Tenant Act 1927, s.19(1A) to (1E), inserted by Covenants Act, s.22.

introduced, and which interrelationship is made explicit by the language of the anti-avoidance provision itself.[7]

After considering the general terms of the anti-avoidance provision and the exceptions to it, three areas of debate, only one of which has been authoritatively resolved, will be addressed, which serve to illustrate the difficulties in stating with certainty the effect of the provision.

An agreement relating to a tenancy is an "agreement" for the purposes of the provision, whether or not the agreement is contained in the instrument creating the tenancy, and whether or not it is made before the creation of the tenancy.[8] Thus, any binding collateral agreement between landlord and tenant is subject to the anti-avoidance provision,[9] even if made orally.[10] So also, it seems, is an agreement between a tenant and a third party,[11] for the provision is not limited to agreements between landlord and tenant but applies to any agreement "relating to a tenancy". Although the section is not clearly expressed to include agreements made *after* the creation of the tenancy,[12] it is considered that the sense of the provision is that such agreements must fall within it.[13] **23.04**

To the extent that[14] any such agreement does one or more of the matters set out in paragraph 23.02 above, it is void. It is considered that "void" means void for all purposes to that extent, and not merely voidable **23.05**

[7] Covenants Act, s.25(2).

[8] *ibid.*, s.25(4).

[9] If the "agreement" is not binding in any event, there is no need for the anti-avoidance provision to apply, for the tenant's rights cannot be affected by such agreement. *Quaere* whether an estoppel binding the tenant in equity can be "an agreement" within the meaning of the section.

[10] Although an oral agreement could not *vary* the terms of a lease made under seal, an oral agreement made for consideration which imposed some other obligation or restriction not inconsistent with the lease could be such a binding agreement.

[11] e.g. a superior landlord; see above, para.22.43.

[12] Compare the definition of "collateral agreement" in Covenants Act, s.28(1).

[13] This is one construction of Covenants Act, s.25(4), but the juxtaposition of "made before the creation of the tenancy" with the words "contained in the instrument creating the tenancy" does give rise to the argument that the provision applies if the agreement is made before *or at the time of* the creation of the tenancy, and not if it is made afterwards. But it is difficult to see why the Act should have been intended to allow the landlord to exploit his dominant position after the tenancy had been granted, e.g. upon the negotiation of a rent review, or upon the tenant's application for a change of use.

[14] But not further; the void part of an agreement may therefore be severed from it, and the remainder of the agreement stand. Thus, even if both parties to a tenancy have negotiated on a fully informed basis and where no inequality of bargaining power was experienced, some (perhaps a substantial part) of the consideration for the tenancy agreement will be excised from the agreement without any compensation or opportunity to renegotiate for the party deprived of that benefit.

at the instance of the party affected, bound or penalised by the agreement, as the case may be. The fact that an agreement is void to a particular extent does not necessarily mean that the offending words must be excised for all purposes; the words would have to be read as not applying to matters to the extent that such matters infringed the anti-avoidance provisions of the Covenants Act.

3. The three limbs of the provision

23.06 The core of the anti-avoidance provision is modelled on a similar "contracting out" subsection in Pt II of the Landlord and Tenant Act 1954,[15] which applies to business tenancies. The cases decided under that statutory provision may, therefore, afford some assistance in construing the anti-avoidance provision[16]; though in some instances the language of the latter has been changed to reflect judicial interpretation of the subsection in the Act of 1954.[17] Each of the limbs must be addressed separately in considering whether an agreement relating to a tenancy is void to any extent.

Limb (a)

23.07 Any agreement relating to a tenancy is void to the extent that it would, but for the anti-avoidance provision, have effect to exclude, modify or otherwise frustrate the operation of any provision of the Covenants Act.[18] Thus, a term of a lease that a guarantor for the lessee should remain liable on all the tenant covenants in the lease, however varied during the term granted, and for the duration of the term notwithstanding any assignment, would be void on account of the provisions of the Covenants Act relating to release of guarantors and non-liability for the conse-

[15] Landlord and Tenant Act 1954, s.38(1), now amended by the Regulatory Reform (Business Tenancies) (England and Wales) Order 2003 (SI 2003/3096), printed below, p.391.

[16] For a commentary on them, see *Woodfall's Law of Landlord and Tenant* (28th (looseleaf) ed.), para.22.038. In particular, the provisions of the Act of 1954 apply only to executory agreements, so that an agreement to surrender is unenforceable but an executed surrender is effective. It is uncertain whether the anti-avoidance provisions in the Covenants Act were intended to act similarly, so that, e.g. an executed sub-guarantee of a former tenant's AGA is valid. See above, paras 18.18 *et seq.*

[17] That subsection provided for an agreement relating to a tenancy to be void in so far as it "purported" to preclude the tenant from exercising his statutory rights. The Court of Appeal in *Joseph v Joseph* [1967] Ch. 78 held that the word "purports" in that context means "has the effect of"; and that is now the language used in the Covenants Act.

[18] Covenants Act, s.25(1)(a).

quences of post-assignment variations.[19] Similarly, an agreement expressly limiting the applicability of one or more of the sections of the Covenants Act would be void because it would have effect to modify the operation of the Act. Limb (a) goes yet further, seemingly for the avoidance of any doubt, and makes void any agreement which would "otherwise frustrate" the operation of any provision of the Act. It is not obvious how an agreement which does not have effect to exclude or modify the operation of any provision of the Act can frustrate the operation of any such provision; but it is possible that it was intended to catch an agreement delaying the operation of provisions of the Act.

The Covenants Act does not provide for landlords to remain liable on their covenants after assignment of the reversion; it provides that, in certain circumstances, a landlord can be released from any such continuing liability. Accordingly, a term of a lease that provides for the landlord's liability under his covenants to terminate upon an assignment of the reversion is not void under the anti-avoidance provision, even though in one sense (though not the relevant sense) it could be said to "frustrate" the operation of ss.6, 7 and 8 of the Act.[20] In seeking to identify whether a term of an agreement is void under the anti-avoidance provision, it is essential to bear in mind the mischief that the Act was passed to remedy.[21] *Semble* an agreement that has an effect that is not contrary to the purposes of the Covenants Act, even though some of the Act's provisions are thereby rendered otiose, is not void under the anti-avoidance provision, even though it could be said to modify the way in which the Act would otherwise apply to the tenancy. The same should logically apply in respect of an agreement that goes further that the provisions of the Act in seeking to implement its purposes, provided that it does not thereby deprive the other party of protection that the Act intended that he should have. But a purported retention, upon a transfer of the reversion, of the right to receive future rent is void under this provision because the Act provides that the benefit of the tenant covenants is annexed to the reversion.[22] **23.08**

[19] *ibid.*, ss.24(2) and 18(3) respectively. Because the term would otherwise have effect to exclude the operation of those sections, it is void to that extent. *Quaere* whether the term remains so as to make the guarantor liable in respect of variations agreed by the lessee as current tenant, as opposed to former tenant. It ought to, because it is only to the extent that the term relates to post-assignment liability and variations that it has effect to exclude the operation of the Act.

[20] *London Diocesan Fund v Phithwa* [2005] 1 W.L.R. 3956.

[21] *ibid.*

[22] *Property Co v Inspector of Taxes* [2005] S.T.C. (SCD) 59, para.56 (*sed quaere*: the chose in action could always be re-assigned by the transferee after the transfer: see *I.R.C. v John Lewis Properties Plc* [2002] 1 W.L.R. 35 (upheld on appeal on a different basis) for a discussion of the nature of the chose in action in relation to an old tenancy).

Limb (b)

23.09 Any agreement relating to a tenancy is void to the extent that it provides for the termination or surrender of the tenancy, or for the imposition on the tenant of any penalty, disability or liability, in the event of the operation of any provision of the Covenants Act.[23] Unlike limb (a), which is concerned with cases where the full operation of the provisions of the Act is in some way fettered, limb (b) is concerned with cases where the provisions of the Act are not prevented from operating fully, but their operation is the trigger for some further liability or obligation arising. Thus, an agreement by the landlord and the tenant that, in the event of the tenant objecting in writing to the release of the landlord from further liability under the landlord covenants of the tenancy,[24] the tenant shall be bound to surrender the tenancy, would fall within this limb and be void. So would an agreement by the tenant to pay additional rent to the former landlord in such circumstances. The words "penalty, disability or liability" are wider than the words "penalty or disability" in the contracting out provisions applicable to business tenancies,[25] and are apt to cover any agreement imposing obligations in such circumstances.

Limb (c)

23.10 Any agreement relating to a tenancy is void to the extent that it provides for the termination or surrender of the tenancy or the imposition of any penalty, disability or liability, and does so (whether expressly or otherwise) in connection with, or in consequence of, the operation of any provision of the Act.[26] This limb is closely related to, though apparently even wider than, limb (b). It extends to implicit as well as express provision for any of these matters[27]; and it covers provision for any such matters in connection with, or in consequence of, the operation of any provision of the Act, and not merely in the event of such operation. These

[23] Covenants Act, s.25(1)(b).

[24] Under *ibid.*, s.8(2)(b).

[25] Landlord and Tenant Act 1954, s.38(1), as amended. The words of that subsection have been held to include any provision which would have the effect of deterring the tenant from exercising the rights he would otherwise have had under that Act: *Stevenson & Rush (Holdings) Ltd v Langdon* (1979) 38 P. & C.R. 208.

[26] Covenants Act, s.25(1)(c).

[27] Perhaps an obligation to vacate and deliver up the lease and keys to the demised premises, which could give rise to a surrender by operation of law, would be covered by limb (c) where it might not fall within the words "provides for . . . the . . . surrender of the tenancy" in limb (b).

are fine distinctions, but perhaps the draftsman had in mind indirect consequences of the operation of the Act, rather than direct ones.[28]

4. The exceptions

The principal reform introduced by the Covenants Act is the termination of the lessee's continuing liability resulting from privity of contract, and the anti-avoidance provisions are clearly intended, inter alia, to protect the automatic termination of the lessee's liability upon a lawful assignment of the tenancy *inter vivos*.[29] But the anti-avoidance provision would prima facie make void any tenant's covenant restricting assignment of the tenancy, as such covenant would have effect to exclude or (if the covenant is qualified) otherwise frustrate the operation of the automatic release provisions of the Act. Similarly, a requirement as a condition of an assignment that the assigning tenant enter into an authorised guarantee agreement[30] is prima facie[31] void under limbs (a) and (b) of the anti-avoidance provision. The Act therefore makes special provision for these two cases by way of exceptions to the anti-avoidance provision. **23.11**

(a) *Covenants against assignment*

To the extent that an agreement relating to a tenancy constitutes a covenant (whether absolute or qualified) against the assignment, or parting with possession, of the premises demised by the tenancy or any part of them, the agreement is not void by virtue of the anti-avoidance provision by reason only of the fact that, as such, the covenant prohibits or restricts any such assignment or parting with possession.[32] Thus, a complete bar on assignment or other parting with possession is perfectly lawful and effective under the Covenants Act. But a qualified covenant against assignment, which permits assignment in certain circumstances but prohibits it in others, is a more complicated case. **23.12**

A standard-form qualified covenant, which permits assignment with the landlord's written consent, not to be unreasonably withheld, restricts assignment of the demised premises in circumstances where it is reasonable for the landlord to withhold consent, for example where the proposed assignee is an undesirable person to be the tenant; and the mere fact that it thus restricts assignment does not make the covenant void **23.13**

[28] It is rather difficult to envisage an agreement which falls within limb (c) but not within either limb (a) or limb (b), as limb (a) is likely to be given the same purposive construction as Landlord and Tenant Act 1954, s.38(1): see *Joseph v Joseph* [1967] Ch. 78.

[29] Under Covenants Act, s.5; see above, paras 14.03 *et seq*.

[30] Under *ibid*., s.16.

[31] But see also the express saving in *ibid*., s.16(1).

[32] *ibid*., s.25(2)(a).

under the anti-avoidance provision, even if the landlord does in fact unreasonably withhold consent. But the Act does not exempt all agreements restricting assignment from the anti-avoidance provision; it is just that the mere fact that an agreement restricts assignment does not make the agreement void.[33]

23.14 Whether or not a particular covenant against assignment is void to any extent depends on its terms; and the anti-avoidance provision is otherwise unaffected in relation to the agreement.[34] In particular, it is not precluded from applying to the covenant to the extent that it purports to regulate the giving of, or the making of any application for, consent to any such assignment or parting with possession.[35] Thus, in any given case, whether or not the particular covenant is void to any extent will depend on the manner in which the covenant purports to restrict the right to assign. And a covenant which restricts the tenant's right to apply for consent, for example, by requiring the tenant first to offer to surrender the tenancy to the landlord,[36] or which purports to allow the landlord to impose terms on the granting of consent, for example requiring the tenant to act as guarantor for all future assignees for the residue of the term,[37] will be void to that extent in that those terms have effect to exclude, modify or otherwise frustrate the operation of the Act. The landlord must therefore in reality choose whether to prohibit assignment altogether (and take any concomitant disadvantages such as diminished rental value), or to restrict the tenant's right to assign but do so in a way which does not infringe the anti-avoidance provision. The application of the anti-avoidance provision to covenants against assignment is related to the circumstances in which a landlord may reasonably withhold consent to a proposed assignment or the conditions subject to which such consent may be granted,[38] and this aspect is considered further in the next Chapter dealing with assignment of tenancies.[39]

(b) *Authorised guarantee agreements*[40]

23.15 Nothing in the anti-avoidance provision applies to any agreement to the extent that it is an authorised guarantee agreement[41]; and nothing else in

[33] *Cf.* the words "by reason only of the fact that as such" in subs.(2)(a).
[34] Covenants Act, s.25(2)(b).
[35] *ibid.*
[36] See *Allnatt London Properties Ltd v Newton* [1984] 1 All E.R. 423.
[37] As to the extent to which an assignor tenant can lawfully be required to guarantee his assignee's liabilities, see below.
[38] As a result of the amendment of Landlord and Tenant Act 1927, s.19(1) made by the Covenants Act.
[39] Below, para.24.07.
[40] See Ch.16, above.
[41] Covenants Act, s.25(3).

the Covenants Act precludes a tenant who is to any extent released from a tenant covenant of a tenancy by virtue of the Act from entering into an authorised guarantee agreement.[42] But an authorised guarantee agreement is restricted to an agreement with respect to the performance by the immediate assignee of the tenant covenants from which the tenant is released.[43] To the extent that an agreement purports to impose on the tenant any requirement to guarantee the performance of the relevant covenant by any person other than the immediate assignee, or to impose on the tenant any liability, restriction or other requirement (of whatever nature) in relation to any time after that assignee is released from the relevant covenant by virtue of the Act, that agreement is not an authorised guarantee agreement and is void.[44] The application of the exception is therefore straightforward in principle: if the agreement is an authorised guarantee agreement it is *ipso facto* not void pursuant to the anti-avoidance provision. The relevant question is whether the agreement satisfies the requirements for an authorised guarantee agreement; if it is a guarantee agreement but does not satisfy those requirements, it is void to that extent. As explained below, one particular difficulty of interpretation has arisen in this regard.

5. Three uncertainties

(a) *Contractual stipulation for release*

In the county court and in the Court of Appeal, a term of a lease—that upon assignment of the reversion the lessor was released from further liability under the landlord covenants—was held plainly void, on the basis that it excluded the operation of the landlord release provisions of the Covenants Act.[45] The parties had made their bargain in such terms that the provisions of the Act were not applicable, and accordingly the tenant was deprived of the opportunity to argue that it was not reasonable for the lessor to be released. On the facts of the case, the tenant would almost certainly have succeeded in such an argument against release; and this, and the unhappy facts of the case generally, undoubtedly influenced the decisions in the lower courts. In the House of Lords, however, the agreement was held valid,[46] on the basis that it was no purpose of the Covenants Act to prevent consensual release, but rather to provide for **23.16**

[42] *ibid.*, s.16(1).

[43] And must otherwise satisfy the requirements of *ibid.*, s.16(2), as to which see above, paras 18.04 *et seq.*

[44] *ibid.*, ss.16(4) and 25(3).

[45] CA judgment reported *sub nom. Avonridge Property Co. Ltd v Mashru* [2005] 1 E.G.L.R. 15.

[46] *London Diocesan Fund v Phithwa*, above.

release where the parties to the lease would otherwise not have been released.[47] This point at least has been settled on the highest authority. The parties are therefore free to make their bargain so that the terms of the Covenants Act do not apply to it,[48] provided that they do not subvert the purpose of the Act in so doing (e.g. by agreeing that the Act will not apply to the tenancy, or by excluding any of its provisions). It is imperative to consider the mischief at which the Covenants Act was aimed before applying the broad terms of the anti-avoidance provision to the facts of a given case.

(b) *Authorised guarantee agreements*

23.17 A difficult question has arisen here, namely whether, as a condition of the grant of a licence to assign a new tenancy, a landlord can stipulate for the tenant's guarantor(s) to stand as guarantor(s) of the tenant's obligations under an authorised guarantee agreement. Lest this be held to be an unreasonable condition to impose at the time of the request for licence to assign, the prescient landlord will have expressly provided for the right to do so in the terms of the covenant against assignment.[49] But in the absence of any express provision in the Covenants Act, equivalent to that legitimising authorised guarantee agreements by former tenants, for sureties of former tenants to remain liable, it is arguable that any such agreement is void to that extent by virtue of the anti-avoidance provisions of the Act. The rival arguments have been set out in detail in the Chapter concerned with authorised guarantee agreements,[50] and there is no recorded judicial pronouncement on their respective merits to date. Resolution of this particular matter must be left to the court, but it is an example of how the very wide terms of the anti-avoidance provision may make void an agreement which the promoters of the Covenants Bill, and Parliament, might not have thought objectionable.[51]

[47] *ibid., per* Lord Nicholls of Birkenhead at paras 16, 17.

[48] In the same way, in *BHP Petroleum v Chesterfield Properties*, above, n.4, the parties were held free to agree that covenants would be personal, and Covenants Act, s.25(2)(a) entitles the parties to agree that the lease is non-assignable.

[49] Taking advantage of the ability in relation to new tenancies to specify conditions subject to which licence may be granted, pursuant to Landlord and Tenant Act 1927, s.19(1A), inserted by Covenants Act, s.22: see below, para.24.05.

[50] Above, paras 18.18 to 18.20.

[51] In the sense that commonly, upon the grant of a lease, the covenant of a new trading company tenant is required to be backed by the guarantee of the established and substantial parent company, and in such circumstances the tenant's guarantee alone of the assignee's liabilities might worthless.

(c) *Executory and executed agreements*

Another uncertainty is whether the anti-avoidance provision applies at all to executed agreements, such as a further guarantee executed by the guarantor of a former tenant upon an assignment of the lease, as opposed to executory agreements only.[52] Some support for the latter can be derived from the language of the provisions of the Covenants Act dealing with fixed charges and variations in tenant covenants after assignment,[53] which imply that such guarantees are in principle enforceable rather than void, as well as from the origins of the anti-avoidance provision in the Landlord and Tenant Act 1954,[54] which has no application to executed agreements. There is also a strong commercial case to be made for this conclusion. A landlord, who would be entitled to refuse an assignment of a lease to a company of poor standing if its covenant would only be bolstered by an authorised guarantee agreement made by the former tenant, a single purpose vehicle with no substantial assets, might be willing to agree the assignment on the basis that the SPV's guarantor further guarantee the SPV's authorised guarantee agreement. If the transaction were to proceed consensually on that basis, thereby conferring a benefit on all parties involved, it would seem unjust for the further guarantee to be struck down *ex post facto*, leaving the landlord with unsatisfactory covenants to which he would never have consented without more security.[55] **23.18**

Despite these arguments, there are countervailing arguments and pointers suggesting that the anti-avoidance provisions were intended to apply to executed agreements too. In the first place, the mischief against which the substantive provisions of the Covenants Act are directed is different in kind from that underlying the anti-avoidance provisions of the Landlord and Tenant Act 1954. In the former case, it is the inability of tenants and their sureties to escape from continuing liability after assignment of the term of years, i.e. after the tenant is no longer the tenant; in the latter case, it is the risk that landlords would use their stronger negotiating position to induce tenants to agree terms that nullified the security of tenure provided by the Act of 1954, i.e. affecting them when they are still the tenant. The former is concerned with the vulnerability of the tenant during as well as at the outset of the lease, with particular emphasis on the ability of the landlord to frustrate or negate the **23.19**

[52] A number of articles in professional journals have argued that it applies only to executory agreements.

[53] Covenants Act, ss.17(1)(a), (3), 18(1)(a), (3), above, para.18.20, n.50.

[54] Above, para.23.06.

[55] It could be argued that the right course for the landlord is simply to refuse his consent, but the consequential stagnation of the parties' interests and the vacation of the demised premises is unlikely to be to any party's commercial advantage.

benefit of the assignment of the lease at some point during its term. The latter is more focused on the time of grant of the lease and the terms in which it is granted, because thereafter the tenant has his security of tenure. It is may therefore be inappropriate to carry too far the analogy with the effect of the provisions of the Act of 1954.

23.20 A term of the lease excluding the effect of the release provisions of the Act in relation to the tenancy is executed, not executory, but the anti-avoidance provisions of the Act must apply to strike down such an agreement. Moreover, the particular protection needed by the tenant at the time of his requesting licence to assign the lease suggests that agreements to the same effect executed at that time should be subject to equivalent protection under the anti-avoidance provision. An agreement in the lease that upon assignment of the term of years the tenant must enter into a guarantee of the tenant covenants for the duration of the term of years (an executory agreement) would also be void to the extent that it goes beyond an authorised guarantee agreement.[56] If, in a case where no such agreement was contained in the lease, the landlord gave consent to the assignment conditionally on the tenant executing such a deed of guarantee, would such an executed guarantee not also be void to the same extent? The fact that the simplest means of extending tenant liability beyond the bounds permitted by the Covenants Act is an executed agreement, *sc.* a guarantee of the liability of all successive assignees, would suggest that such agreements were intended to come within the scope of the anti-avoidance provision. Moreover, an authorised guarantee agreement, which in many if not all cases will be executed rather than executory, is specifically made an exception to the anti-avoidance provision,[57] implying that such executed agreement would otherwise fall within its scope. And the ability to review whether or not the condition of making an authorised guarantee agreement was lawfully imposed, failing which the agreement is not an authorised guarantee agreement,[58] suggests that the fact that the agreement has been executed is not a simple answer to the question whether it is enforceable notwithstanding the provisions of the Act.

Once again, resolution of this difficulty must await judicial interpretation.

[56] Such an agreement is clearly executory rather than executed.

[57] Covenants Act, s.25(3). It is of course likely that many such agreements also contain executory terms, such as the contingent obligation to take up a new lease upon disclaimer.

[58] *ibid.*, s.16(2)(b),(3)(b).

CHAPTER 24

Landlord's Consent to Assignment, etc. of Tenancy

1. The law before the Covenants Act

24.01 At common law, a tenant may assign the benefit of his tenancy or grant a sub-tenancy.[1] That right is, in some or all cases, qualified, restricted or excluded by statute[2]; but it is also bolstered by the doctrine of privity of estate and by statute,[3] so that the burden of the tenancy also passes on assignment. The right of a tenant to assign his tenancy or grant a sub-lease is also commonly qualified, restricted or excluded as a matter of contract between lessor and lessee.[4] In some cases, the right so to act is excluded altogether; in most cases, however, the right is qualified by making the proposed disposition subject to the landlord's licence or consent, and often to other specific requirements and pre-conditions. Even if the lease does not expressly provide that the landlord's licence or consent is not to be unreasonably withheld, all leases requiring such licence or consent to an assignment or sub-letting[5] are subject to a proviso (notwithstanding any express provision to the contrary) that the licence or consent is not to be unreasonably withheld.[6] The landlord may require the payment of a reasonable sum in respect of any legal or other expenses incurred in connection with the licence or consent[7]; but (unless the lease expressly

[1] For a discussion of the effect of the grant of a tenancy being to create an estate in land as well as a contract, and of the consequences of that, see *Old Grovebury Manor Farm v W. Seymour Plant Sales & Hire (No.2)* [1979] 1 W.L.R. 1379.

[2] A statutory qualification is the requirement of formality in Law of Property Act 1925, ss.52–54; an example of a statutory restriction is the prohibition on assignment or sub-letting of an assured tenancy which is a periodic tenancy without the landlord's consent (which may be unreasonably withheld): Housing Act 1988, s.15(1), (2).

[3] In relation to old tenancies, Law of Property Act 1925, s.141; in relation to new tenancies, Covenants Act, s.3(1), (2).

[4] For a brief historical overview, see [2006] 70 Conv. 37.

[5] Save where statute otherwise provides: see, e.g. Housing Act 1988, s.15(2).

[6] Landlord and Tenant Act 1927, s.19(1)(a). For a detailed treatment of the circumstances in which it will or will not be reasonable for a landlord to withhold consent or licence, see *Woodfall's Law of Landlord and Tenant* (28th ed.), paras 11.138 *et seq*.

[7] *ibid*.

otherwise provides) no fine or sum of money in the nature of a fine shall otherwise be payable for or in respect of such licence or consent.[8]

With effect from September 29, 1988, a landlord under a tenancy containing a qualified[9] covenant against assignment, etc. came under a statutory duty (breach of which sounds in damages) to give consent in writing to an assignment, etc. except in a case where it was reasonable for him to withhold consent, and to give it subject only to such conditions as could reasonably be imposed.[10] The onus of proof on the questions whether consent was reasonably withheld, or whether conditions were reasonably imposed, was placed on the landlord.[11]

24.02 As has been seen,[12] the grant by the landlord of licence to assign an old tenancy, and the subsequent assignment pursuant to the licence, did not affect the continuing liability of the lessee under the doctrine of privity of contract to pay the rent and comply with the covenants in the lease. Similarly, where an assignee of the lease who had covenanted directly with the landlord to perform all the tenant's covenants throughout the remainder of the term further assigned the tenancy, that assignee too remained liable to the landlord on his contract. Thus, after several assignments of the tenancy, the landlord often had several tenants or former tenants (and sometimes guarantors too) to whom he could look for payment of the rent and other sums due under the lease. When faced with an application by the tenant to assign the tenancy, the landlord could therefore take some comfort from the fact that he could continue to look to the original lessee or intermediate assignee(s) for the rent, etc. even if the new assignee turned out to be a man of straw. Although it has been held that, as a matter of law, the landlord in such circumstances is entitled to be satisfied that the proposed assignee is himself a responsible and substantial person and otherwise suitable to be the tenant under the lease,[13] it is indisputable that landlords and their agents did have regard to the security of the original tenant's and intermediate assignees' covenants when considering whether or not to give a licence for the lease to be assigned. It is also inherently likely that a licence to assign was granted in many cases on the back of an existing "blue chip" covenant.

24.03 The likely effect on assignments of the proposals in Peter Thurnham M.P.'s original bill abolishing "original tenant liability" was immediately apparent. A landlord would seek to refuse consent to assign in all cases

[8] Law of Property Act 1925, s.144.

[9] i.e. qualified by a provision that the tenancy should not be assigned, etc. without the landlord's consent or licence.

[10] Landlord and Tenant Act 1988, ss.1(3), 4.

[11] *ibid.*, s.1(6).

[12] Above, para.3.02.

[13] See *Ponderosa International Development Ltd v Pengap Securities (Bristol) Ltd* [1986] 1 E.G.L.R. 66; *Warren v Marketing Exchange for Africa* [1988] 2 E.G.L.R. 247.

except where the proposed assignee was of equivalent financial standing tos the current tenant at least, and might well be held to be acting reasonably in so doing. Eventually, the British Property Federation (for landlords) and the British Retail Consortium (for tenants) worked out the compromise which is embodied in the Covenants Act. The essential ingredients of that compromise were to offer landlords the assigning tenant's guarantee of his assignee's liabilities and a greater measure of control over assignments in return for the all-important abolition of privity of contract which the original Bill had sought to promote. The provisions of the Act providing for authorised guarantee agreements have already been considered[14]; the remainder of this chapter is concerned with the amendments to s.19(1) of the Landlord and Tenant Act 1927, which were intended to allow landlords a greater measure of control over assignments of tenancies by agreeing in advance circumstances in which it will be reasonable for the landlord to withhold his consent, or conditions subject to which consent may reasonably be given, or both.

2. The amendment to Landlord and Tenant Act 1927, s.19(1)

(a) *Application*

The Covenants Act inserts a series of new subsections (1A) to (1E), into **24.04**
the well-known s.19 of the Act of 1927. The amendment only applies to what are termed "qualifying leases". A qualifying lease is any lease which is a new tenancy for the purposes of s.1 of the Covenants Act other than a residential lease. A residential lease is, for these purposes, a lease by which a building or part of a building is let wholly or mainly as a single private residence.[15] There is no definition of "building" for the purposes of the Act, and the usual difficulties about sheds, shelters, huts, caravans, mobile homes and connected developments may arise. Some guidance on what the building or part of the building is let "as" may be obtained from the Rent Act cases on the meaning of "let *as* a separate dwelling".[16] The Covenants Act does not, however, distinguish between tenancies on the basis of whether the Rent Acts or the Housing Act 1988 or Pt II of the Landlord and Tenant Act 1954 applies. A building or part of a building may be let mainly as a private residence and yet be subject to the security of tenure regime of the Act of 1954 if business use is a significant purpose of the tenant's occupation of the demised premises.[17] "Significant" means

[14] See above, Ch.16 and para.23.15.

[15] Landlord and Tenant Act 1927, s.19(1E)(a), inserted with effect from January 1, 1996 by Covenants Act, s.22.

[16] See *Megarry's The Rent Acts* (11th ed.), Vol.1, Ch.5, section 2, and Third Cumulative Supplement to the Text.

[17] See Landlord and Tenant Act 1954, s.23(1); Rent Act 1977, s.24(3); Housing Act 1988, s.1(2), Sch.1, Pt I, para.4.

more than merely incidental to the residential purpose.[18] Thus, a tenancy which falls within the 1954 Act might still be let mainly as a single private residence. The words "a single private residence" are used to distinguish such a building from a building or part of a building used for residential purposes but in multiple occupation, and denote premises let as a residence for a single unit or family of persons.[19]

(b) *The principal provision*

24.05 The provision applies where the landlord and the tenant, under a qualifying lease, have entered into an agreement specifying for these purposes[20]: (i) any circumstances in which the landlord may withhold his licence or consent to an assignment of the demised premises or any part of them; or (ii) any conditions subject to which any such licence or consent may be granted. In such cases, the landlord shall not be regarded as unreasonably withholding his licence or consent to any such assignment if he withholds it on the ground (and it is the case) that any such specified circumstances exist; and if he gives the licence or consent subject to any such conditions, he shall not be regarded as giving it subject to unreasonable conditions.[21] Thus, provided that the circumstances or conditions have been agreed in advance (and in the case of the circumstances, exist at the time of the request for licence or consent), the landlord may withhold consent or impose the conditions as the case might be, regardless of whether it is in fact reasonable to do so at the time when the application for licence or consent is considered. Further, the statutory duty imposed by s.1 of the Landlord and Tenant Act 1988 has effect subject to these provisions, and so in such circumstances the landlord cannot be in breach of statutory duty either.[22] "Assignment" for these purposes includes parting with possession on assignment.[23] Thus,

[18] *Cheryl Investments Ltd v Saldanha* [1978] 1 W.L.R. 1329. *Sed quaere*: see also *Gurton v Parrott* [1991] 1 E.G.L.R. 98, and *Wright v Mortimer* [1996] E.G.C.S. 51, leaning towards a test of which is the predominant purpose.

[19] So, e.g. there is no reason why a flat let to three students jointly, each of whom has his own bedroom but who share the sitting room, kitchen and bathroom, should not fall within the definition of residential lease.

[20] i.e. for the purposes of Landlord and Tenant Act 1927, s.19(1A).

[21] *ibid.*, s.19(1A), inserted with effect from January 1, 1996 by Covenants Act, s.22.

[22] *ibid.* The same conclusion was reached apart from these provisions in *Allied Dunbar Assurance Plc v Homebase Ltd* [2002] 2 E.G.L.R. 23 (underlease contained terms contrary to stipulations in alienation covenant in lease: landlord entitled to refuse consent regardless of effect of Landlord and Tenant Act 1988). *Cf. NCR Ltd v Riverland Portfolio No1 Ltd (No.1)* [2004] EWHC 921 (Ch), where the wording of the lease permitted a different conclusion.

[23] Landlord and Tenant Act 1927, s.19(1E)(b), inserted with effect from January 1, 1996 by Covenants Act, s.22.

e.g. if the covenant against assignment, etc., were to provide that the landlord might withhold consent if the profit and loss account in the audited accounts filed with the most recent annual return of any limited company proposed as assignee showed a net loss for the year in question, the landlord could lawfully withhold consent if such was in fact the case at the time of the request for licence to assign to a limited company. Similarly, if the covenant provided that the landlord might always impose a condition that the assignor enter into an authorised guarantee agreement, such a condition could never be unreasonable.

24.06 It is not clear whether the agreement between the landlord and the tenant need state in terms that the agreement is made for the purposes of subs.(1A) of s.19 of the Landlord and Tenant Act 1927.[24] But the provision in that subsection applies whether or not it is contained in the lease, and whether it is made at the time when the lease is granted or at any other time falling before the application for the landlord's licence or consent is made.[25] There is no express requirement that the agreement be made in writing, though if its effect is to vary the terms of a lease made by deed then it must be in writing to be effective.[26] If made before the lease was granted as a collateral agreement supported by consideration, it can be effective notwithstanding the subsequent grant of the lease.[27] An agreement made after the grant of the lease but before the application for licence to assign, e.g. upon the grant of an earlier licence to assign, is clearly within this statutory provision.

But the mere fact that an agreement falls within the terms of subs.(1A) of s.19 of the Landlord and Tenant Act 1927 does not mean that the landlord can with impunity persuade the tenant to agree any circumstances or conditions in advance of an application for licence to assign. His ability to do so is restricted by two matters: first, the anti-avoidance provisions of the Covenants Act, and secondly, the express limitation on such agreements within s.19(1C) of the Landlord and Tenant Act 1927.

[24] Probably not: it is the circumstances or conditions that are required to be specified, not the subsection for the purpose of which the agreement is made.

[25] Landlord and Tenant Act 1927, s.19(1B), inserted with effect from January 1, 1996 by Covenants Act, s.22.

[26] *Goss v Lord Nugent* (1833) 5 B.& Ad. 58; *Morris v Baron & Co.* [1918] A.C. 1.

[27] See, e.g. *City and Westminster Properties (1934) v Mudd* [1959] Ch. 129. Even if the lease was preceded by an agreement for lease which did not include the agreement specifying circumstances or conditions for the purpose of s.19(1A), Law of Property (Miscellaneous Provisions) Act 1989, s.2 is no bar to enforcement of that agreement because it is not itself an agreement for the sale or other disposition of an interest in land: *Tootal Clothing Ltd v Guinea Properties Management Ltd* [1992] 2 E.G.C.S. 80. But see *Grossman v Hooper* [2001] 2 E.G.L.R. 82 for the limits of this approach. The test is whether the totality of the terms agreed are part of a single bargain that are intended to stand or fall together. See also *Wright v Robert Leonard Developments Ltd* [1994] E.G.C.S. 69.

3. Relationship with anti-avoidance provision

24.07 As has been seen,[28] the mere fact that an agreement prohibits or restricts the assignment or parting with possession of the premises demised by a tenancy does not make it void pursuant to the anti-avoidance provision of the Act. But the anti-avoidance provision does nonetheless apply to such an agreement,[29] and if the terms in which the agreement restricts the lawful assignment of the tenancy themselves contravene the anti-avoidance provision, the agreement will to that extent be void. The distinction is a difficult one to draw precisely; but the essence of it is that there must be something in the agreement, more than just the fact that a qualified covenant against assignment inevitably restricts the tenant's right to assign the lease or part with possession of the premises, which contravenes the anti-avoidance provision. Thus, e.g. although a covenant whereby the landlord may withhold consent if it is reasonable to do so is not void, an agreement requiring the assignee to make a formal offer to surrender the tenancy as a condition of the grant of a licence to assign is probably void.[30] One specific, expressed exception to the anti-avoidance provision is an authorised guarantee agreement; and thus it seems that a landlord and a tenant may validly agree that it shall be a condition of any permitted assignment that the assignor shall enter into an authorised guarantee agreement.[31] The borderline between a valid agreement, which merely restricts in some specific way the entitlement of the tenant to assign his lease, and an agreement that regulates the giving of consent in such a way as to infringe the anti-avoidance provisions, will in some cases be unclear. But the question is whether there is anything in the agreement, other than the mere fact that it is a covenant restricting assignment, which infringes any of the limbs of the anti-avoidance provision. If so, the agreement is void.

4. The limitation on the principal provision

(a) *The limitation*

24.08 Subsection (1A) of s.19 of the Act of 1927 does not apply to any agreement specifying circumstances or conditions in connection with the

[28] Above, Ch.23, paras 23.12 *et seq.*
[29] Covenants Act, s.25(2)(b).
[30] See below, para.24.12.
[31] Covenants Act, ss.16(1), 25(3). The Act does not so provide in terms: it provides that the anti-avoidance provisions do not prevent a tenant entering into, nor do they apply to, an authorised guarantee agreement. But if the authorised guarantee agreement is itself unobjectionable, it is difficult to see why an agreement that an authorised guarantee agreement shall be entered into should be struck down, and the draftsman obviously did not intend such a result.

refusal or grant of consent, to the extent that any circumstances or conditions specified in it are framed by reference to any matter falling to be determined by the landlord, or by any other person, for the purposes of the agreement, unless certain conditions are satisfied. These conditions are that either that person's power to determine that matter is required to be exercised reasonably, or that the tenant is given an unrestricted right to have any such determination reviewed by a person independent of both landlord and tenant, whose identity is ascertainable by reference to the agreement. In the second of these alternatives, the agreement must provide for the determination made by any such independent person on review to be conclusive as to the matter in question.[32] This restriction is of central importance in the balance which the Act attempts to maintain between legitimate interests of landlords and tenants. Before turning to some of the more difficult points of construction, some straightforward examples will illustrate how the limitation is designed to work.

(b) *Examples:*

(1) The alienation covenant provides that the landlord may not unreasonably withhold consent to an assignment of the lease. This standard provision is entirely unobjectionable. There is no agreement specifying circumstances or conditions within the meaning of subs.(1A). It is a term which allows assignment in certain circumstances, and as such does not infringe the anti-avoidance provision of the Act. **24.09**

(2) The alienation covenant provides that the landlord may not unreasonably withhold consent, and that it shall be reasonable for him to withhold consent to an assignment to a proposed corporate assignee if the proposed assignee is balance-sheet insolvent on its most recent filed accounts. This is an agreement specifying circumstances within the meaning of subs.(1A), but it is unobjectionable because the circumstances are not framed by reference to any matter falling to be determined by the landlord or by any other person for the purposes of the agreement; the circumstances are capable of ascertainment as a matter of objective fact. Subsection (1A) therefore applies, and the agreement is not void pursuant to the anti-avoidance provision.

(3) The alienation covenant provides that the landlord shall not unreasonably withhold consent, but that it shall be reasonable for the landlord to withhold consent if his managing agent forms the view and certifies in writing that the proposed assignee is unlikely to be a sufficiently respectable tenant of the demised premises.

[32] Landlord and Tenant Act 1927, s.19(1C), inserted with effect from January 1, 1996 by Covenants Act, s.22.

This is an agreement specifying circumstances, but subs.(1A) does not apply to it. The circumstances are framed by reference to a matter falling to be determined by a person, namely the managing agent, for the purposes of the agreement, but the managing agent is not required to determine the matter reasonably, nor is there any provision for independent review. Accordingly, subs.(1A) does not apply by virtue of subs.(1C). The part of the alienation covenant specifying those circumstances is also probably void pursuant to the anti-avoidance provision because it would otherwise have effect to exclude the operation of a provision of the Covenants Act, namely the release of the tenant from liability under the tenant covenants of the Act upon the proposed assignment, based on the *ipse dixit* of a stranger to the lease. Accordingly, the alienation covenant remains as a standard qualified covenant, and if, upon an objective assessment capable of adjudication by the court, the proposed assignee is in fact not a sufficiently respectable person, it will be reasonable for the landlord to withhold consent.

(4) The alienation covenant provides that the landlord may, in giving consent to any proposed assignment, make it a condition of the assignment that any corporate assignee provide at least one individual guarantor of the obligations of the assignee. This is an agreement specifying a condition within the meaning of subs.(1A), and it is not one framed by reference to any matter falling to be determined by the landlord or any other person, and so it is valid for the purposes of the Act of 1927, and the landlord cannot be regarded for the purposes of that Act as having given his consent subject to an unreasonable condition. But it is not clear that the agreement does not infringe the anti-avoidance provision. No sane landlord would require a guarantor for an assignment of a lease to Marks & Spencer Plc, and that company (and many like it) would almost certainly refuse to provide one. In this respect, the terms of the covenant effectively prevent the tenant from being able lawfully to assign his lease to such a company, a wholly unobjectionable assignment, and so are probably void to that extent.

(5) The alienation covenant provides that the landlord may make it a condition of the grant of a licence to assign that the assignee covenant with the landlord to carry out within three months of the assignment such repairs as the landlord shall specify as being required to be done in accordance with the tenant's repairing covenant in the lease. This condition does not fall within subs.(1A) because the condition is framed by reference to a matter falling to be determined by the landlord, and the agreement does not provide for the tenant an unrestricted right to have the

landlord's determination independently reviewed. If it had done, and an independent surveyor's assessment of the necessary repairs was provided to be conclusive as to the matter, the agreement would have been within subs.(1A); but it is not absolutely clear that such a provision escapes the anti-avoidance provision.

(6) The alienation covenant provides that the landlord may grant consent to an assignment subject to a condition that the tenant enter into a guarantee agreement in relation to the liabilities of all successive tenants until the end of the term granted by the lease. Although this condition is specified, and does not depend on any person's subjective judgment, it is self-evidently contrary to the anti-avoidance provision, and must be void.

(c) *The ambit of the limitation*

The limitation on the application of subs.(1A) is concerned with circumstances or conditions "framed by reference to any matter falling to be determined by the landlord or any other person". This is assumed to mean where the circumstances or conditions specified in the agreement in question have, or refer to, or otherwise depend on, some element which is incapable of objective verification, but requires a degree of judgement or interpretation or choice by an individual. So, whereas the book value of a limited company may be capable of objective proof, the creditworthiness of an individual or the quality of appearance of a style of shop front generally are not, and it is to the latter type of case that the limitation is directed. The limitation is concerned to prevent the landlord being able to rely on a prior agreement to justify a refusal of consent (or the imposition of some condition) where the agreement is based on a matter of which either the landlord himself, or some other person who is not required to act reasonably, whose determination is therefore not amenable to review by the court because no objective standard is imposed, is the final arbiter. So the subsection permits a determination by the landlord provided there is some independent and binding review process by which the tenant can challenge the landlord's decision; and it permits a determination by another person provided either that that determination is subject to such a review process, or that that person is required to exercise reasonably his power to determine the matter in question. What the subsection does not on its terms make provision for is for the matter in question to be determined by the landlord acting reasonably,[33] perhaps because it was 24.10

[33] "[T]hat person" in subs.(1C), para.(a) must refer back only to "any other person" and not to "the landlord . . . or any other person".

considered that such a provision would not add much to the landlord's entitlement (under a qualified alienation covenant) reasonably to withhold consent in any event.[34]

24.11 The review contemplated by the new provisions seems to be more in the nature of an expert determination than an award by an arbitrator, because the review by the independent person must be conclusive of the matter; under the Arbitration Act 1996, a party to an arbitration has a limited right in various respects to seek to challenge or reopen an arbitration award. "A person" is not apt to include the Court, so it could not be argued that the inclusion of the criterion of reasonableness satisfied the requirement for a review procedure. The identity of the independent person only needs to be "ascertainable", and not ascertained, and so workable machinery[35] to enable such a person to be identified will suffice. The tenant's right to a review procedure might not be "unrestricted" if, e.g. the terms of the agreement provided for the tenant to bear the costs of the review in any event.[36]

24.12 One particular difficulty of interpretation arises under these new subsections of the Landlord and Tenant Act 1927. It arises in the case where the alienation covenant purports to specify for the purposes of s.19(1A) of the Landlord and Tenant Act 1927 the following condition: that the landlord may, upon receipt of an application for licence to assign a lease, require that the assignor first offer to surrender the lease to the landlord, with the landlord to be entitled to accept that offer during a period of (say) 14 days from the date it is made, and only if such offer is made but not accepted that the landlord shall not unreasonably withhold consent to the proposed assignment. Does this agreement amount either to specifying circumstances in which the landlord may withhold his consent, or alternatively to specifying conditions subject to which

[34] Though it would mean that the landlord would have to prove that he was acting reasonably in general, whereas if he could specify in the covenant circumstances in which, dependent only on his acting reasonably in determining any matter, he would be entitled pursuant to subs.(1A) to withhold consent, he would only have to prove that he acted reasonably in determining that one matter so if the covenant provided that the landlord was entitled to withhold consent if in his reasonable opinion the proposed assignee's mode of use of the premises might prejudice his (the landlord's) ability to market other adjoining premises which he owned, the landlord would only have to prove that his opinion as to that possible prejudice was reasonably formed in the circumstances.

[35] Such as the right for the tenant to apply to the President for the time being of the Law Society or of the Royal Institution of Chartered Surveyors for the appointment of a person to determine the matter in question.

[36] *Quaere* what the position would be if the agreement provided that the tenant should bear his own costs of the review and pay one half of the independent reviewer's costs, or if there was only a limited time in which to initiate the review process.

consent may be granted?[37] It is arguable that this is neither "circumstances" in which a landlord may withhold his consent[38] nor a "condition" subject to which the licence is granted within the meaning of subs.(1A), but rather a pre-condition to the consideration of the question whether consent should be granted, and if so on what terms.[39] If it is a "condition" within the meaning of subs.(1A), then it is not excluded from that subsection by virtue of subs.(1C), and so if the landlord gives consent to the assignment subject to the requirement that the tenant must first offer to surrender, he is not to be regarded as having given it subject to an unreasonable condition. Yet, apart from s.19(1A), the agreement might be held to be void under the anti-avoidance provision of the Covenants Act, because it has effect (if the landlord accepts the offer to surrender) to exclude the operation of the assignment and release provisions of the Act upon the assignment of the lease, or alternatively provides for the surrender of the tenancy in connection with the operation of those provisions, or both.[40]

It is tempting to try to analyse the relationship between the new provisions of the Act of 1927 and the anti-avoidance provision of the Covenants Act thus: that any circumstances or conditions that are validly specified under subs.(1A) of the Act of 1927, and which may therefore entitle the landlord in the future reasonably to withhold consent in the circumstances specified, or to grant it subject to the conditions specified, do not infringe the anti-avoidance provisions of the Covenants Act. The argument would be that a provision cannot be both lawfully imposed for the purposes of one statute, so as to justify a withholding of consent or conditions imposed upon the giving of consent, yet be void under a **24.13**

[37] It should be noted at the outset that this question might not often arise, in that most qualifying leases will be business tenancies to which Landlord and Tenant Act 1954, Pt II applies, and so the agreement will be void under the contracting out provisions in s.38(1) of that Act unless the "contracting out" procedure in *ibid.*, s.38A has been complied with: see *Allnatt London Properties Ltd v Newton* [1984] 1 All E.R. 423. But this will not always be the case, and the problem does pose interesting questions about the way in which, and the extent to which, the provisions of Landlord and Tenant Act 1927, s.19(1A),(1C) are intended to marry with the anti-avoidance provision in Covenants Act, s.25.

[38] Although the effect of an offer to surrender and acceptance would surely mean that the landlord would refuse consent.

[39] The argument is not wholly convincing.

[40] Though applying the reasoning underlying the decision of the House of Lords in *London Diocesan Fund v Phithwa* [2005] 1 W.L.R. 3956, the surrender condition may not be void under the Covenants Act, on the basis that it is no policy of that Act to prevent a tenant from surrendering his lease, thereby terminating his continuing liability under the tenant covenants. The mischief inherent in the requirement to surrender is more a matter for the Landlord and Tenant Act 1954 (if applicable: see n.37, above) or the Landlord and Tenant Act 1988.

second statute.[41] But this analysis cannot be correct, for a condition such as "the assignee shall agree in the licence to assign to pay to the landlord £10,000 on completion of the assignment" would be within s.19(1A) of the Act of 1927, yet would clearly be void under the Covenants Act. The conclusion therefore seems to be that, for these purposes, the Act of 1927 and the anti-avoidance provisions of the Covenants Act work independently, and that both must be satisfied if a landlord is to be able to take advantage of the circumstances and conditions specified in an alienation covenant of a tenancy.

5. Supplementary provision

24.14 The second part of the well-known s.19(1) of the Landlord and Tenant Act 1927 provides (in rather less well-known terms) for the further qualification of the alienation covenant in most building leases of more than 40 years' duration. It is in the following breathless terms:

> "In all leases whether made before or after the commencement of this Act containing a covenant condition or agreement against assigning, under-letting, charging or parting with possession of demised premises or any part thereof without licence or consent, such covenant condition or agreement shall, notwithstanding any express agreement to the contrary, be deemed to be subject . . . (if the lease is for more than 40 years, and is made in consideration wholly or partially of the erection, or the substantial improvement, addition or alteration of buildings, and the lessor is not a Government department or local or public authority, or a statutory or public utility company) to a proviso to the effect that in the case of any assignment, under-letting, charging or parting with the possession (whether by the holders of the lease or any under-tenant whether immediate or not) effected more than seven years before the end of the term no consent or licence shall be required, if notice in writing of the transaction is given to the lessor within six months after the transaction is effected."[42]

In the case of a qualifying lease,[43] subs.(1)(b) of s.19 of the Landlord and Tenant Act 1927 does not have effect in relation to any assignment of the lease.[44] Thus, if so provided, consent or licence is required for the

[41] Particularly where the provision of the first statute was inserted by a section of the second.

[42] Landlord and Tenant Act 1927, s.19(1)(b).

[43] For the definition of "qualifying lease", see above, para.24.04.

[44] Landlord and Tenant Act 1927, s.19(1D), inserted with effect from January 1, 1996 by Covenants Act, s.22.

assignment at any time during the term of a long building lease (other than a residential building lease) which is a new tenancy. "Assignment" includes parting with possession on assignment.[45] But in the case of such a lease, the landlord cannot unreasonably withhold consent to the assignment because the well-known proviso in s.19(1)(a) of the Landlord and Tenant Act 1927 does apply.

6. Analysis

The balance sought to be struck by the amendments to s.19(1) of the Landlord and Tenant Act 1927 is theoretically attractive. As compensation for the loss of the original lessee's covenant throughout the term, the landlord can seek[46] to stipulate for circumstances in which it will be reasonable for him to refuse consent to an assignment that will result in loss of that covenant, and for conditions of granting consent to an assignment which will have that consequence. He can thus seek to ensure that he is not adversely affected by the loss of the covenant; but he can only stipulate in respect of circumstances or conditions that do not depend on the subjective judgement of himself or any other person except an independent arbiter. **24.15**

In practice, this ability to seek to stipulate for such circumstances or conditions gave rise initially to some excessively lengthy and complicated alienation covenants being drafted. They sought to provide for a great variety of anticipated and imagined circumstances that might arise during the term of the lease, and for conditions (including of course the requirement for the assignor to enter into an authorised guarantee agreement) subject to which consent might be granted. The mood seems to have settled to some extent, and landlords, perhaps aware or advised of the risk of such restrictive clauses coming back to haunt them on rent reviews, or perhaps meeting zealous opposition from solicitors and surveyors for would-be tenants, seem to be more content to rely on the pre-Covenants Act criterion of reasonableness at the time of the application for consent. The consistent exceptions to this are that landlords do generally require a stipulation that the assigning tenant enter into an authorised guarantee agreement and do often require the assignee to satisfy an objective criterion of financial soundness by reference to its audited accounts. In that this was the main "price" for the release from privity of contract, the balance between landlord and tenant seems to be working out fairly in practice.

[45] Landlord and Tenant Act 1927, s.19(1E)(b), inserted with effect from January 1, 1996 by Covenants Act, s.22.

[46] It does of course depend on the willingness of the intending tenant to agree such terms.

PART VI

Repeals and Amendments

CHAPTER 25

Repeals and Amendments

The Covenants Act made a number of important amendments and repeals to existing property law statutes, some in relation to the law applicable to new tenancies only and others more generally. They are considered briefly below.

1. Implied covenants of indemnity

Section 77(1)(C),(D) of and Pts IX and X of Sch.2 to the Law of Property Act 1925 (implied covenants in conveyances subject to rents), and s.24(1)(b), (2) of the Land Registration Act 1925 (implied covenants on transfers of leaseholds), ceased to have effect and were repealed as from January 1, 1996[1]; but the repeals do not affect the operation of those provisions in relation to tenancies which are not new tenancies.[2] In relation to such tenancies, the Land Registration Act 2002 provides new implied covenants for transfers taking effect after October 13, 2003.[3] Save for the case of an excluded assignment, no covenant of indemnity by an assignee of a lease which is a new tenancy is needed. The significance and effect of these repeals is fully considered in Pt II of the text.[4] **25.01**

2. Benefit and burden of covenants

Nothing in ss.78 and 79 of the Law of Property Act 1925 (benefit and burden of covenants relating to land) and in ss.141 and 142 of that Act (running of benefit and burden of covenants with reversion) applies in relation to new tenancies.[5] The significance and effect of this provision is fully considered in Pt III of the text.[6] It creates difficulties in relation to concurrent leases and restrictive covenants made by the landlord. **25.02**

[1] Covenants Act, ss.14, 30(2), 31(1); SI 1995/2963.
[2] *ibid.*, ss.1(1), 30(3).
[3] Land Registration Act 2002, s.134(2), Sch.12, para.20; printed below, p.427.
[4] Above, paras 7.18 *et seq.*, 16.08.
[5] Covenants Act, s.30(4).
[6] Above, paras 12.19 *et seq.*

3. Conveyance of land subject to rent or a rentcharge

25.03 Section 77(2) of the Law of Property Act 1925 provided for alterations in the covenants implied under s.77(1) where part of land affected by a rentcharge or comprised in a lease was, without the consent of the owner of the rentcharge or of the lessor, expressed to be conveyed either subject to or charged with the entire rent or discharged or exonerated from the entire rent. In relation to tenancies which are not new tenancies, s.77(2) continues to apply unamended.[7] In all other cases, s.77(2) is amended by substituting two new subsections dealing with conveyances of land affected by a rentcharge and expressed to be conveyed either subject to or charged with, or discharged or exonerated from, the entire rent.[8] In view of the repeal of s.77(1)(C), (D) for such cases, the provisions relating to leases have not been repeated. A further consequential repeal of part of s.77(7) is made.[9]

4. Covenants not to assign, etc. without licence or consent

25.04 Section 19 of the Landlord and Tenant Act 1927 is amended by the insertion of subss.(1A) to (1E), providing that, in relation to non-residential new tenancies, the landlord and the tenant can agree in advance circumstances in which the landlord may withhold his consent to an assignment or conditions subject to which such consent may be given.[10] The significance and effect of this amendment is considered in Pt V of the text.[11]

5. Rent and terms of new business tenancies

(a) *Rent*

25.05 Where the court has to determine the rent payable under a new business tenancy, pursuant to the renewal provisions of Pt II of the Landlord and Tenant Act 1954, it is required to determine the rent at which, having regard to the terms of the tenancy (other than those relating to rent), the holding might reasonably be expected to be let in the open market by a willing lessor, there being disregarded various matters.[12] The valuation date is, in principle, the date when the renewed tenancy is to begin, but as this is three months and three weeks after the court's determination, in

[7] Covenants Act, s.30(1), (3).
[8] *ibid.*, s.30(1), Sch.1, para.2; for the text of the new subsections, see below, App.2, p.363.
[9] *ibid.*, s.30(2), Sch.2.
[10] *ibid.*, s.22.
[11] Above, paras 24.04 *et seq.*
[12] Landlord and Tenant Act 1954, s.34(1).

practice the date of the hearing is taken as the valuation date.[13] Any renewed tenancy granted on or after January 1, 1996 other than pursuant to a court order made before that date will be a new tenancy for the purposes of the Covenants Act.[14] The question of whether the rent for the renewed tenancy should reflect any valuation impact of the tenancy being a new tenancy is resolved by the insertion of a new subsection into s.34 of the Act of 1954, declaring that the court is to take into account any such effect on rent.[15]

(b) *Terms*

In determining the terms of a renewal tenancy, the court is directed to have regard to the terms of the current tenancy and "to all relevant circumstances".[16] That provision is amended by the Covenants Act such that the words "all relevant circumstances" includes a reference to the operation of the provisions of the Covenants Act.[17] Prima facie, the terms of the renewal tenancy are those of the continuing tenancy, and the onus of proof lies on that party seeking to alter the terms to satisfy the court that the change proposed is a reasonable one.[18] But the Covenants Act has effected a "sea change" in what had been common practice and in what the landlord can require, both on assignment and on renewal.[19] A landlord is not entitled to a term, on renewal, that gives him an absolute right to make an authorised guarantee agreement a condition of the assignment of the lease.[20] In view of the very different provisions drafted for new tenancies under the Covenants Act, as compared with old tenancies, this provision is likely to give rise to many disputed applications for new tenancies.[21] **25.06**

6. Contribution

For the purpose of providing for contribution between persons who, by virtue of the Covenants Act, are bound jointly and severally by a **25.07**

[13] *Lovely and Orchard (Services) Ltd v Daejan Investments (Grove Hall) Ltd* [1978] 1 E.G.L.R. 44.

[14] Covenants Act, s.1(3)(b); see above, paras 2.11 *et seq*.

[15] Landlord and Tenant Act 1954, s.34(4), inserted by Covenants Act, s.30(1), Sch.1, para.3. For the terms of the amendment, see below, App.2, p.390.

[16] Landlord and Tenant Act 1954, s.35(1).

[17] *ibid*., s.35(2), inserted by Covenants Act, s.30(1), Sch.1, para.4.

[18] *O'May v City of London Real Property Co. Ltd* [1982] 2 A.C. 726.

[19] *Wallis Fashion Group Ltd v CGU Life Assurance* (2000) 81 P.&C.R. 393, *per* Neuberger J.

[20] *ibid.*

[21] A similarly interesting issue arises under rent review clauses in existing leases: is the hypothetical tenancy which has to be valued on a date after January 1, 1996 a new tenancy or an old tenancy, and if the former, what (if any) changes from the terms of the actual lease will be permissible in the hypothetical lease?

covenant of a new tenancy, the Civil Liability (Contribution) Act 1978 has effect as if—

(1) liability to a person under a covenant were liability in respect of damage suffered by that person;
(2) references to damage accordingly included a breach of a covenant of a tenancy, and
(3) section 7(2) of that Act were omitted.[22]

Thus, where, consequent on an assignment of a new tenancy not giving rise to the release of the assignor from the tenant covenants, and where no express covenant of indemnity was given by the assignee, the assignor is held liable to the landlord, there is now a statutory basis for the assignor's being able to claim contribution from the assignee.[23]

7. Protection against personal liability of trustee or personal representative in respect of rent and covenants

25.08 Section 26(1) of the Trustee Act 1925 limits the personal liability of a personal representative or trustee (where the personal representative or trustee is liable as such for the rent or under a covenant or agreement in a lease) for, inter alia, any rent, covenant or agreement reserved by or contained in any lease, thereby permitting a full distribution of the estate. The Covenants Act extends the protection afforded to such a personal representative or trustee to a case where, as such, he had been required to enter into an authorised guarantee agreement with respect to any lease comprised in the estate. Provided he has met any accrued liabilities under the agreement, he may distribute the estate in full, and is not personally liable in respect of any subsequent claim under the agreement.[24] This new provision, like the old, does not prejudice any right of the lessor to follow the estate into the hands of the beneficiaries.[25]

[22] Covenants Act, s.13(3).
[23] But see above, paras 16.07 *et seq.*, for other remedies available to the assignor in such circumstances.
[24] Trustee Act 1925, s.26(1A), inserted by Covenants Act, s.30(1), Sch.1, para.1.
[25] Trustee Act 1925, s.26(2).

Part VII

Enforcement of Covenants

CHAPTER 26

Enforcement of Landlord and Tenant Covenants

This book is principally concerned with identifying the rights of various persons connected with a lease to enforce its terms and the liability of others to have them enforced against them, rather than with the methods of enforcement. To some extent there is an overlap: any value in a right to enforce presupposes an ability to do so, and in the absence of a remedy the right is worthless. Various issues relating to enforcement have been addressed in the course of the earlier parts of the text. This chapter addresses, briefly, the ways in which those who have a right to enforce landlord or tenant (or third party) covenants can do so. Its purpose is not to rival the many and learned works on contractual and equitable remedies by providing a comprehensive analysis, but to identify the basic methods of enforcement and to highlight some principles of general application to leasehold covenants and of particular application to the scheme introduced by the Covenants Act. **26.01**

1. Debt

(a) *Nature of claim in debt*

A claim in debt exists where a person is liable to pay a liquidated sum of money to another. The other may issue a claim in debt for the money due and interest, either under the terms of the lease or under the statutory power of the court to award interest on judgment sums. There is no material distinction between a claim brought by a landlord, a tenant or another person, whether a party to the lease or a non-party, nor between old tenancies and new tenancies.[1] The relevant question is always whether the liability to pay a liquidated sum to the claimant has accrued. In the case of a claim made against a surety, the liability of the surety is in damages[2] and not in debt unless the terms of the surety covenant impose an obligation to make payment in the event that the principal does not, or **26.02**

[1] The law considered previously in Pts II, III and IV of the text determines who has the right to bring the claim.

[2] For breach of the covenant whereby the surety guarantees that the tenant (or landlord) will pay or otherwise perform: above, para.10.02

to make payment in respect of losses suffered by the creditor.[3] In other (non-surety) cases it may be important to distinguish a claim in debt from a claim for damages, for the latter may be subject to a statutory restriction on the ability to recover damages. Thus, in the case of most leases for more than seven years, a claim by a landlord against a tenant for damages for non-terminal dilapidations requires the leave of the court before the claim for damages can be pursued[4]; and a claim by a landlord for terminal dilapidations is restricted in amount to the diminution in the value of the reversion caused by the disrepair.[5] Tenant covenants are deliberately crafted to avoid these restrictions, where possible, enabling a claim in debt to be pursued.[6]

(b) *Suspension or extinction of creditor's remedy*

26.03 In certain circumstances, rent or other sums payable under a tenancy that would otherwise be due (whether a new tenancy or an old tenancy) are treated as not due to the landlord. This may occur at the outset of a tenancy of premises which consist of or include a dwelling and to which Pt II of the Landlord and Tenant Act 1954 does not apply, if the landlord fails to serve an appropriate notice on the tenant furnishing an address in England and Wales at which the tenant may serve notices on him[7]; or during the term of a similar tenancy when a landlord serves a demand for rent or service charge without including in the demand the landlord's name and address[8]; or where the reversion on such a tenancy is assigned during the term without the new landlord's name and address and notice of the assignment having been provided by him.[9] In the latter case, the assignor landlord's liability is continued under a new tenancy, even if it would otherwise have terminated pursuant to the release provisions of the Covenants Act.[10] The bar to recovery of the rent or service charge is suspensory, not extinctive of the right, and so once the appropriate notice is served all arrears are thereupon due.[11] Under the Covenants Act, however, where no notice is served on a former landlord or his guarantor within six months of a fixed charge becoming due, the landlord's remedy

[3] This is often the case with modern covenants of guarantee: see above, para. 10.02.

[4] Leasehold Property (Repairs) Act 1938, s.1(2),(5), as explained in *Associated British Ports v C.H. Bailey Plc* [1990] 2 A.C. 703.

[5] Landlord and Tenant Act 1927, s.18(1).

[6] See, in the former case, *Jervis v Harris* [1996] Ch. 195 (costs incurred by landlord in entering and performing repairs: debt not damages).

[7] Landlord and Tenant Act 1987, s.48.

[8] *ibid.*, s.47.

[9] Landlord and Tenant Act 1985, s.3; above, para.14.30.

[10] Covenants Act, s.26(2); above, para.14.30.

[11] *Dallhold Estates (UK) Pty Ltd v Lindsey Trading Properties Inc.* [1994] 1 E.G.L.R. 93; *Rogan v Woodfield Building Services Ltd* [1995] 1 E.G.L.R. 72.

is extinguished[12]; and a former landlord's or guarantor's liability may be limited in amount by the other substantive provisions of the Act already considered.[13]

(c) *Defence of set-off*

A defendant will frequently seek to set off against a claim in debt a cross-claim for damages for breach of covenant by the claimant. The most common manifestation is a tenant's cross-claim for disrepair in the face of a landlord's claim for rent. At law, such a set-off is not permitted because the cross-claim is not for a debt nor in reduction of the amount to which the landlord is entitled[14]; but equity allows such a claim to lie in diminution or extinction of the claimant's claim, when brought, where the connection between claim and cross-claim is so close that the cross-claim can be said to "impeach" the claimant's claim.[15] Moreover, where a claimant sues as assignee of a debt, the debtor is entitled to rely on all equities that he could have asserted against the original creditor.[16] Here, particular issues arise in connection with successors in title to the original parties to the lease. Where, in the case of an old tenancy, the successor landlord sues for rent that originally accrued due to the previous landlord,[17] the tenant can set off against such claim any equitable set-off that he would have had to a claim by the previous landlord.[18] But if the new landlord sues only for rent accruing due after the date of the assignment, such equitable set-off cannot be maintained against him.[19] This is because the new landlord is claiming in right of his ownership of the reversion and not as assignee of the rent itself. The same principle would apply to a claim by a tenant against the landlord: the landlord could only set off a cross-claim against the tenant's claim if the cross-claim related to breaches or sums accruing due after the assignment of the term of years, or if the tenant sued as express assignee of the previous 26.04

[12] Covenants Act, s.17; above, Ch.20.

[13] Above, Ch.21.

[14] Under the principle of abatement in *Mondel v Steel* (1841) 8 M. & W. 858, discussed in *Hanak v Green* [1958] 2 Q.B. 9.

[15] *British Anzani (Felixstowe) Ltd v International Marine Management (UK) Ltd* [1980] 1 Q.B. 137.

[16] Law of Property Act 1925, s.136, preserving the common law rule that applied where the assignee had to sue in the name of the assignor: *E Pfeiffer Weinkellerei-Weineinkauf GmbH & Co v Arbuthnot Factors Ltd* [1988] 1 W.L.R. 150 at 162–163.

[17] The effect of Law of Property Act 1925, s.141 being to transfer the right to recover such arrears to the assignee of the reversion: see above, paras 4.19 *et seq*.

[18] *Muscat v Smith* [2003] 1 W.L.R. 2853. Section 141 effects a statutory assignment of the arrears.

[19] *Edlington Properties Ltd v J.H. Fenner & Co Ltd* [2006] 1 W.L.R. 1583.

tenant's right of action.[20] In the case of a new tenancy, a cross-claim that originally accrued against the landlord cannot be raised by way of set-off against his successor in title unless the latter sued as express assignee of the former: the Covenants Act does not effect a transfer to the assignee of the reversion of the assignor's rights in the way that the Law of Property Act 1925 did for old tenancies.[21]

(d) *Concurrent rights and liabilities*

26.05 Problems can arise where a person suing or sued has a concurrent right or liability with some other person in respect of the debt. Under an old tenancy, tenants or landlords and their assignees are severally but non-cumulatively liable under the covenants of the lease. Accordingly, payment by, but *not* a release of, one of the concurrent obligors would discharge the other(s).[22] Under a new tenancy, there will either be no concurrent liability, because the assignor will have been released pursuant to the Act, or, e.g. upon an excluded assignment,[23] the assignor and assignee will be jointly and severally liable on the covenants.[24] In such a case, a release of one obligor is, by statute, not a release of his co-obligor(s),[25] but payment by one will discharge all, and the claimant may choose whom (or how many) to sue. These cases fall to be distinguished from the case of joint tenants or joint landlords where, in general, absent some contrary provision, both (or all) persons who jointly constitute the tenant or landlord must sue and be sued.[26]

26.06 The position where two or more persons are severally entitled to the benefit of a landlord or tenant covenant is less clear. This rarely became an issue in relation to old tenancies,[27] but the Covenants Act itself creates circumstances in which two or more persons or groups of persons are entitled to enforce covenants of the counterparty. These are where an

[20] There is no equivalent provision to Law of Property Act 1925, s.141 that transfers to an assignee tenant his assignor's claims against the landlord under the lease.

[21] *Edlington v Fenner*, above. See also above, paras 12.22 and 12.23.

[22] See *Sun Life Assurance Society Plc v Tantofex (Engineers) Ltd* [1999] 2 E.G.L.R. 135.

[23] See Ch.16, above.

[24] Covenants Act, s.13(1); above, paras 16.06 *et seq.*

[25] *ibid.*, s.13(2).

[26] This common law rule has been abrogated generally in relation to a claim brought in a county court against one or more of a number of persons jointly liable: County Courts Act 1984, s.48(1). Both the High Court and the county courts have power, under CPR Pt 19, to ensure that all appropriate parties are joined.

[27] Partly because of the effect of Law of Property Act 1925, s.141, which does not apply to new tenancies, and partly because lessees who had ceased to be the tenant rarely have an interest in enforcing the lessor's covenants.

excluded assignment of the reversion or of the term of years occurs,[28] where the former landlord has not obtained a release,[29] where a concurrent lease of the reversion is granted,[30] and where a mortgagee is in possession of the reversion or of the term of years.[31] No provision of the Covenants Act regulates how covenants may be enforced in such circumstances, but on the basis that the right cannot, in the absence of some express provision, be joint or joint and several, it appears that any of the obligees may (vis-à-vis the obligor) sue on the covenant in question. Subject to the co-obligee(s) intervening in proceedings, it seems that a tenant would therefore have no defence to a claim to rent by a former landlord or a concurrent lessor, and that payment pursuant to a judgment obtained by such a person should be a defence to a subsequent claim by the co-obligee.[32] The result is surprising, and the tenant (or landlord) faced with such an unusual situation would be well advised to inform the other persons entitled to the benefit of the covenant so that they can intervene as appropriate.

(e) *Limitation*

Actions for rent or for damages in respect of arrears of rent attract a limitation period of six years, regardless of whether the lease is executed as a deed.[33] **26.07**

2. Damages

(a) *Nature of remedy*

In the absence of a claim for specific performance of a covenant, damages will generally be the appropriate remedy for its breach. A claim for damages for breach of covenant is one means of enforcing the covenant. In commercial terms, a contract is understood as giving rise to an obligation to perform or alternatively to pay damages for failure to do so,[34] and non-residential lease at least are commercial contracts. Even where the landlord and tenant in question have not made a contract, e.g. **26.08**

[28] Covenants Act, ss.5(2), (3), 6(2), (3), 11(2), (3).
[29] *ibid.*, s.6(2).
[30] *ibid.*, s.15(1)(a).
[31] *ibid.*, s.15(1)(b), (3).
[32] The assignee landlord, the concurrent lessee or the mortgage in possession, as the case may be, would then have to pursue its claim against the judgment creditor for recoupment.
[33] Limitation Act 1980, s.19; *Romain v Scuba TV Ltd* [1997] Q.B. 887.
[34] See *per* Lord Hobhouse of Woodborough in *Attorney-General v Blake* [2001] 1 A.C. 268 at 297–298, citing Lord Diplock in *Photo Productions Ltd v Securicor Transport Ltd* [1980] A.C. 827.

where they stand in a relationship of privity of estate or where by virtue of the Covenants Act they are bound by the landlord and tenant covenants respectively, they are treated for most purposes as if they had made a contract, and the covenants may be enforced as if they had. Under the law relating to old tenancies, it was a matter of routine for assignee tenants to make a new contract with the landlord, for the purposes of creating a contractual liability for the duration of the term. This also had the effect of making the assignee liable under any covenants that did not touch and concern the demised premises. But apart from these considerations, the express contract did not alter the nature of the landlord's remedy in damages for breach of covenant. In relation to new tenancies, all landlord or tenant covenants except personal and non-registered covenants[35] will pass with the term and the reversion, and the assignee is "bound by the covenants" and entitled to the benefit.[36] So the potential liability and the remedy of damages for breach of covenant will pass to the respective assignees. Although loss is not a necessary ingredient of the cause of action for breach of contract, damages will only be recovered in respect of loss caused by the breach, on established principles of the law of contract.

(b) *Third parties and non-parties*

26.09 Damages will often be the appropriate remedy where a surety is sued, though modern surety covenants are drafted with a view to making the surety liable in debt, at least where the subject-matter of the claim is a liquidated sum of money. Third parties and non-parties who have the benefit of a landlord or tenant covenant will have the same remedies, and third parties who are subject to the burden of a covenant in a lease are liable to have the covenant enforced against them in the same way. In relation to old tenancies, a non-party to the lease cannot be liable under its covenants in the absence of a consensual novation[37]; but the Covenants Act creates the possibility of non-parties being sued on landlord or tenant covenants.[38] In the case of concurrent lessees of the reversion and mortgagees of the landlord's or tenant's interest, the Act expressly provides that covenants enforceable against the landlord or tenant, as the case may be, will also be enforceable against such a concurrent lessee or any mortgage in possession[39]; and in principle this must include a remedy in damages for breach of the covenant, even though the non-party made no such contract.

[35] Above, paras 12.03 to 12.09
[36] Covenants Act, s.5(2), (3).
[37] See above, para.10.10.
[38] Above, paras 17.17 *et seq.*
[39] Covenants Act, s.15(2), (4).

In the case of a restrictive covenant, owners and occupiers of the demised premises will be liable to have the covenant enforced against them. The Covenants Act creates its own code for enforcement of such leasehold covenants relating to the demised premises themselves: the covenant can be enforced against later owners and occupiers whether or not the lease provides that the covenant will bind such persons.[40] Under the general law of restrictive covenants, such persons are only bound in equity, and therefore cannot be sued for damages for breach of covenant, just damages in lieu of injunctive relief. Whether or not the express provision of the Covenants Act changes this position is unclear: the language used ("... shall be capable of being enforced against any other person ... ") is slightly different from that used in the case of concurrent lessees and mortgagees in possession ("... it shall also be so enforceable against ... "), though perhaps a clearer indication would have been given had the Act been intended only to replicate the effect of the general law in the case of covenants between lessor and lessee. It is tentatively suggested that a change in the law in this regard probably was intended, and that accordingly licencees of the landlord and sub-tenants of the tenant may be liable in damages for breach of the restrictive covenant. **26.10**

(c) *Defences*

Apart from a denial of breach and an allegation that no loss was caused thereby,[41] an equitable set-off will be a defence *pro tanto* to a claim for damages for breach of contract as it is to a claim in debt, and the discussion in section 1, above,[42] applies equally here. Liability under landlord and tenant covenants of a new tenancy is generally restricted to the time when the reversion or term of years is vested in the defendant,[43] though there are a number of complex exceptions to this principle built into the scheme of the Covenants Act. Similarly, the right to sue on the covenants is (absent an express assignment of the chose in action) restricted to breaches occurring during the time when the claimant was the landlord or tenant.[44] Specific statutory defences or limitations exist in relation to claims on particular types of covenant,[45] and reference should be made to more general landlord and tenant texts for commentary on those covenants, which is beyond the scope of this book. For the defence of limitation, see below. **26.11**

[40] *ibid.*, s.3(5).

[41] Which, as stated, is not as such a defence to the breach, but if proven will usually entitle the defendant to the costs of the claim.

[42] para.26.04, above.

[43] Covenants Act, ss.3(2), (3), 24(1), (3).

[44] *ibid.*, s.24(4).

[45] e.g. nn.4, 5, above.

(d) *Concurrent rights and liabilities*

26.12 As with claims in debt, situations can arise under old and new tenancies where one or more persons may sue or be sued for damages on landlord or tenant covenants. No particular problem arises in the case of concurrent liability, where the more difficult issues are likely to be ones of contribution or indemnity between co-obligors.[46] The Covenants Act does to a large extent exclude circumstances of concurrent liability by its machinery of release on assignment; but it does create some potentially difficult issues where the right to sue on landlord or tenant covenants is apparently vested in more than one person. In this regard, the commentary in s.1, above,[47] applies equally to claims for damages, though with the additional consideration that recovery of damages will involve proving loss caused by the breach. On established principles, it seems unlikely that a defendant can rely on *jus tertii*, so that a claim for damages by a former landlord who has not been released from the landlord covenants cannot be defended on the basis that the assignee of the reversion has the better right to sue as between assignor and assignee. But if the breach of covenant in question relates to, say, the condition of the demised premises, which are no longer owned by the assignor and over which the assignor has no proprietary rights, it will be difficult for the assignor to prove loss; whereas if the breach is of a covenant to confer on the landlord a financial or other benefit unconnected with ownership of the reversion then the claim may well succeed. In the case of a tenant's repairing covenant, both concurrent lessor and concurrent lessee may have different claims for the same breach, depending on the length and terms of the concurrent lease,[48] though the tenant cannot be liable twice over for the same loss.

(e) *Tort and statutory duties*

26.13 Where a contractual or a statutory basis of enforcement of rights and obligations exists, there is no need for a tortious remedy and generally none exists. So, e.g. the old torts of waste and those associated with the law of negligence rarely have any application in the modern law of landlord and tenant, though the law of nuisance is of general application and may well apply where the landlord owns other property in the

[46] See below, section 4(c), for some of these relating to enforcement.

[47] paras 26.05, 26.06, above.

[48] See, e.g., *Family Management Ltd v Gray* [1980] 1 E.G.L.R. 46; *Crown Estate Commissioners v Town Investments Ltd* [1992] 1 E.G.L.R. 61, where the existence of a sub-tenancy affected the quantification of damages for breach.

vicinity of the demised premises.[49] The old torts associated with the law of distress apply to new and old tenancies alike, subject to the exclusion of the right to levy distress in the case of most residential tenancies, but the levying of distress is now relatively unusual.

The tort of unlawfully inducing a breach of contract does from time to time appear in the context of a contractual landlord and tenant relationship, and can be of value in supplementing the restrictions contained in a standard alienation covenant. This is mostly in circumstances in which a remedy in damages for breach of covenant is *not* sufficient for the landlord rather than as an alternative basis for a damages claim, and as such will be discussed further under the heading of Injunctions.[50] But the cause of action for damages for unlawfully procuring a breach of contract will provide a financial remedy against an unlawful assignee or subtenant, whereas the tenant covenants would only provide a remedy against the tenant. Also in connection with alienation, the statutory duty imposed by s.1 of the Landlord and Tenant Act 1988[51] is a frequent source of litigation, and damages for breach of the statutory duty may include aggravated and exemplary damages as well as damages to compensate actual losses suffered by the claimant.[52] The Covenants Act itself creates one statutory tort to which the same principles will apply, that of failing on request within a reasonable time to grant an overriding lease.[53] Loss is a necessary ingredient of a cause of action in these statutory torts. **26.14**

(f) *Limitation*

Apart from a claim for damages in respect of arrears of rent, where the limitation period is always six years,[54] the limitation period is probably 12 years for any lease executed as a deed, being a specialty for the purposes of the Limitation Act 1980,[55] and otherwise six years. **26.15**

[49] For a general discussion, see *Southwark LBC v Mills* [2001] 1 A.C. 1.

[50] para.26.18, below.

[51] Essentially, to give consent promptly to a request for consent to an assignment or sub-letting, save where it is reasonable to refuse such consent, and to give written notice of the decision and any conditions and of any reasons for a refusal.

[52] *Design Progression Ltd v Thurloe Properties Ltd* [2005] 1 W.L.R. 1.

[53] Covenants Act, ss.19(6)(a), 20(3).

[54] Limitation Act 1980, s.19.

[55] *ibid.*, s.8(1). The doubt expressed in the text reflects the case of mortgage deed that is signed but not executed under seal: is this a "specialty" within the meaning of the Act? Previous cases established that a document executed under seal is a specialty, but in view of changes made by the Law of Property (Miscellaneous Provisions) Act 1989, the Companies Act 1989 and the Regulatory Reform (Execution of Deeds and Documents) Order 2005, it will now be more common for deeds to be executed without a seal: see above, para.1.01.

3. Specific enforcement and injunctive relief

(a) *Positive obligations*

26.16 The equitable remedy of specific enforcement will lie, to enforce a landlord or tenant covenant as much as any other contractual obligation, and the usual limitations on this remedy will apply, namely that specific performance will not be granted where damages will be an adequate remedy for the covenantor's breach of contract or where such an order would be oppressive. In many cases, the courts have established a working practice in relation to particular kinds of covenant, so that e.g. a tenant's covenant to repair the demised premises was rarely enforced, whereas a landlord's covenant would in principle be enforced by an order of specific performance.[56] And an assignee's covenant to perform and observe the covenants on the part of the lessee is regarded as a covenant of indemnity only, so that specific performance will not be ordered,[57] whereas a tenant's covenant in an underlease to perform covenants in the headlease is a covenant to be performed and may be specifically enforced.[58] In more recent times, however, some of these practices and presumptions have been questioned and a more general test applied, namely what in all the circumstances is the most appropriate remedy.[59] The broader test suffers from the disadvantage of relative uncertainty but may have the advantage of greater fairness, and as a result vehement disagreements sometimes occur between courts as to the appropriateness or otherwise of specific enforcement.[60]

The best guidance that can be given is that specific performance of a positive obligation will not be ordered if damages for breach of covenant will be an adequate remedy, but subject to that if what must be done is adequately defined and it is just and equitable in all the circumstances to enforce the obligation it will be enforced. It will not be just and equitable to enforce in a case where the covenantor will suffer exceptional hardship by having to perform the obligation. Specific performance will not be ordered where the defendant *cannot* perform, e.g. against a former landlord or former tenant who remains bound by the repairing covenants of the lease but who has no right of access to the demised premises to

[56] *Jeune v Queen's Cross Properties Ltd* [1974] Ch. 97.

[57] *Harris v Boots, Cash Chemists (Southern) Ltd* [1904] 2 Ch. 376.

[58] *Ayling v Wade* [1961] 2 Q.B. 228, distinguishing *Harris v Boots*, above.

[59] So, in *Rainbow Estates Limited v Tokenhold Ltd* [1999] Ch. 64, the rule of practice stated in *Jeune v Queen's Cross*, above, was doubted.

[60] See, e.g. the comments in the House of Lords about the Court of Appeal's decision to enforce a "keep open" covenant: *Cooperative Insurance Society Ltd v Argyll Stores (Holdings) Ltd* [1998] A.C. 1.

perform the obligation,[61] or against a person who does not have the financial resources to perform. Although a claim for specific performance presupposes that a contract exists[62] and that therefore a remedy of damages at common law will be available, the court can supplement this remedy where appropriate by an award of damages in lieu of specific performance, enabling the financial compensation to be assessed on a different footing.[63]

(b) *Negative obligations*

A different approach is generally applied in relation to negative covenants. The courts take the view that they are doing no more than enforcing the parties' contractual agreement in such a way as to require the defendant only to desist from doing something, rather than to take any positive steps.[64] But where a party is bound in equity only and not as a matter of contract, e.g. under a restrictive covenant, the grant or refusal of an injunction to restrain a breach is discretionary, although the discretion is exercised on well-established principles. Of these, the principle that a person should not be able compulsorily to purchase a proprietary right by offering to pay damages instead,[65] and the principle that equity will not grant injunctive relief where financial compensation is an adequate remedy, potentially conflict. There may be a trend away from the former and towards the latter, at least where there is evidence that the proprietary right has only a financial value.[66] Under the Covenants Act, a restrictive covenant in a new tenancy binds owners and occupiers of the demised premises under the statutory scheme.[67] As such, the covenant is enforceable neither as a contractual stipulation nor solely **26.17**

[61] Though it has been held in one case that concurrent obligors under the same instrument have the right, each as against the other, to do what is necessary to perform the obligation and so to exonerate themselves: see *Stroude v Beazer Homes Ltd* [2006] 2 P. & C.R. 6.

[62] In two respects: first that there is a specified obligation to enforce; and secondly that the party claiming specific performance has provided consideration for the obligation in question, since specific performance will not be granted in favour of a volunteer; see above, para.17.13, n.49, for the position under the Contracts (Rights of Third Parties) Act 1999.

[63] i.e what the defendant would reasonably have to pay to obtain a release from the obligation: see *AMEC Developments Ltd v Jury's Hotel Management (UK) Ltd* (2001) 82 P.& C.R. 22 (compensation for construction of hotel on land not belonging to hotel owner reflecting value of extended development).

[64] Based on the *dicta* of Lord Cairns L.C. in *Doherty v Allman* (1878) 3 App. Cas. 709.

[65] *Shelfer v City of London Electric Lighting Co. Ltd* [1895] 1 Ch. 287, *per* A.L. Smith L.J.

[66] See *Midtown Ltd v City of London Real Property Co. Ltd* [2005] 1 E.G.L.R. 65.

[67] Covenants Act, s.3(5).

in equity, and it is therefore unclear to what extent equitable considerations will apply where a claimant seeks injunctive relief.[68]

(c) *Injunctions*

26.18 An injunction may be granted, whether prohibitory or mandatory, to protect the rights of a claimant who cannot rely on a specific contractual stipulation against the defendant. So, e.g. an injunction will be needed where something done but forbidden by the lease needs to be undone, or where a particular breach of a general negative stipulation is threatened, or where a non-party threatens to interfere unlawfully with a party's rights or interests. Where the court could grant an injunction (i.e. where the claimant has not disentitled himself on equitable grounds from claiming injunctive relief) but an injunction is withheld as an exercise of discretion, damages in lieu of injunctive relief will generally be awarded.[69] But where a tenant assigns the lease or grants a sub-lease in breach of the terms of the alienation covenant, so that a one-off breach has already occurred, the court has shown itself ready to order the tenant and his assignee or sub-tenant to undo the disposition where it can be shown that the assignee or sub-tenant knew that the disposition would be a breach of covenant.[70] Thus, even though the disposition has been completed and registered, the court has jurisdiction to compel the disponee to undo the transaction as a remedy in tort for unlawfully procuring a breach of contract by the tenant. Damages would not be an adequate remedy if they left the landlord with the alternatives of forfeiting the lease, contrary to its commercial interests, or accepting an unsuitable tenant in occupation of the premises.

(d) *Limitation*

26.19 The equitable remedies of specific performance and injunction are not subject to most of the relevant statutory time limits in the Limitation Act 1980, except to the extent and in the manner that time limits were applied "by analogy" before the equivalent time limits of the Limitation Act 1939

[68] In principle, the position should be no different from that of a restrictive covenant enforceable in equity because the court is not enforcing an agreement made by the defendant with the claimant; but the Act arguably requires such third parties to be treated as if they are contractually bound: see para.26.10, above.

[69] See *Jaggard v Sawyer* [1995] 1 W.L.R. 269 and *AMEC v Jury's Hotel*, above. The principles on which damages may be awarded in such cases were reviewed by the House of Lords in *Attorney-General v Blake* [2001] 1 A.C. 268, approving *Jaggard v Sawyer.*

[70] *Hemingway Securities Ltd v Dunraven Ltd* (1996) 71 P. & C.R. 30; *Crestfort Ltd v Tesco Stores Ltd* [2005] 3 E.G.L.R. 25.

came into effect on July 1, 1940.[71] The one relevant provision that is not excepted is the six-year limitation on actions to recover arrears of rent or for damages in respect of rent arrears, but since a claim for equitable relief in relation to rent arrears is unlikely to be brought[72] this omission has no practical significance. Instead of the statutory time limits, the equitable doctrines of laches and acquiescence will apply to determine whether a claimant is disqualified in equity from claiming such relief.[73]

4. Indirect enforcement

(a) *Methods of indirect enforcement*

Sometimes, there are tactical advantages or other good reasons for seeking to enforce a landlord or tenant covenant indirectly; sometimes a claimant will have no other course available to him. Apart from the remedies of debt, damages and specific enforcement just considered, the benefit secured by a covenant may be able to be obtained by threatening or claiming forfeiture, threatening or levying distress, entry to perform the obligation, a claim for an indemnity, contribution, recoupment or performance, or merely for declaratory relief. So, e.g. a landlord to whom rent is owed by the lessee but who cannot claim the arrears from the assignee tenant can forfeit the lease and require the tenant to pay all arrears as a condition of relief from forfeiture, or levy distress against the goods of the tenant or even goods of a sub-tenant, subject to the statutory rights conferred on third parties to prevent distress and to recover impounded goods.[74] Often the threat of forfeiture or of levying distress will be sufficient to persuade the tenant to make payment of the arrears. The law of forfeiture and of distress is beyond the scope of this book and reference should be made to general texts of the law of landlord and tenant. **26.20**

(b) *Entry and performance*

Where a landlord or tenant defaults on a covenant in the lease, the best remedy may be for the other party to perform the obligation himself and then recover the cost of doing so from the defaulting party. In most cases, this will be a more effective and cheaper remedy that pursuing a claim for specific enforcement, and a forfeiture of the lease will often be inappropriate for commercial reasons. Where the landlord fails to repair the **26.21**

[71] Limitation Act 1980, s.36(1). This obscure body of law has no general application under the modern law.

[72] With the possible exception of a guarantor's *quia timet* action to compel payment by a tenant.

[73] Limitation Act 1980, s.36(2).

[74] Law of Distress Amendment Act 1908, s.1.

demised premises, the tenant is entitled to perform the repairs himself and deduct the cost from the rent payable.[75] The landlord has no equivalent right as a matter of law, but a well-drawn lease will usually include a contractual right of entry to perform the repairs on which the tenant has defaulted and then recover the cost as a debt.[76] A right of entry of this kind is different in kind from a right of re-entry and is not subject to the restrictions on forfeiture contained in the Law of Property Act 1925 or in the Leasehold Property (Repairs) Act 1938.[77]

(c) *Enforcement as between assignor and assignee*

26.22 Difficulties of enforcement often arise between persons in the same right or interest under a lease, as well as between opposite parties. It is usually in an assignor's interest for an assignee to perform the landlord or tenant covenants of the lease, and in many cases the assignor will wish to be able to compel such performance, so as to avoid being itself in breach of covenant or liable under an authorised guarantee agreement. Even with new tenancies and apart from such agreements, cases of concurrent liability under landlord or tenant covenants may exist,[78] and this is the normal state of affairs for old tenancies. As noted above,[79] the usual covenant by an assignee of the reversion or of the term of years of an old tenancy to perform the landlord or tenant covenants of the lease and to indemnify the assignor does not entitle the assignor to an order compelling the assignee to perform his obligation.[80] So where a lessee sought to compel his insolvent assignee to compel a further assignee to pay arrears of rent the claim was rejected.[81] But no such covenants are implied in the case of an assignment of the reversion or terms of years of a new tenancy, and any concurrent liability that does arise upon an assignment is on the basis of joint and several liability.[82]

26.23 So can a lessor or lessee who has assigned his interest but who remains liable under (say) a covenant to repair enforce against the assignee his

[75] *Lee-Parker v Izzet (No.1)* [1971] 1 W.L.R. 1688. More accurately, the expenditure is treated as payment of rent itself, not a cross-claim to be set off against the rent.

[76] *Jervis v Harris* [1996] Ch. 195.

[77] *ibid.*

[78] Excluded assignments, former landlords who are not released from the landlord covenants, concurrent leases.

[79] para.26.16, above.

[80] *Harris v Boots*, above.

[81] *RPH Ltd v Mirror Group (Holdings) Ltd* [1993] 1 E.G.L.R. 74. The landlord would not sue the further assignee rather than the lessee because they were in the same group of companies, and the lessee had no restitutionary claim against the further assignee because it was not the current tenant at the time when the arrears accrued.

[82] Covenants Act, s.13(1).

right to enter and carry out the repair? In the case of an old tenancy, the answer is presumably that he cannot, on the basis that the implied covenant is construed as a covenant of indemnity only, and so would not extend to allow indirect enforcement of an obligation to perform. But in the case of a new tenancy, where a joint and several liability to perform exists but no covenant of indemnity is implied, there would seem to be a good argument for the implication of such a right, and support can be derived from a recent case in which one co-obligor under the terms of a planning agreement was held entitled to compel performance directly or indirectly by the other and to enter his land for that purpose.[83] As against the counterparty, the assignor would be entitled to perform because he remains subject to an obligation to do so. In the absence of such a right, the assignor would in principle have a restitutionary claim against the current landlord or tenant, as the case may be, or a claim to contribution under the terms of the Covenants Act.[84] It is possible, though very unusual, for performance by an assignee to be secured by a right of re-entry reserved to the assignor[85]; and a right to security of a similar kind is created by the Covenants Act, which entitles a former tenant or his guarantor who is called upon to pay a fixed charge to take an overriding lease of the demised premises.[86] This in turn would entitle it to forfeit the lease under which the tenant has defaulted.

[83] *Stroude v Beazer Homes* [2006] 2 P. & C.R. 6. The right was held to be implicit where the same obligation was accepted jointly and severally by two parties in the same agreement.

[84] Covenants Act, s.13(3).

[85] See *Shiloh Spinners, Ltd v Harding* [1973] A.C. 691.

[86] Covenants Act, s.19; above, Ch.22.

APPENDICES

APPENDIX ONE

LANDLORD AND TENANT (COVENANTS) ACT 1995

CONTENTS

LANDLORD AND TENANT (COVENANTS) ACT 1995
(c. 30)

An Act to make provision for persons bound by covenants of a tenancy to be released from such covenants on the assignment of the tenancy, and to make other provision with respect to rights and liabilities arising under such covenants; to restrict in certain circumstances the operation of rights of re-entry, forfeiture and disclaimer; and for connected purposes.

[19th July 1995]

Preliminary

Tenancies to which the Act applies

1.—(1) Sections 3 to 16 and 21 apply only to new tenancies.

(2) Sections 17 to 20 apply to both new and other tenancies.

(3) For the purposes of this section a tenancy is a new tenancy if it is granted on or after the date on which this Act comes into force otherwise than in pursuance of—

(a) an agreement entered into before that date, or
(b) an order of a court made before that date.

(4) Subsection (3) has effect subject to section 20(1) in the case of overriding leases granted under section 19.

(5) Without prejudice to the generality of subsection (3), that subsection applies to the grant of a tenancy where by virtue of any variation of a tenancy there is a deemed surrender and regrant as it applies to any other grant of a tenancy.

(6) Where a tenancy granted on or after the date on which this Act comes into force is so granted in pursuance of an option granted before that date, the tenancy shall be regarded for the purposes of subsection (3) as granted in pursuance of an agreement entered into before that date (and accordingly is not a new tenancy), whether or not the option was exercised before that date.

(7) In subsection (6) "option" includes right of first refusal.

Covenants to which the Act applies

2.—(1) This Act applies to a landlord covenant or a tenant covenant of a tenancy—

(a) whether or not the covenant has reference to the subject matter of the tenancy, and
(b) whether the covenant is express, implied or imposed by law,

but does not apply to a covenant falling within subsection (2).

(2) Nothing in this Act affects any covenant imposed in pursuance of—

(a) section 35 or 155 of the Housing Act 1985 (covenants for repayment of discount on early disposals);
(b) paragraph 1 of Schedule 6A to that Act (covenants requiring redemption of landlord's share); or
(c) [section 11 or 13 of the Housing Act 1996 or] paragraph 1 or 3 of Schedule 2 to the Housing Associations Act 1985 (covenants for repaying of discount on early disposals or for restricting disposals).

ANNOTATION

The words in square brackets in subs.(2)(c) were inserted with effect from October 1, 1996 by The Housing Act 1996 (Consequential Provisions) Order 1996 (S.I. 1996 No. 2325), arts 1(2), 5(1), Sch.2, para.22.

Transmission of Covenants

Transmission of benefit and burden of covenants

3.—(1) The benefit and burden of all landlord and tenant covenants of a tenancy—

- (a) shall be annexed and incident to the whole, and to each and every part, of the premises demised by the tenancy and of the reversion in them, and
- (b) shall in accordance with this section pass on an assignment of the whole or any part of those premises or of the reversion in them.

(2) Where the assignment is by the tenant under the tenancy, then as from the assignment the assignee—

- (a) becomes bound by the tenant covenants of the tenancy except to the extent that—
  - (i) immediately before the assignment they did not bind the assignor, or
  - (ii) they fall to be complied with in relation to any demised premises not comprised in the assignment; and
- (b) becomes entitled to the benefit of the landlord covenants of the tenancy except to the extent that they fall to be complied with in relation to any such premises.

(3) Where the assignment is by the landlord under the tenancy, then as from the assignment the assignee—

- (a) becomes bound by the landlord covenants of the tenancy except to the extent that—
  - (i) immediately before the assignment they did not bind the assignor, or
  - (ii) they fall to be complied with in relation to any demised premises not comprised in the assignment; and
- (b) becomes entitled to the benefit of the tenant covenants of the tenancy except to the extent that they fall to be complied with in relation to any such premises.

(4) In determining for the purposes of subsection (2) or (3) whether any covenant bound the assignor immediately before the assignment, any waiver or release of the covenant which (in whatever terms) is expressed to be personal to the assignor shall be disregarded.

(5) Any landlord or tenant covenant of a tenancy which is restrictive of the user of land shall, as well as being capable of enforcement against an assignee, be capable of being enforced against any other person who is the owner or occupier of any demised premises to which the covenant relates, even though there is no express provision in the tenancy to that effect.

(6) Nothing in this section shall operate—

- (a) in the case of a covenant which (in whatever terms) is expressed to be personal to any person, to make the covenant enforceable by or (as the case may be) against any other person; or
- (b) to make a covenant enforceable against any person if, apart from this section, it would not be enforceable against him by reason of its

not having been registered under the Land Registration Act *1925* [2002] or the Land Charges Act 1972.

ANNOTATION

The words in square brackets in subs.(6)(b) were substituted for the words in italics with effect from October 13, 2003 by Land Registration Act 2002, s.133, Sch. 11, para.33(1),(2); S.I. 2003 No. 1725, art.2(1).

(7) To the extent that there remains in force any rule of law by virtue of which the burden of a covenant whose subject matter is not in existence at the time when it is made does not run with the land affected unless the covenantor covenants on behalf of himself and his assigns, that rule of law is hereby abolished in relation to tenancies.

Transmission of rights of re-entry

4. The benefit of a landlord's right of re-entry under a tenancy—

(a) shall be annexed and incident to the whole, and to each and every part, of the reversion in the premises demised by the tenancy, and

(b) shall pass on an assignment of the whole or any part of the reversion in those premises.

Release of Covenants on Assignment

Tenant released from covenants on assignment of tenancy

5.—(1) This section applies where a tenant assigns premises demised to him under a tenancy.

(2) If the tenant assigns the whole of the premises demised to him, he—

(a) is released from the tenant covenants of the tenancy, and

(b) ceases to be entitled to the benefit of the landlord covenants of the tenancy,

as from the assignment.

(3) If the tenant assigns part only of the premises demised to him, then as from the assignment he—

(a) is released from the tenant covenants of the tenancy, and

(b) ceases to be entitled to the benefit of the landlord covenants of the tenancy,

only to the extent that those covenants fall to be complied with in relation to that part of the demised premises.

(4) This section applies as mentioned in subsection (1) whether or not the tenant is tenant of the whole of the premises comprised in the tenancy.

Landlord may be released from covenants on assignment of reversion

6.—(1) This section applies where a landlord assigns the reversion in premises of which he is the landlord under a tenancy.

(2) If the landlord assigns the reversion in the whole of the premises of which he is the landlord—

(a) he may apply to be released from the landlord covenants of the tenancy in accordance with section 8; and

(b) if he is so released from all of those covenants, he ceases to be entitled to the benefit of the tenant covenants of the tenancy as from the assignment.

(3) If the landlord assigns the reversion in part only of the premises of which he is the landlord—

(a) he may apply to be so released from the landlord covenants of the tenancy to the extent that they fall to be complied with in relation to that part of those premises; and

(b) if he is, to that extent, so released from all of those covenants, then as from the assignment he ceases to be entitled to the benefit of the tenant covenants only to the extent that they fall to be complied with in relation to that part of those premises.

(4) This section applies as mentioned in subsection (1) whether or not the landlord is landlord of the whole of the premises comprised in the tenancy.

Former landlord may be released from covenants on assignment of reversion

7.—(1) This section applies where—

(a) a landlord assigns the reversion in premises of which he is the landlord under a tenancy, and

(b) immediately before the assignment a former landlord of the premises remains bound by a landlord covenant of the tenancy ("the relevant covenant").

(2) If immediately before the assignment the former landlord does not remain the landlord of any other premises demised by the tenancy, he may apply to be released from the relevant covenant in accordance with section 8.

(3) In any other case the former landlord may apply to be so released from the relevant covenant to the extent that it falls to be complied with in relation to any premises comprised in the assignment.

(4) If the former landlord is so released from every landlord covenant by which he remained bound immediately before the assignment, he ceases to be entitled to the benefit of the tenant covenants of the tenancy.

(5) If the former landlord is so released from every such landlord covenant to the extent that it falls to be complied with in relation to any premises comprised in the assignment, he ceases to be entitled to the benefit of the tenant covenants of the tenancy to the extent that they fall to be so complied with.

(6) This section applies as mentioned in subsection (1)—

(a) whether or not the landlord making the assignment is landlord of the whole of the premises comprised in the tenancy; and

(b) whether or not the former landlord has previously applied (whether under section 6 or this section) to be released from the relevant covenant.

Procedure for seeking release from a covenant under section 6 or 7

8.—(1) For the purposes of section 6 or 7 an application for the release of a covenant to any extent is made by serving on the tenant, either before or within the period of four weeks beginning with the date of the assignment in question, a notice informing him of—

(a) the proposed assignment or (as the case may be) the fact that the assignment has taken place, and

(b) the request for the covenant to be released to that extent.

(2) Where an application for the release of a covenant is made in accordance with subsection (1), the covenant is released to the extent mentioned in the notice if—

(a) the tenant does not, within the period of four weeks beginning with the day on which the notice is served, serve on the landlord or former landlord a notice in writing objecting to the release, or

(b) the tenant does so serve such a notice but the court, on the application of the landlord or former landlord, makes a declaration that it is reasonable for the covenant to be so released, or

(c) the tenant serves on the landlord or former landlord a notice in writing consenting to the release and, if he has previously served a notice objecting to it, stating that that notice is withdrawn.

(3) Any release from a covenant in accordance with this section shall be regarded as occurring at the time when the assignment in question takes place.

(4) In this section—

(a) "the tenant" means the tenant of the premises comprised in the assignment in question (or, if different parts of those premises are held under the tenancy by different tenants, each of those tenants);

(b) any reference to the landlord or the former landlord is a reference to the landlord referred to in section 6 or the former landlord referred to in section 7, as the case may be; and

(c) "the court" means a county court.

Apportionment of Liability between Assignor and Assignee

Apportionment of liability under covenants binding both assignor and assignee of tenancy or reversion

9.—(1) This section applies where—

(a) a tenant assigns part only of the premises demised to him by a tenancy;

(b) after the assignment both the tenant and his assignee are to be bound by a non-attributable tenant covenant of the tenancy; and

(c) the tenant and his assignee agree that as from the assignment liability under the covenant is to be apportioned between them in such manner as is specified in the agreement.

(2) This section also applies where—

(a) a landlord assigns the reversion in part only of the premises of which he is the landlord under a tenancy;

(b) after the assignment both the landlord and his assignee are to be bound by a non-attributable landlord covenant of the tenancy; and

(c) the landlord and his assignee agree that as from the assignment liability under the covenant is to be apportioned between them in such manner as is specified in the agreement.

(3) Any such agreement as is mentioned in subsection (1) or (2) may apportion liability in such a way that a party to the agreement is exonerated from all liability under a covenant.

(4) In any case falling within subsection (1) or (2) the parties to the agreement may apply for the apportionment to become binding on the appropriate person in accordance with section 10.

(5) In any such case the parties to the agreement may also apply for the apportionment to become binding on any person (other than the appropriate person) who is for the time being entitled to enforce the covenant in question; and section 10 shall apply in relation to such an application as it applies in relation to an application made with respect to the appropriate person.

(6) For the purposes of this section a covenant is, in relation to an assignment, a "non-attributable" covenant if it does not fall to be complied with in relation to any premises comprised in the assignment.

(7) In this section "the appropriate person" means either—

(a) the landlord of the entire premises referred to in subsection (1)(a) (or, if different parts of those premises are held under the tenancy by different landlords, each of those landlords), or

(b) the tenant of the entire premises referred to in subsection (2)(a) (or, if different parts of those premises are held under the tenancy by different tenants, each of those tenants),

depending on whether the agreement in question falls within subsection (1) or subsection (2).

Procedure for making apportionment bind other party to lease

10.—(1) For the purposes of section 9 the parties to an agreement falling within subsection (1) or (2) of that section apply for an apportionment to become binding on the appropriate person if, either before or within the period of four weeks beginning with the date of the assignment in question, they serve on that person a notice informing him of—

(a) the proposed assignment or (as the case may be) the fact that the assignment has taken place;

(b) the prescribed particulars of the agreement; and

(c) their request that the apportionment should become binding on him.

(2) Where an application for an apportionment to become binding has been made in accordance with subsection (1), the apportionment becomes binding on the appropriate person if—

(a) he does not, within the period of four weeks beginning with the day on which the notice is served under subsection (1), serve on the parties to the agreement a notice in writing objecting to the apportionment becoming binding on him, or

(b) he does so serve such a notice but the court, on the application of the parties to the agreement, makes a declaration that it is reasonable for the apportionment to become binding on him, or

(c) he serves on the parties to the agreement a notice in writing consenting to the apportionment become binding on him and, if he has previously served a notice objecting thereto, stating that the notice is withdrawn.

(3) Where any apportionment becomes binding in accordance with this section, this shall be regarded as occurring at the time when the assignment in question takes place.

(4) In this section—

"the appropriate person" has the same meaning as in section 9;

"the court" means a county court;

"prescribed" means prescribed by virtue of section 27.

Excluded Assignments

Assignments in breach of covenant or by operation of law

11.—(1) This section provides for the operation of sections 5 to 10 in relation to assignments in breach of a covenant of a tenancy or assignments by operation of law ("excluded assignments").

(2) In the case of an excluded assignment subsection (2) or (3) of section 5—

(a) shall not have the effect mentioned in that subsection in relation to the tenant as from that assignment, but

(b) shall have that effect as from the next assignment (if any) of the premises assigned by him which is not an excluded assignment.

(3) In the case of an excluded assignment subsection (2) or (3) of section 6 or 7—

(a) shall not enable the landlord or former landlord to apply for such a release as is mentioned in that subsection as from that assignment, but

(b) shall apply on the next assignment (if any) of the reversion assigned by the landlord which is not an excluded assignment so as to enable the landlord or former landlord to apply for any such release as from that subsequent assignment.

(4) Where subsection (2) or (3) of section 6 or 7 does so apply—

(a) any reference in that section to the assignment (except where it relates to the time as from which the release takes effect) is a reference to the excluded assignment; but

(b) in that excepted case and in section 8 as it applies in relation to any application under that section made by virtue of subsection (3) above, any reference to the assignment or proposed assignment is a reference to any such subsequent assignment as is mentioned in that subsection.

(5) In the case of an excluded assignment section 9—

(a) shall not enable the tenant or landlord and his assignee to apply for an agreed apportionment to become binding in accordance with section 10 as from that assignment, but

(b) shall apply on the next assignment (if any) of the premises or reversion assigned by the tenant or landlord which is not an excluded assignment so as to enable him and his assignee to apply for such an apportionment to become binding in accordance with section 10 as from that subsequent assignment.

(6) Where section 9 does so apply—

(a) any reference in that section to the assignment or the assignee under it is a reference to the excluded assignment and the assignee under that assignment; but

(b) in section 10 as it applies in relation to any application under section 9 made by virtue of subsection (5) above, any reference to the assignment or proposed assignment is a reference to any such subsequent assignment as is mentioned in that subsection.

(7) If any such subsequent assignment as is mentioned in subsection (2), (3) or (5) above comprises only part of the premises assigned by the tenant or (as the case may be) only part of the premises the reversion in which was assigned by the landlord on the excluded assignment—

(a) the relevant provision or provisions of section 5, 6, 7 or 9 shall only have the effect mentioned in that subsection to the extent that the covenants or covenant in question fall or falls to be complied with in relation to that part of those premises; and

(b) that subsection may accordingly apply on different occasions in relation to different parts of those premises.

Third Party Covenants

Covenants with management companies etc.

12.—(1) This section applies where—

(a) a person other than the landlord or tenant ("the third party") is under a covenant of a tenancy liable (as principal) to discharge any function with respect to all or any of the demised premises ("the relevant function"); and

(b) that liability is not the liability of a guarantor or any other financial liability referable to the performance or otherwise of a covenant of the tenancy by another party to it.

(2) To the extent that any covenant of the tenancy confers any rights against the third party with respect to the relevant function, then for the purposes of the transmission of the benefit of the covenant in accordance with this Act it shall be treated as if it were—

(a) a tenant covenant of the tenancy to the extent that those rights are exercisable by the landlord; and

(b) a landlord covenant of the tenancy to the extent that those rights are exercisable by the tenant.

(3) To the extent that any covenant of the tenancy confers any rights exercisable by the third party with respect to the relevant functions, then for the purposes mentioned in subsection (4), it shall be treated as if it were—

(a) a tenant covenant of the tenancy to the extent that those rights are exercisable against the tenant; and

(b) a landlord covenant of the tenancy to the extent that those rights are exercisable against the landlord.

(4) The purposes mentioned in subsection (3) are—

(a) the transmission of the burden of the covenant in accordance with this Act; and

(b) any release from, or apportionment of liability in respect of, the covenant in accordance with this Act.

(5) In relation to the release of the landlord from any covenant which is to be treated as a landlord covenant by virtue of subsection (3), section 8 shall apply as if any reference to the tenant were a reference to the third party.

Joint Liability under Covenants

Covenants binding two or more persons

13.—(1) Where in consequence of this Act two or more persons are bound by the same covenant, they are so bound both jointly and severally.

(2) Subject to section 24(2), where by virtue of this Act—

(a) two or more persons are bound jointly and severally by the same covenant, and

(b) any of the persons so bound is released from the covenant,

the release does not extend to any other of those persons.

(3) For the purpose of providing for contribution between persons who, by virtue of this Act, are bound jointly and severally by a covenant, the Civil Liability (Contribution) Act 1978 shall have effect as if—

(a) liability to a person under a covenant were liability in respect of damage suffered by that person;

(b) references to damage accordingly included a breach of a covenant of a tenancy; and

(c) section 7(2) of that Act were omitted.

Abolition of indemnity covenants implied by statute

14. The following provisions (by virtue of which indemnity covenants are implied on the assignment of a tenancy) shall cease to have effect—

(a) subsections (1)(C) and (D) of section 77 of the Law of Property Act 1925; and

(b) subsections (1)(b) and (2) of section 24 of the Land Registration Act 1925.

Enforcement of Covenants

Enforcement of covenants

15.—(1) Where any tenant covenant of a tenancy, or any right of re-entry contained in a tenancy, is enforceable by the reversioner in respect of any premises demised by the tenancy, it shall also be so enforceable by—

(a) any person (other than the reversioner) who, as the holder of the immediate reversion in those premises, is for the time being entitled to the rents and profits under the tenancy in respect of those premises, or

(b) any mortgagee in possession of the reversion in those premises who is so entitled.

(2) Where any landlord covenant of a tenancy is enforceable against the reversioner in respect of any premises demised by the tenancy, it shall also be enforceable against any person falling within subsection (1)(a) or (b).

(3) Where any landlord covenant of a tenancy is enforceable by the tenant in respect of any premises demised by the tenancy, it shall also be so enforceable by any mortgagee in possession of those premises under a mortgage granted by the tenant.

(4) Where any tenant covenant of a tenancy, or any right of re-entry contained in a tenancy, is enforceable against the tenant in respect of any premises demised by the tenancy, it shall also be so enforceable against any such mortgagee.

(5) Nothing in this section shall operate—

(a) in the case of a covenant which (in whatever terms) is expressed to be personal to any person to make the covenant enforceable by or (as the case may be) against any other person; or

(b) to make a covenant enforceable against any person if, apart from this section, it would not be enforceable against him by reason of its not having been registered under the Land Registration Act *1925* [2002] or the Land Charges Act 1972.

ANNOTATION

The words in square brackets in subs.(5)(b) were substituted for the words in italics with effect from October 13, 2003 by Land Registration Act 2002, s.133, Sch.11, para.33(1),(2); S.I. 2003 No. 1725, art.2(1).

(6) In this section—

"mortgagee" and "mortgage" include "chargee" and "charge" respectively;

"the reversioner", in relation to a tenancy, means the holder for the time being of the interest of the landlord under the tenancy.

Liability of Former Tenant etc. in respect of Covenants

Tenant guaranteeing performance of covenant by assignee

16.—(1) Where on an assignment a tenant is to any extent released from a tenant covenant of a tenancy by virtue of this Act ("the relevant covenant"), nothing in this Act (and in particular section 25) shall preclude him from entering into an authorised guarantee agreement with respect to the performance of that covenant by the assignee.

(2) For the purposes of this section an agreement is an authorised guarantee agreement if—

(a) under it the tenant guarantees the performance of the relevant covenant to any extent by the assignee; and
(b) it is entered into in the circumstances set out in subsection (3); and
(c) its provisions conform with subsections (4) and (5).

(3) Those circumstances are as follows—

(a) by virtue of a covenant against assignment (whether absolute or qualified) the assignment cannot be effected without the consent of the landlord under the tenancy or some other person;
(b) any such consent is given subject to a condition (lawfully imposed) that the tenant is to enter into an agreement guaranteeing the performance of the covenant by the assignee; and
(c) the agreement is entered into by the tenant in pursuance of that condition.

(4) An agreement is not an authorised guarantee agreement to the extent that it purports—

(a) to impose on the tenant any requirement to guarantee in any way the performance of the relevant covenant by any person other than the assignee; or
(b) to impose on the tenant any liability, restriction or other requirement (of whatever nature) in relation to any time after the assignee is released from that covenant by virtue of this Act.

(5) Subject to subsection (4), an authorised guarantee agreement may—

(a) impose on the tenant any liability as sole or principal debtor in respect of any obligation owed by the assignee under the relevant covenant;
(b) impose on the tenant liabilities as guarantor in respect of the assignee's performance of that covenant which are no more onerous than those to which he would be subject in the event of his being liable as sole or principal debtor in respect of any obligation owed by the assignee under that covenant;

(c) require the tenant, in the event of the tenancy assigned by him being disclaimed, to enter into a new tenancy of the premises comprised in the assignment—
   (i) whose term expires not later than the term of the tenancy assigned by the tenant, and
   (ii) whose tenant covenants are no more onerous than those of that tenancy;
(d) make provision incidental or supplementary to any provision made by virtue of any of paragraphs (a) to (c).

(6) Where a person ("the former tenant") is to any extent released from a covenant of a tenancy by virtue of section 11(2) as from an assignment and the assignor under the assignment enters into an authorised guarantee agreement with the landlord with respect to the performance of that covenant by the assignee under the assignment—
(a) the landlord may require the former tenant to enter into an agreement under which he guarantees, on terms corresponding to those of that authorised guarantee agreement, the performance of that covenant by the assignee under the assignment; and
(b) if its provisions conform with subsections (4) and (5), any such agreement shall be an authorised guarantee agreement for the purposes of this section; and
(c) in the application of this section in relation to any such agreement—
   (i) subsections (2)(b) and (c) and (3) shall be omitted, and
   (ii) any reference to the tenant or to the assignee shall be read as a reference to the former tenant or to the assignee under the assignment.

(7) For the purposes of subsection (1) it is immaterial that—
(a) the tenant has already made an authorised guarantee agreement in respect of a previous assignment by him of the tenancy referred to in that subsection, it having been subsequently revested in him following a disclaimer on behalf of the previous assignee, or
(b) the tenancy referred to in that subsection is a new tenancy entered into by the tenant in pursuance of an authorised guarantee agreement;

and in any such case subsections (2) to (5) shall apply accordingly.

(8) It is hereby declared that the rules of law relating to guarantees (and in particular those relating to the release of sureties) are, subject to its terms, applicable in relation to any authorised guarantee agreement as in relation to any other guarantee agreement.

Restriction on liability of former tenant or his guarantor for rent or service charge etc.

17.—(1) This section applies where a person ("the former tenant") is as a result of an assignment no longer a tenant under a tenancy but—
(a) (in the case of a tenancy which is a new tenancy) he has under an authorised guarantee agreement guaranteed the performance by his assignee of a tenant covenant of the tenancy under which any fixed charge is payable; or
(b) (in the case of any tenancy) he remains bound by such a covenant.

(2) The former tenant shall not be liable under that agreement or (as the case may be) the covenant to pay any amount in respect of any fixed charge payable

under the covenant unless, within the period of six months beginning with the date when the charge becomes due, the landlord serves on the former tenant a notice informing him—

(a) that the charge is now due; and
(b) that in respect of the charge the landlord intends to recover from the former tenant such amount as is specified in the notice and (where payable) interest calculated on such basis as is so specified.

(3) Where a person ("the guarantor") has agreed to guarantee the performance by the former tenant of such a covenant as is mentioned in subsection (1), the guarantor shall not be liable under the agreement to pay any amount in respect of any fixed charge payable under the covenant unless, within the period of six months beginning with the date when the charge becomes due, the landlord serves on the guarantor a notice informing him—

(a) that the charge is now due; and
(b) that in respect of the charge the landlord intends to recover from the guarantor such amount as is specified in the notice and (where payable) interest calculated on such basis as is so specified.

(4) Where the landlord has duly served a notice under subsection (2) or (3), the amount (exclusive of interest) which the former tenant or (as the case may be) the guarantor is liable to pay in respect of the fixed charge in question shall not exceed the amount specified in the notice unless—

(a) his liability in respect of the charge is subsequently determined to be for a greater amount,
(b) the notice informed him of the possibility that that liability would be so determined, and
(c) within the period of three months beginning with the date of the determination, the landlord serves on him a further notice informing him that the landlord intends to recover that greater amount from him (plus interest, where payable).

(5) For the purposes of subsection (2) or (3) any fixed charge which has becomes due before the date on which this Act comes into force shall be treated as becoming due on that date; but neither of those subsections applies to any such charge if before that date proceedings have been instituted by the landlord for the recovery from the former tenant of any amount in respect of it.

(6) In this section—

"fixed charge", in relation to a tenancy, means—

(a) rent,
(b) any service charge as defined by section 18 of the Landlord and Tenant Act 1985 (the words "of a dwelling" being disregarded for this purpose), and
(c) any amount payable under a tenant covenant of the tenancy providing for the payment of a liquidated sum in the event of a failure to comply with any such covenant;

"landlord", in relation to a fixed charge, includes any person who has a right to enforce payment of the charge.

Restriction of liability of former tenant or his guarantor where tenancy subsequently varied

18.—(1) This section applies where a person ("the former tenant") is as a result of an assignment no longer a tenant under a tenancy but—

(a) (in the case of a new tenancy) he has under an authorised guarantee agreement guaranteed the performance by his assignee of any tenant covenant of the tenancy; or

(b) (in the case of any tenancy) he remains bound by such a covenant.

(2) The former tenant shall not be liable under the agreement or (as the case may be) the covenant to pay any amount in respect of the covenant to the extent that the amount is referable to any relevant variation of the tenant covenants of the tenancy effected after the assignment.

(3) Where a person ("the guarantor") has agreed to guarantee the performance by the former tenant of a tenant covenant of the tenancy, the guarantor (where his liability to do so is not wholly discharged by any such variation of the tenant covenants of the tenancy) shall not be liable under the agreement to pay any amount in respect of the covenant to the extent that the amount is referable to any such variation.

(4) For the purposes of this section a variation of the tenant covenants of a tenancy is a "relevant variation" if either—

(a) the landlord has, at the time of the variation, an absolute right to refuse to allow it; or

(b) the landlord would have had such a right if the variation had been sought by the former tenant immediately before the assignment by him but, between the time of that assignment and the time of the variation, the tenant covenants of the tenancy have been so varied as to deprive the landlord of such a right.

(5) In determining whether the landlord has or would have had such a right at any particular time regard shall be had to all the circumstances (including the effect of any provision made by or under any enactment).

(6) Nothing in this section applies to any variation of the tenant covenants of a tenancy effected before the date on which this Act comes into force.

(7) In this section "variation" means a variation whether effected by deed or otherwise.

Overriding Leases

Right of former tenant or his guarantor to overriding lease

19.—(1) Where in respect of any tenancy ("the relevant tenancy") any person ("the claimant") makes full payment of an amount which he has been duly required to pay in accordance with section 17, together with any interest payable, he shall be entitled (subject to and in accordance with this section) to have the landlord under that tenancy grant him an overriding lease of the premises demised by the tenancy.

(2) For the purposes of this section "overriding lease" means a tenancy of the reversion expectant on the relevant tenancy which—

(a) is granted for a term equal to the remainder of the term of the relevant tenancy plus three days or the longest period (less than three days) that will not wholly displace the landlord's reversionary interest expectant on the relevant tenancy, as the case may require; and

(b) (subject to subsections (3) and (4) and to any modifications agreed to by the claimant and the landlord) otherwise contains the same covenants as the relevant tenancy, as they have effect immediately before the grant of the lease.

(3) An overriding lease shall not be required to reproduce any covenant of the relevant tenancy to the extent that the covenant is (in whatever terms) expressed to be a personal covenant between the landlord and the tenant under that tenancy.

(4) If any right, liability or other matter arising under a covenant of the relevant tenancy falls to be determined or otherwise operates (whether expressly or otherwise) by reference to the commencement of that tenancy—

(a) the corresponding covenant of the overriding lease shall be so framed that that right, liability or matter falls to be determined or otherwise operates by reference to the commencement of that tenancy; but

(b) the overriding lease shall not be required to reproduce any covenant of that tenancy to that extent that it has become spent by the time that that lease is granted.

(5) A claim to exercise the right to an overriding lease under this section is made by the claimant making a request for such a lease to the landlord; and any such request—

(a) must be made to the landlord in writing and specify the payment by virtue of which the claimant claims to be entitled to the lease ("the qualifying payment"); and

(b) must be so made at the time of making the qualifying payment or within the period of 12 months beginning with the date of that payment.

(6) Where the claimant duly makes such a request—

(a) the landlord shall (subject to subsection (7)) grant and deliver to the claimant an overriding lease of the demised premises within a reasonable time of the request being received by the landlord; and

(b) the claimant—

(i) shall thereupon deliver to the landlord a counterpart of the lease duly executed by the claimant, and

(ii) shall be liable for the landlord's reasonable costs of and incidental to the grant of the lease.

(7) The landlord shall not be under any obligation to grant an overriding lease of the demised premises under this section at a time when the relevant tenancy has been determined; and a claimant shall not be entitled to the grant of such a lease if at the time when he makes his request—

(a) the landlord has already granted such a lease and that lease remains in force; or

(b) another person has already duly made a request for such a lease to the landlord and that request has been neither withdrawn nor abandoned by that person.

(8) Where two or more requests are duly made on the same day, then for the purposes of subsection (7)—

(a) a request made by a person who was liable for the qualifying payment as a former tenant shall be treated as made before a request made by a person who was so liable as a guarantor; and

(b) a request made by a person whose liability in respect of the covenant in question commenced earlier than any such liability of another person shall be treated as made before a request made by that other person.

(9) Where a claimant who has duly made a request for an overriding lease under this section subsequently withdraws or abandons the request before he is granted such a lease by the landlord, the claimant shall be liable for the

landlord's reasonable costs incurred in pursuance of the request down to the time of its withdrawal or abandonment; and for the purposes of this section—

(a) a claimant's request is withdrawn by the claimant notifying the landlord in writing that he is withdrawing his request; and

(b) a claimant is to be regarded as having abandoned his request if—

(i) the landlord has requested the claimant in writing to take, within such reasonable period as is specified in the landlord's request, all or any of the remaining steps required to be taken by the claimant before the lease can be granted, and

(ii) the claimant fails to comply with the landlord's request, and is accordingly to be regarded as having abandoned it at the time when that period expires.

(10) Any request or notification under this section may be sent by post.

(11) The preceding provisions of this section shall apply where the landlord is the tenant under an overriding lease granted under this section as they apply where no such lease has been granted; and accordingly there may be two or more such leases interposed between the first such lease and the relevant tenancy.

Overriding leases: supplementary provisions

20.—(1) For the purposes of section 1 an overriding lease shall be a new tenancy only if the relevant tenancy is a new tenancy.

(2) Every overriding lease shall state—

(a) that it is a lease granted under section 19, and

(b) whether it is or is not a new tenancy for the purposes of section 1; and any such statement shall comply with such requirements as may be prescribed by *rules made in pursuance of section 144 of the Land Registration Act 1925 (power to make general rules)* [land registration rules under the Land Registration Act 2002].

ANNOTATION

The words in square brackets in subs.(2)(b) were substituted for the words in italics with effect from October 13, 2003 by Land Registration Act 2002, s.133, Sch.11, para.33(1),(3); S.I. 2003 No. 1725, art.2(1).

(3) A claim that the landlord has failed to comply with subsection (6)(a) of section 19 may be made the subject of civil proceedings in like manner as any other claim in tort for breach of statutory duty; and if the claimant under that section fails to comply with subsection (6)(b)(i) of that section he shall not be entitled to exercise any of the rights otherwise exercisable by him under the overriding lease.

(4) An overriding lease—

(a) shall be deemed to be authorised as against the persons authorised in any mortgage of the landlord's interest (however created or arising); and

(b) shall be binding on any such persons;

and if any such person is by virtue of such a mortgage entitled to possession of the documents of title relating to the landlord's interest—

(i) the landlord shall within one month of the execution of the lease deliver to that person the counterpart executed in pursuance of section 19(6)(b)(i); and

(ii) if he fails to do so; the instrument creating or evidencing the mortgage shall apply as if the obligation to deliver a counterpart were included in the terms of the mortgage as set out in that instrument.

(5) It is hereby declared—

(a) that the fact that an overriding lease takes effect subject to the relevant tenancy shall not constitute a breach of any covenant of the lease against subletting or parting with possession of the premises demised by the lease or any part of them; and

(b) that each of sections 16, 17 and 18 applies where the tenancy referred to in subsection (1) of that section is an overriding lease as it applies in other cases falling within that subsection.

(6) No tenancy shall be registrable under the Land Charges Act 1972 or be taken to be an estate contract within the meaning of that Act by reason of any right or obligation that may arise under section 19, and any right arising from a request made under that section shall not be *an overriding interest within the meaning of the Land Registration Act 1925* [capable of falling within paragraph 2 of Schedules 1 or 3 to the Land Registration Act 2002]; but any such request shall be registrable under the Land Charges Act 1972, or may be the subject of a notice *or caution under the Land Registration Act 1925* [under the Land Registration Act 2002], as if it were an estate contract.

ANNOTATION

The words in the first set of square brackets in subs.(6) were substituted for the immediately preceding words in italics, and the words in the second set of square brackets were substituted for the immediately preceding words in italics, both with effect from October 13, 2003 by Land Registration Act 2002, s.133, Sch.11, para.33(1),(4); S.I. 2003 No. 1725, art.2(1).

(7) In this section—

(a) "mortgage" includes "charge"; and

(b) any expression which is also used in section 19 has the same meaning as in that section.

Forfeiture and Disclaimer

Forfeiture or disclaimer limited to part only of demised premises

21.—(1) Where—

(a) as a result of one or more assignments a person is the tenant of part only of the premises demised by a tenancy, and

(b) under a proviso or stipulation in the tenancy there is a right of re-entry or forfeiture for a breach of a tenant covenant of the tenancy, and

(c) the right is (apart from this subsection) exercisable in relation to that part and other land demised by the tenancy,

the right shall nevertheless, in connection with a breach of any such covenant by that person, be taken to be a right exercisable only in relation to that part.

(2) Where—

(a) a company which is being wound up, or a trustee in bankruptcy, is as a result of one or more assignments the tenant of part only of the premises demised by a tenancy, and

(b) the liquidator of the company exercises his power under section 178 of the Insolvency Act 1986, or the trustee in bankruptcy exercises his power under section 315 of that Act, to disclaim property demised by the tenancy, the power is exercisable only in relation to the part of the premises referred to in paragraph (a).

Landlord's Consent to Assignments

Imposition of conditions regulating giving of landlord's consent to assignments

22. After subsection (1) of section 19 of the Landlord and Tenant Act 1927 (provisions as to covenants not to assign etc. without licence or consent) there shall be inserted—

"(1A) Where the landlord and the tenant under a qualifying lease have entered into an agreement specifying for the purposes of this subsection—

(a) any circumstances in which the landlord may withhold his licence or consent to an assignment of the demised premises of any part of them, or

(b) any conditions subject to which any such licence or consent may be granted,

then the landlord—

(i) shall not be regarded as unreasonably withholding his licence or consent to any such assignment if he withholds it on the ground (and it is the case) that any such circumstances exist, and

(ii) if he gives such licence or consent subject to any such conditions, shall not be regarded as giving it subject to unreasonable conditions;

and section 1 of the Landlord and Tenant Act 1988 (qualified duty to consent to assignment etc.) shall have effect subject to the provisions of this subsection.

(1B) Subsection (1A) of this section applies to such an agreement as is mentioned in that subsection—

(a) whether it is contained in the lease or not, and

(b) whether it is made at the time when the lease is granted or at any other time falling before the application for the landlord's licence or consent is made.

(1C) Subsection (1A) shall not, however, apply to any such agreement to the extent that any circumstances or conditions specified in it are framed by reference to any matter falling to be determined by the landlord or by any other person for the purposes of the agreement, unless under the terms of the agreement—

(a) that person's power to determine that matter is required to be exercised reasonably, or

(b) the tenant is given an unrestricted right to have any such determination reviewed by a person independent of both landlord and tenant whose identity is ascertainable by reference to the agreement,

and in the latter case the agreement provides for the determination made by any such independent person on the review to be conclusive as to the matter in question.

(1D) In its application to a qualifying lease, subsection (1)(b) of this section shall not have effect in relation to any assignment of the lease.

(1E) In subsections (1A) and (1D) of this section—

(a) "qualifying lease" means any lease which is a new tenancy for the purposes of section 1 of the Landlord and Tenant (Covenants) Act 1995 other than a residential lease, namely a lease by which a building or part of a building is let wholly or mainly as a single private residence; and

(b) references to assignment include parting with possession on assignment."

Supplemental

Effects of becoming subject to liability under, or entitled to benefit of, covenant etc.

23.—(1) Where as a result of an assignment a person becomes by virtue of this Act, bound by or entitled to the benefit of a covenant, he shall not by virtue of this Act have any liability or rights under the covenant in relation to any time falling before the assignment.

(2) Subsection (1) does not preclude any such rights being expressly assigned to the person in question.

(3) Where as a result of an assignment a person becomes, by virtue of this Act, entitled to a right of re-entry contained in a tenancy, that right shall be exercisable in relation to any breach of a covenant of the tenancy occurring before the assignment as in relation to one occurring thereafter, unless by reason of any waiver or release it was not so exercisable immediately before the assignment.

Effects of release from liability under, or loss of benefit of, covenant

24.—(1) Any release of a person from a covenant by virtue of this Act does not affect any liability of his arising from a breach of the covenant occurring before the release.

(2) Where—

(a) by virtue of this Act a tenant is released from a tenant covenant of a tenancy, and

(b) immediately before the release another person is bound by a covenant of the tenancy imposing any liability or penalty in the event of a failure to comply with that tenant covenant,

then, as from the release of the tenant, that other person is released from the covenant mentioned in paragraph (b) to the same extent as the tenant is released from that tenant covenant.

(3) Where a person bound by a landlord or tenant covenant of a tenancy—

(a) assigns the whole or part of his interest in the premises demised by the tenancy, but

(b) is not released by virtue of this Act from the covenant (with the result that subsection (1) does not apply),

the assignment does not affect any liability of his arising from a breach of the covenant occurring before the assignment.

(4) Where, by virtue of this Act a person ceases to be entitled to the benefit of a covenant, this does not affect any rights of his arising from a breach of the covenant occurring before he ceases to be so entitled.

Agreement void if it restricts operation of the Act

25.—(1) Any agreement relating to a tenancy is void to the extent that—

(a) it would apart from this section have effect to exclude, modify or otherwise frustrate the operation of any provision of this Act, or

(b) it provides for—

(i) the termination or surrender of the tenancy, or

(ii) the imposition on the tenant of any penalty, disability or liability,

in the event of the operation of any provision of this Act, or

(c) it provides for any of the matters referred to in paragraph (b)(i) or (ii) and does so (whether expressly or otherwise) in connection with, or in consequence of, the operation of any provision of this Act.

(2) To the extent that an agreement relating to a tenancy constitutes a covenant (whether absolute or qualified) against the assignment, or parting with the possession, of the premises demised by the tenancy or any part of them—

(a) the agreement is not void by virtue of subsection (1) by reason only of the fact that as such the covenant prohibits or restricts any such assignment or parting with possession; but

(b) paragraph (a) above does not otherwise affect the operation of that subsection in relation to the agreement (and in particular does not preclude its application to the agreement to the extent that it purports to regulate the giving of, or the making of any application for, consent to any such assignment or parting with possession).

(3) In accordance with section 16(1) nothing in this section applies to any agreement to the extent that it is an authorised guarantee agreement; but (without prejudice to the generality of subsection (1) above) an agreement is void to the extent that it is one falling within section 16(4)(a) or (b).

(4) This section applies to an agreement relating to a tenancy whether or not the agreement is—

(a) contained in the instrument creating the tenancy; or

(b) made before the creation of the tenancy.

Miscellaneous savings etc.

26.—(1) Nothing in this Act is to be read as preventing—

(a) a party to a tenancy from releasing a person from a landlord covenant or a tenant covenant of the tenancy; or

(b) the parties to a tenancy from agreeing to an apportionment of liability under such a covenant.

(2) Nothing in this Act affects the operation of section 3(3A) of the Landlord and Tenant Act 1985 (preservation of former landlord's liability until tenant notified of new landlord).

(3) No apportionment which has become binding in accordance with section 10 shall be affected by any order or decision made under or by virtue of any enactment not contained in this Act which relates to apportionment.

Notices for the purposes of the Act

27.—(1) The form of any notice to be served for the purposes of section 8, 10, or 17 shall be prescribed by regulations made by the Lord Chancellor by statutory instrument.

(2) The regulations shall require any notice served for the purposes of section 8(1) or 10(1) ("the initial notice") to include—

(a) an explanation of the significance of the notice and the options available to the person on whom it is served;

(b) a statement that any objections to the proposed release, or (as the case may be) to the proposed effect of the apportionment, must be made by notice in writing served on the person or persons by whom the initial notice is served within the period of four weeks beginning with the day on which the initial notice is served; and

(c) an address in England and Wales to which any such objections may be sent.

(3) The regulations shall require any notice served for the purposes of section 17 to include an explanation of the significance of the notice.

(4) If any notice purporting to be served for the purposes of section 8(1), 10(1) or 17 is not in the prescribed form, or in a form substantially to the same effect, the notice shall not be effective for the purposes of section 8, section 10 or section 17 (as the case may be).

(5) Section 23 of the Landlord and Tenant Act 1927 shall apply in relation to the service of notices for the purposes of section 8, 10 or 17.

(6) Any statutory instrument made under this section shall be subject to annulment in pursuance of a resolution of either House of Parliament.

Interpretation

28.—(1) In this Act (unless the context otherwise requires)—

"assignment" includes equitable assignment and in addition (subject to section 11) assignment in breach of a covenant of a tenancy or by operation of law;

"authorised guarantee agreement" means an agreement which is an authorised guarantee agreement for the purposes of section 16;

"collateral agreement", in relation to a tenancy, means any agreement collateral to the tenancy, whether made before or after its creation;

"consent" includes licence;

"covenant" includes term, condition and obligation, and references to a covenant (or any description of covenant) of a tenancy include a covenant (or a covenant of that description) contained in a collateral agreement;

"landlord" and "tenant", in relation to a tenancy, mean the person for the time being entitled to the reversion expectant on the term of the tenancy and the person so entitled to that term respectively;

"landlord covenant", in relation to a tenancy, means a covenant falling to be complied with by the landlord of premises demised by the tenancy;

"new tenancy" means a tenancy which is a new tenancy for the purposes of section 1;

"reversion" means the interest expectant on the termination of a tenancy;

"tenancy" means any lease or other tenancy and includes—

(a) a sub-tenancy, and

(b) an agreement for a tenancy,

but does not include a mortgage term;

"tenant covenant", in relation to a tenancy, means a covenant falling to be complied with by the tenant of premises demised by the tenancy.

(2) For the purposes of any reference in this Act to a covenant falling to be complied with in relation to a particular part of the premises demised by a tenancy, a covenant falls to be so complied with if—

(a) it in terms applies to that part of the premises, or

(b) in its practical application it can be attributed to that part of the premises (whether or not it can also be so attributed to other individual parts of those premises).

(3) Subsection (2) does not apply in relation to covenants to pay money; and, for the purposes of any reference in this Act to a covenant falling to be complied with in relation to a particular part of the premises demised by a tenancy, a covenant of a tenancy which is a covenant to pay money falls to be so complied with if—

(a) the covenant in terms applies to that part; or

(b) the amount of the payment is determinable specifically by reference—

(i) to that part, or

(ii) to anything falling to be done by or for a person as tenant or occupier of that part (if it is a tenant covenant), or

(iii) to anything falling to be done by or for a person as landlord of that part (if it is a landlord covenant).

(4) Where two or more persons jointly constitute either the landlord or the tenant in relation to a tenancy, any reference in this Act to the landlord or the tenant is a reference to both or all of the persons who jointly constitute the landlord or the tenant, as the case may be (and accordingly nothing in section 13 applies in relation to the rights and liabilities of such persons between themselves).

(5) References in this Act to the assignment by a landlord of the reversion in the whole or part of the premises demised by a tenancy are to the assignment by him of the whole of his interest (as owner of the reversion) in the whole or part of those premises.

(6) For the purposes of this Act—

(a) any assignment (however effected) consisting in the transfer of the whole of the landlord's interest (as owner of the reversion) in any premises demised by a tenancy shall be treated as an assignment by the landlord of the reversion in those premises even if it is not effected by him; and

(b) any assignment (however effected) consisting in the transfer of the whole of the tenant's interest in any premises demised by a tenancy shall be treated as an assignment by the tenant of those premises even if it is not effected by him.

Crown application

29. This Act binds the Crown.

Consequential amendments and repeals

30.—(1) The enactments specified in Schedule 1 are amended in accordance with that Schedule, the amendments being consequential on the provisions of this Act.

(2) The enactments specified in Schedule 2 are repealed to the extent specified.

(3) Subsections (1) and (2) do not affect the operation of—

(a) section 77 of, or Part IX or X of Schedule 2 to, the Law of Property Act 1925, or

(b) section 24(1)(b) or (2) of the Land Registration Act 1925,

in relation to tenancies which are not new tenancies.

(4) In consequence of this Act nothing in the following provisions, namely—

(a) sections 78 and 79 of the Law of Property Act 1925 (benefit and burden of covenants relating to land), and

(b) sections 141 and 142 of that Act (running of benefit and burden of covenants with reversion),

shall apply in relation to new tenancies.

(5) The Lord Chancellor may by order made by statutory instrument make, in the case of such enactments as may be specified in the order, such amendments or repeals in, or such modifications of, those enactments as appear to him to be necessary or expedient in consequence of any provision of this Act.

(6) Any statutory instrument made under subsection (5) shall be subject to annulment in pursuance of a resolution of either House of Parliament.

Commencement

31.—(1) The provisions of this Act come into force on such day as the Lord Chancellor may appoint by order made by statutory instrument.

(2) An order under this section may contain such transitional provisions and savings (whether or not involving the modification of any enactment) as appear to the Lord Chancellor necessary or expedient in connection with the provisions brought into force by the order.

Short title and extent

32.—(1) This Act may be cited as the Landlord and Tenant (Covenants) Act 1995.

(2) This Act extends to England and Wales only.

* * * *

SCHEDULE 1

Section 30(1)

CONSEQUENTIAL AMENDMENTS

Trustee Act 1925 (c. 19)

1. In section 26 of the Trustee Act 1925 (protection against lability in respect of rents and covenants), after subsection (1) insert—

"(1A) Where a personal representative or trustee has as such entered into, or may as such be required to enter into, an authorised guarantee agreement with respect to any lease comprised in the estate of a deceased testator or intestate or a trust estate (and, in a case where he has entered into such an agreement, he has satisfied all liabilities under it which may have accrued and been claimed up to the date of distribution)—

(a) he may distribute the residuary real and personal estate of the deceased testator or intestate, or the trust estate, to or amongst the persons entitled thereto—
(i) without appropriating any part of the estate of the deceased, or the trust estate, to meet any future liability (or, as the case may be, any liability) under any such agreement, and
(ii) notwithstanding any potential liability of his to enter into any such agreement; and
(b) notwithstanding such distribution, he shall not be personally liable in respect of any subsequent claim (or, as the case may be, any claim) under any such agreement.
In this subsection "authorised guarantee agreement" has the same meaning as in the Landlord and Tenant (Covenants) Act 1995."

Law of Property Act 1925 (c. 20)

2. In section 77 of the Law of Property Act 1925 (implied covenants in conveyances subject to rents), for subsection (2) substitute—

"(2) Where in a conveyance for valuable consideration, other than a mortgage, part of land affected by a rentcharge is, without the consent of the owner of the rentcharge, expressed to be conveyed subject to or charged with the entire rent, paragraph (B)(i) of subsection (1) of this section shall apply as if, in paragraph (i) of Part VIII of the Second Schedule to this Act—
(a) any reference to the apportioned rent were to the entire rent; and
(b) the words "(other than the covenant to pay the entire rent)" were omitted.

(2A) Where in a conveyance for valuable consideration, other than a mortgage, part of land affected by a rentcharge is, without the consent of the owner of the rentcharge, expressed to be conveyed discharged or exonerated from the entire rent, paragraph (B)(ii) of subsection (1) of this section shall apply as if, in paragraph (ii) of Part VIII of the Second Schedule to this Act—
(a) any reference to the balance of the rent were to the entire rent; and
(b) the words ", other than the covenant to pay the entire rent," were omitted."

Landlord and Tenant Act 1954 (c. 56)

3. At the end of section 34 of the Landlord and Tenant Act 1954 (rent under new tenancy) insert—

"(4) It is hereby declared that the matters which are to be taken into account by the court in determining the rent include any effect on rent of the operation of the provisions of the Landlord and Tenant (Covenants) Act 1995."

4.—(1) The existing provisions of section 35 of that Act (other terms of new tenancy) shall constitute subsection (1) of that section.

(2) After those provisions insert—

"(2) In subsection (1) of this section the reference to all relevant circumstances includes (without prejudice to the generality of that reference) a reference to the operation of the provisions of the Landlord and Tenant (Covenants) Act 1995."

SCHEDULE 2

Section 30(2)

Chapter	Short title	Extent of repeal
15 & 16 Geo. 5 (c. 20)	Law of Property Act 1925.	In section 77, subsection (1)(C) and (D) and, in subsection (7), paragraph (c) and the "or" preceding it. In Schedule 2, Parts IX and X.
15 & 16 Geo. 5 (c. 21)	Land Registration Act 1925.	Section 24(1)(b) and (2).

APPENDIX TWO

STATUTES

CONTENTS

LAW OF PROPERTY ACT 1925

(15 & 16 Geo.5, c.20)

An Act to consolidate the enactments relating to Conveyancing and the Law of Property in England and Wales.

[9th April 1925]

* * * *

Conveyances and other Instruments

Lands lie in grant only

51.—(1) All lands and all interests therein lie in grant and are incapable of being conveyed by livery or livery and seisin, or by feoffment, or by bargain and sale; and a conveyance of an interest in land may operate to pass the possession or right to possession thereof, without actual entry, but subject to all prior rights thereto.

(2) The use of the word grant is not necessary to convey land or to create any interest therein.

Conveyances to be by deed

52.—(1) All conveyances of land or of any interest therein are void for the purpose of conveying or creating a legal estate unless made by deed.

(2) This section does not apply to—

(a) assents by a personal representative;

(b) disclaimers made in accordance with [sections 178 to 180 or sections 315 to 319 of the Insolvency Act 1986], or not required to be evidenced in writing;

(c) surrenders by operation of law, including surrenders which may, by law, be effected without writing;

(d) leases or tenancies or other assurances not required by law to be made in writing;

(e) receipts not required by law to be under seal;

(f) vesting orders of the court or other competent authority;

(g) conveyances taking effect by operation of law.

ANNOTATION

The words in square brackets in subsection (2)(b) were substituted on December 29, 1986 by Insolvency Act 1986, ss.439(2), 443, Sch.14 (S.I. 1986 No. 1924).

Instruments required to be in writing

53.—(1) Subject to the provisions hereinafter contained with respect to the creation of interests in land by parol—

(a) no interest in land can be created or disposed of except by writing signed by the person creating or conveying the same, or by his agent thereunto lawfully authorised in writing, or by will, or by operation of law;

(b) a declaration of trust respecting any land or any interest therein must be manifested and proved by some writing signed by some person who is able to declare such trust or by his will;

(c) a disposition of an equitable interest or trust subsisting at the time of the disposition, must be in writing signed by the person disposing of the same, or by his agent thereunto lawfully authorised in writing or by will.

(2) This section does not affect the creation or operation of resulting, implied or constructive trusts.

Creation of interests in land by parol

54.—(1) All interests in land created by parol and not put in writing and signed by the persons so creating the same, or by their agents thereunto lawfully authorised in writing, have notwithstanding any consideration having been given for the same, the force and effect of interests at will only.

(2) Nothing in the foregoing provisions of this Part of this Act shall affect the creation by parol of leases taking effect in possession for a term not exceeding three years (whether or not the lessee is given power to extend the term) at the best rent which can be reasonably obtained without taking a fine.

Savings in regard to last two sections

55.—(1) Nothing in the last two foregoing sections shall—

(a) invalidate dispositions by will; or

(b) affect any interest validly created before the commencement of this Act; or

(c) affect the right to acquire an interest in land by virtue of taking possession; or

(d) affect the operation of the law relating to part performance.

* * * *

Execution of instruments by or on behalf of corporations

74.—[(1) In favour of a purchaser an instrument shall be deemed to have been duly executed by a corporation aggregate if a seal purporting to be the corporation's seal purports to be affixed in the presence of and attested by—

(a) two members of the board of directors, council or other governing body of the corporation, or

(b) one such member and the clerk, secretary or other permanent officer of the corporation or his deputy.]

ANNOTATION

Subs.(1) was substituted for the original subs. with effect from September 15, 2005 by The Regulatory Reform (Execution of Deeds and Documents) Order 2005 (S.I. 2005 No. 1906), arts 1(1), 3. The amendment does not apply in relation to any instrument executed before that date: *ibid.*, art.1(1),(2).

[(1A) Subsection (1) of this section applies in the case of an instrument purporting to have been executed by a corporation aggregate in the name of or on behalf of another person whether or not that person is also a corporation aggregate.]

ANNOTATION

Subsection (1A) was inserted on September 15, 2005 by The Regulatory Reform (Execution of Deeds and Documents) Order 2005 (S.I. 2005 No. 1906), arts 1(1), 7(1). The amendment does not apply in relation to any instrument executed before that date: *ibid.*, art.1(1),(2).

[(1B) For the purposes of subsection (1) of this sectionh, a seal purports to be affixed in the presence of and attested by an officer of the corporation, in the case of an officer which is not an individual, if it is affixed in the presence of and attested by an individual authorised by the officer to attest on its behalf.]

ANNOTATION

Subsection (1B) was inserted on September 15, 2005 by The Regulatory Reform (Execution of Deeds and Documents) Order 2005 (S.I. 2005 No. 1906), arts 1(1), 10(1), Sch.1, paras 1, 2. The amendment does not apply in relation to any instrument executed before that date: *ibid.*, art.1(1),(2).

(2) The board of directors, council or other governing body of a corporation aggregate may, by resolution or otherwise, appoint an agent either generally or in any particular case, to execute on behalf of the corporation any agreement or other instrument [which is not a deed] in relation to any matter within the powers of the corporation.

ANNOTATION

The words in square brackets in subsection (2) were inserted on July 31, 1990 by Law of Property (Miscellaneous Provisions) Act 1989, ss.1(8), 5(1),(2)(a), Sch.1, para.3; S.I. 1990 No. 1175.

(3) Where a person is authorised under a power of attorney or under any statutory or other power to convey any interest in property in the name of or on behalf of a corporation sole or aggregate, he may as attorney execute the conveyance by signing the name of the corporation in the presence of at least one witness [who attests the signature], *and in the case of a deed by affixing his own seal,* and such execution shall take effect and be valid in like manner as if the corporation had executed the conveyance.

ANNOTATION

The words in italics were repealed on July 31, 1990 by Law of Property (Miscellaneous Provisions) Act 1989, ss.4, Sch.2; S.I. 1990 No. 1175. The words in square brackets were inserted with effect from September 15, 2005 by The Regulatory Reform (Execution of Deeds and Documents) Order 2005 (S.I. 2005 No. 1906), arts 1(1), 10(1), Sch.1, paras 1, 3. The latter amendment does not apply in relation to any instrument executed before September 15, 2005: *ibid.*, art.1(1),(2).

(4) Where a corporation aggregate is authorised under a power of attorney or under any statutory or other power to convey any interest in property in the name or on behalf of any other person (including another corporation), an officer appointed for that purpose by the board of directors, council or other governing body of the corporation by resolution or otherwise, may execute the [instrument by signing it] in the name of such other person [or, if the instrument is to be a deed, by so signing it in the presence of a witness who attests the signature]; and where an instrument appears to be executed by an officer so appointed, then in favour of a purchaser the instrument shall be deemed to have been executed by an officer duly authorised.

ANNOTATION

The words in the first set of square brackets were substituted and the words in the second set of square brackets were inserted with effect from September 15, 2005 by The Regulatory Reform (Execution of Deeds and Documents) Order 2005 (S.I. 2005 No. 1906), arts 1(1), 10(1), Sch.1, paras 1, 4(a) and 4(b) respectively. The amendments do not apply in relation to any instrument executed before September 15, 2005: *ibid.*, art.1(1),(2).

(5) The foregoing provisions of this section apply to transactions wherever effected, but only to deeds and instruments executed after the commencement of this Act, except that, in the case of powers or appointments of an agent or officer, they apply whether the power was conferred or the appointment was made before or after the commencement of this Act or by this Act.

(6) Notwithstanding anything contained in this section, any mode of execution or attestation authorised by law or by practice or by the statute, charter, memorandum or articles, deed of settlement or other instrument constituting the corporation or regulating the affairs thereof, shall (in addition to the modes authorised by this section) be as effectual as if this section had not been passed.

[Execution of instrument as a deed

74A. —(1) An instrument is validly executed by a corporation aggregate as a deed for the purposes of section 1(2)(b) of the Law of Property (Miscellaneous Provisions) Act 1989, if and only if—

(a) it is duly executed by the corporation, and

(b) it is delivered as a deed.

(2) An instrument shall be presumed to be delivered for the purposes of section (1)(b) of this section upon its being executed, unless a contrary intention is proved.]

ANNOTATION

Section 74A was inserted with effect from September 15, 2005 by The Regulatory Reform (Execution of Deeds and Documents) Order 2005 (S.I. 2005 No. 1906), arts 1(1), 4. The section does not apply in relation to any instrument executed before September 15, 2005: *ibid.*, art.1(1),(2).

* * * *

Covenants

76. Covenants for title

(1) In a conveyance there shall, in the several cases in this section mentioned, be deemed to be included, and there shall in those several cases, by virtue of this Act, be implied, a covenant to the effect in this section stated, by the person or by each person who conveys, as far as regards the subject-matter or share of subject-matter expressed to be conveyed by him, with the person, if one, to whom the conveyance is made, or with the persons jointly, if more than one, to whom the conveyance is made as joint tenants, or with each of the persons, if more than one, to whom the conveyance is (when the law permits) made as tenants in common, that is to say:

(A) In a conveyance for valuable consideration, other than a mortgage, a covenant by a person who conveys and is expressed to convey as

beneficial owner in the terms set out in Part I of the Second Schedule to this Act;

(B) In a conveyance of leasehold property for valuable consideration, other than a mortgage, a further covenant by a person who conveys and is expressed to convey as beneficial owner in the terms set out in Part II of the Second Schedule to this Act;

(C) In a conveyance by way of mortgage (including a charge) a covenant by a person who conveys or charges and is expressed to convey or charge as beneficial owner in the terms set out in Part III of the Second Schedule to this Act;

(D) In a conveyance by way of mortgage (including a charge) of freehold property subject to a rent or of a leasehold property, a further covenant by a person who conveys or charges and is expressed to convey or charge as beneficial owner in the terms set out in Part IV of the Second Schedule to this Act;

(E) In a conveyance by way of settlement, a covenant by a person who conveys and is expressed to convey as settlor in the terms set out in Part V of the Second Schedule to this Act;

(F) In any conveyance, a covenant by every person who conveys and is expressed to convey as trustee or mortgagee, or as personal representative of a deceased person, . . . or under an order of the court, in the terms set out in Part VI of the Second Schedule to this Act, which covenant shall be deemed to extend to every such person's own acts only, and may be implied in an assent by a personal representative in like manner as in a conveyance by deed.

(2) Where in a conveyance it is expressed that by direction of a person expressed to direct as beneficial owner another person conveys, then, for the purposes of this section, the person giving the direction, whether he conveys and is expressed to convey as beneficial owner or not, shall be deemed to convey and to be expressed to convey as beneficial owner the subject-matter so conveyed by his direction; and a covenant on his part shall be implied accordingly.

(3) Where a wife conveys and is expressed to convey as beneficial owner, and the husband also conveys and is expressed to convey as beneficial owner, then, for the purposes of this section, the wife shall be deemed to convey and to be expressed to convey by direction of the husband, as beneficial owner; and, in addition to the covenant implied on the part of the wife, there shall also be implied, first, a covenant on the part of the husband as the person giving that direction, and secondly, a covenant on the part of the husband in the same terms as the covenant implied on the part of the wife.

(4) Where in a conveyance a person conveying is not expressed to convey as beneficial owner, or as settlor, or as trustee, or as mortgagee, or as personal representative of a deceased person, . . . or under an order of the court, or by direction of a person as beneficial owner, no covenant on the part of the person conveying shall be, by virtue of this section, implied in the conveyance.

(5) In this section a conveyance does not include a demise by way of lease at a rent, but does include a charge and "convey" has a corresponding meaning.

(6) The benefit of a covenant implied as aforesaid shall be annexed and incident to, and shall go with, the estate or interest of the implied covenantee, and shall be capable of being enforced by every person in whom that estate or interest is, for the whole or any part thereof, from time to time vested.

(7) A covenant implied as aforesaid may be varied or extended by a deed or an assent, and, as so varied or extended, shall, as far as may be, operate in the like manner, and with all the like incidents, effects, and consequences, as if such variations or extensions were directed in this section to be implied.

(8) This section applies to conveyances made after the thirty-first day of December, eighteen hundred and eighty-one, but only to assents by a personal representative made after the commencement of this Act.

ANNOTATION

The section was repealed on July 1, 1995 by Law of Property (Miscellaneous Provisions) Act 1994, ss.10, 21(2), 23(1), Sch.2 (S.I. 1995 No. 1317). The repeal is subject to transitional provisions for dispositions made before, or pursuant to contracts made before, July 1, 1995: *ibid.*, s.21(3).

77. Implied covenants in conveyance subject to rents

(1) In addition to the covenants implied under [Part I of the Law of Property (Miscellaneous Provisions) Act 1994], there shall in the several cases in this section mentioned, be deemed to be included and implied, a covenant to the effect in this section stated, by and with such persons as are hereinafter mentioned, that is to say:—

(A) In a conveyance for valuable consideration, other than a mortgage, of the entirety of the land affected by a rentcharge, a covenant by the grantee or joint and several covenants by the grantees, if more than one, with the conveying parties and with each of them, if more than one, in the terms set out in Part VII of the Second Schedule to this Act. Where a rentcharge has been apportioned in respect of any land, with the consent of the owner of the rentcharge, the covenants in this paragraph shall be implied in the conveyance of that land in like manner as if the apportioned rentcharge were the rentcharge referred to, and the document creating the rentcharge related solely to that land:

(B) In a conveyance for valuable consideration, other than a mortgage, of part of land affected by a rentcharge, subject to a part of that rentcharge which has been or is by that conveyance apportioned (but in either case without the consent of the owner of the rentcharge) in respect of the land conveyed–

(i) A covenant by the grantee of the land or joint and several covenants by the grantees, if more than one, with the conveying parties and with each of them, if more than one, in the terms set out in paragraph (i) of Part VIII of the Second Schedule to this Act;

(ii) A covenant by a person who conveys or is expressed to convey as beneficial owner, or joint and several covenants by the persons who so convey or are expressed to so convey, if at the date of the conveyance any part of the land affected by such rentcharge is retained, with the grantees of the land and with each of them (if more than one) in the terms set out in paragraph (ii) of Part VIII of the Second Schedule to this Act:

(C) In a conveyance for valuable consideration, other than a mortgage, of the entirety of the land comprised in a lease, for the residue of the term or interest created by the lease, a covenant by the assignee or joint and several covenants by the assignees (if more than one) with the conveying parties and with each of them (if more than one) in the

terms set out in Part IX of the Second Schedule to this Act. Where a rent has been apportioned in respect of any land, with the consent of the lessor, the covenants in this paragraph shall be implied in the conveyance of that land in like manner as if the apportioned rent were the original rent reserved, and the lease related solely to that land:

(D) In a conveyance for valuable consideration, other than a mortgage, of part of the land comprised in a lease, for the residue of the term or interest created by the lease, subject to a part of the rent which has been or is by the conveyance apportioned (but in either case without the consent of the lessor) in respect of the land conveyed–

(i) A covenant by the assignee of the land, or joint and several covenants by the assignees, if more than one, with the conveying parties and with each of them, if more than one, in the terms set out in paragraph (i) of Part X of the Second Schedule to this Act;

(ii) A covenant by a person who conveys or is expressed to convey as beneficial owner, or joint and several covenants by the persons who so convey or are expressed to so convey, if atthe date of the conveyance any part of the land comprised in the lease is retained, with the assignees of the land and with each of them (if more than one) in the terms set out in paragraph (ii) of Part X of the Second Schedule to this Act.

ANNOTATION

The words in square brackets were substituted on July 1, 1995 (subject to transitional provision) for the words "the last preceding section" by Law of Property (Miscellaneous Provisions) Act 1994, ss.21(1), 21(4), 23(1), Sch.1, para.1 (S.I. 1995 No. 1317). Subsections (1)(C) and (1)(D) were repealed on January 1, 1996 by Landlord and Tenant (Covenants) Act 1995, ss.30(2), 31(1), Sch.2 (S.I. 1995 No. 2963). The repeal does not affect the operation of those subs. in relation to tenancies which are not new tenancies within the meaning of the Act: *ibid.*, s.30(3).

(2) Where in a conveyance for valuable consideration, other than a mortgage, part of land affected by a rentcharge, or part of land comprised in a lease is, without the consent of the owner of the rentcharge or of the lessor, as the case may be, expressed to be conveyed—

(i) subject to or charged with the entire rent—
then paragraph (B)(ii) or (D)(i) of the last subsection, as the case may require shall have effect as if the entire rent were the apportioned rent; or

(ii) discharged or exonerated from the entire rent—
then paragraph (B)(ii) or (D)(ii) of the last subsection, as the case may require, shall have effect as if the entire rent were the balance of the rent, and the words "other than the covenant to pay the entire rent" had been omitted.

[(2) Where in a conveyance for valuable consideration, other than a mortgage, part of land affected by a rentcharge is, without the consent of the owner of the rentcharge, expressed to be conveyed subject to or charged with the entire rent, paragraph (B)(i) of subsection (1) of this section shall apply as if, in paragraph (i) of Part VIII of the Second Schedule to this Act—

(a) any reference to the apportioned rent were to the entire rent; and

(b) the words "(other than the covenant to pay the entire rent)" were omitted.

(2A) Where in a conveyance for valuable consideration, other than a mortgage, part of land affected by a rentcharge is, without the consent of the owner of the rentcharge, expressed to be conveyed discharged or exonerated from the entire rent, paragraph (B)(ii) of subsection (1) of this section shall apply as if, in paragraph (ii) of Part VIII of the Second Schedule to this Act—

(a) any reference to the balance of the rent were to the entire rent; and

(b) the words ", other than the covenant to pay the entire rent," were omitted.]

ANNOTATION

The new subs.(2) and (2A) were substituted for the old subs.(2) on January 1, 1996 by Landlord and Tenant (Covenants) Act 1995, ss.30(1), 31(1), Sch.1, para.2 (S.I. 1995 No. 2963). This amendment does not affect the operation of the old subs.(2) in relation to tenancies which are not new tenancies within the meaning of the Act: *ibid.*, s.30(3).

(3) In this section "conveyance" does not include a demise by way of lease as a rent.

(4) Any covenant which would be implied under this section by reason of a person conveying or being expressed to convey as beneficial owner may, by express reference to this section, be implied, with or without variation, in a conveyance, whether or not for valuable consideration, by a person who conveys or is expressed to convey as settlor, or as trustee, or as mortgagee, or as personal representative of a deceased person, . . . or under an order of the court.

(5) The benefit of a covenant implied as aforesaid shall be annexed and incident to, and shall go with, the estate or interest of the implied covenantee, and shall be capable of being enforced by every person in whom that estate or interest is, for the whole or any part thereof, from time to time vested.

(6) A covenant implied as aforesaid may be varied or extended by deed, and, as so varied or extended, shall, as far as may be, operate in the like manner, and with all the like incidents, effects and consequences, as if such variations or extensions were directed in this section to be implied.

(7) In particular any covenant implied under this section may be extended by providing that—

(a) the land conveyed; or

(b) the part of the land affected by the rentcharge which remains vested in the covenantor; *or*

(c) the part of the land demised which remains vested in the covenantor;

shall, as the case may require, stand charged with the payment of all money which may become payable under the implied covenant.

ANNOTATION

The words in italics were repealed on January 1, 1996 by Landlord and Tenant (Covenants) Act 1995, ss.30(2), 31(1), Sch.2 (S.I. 1995 No. 2963). The repeal does not affect the operation of subsection (7) in relation to tenancies which are not new tenancies within the meaning of that Act: *ibid.*, s.30(3).

(8) This section applies only to conveyances made after the commencement of this Act.

Benefit of covenants relating to land

78.—(1) A covenant relating to any land of the covenantee shall be deemed to be made with the covenantee and his successors in title and the persons deriving title under him or them, and shall have effect as if such successors and other persons were expressed.

For the purposes of this subsection in connexion with covenants restrictive of the user of land "successors in title" shall be deemed to include the owners and occupiers for the time being of the land of the covenantee intended to be benefited.

(2) This section applied to covenants made after the commencement of this Act, but the repeal of section fifty-eight of the Conveyancing Act 1881 does not affect the operation of covenants to which that section applied.

Burden of covenants relating to land

79.—(1) A covenant relating to any land of a covenantor or capable of being bound by him, shall, unless a contrary intention is expressed, be deemed to be made by the covenantor on behalf of himself his successors in title and the persons deriving title under him or them, and, subject as aforesaid, shall have effect as if such successors and other persons were expressed.

This subsection extends to a covenant to do some act relating to the land, notwithstanding that the subject-matter may not be in existence when the covenant is made.

(2) For the purposes of this section in connexion with covenants restrictive of the user of land "successors in title" shall be deemed to include the owner and occupiers for the time being of such land.

(3) This section applies only to covenants made after the commencement of this Act.

* * * *

Effect of extinguishment of reversion

139.—(1) Where a reversion expectant on a lease of land is surrendered or merged, the estate or interest which as against the lessee for the time being confers the next vested right to the land, shall be deemed the reversion for the purpose of preserving the same incidents and obligations as would have affected the original reversion had there been no surrender or merger thereof.

(2) This section applies to surrenders or mergers effected after the first day of October, eighteen hundred and forty-five.

Apportionment of conditions on severance

140.—(1) Notwithstanding the severance by conveyance, surrender, or otherwise of the reversionary estate in any land comprised in a lease, and notwithstanding the avoidance or cesser in any other manner of the term granted by a lease as to part only of the land comprised therein, every condition or right of re-entry, and every other condition contained in the lease, shall be apportioned, and shall remain annexed to the severed parts of the reversionary estate as severed, and shall be in force with respect to the term whereon each severed part is reversionary, or the term in the part of the land as to which the term has not been surrendered, or has not been avoided or has not otherwise ceased, in like manner as if the land comprised in each severed part, or the land as to which the term remains subsisting, as the case may be, had alone originally been comprised in the lease.

(2) In this section "right of re-entry" includes a right to determine the lease by notice to quit or otherwise; but where the notice is served by a person entitled to a severed part of the reversion so that it extends to part only of the land demised, the lessee may within one month determine the lease in regard to the rest of the land by giving to the owner of the reversionary estate therein a counter notice expiring at the same time as the original notice.

(3) This section applies to leases made before or after the commencement of this Act and whether the severance of the reversionary estate or the partial avoidance or cesser of the term was effected before or after such commencement:

Provided that, where the lease was made before the first day of January eighteen hundred and eighty-two nothing in this section shall affect the operation of a severance of the reversionary estate or partial avoidance or cesser of the term which was effected before the commencement of this Act.

Rent and benefit of lessee's covenants to run with the reversion

141.—(1) Rent reserved by a lease, and the benefit of every covenant or provision therein contained, having reference to the subject-matter thereof, and on the lessee's part to be observed or performed, and every condition of re-entry and other condition therein contained, shall be annexed and incident to and shall go with the reversionary estate in the land, or in any part thereof, immediately expectant on the term granted by the lease, notwithstanding severance of that reversionary estate, and without prejudice to any liability affecting a covenantor or his estate.

(2) Any such rent, covenant or provision shall be capable of being recovered, received, enforced, and taken advantage of, by the person from time to time entitled, subject to the term, to the income of the whole or any part, as the case may require, of the land leased.

(3) Where that person becomes entitled by conveyance or otherwise, such rent, covenant or provision may be recovered, received, enforced or taken advantage of by him notwithstanding that he becomes so entitled after the condition of re-entry or forfeiture has become enforceable, but this subsection does not render enforceable any condition of re-entry or other condition waived or released before such person becomes entitled as aforesaid.

(4) This section applies to leases made before or after the commencement of this Act, but does not affect the operation of—

(a) any severance of the reversionary estate; or

(b) any acquisition by conveyance or otherwise of the right to receive or enforce any rent covenant or provision;

effected before the commencement of this Act.

Obligation of lessor's covenants to run with reversion

142.—(1) The obligation under a condition or of a covenant entered into by a lessor with reference to the subject-matter of the lease shall, if and as far as the lessor has power to bind the reversionary estate immediately expectant on the term granted by the lease, be annexed and incident to and shall go with that reversionary estate, or the several parts thereof, notwithstanding severance of that reversionary estate, and may be taken advantage of and enforced by the person in whom the term is from time to time vested by conveyance, devolution in law or otherwise; and, if and as far as the lessor has power to bind the person from time to time entitled to that reversionary estate, the obligation aforesaid may be taken advantage of and enforced against any person so entitled.

(2) This section applies to leases made before or after the commencement of this Act, whether the severance of the reversionary estate was effected before or after such commencement:

Provided that, where the lease was made before the first day of January eighteen hundred and eighty-two, nothing in this section shall affect the operation of any severance of the reversionary estate effected before such commencement.

This section takes effect without prejudice to any liability affecting a covenantor or his estate.

Effect of licences granted to lessees

143.—(1) Where a licence is granted to a lessee to do any act, the licence, unless otherwise expressed, extends only—

(a) to the permission actually given; or

(b) to the specific breach of any provision or covenant referred to; or

(c) to any other matter thereby specifically authorised to be done;

and the licence does not prevent any proceeding for any subsequent breach unless otherwise specified in the licence.

(2) Notwithstanding any such licence—

(a) All rights under covenants and powers of re-entry contained in the lease remain in full force and are available as against any subsequent breach of covenant, condition or other matter not specifically authorised or waived, in the same manner as if no licence has been granted; and

(b) The condition or right of entry remains in force in all respects as if the licence had not been granted, save in respect of the particular matter authorised to be done.

(3) Where in any lease there is a power or condition of re-entry on the lessee assigning, subletting or doing any other specified act without a licence, and a licence is granted—

(a) to any one of two or more lessees to do any act, or to deal with his equitable share or interest; or

(b) to any lessee, or to any one of two or more lessees to assign or underlet part only of the property, or to do any act in respect of part only of the property;

the licence does not operate to extinguish the right of entry in case of any breach of covenant or condition by the co-lessees of the other shares or interests in the property, or by the lessee or lessees of the rest of the property (as the case may be) in respect of such shares or interests or remaining property, but the right of entry remains in force in respect of the shares, interests or property not the subject of the licence.

This subsection does not authorise the grant after the commencement of this Act of a licence to create an undivided share in a legal estate.

(4) This section applies to licences granted after the thirteenth day of August, eighteen hundred and fifty-nine.

No fine to be exacted for licence to assign

144. In all leases containing a covenant, condition, or agreement against assigning, underletting, or parting with the possession, or disposing of the land or property leased, without licence or consent, such covenant, condition, or agreement shall, unless the lease contains an express provision to the contrary, be deemed to be subject to a proviso to the effect that no fine or sum of money in the nature of a fine shall be payable for or in respect of such licence or consent; but this proviso does not preclude the right to require the payment of a reasonable sum in respect of any legal or other expense incurred in relation to such licence or consent.

Restrictions on and relief against forfeiture of leases and under-leases

146. (1) A right of re-entry or forfeiture under any proviso or stipulation in a lease for a breach of any covenant or condition in the lease shall not be enforceable, by action or otherwise, unless and until the lessor serves on the lessee a notice—

(a) specifying the particular breach complained of; and

(b) if the breach is capable of remedy, requiring the lessee to remedy the breach; and

(c) in any case, requiring the lessee to make compensation in money for the breach;

and the lessee fails, within a reasonable time thereafter, to remedy the breach, if it is capable of remedy, and to make reasonable compensation in money, to the satisfaction of the lessor, for the breach.

(2) Where a lessor is proceeding, by action or otherwise, to enforce such a right of re-entry or forfeiture, the lessee may, in the lessor's action, if any, or in any action brought by himself, apply to the court for relief; and the court may grant or refuse relief, as the court, having regard to the proceedings and conduct of the parties under the foregoing provisions of this section, and to all the other circumstances, thinks fit; and in case of relief may grant it on such terms, if any, as to costs, expenses, damages, compensation, penalty, or otherwise, including the granting of an injunction to restrain any like breach in the future, as the court, in the circumstances of each case, thinks fit.

(3) A lessor shall be entitled to recover as a debt due to him from a lessee, and in addition to damages (if any), all reasonable costs and expenses properly incurred by the lessor in the employment of a solicitor and surveyor or valuer, or otherwise, in reference to any breach giving rise to a right of re-entry or forfeiture which, at the request of the lessee, is waived by the lessor, or from which the lessee is relieved, under the provisions of this Act.

(4) Where a lessor is proceeding by action or otherwise to enforce a right of re-entry or forfeiture under any covenant, proviso, or stipulation in a lease, or for non-payment of rent, the court may, on application by any person claiming as under-lessee any estate or interest in the property comprised in the lease or any part thereof, either in the lessor's action (if any) or in any action brought by such person for that purpose, make an order vesting, for the whole term of the lease or any less term, the property comprised in the lease or any part thereof in any person entitled as under-lessee to any estate or interest in such property upon such conditions as to execution of any deed or other document, payment of rent, costs, expenses, damages, compensation, giving security, or otherwise, as the court in the circumstances of each case may think fit, but in no case shall

any such under-lessee be entitled to require a lease to be granted to him for any longer term than he had under his original sub-lease.

(5) For the purposes of this section—

- (a) "Lease" includes an original or derivative under-lease; also an agreement for a lease where the lessee has become entitled to have his lease granted; also a grant at a fee farm rent, or securing a rent by condition;
- (b) "Lessee" includes an original or derivative under-lessee, and the persons deriving title under a lessee; also a grantee under any such grant as aforesaid and the persons deriving title under him;
- (c) "Lessor" includes an original or derivative under-lessor, and the persons deriving title under a lessor; also a person making such grant as aforesaid and the persons deriving title under him;
- (d) "Under-lease" includes an agreement for an under-lease where the under-lessee has become entitled to have his under-lease granted;
- (e) "Under-lessee" includes any person deriving title under an under-lessee.

(6) This section applies although the proviso or stipulation under which the right of re-entry or forfeiture accrues is inserted in the lease in pursuance of the directions of any Act of Parliament.

(7) For the purposes of this section a lease limited to continue as long only as the lessee abstains from committing a breach of covenant shall be and take effect as a lease to continue for any longer term for which it could subsist, but determinable by a proviso for re-entry on such a breach.

(8) This section does not extend—

- (i) To a covenant or condition against assigning, underletting, parting with the possession, or disposing of the land leased where the breach occurred before the commencement of this Act; or
- (ii) In the case of a mining lease, to a covenant or condition for allowing the lessor to have access to or inspect books, accounts, records, weighing machines or other things or to enter or inspect the mine or the working thereof.

(9) This section does not apply to a condition for forfeiture on the bankruptcy of the lessee or on taking in execution of the lessee's interest if contained in a lease of—

- (a) Agricultural or pastoral land;
- (b) Mines or minerals;
- (c) A house used or intended to be used as a public-house or beer-shop;
- (d) A house let as a dwelling-house, with the use of any furniture, books, works of art, or other chattels not being in the nature of fixtures;
- (e) Any property with respect to which the personal qualifications of the tenant are of importance for the preservation of the value or character of the property, or on the ground of neighbourhood to the lessor, or to any person holding under him.

(10) Where a condition of forfeiture on the bankruptcy of the lessee or on taking in execution of the lessee's interest is contained in any lease, other than a lease of any of the classes mentioned in the last subsection then—

- (a) if the lessee's interest is sold within one year from the bankruptcy or taking in execution, this section applies to the forfeiture condition aforesaid;
- (b) if the lessee's interest is not sold before the expiration of that year, this section only applies to the forfeiture condition aforesaid during

the first year from the date of the bankruptcy or taking in execution.

(11) This section does not, save as otherwise mentioned, affect the law relating to re-entry or forfeiture or relief in case of non-payment of rent.

(12) This section has effect notwithstanding any stipulation to the contrary.

Relief against notice to effect decorative repairs

147.—(1) After notice is served on a lessee relating to the internal decorative repairs to a house or other building, he may apply to the court for relief, and if, having regard to all the circumstances of the case (including in particular the length of the lessee's term or interest remaining unexpired), the court is satisfied that the notice is unreasonable, it may by order, wholly or partially relieve the lessee from liability for such repairs.

(2) This section does not apply–

- (i) where the liability arises under an express covenant or agreement to put the property in a decorative state of repair and the covenant or agreement has never been performed;
- (ii) to any matter necessary or proper—
  - (a) for putting or keeping the property in a sanitary condition, or
  - (b) for the maintenance or preservation of the structure;
- (iii) to an statutory liability to keep a house in all respects reasonably fit for human habitation;
- (iv) to any covenant or stipulation to yield up the house or other building in a specified state of repair at the end of the term.

(3) In this section "lease" includes an under-lease and an agreement for a lease, and "lessee" has a corresponding meaning and includes any person liable to effect the repairs.

(4) This section applies whether the notice is served before or after the commencement of this Act, and has effect notwithstanding any stipulation to the contrary.

Waiver of a covenant in a lease

148.—(1) Where any actual waiver by a lessor or the persons deriving title under him of the benefit of any covenant or condition in any lease is proved to have taken place in any particular instance, such waiver shall not be deemed to extend to any instance, or to any breach of covenant or condition save that to which such waiver especially relates, nor operate as a general waiver of the benefit of any such covenant or condition.

(2) This section applies unless a contrary intention appears and extends to waivers effected after the twenty-third day of July, eighteen hundred and sixty.

Abolition of interesse termini, and as to reversionary leases and leases for lives

149.—(1) The doctrine of interesse termini is hereby abolished.

(2) As from the commencement of this Act all terms of years absolute shall, whether the interest is created before or after such commencement, be capable of taking effect at law or in equity, according to the estate interest or powers of the grantor, from the date fixed for commencement of the term, without actual entry.

(3) A term, at a rent or granted in consideration of a fine, limited after the commencement of this Act to take effect more than twenty-one years from the date of the instrument purporting to create it, shall be void, and any contract made after such commencement to create such a term shall likewise be void; but this subsection does not apply to any term taking effect in equity under a settlement, or created out of an equitable interest under a settlement, or under an equitable power for mortgage, indemnity or other like purposes.

(4) Nothing in subsections (1) and (2) of this section prejudicially affects the right of any person to recover any rent or to enforce or take advantage of any covenants or conditions, or, as respects terms or interests created before the commencement of this Act, operates to vary any statutory or other obligations imposed in respect of such terms or interests.

(5) Nothing in this Act affects the rule of law that a legal term, whether or not being a mortgage term, may be created to take effect in reversion expectant on a longer term, which rule is hereby confirmed.

(6) Any lease or under-lease, at a rent, or in consideration of a fine, for life or lives or for any term of years determinable with life or lives, or on the marriage of the lessee [or on the formation of a civil partnership between the lessee and another person], or any contract therefor, made before or after the commencement of this Act, or created by virtue of Part V of the Law of Property Act, 1922, shall take effect as a lease, under-lease or contract therefor, for a term of ninety years determinable after *the death or marriage* (as the case may be) [the death or marriage of, or the formation of a civil partnership by,] *of* the original lessee or *of* the survivor of the original lessees, by at least one month's notice in writing given to determine the same on one of the quarter days applicable to the tenancy, either by the lessor or the persons deriving title under him, to the person entitled to the leasehold interest, or if no such person is in existence by affixing the same to the premises, or by the lessee or other persons in whom the leasehold interest is vested to the lessor or the persons deriving title under him:

Provided that—

(a) this subsection shall not apply to any term taking effect in equity under a settlement or created out of an equitable interest under a settlement for mortgage, indemnity, or other like purposes;

(b) the person in whom the leasehold interest is vested by virtue of Part V of the Law of Property Act, 1922, shall, for the purposes of this subsection, be deemed an original lessee;

(c) if the lease, under-lease, or contract therefor is made determinable on the dropping of the lives of persons other than or besides the lessees, then the notice shall be capable of being served after the death of any person or of the survivor of any persons (whether or not including the lessees) on the cesser of whose life or lives the lease, under-lease, or contract is made determinable, instead of after the death of the original lessee or of the survivor of the original lessees;

(d) if there are no quarter days specially applicable to the tenancy, notice may be given to determine the tenancy on one of the usual quarter days.

ANNOTATION

The words in square brackets in subs.(6) were substituted for the words in italics with effect from December 5, 2005 by Civil Partnerships Act 2004, s.81, Sch.8, para.1; S.I. 2005 No. 3175.

[(7) Subsection (8) applies where a lease, underlease or contract—
- (a) relates to commonhold land, and
- (b) would take effect by virtue of subsection (6) as a lease, underlease or contract of the kind mentioned in that subsection.

(8) The lease, underlease or contract shall be treated as if it purported to be a lease, underlease or contract of the kind referred to in subsection (7)(b) (and sections 17 and 18 of the Commonhold and Leasehold Reform Act 2002 (residential and non-residential leases) shall apply accordingly).]

ANNOTATION

Subsections (7) and (8) were inserted on September 27, 2004 by Commonhold and Leasehold Reform Act 2002, s.68, Sch.5, para.3; S.I. 2004 No. 1832.

Surrender of a lease, without prejudice to under-leases with a view to the grant of a new lease

150.—(1) A lease may be surrendered with a view to the acceptance of a new lease in place thereof, without a surrender of any underlease derived thereout.

(2) A new lease may be granted and accepted, in place of any lease so surrendered, without any such surrender of an under-lease as aforesaid, and the new lease operates as if all under-leases derived out of the surrendered leases had been surrendered before the surrender of that lease was effected.

(3) The lessee under the new lease and any person deriving title under him is entitled to the same rights and remedies in respect of the rent reserved by and the covenants, agreement and conditions contained in any under-lease as if the original lease had not been surrendered but was or remained vested in him.

(4) Each under-lessee and any person deriving title under him is entitled to hold and enjoy the land comprised in his under-lease (subject to the payment of any rent reserved by and to the observance of the covenants, agreements and conditions contained in the under-lease) as if the lease out of which the under-lease was derived had not been surrendered.

(5) The lessor granting the new lease and any person deriving title under him is entitled to the same remedies, by distress or entry in and upon the land comprised in any such under-lease for rent reserved by or for breach of any covenant, agreement or condition contained in the new lease (so far only as the rents reserved by or the covenants, agreements or conditions contained in the new lease do not exceed or impose greater burdens than those reserved by or contained in the original lease out of which the under-lease is derived) as he would have had—
- (a) If the original lease had remained on foot; or
- (b) If a new under-lease derived out of the new lease had been granted to the under-lessee or a person deriving title under him;

as the case may require.

(6) This section does not affect the powers of the court to give relief against forfeiture.

Provision as to attornments by tenants

151.—(1) Where land is subject to a lease—
- (a) the conveyance of a reversion in the land expectant on the determination of the lease; or

(b) the creation or conveyance of a rentcharge to issue or issuing out of the land;

shall be valid without any attornment of the lessee:

Nothing in this subsection—

(i) affects the validity of any payment of rent by the lessee to the person making the conveyance or grant before notice of the conveyance or grant is given to him by the person entitled thereunder; or

(ii) renders the lessee liable for any breach of covenant to pay rent, on account of his failure to pay rent to the person entitled under the conveyance or grant such notice is given to the lessee.

(2) An attornment by the lessee in respect of any land to a person claiming to be entitled to the interest in the land of the lessor, if made without the consent of the lessor, shall be void.

This subsection does not apply to an attornment—

(a) made pursuant to a judgment of a court of competent jurisdiction; or

(b) to a mortgagee, by a lessee holding under a lease from the mortgagor where the right of redemption is barred; or

(c) to any other person rightfully deriving title under the lessor.

Leases invalidated by reason of non-compliance with terms of powers under which they are granted

152.—(1) Where in the intended exercise of any power of leasing, whether conferred by an Act of Parliament or any other instrument, a lease (in this section referred to as an invalid lease) is granted, which by reason of any failure to comply with the terms of the power is invalid, then—

(a) as against the person entitled after the determination of the interest of the grantor to the reversion; or

(b) as against any other person who, subject to any lease properly granted under the power would have been entitled to the land comprised in the lease;

the lease, if it was made in good faith, and the lessee has entered thereunder, shall take effect in equity as a contract for the grant, at the request of the lessee, of a valid lease under the power, of like effect as the invalid lease, subject to such variations as may be necessary in order to comply with the terms of the power:

Provided that a lessee under an invalid lease shall not, by virtue of any such implied contract, be entitled to obtain a variation of the lease if the other persons who would have been bound by the contract are willing and able to confirm the lease without variation.

(2) Where a lease granted in the intended exercise of such a power is invalid by reason of the grantor not having power to grant the lease at the date thereof, but the grantor's interest in the land comprised therein continues after the time when he might, in the exercise of the power, have properly granted a lease in the like terms, the lease shall take effect as a valid lease in like manner as if it had been granted at that time.

(3) Where during the continuance of the possession taken under an invalid lease the person for the time being entitled, subject to such possession, to the land comprised therein or to the rents and profits thereof, is able to confirm the lease without variation, the lessee, or other person who would have been bound by the lease had it been valid, shall, at the request of the person so able to confirm the lease, be bound to accept a confirmation thereof, and thereupon

the lease shall have effect and be deemed to have had effect as a valid lease from the grant thereof.

Confirmation under this subsection may be by a memorandum in writing signed by or on behalf of the persons respectively confirming and accepting the confirmation of the lease.

(4) Where a receipt or a memorandum in writing confirming an invalid lease is, upon or before the acceptance of rent thereunder, signed by or on behalf of the person accepting the rent, the acceptance shall, as against that person, be deemed to be a confirmation of the lease.

(5) The foregoing provisions of this section do not affect prejudicially—

(a) any right of action or other right or remedy to which, but for those provisions or any enactment replaced by those provisions, the lessee named in an invalid lease would or might have been entitled under any covenant on the part of the grantor for title or quiet enjoyment contained therein or implied thereby; or

(b) any right of re-entry or other right or remedy to which, but for those provisions or any enactment replaced thereby, the grantor or other person for the time being entitled to the reversion expectant on the termination of the lease, would or might have been entitled by reason of any breach of the covenants, conditions or provisions contained in the lease and binding on the lessee.

(6) Where a valid power of leasing is vested in or may be exercised by a person who grants a lease which, by reason of the determination of the interest of the grantor or otherwise, cannot have effect and continuance according to the terms thereof independently of the power, the lease shall for the purposes of this section be deemed to have been granted in the intended exercise of the power although the power is not referred to in the lease.

(7) This section does not apply to a lease of land held on charitable, ecclesiastical or public trusts.

(8) This section takes effect without prejudice to the provision in this Act for the grant of leases in the name and on behalf of the estate owner of the land affected.

* * * *

Application of Part V to existing leases

154. This Part of this Act, except where otherwise expressly provided, applies to leases created before or after the commencement of this Act, and "lease" includes an under-lease or other tenancy.

* * * *

Redemption and Apportionment of Rents, etc.

Equitable apportionment of rents and remedies for non-payment or breach of covenant

190.—(1) Where in a conveyance for valuable consideration, other than a mortgage, of part of land which is affected by a rentcharge, such rentcharge or a part thereof is, without the consent of the owner thereof, expressed to be—

(a) charged exclusively on the land conveyed or any part thereof in exoneration of the land retained or other land; or

(b) charged exclusively on the land retained or any part thereof in exoneration of the land conveyed or other land; or
(c) apportioned between the land conveyed or any part thereof, and the land retained by the grantor or any thereof;

then, without prejudice to the rights of the owner of the rentcharge, such charge or apportionment shall be binding as between the grantor and the grantee under the conveyance and their respective successors in title.

(2) Where—
(a) any default is made in payment of the whole or part of a rentcharge by the person who, by reason of such charge or apportionment as a aforesaid, is liable to pay the same; or
(b) any breach occurs of any of the covenants (other than in the case of an apportionment the covenant to pay the entire rentcharge) or conditions contained in the deed or other document creating the rentcharge, so far as the same relate to the land retained or conveyed, as the case may be;

the owner for the time being of any other land affected by the entire rentcharge who—
(i) pays or is required to pay the whole or part of the rentcharge which ought to have been paid by the defaulter aforesaid; or
(ii) incurs any costs, damages or expenses by reason of the breach of covenant or condition aforesaid;

may enter into and distrain on the land in respect of which the default or breach is made or occurs, or any part of the land, and dispose according to law of any distress found, and may also take possession of the income of the same land until, by means of such distress and receipt of income or otherwise the whole or part of the rentcharge (charged or apportioned as aforesaid) so unpaid and all the costs, damages and expenses incurred by reason of the non-payment thereof or of the breach of the said covenants and conditions, are fully paid or satisfied.

(3) Where in a conveyance for valuable consideration, other than a mortgage, of part of land comprised in a lease, for the residue of the term or interest created by the lease, the rent reserved by such lease or a part thereof, is without the consent of the lessor, expressed to be—
(a) charged exclusively on the land conveyed or any part thereof in exoneration of the land retained by the assignor or other land; or
(b) charged exclusively on the land retained by the assignor or any part thereof in exoneration of the land conveyed or other land; or
(c) apportioned between the land conveyed or any part thereof and the land retained by the assignor or any part thereof;

then, without prejudice to the rights of the lessor, such charge or apportionment shall be binding as between the assignor and the assignee under the conveyance and their respective successors in title.

(4) Where—
(a) any default is made in payment of the whole or part of a rent by the person who, by reason of such charge or apportionment as aforesaid, is liable to pay the same; or
(b) any breach occurs of any of the lessee's covenants (other than in the case of an apportionment the covenant to pay the entire rent) or conditions contained in the lease, as far as the same relate to the land retained or conveyed, as the case may be;

the lessee for the time being of any other land comprised in the lease, in whom, as respects that land, the residue of the term or interest created by the lease is vested, who—

(i) pays or is required to pay the whole or part of the rent which ought to have been paid by the defaulter aforesaid; or
(ii) incurs any costs, damages or expenses by reason of the breach of covenant or condition aforesaid;

may enter into and distrain on the land comprised in the lease in respect of which the default or breach is made or occurs, or any part of the land, and dispose according to law of any distress found, and may also take possession of the income of the same land until (so long as the term or interest created by the lease is subsisting) by means of such distress and receipt of income or otherwise, the whole or part of the rent (charged or apportioned as aforesaid) so unpaid and all costs, damages and expenses incurred by reason of the non-payment thereof or of the breach of the said covenants and conditions, are fully paid or satisfied.

(5) The remedies conferred by this section take effect so far only as they might have been conferred by the conveyance whereby the rent or any part thereof is expressed to be charged or apportioned as aforesaid, but a trustee, personal representative, mortgagee or other person in a fiduciary position has, and shall be deemed always to have had, power to confer the same or like remedies.

(6) This section applies only if and so far as a contrary intention is not expressed in the conveyance whereby the rent or any part thereof is expressed to be charged or apportioned as aforesaid, and takes effect subject to the terms of the conveyance and to the provisions therein contained.

(7) The remedies conferred by this section apply only where the conveyance whereby the rent or any part thereof is expressed to be charged or apportioned is made after the commencement of this Act, and do not apply where the rent is charged exclusively as aforesaid or legally apportioned with the consent of the owner or lessor.

(8) The rule of law relating to perpetuities does not affect the powers or remedies conferred by this section or any like powers or remedies expressly conferred, before or after the commencement of this Act, by an instrument.

* * * *

Notices

Regulations respecting notices

196.—(1) Any notice required or authorised to be served or given by this Act shall be in writing.

(2) Any notice required or authorised by this Act to be served on a lessee or mortgagor shall be sufficient, although only addressed to the lessee, or mortgagor by that designation, without his name, or generally to the persons interested, without any name, and notwithstanding that any person to be affected by the notice is absent under disability, unborn, or unascertained.

(3) Any notice required or authorised by this Act to be served shall be sufficiently served if it is left at the last-known place of abode or business in the United Kingdom of the lessee, lessor, mortgagee, mortgagor, or other person to be served, or, in case of a notice required or authorised to be served on a lessee or mortgagor, is affixed or left for him on the land or any house or building comprised in the lease or mortgage, or, in the case of a mining lease, is left for the lessee at the office or counting-house of the mine.

(4) Any notice required or authorised by this Act to be served shall also be sufficiently served, if it is sent by post in a registered letter addressed to the

lessee, lessor, mortgagee, mortgagor, or other person to be served, by name, at the aforesaid place of abode or business, office, or counting-house, and if that letter is not returned through the post-office undelivered; and that service shall be deemed to be made at the time at which the registered letter would in the ordinary course be delivered.

(5) The provisions of this section shall extend to notices required to be served by any instrument affecting property executed or coming into operation after the commencement of this Act unless a contrary intention appears.

(6) This section does not apply to notices served in proceedings in the court.

* * * *

SECOND SCHEDULE

Sections 76 and 77

Implied Covenants

Part I

Covenant Implied in a Conveyance for valuable Consideration, other than a Mortgage, by a Person who Conveys and is expressed to Convey as Beneficial Owner

That, notwithstanding anything by the person who so conveys or any one through whom he derives title otherwise than by purchase for value, made, done, executed, or omitted, or knowingly suffered, the person who so conveys has, with the concurrence of every other person, if any, conveying by his direction, full power to convey the subject-matter expressed to and be conveyed, subject as, if so expressed, and in the manner in which, it is expressed to be conveyed, and that, notwithstanding anything as aforesaid, that subject-matter shall remain to and be quietly entered upon, received, and held, occupied, enjoyed, and taken by the person to whom the conveyance is expressed to be made, and any person deriving title under him, and the benefit thereof shall be received and taken accordingly, without any lawful interruption or disturbance by the person who so conveys or any person conveying by his direction, or rightfully claiming or to claim by, through, under, or in trust for the person who so conveys or any person conveying by his direction, or by, through, or under any one (not being a person claiming in respect of an estate or interest subject whereto the conveyance is expressly made), through whom the person who so conveys, derives title, otherwise than by purchase for value:

And that, freed and discharged from, or otherwise by the person who so conveys sufficiently indemnified against, all such estates, incumbrances, claims, and demands, other than those subject to which the conveyance is expressly made, as, either before or after the date of the conveyance, have been or shall be made, occasioned, or suffered by that person or by any person conveying by his direction, or by any person rightfully claiming by, through, under, or in trust for the person who so conveys, or by, through, or under any person conveying by his direction, by, through, or under any one through whom the person who so conveys derives title, otherwise than by purchase for value:

And further, that the person who so conveys, and any person conveying by his direction, and every other person having or rightfully claiming any estate or interest in the subject-matter of conveyance, other than an estate or interest subject whereto the conveyance is expressly made, by, through, under, or in trust for the person who so conveys, or by, through, or under any person conveying by his direction, or by, through, or under any one through whom the person who so conveys derives title, otherwise than by purchase for value, will, from time to time and at all times after the date of the conveyance, on the request and at the cost of any person to whom the conveyance is expressed to be made, or of any person deriving title under him, execute and do all such lawful assurances and things for further or more perfectly assuring the subject-matter of the conveyance to the person to whom the conveyance is made, and to those deriving title under him, subject as, if so expressed, and in the manner in which the conveyance is expressed to be made, as by him or them or any of them shall be reasonably required.

In the above covenant a purchase for value shall not be deemed to include a conveyance in consideration of marriage.

ANNOTATION

Part I was repealed on July 1, 1995 by Law of Property (Miscellaneous Provisions) Act, ss.21(2), 23(1), Sch.2 (S.I. 1995 No. 1317). The repeal is subject to transitional provisions: *ibid.*, s.21(3).

PART II

FURTHER COVENANT IMPLIED IN A CONVEYANCE OF LEASEHOLD PROPERTY FOR VALUABLE CONSIDERATION, OTHER THAN A MORTGAGE, BY A PERSON WHO CONVEYS AND IS EXPRESSED TO CONVEY AS BENEFICIAL OWNER

That, notwithstanding anything by the person who so conveys, or any one through whom he derives title, otherwise than by purchase for value, made, done, executed, or omitted, or knowingly suffered, the lease or grant creating the term or estate for which the land is conveyed is, at the time of conveyance, a good, valid, and effectual lease or grant of the property conveyed, and is in full force, unforfeited, unsurrendered, and has in nowise become void or voidable, and that, notwithstanding anything as aforesaid, all the rents reserved by, and all the covenants, conditions, and agreements contained in, the lease or grant, and on the part of the lessee or grantee and the persons deriving title under him to be paid, observed, and performed, have been paid, observed, and performed up to the time of conveyance.

In the above covenant a purchase for value shall not be deemed to include a conveyance in consideration of marriage.

ANNOTATION

Part II was repealed on July 1, 1995 by Law of Property (Miscellaneous Provisions) Act 1994, ss.21(2), 23(1), Sch.2 (S.I. 1995 No. 1317). The repeal is subject to transitional provisions: *ibid.*, s.21(3).

* * * *

PART IX

COVENANT IN A CONVEYANCE FOR VALUABLE CONSIDERATION, OTHER THAN A MORTGAGE, OF THE ENTIRETY OF THE LAND COMPRISED IN A LEASE FOR THE RESIDUE OF THE TERM OR INTEREST CREATED BY THE LEASE

That the assignees, or the persons deriving title under them, will at all times, from the date of the conveyance or other date therein stated, duly pay all rent becoming due under the lease creating the term or interest for which the land is conveyed, and observe and perform all the covenants, agreements and conditions therein contained and thenceforth on the part of the lessees to be observed and performed:

And also will at all times, from the date aforesaid, save harmless and keep indemnified the conveying parties and their estates and effects, from and against all proceedings, costs, claims and expenses on account of any omission to pay the said rent or any breach of any of the said covenants, agreements and conditions.

ANNOTATION

Part IX was repealed on January 1, 1996 by Landlord and Tenant (Covenants) Act 1995, ss.30(2), 31(1), Sch.2 (S.I. 1995 No. 2963). The repeal does not affect the operation of Part IX in relation to tenancies which are not new tenancies within the meaning of the Act: *ibid.*, s.30(3).

PART X

COVENANTS IMPLIED IN A CONVEYANCE FOR VALUABLE CONSIDERATION, OTHER THAN A MORTGAGE, OF PART OF THE LAND COMPRISED IN A LEASE, FOR THE RESIDUE OF THE TERM OR INTEREST CREATED BY THE LEASE, SUBJECT TO A PART (NOT LEGALLY APPORTIONED) OF THAT RENT

(i) That the assignees, or the persons deriving title under them, will at all times, from the date of the conveyance or other date therein stated, pay the apportioned rent and observe and perform all the covenants, other than the covenant to pay the rent, agreements and conditions contained in the lease creating the term or interest for which the land is conveyed, and thenceforth on the part of the lessees to be observed and performed, so far as the same relate to the land conveyed:

And also will at all times from the date aforesaid save harmless and keep indemnified, the conveying parties and their respective estates and effects, from and against all proceedings, costs, claims and expenses on account of any omission to pay the said apportioned rent or any breach of any of the said covenants, agreements and conditions, so far as the same relate as aforesaid.

(ii) That the conveying parties, or the persons deriving title under them, will at all times, from the date of the conveyance, or other date therein stated, pay the balance of the rent (after deducting the apportioned rent aforesaid and any other rents similarly apportioned in respect of land not retained) and observe and perform all the covenants, other than the covenant to pay the entire rent, agreements and conditions contained in the lease and on the part of the lessees to be observed and performed so far as the same relate to the land demised (other than the land comprised in the conveyance) and remaining vested in the convenantors:

And also will at all times, from the date aforesaid, save harmless and keep indemnified, the assignees and their estates and effects, from and against all proceedings, costs, claims and expenses on account of any omission to pay the aforesaid balance of the rent or any breach of any of the said covenants, agreements and conditions so far as they relate as aforesaid.

ANNOTATION

Part X was repealed on January 1, 1996 by Landlord and Tenant (Covenants) Act 1995, ss.30(2), 31(1), Sch.2 (S.I. 1995 No. 2963). The repeal does not affect the operation of Part X in relation to tenancies which are not new tenancies within the meaning of the Act: *ibid*., s.30(3).

* * * *

LAND REGISTRATION ACT 1925

(15 & 16 Geo. 5, c. 21)

An Act to consolidate the Land Transfer Acts and the statute law relating to registered land.

[9th April 1925]

ANNOTATION

Land Registration Act 1925 was repealed in its entirety with effect from October 13, 2003 and replaced by the provisions of Land Registration Act 2002, below, pp.420 *et seq*.,: Land Registration Act 2002, s.135; Sch.13; S.I. 2003 No. 1725. The repeal does not affect the applicability of the sections of the 1925 Act, below, where an application for first registration, or any application that would if completed result in a change to the register, is pending immediately before October 13, 2003: The Land Registration Act 2002 (Transitional Provisions) Order 2003 (S.I. 2003 No. 1953) art.3. Accordingly, these sections of the 1925 Act may have some continuing relevance (subject to earlier repeals) where a transfer or an application for registration of a leasehold or freehold estate was made before October 13, 2003.

* * * *

PART III

REGISTERED DEALINGS WITH REGISTERED LAND

Dispositions of Freehold Land

Powers of disposition of registered freeholds

18.—*(1) Where the registered land is a freehold estate the proprietor may, in the prescribed manner, transfer the registered estate in the land or any part thereof, and, subject to any entry in the register to the contrary, may in the prescribed manner—*

(a) transfer the fee simple in possession of all or any mines or minerals apart from the surface; or of the surface without all or any of the mines and minerals;

(b) grant an annuity or a rentcharge in possession (either perpetual or for a term of years absolute) in any form which sufficiently refers in the prescribed manner to the registered land charged;

(c) grant in fee simple in possession any easement, right, or privilege in, over, or derived from the registered land or any part thereof, in any form which sufficiently refers, in the prescribed manner, to the registered servient tenement and to the dominant tenement, whether being registered land or not;

(d) transfer the fee simple in possession of the registered land or any part thereof, subject to the creation thereout, by way of reservation, in favour of any person of an annuity or a rentcharge in possession (either perpetual or for a term of years absolute), or of any easement, right, or privilege in possession (either in fee simple or for a term of years absolute);

(e) grant (subject or not to the reservation of an easement, right, or privilege) a lease of the registered land or any part thereof, or of all or any mines and minerals apart from the surface, or of the surface without all or any of the mines and minerals, or of an easement, right or privilege in or over the land, or any part thereof, for any term of years absolute for any purpose (but where by way of mortgage subject to the provisions of this Act and the Law of Property Act 1925 relating thereto), and in any form which sufficiently refers, in the prescribed manner, to the registered land.

(2) A perpetual annuity or rentcharge in possession may be granted or reserved to any person with or without a power of re-entry, exercisable at any time, on default of payment thereof, or on breach of covenant, and shall have incidental thereto all the powers and remedies (as varied if at all by the disposition creating the rentcharge) for recovery thereof conferred by the Law of Property Act 1925; and where an easement, right, or privilege is reserved in a registered disposition for a legal estate, the reservation shall operate to create the same for the benefit of the land for the benefit of which the right is reserved.

(3) A lease for a term, not exceeding twenty-one years, to take effect in possession or within one year from the date thereof . . . may be granted and shall take effect under this section notwithstanding that a caution, notice of deposit of a certificate, restriction, or inhibition (other than a bankruptcy inhibition) may be subsisting, but subject to the interests intended to be protected by any such caution, notice, restriction, or inhibition.

(4) The foregoing powers of disposition shall (subject to the express provisions of this Act and of the Law of Property Act 1925 relating to mortgages) apply to dispositions by the registered proprietor by way of charge or mortgage; but no estate, other than a legal estate, shall be capable of being disposed of, or created under, this section.

(5) In this Act "transfer" or "disposition" when referring to registered freehold land includes any disposition authorised as aforesaid; and "transferee" has a corresponding meaning.

ANNOTATION

See general note on repeal of Land Registration Act 1925, above.

Registration of disposition of freeholds

19.—(1) The transfer of the registered estate in the land or part thereof shall be completed by the registrar entering on the register the transferee as the proprietor of the estate transferred, but until such entry is made the transferor shall be deemed to remain proprietor of the registered estate; and, where part only of the land is transferred, notice thereof shall also be noted on the register.

(2) All interests transferred or created by dispositions by the proprietor, other than a transfer of the registered estate in the land, or part thereof, shall, subject to the provisions relating to mortgages, be completed by registration in the same manner and with the same effect as provided by this Act with respect to transfers of registered estates and notice thereof shall also be noted on the register:

Provided that nothing in this subsection—

- *(a) shall authorise the registration of a lease granted for a term not exceeding twenty-one years, or require the entry of a notice of such a lease . . . ; or*
- *(b) shall authorise the registration of a mortgage term where there is a subsisting right of redemption; or*
- *(c) shall render necessary the registration of any easement, right, or privilege except as appurtenant to registered land, or the entry of notice thereof except as against the registered title of the servient land.*

Every such disposition shall, when registered, take effect as a registered disposition, and a lease made by the registered proprietor under the last foregoing section which is not required to be registered or noted on the register shall nevertheless take effect as if it were a registered disposition immediately on being granted.

(3) The general words implied in conveyances under the Law of Property Act 1925 shall apply, so far as applicable thereto, to dispositions of a registered estate.

ANNOTATION

See general note on repeal of Land Registration Act 1925, above.

Effect of registration and dispositions of freeholds

20.—(1) In the case of a freehold estate registered with an absolute title, a disposition of the registered land or of a legal estate therein, including a lease thereof, for valuable consideration shall, when registered, confer on the transferee or grantee an estate in fee simple or the term of years absolute or other legal estate expressed to be created in the land dealt with, together with all rights, privileges, and appurtenances belonging or appurtenant thereto, including (subject to any entry to the contrary in the register) the appropriate rights and interests which would, under the Law of Property Act 1925, have been transferred if the land had not been registered, subject—

- *(a) to the incumbrances and other entries, if any, appearing on the register [and any charge for capital transfer tax subject to which the disposition takes effect under section 73 of this Act]; and*
- *(b) unless the contrary is expressed on the register, to the overriding interests, if any, affecting the estate transferred or created,*

but free from all other estates and interests whatsoever, including estates and interests of His Majesty, and the disposition shall operate in like manner as if the registered transferor or grantor were (subject to any entry to the contrary in the register) entitled to the registered land in fee simple in possession for his own benefit.

(2) In the case of a freehold estate registered with a qualified title a disposition of the registered land or of a legal estate therein, including a lease thereof, for valuable consideration shall, when registered, have the same effect as it would have had if the land had been registered with an absolute title, save that such disposition shall not affect or prejudice the enforcement of any right or interest appearing by the register to be excepted.

(3) In the case of a freehold estate registered with a possessory title, a disposition of the registered land or of a legal estate therein, including a lease thereof, for valuable consideration shall not affect or prejudice the enforcement of any right or interest adverse to or in derogation of the title of the first registered proprietor, and subsisting or capable of arising at the time of the registration of such proprietor; but, save as aforesaid, shall when registered have the same effect as it would have had if the land had been registered with an absolute title.

(4) Where any such disposition is made without valuable consideration, it shall, so far as the transferee or grantee is concerned, be subject to any minor interests subject to which the transferor or grantor held the same, but, save as aforesaid, shall, when registered, in all respects, and in particular as respects any registered dealings on the part of the transferee or grantee, have the same effect as if the disposition had been made for valuable consideration.

ANNOTATION

See general note on repeal of Land Registration Act 1925, above.

Dispositions of Leasehold Land

Powers of disposition of registered leaseholds

21.—*(1) Where the registered land is a leasehold interest the proprietor may, in the prescribed manner, transfer the registered estate in the land or any part thereof, and, subject to any entry in the register to the contrary may in the prescribed manner—*

- *(a) transfer all or any of the leasehold mines and minerals apart from the surface; or the surface without all or any of the leasehold mines and minerals;*
- *(b) grant (to the extent of the registered estate) any annuity or rentcharge in possession, easement, right or privilege in, over, or derived from the registered land or any part thereof, in any form which sufficiently refers, in the prescribed manner, to the registered lease, and to the dominant tenement, whether being registered land or not;*
- *(c) transfer the registered land or any part thereof subject to a reservation to any person of any such annuity, rentcharge, easement, right, or privilege;*
- *(d) grant (subject or not to the reservation of an easement, right or privilege) an underlease of the registered land, or any part thereof, or of all or any mines and minerals apart from the surface, or of the surface without all or any of the mines and minerals, or of an easement, right or privilege, in or over the registered land or any part thereof, for any term of years absolute of less duration than the*

registered estate and for any purpose (but where by way of mortgage, subject to the provisions of this Act and of the Law of Property Act 1925 relating thereto), and in any form which sufficiently refers in the prescribed manner to the registered land, and in the case of an easement, right, or privilege, to the dominant tenement, whether being registered land or not.

(2) A disposition of registered leasehold land may be made subject to a rent legally apportioned in the prescribed manner, or to a rent not so apportioned.

(3) An underlease for a term, not exceeding twenty-one years, to take effect in possession or within one year from the date thereof . . . , may be granted and shall take effect under this section, notwithstanding that a caution, notice of deposit of a certificate, restriction, or inhibition (other than a bankruptcy inhibition) may be subsisting, but subject to the interests intended to be protected by any such caution, notice, restriction or inhibition.

(4) The foregoing powers of disposition shall (subject to the express provisions of this Act and of the Law of Property Act 1925 relating to mortgages) apply to dispositions by the registered proprietor by way of charge or mortgage, but no estate, other than a legal estate, shall be capable of being disposed of or created under this section.

(5) In this Act "transfer" or "disposition" when referring to registered leasehold land includes any disposition authorised as aforesaid and "transferee" has a corresponding meaning.

ANNOTATION

See general note on repeal of Land Registration Act 1925, above.

Registration of dispositions of leaseholds

***22.**—(1) A transfer of the registered estate in the land or part thereof shall be completed by the registrar entering on the register the transferee as proprietor of the estate transferred, but until such entry is made the transferor shall be deemed to remain the proprietor of the registered estate; and where part only of the land is transferred, notice thereof shall also be noted on the register.*

(2) All interests transferred or created by dispositions by the registered proprietor other than the transfer of his registered estate in the land or in part thereof shall (subject to the provisions relating to mortgages) be completed by registration in the same manner and with the same effect as provided by this Act with respect to transfers of the registered estate, and notice thereof shall also be noted on the register in accordance with this Act:

Provided that nothing in this subsection—

(a) shall authorise the registration of an underlease originally granted for a term not exceeding twenty-one years, or require the entry of a notice of such an underlease . . . ; or

(b) shall authorise the registration of a mortgage term where there is a subsisting right of redemption, or

(c) shall render necessary the registration of any easement, right, or privilege except as appurtenant to registered land, or the entry of notice thereof except as against the registered title of the servient land.

Every such disposition shall, when registered, take effect as a registered disposition, and an underlease made by the registered proprietor which is not required to be registered or noted on the register shall nevertheless take effect as if it were a registered disposition immediately on being granted.

(3) The general words implied in conveyances under the Law of Property Act 1925 shall apply, so far as applicable thereto, to transfers of a registered leasehold estate.

ANNOTATION

See general note on repeal of Land Registration Act 1925, above.

Effect of registration of dispositions of leaseholds

23.—*(1) In the case of a leasehold estate registered with an absolute title, a disposition (including a subdemise thereof) for valuable consideration shall, when registered, be deemed to vest in the transferee or underlessee the estate transferred or created to the extent of the registered estate, or for the term created by the subdemise, as the case may require, with all implied or expressed rights, privileges, and appurtenances attached to the estate transferred or created, including (subject to any entry to the contrary on the register) the appropriate rights and interests which would under the Law of Property Act 1925 have been transferred if the land had not been registered, but subject as follows:—*

- *(a) To all implied and express covenants, obligations, and liabilities incident to the estate transferred or created; and*
- *(b) To the incumbrances and other entries (if any) appearing on the register [and any charge for capital transfer tax subject to which the disposition takes effect under section 73 of this Act]; and*
- *(c) Unless the contrary is expressed on the register, to the overriding interests, if any, affecting the estate transferred or created,*

but free from all other estates and interests whatsoever, including estates and interests of His Majesty; and the transfer or subdemise shall operate in like manner as if the registered transferor or sublessor were (subject to any entry to the contrary on the register) absolutely entitled to the registered lease for his own benefit.

(2) In the case of a leasehold estate registered with a good leasehold title, a disposition (including a subdemise thereof) for valuable consideration shall, when registered, have the same effect as it would have had if the land had been registered with an absolute title, save that it shall not affect or prejudice the enforcement of any right or interest affecting or in derogation of the lessor to grant the lease.

(3) In the case of a leasehold estate registered with a qualified title, a disposition (including a subdemise thereof) for valuable consideration shall, when registered, have the same effect as it would have had if the land had been registered with an absolute title, save that such disposition shall not affect or prejudice the enforcement of any right or interest (whether in respect of the lessor's title or otherwise) appearing by the register to be excepted.

(4) In the case of a leasehold estate registered with a possessory title, a disposition (including a subdemise thereof) for valuable consideration shall not affect or prejudice the enforcement of any right or interest (whether in respect of the lessor's title or otherwise) adverse to or in derogation of the title of the first registered proprietor, and subsisting or capable of arising at the time of the registration of such proprietor, but save as aforesaid shall, when registered, have the same effect as it would have had if the land had been registered with an absolute title.

(5) Where any such disposition is made without valuable consideration it shall, so far as the transferee or underlessee is concerned, be subject to any minor interests subject to which the transferor or sublessor held the same; but,

save as aforesaid, shall, when registered, in all respects, and in particular as respects any registered dealings on the part of the transferee or underlessee, have the same effect as if the disposition had been made for valuable consideration.

ANNOTATION

See general note on repeal of Land Registration Act 1925, above.

Implied covenants on transfers of leaseholds

24.—*(1) On the transfer, otherwise than by way of underlease, of any leasehold interest in land under this Act, unless there be an entry on the register negativing such implication, there shall be implied—*

- *(a) on the part of the transferor, a covenant with the transferee that, notwithstanding anything by such transferor done, omitted, or knowingly suffered, the rent, covenants, and conditions reserved and contained by and in the registered lease, and on the part of the lessee to be paid, performed, and observed, have been so paid, performed, and observed up to the date of the transfer; and*
- *(b) on the part of the transferee, a covenant with the transferor, that during the residue of the term the transferee and the persons deriving title under him will pay, perform, and observe the rent, covenants, and conditions by and in the registered lease reserved and contained, and on the part of the lessee to be paid, performed, and observed, and will keep the transferor and the persons deriving title under him indemnified against all actions, expenses, and claims on account of the non-payment of the said rent or any part thereof, or the breach of the said covenants or conditions, or any of them.*

(2) On a transfer of part of the land held under a lease, the covenant implied on the part of the transferee by this section shall be limited to the payment of the apportioned rent, if any, and the performance and observance of the covenants by the lessee and conditions in the registered lease so far only as they affect the part transferred. Where the transferor remains owner of part of the land comprised in the lease, there shall also be implied on his part, as respects the part retained, a covenant with the transferee similar to that implied on the part of the transferee under this subsection.

ANNOTATION

Subsection (1)(a) was repealed on July 1, 1995 by Law of Property (Miscellaneous Provisions) Act 1994, ss.21(2), 23(1), Sch.2 (S.I. 1995 No. 1317). The repeal is subject to transitional provisions: *ibid*., s.21(3).

Subsections (1)(b) and (2) were repealed in relation to new tenancies only on January 1, 1996 by Landlord and Tenant (Covenants) Act 1995, ss.30(2), 31(1), Sch.2 (S.I. 1995 No. 2963), and then repealed further on October 13, 2003 by Land Registration Act 2002, s.135, Sch.13, subject to transitional provisions in *ibid*., s.134, Sch.12, para.20, below, p.427, introducing new indemnity covenants that apply on the transfer of old tenancies on or after October 13, 2003.

See general note on repeal of Land Registration Act 1925, above.

* * * *

LANDLORD AND TENANT ACT 1927

(17 & 18 Geo. 5, c. 36)

An Act to provide for the payment of compensation for improvements and goodwill to tenants of premises used for business purposes, or the grant of a new lease in lieu thereof; and to amend the law of landlord and tenant.

[22nd December 1927]

Part II

General Amendments of the Law of Landlord and Tenant

* * * *

Provisions as to covenants not to assign, etc., without licence or consent

19.—(1) In all leases whether made before or after the commencement of this Act containing a covenant condition or agreement against assigning, under-letting, charging or parting with the possession of demised premises or any part thereof without licence or consent, such covenant condition or agreement shall, notwithstanding any express provision to the contrary, be deemed to be subject—

- (a) to a proviso to the effect that such licence or consent is not to be unreasonably withheld, but this proviso does not preclude the right of the landlord to require payment of a reasonable sum in respect of any legal or other expenses incurred in connection with such licence or consent; and
- (b) (if the lease is for more than forty years, and is made in consideration wholly or partially of the erection, or the substantial improvement, addition or alteration of buildings, and the lessor is not a Government department or local or public authority, or a statutory or public utility company) to a proviso to the effect that in the case of any assignment, under-letting, charging or parting with the possession (whether by the holders of the lease or any under-tenant whether immediate or not) effected more than seven years before the end of the term no consent or licence shall be required, if notice in writing of the transaction is given to the lessor within six months after the transaction is effected.

[(1A) Where the landlord and the tenant under a qualifying lease have entered into an agreement specifying for the purposes of this subsection—

- (a) any circumstances in which the landlord may withhold his licence or consent to an assignment of the demised premises or any part of them, or
- (b) any conditions subject to which any such licence or consent may be granted,

then the landlord—

- (i) shall not be regarded as unreasonably withholding his licence or consent to any such assignment if he withholds it on the ground (and it is the case) that any such circumstances exist, and
- (ii) if he gives any such licence or consent subject to any such conditions, shall not be regarded as giving it subject to unreasonable conditions;

and section 1 of the Landlord and Tenant Act 1988 (qualified duty to consent to assignment etc.) shall have effect subject to the provisions of this subsection.

(1B) Subsection (1A) of this section applies to such an agreement as is mentioned in that subsection—

(a) whether it is contained in the lease or not, and
(b) whether it is made at the time when the lease is granted or at any other time falling before the application for the landlord's licence or consent is made.

(1C) Subsection (1A) shall not, however, apply to any such agreement to the extent that any circumstances or conditions specified in it are framed by reference to any matter falling to be determined by the landlord or by any other person for the purposes of the agreement, unless under the terms of the agreement—

(a) that person's power to determine that matter is required to be exercised reasonably, or
(b) the tenant is given an unrestricted right to have any such determination reviewed by a person independent of both landlord and tenant whose identity is ascertainable by reference to the agreement,

and in the latter case the agreement provides for the determination made by any such independent person on the review to be conclusive as to the matter in question.

(1D) In its application to a qualifying lease, subsection (1)(b) of this section shall not have effect in relation to any assignment of the lease.

(1E) In subsections (1A) and (1D) of this section—

(a) "qualifying lease" means any lease which is a new tenancy for the purposes of section 1 of the Landlord and Tenant (Covenants) Act 1995 other than a residential lease, namely a lease by which a building or part of a building is let wholly or mainly as a single private residence; and
(b) references to assignment include parting with possession on assignment.]

ANNOTATION

Subsections (1A) to (1E) were inserted on January 1, 1996 by Landlord and Tenant (Covenants) Act 1995, s.22 (S.I. 1995 No. 2963).

*   *   *   *

(4) This section shall not apply to leases of agricultural holdings within the meaning of the [Agricultural Holdings Act 1986] [which are leases in relation to which that Act applies, or to farm business tenancies within the meaning of the Agricultural Tenancies Act 1995] and paragraph (b) of subsection (1), subsection (2) and subsection (3) of this section shall not apply to mining leases.

ANNOTATION

The words in the first set of square brackets were substituted by Agricultural Holdings Act 1986, Sch.14, para.15.

The words in the second set of square brackets were inserted on September 1, 1995 by Agricultural Tenancies Act 1995, ss.40, 41(2), Sch., para.6.

*   *   *   *

Part III

General

* * * *

Service of notices

23.—(1) Any notice, request, demand or other instrument under this Act shall be in writing and may be served on the person on whom it is to be served either personally, or by leaving it for him at his last known place of abode in England or Wales, or by sending it though the post in a registered letter addressed to him there, or, in the case of a local or public authority or a statutory or a public utility company, to the secretary or other proper officer at the principal office of such authority or company, and in the case of a notice to a landlord, the person on whom it is to be served shall include any agent of the landlord duly authorised in that behalf.

(2) Unless or until a tenant of a holding shall have received notice that the person theretofore entitled to the rents and profits of the holding (hereinafter referred to as "the original landlord") has ceased to be so entitled, and also notice of the name and address of the person who has become entitled to such rents and profits, any claim, notice, request, demand, or other instrument, which the tenant shall serve upon or deliver to the original landlord shall be deemed to have been served upon or delivered to the landlord of such holding.

* * * *

LANDLORD AND TENANT ACT 1954

(2 & 3 Eliz. 2, c. 56)

An Act to provide security of tenure for occupying tenants under certain leases of residential property at low rents and for occupying sub-tenants of tenants under such leases; to enable tenants occupying property for business, professional or certain other purposes to obtain new tenancies in certain cases; to amend and extend the Landlord and Tenant Act 1927, the Leasehold Property (Repairs) Act 1938, and section eight-four of the Law of Property Act 1925; to confer jurisdiction on the County Court in certain disputes between landlords and tenants; to make provision for the termination of tenancies of derelict land; and for purposes connected with the matters aforesaid.

[30th July 1954]

Part II

Security of Tenure for Business, Professional and other Tenants

* * * *

Rent under new tenancy

34.—[(1)] The rent payable under a tenancy granted by order of the court under this Part of this Act shall be such as may be agreed between the landlord and the tenant or as, in default of such agreement, may be determined by the court to be that at which, having regard to the terms of the tenancy (other than those relating to rent), the holding might reasonably be expected to be let in the open market by a willing lessor, there being disregarded—

(a) any effect on rent of the fact that the tenant has or his predecessors in title have been in occupation of the holding,

(b) any goodwill attached to the holding by reason of the carrying on thereat of the business of the tenant (whether by him or by a predecessor of his in that business),

[(c) any effect on rent of an improvement to which this paragraph applies.]

(d) in the case of a holding comprising licensed premises, any addition to its value attributable to the licence, it it appears to the court that having regard to the terms of the current tenancy and any other relevant circumstances the benefit of the licence belongs to the tenant.

[(2) Paragraph (c) of the foregoing subsection applies to any improvement carried out by a person who at the time it was carried out was the tenant, but only if it was carried out otherwise than in pursuance of an obligation to his immediate landlord and either it was carried out during the current tenancy or the following conditions are satisfied, that is to say,—

(a) that it was completed not more than twenty-one years before the application *for the new tenancy* [to the court] was made; and

(b) that the holding or any part of it affected by the improvement has at all times since the completion of the improvement been comprised in tenancies of the description specified in section 23(1) of this Act; and

(c) that at the termination of each of those tenancies the tenant did not quit.]

[(2A) If this Part of this Act applies by virtue of section 23(1A) of this Act, the reference in subsection (1)(d) above to the tenant shall be construed as including—

(a) a company in which the tenant has a controlling interest, or

(b) where the tenant is a company, a person with a controlling interest in the company.]

(3) Where the rent is determined by the court the court may, if it thinks fit, further determine that the terms of the tenancy shall include such provision for varying the rent as may be specified in the determination.]

[(4) It is hereby declared that the matters which are to be taken into account by the court in determining the rent include any effect on rent of the operation of the provisions of the Landlord and Tenant (Covenants) Act 1995.]

ANNOTATION

Subsections (1)(c), (2) and (3) were inserted by Law of Property Act 1969.

The words in square brackets in subs.(2)(a) were substituted for the words in italics immediately preceding them with effect from June 1, 2004 by The Regulatory Reform (Business Tenancies) (England and Wales) Order 2003 (S.I. 2003 No. 3096), arts 1(3), 2, 9, subject to transitional provisions in *ibid.*, art.29.

Subsection (2A) was inserted on June 1, 2004 by The Regulatory Reform (Business Tenancies) (England and Wales) Order 2003 (S.I. 2003 No. 3096), arts 1(3), 2, 15, subject to transitional provisions in *ibid.*, art.29.

Subsection (4) was inserted on January 1, 1996 by Landlord and Tenant (Covenants) Act 1995, s.30(2), Sch.1, para.3 (S.I. 1995 No. 2963).

Other terms of new tenancy

35.—[(1)] The terms of a tenancy granted by order of the court under this Part of this Act (other than terms as to the duration thereof and as to the rent payable thereunder)[, including, where different persons own interests which fulfil the conditions specified in section 44(1) of this Act in different parts of it, terms as to the apportionment of the rent,] shall be such as may be agreed between the landlord and the tenant or as, in default of such agreement, may be determined by the court; and in determining those terms the court shall have regard to the terms of the current tenancy and to all relevant circumstances.

[(2) In subsection (1) of this section the reference to all relevant circumstances includes (without prejudice to the generality of that reference) a reference to the operation of the provisions of the Landlord and Tenant (Covenants) Act 1995.]

ANNOTATION

The words in square brackets in subs.(1) were inserted on June 1, 2004 by The Regulatory Reform (Business Tenancies) (England and Wales) Order 2003 (S.I. 2003 No. 3096), arts 1(3), 2, 27(3), subject to transitional provisions in *ibid.*, art.29.

Subsection (2) was inserted on January 1, 1996 by Landlord and Tenant (Covenants) Act 1995, s.30(1), Sch.1, para.4 (S.I. 1995 No. 2963).

* * * *

Restriction on agreements excluding provisions of Part II

38.—(1) Any agreement relating to a tenancy to which this Part of this Act applies (whether contained in the instrument creating the tenancy or not) shall be void [(except as provided by *subsection (4) of this section* [section 38A of this Act])] in so far as it purports to preclude the tenant from making an application or request under this Part of this Act or provides for the termination or the surrender of the tenancy in the event of his making such an application or request or for the imposition of any penalty or disability on the tenant in that event.

* * * *

[*(4) The court may—*

(a) on the joint application of the persons who will be the landlord and the tenant in relation to a tenancy to be granted for a term of years certain which will be a tenancy to which this part of this Act applies, authorise an agreement excluding in relation to that tenancy the provisions of section 24 to 28 of this Act; and

(b) on the joint application of the persons who are the landlord and the tenant in relation to a tenancy to which this Part of this Act applies, authorise an agreement for the surrender of the tenancy on such date or in such circumstances as may be specified in the agreement and on such terms (if any) as may be so specified;

if the agreement is contained in or endorsed on the instrument creating the tenancy or such other instrument as the court may specify; and an agreement contained in or endorsed on an instrument in pursuance of an authorisation given under this subsection shall be valid notwithstanding anything in the preceding provisions of this section.]

ANNOTATION

The words in the first set of square brackets in subsection (1) were inserted, and subs.(4) was added, by Law of Property Act 1969, s.5.

The words in the second set of square brackets in subs.(1) were substituted for the words in italics immediately preceding them with effect from June 1, 2004 by The Regulatory Reform (Business Tenancies) (England and Wales) Order 2003 (S.I. 2003 No. 3096), arts 1(3), 2, 21(1), subject to transitional provisions in *ibid.*, art.29.

Subsection (4) was repealed on June 1, 2004 by The Regulatory Reform (Business Tenancies) (England and Wales) Order 2003 (S.I. 2003 No. 3096), arts 1(3), 2, 21(2), 28(2), Sch.6, subject to transitional provisions in *ibid.*, art.29.

* * * *

[Agreements to exclude provisions of Part 2

38A.—(1) The persons who will be the landlord and the tenant in relation to a tenancy to be granted for a term of years certain which will be a tenancy to which this Part of this Act applies may agree that the provisions of sections 24 to 28 of this Act shall be excluded in relation to that tenancy.

(2) The persons who are the landlord and the tenant in relation to a tenancy to which this Part of this Act applies may agree that the tenancy shall be surrendered on such date or in such circumstances as may be specified in the agreement and on such terms (if any) as may be so specified.

(3) An agreement under subsection (1) above shall be void unless—

(a) the landlord has served on the tenant a notice in the form, or substantially in the form, set out in Schedule 1 to the Regulatory Reform (Business Tenancies) (England and Wales) Order 2003 ("the 2003 Order"); and

(b) the requirements specified in Schedule 2 to that Order are met.

(4) An agreement under subsection (2) above shall be void unless—

(a) the landlord has served on the tenant a notice in the form, or substantially in the form, set out in Schedule 3 to the 2003 Order; and

(b) the requirements specified in Schedule 4 to that Order are met.]

ANNOTATION

Section 38A was added on June 1, 2004 by The Regulatory Reform (Business Tenancies) (England and Wales) Order 2003 (S.I. 2003 No. 3096), arts 1(3), 2, 22(1), subject to transitional provisions in *ibid.*, art.29.

* * * *

CIVIL LIABILITY (CONTRIBUTION) ACT 1978

(c. 47)

An Act to make new provision for contribution between persons who are jointly or severally, or both jointly and severally, liable for the same damage and in certain other similar cases where two or more persons have paid or may be required to pay compensation for the same damage; and to amend the law relating to proceedings against persons jointly liable for the same debt or jointly or severally, or both jointly and severally, liable for the same damage.

[31st July 1978]

Proceedings for contribution

Entitlement to contribution

1.—(1) Subject to the following provisions of this section, any person liable in respect of any damage suffered by another person may recover contribution from any other person liable in respect of the same damage (whether jointly with him or otherwise).

(2) A person shall be entitled to recover contribution by virtue of subsection (1) above notwithstanding that he has ceased to be liable in respect of the damage in question since the time when the damage occurred, provided that he was so liable immediately before he made or was ordered or agreed to make the payment in respect of which the contribution is sought.

(3) A person shall be liable to make contribution by virtue of subsection (1) above notwithstanding that he has ceased to be liable in respect of the damage in question since the time when the damage occurred, unless he ceased to be liable by virtue of the expiry of a period of limitation or prescription which extinguished the right on which the claim against him in respect of the damage was based.

(4) A person who has made or agreed to make any payment in bona fide settlement or compromise of any claim made against him in respect of any damage (including a payment into court which has been accepted) shall be entitled to recover contribution in accordance with this section without regard to whether or not he himself is or ever was liable in respect of the damage, provided, however, that he would have been liable assuming that the factual basis of the claim against him could be established.

(5) A judgment given in any action brought in any part of the United Kingdom by or on behalf of the person who suffered the damage in question against any person from whom contribution is sought under this section shall be conclusive in the proceedings for contribution as to any issue determined by that judgment in favour of the person from whom the contribution is sought.

(6) References in this section to a person's liability in respect of any damage are references to any such liability which has been or could be established in an action brought against him in England and Wales or by or on behalf of the person who suffered the damage; but it is immaterial whether any issue arising in any such action was or would be determined (in accordance with the rules of private international law) by reference to the law of a country outside England and Wales.

Assessment of contribution

2.—(1) Subject to subsection (3) below, in any proceedings for contribution under section 1 above the amount of the contribution recoverable from any person shall be such as may be found by the court to be just and equitable having regard to the extent of that person's responsibility for the damage in question.

(2) Subject to subsection (3) below, the court shall have power in any such proceedings to exempt any person from liability to make contribution, or to direct that the contribution to be recovered from any person shall amount to a complete indemnity.

(3) Where the amount of the damages which have or might have been awarded in respect of the damage in question in any action brought in England and Wales by or on behalf of the person who suffered it against the person from whom the contribution is sought was or would have been subject to—

(a) any limit imposed by or under any enactment or by any agreement made before the damage occurred;

(b) any reduction by virtue of section 1 of the Law Reform (Contributory Negligence) Act 1945 or section 5 of the Fatal Accidents Act 1976; or

(c) any corresponding limit or reduction under the law of a country outside England and Wales;

the person from whom the contribution is sought shall not by virtue of any contribution awarded under section 1 above be required to pay in respect of the damage a greater amount than the amount of those damages as so limited or reduced.

Proceedings for the Same Debt or Damage

Proceedings against persons jointly liable for the same debt or damage

3. Judgment recovered against any person liable in respect of any debt or damage shall not be a bar to an action, or to the continuance of an action, against any other person who is (apart from any such bar) jointly liable with him in respect of the same debt or damage.

Successive actions against persons liable (jointly or otherwise) for the same damage

4. If more than one action is brought in respect of any damage by or on behalf of the person by whom it was suffered against persons liable in respect of the damage (whether jointly or otherwise) the plaintiff shall not be entitled to costs in any of those actions, other than that in which judgment is first given, unless the court is of the opinion that there was reasonable ground for bringing the action.

Supplemental

Application to the Crown

5. Without prejudice to section 4(1) of the Crown Proceedings Act 1947 (indemnity and contribution) this Act shall bind the Crown, but nothing in this Act shall be construed as in any way affecting Her Majesty in Her private capacity (including in right of Her Duchy of Lancaster) or the Duchy of Cornwall.

Interpretation

6.—(1) A person is liable in respect of any damage for the purposes of this Act if the person who suffered it (or anyone representing his estate or dependants) is entitled to recover compensation from him in respect of that damage (whatever the legal basis of his liability whether tort, breach of contract, breach of trust or otherwise).

(2) References in this Act to an action brought by or on behalf of the person who suffered any damage include references to an action brought for the benefit of his estate or dependants.

(3) In this Act "dependants" has the same meaning as in the Fatal Accidents Act 1976.

(4) In this Act, except in section 1(5) above, "action" means an action brought in England and Wales.

Savings

7.—(1) Nothing in this Act shall affect any case where the debt in question became due or (as the case may be) the damage in question occurred before the date on which it comes into force.

(2) A person shall not be entitled to recover contribution or liable to make contribution in accordance with section 1 above by reference to any liability based on breach of any obligation assumed by him before the date on which this Act comes into force.

(3) The right to recover contribution in accordance with section 1 above supersedes any right, other than an express contractual right, to recover contribution (as distinct from indemnity) otherwise than under this Act in corresponding circumstances; but nothing in this Act shall affect—

(a) any express or implied contractual or other right to indemnity; or
(b) any express contractual provision regulating or excluding contribution;

which would be enforceable apart from this Act (or render enforceable any agreement for indemnity or contribution which would not be enforceable apart from this Act).

* * * *

COMPANIES ACT 1985

(c. 8)

PART I

CHAPTER III—A COMPANY'S CAPACITY; FORMALITIES OF CARRYING ON BUSINESS

* * * *

[Execution of documents: England and Wales

36A.—(1) Under the law of England and Wales the following provisions have effect with respect to the execution of documents by a company.

(2) A document is executed by a company by the affixing of its common seal.

(3) A company need not have a common seal, however, and the following subsections apply whether it does or not.

(4) A document signed by a director and the secretary of a company, or by two directors of a company, and expressed (in whatever form of words) to be executed by the company has the same effect as if executed under the common seal of the company.

[(4A) Where a document is to be signed by a person as a director or the secretary of more than one company, it shall not be taken to be duly signed by that person for the purposes of subsection (4) unless the person signs it separately in each capacity.]

(5) . . . . . .

(6) In favour of a purchaser a document shall be deemed to have been duly executed by a company if it purports to be signed by a director and the secretary of the company, or by two directors of the company, ...

A "purchaser" means a purchaser in good faith for valuable consideration and includes a lessee, mortgage or other person who for valuable consideration acquires an interest in property.

[(7) This section applies in the case of a document which is (or purports to be) executed by a company in the name of or on behalf of another person whether or not that other person is also a company.]

[(8) For the purposes of this section, a document is (or purports to be) signed, in the case of a director or the secretary of a company which is not an individual, if it is (or purports to be) signed by an individual authorised by the director or secretary to sign on its behalf.]]

ANNOTATION

The section was originally inserted by the Companies Act 1989, s.130(2).

Subsection (4A) was inserted on September 15, 2005 by The Regulatory Reform (Execution of Deeds and Documents) Order 2005 (S.I. 2005 No. 1906), arts.1(1), 10(1), Sch.1, paras 9, 10. The amendments do not apply in relation to any instrument executed before September 15, 2005: *ibid.*, art.1(1),(2).

Subsection (5) was repealed on September 15, 2005 by The Regulatory Reform (Execution of Deeds and Documents) Order 2005 (S.I. 2005 No. 1906), arts 1(1), 5, 10(2), Sch.2. The amendments do not apply in relation to any instrument executed before September 15, 2005: *ibid.*, art.1(1),(2).

The words omitted from subs.(6) were repealed on September 15, 2005 by The Regulatory Reform (Execution of Deeds and Documents) Order 2005 (S.I. 2005 No. 1906), arts 1(1), 10(2), Sch.2. The amendments do not apply in relation to any instrument executed before September 15, 2005: *ibid.*, art.1(1),(2).

Subsections (7) and (8) were added on September 15, 2005 by The Regulatory Reform (Execution of Deeds and Documents) Order 2005 (S.I. 2005 No. 1906), arts 1(1), 7(2) 10(1), Sch.1, paras 9, 11. The amendments do not apply in relation to any instrument executed before September 15, 2005: *ibid.*, art.1(1),(2).

[Execution of deeds: England and Wales

36AA.—(1) A document is validly executed by a company as a deed for the purposes of section 1 of the Law of Property (Miscellaneous Provisions) Act 1989, if and only if—

(a) it is duly executed by the company, and

(b) it is delivered as a deed.

(2) A document shall be presumed to be delivered for the purposes of subsection (1)(b) upon its being executed, unless a contrary intention is proved.]

ANNOTATION

The section was inserted on September 15, 2005 by The Regulatory Reform (Execution of Deeds and Documents) Order 2005 (S.I. 2005 No. 1906), arts 1(1), 6. The amendments do not apply in relation to any instrument executed before September 15, 2005: *ibid.*, art.1(1),(2).

* * * *

LANDLORD AND TENANT ACT 1985

(c. 70)

Information to be Given to Tenant

* * * *

Duty to inform tenant of assignment of landlord's interest

3.—(1) If the interest of the landlord under a tenancy of premises which consist of or include a dwelling is assigned, the new landlord shall give notice in writing of the assignment, and of his name and address, to the tenant not later than the next day on which rent is payable under the tenancy or, of that is within two months of the assignment, the end of that period of two months.

(2) If trustees constitute the new landlord, a collective description of the trustees as the trustees of the trust in question may be given as the name of the landlord, and where such a collective description is given—

(a) the address of the new landlord may be given as the address from which the affairs of the trust are conducted, and

(b) a change in the persons who are for the time being the trustees of the trust shall not be treated as an assignment of the interest of the landlord.

(3) A person who is the new landlord under a tenancy falling within subsection (1) and who fails, without reasonable excuse, to give the notice required by that subsection, commits a summary offence and is liable on conviction to a fine not exceeding level 4 on the standard scale.

[(3A) The person who was the landlord under the tenancy immediately before the assignment ("the old landlord") shall be liable to the tenant in respect of any breach of any covenant, condition or agreement under the tenancy occurring before the end of the relevant period in like manner as if the interest assigned were still vested in him; and where the new landlord is also liable to the tenant in respect of any such breach occurring within that period, he and the old landlord shall be jointly and severally liable in respect of it.

(3B) In subsection (3A) "the relevant period" means the period beginning with the date of the assignment and ending with the date when—

(a) notice in writing of the assignment, and of the new landlord's name and address, is given to the tenant by the new landlord (whether in accordance with subsection (1) or not), or

(b) notice in writing of the assignment, and of the new landlord's name and last-known address, is given to the tenant by the old landlord,

whichever happens first.]

ANNOTATION

Subsections (3A) and (3B) were inserted by Landlord and Tenant Act 1987, ss.50 and 62(2), with effect from February 1, 1988 (S.I. 1987 No. 2177).

(4) In this section—
- (a) "tenancy" includes a statutory tenancy, and
- (b) references to the assignment of the landlord's interest include any conveyance other than a mortgage or charge.

* * * *

INSOLVENCY ACT 1986

(c. 45)

Disclaimer (England and Wales Only)

Power to disclaim onerous property

178.—(1) This and the next two sections apply to a company that is being wound up in England and Wales.

(2) Subject as follows, the liquidator may, by the giving of the prescribed notice, disclaim any onerous property and may do so notwithstanding that he has taken possession of it, endeavoured to sell it, or otherwise exercised rights of ownership in relation to it.

(3) The following is onerous property for the purposes of this section—
- (a) any unprofitable contract, and
- (b) any other property of the company which is unsaleable or not readily saleable or is such that it may give rise to a liability to pay money or perform any other onerous act.

(4) A disclaimer under this section—
- (a) operates so as to determine, as from the date of the disclaimer, the rights, interests and liabilities of the company in or in respect of the property disclaimed; but
- (b) does not, except so far as is necessary for the purpose of releasing the company from any liability, affect the rights or liabilities of any other person.

(5) A notice of disclaimer shall not be given under this section in respect of any property if—
- (a) a person interested in the property has applied in writing to the liquidator or one of his predecessors as liquidator requiring the liquidator or that predecessor to decide whether he will disclaim or not, and
- (b) the period of 28 days beginning with the day on which that application was made, or such longer period as the court may allow, has expired without a notice of disclaimer having been given under this section in respect of that property.

(6) Any person sustaining loss or damage in consequence of the operation of a disclaimer under this section is deemed a creditor of the company to the extent of the loss or damage and accordingly may prove for the loss or damage in the winding up.

Disclaimer of leaseholds

179.—(1) The disclaimer under section 178 of any property of a leasehold nature does not take effect unless a copy of the disclaimer has been served (so far as the liquidator is aware of their addresses) on every person claiming under the company as underlessee or mortgagee and either—

(a) no application under section 181 below is made with respect to that property before the end of the period of 14 days beginning with the day on which the last notice served under this subsection was served; or

(b) where such an application has been made, the court directs that the disclaimer shall take effect.

(2) Where the court gives a direction under subsection (1)(b) it may also, instead of or in addition to any order it makes under section 181, make such orders with respect to fixtures, tenant's improvements and other matters arising out of the lease as it thinks fit.

Land subject to rentcharge

180.—(1) The following applies where, in consequence of the disclaimer under section 178 of any land subject to a rentcharge, that land vests by operation of law in the Crown or any other person (referred to in the next subsection as "the proprietor").

(2) The proprietor and the successors in title of the proprietor are not subject to any personal liability in respect of any sums becoming due under the rentcharge except sums becoming due after the proprietor, or some person claiming under or through the proprietor, has taken possession or control of the land or has entered into occupation of it.

Powers of court (general)

181.—(1) This section and the next apply where the liquidator has disclaimed property under section 178.

(2) An application under this section may be made to the court by—

(a) any person who claims an interest in the disclaimed property, or

(b) any person who is under any liability in respect of the disclaimed property, not being a liability discharged by the disclaimer.

(3) Subject as follows, the court may on the application make an order, on such terms as it thinks fit, for the vesting of the disclaimed property in, or for its delivery to—

(a) a person entitled to it or a trustee for such a person, or

(b) a person subject to such a liability as is mentioned in subsection (2)(b) or a trustee for such a person.

(4) The court shall not make an order under subsection (3)(b) except where it appears to the court that it would be just to do so for the purpose of compensating the person subject to the liability in respect of the disclaimer.

(5) The effect of any order under this section shall be taken into account in assessing for the purpose of section 178(6) the extent of any loss or damage sustained by any person in consequence of the disclaimer.

(6) An order under this section vesting property in any person need not be completed by conveyance, assignment or transfer.

Powers of court (leaseholds)

182.—(1) The court shall not make an order under section 181 vesting property of a leasehold nature in any person claiming under the company as underlessee or mortgagee except on terms making that person—

(a) subject to the same liabilities and obligations as the company was subject to under the lease at the commencement of the winding up, or

(b) if the court thinks fit, subject to the same liabilities and obligations as that person would be subject to if the lease had been assigned to him at the commencement of the winding up.

(2) For the purposes of an order under section 181 relating to only part of any property comprised in a lease, the requirements of subsection (1) apply as if the lease comprised only the property to which the order relates.

(3) Where subsection (1) applies and no person claiming under the company as underlessee or mortgagee is willing to accept an order under section 181 on the terms required by virtue of that subsection, the court may, by order under that section, vest the company's estate or interest in the property in any person who is liable (whether personally or in a representative capacity, and whether alone or jointly with the company) to perform the lessee's covenants in the lease.

The court may vest that estate and interest in such a person freed and discharged from all estates, incumbrances and interests created by the company.

(4) Where subsection (1) applies and a person claiming under the company as underlessee or mortgagee declines to accept an order under section 181, that person is excluded from all interest in the property.

* * * *

Protection of Bankrupt's Estate and Investigation of His Affairs

Definition of bankrupt's estate

283.—(1) Subject as follows, a bankrupt's estate for the purposes of any of this Group of Parts comprises—

(a) all property belonging to or vested in the bankrupt at the commencement of the bankruptcy, and

(b) any property which by virtue of any of the following provisions of this Part is comprised in that estate or is treated as falling within the preceding paragraph.

(2) Subsection (1) does not apply to—

(a) such tools, books, vehicles and other items of equipment as are necessary to the bankrupt for use personally by him in his employment, business or vocation;

(b) such clothing, bedding, furniture, household equipment and provisions as are necessary for satisfying the basic domestic needs of the bankrupt and his family.

This subsection is subject to section 308 in Chapter IV (certain excluded property reclaimable by trustee).

(3) Subsection (1) does not apply to—

(a) property held by the bankrupt on trust for any other person, or

(b) the right of nomination to a vacant ecclesiastical benefice.

[(3A) Subject to section 308A in Chapter IV, subsection (1) does not apply to—

(a) a tenancy which is an assured tenancy or an assured agricultural occupancy, within the meaning of Part I of the Housing Act 1988, and the terms of which inhibit an assignment as mentioned in section 127(5) of the Rent Act 1977, or

(b) a protected tenancy, within the meaning of the Rent Act 1977, in respect of which, by virtue of any provision of Part IX of that Act, no premium can lawfully be required as a condition of assignment, or

(c) a tenancy of a dwelling-house by virtue of which the bankrupt is, within the meaning of the Rent (Agriculture) Act 1976, a protected occupier of the dwelling-house, and the terms of which inhibit an assignment as mentioned in section 127(5) of the Rent Act 1977, or

(d) a secure tenancy, within the meaning of Part IV of the Housing Act 1985, which is not capable of being assigned, except in the cases mentioned in section 91(3) of that Act.]

ANNOTATION

Subsection (3A) was inserted on January 15, 1989 by Housing Act 1988, ss.117(1), 141(3).

(4) References in any of this Group of Parts to property, in relation to a bankrupt, include references to any power exercisable by him over or in respect of property except in so far as the power is exercisable over or in respect of property not for the time being comprised in the bankrupt's estate and—

(a) is so exercisable at a time after either the official receiver has had his release in respect of that estate under section 299(2) in Chapter III or a meeting summoned by the trustee of that estate under section 331 in Chapter IV has been held, or

(b) cannot be so exercised for the benefit of the bankrupt;

and a power exercisable over or in respect of property is deemed for the purposes of any of this Group of Parts to vest in the person entitled to exercise it at the time of the transaction or event by virtue of which it is exercisable by that person (whether or not it becomes so exercisable at that time).

(5) For the purposes of any such provision in this Group of Parts, property comprised in a bankrupt's estate is so comprised subject to the rights of any person other than the bankrupt (whether as a secured creditor or the bankrupt or otherwise) in relation thereto, but disregarding—

(a) any rights in relation to which a statement such as is required by section 269(1)(a) was made in the petition on which the bankrupt was adjudged bankrupt, and

(b) any rights which have been otherwise given up in accordance with the rules.

(6) This section has effect subject to the provisions of any enactment not contained in this Act under which any property is to be excluded from a bankrupt's estate.

* * * *

Acquisition, Control and Realisation of Bankrupt's Estate

Vesting of bankrupt's estate in trustee

306.—(1) The bankrupt's estate shall vest in the trustee immediately on his appointment taking effect or, in the case of the official receiver, on his becoming trustee.

(2) Where any property which is, or is to be, comprised in the bankrupt's estate vests in the trustee (whether under this section or under any other

provision of this Part), it shall so vest without any conveyance, assignment or transfer.

* * * *

Vesting in trustee of certain items of excess value

308.—(1) Subject to [section 309], where—

(a) property is excluded by virtue of section 283(2) (tools of trade, household effects, etc.) from the bankrupt's estate, and

(b) it appears to the trustee that the realisable value of the whole or any part of that property exceeds the cost of a reasonable replacement for that property or that part of it.

the trustee may by notice in writing claim that property or, as the case may be, that part of it for the bankrupt's estate.

ANNOTATION

The words "section 309" in subsection (1) were substituted for the words "the next section" by Housing Act 1988, s.140(1), Sch.17, para.73, as from January 2, 1989 (S.I. 1988 No. 2152).

(2) Upon the service on the bankrupt of a notice under this section, the property to which the notice relates vests in the trustee as part of the bankrupt's estate; and, except against a purchaser in good faith, for value and without notice of the bankruptcy, the trustee's title to that property has relation back to the commencement of the bankruptcy.

(3) The trustee shall apply funds comprised in the estate to the purchase by or on behalf of the bankrupt of a reasonable replacement for any property vested in the trustee under this section; and the duty imposed by this subsection has priority over the obligation of the trustee to distribute the estate.

(4) For the purposes of this section property is a reasonable replacement for other property if it is reasonably adequate for meeting the needs met by the other property.

[Vesting in trustee of certain tenancies

308A. Upon the service on the bankrupt by the trustee of a notice in writing under this section, any tenancy—

(a) which is excluded by virtue of section 283(3A) from the bankrupt's estate, and

(b) to which the notice relates,

vests in the trustee as part of the bankrupt's estate; and, except against a purchaser in good faith, for value and without notice of the bankruptcy, the trustee's title to that tenancy has relation back to the commencement of the bankruptcy.]

ANNOTATION

Section 308A was inserted on January 15, 1989 by Housing Act 1988, ss.117(2) and 141(3).

* * * *

Disclaimer (general power)

315.—(1) Subject as follows, the trustee may, by the giving of the prescribed notice, disclaim any onerous property and may do so notwithstanding that he has taken possession of it, endeavoured to sell it or otherwise exercised rights of ownership in relation to it.

(2) The following is onerous property for the purposes of this section, that is to say—

(a) any unprofitable contract, and

(b) any other property comprised in the bankrupt's estate which is unsaleable or not readily saleable, or is such that it may give rise to a liability to pay money or perform any other onerous act.

(3) A disclaimer under this section—

(a) operates so as to determine, as from the date of the disclaimer, the rights, interests and liabilities of the bankrupt and his estate in or in respect of the property disclaimed, and

(b) discharges the trustee from all personal liability in respect of that property as from the commencement of his trusteeship,

but does not, except so far as is necessary for the purpose of releasing the bankrupt, the bankrupt's estate and the trustee from any liability, affect the rights or liabilities of any other person.

(4) A notice of disclaimer shall not be given under this section in respect of any property that has been claimed for the estate under section 307 (after-acquired property) or 308 (personal property of bankrupt exceeding reasonable replacement value) [or 308A], except with the leave of the court.

ANNOTATION

The words "or 308A" were inserted as from January 15, 1989 by Housing Act 1988, ss.117(4), 141(3).

(5) Any person sustaining loss or damage in consequence of the operation of a disclaimer under this section is deemed to be a creditor of the bankrupt to the extent of the loss or damage and accordingly may prove for the loss or damage as a bankruptcy debt.

Notice requiring trustee's decision

316.—(1) Notice of disclaimer shall not be given under section 315 in respect of any property if—

(a) a person interested in the property has applied in writing to the trustee or one of his predecessors as trustee requiring the trustee or that precedessor to decide whether he will disclaim or not, and

(b) the period of 28 days beginning with the day on which that application was made has expired without a notice of disclaimer having been given under section 315 in respect of that property.

(2) The trustee is deemed to have adopted any contract which by virtue of this section he is not entitled to disclaim.

Disclaimer of leaseholds

317.—(1) The disclaimer of any property of a leasehold nature does not take effect unless a copy of the disclaimer has been served (so far as the trustee is aware of their addresses) on every person claiming under the bankrupt as underlessee or mortgagee and either—

(a) no application under section 320 below is made with respect to the property before the end of the period of 14 days beginning with the day on which the last notice served under this subsection was served, or

(b) where such an application has been made, the court directs that the disclaimer is to take effect.

(2) Where the court gives a direction under subsection (1)(b) it may also, instead of or in addition to any order it makes under section 320, make such orders with respect to fixtures, tenant's improvements and other matters arising out of the lease as it thinks fit.

Disclaimer of dwelling house

318. Without prejudice to section 317, the disclaimer of any property in a dwelling house does not take effect unless a copy of the disclaimer has been served (so far as the trustee is aware of their addresses) on every person in occupation of or claiming a right to occupy the dwelling house and either—

(a) no application under section 320 is made with respect to the property before the end of the period of 14 days beginning with the day on which the last notice served under this section was served, or

(b) where such an application has been made, the court directs that the disclaimer is to take effect.

Disclaimer of land subject to rentcharge

319.—(1) The following applies where, in consequence of the disclaimer under section 315 of any land subject to a rentcharge, that land vests by operation of law in the Crown or any other person (referred to in the next subsection as "the proprietor").

(2) The proprietor, and the successors in title of the proprietor, are not subject to any personal liability in respect of any sums becoming due under the rentcharge, except sums becoming due after the proprietor, or some person claiming under or through the proprietor, has taken possession or control of the land or has entered into occupation of it.

Court order vesting disclaimed property

320.—(1) This section and the next apply where the trustee has disclaimed property under section 315.

(2) An application may be made to the court under this section by—

(a) any person who claims an interest in the disclaimed property,

(b) any person who is under any liability in respect of the disclaimed property, not being a liability discharged by the disclaimer, or

(c) where the disclaimed property is property in a dwelling house, any person who at the time when the bankruptcy petition was presented was in occupation of or entitled to occupy the dwelling house.

(3) Subject as follows in this section and the next, the court may, on an application under this section, make an order on such terms as it thinks fit for the vesting of the disclaimed property in, or for its delivery to—

(a) a person entitled to it or a trustee for such a person,

(b) a person subject to such a liability as is mentioned in subsection (2)(b) or a trustee for such a person, or

(c) where the disclaimed property is property in a dwelling house, any person who at the time when the bankruptcy petition was presented was in occupation of or entitled to occupy the dwelling house.

(4) The court shall not make an order by virtue of subsection (3)(b) except where it appears to the court that it would be just to do so for the purpose of compensating the person subject to the liability in respect of the disclaimer.

(5) The effect of any order under this section shall be taken into account in assessing for the purposes of section 315(5) the extent of any loss or damage sustained by any person in consequence of the disclaimer.

(6) An order under this section vesting property in any person need not be completed by any conveyance, assignment or transfer.

Order under section 320 in respect of leaseholds

321.—(1) The court shall not make an order under section 320 vesting property of a leasehold nature in any person, except on terms making that person—

(a) subject to the same liabilities and obligations as the bankrupt was subject to under the lease on the day the bankruptcy petition was presented, or

(b) if the court thinks fit, subject to the same liabilities and obligations as that person would be subject to if the lease had been assigned to him on that day.

(2) For the purposes of an order under section 320 relating to only part of any property comprised in a lease, the requirements of subsection (1) apply as if the lease comprised only the property to which the order relates.

(3) Where subsection (1) applies and no person is willing to accept an order under section 320 on the terms required by that subsection, the court may (by order under section 320) vest the estate or interest of the bankrupt in the property in any person who is liable (whether personally or in a representative capacity and whether alone or jointly with the bankrupt) to perform the lessee's covenants in the lease.

The court may by virtue of this subsection vest that estate and interest in such a person freed and discharged from all estates, incumbrances and interests created by the bankrupt.

(4) Where subsection (1) applies and a person declines to accept any order under section 320, that person shall be excluded from all interest in the property.

* * * *

LAW OF PROPERTY (MISCELLANEOUS PROVISIONS) ACT 1989

(c. 34)

An Act to make new provisions with respect to deeds and their execution and contracts for the sale or other disposition of interests in land; and to abolish the rule of law known as the rule in Bain v. Fothergill.

[27th July, 1989]

* * * *

Deeds and their execution

1.—(1) Any rule of law which—

(a) restricts the substances on which a deed may be written;

(b) requires a seal for the valid execution of an instrument as a deed by an individual; or

(c) requires authority by one person to another to deliver an instrument as a deed on his behalf to be given by deed, is abolished.

(2) An instrument shall not be a deed unless—

(a) it makes it clear on its face that it is intended to be a deed by the person making it or, as the case may be, by the parties to it (whether by describing itself as a deed or expressing itself to be executed or signed as a deed or otherwise); and

(b) it is validly executed as a deed *by that person or, as the case may be, one or more of those parties*[–

(i) by that person or a person authorised to execute it in the name or on behalf of that person, or

(ii) by one or more of those parties or a person authorised to execute it in the name or on behalf of one or more of those parties].

ANNOTATION

The words in square brackets in subs.(2)(b) were substituted for the words in italics immediately preceding them on September 15, 2005 by The Regulatory Reform (Execution of Deeds and Documents) Order 2005 (S.I. 2005 No. 1906), arts 1(1), 7(3). The amendment does not apply in relation to any instrument executed before September 15, 2005: *ibid.*, art.1(1),(2).

[(2A) For the purposes of subsection (2)(a) above, an instrument shall not be taken to make it clear on its face that it is intended to be a deed merely because it is executed under seal.]

ANNOTATION

Subsection (2A) was inserted on September 15, 2005 by The Regulatory Reform (Execution of Deeds and Documents) Order 2005 (S.I. 2005 No. 1906), arts 1(1), 8. The amendment does not apply in relation to any instrument executed before September 15, 2005: *ibid.*, art.1(1),(2).

(3) An instrument is validly executed as a deed by an individual if, and only if—

(a) it is signed—

(i) by him in the presence of a witness who attests the signature; or

(ii) at his direction and in his presence and the presence of two witnesses who each attest the signature; and

(b) it is delivered as a deed *by him or a person authorised to do so on his behalf.*

ANNOTATION

The words in italics were repealed on September 15, 2005 by The Regulatory Reform (Execution of Deeds and Documents) Order 2005 (S.I. 2005 No. 1906), arts 1(1), 10(2), Sch.2. The amendment does not apply in relation to any instrument executed before September 15, 2005: *ibid.*, art.1(1),(2).

(4) In subsections (2) and (3) above "sign", in relation to an instrument, includes *making one's mark on the instrument and "signature" is to be construed accordingly* [–

(a) an individual signing the name of the person or party on whose behalf he executes the instrument; and

(b) making one's mark on the instrument,

and "signature" is to be construed accordingly].

ANNOTATION

The words in square brackets were substituted for the words in italics immediately preceding them on September 15, 2005 by The Regulatory Reform (Execution of Deeds and Documents) Order 2005 (S.I. 2005 No. 1906), arts 1(1), 10(1), Sch.1, paras 13, 14. The amendment does not apply in relation to any instrument executed before September 15, 2005: *ibid.*, art.1(1),(2).

[(4A) Subsection (3) above applies in the case of an instrument executed by an individual in the name or on behalf of another person whether or not that person is also an individual.]

ANNOTATION

Subsection (4A) was inserted on September 15, 2005 by The Regulatory Reform (Execution of Deeds and Documents) Order 2005 (S.I. 2005 No. 1906), arts 1(1), 7(4). The amendment does not apply in relation to any instrument executed before September 15, 2005: *ibid.*, art.1(1),(2).

(5) Where a solicitor[, duly certificated notary public] or licensed conveyancer, or an agent or employee of a solicitor[, duly certificated notary public] or licensed conveyancer, in the course of or in connection with a transaction *involving the disposition or creation of an interest in land*, purports to deliver an instrument as a deed on behalf of a party to the instrument, it shall be conclusively presumed in favour of a purchaser that he is authorised so to deliver the instrument.

ANNOTATION

The words in both sets of square brackets were inserted by Courts and Legal Services Act 1990, s.125(2), Sch.17, para.20. The words in italics were repealed on September 15, 2005 by The Regulatory Reform (Execution of Deeds and Documents) Order 2005 (S.I. 2005 No. 1906), arts 1(1), 10(2), Sch.2. The repeal does not apply in relation to any instrument executed before September 15, 2005: *ibid.*, art.1(1),(2).

(6) In subsection (5) above—

"disposition" and "purchaser" have the same meanings ["purchaser" has the same meaning] as in the Law of Property Act 1925;

["duly certificated notary public" has the same meaning as it has in the Solicitors Act 1974 by virtue of section 87 of that Act;]

"interest in land" means any estate, interest or charge in or over land or in or over the proceeds of sale of land.

ANNOTATION

The words in the first set of square brackets were substituted for the words in italics immediately preceding them on September 15, 2005 by The Regulatory Reform (Execution of Deeds and Documents) Order 2005 (S.I. 2005 No. 1906), arts 1(1), 10(1), Sch.1, paras 13, 15. The amendment does not apply in relation to any instrument executed before September 15, 2005: *ibid.*, art.1(1),(2).

The definition in the second set of square brackets was inserted by Courts and Legal Services Act 1990, s.125(2), Sch.17, para.20.

The definition in italics was repealed on September 15, 2005 by The Regulatory Reform (Execution of Deeds and Documents) Order 2005 (S.I. 2005 No. 1906), arts 1(1), 10(2), Sch.2. The repeal does not apply in relation to any instrument executed before September 15, 2005: *ibid.*, art.1(1),(2).

(7) Where an instrument under seal that constitutes a deed is required for the purposes of an Act passed before this section comes into force, this section shall have effect as to signing, sealing or delivery of an instrument by an individual in place of any provision of that Act as to signing, sealing or delivery.

(8) The enactments mentioned in Schedule 1 to this Act (which in consequence of this section require amendments other than those provided by subsection (7) above) shall have effect with the amendments specified in that Schedule.

(9) Nothing in subsection (1)(b), (2), (3), (7) or (8) above applies in relation to deeds required or authorised to be made under—

- (a) the seal of the county palatine of Lancaster;
- (b) the seal of the Duchy of Lancaster; or
- (c) the seal of the Duchy of Cornwall.

(10) The references in this section to the execution of a deed by an individual do not include execution by a corporation sole and the reference in subsection (7) above to signing, sealing or delivery by an individual does not include signing, sealing or delivery by such a corporation.

(11) Nothing in this section applies in relation to instruments delivered as deeds before this section comes into force.

ANNOTATION

Section 1 came into force on July 31, 1990: Law of Property (Miscellaneous Provisions) Act 1989, s.5(1), (2); S.I. 1990 No. 1175.

Contracts for sale etc of land to be made by signed writing

2.—(1) A contract for the sale or other disposition of an interest in land can only be made in writing and only by incorporating all the terms which the parties have expressly agreed in one document or, where contracts are exchanged, in each.

(2) The terms may be incorporated in a document either by being set out in it or by reference to some other document.

(3) The document incorporating the terms or, where contracts are exchanged, one of the documents incorporating them (but not necessarily the same one) must be signed by or on behalf of each party to the contract.

(4) Where a contract for the sale or other disposition of an interest in land satisfies the conditions of this section by reason only of the rectification of one or more documents in pursuance of an order of a court, the contract shall come into being, or be deemed to have come into being, at such time as may be specified in the order.

(5) This section does not apply in relation to—

- (a) a contract to grant such a lease as is mentioned in section 54(2) of the Law of Property Act 1925 (short leases);
- (b) a contract made in the course of a public auction; or

(c) *a contract regulated under the Financial Services Act 1986* [a contract regulated under the Financial Services and Markets Act 2000, other than a regulated mortgage contract];

and nothing in this section affects the creation or operation of resulting, implied or constructive trusts.

ANNOTATION

The words in square brackets were substituted for the words in italics immediately preceding them on December 1, 2001 by The Financial Services and Markets Act 2000 (Consequential Amendments and Repeals) Order 2001 (S.I. 2001 No. 3649), art.317(1),(2).

(6) In this section—

"disposition" has the same meaning as in the Law of Property Act 1925;

"interest in land" means any estate, interest or charge in or over land *or in or over the proceeds of sale of land*;

["regulated mortgage contract" must be read with—

(a) section 22 of the Financial Services and Markets Act 2000,

(b) any relevant order under that section, and

(c) Schedule 2 to that Act].

ANNOTATION

The words in italics were repealed on January 1, 1997 by Trusts of Land and Appointment of Trustees Act 1996, s.25(2), Sch.4; S.I. 1996 No. 2974.

The definition in square brackets was inserted on December 1, 2001 by The Financial Services and Markets Act 2000 (Consequential Amendments and Repeals) Order 2001 (S.I. 2001 No. 3649), art.317(1),(3).

(7) Nothing in this section shall apply in relation to contracts made before this section comes into force.

(8) Section 40 of the Law of Property Act 1925 (which is superseded by this section) shall cease to have effect.

ANNOTATION

Section 2 came into force on September 27, 1989: Law of Property (Miscellaneous Provisions) Act 1989, s.5(3), (4).

* * * *

LAW OF PROPERTY (MISCELLANEOUS PROVISIONS) ACT 1994

(c. 36)

PART I

IMPLIED COVENANTS FOR TITLE

The Covenants

Covenants to be implied on a disposition of property

1.—(1) In an instrument effecting or purporting to effect a disposition of property there shall be implied on the part of the person making the disposition, whether or not the disposition is for valuable consideration, such of the covenants specified in sections 2 to 5 as are applicable to the disposition.

(2) Of those sections—

(a) sections 2, 3(1) and (2), 4 and 5 apply where dispositions are expressed to be made with full title guarantee; and

(b) sections 2, 3(3), 4 and 5 apply where dispositions are expressed to be made with limited title guarantee.

(3) Sections 2 to 4 have effect subject to section 6 (no liability under covenants in certain cases); and sections 2 to 5 have effect subject to section 8(1) (limitation or extension of covenants by instrument effecting the disposition).

(4) In this Part—

"disposition" includes the creation of a term of years;

"instrument" includes an instrument which is not a deed; and

"property" includes a thing in action, and any interest in real or personal property.

Right to dispose and further assurance

2.—(1) If the disposition is expressed to be made with full title guarantee or with limited title guarantee there shall be implied the following covenants—

(a) that the person making the disposition has the right (with the concurrence of any other person conveying the property) to dispose of the property as he purports to, and

(b) that that person will at his own cost do all that he reasonably can to give the person to whom he disposes of the property the title he purports to give.

(2) The latter obligation includes—

(a) in relation to a disposition of an interest in land the title to which is registered, doing all that he reasonably can to ensure that the person to whom the disposition is made is entitled to be registered as proprietor with at least the class of title registered immediately before the disposition; and

(b) in relation to a disposition of an interest in land the title to which is required to be registered by virtue of the disposition, giving all reasonable assistance fully to establish to the satisfaction of the Chief Land Registrar the right of the person to whom the disposition is made to registration as proprietor.

(3) In the case of a disposition of an existing legal interest in land, the following presumptions apply, subject to the terms of the instrument, in ascertaining for the purposes of the covenants implied by this section what the person making the disposition purports to dispose of—

(a) where the title to the interest is registered, it shall be presumed that the disposition is of the whole of that interest;

(b) where the title to the interest is not registered, then—

(i) if it appears from the instrument that the interest is a leasehold interest, it shall be presumed that the disposition is of the property for the unexpired portion of the term of years created by the lease; and

(ii) in any other case, it shall be presumed that what is disposed of is the fee simple.

Charges, incumbrances and third party rights

3.—(1) If the disposition is expressed to be made with full title guarantee there shall be implied a covenant that the person making the disposition is disposing of the property free—

(a) from all charges and incumbrances (whether monetary or not), and

(b) from all other rights exercisable by third parties,

other than any charges, incumbrances or rights which that person does not and could not reasonably be expected to know about.

(2) In its application to charges, incumbrances and other third party rights subsection (1) extends to liabilities imposed and rights conferred by or under any enactment, except to the extent that such liabilities and rights are, by reason of—

(a) being, at the time of the disposition, only potential liabilities and rights in relation to the property, or

(b) being liabilities and rights imposed or conferred in relation to property generally,

not such as to constitute defects in title.

(3) If the disposition is expressed to be made with limited title guarantee there shall be implied a covenant that the person making the disposition has not since the last disposition for value—

(a) charged or incumbered the property by means of any charge or incumbrance which subsists at the time when the disposition is made, or granted third party rights in relation to the property which so subsist, or

(b) suffered the property to be so charged or incumbered or subjected to any such rights,

and that he is not aware that anyone else has done so since the last disposition for value.

Validity of lease

4.—(1) Where the disposition is of leasehold land and is expressed to be made with full title guarantee or with limited title guarantee, the following covenants shall also be implied—

(a) that the lease is subsisting at the time of the disposition, and

(b) that there is no subsisting breach of a condition or tenant's obligation, and nothing which at that time would render the lease liable to forfeiture.

(2) If the disposition is the grant of an underlease, the references to "the lease" in subsection (1) are references to the lease out of which the underlease is created.

Discharge of obligations where property subject to rentcharge or leasehold land

5.—(1) Where the disposition is a mortgage of property subject to a rentcharge, *or of leasehold land* [of leasehold land or of a commonhold unit], and is expressed to be made with full title guarantee or with limited title guarantee, the following covenants shall also be implied.

ANNOTATION

The words in square brackets were substituted for the words in italics immediately preceding them on September 27, 2004 by Commonhold and Leasehold Reform Act 2002, s.68, Sch.5, para.7(1),(2); S.I. 2004 No. 1832.

(2) If the property is subject to a rentcharge, there shall be implied a covenant that the mortgagor will fully and promptly observe and perform all the obligations under the instrument creating the rentcharge that are for the time being enforceable with respect to the property by the owner of the rentcharge in his capacity as such.

(3) If the property is leasehold land, there shall be implied a covenant that the mortgagor will fully and promptly observe all the obligations under the lease subject to the mortgage that are for the time being imposed on him in his capacity as tenant under the lease.

[(3A) If the property is a commonhold unit, there shall be implied a covenant that the mortgagor will fully and promptly observe and perform all the obligations under the commonhold community statement that are for the time being imposed on him in his capacity as a unit-holder or a joint unit-holder.]

ANNOTATION

Subsection (3A) was inserted on September 27, 2004 by Commonhold and Leasehold Reform Act 2002, s.68, Sch.5, para.7(1),(3); S.I. 2004 No. 1832.

(4) *In this section "mortgage" includes charge, and "mortgagor" shall be construed accordingly.* [In this section—

- (a) "commonhold community statement", "commonhold unit", "joint unit-holder" and "unit-holder" have the same meaning as in the Commonhold and Leasehold Reform Act 2002, and
- (b) "mortgage" includes charge, and "mortgagor" shall be construed accordingly.]

ANNOTATION

The words in square brackets were substituted for the words in italics immediately preceding them on September 27, 2004 by Commonhold and Leasehold Reform Act 2002, s.68, Sch.5, para.7(1),(4); S.I. 2004 No. 1832.

Effect of Covenants

No liability under covenants in certain cases

6.—(1) The person making the disposition is not liable under the covenants implied by virtue of—

- (a) section 2(1)(a) (right to dispose),
- (b) section 3 (charges, incumbrances and third party rights), or
- (c) section 4 (validity of lease),

in respect of any particular matter to which the disposition is expressly made subject.

(2) Furthermore that person is not liable under any of those covenants for anything (not falling within subsection (1))—

- (a) which at the time of the disposition is within the actual knowledge, or

(b) which is a necessary consequence of facts that are then within the actual knowledge,

of the person to whom the disposition is made.

(3) For this purpose section 198 of the Law of Property Act 1925 (deemed notice by virtue of registration) shall be disregarded.

[(4) Moreover, where the disposition is of an interest the title to which is registered under the Land Registration Act 2002, that person is not liable under any of those covenants for anything (not falling within subsection (1) or (2)) which at the time of the disposition was entered in relation to that interest in the register of title under that Act.]

ANNOTATION

Subsection (4) was added on October 13, 2003 by Land Registration Act 2002, s.133, Sch.11, para.31(2); S.I. 2003 No. 1725.

Annexation of benefit of covenants

7. The benefit of a covenant implied by virtue of this Part shall be annexed and incident to, and shall go with, the estate or interest of the person to whom the disposition is made, and shall be capable of being enforced by every person in whom that estate or interest is (in whole or in part) for the time being vested.

Supplementary provisions

8.—(1) The operation of any covenant implied in an instrument by virtue of this Part may be limited or extended by a term of that instrument.

(2) Sections 81 and 83 of the Law of Property Act 1925 (effect of covenant with two or more jointly; construction of implied covenants) apply to a covenant implied by virtue of this Part as they apply to a covenant implied by virtue of that Act.

(3) Where in an instrument effecting or purporting to effect a disposition of property a person is expressed to direct the disposition, this Part applies to him as if he were the person making the disposition.

(4) This Part has effect—

(a) where "gyda gwarant teitl llawn" is used instead of "with full title guarantee", and

(b) where "gyda gwarant teitl cyfyngedig" is used instead of "with limited title guarantee",

as it has effect where the English words are used.

Modifications of statutory forms

9.—(1) Where a form set out in an enactment, or in an instrument made under an enactment, includes words which (in an appropriate case) would have resulted in the implication of a covenant by virtue of section 76 of the Law of Property Act 1925, the form shall be taken to authorise instead the use of the words "with full title guarantee" or "with limited title guarantee" or their Welsh equivalent given in section 8(4).

(2) This applies in particular to the forms set out in Schedule 1 to the Settled Land Act 1925 and Schedules 4 and 5 to the Law of Property Act 1925.

Transitional Provisions

General saving for covenants in old form

10.—(1) Except as provided by section 11 below (cases in which covenants in old form implied on disposition after commencement), the following provisions, namely—

(a) section 76 of the Law of Property Act 1925, and

(b) section 24(1)(a) of the Land Registration Act 1925,

are repealed as regards dispositions of property made after the commencement of this Part.

(2) The repeal of those provisions by this Act accordingly does not affect the enforcement of a covenant implied by virtue of either of them on a disposition before the commencement of this Part.

Covenants in old form implied in certain cases

11.—(1) Section 76 of the Law of Property Act 1925 applies in relation to a disposition of property made after the commencement of this Part in pursuance of a contract entered into before commencement where—

(a) the contract contains a term providing for a disposition to which that section would have applied if the disposition had been made before commencement, and

(b) the existence of the contract and of that term is apparent on the face of the instrument effecting the disposition,

unless there has been an intervening disposition of the property expressed, in accordance with this Part, to be made with full title guarantee.

(2) Section 24(1)(a) of the Land Registration Act 1925 applies in relation to a disposition of a leasehold interest in land made after the commencement of this Part in pursuance of a contract entered into before commencement where—

(a) the covenant specified in that provision would have been implied on the disposition if it had been made before commencement, and

(b) the existence of the contract is apparent on the face of the instrument effecting the disposition,

unless there has been an intervening disposition of the leasehold interest expressed, in accordance with this Part, to be made with full title guarantee.

(3) In subsections (1) and (2) an "intervening disposition" means a disposition after the commencement of this Part to, or to a predecessor in title of, the person by whom the disposition in question is made.

(4) Where in order for subsection (1) or (2) to apply it is necessary for certain matters to be apparent on the face of the instrument effecting the disposition, the contract shall be deemed to contain an implied term that they should so appear.

Covenants in new form to be implied in other cases

12.—(1) This section applies to a contract for the disposition of property entered into before the commencement of this Part where the disposition is made after commencement and section 11 (cases in which covenants in old form to be implied) does not apply because there has been an intervening disposition expressed, in accordance with this Part, to be with full title guarantee.

(2) A contract which contains a term that the person making the disposition shall do so as beneficial owner shall be construed as requiring that person to do so by an instrument expressed to be made with full title guarantee.

(3) A contract which contains a term that the person making the disposition shall do so—

(a) as settlor, or

(b) as trustee or mortgagee or personal representative,

shall be construed as requiring that person to do so by an instrument expressed to be made with limited title guarantee.

(4) A contract for the disposition of a leasehold interest in land entered into at a date when the title to the leasehold interest was registered shall be construed as requiring the person making the disposition for which it provides to do so by an instrument expressed to be made with full title guarantee.

(5) Where this section applies and the contract provides that any of the covenants to be implied by virtue of section 76 of the Law of Property Act 1925 or section 24(1)(a) of the Land Registration Act 1925 shall be implied in a modified form, the contract shall be construed as requiring a corresponding modification of the covenants implied by virtue of this Part.

Application of transitional provisions in relation to options

13. For the purposes of sections 11 and 12 (transitional provisions, implication of covenants in old form in certain cases and new form in others) as they apply in relation to a disposition of property in accordance with an option granted before the commencement of this Part and exercised after commencement, the contract for the disposition shall be deemed to have been entered into on the grant of the option.

* * * *

PART III

GENERAL PROVISIONS

Crown application

20. This Act binds the Crown.

Consequential amendments and repeals

21.—(1) The enactments specified in Schedule 1 are amended in accordance with that Schedule, the amendments being consequential on the provisions of this Act.

(2) The enactments specified in Schedule 2 are repealed to the extent specified.

(3) In the case of section 76 of the Law of Property Act 1925 and section 24(1)(a) of the Land Registration Act 1925, those provisions are repealed in accordance with section 10(1) above (general saving for covenants in old form).

(4) The amendments consequential on Part I of this Act (namely those in paragraphs 1, 2, 5, 7, 9 and 12 of Schedule 1) shall not have effect in relation to any disposition of property to which, by virtue of section 10(1) or 11 above

(transitional provisions), section 76 of the Law of Property Act 1925 or section 24(1)(a) of the Land Registration Act 1925 continues to apply.

* * * *

Commencement

23.—(1) The provisions of this Act come into force on such a day as the Lord Chancellor may appoint by order made by statutory instrument.

(2) Different days may be appointed for different provisions and for different purposes.

ANNOTATION

All material parts of the Act came into force on July 1, 1995: Law of Property (Miscellaneous Provisions) Act 1994 (Commencement No. 2) Order 1995 (S.I. 1995 No. 1317).

* * * *

SCHEDULE 1

Section 21(1)

CONSEQUENTIAL AMENDMENTS

Law of Property Act 1925 (c. 20)

1. In section 77(1) of the Law of Property Act 1925 (implied covenants in conveyances subject to rents), for "the last preceding section" substitute "Part I of the Law of Property (Miscellaneous Provisions) Act 1994".

* * * *

SCHEDULE 2

Section 21(2)

Chapter	Short title	Extent of repeal
15 & 16 Geo. 5 (c. 20)	Law of Property Act 1925.	Section 76. In Schedule 2, Parts I to VI.
15 & 16 Geo. 5 (c. 21)	Land Registration Act 1925.	Section 24(1)(a).
15 & 16 Geo. 5 (c. 23)	Administration of Estates Act 1925.	In section 2(2), the words ", save as otherwise provided as respects trust estates including settled [land] and,". Section 36(3). In section 55(1), paragraph (xv).

Chapter	Short title	Extent of repeal
1964 (c. 63)	Law of Property (Joint Tenants) Act 1964.	In section 1(1), the words "he conveys as beneficial owner or".
1967 (c. 1)	Land Commission Act 1967.	In Schedule 12, paragraph 10(2).
1967 (c. 88)	Leasehold Reform Act 1967.	In section 10(1), from the words "nor to enter into any covenant for title" to the end.
1970 (c. 31)	Administration of Justice Act 1970	In Schedule 2, paragraph 5.
1985 (c. 6)	Companies Act 1985.	Section 209(10)(d).
1985 (c. 68)	Housing Act 1985.	In Schedule 6, paragraph 10.

* * * *

CONTRACTS (RIGHTS OF THIRD PARTIES) ACT 1999

(c. 31)

An Act to make provision for the enforcement of contractual terms by third parties.

[11th November 1999]

Right of third party to enforce contractual term

1.—(1) Subject to the provisions of this Act, a person who is not a party to a contract (a "third party") may in his own right enforce a term of the contract if—

(a) the contract expressly provides that he may, or
(b) subject to subsection (2), the term purports to confer a benefit on him.

(2) Subsection (1)(b) does not apply if on a proper construction of the contract it appears that the parties did not intend the term to be enforceable by the third party.

(3) The third party must be expressly identified in the contract by name, as a member of a class or as answering a particular description but need not be in existence when the contract is entered into.

(4) This section does not confer a right on a third party to enforce a term of a contract otherwise than subject to and in accordance with any other relevant terms of the contract.

(5) For the purpose of exercising his right to enforce a term of the contract, there shall be available to the third party any remedy that would have been

available to him in an action for breach of contract if he had been a party to the contract (and the rules relating to damages, injunctions, specific performance and other relief shall apply accordingly).

(6) Where a term of a contract excludes or limits liability in relation to any matter references in this Act to the third party enforcing the term shall be construed as references to his availing himself of the exclusion or limitation.

(7) In this Act, in relation to a term of a contract which is enforceable by a third party—

"the promisor" means the party to the contract against whom the term is enforceable by the third party, and

"the promisee" means the party to the contract by whom the term is enforceable against the promisor.

Variation and rescission of contract

2.—(1) Subject to the provisions of this section, where a third party has a right under section 1 to enforce a term of the contract, the parties to the contract may not, by agreement, rescind the contract, or vary it in such a way as to extinguish or alter his entitlement under that right, without his consent if–

(a) the third party has communicated his assent to the term to the promisor,

(b) the promisor is aware that the third party has relied on the term, or

(c) the promisor can reasonably be expected to have foreseen that the third party would rely on the term and the third party has in fact relied on it.

(2) The assent referred to in subsection (1)(a)—

(a) may be by words or conduct, and

(b) if sent to the promisor by post or other means, shall not be regarded as communicated to the promisor until received by him.

(3) Subsection (1) is subject to any express term of the contract under which—

(a) the parties to the contract may by agreement rescind or vary the contract without the consent of the third party, or

(b) the consent of the third party is required in circumstances specified in the contract instead of those set out in subsection (1)(a) to (c).

(4) Where the consent of a third party is required under subsection (1) or (3), the court or arbitral tribunal may, on the application of the parties to the contract, dispense with his consent if satisfied—

(a) that his consent cannot be obtained because his whereabouts cannot reasonably be ascertained, or

(b) that he is mentally incapable of giving his consent.

(5) The court or arbitral tribunal may, on the application of the parties to a contract, dispense with any consent that may be required under subsection (1)(c) if satisfied that it cannot reasonably be ascertained whether or not the third party has in fact relied on the term.

(6) If the court or arbitral tribunal dispenses with a third party's consent, it may impose such conditions as it thinks fit, including a condition requiring the payment of compensation to the third party.

(7) The jurisdiction conferred on the court by subsections (4) to (6) is exercisable by both the High Court and a county court.

Defences etc. available to purchaser

3.—(1) Subsections (2) to (5) apply where, in reliance on section 1, proceedings for the enforcement of a term of a contract are brought by a third party.

(2) The promisor shall have available to him by way of defence or set-off any matter that—

(a) arises from or in connection with the contract and is relevant to the term, and

(b) would have been available to him by way of defence or set-off if the proceedings had been brought by the promisee.

(3) The promisor shall also have available to him by way of defence or set-off any matter if—

(a) an express term of the contract provides for it to be available to him in proceedings brought by the third party, and

(b) it would have been available to him by way of defence or set-off if the proceedings had been brought by the promisee.

(4) The promisor shall also have available to him—

(a) by way of defence or set-off any matter, and

(b) by way of counterclaim any matter not arising from the contract,

that would have been available to him by way of defence or set-off or, as the case may be, by way of counterclaim against the third party if the third party had been a party to the contract.

(5) Subsections (2) and (4) are subject to any express term of the contract as to the matters that are not to be available to the promisor by way of defence, set-off or counterclaim.

(6) Where in any proceedings brought against him a third party seeks in reliance on section 1 to enforce a term of a contract (including, in particular, a term purporting to exclude or limit liability), he may not do so if he could not have done so (whether by reason of any particular circumstances relating to him or otherwise) had he been a party to the contract.

Enforcement of contract by promisee

4. Section 1 does not affect any right of the promisee to enforce any term of the contract.

Protection of promisor from double liability

5. Where under section 1 a term of a contract is enforceable by a third party, and the promisee has recovered from the promisor a sum in respect of—

(a) the third party's loss in respect of the term, or

(b) the expense to the promisee of making good to the third party the default of the promisor,

then, in any proceedings brought in reliance on that section by the third party, the court or arbitral tribunal shall reduce any award to the third party to such extent as it things appropriate to take account of the sum recovered by the promisee.

* * * *

Supplementary provisions relating to third party

7.—(1) Section 1 does not affect any right or remedy of a third party that exists or is available apart from this Act.

(2) Section 2(2) of the Unfair Contract Terms Act 1977 (restriction on exclusion etc. of liability for negligence) shall not apply where the negligence consists of the breach of an obligation arising from a term of a contract and the person seeking to enforce it is a third party acting in reliance on section 1.

(3) In sections 5 and 8 of the Limitation Act 1980 the references to an action founded on a simple contract and an action upon a specialty shall respectively include references to an action brought in reliance on section 1 relating to a simple contract and an action brought in reliance on that section relating to a specialty.

(4) A third party shall not, by virtue of section 1(5) or 3(4) or (6), be treated as a party to the contract for the purposes of any other Act (or any instrument made under any other Act).

* * * *

Short title, commencement and extent

10.—(1) This Act may be cited as the Contracts (Rights of Third Parties) Act 1999.

(2) This Act comes into force on the day on which it is passed but, subject to subsection (3), does not apply in relation to a contract entered into before the end of the period of six months beginning with that day.

(3) The restriction in subsection (2) does not apply in relation to a contract which—

(a) is entered into on or after the day on which this Act is passed, and

(b) expressly provides for the application of this Act.

(4) This Act extends as follows—

(a) section 9 extends to Northern Ireland only;

(b) the remaining provisions extend to England and Wales and Northern Ireland only.

* * * *

LAND REGISTRATION ACT 2002

(c. 9)

An Act to make provision about land registration; and for connected purposes.

[26th February 2002]

PART III

DISPOSITIONS OF REGISTERED LAND

Powers of disposition

Owner's powers

23.—(1) Owner's powers in relation to a registered estate consist of—

(a) power to make a disposition of any kind permitted by the general law in relation to an interest of that description, other than a mortgage by demise or sub-demise, and

(b) power to charge the estate at law with the payment of money.

(2) Owner's powers in relation to a registered charge consist of—

(a) power to make a disposition of any kind permitted by the general law in relation to an interest of that description, other than a legal sub-mortgage, and

(b) power to charge at law with the payment of money indebtedness secured by the registered charge.

(3) In subsection (2)(a), "legal sub-mortgage" means—

(a) a transfer by way of mortgage,

(b) a sub-mortgage by sub-demise, and

(c) a charge by way of legal mortgage.

Right to exercise owner's powers

24. A person is entitled to exercise owner's powers in relation to a registered estate or charge if he is—

(a) the registered proprietor, or

(b) entitled to be registered as the proprietor.

Mode of exercise

25.—(1) A registrable disposition of a registered estate or charge only has effect if it complies with such requirements as to form and content as rules may provide.

(2) Rules may apply subsection (1) to any other kind of disposition which depends for its effect on registration.

Protection of disponees

26.—(1) Subject to subsection (2), a person's right to exercise owner's powers in relation to a registered estate or charge is to be taken to be free from any limitation affecting the validity of a disposition.

(2) Subsection (1) does not apply to a limitation—

(a) reflected by an entry in the register, or

(b) imposed by, or under, this Act.

(3) This section has effect only for the purpose of preventing the title of a disponee being questioned (and so does not affect the lawfulness of a disposition).

Dispositions required to be registered

27.—(1) If a disposition of a registered estate or registered charge is required to be completed by registration, it does not operate at law until the relevant registration requirements are met.

(2) In the case of a registered estate, the following are the dispositions which are required to be completed by registration—

(a) a transfer,

(b) where the registered estate is an estate in land, the grant of a term of years absolute—

(i) for a term of more than seven years from the date of the grant,

(ii) to take effect in possession after the end of the period of three months beginning with the date of the grant,

(iii) under which the right to possession is discontinuous,

(iv) in pursuance of Part 5 of the Housing Act 1985 (c. 68) (the right to buy), or

(v) in circumstances where section 171A of that Act applies (disposal by landlord which leads to a person no longer being a secure tenant),

(c) where the registered estate is a franchise or manor, the grant of a lease,

(d) the express grant or reservation of an interest of a kind falling within section 1(2)(a) of the Law of Property Act 1925 (c. 20), other than one which is capable of being registered under the Commons Registration Act 1965 (c. 64),

(e) the express grant or reservation of an interest of a kind falling within section 1(2)(b) or (e) of the Law of Property Act 1925, and

(f) the grant of a legal charge.

(3) In the case of a registered charge, the following are the dispositions which are required to be completed by registration—

(a) a transfer, and

(b) the grant of a sub-charge.

(4) Schedule 2 to this Act (which deals with the relevant registration requirements) has effect.

(5) This section applies to dispositions by operation of law as it applies to other dispositions, but with the exception of the following—

(a) a transfer on the death or bankruptcy of an individual proprietor,

(b) a transfer on the dissolution of a corporate proprietor, and

(c) the creation of a legal charge which is a local land charge.

(6) Rules may make provision about applications to the registrar for the purpose of meeting registration requirements under this section.

(7) In subsection (2)(d), the reference to express grant does not include grant as a result of the operation of section 62 of the Law of Property Act 1925 (c. 20).

Basic rule

28.—(1) Except as provided by sections 29 and 30, the priority of an interest affecting a registered estate or charge is not affected by a disposition of the estate or charge.

(2) It makes no difference for the purposes of this section whether the interest or disposition is registered.

Effect of registered dispositions: estates

29.—(1) If a registrable disposition of a registered estate is made for valuable consideration, completion of the disposition by registration has the effect of postponing to the interest under the disposition any interest affecting the estate immediately before the disposition whose priority is not protected at the time of registration.

(2) For the purposes of subsection (1), the priority of an interest is protected—

(a) in any case, if the interest—

(i) is a registered charge or the subject of a notice in the register,

(ii) falls within any of the paragraphs of Schedule 3, or

(iii) appears from the register to be excepted from the effect of registration, and

(b) in the case of a disposition of a leasehold estate, if the burden of the interest is incident to the estate.

(3) Subsection (2)(a)(ii) does not apply to an interest which has been the subject of a notice in the register at any time since the coming into force of this section.

(4) Where the grant of a leasehold estate in land out of a registered estate does not involve a registrable disposition, this section has effect as if—

(a) the grant involved such a disposition, and

(b) the disposition were registered at the time of the grant.

* * * *

SCHEDULE 2

Section 27

REGISTRABLE DISPOSITIONS: REGISTRATION REQUIREMENTS

PART I

REGISTERED ESTATES

Introductory

1. This Part deals with the registration requirements relating to those dispositions of registered estates which are required to be completed by registration.

Transfer

2. (1) In the case of a transfer of whole or part, the transferee, or his successor in title, must be entered in the register as the proprietor.

(2) In the case of a transfer of part, such details of the transfer as rules may provide must be entered in the register in relation to the registered estate out of which the transfer is made.

Lease of estate in land

3. (1) This paragraph applies to a disposition consisting of the grant out of an estate in land of a term of years absolute.

(2) In the case of a disposition to which this paragraph applies—

(a) the grantee, or his successor in title, must be entered in the register as the proprietor of the lease, and

(b) a notice in respect of the lease must be entered in the register.

Lease of franchise or manor

4. (1) This paragraph applies to a disposition consisting of the grant out of a franchise or manor of a lease for a term of more than seven years from the date of the grant.

(2) In the case of a disposition to which this paragraph applies—

(a) the grantee, or his successor in title, must be entered in the register as the proprietor of the lease, and

(b) a notice in respect of the lease must be entered in the register.

5. (1) This paragraph applies to a disposition consisting of the grant out of a franchise or manor of a lease for a term not exceeding seven years from the date of the grant.

(2) In the case of a disposition to which this paragraph applies, a notice in respect of the lease must be entered in the register.

Creation of independently registrable legal interest

6. (1) This paragraph applies to a disposition consisting of the creation of a legal rentcharge or profit a prendre in gross, other than one created for, or for an interest equivalent to, a term of years absolute not exceeding seven years from the date of creation.

(2) In the case of a disposition to which this paragraph applies—

(a) the grantee, or his successor in title, must be entered in the register as the proprietor of the interest created, and

(b) a notice in respect of the interest created must be entered in the register.

(3) In sub-paragraph (1), the reference to a legal rentcharge or profit a prendre in gross is to one falling within section 1(2) of the Law of Property Act 1925 (c. 20).

Creation of other legal interest

7. (1) This paragraph applies to a disposition which—

(a) consists of the creation of an interest of a kind falling within section 1(2)(a), (b) or (e) of the Law of Property Act 1925, and

(b) is not a disposition to which paragraph 4, 5 or 6 applies.

(2) In the case of a disposition to which this paragraph applies—

(a) a notice in respect of the interest created must be entered in the register, and

(b) if the interest is created for the benefit of a registered estate, the proprietor of the registered estate must be entered in the register as its proprietor.

(3) Rules may provide for sub-paragraph (2) to have effect with modifications in relation to a right of entry over or in respect of a term of years absolute.

Creation of legal charge

8. In the case of the creation of a charge, the chargee, or his successor in title, must be entered in the register as the proprietor of the charge.

* * * *

SCHEDULE 3

Sections 29 and 30

UNREGISTERED INTERESTS WHICH OVERRIDE REGISTERED DISPOSITIONS

Leasehold estates in land

1. A leasehold estate in land granted for a term not exceeding seven years from the date of the grant, except for—

(a) a lease the grant of which falls within section 4(1)(d), (e) or (f);
(b) a lease the grant of which constitutes a registrable disposition.

Interests of persons in actual occupation

2. An interest belonging at the time of the disposition to a person in actual occupation, so far as relating to land of which he is in actual occupation, except for—

(a) an interest under a settlement under the Settled Land Act 1925 (c. 18);
(b) an interest of a person of whom inquiry was made before the disposition and who failed to disclose the right when he could reasonably have been expected to do so;
(c) an interest—
    (i) which belongs to a person whose occupation would not have been obvious on a reasonably careful inspection of the land at the time of the disposition, and
    (ii) of which the person to whom the disposition is made does not have actual knowledge at that time;
(d) a leasehold estate in land granted to take effect in possession after the end of the period of three months beginning with the date of the grant and which has not taken effect in possession at the time of the disposition.

[2A. (1) An interest which, immediately before the coming into force of this Schedule, was an overriding interest under section 70(1)(g) of the Land Registration Act 1925 by virtue of a person's receipt of rents and profits, except for an interest of a person of whom inquiry was made before the disposition and who failed to disclose the right when he could reasonably have been expected to do so.

(2) Sub-paragraph (1) does not apply to an interest if at any time since the coming into force of this Schedule it has been an interest which, had the Land Registration Act 1925 (c. 21) continued in force, would not have been an overriding interest under section 70(1)(g) of that Act by virtue of a person's receipt of rents and profits.]

Easements and profits a prendre

3. (1) A legal easement or profit a prendre, except for an easement, or a profit a prendre which is not registered under the Commons Registration Act 1965 (c. 64), which at the time of the disposition—

(a) is not within the actual knowledge of the person to whom the disposition is made, and
(b) would not have been obvious on a reasonably careful inspection of the land over which the easement or profit is exercisable.

(2) The exception in sub-paragraph (1) does not apply if the person entitled to the easement or profit proves that it has been exercised in the period of one year ending with the day of the disposition.

Customary and public rights

4. A customary right.

5. A public right.

Local land charges

6. A local land charge.

Mines and minerals

7. An interest in any coal or coal mine, the rights attached to any such interest and the rights of any person under section 38, 49 or 51 of the Coal Industry Act 1994 (c. 21).

8. In the case of land to which title was registered before 1898, rights to mines and minerals (and incidental rights) created before 1898.

9. In the case of land to which title was registered between 1898 and 1925 inclusive, rights to mines and minerals (and incidental rights) created before the date of registration of the title.

Miscellaneous

10. A franchise.

11. A manorial right.

12. A right to rent which was reserved to the Crown on the granting of any freehold estate (whether or not the right is still vested in the Crown).

13. A non-statutory right in respect of an embankment or sea or river wall.

14. A right to payment in lieu of tithe.

[15. A right under paragraph 18(1) of Schedule 12.]

[16. A right in respect of the repair of a church chancel.]

ANNOTATION

Paragraph 1 is taken to include an interest which immediately before October 13, 2003 was an overriding interest under Land Registration Act 1925, s.70(1)(k): Land Registration Act 2002, s.134(2), Sch.12, para.12; S.I. 2003 No. 1725.

Paragraph 2A was inserted as a transitional provision with effect from October 13, 2003 by Land Registration Act 2002, s.134(2), Sch.12, para.8; S.I. 2003 No. 1725.

Paragraph 3 had effect for a period of 3 years from October 13, 2003 with the omission of the exception in sub-paragraph (1): Land Registration Act 2002, s.134(2), Sch.12, para.10: S.I. 2003 No. 1725. Further, in relation to an easement or profit which was an overriding interest in relation to a registered estate immediately before that date, but which would not be an overriding interest under para.3 if created on or after that date, Sch.3 applies as if such an interest were not excluded from para.3: Land Registration Act 2002, s.134(2), Sch.12, para.9; S.I. 2003 No. 1725.

Paragraph 6 is taken to include an interest which immediately before October 13, 2003 was an overriding interest under Land Registration Act 1925, s.70(1)(i) and whose status as such was preserved by Local Land Charges Act 1975, s.19(3): Land Registration Act 2002, s.134(2), Sch.12, para.13; S.I. 2003 No. 1725.

Paragraphs 10 to 14 cease to have effect on October 13, 2013: Land Registration Act 2002, s.117(1); S.I. 2003 No. 1725.

Paragraph 15 was added for a transitional period of 3 years from October 13, 2003 by Land Registration Act 2002, s.134(2), Sch.12, para.11; S.I. 2003 No. 1725.

Paragraph 16 was added for a transitional period of 10 years from October 13, 2003 by The Land Registration Act 2002 (Transitional Provisions) (No.2) Order 2003 (S.I. 2003 No. 2431), art.2(2); S.I. 2003 No. 1725.

* * * *

SCHEDULE 12

Section 134

TRANSITION

* * * *

Implied indemnity covenants on transfers of pre-1996 leases

20. (1) On a disposition of a registered leasehold estate by way of transfer, the following covenants are implied in the instrument effecting the disposition, unless the contrary intention is expressed—

(a) in the case of a transfer of the whole of the land comprised in the registered lease, the covenant in sub-paragraph (2), and

(b) in the case of a transfer of part of the land comprised in the lease—

(i) the covenant in sub-paragraph (3), and

(ii) where the transferor continues to hold land under the lease, the covenant in sub-paragraph (4).

(2) The transferee covenants with the transferor that during the residue of the term granted by the registered lease the transferee and the persons deriving title under him will—

(a) pay the rent reserved by the lease,

(b) comply with the covenants and conditions contained in the lease, and

(c) keep the transferor and the persons deriving title under him indemnified against all actions, expenses and claims on account of any failure to comply with paragraphs (a) and (b).

(3) The transferee covenants with the transferor that during the residue of the term granted by the registered lease the transferee and the persons deriving title under him will—

(a) where the rent reserved by the lease is apportioned, pay the rent apportioned to the part transferred,

(b) comply with the covenants and conditions contained in the lease so far as affecting the part transferred, and

(c) keep the transferor and the persons deriving title under him indemnified against all actions, expenses and claims on account of any failure to comply with paragraphs (a) and (b).

(4) The transferor covenants with the transferee that during the residue of the term granted by the registered lease the transferor and the persons deriving title under him will—

(a) where the rent reserved by the lease is apportioned, pay the rent apportioned to the part retained,

(b) comply with the covenants and conditions contained in the lease so far as affecting the part retained, and

(c) keep the transferee and the persons deriving title under him indemnified against all actions, expenses and claims on account of any failure to comply with paragraphs (a) and (b).

(5) This paragraph does not apply to a lease which is a new tenancy for the purposes of section 1 of the Landlord and Tenant (Covenants) Act 1995 (c. 30).

* * * *

APPENDIX THREE

STATUTORY INSTRUMENTS

CONTENTS

THE LANDLORD AND TENANT (COVENANTS) ACT 1995 (COMMENCEMENT) ORDER 1995

(S.I. 1995 No. 2963)

Made .... November 9, 1995

The Lord Chancellor, in exercise of the powers conferred on him by section 31 of the Landlord and Tenant (Covenants) Act 1995 (c. 30) hereby makes the following Order:

1. This Order may be cited as the Landlord and Tenant (Covenants) Act 1995 (Commencement) Order 1995.

2. The Landlord and Tenant (Covenants) Act 1995 shall come into force on 1st January 1996.

[Dated 9th November 1995 Mackay of Clashfern, C.]

* * * *

THE LANDLORD AND TENANT (COVENANTS) ACT 1995 (NOTICES) REGULATIONS 1995

(S.I. 1995 No. 2964)

Made .... 9th November 1995
Laid before Parliament ..... 20th November 1995
Coming into force .... 1st January 1996

The Lord Chancellor, in exercise of the powers conferred on him by section 27 of the Landlord and Tenant (Covenants) Act 1995, hereby makes the following Regulations:

1.—(1) These Regulations may be cited as the Landlord and Tenant (Covenants) Act 1995 (Notices) Regulations 1995 and shall come into force on 1st January 1996.

(2) In these Regulations, "the Act" means the Landlord and Tenant (Covenants) Act 1995, and a form referred to by number means the form so numbered in the Schedule to these Regulations.

2. The forms prescribed for the purposes of the Act shall be as follows, or in each case a form substantially to the like effect:

	PURPOSE OF NOTICE	FORM TO BE USED
(a) (i)	Landlord informing a former tenant or guarantor of such a tenant of an amount payable in respect of a fixed charge under a covenant of the tenancy which the landlord intends to recover from that person under section 17 of the Act	Form 1
(ii)	Landlord informing a former tenant or guarantor of such a tenant of a revised, greater amount payable in respect of a fixed charge under a covenant of the tenancy which the landlord intends to recover from that person under section 17 of the Act	Form 2
(b) (i)	Landlord applying to be released from all the landlord covenants of the tenancy on assignment of his entire interest under sections 6 and 8 of the Act	Whole of Form 3 (landlord to complete Part I only)
(ii)	Tenant objecting to the landlord's release under section 8 of the Act	Part II of Form 3
(iii)	Tenant consenting to the landlord's release and withdrawing a notice objecting to such release under section 8 of the Act	Notice in writing stating that tenant is now consenting and that the notice of objection is withdrawn
(c) (i)	Landlord applying to be released from the landlord covenants of the tenancy to the appropriate extent on assignment of part only of his interest under sections 6 and 8 of the Act	Whole of Form 4 (landlord to complete Part I only)
(ii)	Tenant objecting to the landlord's release under section 8 of the Act	Part II of Form 4
(iii)	Tenant consenting to the landlord's release and withdrawing a notice objecting to such release under section 8 of the Act	Notice in writing stating that tenant is now consenting and that the notice of objection is withdrawn

	PURPOSE OF NOTICE	FORM TO BE USED
(d) (i)	Former landlord applying to be released from all the landlord covenants of the tenancy on a subsequent assignment of the landlord's interest under sections 7 and 8 of the Act	Whole of Form 5 (landlord to complete Part I only)
(ii)	Tenant objecting to the former landlord's release under section 8 of the Act	Part II of Form 5
(iii)	Tenant consenting to the former landlord's release and withdrawing a notice objecting to such release under section 8 of the Act	Notice in writing stating that tenant is now consenting and that the notice of objection is withdrawn
(e) (i)	Former landlord who assigned part only of his interest applying to be released from the landlord covenants of the tenancy to the appropriate extent on a subsequent assignment of the landlord's interest under sections 7 and 8 of the Act	Whole of Form 6 (landlord to complete Part I only)
(ii)	Tenant objecting to the former landlord's release under section 8 of the Act	Part II of Form 6
(iii)	Tenant consenting to the former landlord's release and withdrawing a notice objecting to such release under section 8 of the Act	Notice in writing stating that tenant is now consenting and that the notice of objection is withdrawn
(f) (i)	Tenant and tenant's assignee jointly applying for an apportionment of liability under the covenants of the tenancy to become binding on the appropriate person under sections 9 and 10 of the Act	Whole of Form 7 (tenant and assignee to complete Part I only)
(ii)	Appropriate person objecting to the apportionment becoming binding on that person under section 10 of the Act	Part II of Form 7

	PURPOSE OF NOTICE	FORM TO BE USED
(iii)	Appropriate person consenting to the apportionment becoming binding on that person and withdrawing a notice objecting to the apportionment becoming so binding under section 10 of the Act	Notice in writing stating that appropriate person is now consenting and that the notice of objection is withdrawn
(g) (i)	Landlord and landlord's assignee jointly applying for an apportionment of liability under the covenants of the tenancy to become binding on the appropriate person under sections 9 and 10 of the Act	Whole of Form 8 (landlord and assignee to complete Part I only)
(ii)	Appropriate person objecting to the apportionment becoming binding on that person under section 10 of the Act	Part II of Form 8
(iii)	Appropriate person consenting to the apportionment becoming binding on that person and withdrawing a notice objecting to the apportionment becoming so binding under section 10 of the Act	Notice in writing stating that appropriate person is now consenting and that the notice of objection is withdrawn
Dated 9th November 1995		Mackay of Clashfern, C.

SCHEDULE

FORM 1

NOTICE TO FORMER TENANT OR GUARANTOR OF INTENTION TO RECOVER FIXED CHARGE[1]
(Landlord and Tenant (Covenants) Act 1995, section 17)

To [name and address]: ....

....

IMPORTANT – THE PERSON GIVING THIS NOTICE IS PROTECTING THE RIGHT TO RECOVER THE AMOUNT(S) SPECIFIED FROM YOU NOW OR AT SOME TIME IN THE FUTURE. THERE MAY BE ACTION WHICH YOU CAN TAKE TO PROTECT YOUR POSITION. READ THE NOTICE AND ALL THE NOTES OVERLEAF CAREFULLY. IF YOU ARE IN ANY DOUBT ABOUT THE ACTION YOU SHOULD TAKE, SEEK ADVICE IMMEDIATELY, FOR INSTANCE FROM A SOLICITOR OR CITIZENS ADVICE BUREAU.

1. This notice is given under section 17 of the Landlord and Tenant (Covenants) Act 1995. *{see Note 1 overleaf}*

2. It relates to (address and description of property ....

....

let under a lease dated .... and made between ....

....

....

[of which you were formerly tenant] [in relation to which you are liable as guarantor of a person who was formerly tenant].[2]

3. I/we as landlord[3] hereby give you notice that the fixed charge(s) of which details are set out in the attached Schedule[4] is/are now due and unpaid, and that I/we intend to recover from you the amount(s) specified in the Schedule [and interest from the date and calculated on the basis specified in the Schedule][5]. *{see Notes 2 and 3 overleaf}*

[continued over]

1 The Act defines a fixed charge as (a) rent, (b) any service charge (as defined by section 18 of the Landlord and Tenant Act 1985, disregarding the words "of a dwelling") and (c) any amount payable under a tenant covenant of the tenancy providing for payment of a liquidated sum in the event of failure to comply with the covenant.
2 Delete alternative as appropriate.
3 "Landlord" for these purposes includes any person who has the right to enforce the charge.
4 The Schedule must be in writing, and must indicate in relation to each item the date on which it became payable, the amount payable and whether it is rent, service charge or a fixed charge of some other kind (in which case particulars of the nature of the charge should be given). Charges due before 1 January 1996 are deemed to have become due on that date, but the actual date on which they became due should also be stated.
5 Delete words in brackets if not applicable. If applicable, the Schedule must state the basis on which interest is calculated (for example, rate of interest, date from which it is payable and provision of Lease or other document under which it is payable).

4. [1] There is a possibility that your liability in respect of the fixed charge(s) detailed in the Schedule will subsequently be determined to be for a greater amount. *{see Note 4 below}*

5. All correspondence about this notice should be sent to the landlord/landlord's agent at the address given below.

Date .... Signature of landlord/landlord's agent ....

Name and address of landlord ....

....

....

[Name and address agent ....

....

....]

NOTES

1. The person giving you this notice alleges that you are still liable for the performance of the tenant's obligations under the tenancy to which this notice relates, either as a previous tenant bound by privity of contract or an authorised guarantee agreement, or because you are the guarantor of a previous tenant. By giving you this notice, the landlord (or other person entitled to enforce payment, such as a management company) is protecting his right to require you to pay the amount specified in the notice. There may be other sums not covered by the notice which the landlord can also recover because they are not fixed charges (for example in respect of repairs or costs if legal proceedings have to be brought). If you pay the amount specified in this notice in full, you will have the right to call on the landlord to grant you an "overriding lease", which puts you in the position of landlord to the present tenant. There are both advantages and drawbacks to doing this, and you should take advice before coming to a decision.

Validity of notice

2. The landlord is required to give this notice within six months of the date on which the charge or charges in question became due (or, if it became due before 1 January 1996, within six months of that date). If the notice has been given late, it is not valid and the amount in the notice cannot be recovered from you. The date of the giving of the notice may not be the date written on the notice or the date on which you actually saw it. It may, for instance, be the date on which the notice was delivered through the post to your last address known to the landlord. If you are in any doubt, you should seek advice immediately.

Interest

3. If interest is payable on the amount due, the landlord does not have to state the precise amount of interest, but he must state the basis on which the interest is calculated to enable you to work out the likely amount, or he will not be able to claim interest at all. This does not include interest which may be payable under rules of court if legal proceedings are brought.

Change in amount due

4. Apart from interest, the landlord is not entitled to recover an amount which is more than he has specified in the notice, with one exception. This is where the amount cannot be finally determined within six months after it is due (for example, if there is dispute concerning an outstanding rent review or if the charge is a service charge collected on account and adjusted following final determination). In such a case, if the amount due is eventually determined to be more than originally notified, the landlord may claim the larger amount *if and only if* he completes the paragraph giving notice of the possibility that the amount may change, and gives a further notice specifying the larger amount within three months of the final determination.

---

1 Delete this paragraph if not applicable. If applicable (for example, where there is an outstanding rent review or service charge collected on account) a further notice must be served on the former tenant or guarantor within three (3) months beginning with the date on which the greater amount is determined. If only applicable to one or more charge of several, the Schedule should specify which.

FORM 2

FURTHER NOTICE TO FORMER TENANT OR GUARANTOR OF REVISED AMOUNT DUE IN RESPECT OF A FIXED CHARGE[1]
(Landlord and Tenant (Covenants) Act 1995, section 17)

To [name and address]: ....

....

> IMPORTANT – THE PERSON GIVING THIS NOTICE IN PROTECTING THE RIGHT TO RECOVER THE AMOUNT(S) SPECIFIED FROM YOU NOW OR AT SOME TIME IN THE FUTURE. THERE MAY BE ACTION WHICH YOU CAN TAKE TO PROTECT YOUR POSITION. READ THE NOTICE AND ALL THE NOTES OVERLEAF CAREFULLY. IF YOU ARE IN ANY DOUBT ABOUT THE ACTION YOU SHOULD TAKE, SEEK ADVICE IMMEDIATELY, FOR INSTANCE FROM A SOLICITOR OR CITIZENS ADVICE BUREAU.

1. This notice is given under section 17 of the Landlord and Tenant (Covenants) Act 1995. *{see Note 1 overleaf}*

2. It relates to (address and description of property) ....

....

let under a lease dated .... and made between ....

....

....

[of which you were formerly tenant] [in relation to which you are liable as guarantor of a person who was formerly tenant].[2]

3. You were informed on .... (date of original notice) of the amount due in respect of a fixed charge or charges, and of the possibility that your liability in respect of the charge(s) might subsequently be determined to be for a greater amount.

4. I/we as landlord[3] hereby give you notice that the fixed charge(s) of which details are set out in the attached Schedule[4] has/have now been determined to be for a greater amount than specified in the original notice, and that I/we intend to recover from you the amount(s) specified in the Schedule [and interest from the date and calculated on the basis specified in the Schedule][5]. *{see Notes 2 and 3 overleaf}*

[continued over]

1 The Act defines a fixed charge as (a) rent, (b) any service charge (as defined by section 18 of the Landlord and Tenant Act 1985, disregarding the words "of a dwelling") and (c) any amount payable under a tenant covenant of the tenancy providing for payment of a liquidated sum in the event of failure to comply with the covenant.
2 Delete alternative as appropriate.
3 "Landlord" for these purposes includes any person who has the right to enforce the charge.
4 The Schedule can be in any form, but must indicate in relation to each item the date on which it was revised, the revised amount payable and whether it is rent, service charge or a fixed charge of some other kind (in which case particulars of the nature of the charge should be given).
5 Delete words in brackets if not applicable. If applicable, the Schedule must state the basis on which interest is calculated (for example, rate of interest, date from which it is payable and provision of Lease or other document under which it is payable).

5. All correspondence about this notice should be sent to the landlord/landlord's agent at the address given below.

Date .... Signature of landlord/landlord's agent ....

Name and address of landlord ....

....

....

[Name and address of agent ....

....

....]

NOTES

1. The person giving you this notice alleges that you are still liable for the performance of the tenant's obligations under the tenancy to which this notice relates, either as a previous tenant bound by privity of contract or an authorised guarantee agreement, or because you are the guarantor of a previous tenant. You should already have been given a notice by which the landlord (or other person entitled to enforce payment, such as a management company) protected his right to require you to pay the amount specified in that notice. The purpose of this notice is to protect the landlord's right to require you to pay a larger amount, because the amount specified in the original notice could not be finally determined at the time of the original notice (for example, because there was a dispute concerning an outstanding rent review or if the charge was a service charge collected on account and adjusted following final determination).

Validity of notice

2. The notice is not valid unless the original notice contained a warning that the amount in question might subsequently be determined to be greater. In addition, the landlord is required to give this notice within three months of the date on which the amount was finally determined. If the original notice did not include that warning, or if this notice has been given late, then this notice is not valid and the landlord cannot recover the greater amount, but only the smaller amount specified in the original notice. The date of the giving of this notice may not be the date written on the notice or the date on which you actually saw it. It may, for instance, be the date on which the notice was delivered through the post to your last address known to the person giving notice. If you are in any doubt, you should seek advice immediately.

Interest

3. If interest is chargeable on the amount due, the landlord does not have to state the precise amount of interest, but he must have stated the basis on which the interest is calculated, or he will not be able to claim interest at all.

FORM 3

PART I

LANDLORD'S NOTICE APPLYING FOR RELEASE FROM LANDLORD COVENANTS OF A TENANCY ON ASSIGNMENT OF WHOLE OF REVERSION (Landlord and Tenant (Covenants) Act 1995, sections 6 and 8)

To [name and address]: ....

....

> IMPORTANT – THIS NOTICE IS INTENDED TO RELEASE YOUR LANDLORD FROM HIS OBLIGATIONS WHEN HE TRANSFERS HIS INTEREST TO A NEW LANDLORD. IF YOU CONSIDER THAT THERE IS GOOD REASON FOR YOUR LANDLORD **NOT** TO BE RELEASED, YOU MUST ACT QUICKLY. READ THE NOTICE AND ALL THE NOTES OVERLEAF CAREFULLY. IF YOU ARE IN ANY DOUBT ABOUT THE ACTION YOU SHOULD TAKE, SEEK ADVICE IMMEDIATELY, FOR INSTANCE FROM A SOLICITOR OR CITIZENS ADVICE BUREAU.

1. This notice is given under section 8 of the Landlord and Tenant (Covenants) Act 1995. *{see Note 1 overleaf}*

2. It relates to (address and description of property) ....

....

let under a lease dated .... and made between ....

....

....

of which you are the tenant.

3. I/we [propose to transfer] [transferred on ....][1] the whole of the landlord's interest and wish to be released from the landlord's obligations under the tenancy with effect from the date of the transfer. *{see Note 2 overleaf}*

4. If you consider that it is reasonable for me/us to be released, you do not need to do anything, but it would help me/us if you notify me/us using Part II of this Form. *{see Note 3 overleaf}*

5. If you do **not** consider it reasonable for me/us to be released you **must** notify me/us of your objection, using Part II of this Form, within the period of **FOUR WEEKS** beginning with the giving of this notice, or I/we will be released in any event. You may withdraw your objection at any time by notifying me/us in writing. *{see Notes 4–6 overleaf}*

6. All correspondence about this notice should be sent to the landlord/landlord's agent at the address given below.

Date .... Signature of landlord/landlord's agent ....
Name and address of landlord ....

....

....

[Name and address of agent ....

....

....]

1 Delete alternative as appropriate.

NOTES TO PART I

Release of landlord

1. The landlord is about to transfer his interest to a new landlord, or has just done so, and is applying to be released from the obligations of the landlord under your tenancy. You have a number of options: you may expressly agree to the landlord's being released; you may object to his being released (with the option of withdrawing your objection later); or you may do nothing, in which case the landlord will automatically be released, with effect from the date of the transfer, once four weeks have elapsed from the date of the giving of the notice. If you choose to oppose release, you must act within four weeks of the giving of the notice.

Validity of notice

2. The landlord must give this notice either before the transfer or within the period of four weeks beginning with the date of the transfer. If the notice has been given later, it is not valid. You should read Note 4 below concerning the date of the giving of the notice.

Agreeing to release

3. If you are content for the landlord to be released, you may notify him of this using Part II of this Form, and the landlord will then be released as from the date of the transfer. If you do this, you may not later change your mind and object.

Objecting to release

4. If you think that it is not reasonable for the landlord to be released, you may object to release by notifying the landlord, using Part II of this Form. You must, however, do this within four weeks of the date of the giving of the notice. The date of the giving of the notice may not be the date written on the notice or the date on which you actually saw it. It may, for instance, be the date on which the notice was delivered through the post to your last address known by the landlord. If there has been any delay in your seeing this notice you may need to act very quickly. If you are in any doubt, you should seek advice immediately. If you change your mind after objecting, you may consent instead, at any time, by notifying the landlord *in writing* that you now consent to his being released and that your objection is withdrawn.

5. If you object within the time limit, the landlord will only be released if *either* he applies to a court and the court decides that it is reasonable for him to be released, *or* you withdraw your objection by a notice in writing as explained in Note 4 above.

6. In deciding whether to object, you should bear in mind that if the court finds that it is reasonable for the landlord to be released, or if you withdraw your objection late, you may have to pay costs.

PART II

TENANT'S RESPONSE TO LANDLORD'S NOTICE APPLYING FOR RELEASE FROM LANDLORD COVENANTS OF A TENANCY ON ASSIGNMENT OF WHOLE OF REVERSION (Landlord and Tenant (Covenants) Act 1995, section 8)

To [name and address]: ....

....

1. This notice is given under section 8 of the Landlord and Tenant (Covenants) Act 1995.

2. It relates to (address and description of property) ....

....

let under a lease dated .... and made between ....

....

....

of which you are the landlord or have just transferred the landlord's interest.

3. You [propose to transfer] [transferred on ....][1] the landlord's interest and have applied to be released from the landlord's obligations under the tenancy with effect from the date of the transfer.

4.[2] I/we agree to your being released from the landlord's obligations with effect from the date of the transfer. *{see Note 1 overleaf}*

OR

4. I/we do **not** consider it reasonable that you should be released from the landlord's obligations, and object to the release. *{see Notes 2 and 3 overleaf}*

5. All correspondence about this notice should be sent to the tenant/tenant's agent at the address given below.

Date .... Signature of tenant/tenant's agent ....

Name and address of tenant ....

....

....

[Name and address of agent] ....

....

....]

1 Delete alternative as appropriate.

2 The tenant should select one version of paragraph 4 and cross out the other.

NOTES TO PART II

Agreement to release

1. If the tenant has indicated agreement in paragraph 4 of the notice, you will automatically be released from the landlord's obligations under the tenancy with effect from the date of your transfer of the landlord's interest.

Objection to release

2. If the tenant has indicated an objection in paragraph 4 of the notice, you will not be released unless either the tenant later withdraws his objection *or* you apply to the County Court to declare that it is reasonable for you to be released, and the court so declares. If you are not released, you may still apply for release when the landlord's interest, or part of it, is next transferred, and it may therefore be sensible to make arrangements for the person to whom you are making the transfer to inform you when he intends to transfer the landlord's interest in his turn.

Validity of notice of objection

3. A notice of objection by the tenant is only valid if he has given it to you within the period of four weeks beginning with the date on which you gave him your notice applying for release. If you are in any doubt, you should seek advice before applying to the court.

FORM 4

PART I

LANDLORD'S NOTICE APPLYING FOR RELEASE FROM LANDLORD COVENANTS OF A TENANCY ON ASSIGNMENT OF PART OF REVERSION
(Landlord and Tenant (Covenants) Act 1995, sections 6 and 8)

To [name and address]: ....

....

IMPORTANT – THIS NOTICE IS INTENDED TO RELEASE YOUR LANDLORD PARTLY FROM HIS OBLIGATIONS WHEN HE TRANSFERS PART OF HIS INTEREST TO A NEW LANDLORD. IF YOU CONSIDER THAT THERE IS GOOD REASON FOR YOUR LANDLORD **NOT** TO BE RELEASED, YOU MUST ACT QUICKLY. READ THE NOTICE AND ALL THE NOTES OVERLEAF CAREFULLY. IF YOU ARE IN ANY DOUBT ABOUT THE ACTION YOU SHOULD TAKE, SEEK ADVICE IMMEDIATELY, FOR INSTANCE FROM A SOLICITOR OR CITIZENS ADVICE BUREAU.

1. This notice is given under section 8 of the Landlord and Tenant (Covenants) Act 1995. *{see Note 1 overleaf}*

2. It relates to (address and description of property) ....

....

let under a lease dated .... and made between ....

....

....

of which you are the tenant.

3. I/we [propose to transfer] [transferred on ....][1] part of the landlord's interest, namely

....

and wish to be released from the landlord's obligations under the tenancy, to the extent that they fall to be complied with in relation to that part, with effect from the date of the transfer. *{see Note 2 overleaf}*

4. If you consider that it is reasonable for me/us to be released, you do not need to do anything, but it would help me/us if you notify me/us using Part II of this Form. *{see Note 3 overleaf}*

5. If you do **not** consider it reasonable for me/us to be released, you **must** notify me/us of your objection, using Part II of this Form, within the period of **FOUR WEEKS** beginning with the giving of this notice, or I/we will be released in any event. You may withdraw your objection at any time by notifying me/us in writing. *{see Notes 4–6 overleaf}*

6. All correspondence about this notice should be sent to the landlord/landlord's agent at the address given below.

Date .... Signature of Landlord/Landlord's agent..............

Name and address of landlord ....

....

....

[continued over]

1 Delete alternative as appropriate.

[Name and address of agent ....
....
....]

NOTES TO PART I

Release of landlord

1. The landlord is about to transfer part of his interest to a new landlord, or has just done so, and is applying to be released from the obligations of the landlord under your tenancy, to the extent that they fall to be complied with in relation to that part. You have a number of options: you may expressly agree to the landlord's being released; you may object to his being released (with the option of withdrawing your objection later); or you may do nothing, in which case the landlord will automatically be released, with effect from the date of the assignment, once four weeks have elapsed from the date of the giving of the notice. If you choose to oppose release, you must act within four weeks of the giving of the notice.

Validity of notice

2. The landlord must give this notice either before the transfer or within the period of four weeks beginning with the date of the transfer. If the notice has been given later, it is not valid. You should read Note 4 below concerning the date of the giving of the notice.

Agreeing to release

3. If you are content for the landlord to be released, you may notify him of this using Part II of this Form, and the landlord will then be released as from the date of the transfer. If you do this, you may not later change your mind and object.

Objecting to release

4. If you think that it is not reasonable for the landlord to be released, you may object to release by notifying the landlord, using Part II of this Form. You must, however, do this within four weeks of the date of the giving of the notice. The date of the giving of the notice may not be the date written on the notice or the date on which you actually saw it. It may, for instance, be the date on which the notice was delivered through the post to your last address known to the person giving the notice. If there has been any delay in your seeing this notice you may need to act very quickly. If you are in any doubt, you should seek advice immediately. If you change your mind after objecting, you may consent instead, at any time, by notifying the landlord *in writing* that you now consent to his being released and that your objection is withdrawn.

5. If you object within the time limit, the landlord will only be released if *either* he applies to a court and the court decides that it is reasonable for him to be released, *or* you withdraw your objection by a notice in writing as explained in Note 4 above.

6. In deciding whether to object, you should bear in mind that if the court finds that it is reasonable for the landlord to be released, or if you withdraw your objection late, you may have to pay costs.

PART II

TENANT'S RESPONSE TO LANDLORD'S NOTICE APPLYING FOR RELEASE FROM LANDLORD COVENANTS OF A TENANCY ON ASSIGNMENT OF PART OF REVERSION
(Landlord and Tenant (Covenants) Act 1995, section 8)

To [name and address]: ....

....

1. This notice is given under section 8 of the Landlord and Tenant (Covenants) Act 1995.

2. It relates to (address and description of property) ....

....

let under a lease dated .... and made between ....

....

of which you are the landlord or have just transferred part of the landlord's interest.

3. You [propose to transfer] [transferred on ....][1] part of the landlord's interest, namely

....

and have applied to be released from the landlord's obligations under the tenancy, to the extent that they fall to be complied with in relation to that part, with effect from the date of the transfer.

4.[2] I/we agree to your being released from the landlord's obligations to that extent with effect from the date of the transfer. *{see note 1 overleaf}*

OR

4. I/we do **not** consider it reasonable that you should be released from the landlord's obligations, and object to the release. *{see Notes 2 and 3 overleaf}*

5. All correspondence about this notice should be sent to the tenant/tenant's agent at the address given below.

Date .... Signature of tenant/tenant's agent ....

Name and address of tenant ....

....

....

[Name and address of agent ....

....

....]

1 Delete alternative as appropriate.
2 The tenant should select one version of paragraph 4 and cross out the other.

NOTES TO PART II

Agreement to release

1. If the tenant has indicated agreement in paragraph 4 of the notice, you will automatically be released from the landlord's obligations under the tenancy, to the extent that they fall to be complied with in relation to the part of your interest being transferred, with effect from the date of the transfer.

Objection to release

2. If the tenant has indicated an objection in paragraph 4 of the notice, you will not be released unless *either* the tenant later withdraws his objection *or* you apply to the County Court to declare that it is reasonable for you to be released, and the court so declares. If you are not released, you may still apply for release when the landlord's interest, or part of it, is next transferred, and it may therefore be sensible to make arrangements for the person to whom you are making the transfer to inform you when he intends to transfer the landlord's interest in his turn.

Validity of notice of objection

3. A notice of objection by the tenant is only valid if he has given it to you within the period of four weeks beginning with the date on which you gave him your notice applying for release. If you are in any doubt, you should seek advice before applying to the court.

FORM 5

PART I

FORMER LANDLORD'S NOTICE APPLYING FOR RELEASE FROM LANDLORD COVENANTS OF A TENANCY (Landlord and Tenant (Covenants) Act 1995, sections 7 and 8)

To [name and address]: ....

....

IMPORTANT – THIS NOTICE IS INTENDED TO RELEASE THE FORMER LANDLORD OF THE PROPERTY FROM HIS OBLIGATIONS UNDER YOUR TENANCY. IF YOU CONSIDER THAT THERE IS GOOD REASON FOR THE FORMER LANDLORD **NOT** TO BE RELEASED, YOU MUST ACT QUICKLY. READ THE NOTICE AND ALL THE NOTES OVERLEAF CAREFULLY. IF YOU ARE IN ANY DOUBT ABOUT THE ACTION YOU SHOULD TAKE, SEEK ADVICE IMMEDIATELY, FOR INSTANCE FROM A SOLICITOR OR CITIZENS ADVICE BUREAU.

1. This notice is given under section 8 of the Landlord and Tenant (Covenants) Act 1995. *{see Note 1 overleaf}*

2. It relates to (address and description of property) ....

....

let under a lease dated .... and made between ....

....

....

of which you are the tenant.

3. I/we was/were formerly landlord of the property of which you are tenant and remained bound by the landlord's obligations under the tenancy after transferring the landlord's interest. The landlord's interest, or part of it [is about to be transferred] [was transferred on ....][1]. I/we wish to be released from my/our obligations with effect from the date of that transfer. *{see Note 2 overleaf}*

4. If you consider that it is reasonable for me/us to be released, you do not need to do anything, but it would help me/us if you notify me/us using Part II of this Form. *{see Note 3 overleaf}*

5. If you do **not** consider it reasonable for me/us to be released, you **must** notify me/us of your objection, using Part II of this Form, within the period of **FOUR WEEKS** beginning with the giving of this notice, or I/we will be released in any event. You may withdraw your objection at any time by notifying me/us in writing. *{see Notes 4–6 overleaf}*

6. All correspondence about this notice should be sent to the former landlord/landlord's agent at the address given below.

Date .... Signature of former landlord/agent ....

Name and address of former landlord ....

....

....

[continued over]

1 Delete alternative as appropriate.

[Name and address of agent ....

....

....]

NOTES TO PART I

Release of former landlord

1. Your landlord is about to transfer his interest, or part of it, to a new landlord, or has just done so, and a former landlord of the property is applying to be released from his obligations, from which he was not released when he transferred the landlord's interest himself. You have a number of options: you may expressly agree to the former landlord's being released; you may object to his being released (with the option of withdrawing your objection later); or you may do nothing, in which case the former landlord will automatically be released, with effect from the date of the present transfer, once four weeks have elapsed from the date of the giving of the notice. If you choose to oppose release, you must act within four weeks of the giving of the notice.

Validity of notice

2. The former landlord is required to give this notice either before the transfer by the present landlord takes place or within the period of four weeks beginning with the date of the transfer. If the notice has been given late, it is not valid. You should read Note 4 below concerning the date of the giving of the notice.

Agreeing to release

3. If you are content for the former landlord to be released, you may notify him of this using Part II of this Form, and the former landlord will then automatically be released as from the date of the present transfer. If you do this, you may not later change your mind and object.

Objecting to release

4. If you think that it is not reasonable for the former landlord to be released, you may object to release by notifying the former landlord, using Part II of this Form. You must, however, do this within four weeks of the date of the giving of the notice. The date of the giving of the notice may not be the date written on the notice or the date on which you actually saw it. It may, for instance, be the date on which the notice was delivered through the post to your last address known to the person giving the notice. If there has been any delay in your seeing this notice you may need to act very quickly. If you are in any doubt, you should seek advice immediately. If you change your mind after objecting, you may consent instead, at any time, by notifying the former landlord *in writing* that you now consent to his being released and that your objection is withdrawn.

5. If you object within the time limit, the former landlord will only be released if *either* he applies to a court and the court decides that it is reasonable for him to be released, *or* you withdraw your objection by a notice in writing as explained in Note 4 above.

6. In deciding whether to object, you should bear in mind that if the court finds that it is reasonable for the former landlord to be released, or if you withdraw your objection late, you may have to pay costs.

PART II

TENANT'S RESPONSE TO FORMER LANDLORD'S NOTICE APPLYING FOR RELEASE FROM LANDLORD COVENANTS OF A TENANCY
(Landlord and Tenant (Covenants) Act 1995, section 8)

To [name and address]: ....

....

1. This notice is given under section 8 of the Landlord and Tenant (Covenants) Act 1995.

2. It relates to (address and description of property) ....

....

let under a lease dated .... and made between ....

....

....

of which you were formerly landlord.

3. You have applied to be released from the landlord's obligations under the tenancy with effect from the date of a [proposed transfer] [transfer on .....][1] of the landlord's interest.

4.[2] I/we agree to your being released from the landlord's obligations with effect from the date of that transfer. *{see Note 1 overleaf}*

OR

4. I/we do **not** consider it reasonable that you should be released from the landlord's obligations, and object to your being so released. *{see Notes 2 and 3 overleaf}*

5. All correspondence about this notice should be sent to the tenant/tenant's agent at the address given below.

Date .... Signature of tenant/tenant's agent ....

Name and address of tenant ....

....

....

[Name and address of agent ....

....

....]

1 Delete alternative as appropriate.
2 The tenant should select one version of paragraph 4 and cross out the other.

NOTES TO PART II

Agreement to release

1. If the tenant has indicated agreement in paragraph 4 of the notice, you will automatically be released from the landlord's obligations under the tenancy with effect from the date of the transfer by the present landlord.

Objection to release

2. If the tenant has indicated an objection in paragraph 4 of the notice, you will not be released unless *either* the tenant later withdraws his objection *or* you apply to the County Court to declare that it is reasonable for you to be released, and the court so declares. If you are not released, you may still apply for release when the reversion, or part of it, is next assigned, and it may therefore be sensible to make arrangements for you to be informed when the present landlord's transferee intends to transfer the landlord's interest in his turn.

Validity of notice of objection

3. A notice of objection by the tenant is only valid if he has given it to you within the period of four weeks beginning with the date on which you gave him your notice applying for release. If you are in any doubt, you should seek advice before applying to the court.

FORM 6

PART I

FORMER LANDLORD'S NOTICE APPLYING FOR RELEASE FROM LANDLORD COVENANTS OF A TENANCY (FORMER LANDLORD HAVING ASSIGNED PART OF REVERSION)
(Landlord and Tenant (Covenants) Act 1995, sections 7 and 8)

To [name and address]: ....

....

IMPORTANT – THIS NOTICE IS INTENDED TO RELEASE THE FORMER LANDLORD OF THE PROPERTY PARTIALLY FROM HIS OBLIGATIONS UNDER YOUR TENANCY. IF YOU CONSIDER THAT THERE IS GOOD REASON FOR THE FORMER LANDLORD **NOT** TO BE RELEASED, YOU MUST ACT QUICKLY. READ THE NOTICE AND ALL THE NOTES OVERLEAF CAREFULLY. IF YOU ARE IN ANY DOUBT ABOUT THE ACTION YOU SHOULD TAKE, SEEK ADVICE IMMEDIATELY, FOR INSTANCE FROM A SOLICITOR OR CITIZENS ADVICE BUREAU.

1. This notice is given under section 8 of the Landlord and Tenant (Covenants) Act 1995. *{see Note 1 overleaf}*

2. It relates to (address and description of property) ....

....

let under a lease dated .... and made between ....

....

....

of which you are the tenant.

3. I/we was/were formerly landlord of the property of which you are tenant and remained bound by all the landlord's obligations under the tenancy after transferring part of the landlord's interest, namely...

....

The landlord's interest, or part of it [is about to be transferred] [was transferred on ....][1]. I/we wish to be released from my/our obligations with effect from the date of that transfer. *{see Note 2 overleaf}*

4. If you consider that it is reasonable for me/us to be released, you do not need to do anything, but it would help me/us if you notify me/us using Part II of this Form. *{see Note 3 overleaf}*

5. If you do **not** consider it reasonable for me/us to be released, you **must** notify me/us of your objection, using Part II of this Form, within the period of **FOUR WEEKS** beginning with the giving of this notice, or I/we will be released in any event. You may withdraw your objection at any time by notifying me/us in writing. *{see Notes 4–6 overleaf}*

6. All correspondence about this notice should be sent to the former landlord/former landlord's agent at the address given below.

Date .... Signature of former landlord/agent ....

Name and address of former landlord ....

....

....

[continued over]

1 Delete alternative as appropriate.

[Name and address of agent ....
....
....]

NOTES TO PART I

Release of former landlord

1. Your landlord is about to transfer his interest, or part of it, to a new landlord, or has just done so, and a former landlord of the property is applying to be released from his obligations in relation to part of the landlord's interest, from which he was not released when he transferred that part himself. You have a number of options: you may expressly agree to the former landlord's being released; you may object to his being released (with the option of withdrawing your objection later); or you may do nothing, in which case the former landlord will automatically be released, with effect from the date of the present transfer, once four weeks have elapsed from the date of the giving of the notice. If you choose to oppose release, you must act within four weeks of the giving of the notice.

Validity of notice

2. The former landlord is required to give this notice either before the transfer by the present landlord takes place or within the period of four weeks beginning with the date of the transfer. If the notice has been given late, it is not valid. You should read Note 4 below concerning the date of the giving of the notice.

Agreeing to release

3. If you are content for the former landlord to be released, you may notify him of this using Part II of this Form, and the former landlord will then automatically be released as from the date of the present transfer. If you do this, you may not later change your mind and object.

Objecting to release

4. If you think that it is not reasonable for the former landlord to be released, you may object to release by notifying the former landlord, using Part II of this Form. You must, however, do this within four weeks of the date of the giving of the notice. The date of the giving of the notice may not be the date written on the notice or the date on which you actually saw it. It may, for instance, be the date on which the notice was delivered through the post to your last address known to the person giving the notice. If there has been any delay in your seeing this notice you may need to act very quickly. If you are in any doubt, you should seek advice immediately. If you change your mind after objecting, you may consent instead, at any time, by notifying the former landlord *in writing* that you now consent to his being released and that your objection is withdrawn.

5. If you object within the time limit, the former landlord will only be released if *either* he applies to a court and the court decides that it is reasonable for him to be released, *or* you withdraw your objection by a notice in writing as explained in Note 4 above.

6. In deciding whether to object, you should bear in mind that if the court finds that it is reasonable for the former landlord to be released, or if you withdraw your objection late, you may have to pay costs.

PART II

TENANT'S RESPONSE TO FORMER LANDLORD'S NOTICE APPLYING FOR RELEASE FROM LANDLORD COVENANTS OF A TENANCY (FORMER LANDLORD HAVING ASSIGNED PART OF REVERSION)
(Landlord and Tenant (Covenants) Act 1995, section 8)

To [name and address]: ....

....

1. This notice is given under section 8 of the Landlord and Tenant (Covenants) Act 1995.

2. It relates to (address and description of property) ....

....

let under a lease dated .... and made between ....

....

....

of which you were formerly landlord.

3. You remain bound by the landlord's obligations under the tenancy in relation to a part of the landlord's interest which you previously assigned, namely ....

....
You have applied to be released from those obligations, to the extent that they relate to that part, with effect from the date of a [proposed transfer] [transfer on ....][1] of the landlord's interest.

4.[2] I/we agree to your being released from the landlord's obligations to that effect from the date of that transfer. *{see Note 1 overleaf}*

OR

4. I/we do **not** consider it reasonable that you should be released from the landlord's obligations and object to your being so released. *{see Notes 2 and 3 overleaf}*

5. All correspondence about this notice should be sent to the tenant/tenant's agent at the address given below.

Date .... Signature of tenant/tenant's agent ....

Name and address of tenant ....

....

....

[Name and address of agent ....

....

....]

1 Delete alternative as appropriate.
2 The tenant should select one version of paragraph 4 and cross out the other.

NOTES TO PART II

Agreement to release

1. If the tenant has indicated agreement in paragraph 4 of the notice, you will automatically be released from the landlord's obligations under the tenancy to the appropriate extent with effect from the date of the transfer by the present landlord.

Objection to release

2. If the tenant has indicated an objection in paragraph 4 of the notice, you will not be released unless *either* the tenant later withdraws his objection *or* you apply to the County Court to declare that it is reasonable for you to be released, and the court so declares. If you are not released, you may still apply for release when the reversion, or part of it, is next transferred, and it may therefore be sensible to make arrangements for you to be informed when the present landlord's transferee intends to transfer the landlord's interest in his turn.

Validity of notice of objection

3. A notice of objection by the tenant is only valid if he has given it to you within the period of four weeks beginning with the date on which you gave him your notice applying for release. If you are in any doubt, you should seek advice before applying to the court.

FORM 7

PART I

JOINT NOTICE BY TENANT AND ASSIGNEE FOR BINDING APPORTIONMENT OF LIABILITY UNDER NON-ATTRIBUTABLE TENANT COVENANTS OF A TENANCY ON ASSIGNMENT OF PART OF PROPERTY

(Landlord and Tenant (Covenants) Act 1995, sections 9 and 10)

To [name and address]: ....

....

IMPORTANT – THIS NOTICE IS INTENDED TO AFFECT THE WAY IN WHICH YOU CAN ENFORCE THE TENANT'S OBLIGATIONS UNDER THE TENANCY AS BETWEEN THE TENANT AND THE NEW TENANT. IF YOU CONSIDER THAT THERE IS GOOD REASON WHY YOU SHOULD **NOT** BE BOUND BY THEIR AGREEMENT, YOU MUST ACT QUICKLY. READ THE NOTICE AND ALL THE NOTES OVERLEAF CAREFULLY. IF YOU ARE IN ANY DOUBT ABOUT THE ACTION YOU SHOULD TAKE, SEEK ADVICE IMMEDIATELY, FOR INSTANCE FROM A SOLICITOR OR CITIZENS ADVICE BUREAU.

1. This notice is given under section 10 of the Landlord and Tenant (Covenants) Act 1995. *{see Note 1 overleaf}*

2. It relates to (address and description of property) ....

....

let under a lease dated .... and made between ....

....

....

of which you are the landlord.[1]

3. We are the parties to a [proposed transfer] [transfer on ....][2] of the part of the property comprised in the tenancy, namely ....

....

We are jointly and severally liable to perform the obligation(s) specified in the attached Schedule, and have agreed to divide that liability between us in the manner specified in the Schedule.[3] We wish this agreement to be binding on you as well as between us, with effect from the date of the transfer. *{see Note 2 overleaf}*

4. If you consider that it is reasonable for you to be bound by this agreement, you do not need to do anything, but it would help us if you notify us using Part II of this Form. *{see Note 3 overleaf}*

5. If you do **not** consider it reasonable for you to be bound by this agreement, you **must** notify both of us of your objection, using Part II of this Form, within the period of **FOUR WEEKS** beginning with the giving of this notice. You may withdraw your objection at any time by notifying us in writing. *{see Notes 4–6 overleaf}*

[continued over]

1 "Landlord", for these purposes, includes any person for the time being entitled to enforce the obligations in question (for example, a management company).

2 Delete alternative as appropriate.

3 The Schedule must be in writing, and must specify the nature of the obligation, the term or condition of the Lease or other instrument under which it arises and the manner in which liability to perform it is divided under the agreement (for example, an obligation to pay service charge under a specific provision of the lease might be divided equally). It may be helpful to attach a copy of the agreement to the notice.

6. All correspondence about this notice should be copied, one copy sent to each of the parties to the agreement, at the addresses given below.

Signature of tenant/tenant's agent ....

Name and address of tenant ....

....

....

[Name and address of agent ....

....

....]

Signature of new tenant/agent ....

Name and address of new tenant ....

....

....

[Name and address of agent ....

....

....]

Date ....

NOTES TO PART I

Apportionment of liability

1. The tenant is about to transfer, or has just transferred, part of his interest to a new tenant, but they are jointly and severally liable for a particular obligation or obligations covering the whole of the property. They have agreed to divide that liability between them, and are applying for you as the landlord to be bound as well, so that you can only enforce the liability against each of them as set out in their agreement. If you are bound, any subsequent landlord to whom you may transfer your interest will also be bound. You have a number of options: you may expressly agree to be bound; you may object to being bound (with the option of withdrawing your objection later); or you may do nothing, in which case you will automatically be bound, with effect from the date of the transfer, once four weeks have elapsed from the date of the giving of the notice. If you choose to object, you must act within four weeks of the giving of the notice.

Validity of notice

2. This notice must be given either before the transfer or within the period of four weeks beginning with the date of the transfer. If the notice has been given late, it is not valid. You should read Note 4 below concerning the date of the giving of the notice.

Agreeing to be bound

3. If you are content to be bound, you may notify the tenant and new tenant using Part II of this Form (sending a copy to each of them), and all of you will be bound with effect from the date of the transfer. If you do this, you may not later change your mind and object.

[continued over]

Objecting to being bound

4. If you think that it is not reasonable for you to be bound, you may object by notifying the tenant and new tenant, using Part II of this Form (sending a copy to each of them). You must, however, do this within four weeks of the date of the giving of this notice. The date of the giving of the notice may not be the date written on the notice or the date on which you actually saw it. It may, for instance, be the date on which the notice was delivered through the post to your last address known to the person giving the notice. If there has been any delay in your seeing this notice you may need to act very quickly. If you are in any doubt, you should seek advice immediately. If you change your mind after objecting, you may consent instead, at any time, by notifying *both* the tenant and new tenant *in writing* that you now consent to be bound and that your objection is withdrawn.

5. If you object within the time limit, the apportionment will only bind you if *either* the tenant and new tenant apply to a court and the court decides that it is reasonable for you to be bound, *or* you withdraw your objection by notice in writing as explained in Note 4 above.

6. In deciding whether to object, you should bear in mind that if the court finds that it is reasonable for you to be bound, *or* if you withdraw your objection late, you may have to pay costs.

PART II

LANDLORD'S RESPONSE TO JOINT NOTICE BY TENANT AND ASSIGNEE SEEKING BINDING APPORTIONMENT OF LIABILITY UNDER NON-ATTRIBUTABLE TENANT COVENANTS OF A TENANCY ON ASSIGNMENT OF PART OF PROPERTY (Landlord and Tenant (Covenants) Act 1995, section 10)

To [name and address]: ....

....

And [name and address]: ....

....

1. This notice is given under section 10 of the Landlord and Tenant (Covenants) Act 1995.

2. It relates to (address and description of property) ....

....

let under a lease dated .... and made between ....

....

....

of which I/we am/are the landlord.[1]

3. You have applied for me/us to be bound by your agreement to divide liability between you with effect from the [proposed transfer] [transfer on ....][2] of part of the property comprised in the tenancy.

4.[3] I/we agree to be bound by your agreement with effect from the date of the transfer. *{see Note 1 overleaf}*

OR

4. I/we do **not** consider it reasonable that I/we should be bound by your agreement, and object to being so bound. *{see Notes 2 and 3 overleaf}*

6. All correspondence about this notice should be sent to the landlord/landlord's agent at the address given below.

Date .... Signature of landlord/landlord's agent.............

Name and address of landlord ....

....

....

[Name and address of agent ....

....

....]

[continued overleaf]

1 "Landlord", for these purposes, includes any person for the time being entitled to enforce the obligations in question (for example, a management company).
2 Delete alternative as appropriate.
3 The landlord should select one version of paragraph 4 and cross out the other.

NOTES TO PART II

Agreement to be bound

1. If the landlord has indicated agreement in paragraph 3 of the notice, he will automatically be bound by your agreement, with effect from the date of the transfer. Any subsequent landlord will also be bound.

Objection to being bound

2. If the landlord has indicated an objection in paragraph 3 of the notice, he will not be bound by your agreement unless *either* the landlord later withdraws his objection *or* you apply to the County Court to declare that it is reasonable for him to be bound, and the court so declares.

Validity of notice of objection

3. A notice of objection by the landlord is only valid if he has given it to each of you within the period of four weeks beginning with the date on which you gave him your notice applying for your agreement to become binding on him. If you are in any doubt, you should seek advice before applying to the court.

FORM 8

PART I

JOINT NOTICE BY LANDLORD AND ASSIGNEE FOR BINDING APPORTIONMENT OF LIABILITY UNDER NON-ATTRIBUTABLE LANDLORD COVENANTS OF A TENANCY ON ASSIGNMENT OF PART OF REVERSION

(Landlord and Tenant (Covenants) Act 1995, sections 9 and 10)

To [name and address]: ....

....

IMPORTANT – THIS NOTICE IS INTENDED TO AFFECT THE WAY IN WHICH YOU CAN ENFORCE THE LANDLORD'S OBLIGATIONS UNDER THE TENANCY AS BETWEEN THE LANDLORD AND THE NEW LANDLORD. IF YOU CONSIDER THAT THERE IS GOOD REASON WHY YOU SHOULD **NOT** BE BOUND BY THEIR AGREEMENT, YOU MUST ACT QUICKLY. READ THE NOTICE AND ALL THE NOTES OVERLEAF CAREFULLY. IF YOU ARE IN ANY DOUBT ABOUT THE ACTION YOU SHOULD TAKE, SEEK ADVICE IMMEDIATELY, FOR INSTANCE FROM A SOLICITOR OR CITIZENS ADVICE BUREAU.

1. This notice is given under section 10 of the Landlord and Tenant (Covenants) Act 1995. *{see Note 1 overleaf}*

2. It relates to (address and description of property) ....

....

let under a lease dated .... and made between ....

....

....

of which you are the tenant.

3. We are the parties to a [proposed transfer] [transfer on ....][1] of the landlord's interest in part of the property comprised in the tenancy, namely ....

....

We are jointly and severally liable to perform the obligation(s) specified in the attached Schedule and have agreed to divide that liability between us in the manner specified in the Schedule.[2] We wish this agreement to be binding on you as well as between us, with effect from the date of the transfer. *{see Note 2 overleaf}*

4. If you consider that it is reasonable for you to be bound by this agreement, you do not need to do anything, but it would help us if you notify us using Part II of this Form. *{see Note 3 overleaf}*

5. If you do **not** consider it reasonable for you to be bound by this agreement, you **must** notify both of us of your objection, using Part II of this Form, within the period of **FOUR WEEKS** beginning with the giving of this notice. You may withdraw your objection at any time by notifying us in writing. *{see Notes 4–6 overleaf}*

[continued over]

1 Delete alternative as appropriate.

2 The Schedule must be in writing, and must specify the nature of the obligation, the term or condition of the Lease or other instrument under which it arises and the manner in which liability to perform it is divided under the agreement. It may be helpful to attach a copy of the agreement to the notice.

6. All correspondence about this notice should be copied, and one copy sent to each of the parties to the agreement, at the addresses given below.

Signature of landlord/landlord's agent..

Name and address of landlord ....

....

....

[Name and address of agent ....

....

....]

Signature of new landlord/agent ....

Name and address of new landlord ....

....

....

[Name and address of agent ....

....

....]

Date ....

NOTES TO PART I

Apportionment of liability

1. The landlord is about to transfer, or has just transferred, part of his interest to a new landlord, but they are jointly and severally liable for a particular obligation or obligations covering the whole of the property. They have agreed to divide that liability between them, and are applying for you as tenant to be bound as well, so that you can only enforce the liability against each of them as set out in their agreement. If you are bound, any subsequent tenant to whom you may transfer your interest will also be bound. You have a number of options: you may expressly agree to be bound; you may object to being bound (with the option of withdrawing your objection later); or you may do nothing, in which case you will automatically be bound, with effect from the date of the transfer, once four weeks have elapsed from the date of the giving of the notice. If you choose to object, you must act within four weeks of the giving of the notice.

Validity of notice

2. This notice must be given either before the transfer or within the period of four weeks beginning with the date of the transfer. If the notice has been given later, it is not valid. You should read Note 4 below concerning the date of the giving of the notice.

Agreeing to be bound

3. If you are content to be bound, you may notify the landlord and new landlord using Part II of this Form (sending a copy to each of them), and all of you will be bound with effect from the date of the transfer. If you do this, you may not later change your mind and object.

[continued over]

Objecting to being bound

4. If you think that it is not reasonable for you to be bound, you may object by notifying the landlord and new landlord, using Part II of this Form (sending a copy to each of them). You must, however, do this within four weeks of the date of the giving of the notice. The date of the giving of the notice may not be the date written on the notice or the date on which you actually saw it. It may, for instance, be the date on which the notice was delivered through the post to your last address known to the person giving the notice. If there has been any delay in your seeing this notice you may need to act very quickly. If you are in any doubt, you should seek advice immediately. If you change your mind after objecting, you may consent instead, at any time, by notifying *both* the landlord and new landlord *in writing* that you now consent to be bound and that your objection is withdrawn.

5. If you object within the time limit, the apportionment will only bind you if *either* the landlord and new landlord apply to a court and the court decides that it is reasonable for you to be bound, *or* you withdraw your objection by notice in writing as explained in Note 4 above.

6. In deciding whether to object, you should bear in mind that if the court finds that it is reasonable for you to be bound, *or* if you withdraw your objection late, you may have to pay costs.

PART II

TENANT'S RESPONSE TO JOINT NOTICE BY LANDLORD AND ASSIGNEE SEEKING BINDING APPORTIONMENT OF LIABILITY UNDER NON-ATTRIBUTABLE LANDLORD COVENANTS OF A TENANCY ON ASSIGNMENT OF PART OF REVERSION (Landlord and Tenant (Covenants) Act 1995, section 10)

To [name and address]: ....

....

And [name and address]: ....

....

1. This notice is given under section 10 of the Landlord and Tenant (Covenants) Act 1995.

2. It relates to (address and description of property) ....

....

let under a lease dated .... and made between ....

....

....

of which I/we am/are the tenant.

3. You have applied for me/us to be bound by your agreement to divide liability between you with effect from the [proposed transfer] [transfer on ....][1] of part of the landlord's interest in the property comprised in the tenancy.

4.[2] I/we agree to be bound by your agreement with effect from the date of the transfer. *{see Note 1 overleaf}*

OR

4. I/we do **not** consider it reasonable that I/we should be bound by your agreement, and object to being so bound. *{see Notes 2 and 3 overleaf}*

6. All correspondence about this notice should be sent to the tenant/tenant's agent at the address given below.

Date .... Signature of tenant/tenant's agent ....

Name and address of tenant ....

....

....

[Name and address of agent ....

....

....]

[continued over]

1 Delete alternative as appropriate.
2 The tenant should select one version of paragraph 4 and cross out the other.

NOTES TO PART II

Agreement to be bound

1. If the tenant has indicated agreement in paragraph 3 of the notice, he will automatically be bound by your agreement, with effect from the date of the transfer. Any subsequent tenant will also be bound.

Objection to being bound

2. If the tenant has indicated an objection in paragraph 3 of the notice, he will not be bound by your agreement unless *either* the tenant later withdraws his objection *or* you apply to the County Court to declare that it is reasonable for him to be bound, and the court so declares.

Validity of notice of objection

3. A notice of objection by the tenant is only valid if he has given it to each of you within the period of four weeks beginning with the date on which you gave him your notice applying for your agreement to become binding on him. If you are in any doubt, you should seek advice before applying to the court.

* * * *

THE LAND REGISTRATION (OVERRIDING LEASES) RULES 1995

(S.I. 1995 No. 3154)

Made .... *6th December 1995*
Laid before Parliament .... *6th December 1995*
Coming into force .... *1st January 1996*

The Lord Chancellor, with the advice and assistance of the Rule Committee appointed in pursuance of section 144 of the Land Registration Act 1925, in exercise of the powers conferred on him by that section and by section 20(2) of the Landlord and Tenant (Covenants) Act 1995, hereby makes the following rules:

Citation and commencement

1. These rules may be cited as the Land Registration (Overriding Leases) Rules 1995 and shall come into force on 1st January 1996.

Statement to be inserted in an overriding lease

2. The statement required by section 20(2) of the Landlord and Tenant (Covenants) Act 1995 to be inserted into an overriding lease granted under section 19 of that Act shall in relation to a registrable lease be in the following form:
"This lease is granted under section 19 of the Landlord and Tenant (Covenants) Act 1995 and is (*or* is not) a new tenancy for the purposes of section 1 of that Act."

[Dated 6th December 1995 MacKay of Clashfern, C.]

* * * *

INDEX